UNIVERSAL ECONOMICS

Universal Economics

ARMEN A. ALCHIAN AND WILLIAM R. ALLEN

EDITED BY JERRY L. JORDAN

Foreword by William R. Allen

LIBERTY FUND

This book is published by Liberty Fund, Inc.,
a foundation established to encourage study of the
ideal of a society of free and responsible individuals.

𒂼𒄀

The cuneiform inscription that serves as our logo and
as the design motif for our endpapers is the earliest-known
written appearance of the word "freedom" (*amagi*), or "liberty."
It is taken from a clay document written about 2300 B.C.
in the Sumerian city-state of Lagash.

© 2018 by Pacific Academy for Advanced Studies (PAAS).
Published by permission.

19 20 21 22 C 5 4 3 2
19 20 21 22 P 5 4 3 2

Library of Congress Cataloging-in-Publication Data

Names: Alchian, Armen Albert, 1914–   author. | Allen, William Richard, 1924–   author. |
    Jordan, Jerry L., 1941–   editor.
Title: Universal economics / Armen A. Alchian and William R. Allen ; edited by
    Jerry L. Jordan ; foreword by William R. Allen.
Description: Carmel, Indiana : Liberty Fund, Inc., [2018] | Includes bibliographical references
    and index. | Description based on print version record and CIP data provided by publisher;
    resource not viewed.
Identifiers: LLCN 2017052105 (print) | LCCN 2017054644 (ebook) | ISBN 9781614876571
    (Kindle) | ISBN 9781614872818 (epub) | ISBN 9781614879275 (pdf) | ISBN 9780865979055
    (hardcover : alk. paper) | ISBN 9780865979062 (pbk. : alk. paper)
Subjects: LCSH: Economics.
Classification: LCC HB171.5 (ebook) | LCC HB171.5 .A339 2018 (print) | DDC 330—dc23
LC record available at https://lccn.loc.gov/2017052105

LIBERTY FUND, INC.
11301 North Meridian Street, Carmel, Indiana 46032-4564

CONCISE CONTENTS

DETAILED CONTENTS

FOREWORD

Living is an important activity. And in a world of limitations — faced with scarcities of talent and character and iron ore — living is also difficult. Alternatives must be compared, analyses have to be conducted, decisions inevitably are required. And we often complicate our situation further with personal peculiarities and social arrangements which unduly increase the costs and dilute the rewards of our existence.

Various sorts of observers and self-appointed counselors — theologians, poets, philosophers — have long worked to resolve some of the bittersweet mystery of life. And now we are blessed with economists.

Aristotle, over twenty-four centuries ago, was the most conspicuous of the meditators of antiquity to devote considerable attention to selected aspects of economic conditions and activity. Adam Smith, in the eighteenth century, is the acknowledged father figure in the early development of modern economics. Something resembling current theory began to take shape with the Marginalist Revolution of nearly 150 years ago. A veritable golden age waxed — and perhaps then waned in some respects — in the second half of the twentieth century. In this post–World War II era, there was a considerable band of innovative theorists and applicators of fruitful analytics. Few of these elite were as useful as Armen A. Alchian.

Useful economics relies conspicuously on a toolkit of formal analytic techniques. But tools must be manipulated by competent carpenters. And the carpenters follow building plans prepared by imaginative, inspired, broadly sophisticated architects. Alchian was a master craftsman and contributed additional tools to the kit. And he has been a striking architect. Most rarely, he was anointed with feel for and sense of the nature of individuals and their societies and the mechanisms of the economy on which a community is founded. Further, like many other stalwarts of the economics fraternity, he was motivated to teach.

Milton Friedman observed that "some have a natural instinct for economics and the economic way of reasoning," but "for most, economic reasoning is an acquired skill — and taste." Alchian helped a long stream of talented students to acquire productive skills — and sophisticated intellectual tastes.

A spectacular technical, bravura scholarly exhibition often will be of little value to the general community. A conspicuous Alchian characteristic has been to explain important matters in the most *simple* manner, and he was ingenious in solving questions with use of only the most basic conceptions and constructs. Mark Twain noted that his wife, living along the Mississippi River, learned all the swear words — but not how to carry the tune. In economic analysis, Alchian knew the words well and also splendidly hummed the tune.

Useful economists have learned that elemental, even elementary, economic tools in the hands of an accomplished scholar, teacher, and practitioner can be highly productive. Alain A. Enthoven, while working at the highest levels of policymaking in the Department of Defense, reported: "the tools of analysis that we [in Defense] use are the simplest, most fundamental concepts of economic theory, combined with the simplest quantitative methods. The requirements for success in this line of work are a thorough understanding of and, if you like, belief in the relevance of such concepts as marginal products and marginal costs, and an ability to discover the marginal products and costs in complex situations, combined with a good quantitative sense. The economic theory we are using is the theory most of us learned as sophomores." (*Economic Analysis in the Department of Defense*, American Economic Review, LIII [May 1963], 422.)

Armen and I became UCLA colleagues in 1952. We have collaborated in several ventures, primarily in writing *University Economics* (Wadsworth Publishing Co., 1964, 1967, 1972) and *Exchange and Production* (Wadsworth Publishing Co., 1969, 1977, 1983). This is a new volume, although it bears family resemblance to its predecessors. Like *Exchange and Production*, it is essentially price-and-allocation analysis, along with consideration of inflation and various references to the applicability of microeconomics to the aggregate economy and international implications. Above all, it continues the effort of the earlier volumes to present an exposition of economic analysis with persistent emphasis on empirical validity and meaningfulness. The original manuscript was prepared by Armen over the course of a decade, before deteriorating health ended further work, preventing a polished exposition. Now, belatedly, the draft has been completed, edited, and updated.

Bringing Armen's last project to fruition has required considerable and varied effort. It would not have been completed — if attempted, at all — without Jerry Jordan. Jerry was among a substantial flow of graduate students who were definitively influenced by Armen from the 1950s through the 1980s, and, like many of them, he has had a highly distinguished and conspicuous economics career. Along with prodigious work directly on the manuscript, he has been the chief coordinator of the variety of activities by several people involved in producing such a large publication.

Many scholars across the world, affiliated formally or informally with the UCLA Department of Economics in the Alchian era, have taken an interest in the publication and contributed to the project. Linda Kleiger, another of Alchian's students, has done much both as an administrator and a critic of content. Arline Alchian and Daniel Benjamin preserved the original manuscript and made it available to Jerry and me. Ben Zycher, Courtney Clifford Stone, Rachael Balbach, W. Lee Hoskins, Ken Clarkson, Zhaofeng Xue, and Kam-Ming Wan are among those who have provided guidance and encouragement. Michael Pistone aided greatly in preparing the diagrams and tables; Tsvetelin Tsonevski reformatted the entire manuscript. All who contributed to preparation of the manuscript are gratified that Liberty Fund has committed resources — most of all the time and talents of Laura Goetz, Senior Editor — and prestige to making available this final component of Armen's legacy.

Armen Alchian — a colleague, mentor, coauthor, and virtual older brother of mine — left us, at age ninety-eight, in February 2013.

William R. Allen

PART ONE

DEMAND, EXCHANGE, AND

PROPERTY RIGHTS

CHAPTER 1
WELCOME TO ECONOMICS

Since the discouraging fiasco in the Garden of Eden, all the world has been a place conspicuous in its scarcity of resources, contributing heavily to an abundance of various sorrows and sins. People have had to adjust and adapt to limitations of what is available to satisfy unlimited desires. Some individuals and societies have been much more successful than others in thus making do.

The study of economics deals with this yoke of scarcity and the modes of behavior intended to minimize the pains and maximize the gains of getting along—behavior which is restricted and channeled, sometimes helpfully and efficiently but often hurtfully and wastefully, by the social ground rules and institutions we adopt and have had imposed upon us.

To survive (much less to prosper a bit) in this vale of tears has required enormous, unrelenting effort. The vast variety of economic activity—bidding and offering in the market, producing and consuming currently, and saving and investing for the future—typically entails *coordinated* decision making and labor. But even seemingly simple operations of production and distribution can require contributions by many people, most of whom never meet or directly communicate with each other and are located in scattered corners of the world.

Consider this book. Thousands of people—in addition to the authors—contributed to placing this book in your hands. Some made paper; some made ink and glue; some edited the manuscript; some printed, warehoused, promoted, and distributed the product. No single person completely planned and supervised all that, and no one was a specialist in performing each of the myriad tasks. Yet, you have the book.

The essence of the story is not different for those who have escaped the surly bounds of conventional books to enter the era of e-books, iPads, Kindles, and Nooks. The more technically advanced modes of providing reading material still require elaborate collaboration of many producers. How are such complex, interrelated, varied activities by so many people in so many places organized? We will show how and why the modes of coordination in a basically private property, individualistic society have dominated all others in productivity, growth, and freedom.

This book will help you grasp and gain a working familiarity with, and appreciation for, the most basic, universal concepts, principles, and techniques of Economics. With experience, you will build a sense of and feel for fruitful economic analysis and its worldly applications.

SCARCITY

Motivating nearly all behavior is the inevitable existence of "scarcity"—simply put, our wants and desires exceed what is available to satisfy them. Most of what you enjoy is acquired by your efforts, accompanied by strain, sweat, and anxiety. However, no matter how successful are your efforts, you want even more.

Two apparent devils restrict what you can have—the limited amounts of goods and services available, and the rest of us who also want them. It is important to understand that scarcity does not exist because society produces the "wrong" things (e.g., beer, pop-jazz, TV games) instead of the "right" things (e.g., museums, symphony orchestras, art). Scarcity exists because of our boundless desires for limited goods of all kinds and types.

GOODS: ECONOMIC OR FREE

A "good," as that word is used in Economics, is *anything of which more is preferred to less*. "Goods" includes services as well as physical things—services of doctors, painters, carpenters, and athletes. Fresh chicken eggs are more plentiful than stale eggs. But fresh eggs are scarce; stale eggs are not. Fresh eggs are *economic* goods—goods for which more is desired than is available.

If a good, however desirable, is so abundant that no one wants more of it, it is a "free" good. Hereafter, the word "good" will always mean an "economic" (scarce) good. If we mean "free good," we'll write "free good." But examples are not easy to find. The classic case of a free good, to most of us most of the time, is air: we simply inhale, and there it is, without our sacrificing anything to obtain it. However, air is an economic good to the astronaut and the deep-sea diver, and so is fresh air to the city resident on a smoggy day.

Caution: "free good" does not mean something for which a zero price is charged, like "free education," "freeways," "free public parks," "free libraries," and "free beaches." Those "zero price" goods are scarce (economic) goods. Charging a zero price does not convert an economic good into a free good. As we will see, distributing goods for "free"—at a zero price—paradoxically makes their scarcity seem even greater.

Admittedly, the term "good" creates a psychological bias suggesting that the "good" is good ("beneficial"). In Economics, however, the word "goods" refers to whatever a person wants, no matter why. Maybe you think cigarettes are not "goods" and people would be better off without them. Nevertheless, as long as someone thinks they are desirable and wants more — that makes them "goods."

SELF-INTEREST?

Self-interest, as the concept is used in Economics, means you want more power to control resources, whether for your own or for someone else's benefit. Because we engage in market exchanges, without the intent of aiding other persons, some "philosophical critics" are misled into believing that economic principles presume people are purely and thoroughly selfish. That is incorrect. You often intentionally act in ways to benefit others. You act as a Good Samaritan in emergencies, even though that's costly to you.

More important, economic analysis shows how our market actions benefit other people, even if we are not deliberately trying to help them. Both parties to an exchange must anticipate a gain; otherwise there would be no markets and voluntarily negotiated exchanges of private property. Though we act primarily with our own benefits in mind, others are benefited by market exchanges.

Let Adam Smith, the eighteenth-century Scot, author of the first systematic and classic treatise on economics, *An Inquiry into the Nature and Causes of the Wealth of Nations*, explain the incentive and effect:

> Man has almost constant occasion for the help of his brethren, and it is in vain for him to expect it from their benevolence only. He will be more likely to prevail if he can interest their self-love in his favor, and show them that it is for their own advantage to do for him what he requires of them. . . . Give me that which I want, you shall have this which you want. . . . It is not from the benevolence of the butcher, the brewer, or the baker, that we expect our dinner, but from their regard of their own interest. We address ourselves not to their humanity but to their self-love, and never talk to them of our own necessities but of their advantages.

COMPETITION

Scarcity's inevitable companion is competition with other people for "more." According to a master competitor, the golfer Arnold Palmer, "If you aren't competing, you're dead." To which we add, "If you aren't dead, you must be competing." How? Consider a few ways to compete.

Violence

Violence is a commonly respected mode of competition. Alexander, Caesar, Napoleon, Eisenhower, Lenin, and Mao used it. They were highly respected. To be sure, had Caesar merely roughed up a few Romans, he would have been crucified. Had Lenin been defeated, he would have been liquidated on the spot.

If violence is attempted on a large enough (e.g., national) scale, the perpetrators are condemned only if they fail. The power of violence is the jealously guarded near-monopoly of a "government"—by definition of what a government is. "Near-monopoly" because, within a nation, it is often used by individuals in street demonstrations for access to political power. A government will suppress violence by individuals—except in the realm of contact sports.

A wealthy nation is more likely to be attacked—unless potential aggressors know it is willing and able to impose severe losses on the aggressor. The Iraqi government in 1991 attempted to confiscate wealth from Kuwait via invasion, but was rebuffed by the cooperation of other nations. Some years earlier, the poorer North Koreans attacked the South Koreans, but they also were rebuffed by the aid of richer countries that had taken the precaution to have sufficient defensive armor. In much earlier times, the Vikings, Mongols, and Tartars lived by raiding productive, but less defended, communities. Europeans invaded the South American and Southeastern Asiatic regions to expropriate wealth from the less-ably defended areas. Similar events have occurred throughout history.

Political Power

Governments help maintain security of person and property from violence and theft. In a democracy, that power is directed by political leaders elected by voters who are competing for access to government power for their greater protection as well as to redistribute wealth. When we complain about high government taxes or expenditures, we are commonly complaining about our neighbors whose interests conflict with ours.

Discrimination: Allocations by Authorities

Consider a college that has five thousand students and only two thousand parking spaces. On the assumption that most students desire a parking space, the college has a *rationing* problem: Who gets a parking space? A method of discriminating—to decide who gets spaces—is inevitable. Somehow, some people will get a space, and some will not. There are alternative ways to discriminate. All competition and choice is discriminatory. *Choice* is merely another name for *discrimination*—to rank alternatives according to some attribute. It is not discrimination that is condemned, but "invidious" discrimination — by whatever criteria enough people consider undesirable — such as religion, nationality, and gender.

First Come, First Served

The parking spaces could be allocated on a first come, first served basis. Though the money price would be zero, a competitive cost would be incurred in getting to the campus before dawn in an effort to get a space. Costs need not be in money payments. A zero price does not make something free.

Most Deserving?

The costly scramble to get a space could be avoided by prior assignment to the most "deserving" or "needy." The committee dispensing privileges would ask, "Who, other than professors, are the most deserving, most needy ones?" There is almost no limit to the ingenuity of dispensing committees in rationalizing their favors. Among the criteria may be: distance from campus, age, health, senior status, family size, major of student, grades, and so forth. But one question leads to another. For example, should those who are awarded rights to a parking space be allowed to sell the rights to others?

Jungle or Civilized Competition

You may have heard competition promotes antisocial, jungle-like, irresponsible behavior. That depends on the kind of competition that is tolerated. As we'll see, a society with reliable private property rights and readily available markets for exchange of those rights has proven to be conducive to greater production and civilized behavior than a society that condones violence or brute force in resolving differences of opinions about use of economic resources.

Competitive Cooperation by Exchanges

The primary focus of economic analysis is on (a) competition in exchange of rights to services and goods and (b) coordinated cooperation in creating wealth. Competition by offers of exchange is a form of cooperation. "I'll do this for you if you'll do that for me — at better terms than someone else." Though competing, we also cooperate — in the market, in the family, in firms, and in governments. We cooperate to make the "pie" larger; we compete over how much of the pie each of us gets. Any effective combination of cooperation and competition requires a control of the permissible types of competition so as to not obstruct social cohesion and cooperation.

Differences in amounts of wealth held by the richer and the poorer are not

all results of the rich being winners and the poor being losers in some con-
test for the distribution of a given total. A source of the differences in wealth
is difference in productivity and willingness to save for more wealth. But the
resulting pattern of relative wealth can be so concentrated in a few that the distribution is deliberately altered to attempt to maintain greater social stability.

OUR INTENT

We want your study of economics to be interesting and even enjoyable. But we
promise one unanticipated result: you'll be brainwashed — in the "desirable"
sense of removing erroneous beliefs. You will begin to suspect that a vast majority of what people popularly believe about economic events is at least misleading and often wrong. A few examples of such common errors are:

- price controls prevent higher costs to consumers;
- reducing unemployment necessarily requires creation of more jobs;
- larger incomes for some people require smaller incomes for others;
- free, or low, tuition reduces costs to students;
- all unemployment must be wasteful;
- stockbrokers and investment advisors predict better than the
  alternatives of throwing a dart at a list of stocks or the use of
  horoscopes;
- taxes are borne entirely by consumers of taxed items;
- employers pay for "employer-provided insurance";
- minimum wage legislation helps the unskilled and minorities;
- housing developers drive up the price of land;
- foreign imports reduce the total of domestic jobs;
- "equal pay for equal work" laws aid women, minorities, and the young;
- economic efficiency is a matter only of technology and engineering;
- agricultural and other surpluses stem from productivity outrunning
  demand;
- capitalism requires a social "harmony of interests"—but also
  capitalism is the source of competitiveness and conflict;
- property rights commonly conflict with human rights;
- business people are self-centered and rapacious, while government
  people are self-sacrificing and altruistic;
- labor unions protect the natural brotherhood and collective well-being
  of workers against their natural enemies, employers;
- charging a higher price always increases the seller's profits;
- the American economy is increasingly dominated by monopolists who
  arbitrarily set prices as high and wages as low as they please;

- rent control improves and expands housing;
- there is unemployment because workers outnumber jobs;
- fluctuating prices create wasteful uncertainty and rising prices constitute inflation, so government should make it illegal to raise prices;
- we cannot compete in a world in which most foreign wages are lower than wages paid to domestic workers;

and on and on and on.

Fortunately, societies have progressed despite almost universal ignorance of economic principles. Without an abundance of sophisticated economic analysts, the US economy, over more than two centuries, has generally performed very well, yielding a growth and prosperity that is embarrassingly conspicuous in world history.

The collapse of the socialist Soviet Union and the rise of China and India in world markets was not the result of their sudden awareness of their ignorance of economic principles. Instead, their disappointing economic experiences—in sharp contrast to the economic performance of other nations—showed that the lack of understanding of basic economic principles ultimately creates weaknesses, and motivated their social and market changes accordingly.

SEQUENCE OF EXPOSITION AND
UNSOLICITED ADVICE FOR STUDY

This text starts with the simplest principles and applies them to explain the meaning of the gains from trade and how these gains occur. It may seem silly to develop a method of analysis to explain what's so obvious—that people gain from trade. However, looking at a simple action permits an easy exposition of the very important principles of "demand" and their meaning—without distractions by side details of more complex activities. Also, the initial familiarization with graphs for applications of these principles will ease the later study of more complex events that are far less commonly understood. These results will often be surprising and counterintuitive.

To anticipate briefly, the first thirteen chapters explain and apply the concepts of "property rights," "efficiency," "cost," "marginals," "equalization of marginals to avoid waste," and the principles of personal choice and behavior, which determine the prices and allocation of existing goods. Chapters 14 through 29 introduce the principles of production, specialization, teams, and firms; decision making within organizations is viewed from the perspective of economic analysis. Market pricing tactics of different types of firms in alternative competitive situations are explored. Chapters 30 through 38 extend the exposition and application of financial capital value principles and adaptations to economic risk and wealth creation. Chapters 39 through 41 address issues that arise in labor markets, including search costs in seeking highest-valued employment opportunities. Chapter 42 addresses issues of money, inflation, and their effects on prices.

Economics really is easy — in a subtle sort of way. Rely on application of its analytic principles. Sometimes they supersede dictates of physics. The law of gravity says, "*If you drop a $20 bill on the ground, it will stay there.*" Economics says, "*If you drop a $20 bill on the ground, it will quickly disappear.*"

QUESTIONS AND MEDITATIONS

1) A once popular book states (in essence): "We are trapped by the 'dismal science' — economics, which is dominated by the belief that the achievement of abundance is impossible and that the economic problem is still the distribution of scarce resources. This is nonsense. Abundance has arrived! The United States can produce so much that the basic problems are to see that the potential production is realized and distributed fairly and equitably." Are you inclined to agree or disagree?

Answer:

You are not expected to be able to answer this now. But upon finishing this course, you should be able to show why the concluding sentences are wrong. As for the first sentence, economic science has not trapped us — scarcity has.

2) "If people were reasonable and acted with justice and good faith, there would be no strikes, no economic problems, and no wars." Do you agree?

Answer:

False. It is because people are reasonable and, therefore, act in accord with their own interest that there are economic problems and wars.

3) "A more equal distribution of wealth is socially preferred to a less equal distribution."
    Explain why you agree or disagree.
    What is meant by "socially preferred," as contrasted to "individually preferred"?

Answer:

Until you know what socially preferred means, you cannot answer this question. We do not know what socially preferred means. For example, does it mean that a majority prefer it, or that the most important people prefer it, or that the current rulers of a nation happen to prefer it, or that "everyone" prefers it, or that the speaker thinks everyone *should* prefer it, or that merely the speaker prefers it? Beware of any expression referring to the preference of a group.

4) What do you think is meant by a fair share? Do you think other people will agree with your interpretation? How does your interpretation compare with the idea of students getting "fair" grades?

Answer:

Fair does not mean equal, and even if some asserted that it "should," there is the problem of equal absolute versus equal proportional. It is often hard to know what people mean by equal. Would *fair grades* mean that there should be a minimum grade such as C–? Studies have shown that students who get better grades tend to lead more prosperous lives; but it would be absurd to assert that mandating minimum grades would cause students to be more successful.

5) "Scarcity, competition, and discrimination are inextricably tied together. Any one implies the other two. Furthermore, to think of a society without these is to be a romantic dreamer." Do you agree?

Answer:

Choice of one thing versus another occurs because there is scarcity; competition and discrimination occur even in an imaginary world of no money, no prices, and no markets. As we will see, suppression of market-determined prices of goods and services gives rise to nonmoney forms of competition and discrimination.

6) Name three honored statesmen who obtained their status by successfully competing in the ability to use violence and who, had they failed, would have been punished for treason or crimes against mankind.

Answer:

William the Conqueror, Julius Caesar, Napoleon Bonaparte. You can add scores of others. (Hint: George Washington and every other leader of a successful revolution.)

7) Permissible competition:
What kind of competition is permissible in seeking political office but is not permissible in private business?
What kinds of competition are permissible in seeking admission to college but not permissible for grades in this course?

What kinds of competition are approved for business but not for admission to fraternities?

Answer:

Promises to raise or lower taxes (affect other people's wealth) in order to benefit those who vote for you. But the politician can't (legally) offer to sell services as a businessman can.

Will letters of recommendation help you get a better grade in this course? Does your past record influence the teacher of this course in making grades? Does wealth of parents?

Employees can offer to work for a lower salary to get a job with a favored employer in a preferred town. Will this work in fraternities? How about a candidate's ability to increase the wealth of the fraternity?

8) "Government monopolizes coercive violence." "Government is a social agency for resolving interpersonal conflict."
   Are those two propositions correct and compatible statements of fact?
   What evidence can you cite for your answer?

Answer:

Yes. Until very recently, we know of no institution with the dominant power of coercive violence that is not the government in any country. Government is an institution for enforcing certain rules and procedures for resolving interpersonal conflicts of interest. The making and enforcement of laws and the judicial settlement of disputes are behaviors that support the propositions. (Note that the second statement says government is *an* agency, not the *only* agency. For example, many social disputes are resolved by social ostracism and by agreement to use an arbitrator.)

9) Illegal competition:
   If you had the power to decide, what forms of competition would you declare illegal?
   What forms of competition are made illegal by laws establishing price ceilings, minimum wages, fair-employment practices, pure food and drug standards, private property rights, and by socialism?

Answer:

You should first want to know the behavioral consequence of each kind. More than that we can't yet say.

The only kind of competition made illegal by a price ceiling is that of offering more money than the legal limit as means of offsetting weaknesses in other attributes in competing for goods. Fair-employment laws (prohibiting choice of employees by race, color, creed, or age) prohibit competition in terms of personal attributes. Pure food and drug laws prohibit offers of inferior food at lower prices or of new and possibly better but untested (by government) foods and drugs. Private property rights prohibit competition by violence and involuntary dispossession of goods deemed to be private property. Socialism prohibits competition in terms of offers of types of services and goods that individuals privately prefer, without having to obtain authorization of government officials for propriety of producing the services. These are merely examples of types of competition that are ruled out—not a complete chronicle and certainly not an evaluation of the desirability of the various types.

10) Competition for admission to colleges uses mental ability, athletic ability, good looks, residence, willingness to pay, alumni status of parents, race, sex, and religious belief. Why?

Answer:

Greater use of factors other than willingness to pay is enabled by the fact that most colleges are not privately owned.

11) On the average, who do you think are most honest—politicians, businessmen, or teachers? Why? What is your evidence? Can you think of any reasons why dishonesty would be more surely detected and punished in one of these professions? If successful, would dishonesty be more rewarding in one rather than the others?

Answer:

A predisposition to tell the truth is essential to the long-run viability of a free and democratic society that relies on private property and market-determined prices to allocate scarce resources. A shocking reality of the Soviet Union of the twentieth century was that generations of people learned that it was important to be good at lying—not only to the government, but also to close friends and even one's family.

12) "Under socialism, cooperation will replace competition."
Is the quoted proposition correct?
What evidence can you cite to support your answer?
What is the difference between cooperation and competition?

Answer:

Since scarcity is present in socialism, as in capitalism, competition for control of resources is inescapable. In socialism more is in the form of political avenues of competition (persuasion, favors, personal connections). Competition is the interpersonal striving for more of what is scarce and desired — for production, by purchase, by striving for political power, and so on. Cooperation is a joint activity with mutual striving for a common end.

13) Food is grown, harvested, sorted, processed, packed, transported, assembled in appropriately small bundles, and offered to consumers every day by individuals pursuing personal interests. No authority is responsible for seeing that these functions are performed and that the right amount of food is produced. Yet food is available every day. On the other hand, especially appointed authorities are responsible for seeing that such things as water, education, and electricity are made available. Is it not paradoxical that in the very areas where we consciously plan and control social output, we often find shortages and failure of service? References to classroom shortages and water shortages are rife; but who has heard of a shortage of restaurants, churches, furniture, beer, shoes, or paper? Even further, is it not surprising that privately owned businesses, operating for the private gain of the owners, provide as good, if not better, service to patrons and customers as do the post office, schools, and other publicly owned enterprises? Furthermore, wouldn't you expect public agencies to be less discriminating according to race and creed rather than privately owned business? Yet the fact is that they are not. How do you explain these paradoxes?

Answer:

They will be explained in the course of study. The query is intended to whet your interest in what is coming.

CHAPTER 2
YOUR ECONOMIC SOCIETY

The United States is not the largest country in the world in either number of inhabitants or land area, but its enormous and complex economy produces more annual output than does the economy of any other country. However, reciting a collection of various economic measurements is not analytically very useful, especially when the measurements persistently change over time. Neither would it be highly helpful to tell a first-time viewer of a football game only how many players are on a team, the size of the field, and the typical scores. Without knowing the rules and something about the competitive tactics and strategies, the viewer would be bored or totally confused. The same risk faces you in learning about the competitive game, the "economy." A first step in comprehension is awareness of the rule: private property.

RIGHTS AND PROPERTY RIGHTS

You live in a largely private property society. Whether or not it is in any sense the best type of society is not our question here. We do know that it has evolved and dominated in competition against others. Though most economic resources in the United States are privately owned and managed, some, such as large acreages of land and sophisticated and massive military equipment, are held as government property. Also, while about 80 percent of national income is earned in the private sector, government purchases of goods and services (for example, fire, police, defense, judiciary, education, roads, sanitation) account for the critical other 20 percent.

In every society, each person has various kinds of "rights." A "right" is a person's *socially recognized and supported* authority to do certain things. The community at large will protect you from anyone who tries to interfere. If people saw someone trying to steal your car — violate your right to it — they would usually call the police or alert other bystanders to forestall that attempt. Your property right to the car rests on the willingness and ability of other people, not your ability alone, to protect your control over that resource — your property. But though you may have physical legal possession of an automobile, you don't thereby have an inherent "right" to it. In a pride of lions, the male by dint of sheer physical prowess takes first choice of feeding on prey. That's not what a *right* means here. A right is lacking because lions don't enforce rights of other lions. Instead, there is cowed tolerance of dominant lions.

GOVERNMENT PURCHASES VERSUS
GOVERNMENT EXPENDITURES

How much does the government spend? In the National Income Accounts — which measure the total output or product of an economy — the US government accounts for about 20 percent of everything produced. That is, the Gross Domestic Product (GDP) includes purchases of goods and services by the government along with the consumption spending of households and investment spending of business. Such government spending includes ships for the navy and the salaries of all the employees of the government.

Another measure, government expenditures — everything in the government's budget — includes all such government purchases and much more. Interest payments on the trillions of dollars of government debt are an expense of government, but show up in the national income accounts as interest income earned by the bondholders. Government also makes transfer payments for Social Security, Medicare, Medicaid, food stamps, unemployment insurance, and housing vouchers. Such transfer payments do not directly contribute to the output of the economy, so are not included in the government component of GDP. Instead, the people and businesses that receive transfer payments from government will either spend or save — just as they would earned income from wages and dividends — so GDP components such as consumer spending and private investment are larger as a result of such transfers.

That does not mean the economy is larger or the people are richer because of such transfer payments. Those payments have to be financed either by taxes collected from households and businesses — thereby reducing private consumption and investment spending — or by the issuance of additional government debt — which also reduces household and business spending.

The government expenditure concept that includes transfer payments rose to 30 percent of GDP over thirty years ago and then in the great recession of 2007–2009 shot up to over 35 percent of GDP. The result has been that a large and growing share of the spending by households for consumption and some of the spending by businesses for investment are paid for by transfers from taxpayers or by debt issuance by government.

Donald Marron, Musings on Economics, Finance, and Life, July 2012, "Has Government Gotten Bigger or Smaller? Yes," http://dmarron.com/2012/07/.

Your rights determine your status and potential welfare and your "freedoms"—what the rest of society will let you do. To understand your economy and society, you must know the "rules of the game." The "rights" are part of the rules. In playing a game, the rules are the rights defining actions a player can choose. If you don't know who has what rights, you won't understand behavior in a society.

Comparing socialist and capitalistic nations without knowing the different rights people have to economic goods would suggest that the nature of people differs in the two societies. In their underlying natures, people are everywhere much the same, but in different societies they may act within very different contexts and restraints and incentives—the ground rules differ. That's why we start with a statement of some of the property rights that dominate in a private property nation—often called "capitalistic."

PRIVATE PROPERTY RIGHTS

Private property rights contain three key features: (1) the right to make decisions about the *physical*[1] conditions and uses of *specified* goods, (2) the right to sell the rights of ownership to other people, and (3) the right to enjoy the resulting income and to bear the loss of the use decision. These are exclusive rights; they all belong to the same person. These three elements together constitute the essence of private property rights. If any of the three is missing, private property rights are not present.

Private property rights restrain you from interfering with other peoples' rights. The physical attributes or yields of all resources owned by other persons must not be affected. If you own private property rights to something, you, and only you, may choose its future use and physical condition, or transfer that right to a willing recipient. No other person has a right to alter its *physical* features or uses of the good to which you have the private property right. We refer to "private property *rights*." If you sell something, according to the law, that is interpreted as being a sale of private property *rights*, not the thing itself. Even if the good itself can't be moved, as a tract of land, the rights are transferable to others. Don't be misled by statements that private property rights put rights of property over rights of people. Private property rights are rights of *people* over uses of goods they own.

---

1. The use of the adjective "physical" here should not be confused with "tangible" versus "intangible." The uses and control over "intangible private property" can be physically controlled—that is, others can be constrained from use without permission.

Avoid another confusion. In economics, we are concerned about *constitutionally protected rights*. This is different from some people's claims to rights to education, health care, housing, a good job, and so forth. Such claims would amount to other people being *forced* to provide something that I want. No such constitutional rights exist. Constitutional scholars make a distinction between "negative rights," which limit what governments can do, versus the notion of "positive rights," which would require government actions to benefit some people at the expense of other people.

Physical Attributes, Not Market Values

Private property rights protect your property from *physical*[2] effects caused by other people. I can't legally use my hammer to break your windows. But you are not protected from *market-value* effects caused by a reduced demand for your property. If I build an apartment building and increase the supply of apartments enough to reduce the rental value of your apartment, that's legal. Or if this textbook reduces the sales of a competitor's book, that's legal. It doesn't reduce the offers the competitors can make to potential customers. Nor does it reduce competitors' physical productive potential.

Beware of Presumed Clarity and Definiteness of Private Property Rights

The distinction between physical effects and market-value effects seems clear—at first thought. But consider the following situation. From your land, you have a beautiful view over land owned by someone else who proposes to erect a building obstructing your sight. Would the physical attributes of your land be affected? Yes and no—depending on what is meant by the physical attributes of your land. Physical features might not be interpreted to include the "light rays" reflected onto your land. Usually, but not always, they are excluded from your private property rights. Your neighbor can block your view without violating your private property rights. The moral is: When buying private property rights to something, first identify what the rights include and what is excluded. The less that is included, the lower the market value will be.

Alienability of Private Property Rights

Another essential feature of private property rights is "transferability," often called "alienability." That's the right to sell your rights. And that makes you pay attention to potential market value of what you own. The way you use your

---

2. To repeat, this applies to intangible property. Without my permission, you may not sing (professionally, for money) a song I wrote and copyrighted.

car or house will affect their market values. If you have the right to resell this textbook, you'll take better care of it than if you have no right to sell it. This salability of rights to the resource is a fundamental difference between private property rights and all other forms of property rights over resources.

In England, until about one hundred years ago, major land holdings were not "alienable." They passed from parent to child. All the "owner-occupant" could do was live on it or enjoy its income if rented to someone else. In China, publicly traded companies issue shares of "ownership" that are not resalable without government approval. In Switzerland, until a couple of decades ago, shares in many publicly traded corporations could not be sold to other people unless the buyer was approved by the corporate directors.

Private property rights are transferable to any person *willing to accept it or share in it.* You bear that right until someone else is willing to accept it. You can't just revoke your right and abandon all future responsibility for its subsequent condition. Once you acquire a private property right to some good, you either must transfer it to some other willing recipient or bear it until death. At that inevitable time, without a willing designated recipient (inheritor), the government takes the right.

At your college, if not a privately owned institution, no one has a private property right to the marketable value of the college's resources. Because the administrators are thereby more insulated from changes in market values of the resources, they use those resources less in accord with their highest market-valued uses. This does not mean that private property rights are necessarily always better. There are reasons for not having private property rights in some institutions, such as "not-for-profit" hospitals, colleges, museums, fraternities, and sororities—and we'll see later some of these reasons.

Torts

We note another kind of "property right." A taking or using of another person's property in an emergency is called a "tort." Because this occurs commonly, there is a whole body of law about "torts." In a sudden storm on a lake, if you berth your boat at my dock to save your life (without prior negotiation for my permission), have my "rights" been violated? Or, if you could have attracted my attention and asked for the right to use my dock, could I extract from you a promise to all your wealth to save your life? A more common example of a tort occurs when you berth your boat on my dock (with or without my permission), but because of some *proven* negligence on my part your boat is damaged or you are injured. In such cases, courts may force me to compensate you.

THE RULE AGAINST PERPETUITIES

An important restriction on the scope of private property rights is contained in the *Rule against Perpetuities*. That rule restricts your control of the future uses of what you own now. You might in your will try to restrict the future uses of your enormous wealth, perhaps leaving a parcel of land to a foundation as a permanent refuge for deer.

However, a reason for the ban on your unlimited future control is that it reduces the influence of future market values on the way that resource will then be used. The "dead hand of the past" is not allowed to overrule the "invisible hand" of future generations' market values. The rule against perpetuities permits restrictions on use and salability of resources for only about twenty-one years after the death of persons who were alive at the time of the death of the donor. If that rule were not enforced, resources today would still be used in ways they were generations ago — a potentially unattractive result.

CAPITALIST OR SOCIALIST

A major difference between societies is not whether property rights do or do not exist, but is instead the *extent* to which they apply. Even in formerly communist Russia, private property rights were not totally absent. People owned and could buy and sell furniture and automobiles, as well as vegetables grown in their gardens. However, almost all productive resources — those used to produce goods and services for other people — were "owned" by the government.

An economy with extensive private property rights over most resources is usually called a "capitalist" economy. With salable resources, the anticipated future consequences of present uses of resources are "capitalized" into current market values of the resources, as we'll be examining. Explaining what those capitalized market values reflect, and how they influence our behavior and uses of resources, is one of the basic achievements of economic analysis.

To incorporate anticipation into present values requires establishing and maintaining consistency of actions among the populace. That has to be done in an economy in which decisions and adjustments are independent in the sense that each person makes choices without requiring permission from someone else. Yet, the decisions are *dependent* in that they depend on what other people are expected to do. In a market economy — with restrictive private property rules of the game — individuals make risky decisions and bear the consequences of their decisions.

We have separated the particular "system" from universal "economic principles," because these principles apply to any economic system. They reflect characteristics of individuals' preferences and productive abilities that are found everywhere. We refer to "demand" to identify universal features of people's preferences among types and quantities of goods. We use "supply" to identify the abilities to produce goods and services that are common to all economies. We will start in the next chapter by looking at demand for various amounts and types of goods, assuming initially they already have been produced.

ALERT! FREE SPEECH IS NOT "FREE RESOURCES"

"Economically Free" and "Politically Free" have different meanings. Your private property rights to your land prevent me from encroaching to pitch a tent or dump garbage or hold a meeting without your permission. I would be violating your private property rights to your land. Similarly, if, without prior permission, I took your loudspeaker to talk to people, I would be violating your private property rights to the loudspeaker. I do have a right to free speech, but that does not mean I have a right to take your loudspeaker or land to communicate with others even if they would be willing listeners.

A right of free speech is not an "economically free" right. It uses scarce resources. "Free speech" means the right to communicate with *your own* resources to other *willing* listeners — without political intervention about what you say. I can't force you to hear or read my "speech" any more than I can force you to give me your wealth. I can't take property of others to communicate, nor can I regard the attention of other people as "free" to me. I must use my own, or rented, resources to communicate, and then only to willing persons. Both these critical features, (1) use of one's owned or rented resources by the speaker and (2) a willing listener, are often ignored.

This kind of confusion of "free speech" with a "free right" to use resources, as if they become "free" when the resources are to be used for speech, has confounded many judges and lawmakers and college administrators. Someone sends unwanted email to your computer. You are an unwilling recipient. Both required conditions of free speech are violated. Your computer is being used without your permission, and you are not a willing recipient of the messages. The right of free speech is neither a right to "free" access to resources of other people nor a right to "unwilling listeners."

EFFICIENCY AND THE "CONSTRAINED MAXIMUM" CONCEPT

Within the private property "rules of the game," a person can use resources under his control to produce other assets. An efficiently produced amount of some good is a "constrained maximum" of that good. More of a specified good requires reduced production of some other goods.

The necessity of that trade-off is represented by the production possibility boundary (PPB), as shown in figure 2.1.

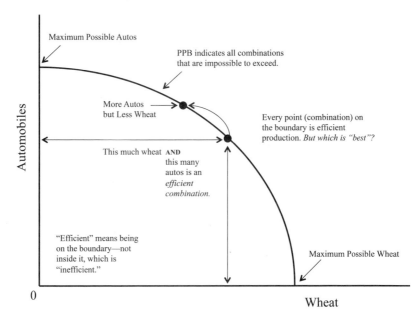

Figure 2.1 *Meaning of "Efficiency" Contrasted to "Maximizing"*

The production possibility boundary (PPB) curve, also called the production possibility curve (PPC), shows the meaning of "efficient" or "efficiency." Think of automobiles and wheat as the only possible alternative goods. The curved boundary line indicates, vertically, the maximum amount of autos that can be produced, given that a specified amount of wheat, measured on the horizontal scale, is to be produced also. Every point on the PPB represents a combination of annual amounts of automobiles produced, measured on the vertical axis, and annual amounts of wheat, measured on the horizontal axis. All points below (inside) the curve represent wasteful, inefficient situations, because more of both autos and wheat could be produced. All points on the curve represent efficient combinations of autos and wheat — meaning you can't then have more of one without less of the other.

The end points (at the vertical scale and at the horizontal scale) are measures of the maximum amounts of a good when only that one good is produced. The negative (downward) slope of the boundary curve represents the fact that more of one good means less of other goods. Moving on the boundary line upward to the left means more of the vertically measured good is produced, but with a necessary reduction in the production of the other good. The boundary line represents all the efficient points — no waste — with the maximum amounts of one good along with minimum necessary reductions in production of other goods. All points on the PPB can be called "cost efficient."

Sometimes some equipment, say a refrigerator, is called "electricity efficient," meaning merely that the refrigerator was constructed so as to use less electricity than some other refrigerator. But the "electricity energy-efficient refrigerator" costs more to produce. Whether the saving in electricity is worth more than the increased cost of production of the refrigerator is the pertinent question, not the fact that less electricity is used.

Again, the concept of "efficient" is different from the concept of an unconstrained, or "unconditional," maximum. More housing could be produced if we didn't care about anything else. That would be maximum housing, with nothing else. We'd all starve in nice homes. Similarly, a maximum of clean air would mean no production of anything that "dirtied" the air. We'd all starve while breathing perfectly clean air. Clearly, we want more than just one good. We want combinations of goods. But more of one means less of others, if we are efficient.

With investment, such as new equipment, buildings, and production techniques, the PPB is expanded outward, in one or more dimensions, though only two are shown in figure 2.1. But the PPB reminds us that at any given moment the production potential is limited.

Is Efficiency Desirable?

"Efficient and inefficient" suggests that it's "bad" or "undesirable" to be inefficient, because more of some goods or desirable things could otherwise be obtained without reduction of the presently available amount of other goods. However, if some of the alternatives are "good" in one person's opinion while being "bad" in another's preferences, disputes will arise. You'll be told you're considering the wrong alternatives, and therefore the efficiency for your set of possible goods is irrelevant. People differ in their preferences and evaluations. You want cleaner air even at the cost of less driving. I want more driving even at the cost of less clean air. Both of us want efficiency with respect to our preferred mixtures. Therefore, "efficiency" is not a basis for choosing among alternative "efficient" combinations.

Incomplete Span of "Components" for Efficiency!

A new refrigerator may be labeled "energy efficient" and uses less energy than required in the old model, but at the cost of having to use a more expensive motor and more expensive insulation. Does efficiency mean the least possible amount of energy is used — regardless of cost of other materials? Reducing the amount of one component, while having to increase the costs of other components even more, is not "cost efficient."

Every point on the production boundary curve is efficient; all points inside the boundary are "inefficient." But which of all the points on the boundary — all the efficient points — is most desirable has not been answered. Furthermore, the location (higher or lower) of the boundary curve depends on the reliability of laws and contracts, government policies, taxes, security of property, work ethic, entrepreneurship, education, access to markets, mobility of resources — a lot more than just the number of people and quantity of physical resources. Those other factors are major features that economic principles help us understand.

We now prepare to learn economic principles and how to use them reliably to understand events in the economy. The set of principles we'll explain is "economic theory." But don't let the label, "theory," mislead you into supposing that it's all "theoretical" and "abstract" rather than practical. There's a difference between theoretical and theory. "Theoretical" suggests it's debatable, conjectural, unproven, and thus not reliable. In fact, the economic principles that form economic theory are very powerful, proven, and reliable.

MEANING OF A "THEORY"

In scientific analysis and interpretation of an event, theory means a set of principles, or propositions, which, when logically used, will guide us to state correctly what will be the consequences of some initial action — a set of concepts and relationships that enables us to deduce what action will lead to what result.

Principles form a "science" if people can deduce from those principles consequences as a result of specified initial events. If those implied consequences happen reliably, that set of principles is a "science." The theory of physics tells us features of the swing of a golf club that reliably will make the ball go straight. That's true no matter who is the player. The theory is reliable, even if the players are not reliable in their performance.

ECONOMIC ANALYSIS IS POSITIVE, NOT NORMATIVE

Economic principles form a "positive," not a "normative," set. It's an "If this, then that" form of analysis. It helps to understand or deduce consequences. It contains NO basis for deciding what is ultimately "good" or "bad," commendable or condemnable.

Principles of chemistry explain what happens if you add iron filings into sulfuric acid, or if you toss a match into a pile of paper, but it does not tell whether you should add the filings or toss the match. Physics does not imply carbon is better than lithium, or that heavier elements are better than lighter.

Economics does not tell us (imply) that governments should be smaller rather than larger, or that taxes should be lower or higher. Economics can foretell some of the consequences of a law or event, and you can then decide for yourself whether the prior action is desirable. Whether some event or consequence is *good* or *bad* is NOT implied, indicated, or deducible solely from economic theory.

INCREASED OR REDUCED PROBABILITY
AND REFUTABLE IMPLICATIONS

To say something "may" or "might" or "could" happen is empty, useless, irrefutable — and worthless! "Could, may, or might" statements permit anything — not what will or will not happen. The world's entire population may suddenly change their behavior and act like angels. You may, might, or could become the world's greatest violinist.

A useful statement indicates (a) what will or will not happen, or b) a probability of the event, or c) what raises, or lowers, the probability. Economic analysis implies that price controls increase the probability of shortages and discrimination by gender, ethnicity, and religion. The collected evidence supports that implication. Since nothing in the world is certain, except probably death and taxes, you should think in terms of increased or lowered probabilities. For brevity, we'll often say that the implied consequence "will" occur. But in life virtually everything is probabilistic.

REPORTED VERSUS VERIFIED EVENT

A research "result" is announced in the news. Later, someone reexamines the data to see how, and how reliably, it was collected and what significant features, if any, were omitted. But by then, if the initial results were misinterpreted, the first wrong impression is hard to remove. Whether in medicine, physics, nutrition, or economics, be careful in placing heavy reliance on first reports.

TRANSIENT LUCKY EVENT VERSUS BASIC DIFFERENCE:
THE UBIQUITOUS REGRESSION EFFECT

Compounding the doubts about unusual events is the "regression effect," which states that there is a higher probability of good luck to be followed by just "normal" luck, than by continued good luck. Of one hundred identical salespeople, some would, by good luck, have higher sales than others in any one week. But in the next week those who were unusually lucky in the first week would more likely get fewer sales, nearer their long-run averages. Similarly, those with very bad luck the first week would not have such bad luck the next week, so in the second week their sales would improve. The very lucky as well as the very unlucky in the first week tend to "regress" toward their longer-run average.

This universal tendency to regress toward the long-run average is the regression effect. One of the classic ways of taking advantage of this effect is to invite people to take some performance test—say a reading test—and to tell those who score below average to take lessons in "reading improvement." After the lessons (which could be nothing more than taking ten deep breaths or blinking their eyes three times) their test performance will on average improve, because their unusually low performance on the first test was at least in part due to unusually bad (nonrepetitive) luck.

ECONOMICS VERSUS ECONOMISTS

What economics says is not always what economists say. An economist (one capable of applying economic analysis logically) may express personal preferences, recommendations, and advice, such as, "Invest more, reduce the size of government, reduce tariffs, and buy this stock." But those normative, prescriptive statements are hardly more reliable or authoritative than if uttered by anyone else. What the economist can do with economic analysis is to deduce some of the consequences of a proposed act, presumably more accurately than a noneconomist. But definitely to assess and appraise whether the consequences of the action are good or bad is, to the economist, forbidden fruit. Yet, like Adam, many economists eat of it.

WHICH ECONOMIC THEORY?

The principles of economics, which form "economic theory," are intended to be reliable, useful guides to understanding economic events. Don't make the intellectual mistake of asking whether the theory (the set of principles) is "true." No theory is perfect. Ask instead, "Is it useful and reliable enough for my purposes? That is, will it lead to generally correct implications and guidance at sufficiently low cost without intolerable error?" That's the question to ask in every discipline, whether Chemistry, Physics, Biology, or Economics.

Every theory is wrong and incomplete with respect to some things—just as with maps. Maps of the same area differ in accord with the purpose of the user. No map, and likewise no theory, is a literally correct representation of every detail. Your useful road map doesn't show all the bumps, traffic signs, overpasses, degrees of traffic congestion to be expected, and so forth. There is a variety of maps, each appropriate for a different purpose—some for travel by car, airplane, or boat, some for surveying land and rivers, and some for building roads. Nevertheless, though the variety differs, all of the maps must be consistent with each other in certain fundamental respects. No valid map of the United States would show the Mississippi River emptying into the San Francisco Bay, though useful maps will differ in the degree of details.

There is not one economic theory for capitalism and another for socialism and another for some other form of economy. The situation parallels biology. The same biological principles hold no matter where animals and people live. In every society, the basic principles of human behavior are the same.

ECONOMICS AND BIOLOGY

Economics is part of "biology"—the study of life. "Economics" concentrates on the activities that are dominant in the "market" for the production and distribution of desired goods and services. Other actions, such as the social activities within the family and in social groups, or in governments, are studied in sociology and political science—although economics increasingly is being used to explain these actions as well.

THE BASIC UNIT OF ANALYSIS IS THE
INDIVIDUAL, NOT A GROUP

Economics assumes that choices are made by individuals, not by a group, family, business, or government. We don't inquire about why some "firm" or "union" or "government" does something. Always, it is some *person* who is doing something. That's why we'll always look at the choices individuals make, whether when isolated or in organizations. However, this does not mean people make choices with only their own narrow interests in mind. Effects on other people are not excluded from a person's interests. But our focus is on an individual's chosen action.

QUESTIONS AND MEDITATIONS

1) What does "equality of opportunity" mean? How could you determine whether it exists? What is the difference between increasing opportunity and equalizing it?

Answer:

We don't know. It depends upon your point of view and what you think is "equal" or "fair." Does it mean starting with the same amount? Then what about the differences in people's natural abilities or ability to learn? Does it mean ending with the same amount? What if people value the same amount differently? Economics doesn't answer subjective issues. The purpose of this question is to make you aware of the ambiguities in such questions.

2) When you purchase a car, what is it that you are actually buying?

Answer:

> You are purchasing the rights to exclusive use of that car provided you do not violate the rights of others to use their resources. By "owning" the car you also possess the rights to transfer (sell) the exclusive rights of usage to another person, something you cannot do if the car is rented, leased, or "owned" by the community.

3) "The free-enterprise, capitalist system is free in that it involves no imposition of force or compulsion." Do you agree? Explain your answer.

Answer:

> All societies use force and compulsion. The pertinent issue is: What kinds of coercion and force do various economic, political, and social systems use? The capitalist system uses the force of self-interest; it is impersonal in its market effects. The effects of decisions are borne by the owner of a resource. Someone who produces at a loss bears the effect and is forced out of business into some other task, perhaps with less compassion than under a socialist dictator, who might spread the loss to other people instead of concentrating the effect on one person, the owner.
>
> More sensible than the question of which system uses less force is the question of what effects the various kinds of forces (incentives, rewards, signals, orders, and penalties) have on individuals' economic, cultural, and political behavior. For example, how does the economic system affect freedom of speech, job mobility, social fluidity, individual dignity, worship, search for the truth, and so on? The effects on all the various goals of a person must be considered. Not even reference to the use of the rule of law versus the rule of arbitrary dictators is a basis for ultimate judgment. Here too, the question is: What law and what rules will be enforced? Will it be the rule of private property rights, the rule of socialism, or some other?

4) "The free-enterprise, capitalist system is good because it gives individuals more opportunity or freedom to choose for themselves than other systems." Do you agree? Why?

Answer:

> Economics cannot make value judgments and answer the question of what is "good." Differences are implied about the kinds of opportunities or "freedoms" provided to individuals living under each system. The implications are that a free-enterprise, market economy gives individuals a

greater range of consumption patterns or goods from which to choose. Whether it is "good" that individuals should have such a range of options to explore is a question that economic theory cannot answer. A greater range of choice can be regarded as a greater range of temptation, risk, error, regret, and deviant behavior. Just as parents restrain children's choices for their own good, we may prefer to restrain the choices of adults because everyone retains some childlike impulses. Whether you wish to regard one system or the other as giving more freedom depends upon your meaning of "freedom." In one sense, freedom can include protection from the costs of temptation and unfortunate choices; in another sense, freedom might include the right to bear those costs and to make those choices and explore tempting alternatives. The implications derived from economic theory about the factual consequences of different systems will be helpful in forming a judgment.

5) "The college football team has a goal."
   a. Is it the social goal of the "team," or is it the common individual goal of each member of the team?
   b. Are you sure that each member has only that goal?
   c. Is it helpful to talk of one goal being preferred over another?

Answer:
   a. Each team member has a goal. In analyzing problems look at the individual. Individuals make decisions, not entities such as "teams, firms, governments."
   b. We're not sure; some members may have more goals.
   c. No. It's a matter of fulfilling some of one goal and some of the next.

6) In trying to understand some policy enforced at your college, why may it be misleading to ask why the college adopts that policy?

Answer:
   Individuals, not abstract things called "colleges," make decisions.

7) If you don't smoke, is tobacco a good? Are purchase and sale necessary for something to be considered a good?

Answer:
   Although you do not smoke, there are others who want more tobacco products than are available at a zero price. They are willing to trade some amount of other goods to acquire a given amount of tobacco. Tobacco is an economic good, even if you do not think it is good to use tobacco.

8) "Economic theory is built on an idealization of people: that they have tremendous computational power, a detailed knowledge of their desires and needs, a thorough understanding of their environment and its causal relationships, a resistance to acting on impulse or by habit." Explain why this statement incorrectly characterizes economic theory.

Answer:

It is theory and its structure that are logical. The predictable regularities of people's responses to changes in their environment do not require their rationality any more than the response of water to a slope requires rationality by each molecule of water.

9) Suppose it were claimed that a denial of college facilities to some speaker is a denial of the right of free speech. Show how that argument confuses free resources with free speech.

Answer:

Free speech means a right to speak or communicate with others who are willing to listen, free of intervention or prohibition. It is not a right to take resources of other people for one's own purposes of communication. To use college property without permission of the college authorities is not a right of free speech; it is simply appropriation of property as if the property were free for the taking. Nor is it a denial of free speech if a college or anyone else denies the use of resources under its or his control which others would like to use for their own purposes. This does not mean that colleges ought to refuse to others all uses of their resources for communication of popular or unpopular ideas; it is a clarification of the difference between free speech and the proposition that resources are "free" to anyone for the taking to be used for communication.

10) Evaluate the statement: "When property rights conflict with human rights, property rights must give way."

Answer:

The statement is vacuous. Human rights are the rights of people to use scarce resources. The property itself has no rights.

11) What is nonsensical about the proposition, "A good economic system maximizes the welfare of the maximum number of people"?

Answer:

Only one quantity can be maximized subject to all others being held at specified levels. You can maximize the welfare of one person provided that the welfare of each of the other people is unchanged.

12) What are theories, and why are they useful? What is logical validity of a theory? What is empirical validity of a theory? Does either imply the other?

Answer:

Theories provide a coherent and facilitating framework for explaining and predicting events in the world. Theories have two aspects — logical and empirical. A theory interprets events in terms of a general framework, using principles considered to be true. Using logic and the principles on which a theory is based, one can draw implications. If the principles and the derived implications are logical, the theory is logically valid. Second, useful implications are those which can be tested empirically against events in the world and shown to be wrong or "refuted." If the implications are not refuted by empirical testing — that is, by events in the world — the theory is empirically valid or conditionally confirmed. Logical and empirical validity do not imply each other. In short, use of theory and empirical testing is a way to increase the probability of making more accurate predictions or reduce the probability of making erroneous predictions.

13) Can a theory be proven true?

Answer:

No. Logically it's impossible to prove a theory. A theory says that an assertion or proposition X logically implies some event Y. Empirically, if we observe event X and then the event Y, we can't infer that X caused Y to occur, because there may be something else (Z, which we may not be aware of) that caused Y to occur. We can say that the evidence supports the theory. "Confirmed" or "validated" however do not here mean "proven."

14) "The assumptions or principles underlying the theory are too simplistic or unrealistic, so the theory is not useful or won't work." Do you agree?

Answer:

No. The usefulness of a theory depends upon its simplicity (how easy it is to use) and predictive power (how accurately it predicts events in the world). A theory with complicated "realistic" assumptions may generate implications which are not supported or confirmed by events (it predicts very poorly) while a theory with simplistic assumptions may generate implications that are largely realized by events (it predicts well). Use the theory that predicts best — even though its assumptions are simplistic. The predictive power or empirical validity of a theory does not depend upon the complexity (or realism) of the theory's underlying assumptions, propositions, or assertions.

15) "It's better in theory than in practice." What do you think this means? Do you agree?

Answer:

"It's a good theory but it predicts badly." Disagree. If the theory predicts badly, it's not a useful theory. A useful theory predicts well — the theory makes implications that are confirmed or supported by events.

16) What is meant by (a) the logical validity of a theory? (b) the empirical validity? Does either imply the other?

Answer:

A theory is logically valid if all its elements are *logically* consistent with each other or with some broader theory with which it is associated. It is empirically valid if its implications about observable phenomena are consistent with the observed phenomena. Neither implies the other.

CHAPTER 3

CHOICE AND COST

A candy-store owner told Annie: "I want to give you some candy for free. Select whichever one you want." She responded, "Thank you. But it's not free!" Annie's smart! She recognized that choosing her favorite, Snickers, is costly. She would have to give up her next best-liked candy, a bag of M&Ms — her alternate personal highest-worth good. Costs can occur in several forms, and some things that are not costs are often called costs.

DEFINITION OF COST OF A CHOSEN ACTION

The cost of an action is the best alternative you otherwise would have chosen. Cost is what you forgo. When Annie chose the Snickers, she gave up one of the several other kinds of candy she could have had. The best — the highest valued — alternative in her opinion was the M&Ms. So for Annie, the cost of the Snickers was the M&Ms. "Opportunity" is sometimes used with "cost" — "opportunity cost" — to emphasize that the cost of an act is the best of the forgone opportunities.

Annie did get the *right* to choose some candy. Getting that right didn't cost her anything. The cost occurred when she had to choose to have this rather than that. We must recognize the difference between (a) the gift of the *right to choose* among the specified items and (b) the *act* of choosing among them. Though the right to choose some candy was obtained without payment, the choice itself was not free.

PERSONAL WORTH

When Annie was then asked if she would rather have the Snickers over *two* bags of M&M's, she replied, "No, I'd still choose the Snickers. But I would have a hard time deciding whether one Snickers was worth to me as much as three bags of M&Ms. I'd let you choose whether I obtained a Snickers or three bags of M&Ms." She could have added, "My personal worth of a Snickers is the most bags of M&Ms I'd be willing to give up to get a Snickers. Cost is what you *must* pay to get something. Personal worth is the highest value you'd be *willing* to pay. For any action, if your personal worth exceeds your cost, you'll do it. If your cost exceeds your personal worth for it, you'll not do it."

SOME CONFUSIONS THAT MUST BE AVOIDED

Consequences of Act versus Cost

Distinguish between (a) the *cost* of a chosen act and (b) the "bad" *consequences* of that act. Undesirable features of choices are not the "cost." People say that the cost of playing tennis is the resulting sore arm, or that the cost of studying is eyestrain. The eyestrain is a consequence, or part of the act, of studying; the sore arm is a consequence, or part of the act, of playing tennis. Don't confuse the undesirable features of a chosen act with its cost — the best alternative given up. The cost of "studying and getting a headache" is the "best opportunity" thereby given up, which may be the two hours of playing video games you give up in order to study.

Purchases versus Use — Explicit and Implicit Costs

Another distinction is between the cost of *getting* some good and the cost of *using* that good. When you buy something, you trade rights, giving up rights to one good in exchange for rights to what you bought. What you paid is a cost of *getting* what you bought. But when you use something you already own, you incur a cost — giving up the next best *use* of the object. You might call that a cost of "use." Whatever it's called, cost can occur without giving up some good in exchange.

If I use my garage as a workshop, there's a cost of using the garage in that way — the loss of storage space for my car. Because no rights are transferred or goods given up to someone else, the cost is called an "implicit" cost. The implicit cost here is the best forgone *use* of goods I already have. Thus, even already owned resources are not costless to use, because their *use* for "this" means giving up the opportunity to *use* them for "that." The label "implicit" is a way of reminding us that a *forgone opportunity* is a cost. Every cost is appropriately called an "opportunity" cost, to emphasize the opportunity forgone, whether as a payment or as some alternative use.

Precisely What Is the Action?

Consider three related activities concerning an auto: (1) purchase of its title, the ownership; (2) continued ownership of the car; and (3) use of the car. Each of these acts has its cost. Suppose a car with a purchase price of $20,000 could immediately be resold for $19,000. What is the cost of purchasing title to the car? Is it $1,000 or is it $20,000? The cost is $1,000, because your wealth is reduced by only $1,000 when you purchase the car ($1,000 = $20,000 minus the immediate resale value of $19,000). Only $1,000 is initially forsaken. But immediately there is a cost of continuing to own the car. And there will be costs of driving the car.

Price versus Full Cost

More than money payments are involved in the costs of most acts. Suppose you spend an hour shopping for a movie on DVD you then purchase for $10. That's an hour of time otherwise available for some other activity, like working at $8 per hour. The full cost of the purchase is $18, the $10 money payment plus the $8 value of what you could have done with that time. Suppose, instead, you hired an agent to do the shopping, purchasing, and delivery for a total money price of $15 ($10 price of the DVD plus the $5 cost of the agent's services). That would have been cheaper, though the money price was higher — the $18 full cost without the agent compared to $15 with the agent.

The value of your time is one reason you don't drive across town to purchase at a lower money price — but at higher full price. The relatively high value of time for some customers is why convenience stores thrive. Richer people (who have higher-valued alternative uses for their time) typically pay higher money prices to get faster service. They don't shop around to save a dollar waiting in lines as long as do people with lower hourly earnings. Wealthy people pay higher greens fees on golf courses or higher fees for tennis courts that have less waiting time or faster play; they insist that sellers of service (restaurants, hair stylists, tailors, lawyers, doctors, auto mechanics) provide reservations and faster service. The rich pay a higher dollar price for the faster service, because the greater value of time saved reduces the full cost for them. Conclusion: Do not regard the money price as the full cost. Consider all components of cost.

Expenditures versus Purchases

An expenditure (payment of money) is not a cost if you are already obligated to make the payment, as when you repay a debt. After you buy an automobile under an installment payment plan, the later expenditures, when made, are not costs. You incurred the cost at the moment you agreed to the installment plan. At that moment, you gave up your right to the stipulated amount of future income to be used for other things. When making the installment payments, you are fulfilling an obligation. Those contracted expenditures are not costs — and some costs are not expenditures, as we'll see next.

Changes in Implicit Costs

Depreciation is a reduction of current value, not of initial purchase price. Suppose you have just purchased a used car for $15,000 to use in a limousine service business. You contemplate a 100,000 mile service life, with zero final resale value. The depreciation due to use of the auto would be $.15 a mile (= $15,000/100,000 miles).

The day after you bought the car, you discover it has been owned by a celebrity and therefore could be resold for $100,000! You've just gained $85,000 in wealth. But at the same time, the rate of depreciation of the car has increased from $.15 a mile to $1 a mile (= $100,000/100,000 miles). You have become wealthier. But you now lose more of that greater wealth with each unit of use. Depreciation always must be based on the pro-rata share of its *current* value — not its initial purchase price.

Misfortune can make us understand the world more clearly. You buy a used car for $15,000 for a limousine service, and the next day you discover some defects in it, which reduce the value of the car to $5,000. You've suffered a wealth loss of $10,000. However, the depreciation per mile of use of the car falls to $.05 per mile (= $5,000/100,000 miles), assuming the car will still render 100,000 miles of service. Again, the point is that the depreciation of an asset is the decrease in its *current* value, not in the *initial* value at the time of purchase.

"Sunk Cost" Is No Longer a Cost

The concept "sunk costs" is important in many decisions. You are writing a term paper and have already spent twenty hours on it. Someone says you could write a paper on a different topic and get a better grade. Would your decision depend upon how much time and effort you have already spent on the present topic? We hope not! That time spent is sunk, gone, and unaffected by any future actions.

A sunk cost is the cost of a past act. It is not a cost of any present or future action. It may provoke tears, sadness, and regret. But costs of past acts are bygones, sunk and irrelevant for present acts. However, at the earlier time of initial action, the contemplated act's foreseen (but not yet incurred) sunk cost is of prime relevance in deciding whether to undertake the act.

Time Used versus Time of Use

Time passes no matter what you do. It can't be saved and accumulated; there is no *choice* about delaying or speeding up time. Therefore, the time required to do something cannot itself be a cost. Instead, the cost is the *alternative* act that otherwise would have been accomplished within that amount of time — possibly later and not just at the present moment.

EXTERNALITIES: UNCOMPENSATED
EFFECTS BORNE BY OTHER PEOPLE

"Externalities" are effects on other people to whom adequate — mutually agreeable — compensation is not made. If compensation for effects on another person were made, that would be a "purchase." Theft has an external effect, but if you had bought the item, that would not be said to result in an externality. So long as mutually agreeable compensation is made to those who would otherwise be harmed, that's not an externality.

You will not always bear all the costs of your action. You may impose some losses on the property of other people. That would happen if you stole some of the resources you were going to use. Or your action might inadvertently harm someone. If I eat a hamburger with onions during a close conversation with you, that's legal, even though I have polluted the air you breathe.

If I turn up my sound system and annoy neighbors, or throw litter on their land, or drive my noisy motorcycle near their land, I am abusing — reducing — the benefits they receive from their property rights in land. But often the actor abuses resources that aren't clearly owned by anyone. If a steel mill discharges polluted water, or if a refinery emits pollutants and reduces the quality of air, these acts change the physical characteristics of resources over which no one seems to have unambiguous enforceable and transferable property rights.

Actions that are legal but incidentally impose costs or losses on other people are "externalities." Whether such actions would be illegal usually depends on the cost of assigning and protecting property rights over the abused resources. If declared illegal, they are punishable by government power.

Trivial harms to other people's property are permitted if the harm is a side effect of some productive action, or if its prohibition is too expensive relative to the benefits of initiating action. Many external effects typically are tolerated because the costs of prevention by laws would exceed the benefits of prevention. Smoke from a neighbor's bonfire of leaves in the fall season may be legally "dumped" on neighboring property. The same is true for typical traffic noises. In many situations, social customs, rules of etiquette, and ostracism help control our behavior.

If you owned well-defined and enforceable property rights to air over your land, I would have to compensate you for the right to dump smoke on your property. Then I would have to take those costs into account when deciding whether to burn leaves or haul them to a dump. The costs would be "internalized" (borne by me). But since complete private property rights are not perfectly enforceable over all resources, people aren't forced to take account of, or bear, all the costs. As another example, an employee strains and suffers in his work. That would be an external effect imposed on the employee by the employer — if the employer hadn't agreed to pay enough to the employee for the right to have the employee do that work.

Environmental Pollution

What is called "pollution" is the use of a nonowned resource without compensation. In some situations, there are no private owners, as with the air. If there were, they could demand compensation for permission to use the resources, as with ordinary purchases. The consequences would be "internalized" on the responsible person, and pollution might be avoided or reduced.

Complete, exhaustive private property rights are difficult to specify and enforce. Does a right to the view across the parcel of land neighboring your property belong to you or to the neighbor? If someone did own the view and that ownership was salable, as land is bought or an employer buys one's labor, the effects and costs and benefits would be "internalized" on the actor, and the resources would be used accordingly.

Inducing Beneficial Externalities

Some of your actions improve the resources or environment of other people, increasing the benefits they derive from their property, though you weren't paid to do that. Examples are better hygiene, prettier gardens, politeness, and so forth. How are we persuaded to do that when we are not paid to do so, or no reward can be forced from the beneficiaries? Social pressures, social approbation, ethics — such as "Keep up the neighborhood" or "Neighborhood Watch" — are sometimes influential. Also government rules and regulations are applied, as in compulsory vaccination.

Pecuniary Externalities

All these examples of externalities are "physical" externalities, pertaining to the *physical* attributes or uses of a resource. There are also "pecuniary"— market value — external effects, without any physical impact. An example of a pure pecuniary externality is provided by the book in your hands. When this textbook was published, it lowered the market value of competing texts. Other text publishers did not have to be compensated for the loss in the market value of their texts. No one has rights to *particular market values* of resources. The market value depends on offers of other people. No one has the right to make other people continue to buy something and to do so at a specified price. That kind of "right" is not part of private property rights. Only governments have that right — mainly in the power of taxation.

COSTS AND EFFECTS OF ACTIONS

The distinctions among costs, losses, rights, and externalities are not hair-splitting trivial distinctions. Let's review some of these key concepts.

- Definition of Cost: The cost of a chosen act is the best of the alternative actions forgone. The chosen act is the one most preferred of all options.
- Full Cost: Money plus other resource costs.
- Implicit Cost: Best alternative use value of already possessed resources.
- Explicit Cost: Transfer, or reduction in value, of property rights in an exchange.
- External Cost: Reduction of options of uses of resources owned by other people and for which no compensation is made to the other people.
- Sunk Cost: Past cost of a past action; not a cost of current or future choice.

CHOICES REFLECT PRINCIPLES OF PERSONAL PREFERENCES

Individuals Are the Choosers

If you couldn't choose, you'd have no costs! But when free to choose, you don't choose at random. Your choices reflect patterns of preferences. We will always look at the behavior and choices of individuals. If you ask, "Why does the government or General Electric or some union behave as it does?" you should ask instead, "Why do the decision makers decide as they do?" This direction of attention to individuals does not mean that people are solely self-interested and self-seeking without regard to other people. But we regard individuals as the basic units of choice, no matter what are a person's motives or ultimate objectives.

The likelihood of a particular choice depends on its cost and personal worth. And a bigger "basket" will, at the same cost, be chosen over a smaller one. "More is preferred to less." But our choices aren't typically the easy choices between bigger and smaller baskets. Instead, we must choose between *combinations* of goods. They differ in the relative amounts of various goods. One has more "oranges" but fewer "apples." One area has nicer indoor living, while another has better outdoor activities. The fundamental premise is that for each person there are several other equally preferred and equally costly (affordable) *combinations of goods or activities* among which he can choose. If the cost of any of the components in that combination should change, you'd shift to a new equally costly, but possibly better or worse, combination. In other words, you'd alter your lifestyle, behavior, and the goods you buy.

If we know of some reliable regularities in personal preferences, we can deduce the adjustments to changes in costs and opportunities, whether in domestic or in business activities. Some reliably consistent features, called a "pattern of personal preferences," have been identified. The preferences are about *more of one good relative to more of other goods.*

The principles are not about which goods we prefer over other goods. No such absolute ranking of goods according to importance or purpose is known. Instead, what is known are some preferences for amounts of one good *relative* to other goods — how *much* more or less of one good is substitutable for how much more or less of other goods. These principles apply to people living in socialist, as well as to those in capitalist, systems. And they apply to all living objects — people, animals, and even plants.

THE PERSONAL PREFERENCE PRINCIPLES

Principle 1: For Every Good You Desire More

You want more of this and more of that. You want also to accomplish more than one goal. But we live in a world of scarcity and limitations. Choices must be made.

Principle 2: You Are Willing to Forgo Some of One Good for More of Other Goods

You do not wait until you have obtained some "necessary minimum" of one good, say food, before you want to have some clothes. And you don't then wait until you have some minimum necessary amount of clothes before you want some of other things. There is no hierarchical ranking of goods as "needs." You prefer combinations of goods, rather than a successive fulfillment of essential goods. This is described by the principle of *marginal substitutability* among all goods. The principle asserts that you are willing to give up *some* (not necessarily all) of *any* good, if you are able to get *enough* of other goods in return.

Principle 3: The More You Have of Some Good, the Less of Other Goods You Are Willing to Give Up to Get an Additional Unit

To obtain one *more* pint of ice cream a week, you would be willing to pay only a lower price if you are already consuming much, than if you are consuming little. An extra pint has less added worth to you, the more you have. Some would call that "diminishing marginal utility" at larger amounts of a good. The larger the amount of a good a person possesses or controls, the lower is its *marginal* personal worth to that person.

We use the word "worth" rather than "utility," because we don't know how to measure utility or if it means anything other than "personal worth."

This principle can be called "diminishing marginal rate of substitution." The amount you'd be willing to pay (give up) for an additional unit diminishes the more you have of the good. We always refer to *personal worth*, because it reflects each person's own personal opinion and judgment. Often we'll write just "worth," instead of "personal worth." But "worth" always will refer to one's personal worth, not the *market value*.

We take the following "observations" to be true:

OBSERVATION 1: PREFERENCE PATTERNS DIFFER
Preferences differ among people, and they are different for any given individual at different times and different circumstances. Though the three "principles of *patterns* of preferences" apply to everyone, not everyone has exactly the same numerical magnitudes in their trade-offs among relative amounts of goods.

OBSERVATION 2: PEOPLE ARE INNOVATIVE
People innovate and experiment in attempting to improve their situation, at the risk of ending up worse off. This does not mean people like risk and uncertainty; instead, in the prospect of a (sufficiently large) gain, they are willing to incur some risk of loss.

OBSERVATION 3: PEOPLE ARE CHARITABLE, BUT NOT IN MARKETS
People are not purely selfish, without interest in the welfare of other persons. An enormous amount of philanthropy and charitable activity occurs. This is consistent with the principle that a person prefers command over more rather than less goods and wealth: one can want such power in order to help others as well as one's self. But people are not charitable in all their actions. The market (wherein people exchange property rights in arranging for consumption, earning incomes, and investing) is not the place to expect charity. Charity begins outside the market.

OBSERVATION 4: ETHICS IN MARKET BEHAVIOR
Ethical, honest, reliable, and moral behavior is generally a survival behavior and wealth-enhancing characteristic in the market. Not only are violations of ethics more likely to prevent successful market activities but they are arguably more powerful in the economic market than in the markets of political and social exchange. Ask whether a seller/supplier or a politician tends to make more reliable promises. Which will suffer most, and most quickly, if caught being dishonest or evasive?

OBSERVATION 5: GOODS AND PRINCIPLES—
THE GENERALITY AND SCOPE OF MEANING

The three personal preference principles apply to all goods and all desired attributes of life. Living in Los Angeles or Miami provides some combinations of conditions and attributes more cheaply than does living in some other area. There are combinations in Omaha that are equally desired, possibly involving larger homes on more land with more wide roads and security, but with poorer climate and cosmopolitan variety. We "trade" some amount of one desirable attribute for more of another.

These trade-offs (substitutions on the margin) apply to ideals and even to honesty. Each of us on occasion sacrifices or risks some small degree of our integrity, of our fidelity to an ideal or principle, for some sufficient increase in income or safety or popularity or power. (Imagine a world in which no one ever told the slightest "white lie," such as "I've had a wonderful time," when you were bored stiff, or hid the slightest truth when commenting on someone's new clothes or hairstyle.) Goals and ideals, like ordinary goods, are competitive and substitutable in degrees of attainment and fulfillment, where the tradeoff is between *more* or *less*, not between *all* or *none*.

QUESTIONS AND MEDITATIONS

1) If there is more than one opportunity to be forsaken, which forsaken opportunity is the cost?
   a. How are opportunities made comparable so that one can determine which one is the cost?
   b. Can there be production without cost?

Answer:

   The highest-valued opportunity is the cost.

   Expressed in a common denominator or measure of value.

   In general, no. Not if more than one thing could have been produced — including leisure.

2) "The *time* involved in purchasing something cannot be considered part of the cost since the time would have passed anyway. It is an error to count the value of time as part of the cost of any action." Evaluate: What is meant by the value (or cost) of time?

Answer:

   The first statement is true, but the second is false. The *value* of an hour is the highest-valued use one could have made of that hour. Hence the cost of an act taking an hour is the value of the best alternative action forsaken during that hour. (A common, though not always accurate, measure of the value of time is the earnings one could have obtained during the time.)

3) "Joe builds a garage next to his house. Later, he decides to park his vehicle on the street and use the garage for storing miscellaneous items. Since the garage has already been built and paid for, it costs nothing to use it for general storage." What is "cost"? Is using the garage for storage "costless"?

Answer:

Cost is the most valuable of options forgone. Joe cannot use the garage for both housing his chariot and storage: he must make a choice. Evidently, he values the garage for storage more than for coddling the car, but that treatment of the car is the cost of the storage capacity, even though Joe now makes no money payment.

4) "In an open market, with buyers and sellers unrestricted in coming to agreements on transactions, the money price of the traded object is the *full* price: the specified market price is not greater than the personal valuation of the buyer." Right? Or are there nonprice ways in which consumers compete in obtaining commodities? Are there costs to the buyer in addition to the money expenditure directly for the good?

Answer:

There are exertions, time expenditures, uncertainties and frustrations, and money outlays in buying almost anything — put on your shoes, drive to the store, park and deal with clerks who may be inept, gamble on the quality of products, and pay the babysitter. All this is part of the "full" price.

5) Are costs the same thing as the undesirable consequences of some action? Explain why not.

Answer:

Costs are not the undesirable consequences of an act; they are the highest-valued forsaken opportunity. Anticipated unattractive consequences of a possible action may well play a role in deciding whether or not to pursue the activity or in determining how far to pursue it, but they are not formally a "cost" of the venture.

6) What is meant by equality between private and social costs?

Answer:

All costs are private. Social costs are simply the total of all private costs. If a person does not bear all the costs of his action, then the social costs exceed the total of the costs he bears, because some of the costs are borne by others. With equality of private with social costs, all costs of a decision are then borne by the decision maker.

7) "Cost is an opportunity concept and exists wherever a choice exists." Explain.

Answer:

A choice is an opportunity among two or more options. The *cost* of the chosen alternative is the most valuable option given up.

8) What is the relation between opportunity costs and compensation for work?

Answer:

If my rights to myself and my labor are protected, I cannot be forced to work. But I can be induced to work if paid at least the costs of my doing the work — the value of what I otherwise could have done. If I had been forced to work without regard to my rights, then I would be suffering the externalities of the actions by the person who forced me to work. But if I'm compensated by a negotiated wage, the "externality" has been "internalized." The employer bears the cost. We could use the term "uncompensated externality" to mean "taking without compensation" or theft, while reserving the term "compensated externality" or "internalized externality" for an ordinary purchase and sale of goods and labor. But we already have such standard terms as "purchase," "sale," "wages," and so forth. Later we'll examine some important examples of existing externalities.

APPENDIX TO CHAPTER 3: INDIFFERENCE CURVES

The principles of choice and behavior can be described by so-called preference maps. In figure 3.1, point A denotes a combination of two goods, X and Y. The amount of X is measured by the horizontal distance to the right from the vertical axis, and the amount of Y by the vertical distance upward from the horizontal axis. Point B contains more Y, but no more X, than does combination A. Combination C contains more X than point A, but no more Y.

If point B is preferred to A, Y must be an economic good. If point C is preferred to A, X must be an economic good. If B were not preferred to A, the good Y must either be a free good or a "bad" (rather than a "good"). But we have defined X and Y to be economic goods, meaning they are not so plentiful as to make no more wanted even at a zero price.

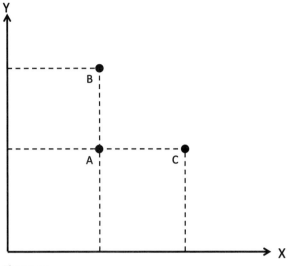

Figure 3.1

How could you portray the personal worth of an additional (marginal) unit of X at point A? Since "personal worth" of a good is defined and *measured* only in terms of an added amount of some other substitutable good that would offset one unit of X, that personal worth depends on the amount of X that is held. The greater the initial amount of X, the less the amount of Y that will be offered for one unit more (preference principle #3).

Combination B has more Y, and no less X than at A, so more Y will be offered for an X if that person is initially at B than if at A. A person at B would offer more Y to get an X than if that person were at C, for the more Y held, the less each is worth relative to other goods.

In figure 3.2, points B and C are on the same indifference curve I_2, meaning either is as preferred as the other. And point A is less preferred than C or B or any other point on I_2. The two lines become flatter as they extend to the right to more X. The resulting shape of the line connecting all combinations (points) that are *equally* preferred (indifferent) is curved, and sags in toward the origin. (In chapter 2, the production possibility boundary [PPB] also was not a straight line, but it bulged out from the origin.) The slope of curve I_2 is (negatively) "steeper" at B than at C; I_2 is "steeper" at B than is I_1 at A; and I_1 is "steeper" at A than is I_2 at C. For example, one more unit of Y (vertical movement) is worth more X forgone (leftward horizontal movement) when starting at C than when starting at A.

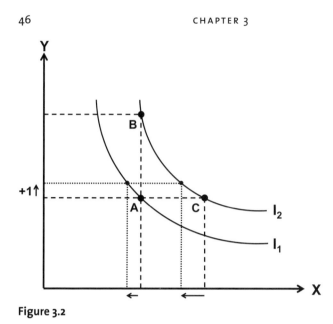

Figure 3.2

Meaning and Measures of Marginal "Personal Worth"

A *marginal* personal worth of a unit more of a good, X, is the amount of other goods (here denoted by Y) that a person is willing to give up to get the added unit of X. The curvature of an indifference curve reflects the *diminishing* marginal personal worth at *more* units of a good (measured on one axis) and with less of another good (measured on the other axis). If an indifference line were straight from upper left to lower right, the *relative* marginal personal worth of the two goods would be constant regardless of the relative amounts of the two goods. That would not be consistent with reality. The marginal rate of substitution of X for Y can be expressed: $MRS_{xy} = -\Delta Y/\Delta X$ (where Δ denotes the quantity change). The ratio is negative, for X and Y change in opposite directions as we substitute a little more of one for a little less of the other. And the numerical value decreases as we move to the right on an indifference curve, for we must gain ever larger amounts of X to compensate for a given reduction in Y.

We use a smooth curved line for simplicity, though a realistic curve could be kinked with straight-line segments, but the slope becomes *successively flatter*, meaning that the less of a good a person has, the more of other goods that must be obtained for further unit reduction in the good.

The meaning of the first principle, "More of a good is preferred to less," is represented by a choice of a point on a *higher* indifference curve. Being at any point on the higher indifference curve is preferred to being on any of the points on a lower indifference curve. In figure 3.2, the higher curve, above and

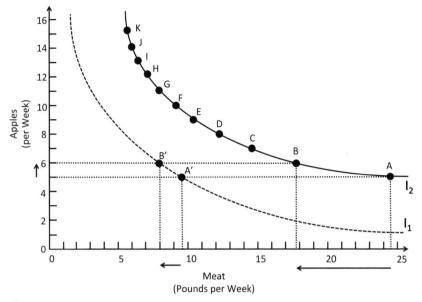

Figure 3.3

to the right, represents a set of baskets that are: (1) each of the same worth to a person, and (2) each preferred (superior) to each basket on the lower curve.

Higher and Lower Indifference Curves

All points on an indifference curve represent equally preferred alternative combinations. Combination A and B on curve I_2 are equally preferred, as are points A′ and B′ on curve I_1, and any point of the higher curve, I_2, is preferred to any on the lower.

All three preference principles are summarized graphically in figure 3.3. (1) The upper indifference curve, representing combinations preferred to those on the lower indifference curve, portrays the first proposition — *more is preferred to less.* (2) The *negative* slope portrays proposition 2 — the principle of *substitution on the margin.* (3) Sagging toward the origin, and becoming flatter as one moves from left to right, portrays proposition 3 — diminishing rates of marginal substitutability of X for Y at larger amounts of X relative to Y along a given indifference curve.

We can think of "personal worth" of this versus that good or action without having to make psychological comparisons with any other person. The comparison is "before" and "after" for the same person. Personal worth means how much a person is willing to pay for something, not measures of psychological satisfaction or distress of some action. For each person, personal worth of one action is compared with that person's personal worth of an alternative action, measured in market value of what is given up.

An indifference curve is sometimes called a "constant utility" curve. That doesn't define what "utility" is. It means only that, no matter what you mean by the word "utility," its amount is constant—the same at every combination on an indifference curve.

ARITHMETIC

Table 3.1 lists alternative, equally preferred combinations—baskets—of amounts of meat and apples for Adam. Adam is indifferent in his preference among these alternative baskets. That is to say, "Each alternative is equally preferred." Or, "Adam is *indifferent* among those baskets—he doesn't care which one is obtained. Or, "Adam would let even his worst enemy choose which of those combinations Adam gets!"

If Adam initially had basket D, representing a weekly rate of consumption of eight apples and thirteen pounds of meat, Adam would be neither helped nor hurt (as judged by Adam) by having basket E instead—with two fewer pounds of meat (eleven versus thirteen) but one more apple (nine versus eight). Two fewer pounds of meat for one more apple is a "*marginal rate of substitution*" between apples and meat that would leave Adam no better or worse off than before, according to his own opinion.

Table 3.1 *Adam's Equally Preferred Combinations of Apples and Meat*

Basket	Apples	Meat	Meat given up for additional apple
A	5	24.5	
B	6	18.5	6.0
C	7	15.5	3.0
D	8	13.0	2.5
E	9	11.0	2.0
F	10	9.3	1.7
G	11	8.0	1.3
H	12	7.0	1.0
I	13	6.2	0.8
J	14	5.6	0.6
K	15	5.2	0.4

The adjective "marginal" means two more pounds of meat is the personal worth of one *more* apple, *not* the personal worth of *all* nine apples.

Why is the marginal personal worth of another apple lower between E and F (1.7 pounds of meat) than between D and E (two pounds)? Adam has more apples at E than D, and less meat. An additional apple is not worth as much to him when more apples are possessed. The marginal personal worth of an apple (or of any good) falls the more one has of the good. He is willing to give up less meat (only 1.7 pounds) for another apple between combinations E and F, where more apples are possessed.

As we move to more apples and less meat for Adam, the amount of meat that would be given up for one more apple diminishes. The larger the ratio of the amount of one good possessed relative to other goods, the lower is the marginal personal worth of the first good. The greater is the amount of a good relative to other goods in one's consumption pattern, the less is the amount of other goods one will be willing to give up for one more unit of the first good.

If the amount of apples and the amount of meat were both twice as large as in the initial situation, we don't know how that doubling of wealth would affect the marginal personal worth of apples relative to meat. We don't know how wealth (having more apples *and* more meat) affects your willingness to substitute among the goods. But we can be sure that at larger amounts of a good, its marginal rate of substitution with any other good will fall. Note also, in accord with our earlier observation 1, that one person's marginal personal worth of apples may be different from another person's even though both have the same combination of all goods.

You can move up the table and discover the marginal personal worth of meat, instead of the marginal personal worth of apples. Between baskets I and H, the marginal substitution ratio is one apple for .8 pounds of meat. So the marginal personal worth of one pound of meat is 1.25 apples (= 1 apple/.8 pounds of meat). Between E and D, the marginal personal worth of one pound of meat is .5 of an apple (= 1 apple/2 pounds of meat), or the marginal personal worth of one apple is two pounds of meat.

CHAPTER 4

GAINS FROM EXCHANGE

It's been going on for thousands of years. Long ago, flint arrowheads were traded for olive oil and fish. Today, it's crude oil for fish. But there is much misunderstanding about why we trade. Sometimes, trading is (wrongly) called a *zero-sum* activity, in the sense that what one person gets another gives up—with no net change in the total.

Trading (or exchanging) is a *positive-sum* activity in that both participants end in preferred situations. In some exchanges, both traders may end up with fewer goods—even though they both gain. To see how, we'll look at exchange in an imaginary refugee camp.

TRADE IN A REFUGEE CAMP

We visit a camp where hurricane refugees are housed. Monthly, each receives Red Cross parcels containing, among other things, twenty bottled waters and twenty granola bars (shown as basket A in tables 4.1 and 4.2). Into the camp comes a newcomer, who does not receive a gift parcel. The wily newcomer offers Sam ten bottled waters in exchange for seven granola bars: "If you'll give me seven granola bars, I'll be back in a moment with the ten bottled waters." Sam is *willing* to give as many as eight granola bars for the extra ten bottled waters. So Sam agrees.

Sam started with basket A. The hypothetical basket B1 is equal to basket A in terms of Sam's preferences: he is indifferent between baskets A and B1 in table 4.1. Now, we'll see exchanges among all three—Sam, Joe, and newcomer—improve *everyone's* situation despite the fact that Sam and Joe end up with less water and granola between them, because some are taken by the newcomer.

The newcomer dashes to Joe and offers five granola bars in exchange for ten bottled waters. Joe would have been indifferent to selling the ten bottled waters for as few as four granola bars (basket B1 in table 4.2). Being offered five granola bars, Joe agrees to the trade.

The newcomer pays Joe five granola bars and delivers the promised ten bottled waters to Sam (baskets B2 in tables 4.1 and 4.2). Both Sam and Joe are pleased by the improvements in their situations; for each, basket B2 is better

Table 4.1 *Sam's Equivalent and Preferred Baskets (to Basket A)*

	Water	Granola	Baskets
Basket A	20	20	Original
Changes from A to B1	*(+10)*	*(−8)*	*Changes from A*
Basket B1	30	12	Indifferent to A
Changes from A to B2	*(+10)*	*(−7)*	*Changes from A*
Basket B2	30	13	Preferred to A

Table 4.2 *Joe's Equivalent and Preferred Baskets (to Basket A)*

Baskets	Water	Granola	Baskets
Basket A	20	20	Original Basket
Changes from A to B1	*(−10)*	*(+4)*	*Changes from A*
Basket B1	10	24	Indifferent to A
Changes from A to B2	*(−10)*	*(+5)*	*Changes from A*
Basket B2	10	25	Preferred to A

than basket B1. The newcomer, too, is happy, having acquired a profit of two granola bars by selling water to Sam at a price of seven granola bars after buying from Joe for only five.

LESS IS MORE: FEWER GOODS, MORE SATISFACTION

The total of goods left to Sam and the Joe has been reduced! The newcomer has taken two granola bars from them. Yet, each thought the trade to be a good deal. Has the wily newcomer confused them or exploited their irrationality? No, *everyone* is better off. The newcomer explains:

"You have not been cheated. In fact, you are both better off. You both obtained something worth more to you than what you paid. Sam, table 4.1 shows that you accepted my offer of ten bottled waters for seven granola bars as a good deal. You were willing to pay as many as eight granola bars for ten additional bottled waters, but I accepted a price of only seven. That trade was worth as much to you as a gift of one granola bar. And Joe, you paid ten waters and received five granola bars, which gave you one more granola bar than your value of the ten bottled waters you paid. You received a benefit equal to a gift of one granola bar.

"You both benefited. I kept two granola bars as payment for my services. True, I didn't do this only because I liked you. I was interested also in helping myself.

In helping you, I helped myself—or if you wish, in helping myself, I helped you. Furthermore, admit it—each of you thought you were outwitting and exploiting me, because you were each prepared to give up more (or receive less) than you did. Of course, you would have benefited more if I had traded on less favorable terms to myself, and kept fewer than two granola bars. Yet, there is no denying that you are now better off. None of us has been foolish."

THINKING ABOUT THE TRADE

1) What made the trade mutually beneficial?

    When two individuals have different *personal worths* of a good, each can gain from a trade. Sam's personal worth of ten bottles of water was eight granola bars; Joe's was four granola bars.

2) Which is the direction of the trade? That is, who gives up water, and who receives it in the trade?

    Sam has a higher personal worth of bottled water *in terms of granola bars*, so Sam buys water, and Joe sells it.

3) What is the *maximum* possible payment to the wily newcomer (intermediary) that would leave neither Sam nor Joe better or worse off?

    At the limit, the intermediary could receive four granola bars per ten bottles of water traded. This is the difference between Sam's personal worth of ten bottles of water (eight granola bars) and Joe's personal worth of the bottled water (four granola bars).

4) Who has a higher personal worth of granola bars in terms of bottled water?

    Sam's personal worth of a granola bar is 1.25 bottles (ten bottles/ eight granola bars = 1.25 bottles per granola bar). Joe's personal worth of a granola bar is 2.5 bottled waters (ten bottles/four granola bars = 2.5 bottles per granola bar). Joe's personal value of granola bars is greater than Sam's.

5) Arranging trades can sometimes be very costly. Suppose the cost of arranging the trade of ten bottled waters amounted to six granola bars. Would the trade still occur?

    The cost of setting up the trade would exceed the difference between Sam's and Joe's personal worths of bottled water. The trade would not occur because the costs exceed any possible gains from trading.

6) What would be the *final* achieved combinations of bottled water and granola bars for each person at which no further trades would be

mutually acceptable? How far might the trading go between Sam and Joe?

The answer depends on a more complete understanding of personal worth, which later chapters explain.

MORE ABOUT PERSONAL WORTH

The intermediary, or "middleman," did not ask if Sam likes bottled water more than Joe. One of them may regard both granola and water as barely desirable, while the other may drool at the thought of each. Instead, what was important for the exchange to occur was each person's personal worth — the value of one good *relative to another*.

Nor did either Sam or Joe have a "surplus" or too much of the good traded away. The critical feature is that the two persons had *different personal worths* of bottled water and of granola. Trade can benefit both if their personal worths for a good differ.

Personal Worth: The Most of Other Goods a
Person Is Willing to Pay to Get a Good

While people do barter some goods for others, "most of other goods" are typically measured in terms of their dollar value. The largest dollar amount a person would be willing to pay for a good is a measure of its personal worth to that person. If you are willing to give at most $100 for a fancy pair of shoes, your personal worth of those shoes is measured at $100. You'd prefer to get them for less. But if you wouldn't pay the $100, then your personal worth must, by definition, be less than $100. Or, in reverse, a person's personal worth is the smallest amount of other goods for which that person would sell a good. If you already owned a good and would not sell it for less than $120, then $120 is a measure of its personal worth to you.

Personal worth doesn't refer to an emotional or psychological concept. Mere words, wishes, or assertions of desires say nothing about one's personal worth for a good. Actions are what count — how much of other goods one is willing and able to pay to get more of a good.

Economic analysis doesn't rest on any presumptions of why a good is desired. You may believe that someone is foolish, or ill informed, in placing high personal worth on some good, such as opera tickets, tofu, or a round of golf. Personal worth differs for each of us because we make different judgments and have different preferences or whims. Certainly, one's opinion may be influenced by the arguments, pleadings, and behavior of other people. And a parent may regard a child's personal worth for a good (e.g., candy) as "improperly and inappropriately" high. The parent might not allow the child to have the candy, but that wouldn't alter the child's personal worth for it. That would merely restrict the child's right to make exchanges.

Presumably, a person becomes an adult when one has a right to choose according to one's own personal worth. By law, that comes for most goods and services at the age of eighteen in the United States. Nevertheless, you can't buy some kinds of medication without the approval of a physician, reflecting that physician's judgment of what the personal worth of the medication should be for you. We will hereafter ignore those restrictions and deal with goods and services you may choose on the basis of your own personal worth.

Distinguish between a) an individual's *personal worth* of a good (the most that person is willing to pay, or the least that would be accepted for its sale) and b) the good's *market value* (its market price). In any exchange, the buyer's anticipated personal worth of a good exceeds its market value (price), or the purchase would not be made. And the reverse is true for the seller, whose personal worth of the good is less than its market value (price).

TO HAVE?

"The most that a person is willing to pay to have more of a good." What is meant by "have"? When buying some land, what does it mean to "have" the land — which may be located far away? We will mean by "have" the possession of the private property rights to the good. In any exchange, one obtains the private property rights to goods. If some other exchange is meant — like rental, or loan, or permission to use without ownership — we'll say so.

BACK AT THE REFUGEE CAMP, COMPETITION DEVELOPS

Back in the hurricane refugee camp, a competing copycat dissipates the newcomer's profits. She offers to sell Sam ten bottles of water at a price of 6.5 granola bars for ten bottles — a price 0.5 bottles below the former price of seven bottles. Sam accepts, saving 0.5 granola bars per ten bottles bought.

In turn, the new dealer offers to pay Joe a higher price, 5.5 granola bars, rather than the five paid by the first dealer, who argues that the new dealer is unreliable and will not deliver granola bars as promised, or will deliver dry, old granola and sell impure water. But Joe takes a chance and trades with the new dealer. Both Joe and Sam benefit. Buyers like lower prices, and sellers like higher prices. Joe and Sam now are even better off than they were with only one intermediary.

Competition between the two dealers decreases the dealer gains by reducing

Table 4.3 *Achieved Baskets after Competition among Dealers*

	Water	Granola
Sam		
Before Trade	20	20
After Trade with Only One Dealer	30	13
After Trade with Second Dealer	30	13.5
Gain is equivalent of 0.5 bar.		+0.5 bar
Joe		
Before Trade	20	20
After Trade with Only One Dealer	10	25
After Trade with Second Dealer	10	25.5
Gain is equivalent of 0.5 bar.		+0.5 bar

the spread between the buying and selling prices of the goods. The consumer/buyer pays less to the intermediary dealer, and the supplier/seller gets a higher price. The spread between the buying and selling price for bottled water is narrowed from .2 bars (two bars/ten bottles) to .1 bars (one bar/ten bottles), and the gain to the new dealer is one bar instead of the two formerly obtained by the initial dealer.

Competition among actual and potential intermediary dealers reduces the price spread to where it just covers the costs of providing the service customers demand. A larger spread would attract new dealers, while a loss would force some people out of business into other, more useful tasks. Competition that reduces prices to buyers and raises prices to sellers is competition of intermediaries against each other. Intermediaries do not compete against consumers or against suppliers; they compete against other intermediaries.

It is often argued that intermediaries like wholesalers, retailers, sales agents, and advertisers exploit the ignorance of customers. That is true in the same way a teacher exploits the ignorance of students, doctors exploit the ignorance of patients, and authors the ignorance of readers. Intermediaries exist (survive) because they reduce the costs of exchange. Imagine what it would cost you to obtain the products you normally buy from their producers. You'd have to know who and where they are; you'd have to travel and communicate with producers; you'd have to inspect their offerings; you'd have to know enough about each product to be able to judge quality; and you'd have to arrange for components to be assembled properly and delivered. Instead, you rely on retailers — intermediaries who supply goods they think customers will prefer and will value at more than the cost of supplying them.

PROMISES AND DEPENDENCIES

The intermediary in our story has the opportunity to take the offered goods and not return with the promised goods. But intermediaries rarely disappoint customers. When an intermediary receives ten bottles and promises to return promptly with granola bars, it happens. The intermediary is swift to pay even the most timid and weak of customers. Why? Why not "hold-up" a customer by promising the 6.5 granola bars, but later pay less and keep the difference? Or perhaps the intermediary might mix sawdust with the granola, diluting quality and retaining an extra portion of granola. The customer wouldn't discover the loss until later.

Intermediaries don't tend to cheat customers because intermediaries have valuable reputations to protect. A customer treated unfairly would not only refuse to patronize the intermediary again but would broadcast the intermediary's dishonest behavior. While the intermediary might have made a one-time gain by cheating a customer, the lost reputation implies a loss of future profitable business. But what about an aging intermediary who is growing too weak to run between customers? Why not hold up all customers and make a final profit before retiring — known as the "end problem"?

There are at least two restraints against that. One is that a retiring intermediary often can do better. He can sell the business to a young protégé for a share of future profits, vouching for the reliability of the protégé. Another powerful restraint on cheating "at the end" is the force of a personal sense of shame. This is considered more fully in chapter 34. Here, we say merely that you will render help to someone in an accident or emergency because you "want to." If you did not, and even if no one else knows, you still would suffer qualms of conscience from your unethical behavior. Ethics commonly are effective, widespread, and desirable in a harmonious, productive, and civilized society.

RELIABLE *GENERAL* DEPENDENCY:
ESSENTIAL IN EVERY ECONOMY AND SOCIETY

You depend in general on other people to play an important part in your welfare, so long as you make an attractive offer. You depend also on specific other persons. This distinction between "general" and "specific" dependency is important. When you shop for goods, you depend on the rest of the world to supply you. But once you decide to buy from a specific seller, you become dependent on *that* seller.

In many situations, such as marriage or as an employee in a firm, you will continue to be dependent on the behavior of *specific* other persons. Much of economics is about methods of assuring reliabilities of dependencies on specific other persons.

TRADE BENEFITS BOTH PARTIES, NOT JUST ONE AT THE EXPENSE OF THE OTHER

We've considered a) the *conditions* for mutually preferred trade, b) the *direction* of trade, c) the nature of the *gain* from trade, and d) the extent of trade. Trade is not a matter of one person gaining at the expense of the other. Instead, it supplies a gain to both — each moves to a new combination of goods preferred to the prior combination.

Trade provides more personal worth to *each* party. What may lead many to think a trade results merely in a transfer from one person to another is the presence of "haggling, dickering, and bargaining" about the terms of trade. That haggling is a zero-sum activity, in which one person gets a greater share of the *gains of trade at the other's expense*. But the trade itself is a positive-sum activity in which both sides gain.

In the next chapter, we will flesh out the nature and extent of the gains from trade. To do that, we will define and explain *marginal* personal worth and show why *marginal* is a critical concept in economics and in *all* sciences. You will learn, for example, how marginal underlies the basic principle of *demand*.

QUESTIONS AND MEDITATIONS

1) The left half of the table shows three combinations of vegetables and meat among which Linus would have been indifferent if he had been offered a choice; that is, all three are equally desirable to him. The right half shows three combinations among which Charlie would have been indifferent.

   a. If Linus has combination B, what is his highest and lowest personal worth of vegetables? What is his highest and lowest personal worth of meat?

Table 4.4

	Linus				Charlie		
Options	Vegetables		Meat	Options	Vegetables		Meat
A	10	and	14	A	40	and	16
B	13	and	13	B	45	and	15
C	17	and	12	C	52	and	14

b. If Charlie has combination B, what is his highest and lowest personal worth of vegetables? What is his highest and lowest personal worth of meat?

c. In what sense is it impossible to say who likes vegetables more, Linus or Charlie? In what sense is it possible?

d. If Linus and Charlie each have their combinations designated B, does any possible trade exist whereby each could reach a preferred combination? If so, give an example.

e. What must be true about personal worth of two individuals if they are to gain by trading with one another, even though they lose part of their goods in the process?

Answers:

a. Between .25 and .33 meat for one unit of vegetables. Between three and four vegetables for one unit of meat.

b. Between .14 and .2 units of meat for one unit of vegetables. Between five and seven vegetables for one unit of meat.

c. We don't know who gets more psychological satisfaction or utility from each good considered separately. We can measure only their value of one good in terms of the other — their personal worths. Linus values vegetables more than Charlie in the sense that his personal worth of vegetables is higher. And Charlie values meat more than Linus because his personal worth for meat is higher.

d. Linus would be willing to move to combination C, giving up no more than one meat for four vegetables; Charlie would be willing to give up as many as five vegetables to gain one meat in a move to combination A. They both have an incentive to arrange a trade in which one unit of meat is traded for between four and five units of vegetables. The trade would make each of them better off.

e. The personal worths of both individuals must differ if exchange is to be mutually acceptable.

2) Suppose that Charlie and Linus have the following initial personal worths:
Charlie: 7 meat = 1 fruit
Linus: 3 meat = 1 fruit

a. Compared to Linus, is Charlie fonder of fruit or meat?

b. If the government makes it illegal to trade fruit for meat, always assuming that the law is obeyed, who gains and who loses? Why?

c. Now, the government relents and allows trade, but makes it illegal for anyone to trade at any exchange ratio other than one meat for one fruit. Explain the likely consequences of this new ruling.

    d. Next, suppose the government relents even more, but in order to protect fruit consumers a price ceiling is put on fruit. The maximum price of one unit of fruit is set at four meats. Who is likely to gain, and who is likely to lose by this price control? Explain.

    e. Finally, imagine that the government takes off all restrictions on the trade of meat and fruit. Introduce a middleman who conducts the trade between Charlie and Linus. What is the *maximum* cut the middleman can take in the form of meat? Or of fruit?

Answers:

    a. Fruit.

    b. Both lose because both could be better off if permitted to trade.

    c. No trade will occur; neither is willing to give up 1 fruit for only 1 meat.

    d. Neither will be as well off as they would be under free trade; however, there is opportunity for trade because Charlie would be willing to give up 7 meats for 1 fruit, while Linus demands only 3 meats in exchange for 1 fruit.

    e. With free trade, a middleman can offer Linus 3 meats for 1 fruit, then trade 1 fruit to Charlie for 7 meats, keeping 4 meats for his efforts.

3) You obtain a permit for one of a limited number of parking spaces allotted by your college; a friend is allotted a desk in the library stacks. Suppose that you would each be better off if you were to trade your parking permit for your friend's desk space.

    a. This kind of trading is almost invariably prohibited by the college authorities. Why?

    b. If you were the college president, why would you prohibit it?

    c. Would you consider solving the whole problem by simply selling parking space to one and all, like a private downtown parking garage? Why?

Answer:

    a. College authorities cannot pocket the money from the sale of the parking space since it is not their private property. However, the power to control who gets the use of the parking space is a valuable good, so the authorities could capture that value in nonmonetary forms.

    b. Since the president cannot pocket money from the sale of parking spaces, nonmonetary forms of competition for the parking space become more important. He can capture the value of the space in non-monetary forms, such as from commitments to help raise funds for the college, from speeches to promote the college, or from personal favors.

c. The value of the parking space can be captured in either monetary or nonmonetary forms. If decision makers cannot receive money for the space, nonmonetary forms of payment become more important. (As a student, would you prefer the parking space be sold, or would you prefer to have the college authorities decide how the space is distributed?)

4) "Economic analysis implies that permitting trade is better than prohibiting it." Does it?

Answer:

No. It does not imply what is good, bad, better, or worse. It implies what will be observed in the real world. Individual economists, however, often assert that trade in various circumstances is good or bad.

5) "Trade between the Mediterranean and the Baltic developed when each area produced a surplus of some good." What do you think this quotation from a history text means? Can you propose an alternative explanation of that trade?

Answer:

If it is supposed to mean that one area had more of some good than it wanted (could possibly use at all), the statement is wrong. And we can't think of anything else it might mean. We propose that the relative supplies were different, so the relative values (personal worths) were different, leading to mutually preferred exchange and reallocation of goods among Mediterranean and Baltic people.

6) "Middlemen and the do-it-yourself principle are incompatible." Explain.

Answer:

Middlemen facilitate exchange and specialization, while "do-it-yourself" is a reduction of specialization and exchange — "eliminating the middleman" who economizes on transactions costs and doing it yourself is not necessarily cheaper. (This doesn't mean that it's not ever cheaper to "do it yourself"— to the contrary, look at the home improvement industry.)

7) Based on tables 4.1 and 4.2, what is the value of the combined gains of trade to Sam and Joe measured in bottled water? What is the combined

value, measured in granola bars, of the gains of trade to Sam, Joe, and the newcomer?

Answer:

Sam gained an additional 10 bottled waters worth 8 granola bars but paid only 7. To Sam, therefore, the gains were 1 granola bar, worth 1.25 bottles of water. Joe paid 10 bottles worth 4 granola bars but received 5 granola bars. To Joe, the gain was 1 granola bar, worth 2.5 bottles of water. So the combined gains to both Sam and Joe were worth 3.75 bottled waters (or 2 granola bars).

The newcomer gained 2 granola bars from the trade, so the combined worth of the exchange to all three participants (its social gain) was: 1 granola bar + 1 granola bar + 2 granola bars = 4 granola bars. Everyone gained from the trade, even though Sam and Joe ended up with 2 fewer granola bars between them.

Can we also measure the social gain in terms of bottled water? No, because we don't know the newcomer's personal value of granola bars in terms of bottled water.

CHAPTER 5

DEMANDS AND THE LAWS OF DEMAND

We don't live in refugee camps. We live in economies with markets, where we can compare goods and offers and can buy and sell. So widely recognized are the advantages of markets that "primitive" tribes have truces on market days. Several medieval political leaders amassed fortunes by fostering marketplaces (fairs) in their favorite cities and inviting foreign merchants to attend—for a modest fee. And doubtless merchants recognized one general economic law: the "First Law of Demand."

FIRST LAW OF DEMAND

The First Law of Demand says, "Less is demanded at a higher price." No matter what the amount demanded at the current price, there is a higher price at which less would be demanded. Or, in the opposite direction, "The amount demanded is larger at a lower price." We will be explaining two demand functions. One is the demand by one person; the second is the demand aggregated over a population.

Demand Function Relates Amounts Demanded to Prices: The word "function" is a way of indicating that the amount demanded depends on—is a function of—something. Here, it's the price. Sometimes we'll refer to a demand curve or schedule (when imagining the demand function in a graph). "Demand" will mean the whole curve, schedule, or function—not just the amount demanded at some specific price.

Simplicity Is a Virtue: Realistic Data Are a Burden: Concepts and principles will be explained with simple, seemingly unrealistic numbers. Don't assume that the simplicity weakens the analysis. And we use "quantity demanded" and "amount demanded" interchangeably.

Arithmetic Example of a Demand Function: Table 5.1 shows the typical feature of a demand function. Here, the commodity is quarts of milk per week. The demand function, or demand schedule, lists the number of quarts demanded per week for each price. In table 5.1, at the price $.70, the quantity demanded is four quarts per week.

Table 5.1 *Demand Function (Schedule) for Quarts of Milk Weekly*

Price of a Quart	Weekly Demanded
$1.00	1
.90	2
.80	3
.70	4
.60	5
.50	6
.40	7
.30	8
.20	9
.10	10

"QUANTITY DEMANDED" VERSUS "DEMAND"

It is analytically sinful to confuse (a) the whole schedule of amounts demanded at various prices, such as shown in table 5.1, with (b) one of the amounts demanded at a specific price, like six units at $.50. In figure 5.1, the demand schedule is represented by a graph. The line on the graph is the "demand curve." The "amount demanded at a particular price" is represented by one point on the demand curve.

Graph of the Principle of Demand — Demand Curve

The data of table 5.1 are plotted in figure 5.1, with the points identifying the combinations of price and quantity being linked with a smoothed line. It is conventional to measure price along the vertical scale and quantity along the horizontal scale.

The "quantity demanded" is the amount demanded at any one of the prices in the schedule. An increase in "demand" means the whole schedule of listed quantities has increased. A person's wealth may have increased, so that at each possible price more is now demanded.

Quantity: Rate or Stock?

For some storable or durable goods like tennis rackets, shoes, or automobiles, the number demanded at a particular price may mean the number of items kept on hand as a stock. At some price of milk, you might wish to keep consistently about two quarts on hand, replenishing your supply at convenient shopping times, while consuming at a relatively steady daily rate. So there are

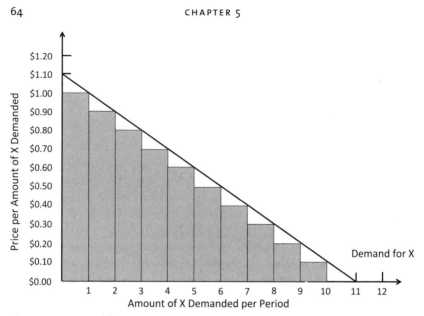

Figure 5.1 *Demand for X*

This is a bar graph of the demand schedule in table 5.1. A smoothed line, or demand curve, has been superimposed, because a simple line is easier for graphic techniques. The demand curve can be read: "At any specified price, the horizontal distance indicates the quantity demanded." Or it could be read: "For a given quantity demanded, the height indicates the marginal personal worth at that quantity, expressed as a price."

two measures of the "amount demanded." One is the stock of milk on hand, say, generally two quarts. The other is the flow or rate of consumption of milk per week. Even though at any moment there are only some two quarts in the refrigerator, the demand measured as a rate of consumption (or use) might be six quarts per week.

The demand function does not require that the amounts demanded have to adjust continuously and smoothly to every tiny change in price. A slightly higher price might have no discernible effect on the current quantity demanded; nevertheless, at some sufficiently higher price, or threshold, the quantity demanded will be reduced. The quantity of gasoline you demand at $3.50 per gallon might be the same as at $3.40 a gallon. But at some higher price, say, $4.00, you would buy less. You'd cut back on the gasoline to minimize reductions in everything else.

At some higher price of a good, less will be demanded, and at some lower price more will be demanded. That's the First Law of Demand.

Examples of possible shapes of demand curves are shown in figure 5.2. Each of these demand curves "slopes downward." At lower prices more is de-

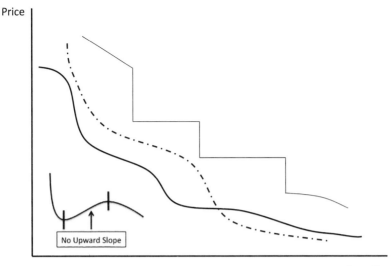

Fig. 5.2 *Possible Demand Curves*

Any line, whether smooth or stepped, straight or curved, is an acceptable representation of the relationships among marginal personal worth, price, and the quantity demanded. We'll often use a straight line because it's easy to read. The line is assumed not to have any upward sloping portion (a possible exception will be discussed much later).

manded, and at higher prices less is demanded. The amount demanded and a price are "negatively" related.

NEGATIVELY SLOPED DEMAND

While the demand curve can have many shapes and slopes, it will not have an upward (positive) sloping segment — unless an unusual "wealth effect" occurs. A demand curve can be vertical in a range of prices, indicating that within that range, the quantity demanded doesn't change. But at a sufficiently higher price, the amount demanded will be decreased. The principle of demand is possibly the most reliable and most important principle in Economics.

SLIDE VERSUS SHIFT

Though many other things affect the quantity demanded — income, health, age, sex, family size, past personal experience, prices of other goods — they are assumed to be unchanged during the time the demand schedule is used. The effects of changes in any factor other than the price of the good are represented by a changed demand — a shift in the demand, which means that at a given price the quantity demanded has changed.

"Change in demand" means the whole demand schedule has shifted. "Change in amount demanded" means a change in quantity demanded because of a change in price with no change in the demand schedule. Always distinguish between: (1) a change in the quantity demanded because of a price change (a slide along the demand schedule) and (2) a change in demand (a shift in the entire demand schedule due to a change in some factor other than the price).

Demand depends in large part on a demander's income or wealth. In figure 5.3B, the lower demand is associated with a lower income. Shifting the demand curve shows the effect of a higher income.

By common terminology, the quantity demanded of a "normal" good increases or decreases with increases or decreases in income. "Income elasticity of demand"—the proportionate change in quantity demanded relative to the proportionate change in income—is positive, but not necessarily unitary. If less of the good is bought as a result of greater income, the good is designated as "inferior." Our attention is generally directed to demand responses to income changes of "normal" goods, that is, goods with positive income elasticity of demand.

Relative Prices

We've looked at the price of just one good, without regard for the prices of other goods. However, if the dollar price of eggs was $13 a dozen and gasoline was $29 a gallon and a hair styling was $100 and a hamburger was $16, you'd probably consider a $1 price of bread to be "low"—relative to prices of other goods. The price of just one good is not sufficient to discern the true cost of buying a good. The *relative* price of a good is important in determining its "real" price in deciding whether to buy and how much to buy.

During inflation, when almost all prices rise, there's an extra complication. A rise in the price of one good doesn't mean its price has risen relative to prices of other goods. Others may have gone up even more. You've got to look at many other prices, more than if there were no inflation. More mistakes of computation and comparison are then made. This confusion is a major reason inflation tends to reduce "productivity" of the economy. The effects of inflation on money prices are discussed further in chapter 42.

ASSUMPTIONS ABOUT ACTIONS, NOT ABOUT THOUGHT PROCESSES

We are not presuming people consciously think in terms of explicit demand curves. You may never have heard of the "demand function," yet you behave in accord with what the demand curve concept implies. Atoms and rocks have

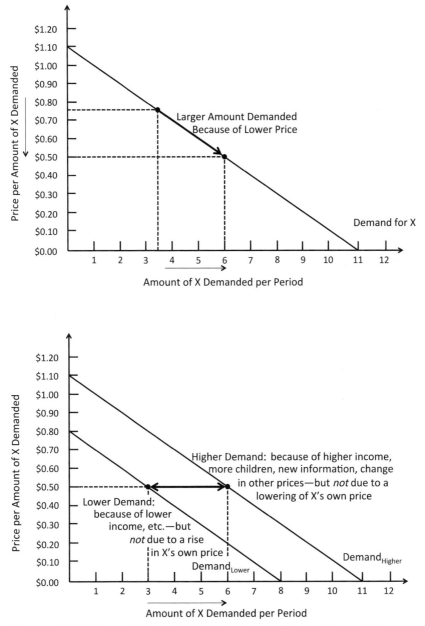

Figure 5.3A & B *Change in Amount Demanded versus Changed Demand Curve*

Figure 5.3A shows a change in the "amount demanded" in response to a change in X's own price. That's shown as a slide along a given unchanged demand curve to the new amount at the new price. Figure 5.3B shows a change in "demand," meaning the whole demand curve has shifted consequent to a change in something other than its own price, say the price of a substitute or an individual's income. Thus, a "demand change" means a shift in the demand curve, say from Demand Lower to Demand Higher in Figure 5.3B.

never heard of the laws of physics, yet their behavior is consistent with —
implied by — the laws of physics. We use those laws and principles to deduce
behavior — not to deduce or characterize some process of thought.

Interpretation of a Person's Demand Function with "Personal Worth"

If you buy two quarts of milk per week, we'll assume you do so because the
milk is worth to you at least the price to be paid. Your total personal worth
of the 2 quarts of milk per week is the total amount of other goods you'd be
willing to give up, or pay, to get the 2 quarts. The measure of the "amount of
other goods" we'll use is a generalized measure — the dollar purchase cost of
the other goods. If you were willing to pay $7 for 2 quarts per week, your total
personal worth of 2 quarts per week would be $7. We don't have to ask why
the milk is wanted. It's sufficient for our purposes that you are willing to give
up something to get it. And people accept options and exchanges that have a
personal worth to them at least equal to the price to be paid.

In table 5.2, we interpret the demand function (schedule) in terms of "personal worths."

Total and Marginal Personal Worth

The first two columns of table 5.2 describe the demand function (schedule).
Because one unit per day is demanded at $1.00, we interpret that to mean
that having one unit daily has a personal worth at least equal to $1.00 to the
buyer — or else the buyer wouldn't have bought it.

Looking at two units, the data indicate that if the price were $.90, two units
are demanded. A second unit must have an added (marginal) personal worth

Table 5.2 *The Demand Schedule and Personal Worths*

Price (1)	Quantity (2)	Marginal Personal Worths (3)	Total Personal Worths (4)
$1.00	1	$1.00	$1.00
.90	2	.90	1.90
.80	3	.80	2.70
.70	4	.70	3.40
.60	5	.60	4.00
.50	6	.50	4.50
.40	7	.40	4.90
.30	8	.30	5.20
.20	9	.20	5.40
.10	10	.10	5.50

of at least $.90 (column 3), or else the buyer would not have purchased a second unit at a price of $.90. The total personal worth of two units daily is $1.90 (column 4). That's the sum of the marginal personal worth of one unit plus the marginal personal worth of a second unit. It is not equal to the price ($.90) multiplied by the quantity purchased (2) at that price.

"Personal worth" identifies the greatest price a person would offer to get that unit of the good. We didn't specify what item or items we'd give up to get the good. We'll think and measure in terms of the most dollars a person would offer to get the good. Fortunately, we're almost always able to buy the good for less — yielding a "gain from trade" whether measured in money or in goods purchasable with that amount of money.

At a price of $.80 per unit, a buyer would buy 3 units each week. We deduce that a fourth must add less than $.80 of personal worth, or the fourth would be demanded at that price. We are presuming that a buyer won't buy a unit whose contribution to the buyer's total personal worth is less than the price of that unit.

Distinguish between the total and the marginal personal worths. The total personal worths increase at larger amounts of the good. This is a generally valid relationship for every good and for every person. In contrast, marginal personal worth decreases at larger amounts of the good. Diminishing marginal personal worths at greater amounts of a good is a universal characteristic of all people for all goods — or so we presume in economic analysis.

DIRECTION OF RELATIONS, NOT EXACT DATA, IS PERTINENT

Two Margins: Marginal Personal Worth and Marginal Units of the Good
"Marginal" applies to a) the added unit of a good, and b) the added amount of "personal worth" associated with that marginal unit of the good. The "marginal personal worth" of a marginal unit of a good is the increase in total personal worth consequent to that additional (marginal) unit of the good. In table 5.2, if the buyer purchases six, instead of five, units, the total personal worth to the buyer increases by $.50. That's a marginal personal worth of $.50 at the sixth unit of the good. Table 5.3 is the same as table 5.2 with two added columns, "market value" and "consumer surplus."

Marginal Units with Marginal, Total, and Surplus Consumer Worths
The sum of marginal worths on the marginal units one through five plus the marginal personal worth at the sixth, the marginal unit, is $4.50 (= $1 + .90 + .80 + .70 + .60 + .50); this is the total personal worth of six units. The consumer surplus is $1.50 (= $4.50 − $3.00, the excess of personal worth over

Table 5.3 *Concepts in the Demand Function*

		Personal Total Worth	Marginal Personal Worth	Total Market Value	Total Consumer Surplus
Price	Quantity				
$1.00	1	$1.00	$1.00	$1.00	$0.00
.90	2	1.90	.90	1.80	0.10
.80	3	2.70	.80	2.40	0.30
.70	4	3.40	.70	2.80	0.60
.60	5	4.00	.60	3.00	1.00
.50	6	4.50	.50	3.00	1.50
.40	7	4.90	.40	2.80	2.10
.30	8	5.20	.30	2.40	2.80
.20	9	5.40	.20	1.80	3.60
.10	10	5.50	.10	1.00	4.50

If the price were $.50, the buyer purchases six units at an expenditure of $3.00 ($.50 × 6), while personally assessing the total personal worth of the six units at the equivalent of $4.50, as illustrated in figure 5.4. The buyer would have achieved a consumer surplus that is the equivalent of obtaining $1.50 (= $4.50 − $3) more of total personal worth.

market value). The quantity demanded brings the marginal personal worth down to equality with the price. That maximizes the "consumer surplus worth" at that price.

Personal Worth or Market Value: Which One Indicates Welfare?

Don't be like a governor of California who—in defending a law that reduced the aggregate quantity of tomatoes harvested in California—bragged that the total market value had increased. (He neglected to mention that the smaller crop had a smaller total personal worth.) The increase in the market value of the entire crop may have made the tomato growers wealthier, but it cost society a reduction in total personal worth.

It is an error to try to leap from total market value of some quantity of a good to an inference about its total personal worth. Both the market value and the total personal worth are shown in figure 5.5. The market value rectangle, formed by the new price and the smaller quantity produced, may be larger at the higher price. But total personal worth, shown by the entire area under the demand curve, is smaller at the smaller quantity. And, more pertinently, the consumer surplus is smaller at that smaller quantity.

The consumer's surplus, not the market value, is usually considered the desirable thing to maximize. How much of the personal worth is obtained by the buyer/consumer or is captured by the seller depends on the pricing tactic

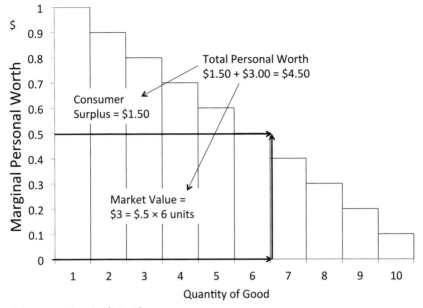

Figure 5.4 *Marginal Worths*

The sum of the marginal personal worths at the 1st, 2nd, 3rd, 4th, and 5th units plus the marginal worth of the marginal unit (the 6th) is the total personal worth of six units. The "market value" of the six units is represented by the area of the rectangle formed by the horizontal distance measuring the quantity demanded (6 units) multiplied by the vertical distance measuring the price ($.50). The consumer (or buyer) surplus is the excess of total personal worths over the prices paid on each unit—the total consumer worth in excess of the market value. The total consumer worth at 6 units is the equivalent of $4.50 (= $1 + .90 + .80 + .70 + .60 + .50). The market value (total cost of purchase) is $3.00 (= 6 × $.50).

of the seller. How much should go to the seller is a source of argument, with no general consensus.

In general, a higher price for a good will reduce the quantity demanded, and therefore will reduce both total personal worth and consumer surplus. But that higher price may cause consumer spending on the good (market value) to rise or fall, so changes in market value of the quantity purchased as the output and price change tell us nothing about changes in consumers' total personal worth.

WHY SO MUCH CONCENTRATION ON "MARGINALS" RATHER THAN TOTALS OR AVERAGES?

When you buy something, you act as if you had made two decisions: 1) whether or not to buy, and then 2) how much of it to buy. Those two become just one if you are considering the purchase of just one unit, say a car, house, or piano—at least for most people!

The amount you'll buy will be interpreted as being the amount that maxi-

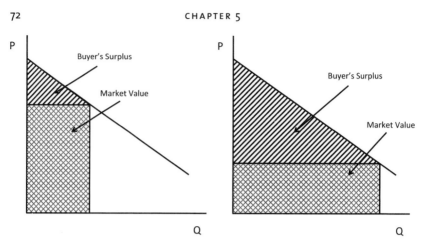

Figure 5.5 *Buyer's Surplus plus Market Value Equals Total Worth*

The left diagram shows consumer's (buyer's) surplus at a small amount of the good. It shows also the smaller total personal worth than in the right diagram, where the price is lower. A smaller quantity of the good always means a smaller total worth and smaller consumer surplus; the market value may be higher or lower depending on the slope of the demand curve. The consumer/buyer's surplus worth — the gains from the purchase — is the excess of total personal worth over the total market value.

mizes your net personal worth (your personal total worth of the good minus the cost). That net total personal worth is "consumer surplus." We assume the most reliable presumption is that people will buy an amount for which the achieved consumer surplus is maximized. You won't buy one more if the added personal worth to you is less than the cost of buying one more. And you will buy more so long as added personal worth to you exceeds the cost of buying one more. The prospective addition to total personal worth is compared to the additional cost of one more. The cost of one more is the "marginal cost." The added personal worth obtained with an additional unit is the "marginal personal worth."

The average personal worths and average costs don't tell how much will be bought. In table 5.2, at the fifth unit, the marginal personal worth is $.60, and the average per unit personal worth of 5 units is $4.00/5, or $.80. However, you wouldn't buy a fifth if it costs more than $.60, its marginal personal worth. Indeed, at any price over $.60 you'd be worse off (less total personal worth net of cost) if you bought more than 5 units, despite their higher average personal worth.

DOLLAR PRICE AND RELATIVE PRICE

When making purchase decisions, you want to know something about the general, or average, level of prices so you can tell whether the price of something is high or low. What counts is the "relative price," not just the "dollar" price. A relative price change occurs, for example, when just one price in dollar terms changes while other prices are constant.

But in the real world, we can't reliably assume other dollar prices are constant. If the dollar price for the product of some business firm falls, the question facing the business manager is: "Is there also a fall in the (dollar) price of all other goods (called deflation) or is it a fall in just this one good's (dollar) price? If it's a fall for this one product, I may not be able to continue to produce profitably. If I were sure it's associated with a fall in the dollar price of all goods, so that the costs of my inputs also will fall, I am more likely to be able to continue profitable production. If I'm not sure which it is, however, I'm going to hesitate in maintaining production and in investing."

The confusion caused by inflation and deflation, which mask relative price changes, reduces productivity of the economy and even causes recessions. People tend to speak in terms of "dollar prices," but act in response to relative prices.

MEANING OF "CHANGE IN PRICE"

When referring to a change in the price of a good, we'll mean that only that good's price changes. Thus, the price of that good has changed relative to the prices of other goods. If, instead, every other price also were to be changed by the same proportion, there'd be no change in prices of one good relative to another. The demand curve shows that more is demanded at a lower dollar price on the assumption other prices aren't changed.

Cross-Price Effects on Demand: Substitutes and Complements

Goods can be substitutes or complements in the sense that the demand for the good depends strongly also on the price of another good. The demand (curve) for margarine depends on the price of butter, as illustrated in figure 5.6. A higher price of butter raises the whole demand for margarine. As a result, at a given price of margarine more will be demanded the higher is the price of butter.

This shift in the demand curve for one good caused by a price change in another is a "cross-price" effect. The goods can be substitutes, in the sense that a higher price of one raises the demand curve for the other, as people shift to purchases of the good whose price has fallen relative to the good whose price was raised. Pairs of goods are "complements" if a higher price of one good reduces the demand curve for the other good. And two goods are "independent" if a change in the price of one has no discernible effect on the demand for the other.

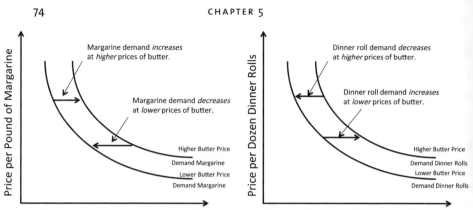

Figure 5.6 *The Cross-Price Effects on a Good's Demands of Changing Prices of Substitutes and Complements*

Changes in the prices of other goods can produce "cross-price" effects on the demand for a good. As the left-hand graph indicates, an increase (decrease) in the price of one good, butter, can cause not only a decrease (increase) in the quantity demanded of that good, butter, but can also cause the quantity demanded of another good, margarine, to increase (decrease) at all prices. Goods related to one another in this way, where a change in the price of one good causes a shift in the same direction in the demand of another good, are "substitutes."

As illustrated in figure 5.6, a rise of the price of butter causes the demand for margarine to shift in the same direction, for margarine and butter are "substitutes in demand." But if a rise in the price of one good causes a reduction in the demand for another good, those are "complements in demand."

On the other hand, as the right-hand diagram indicates, an increase (decrease) in the price of one good, butter, can cause the quantity demanded of another good, dinner rolls, to decrease (increase) at all prices. Goods related to one another such that the change in the price of one good causes a shift in the demand of another good in the opposite direction are "complements." When the change in price of one good causes no discernible change in the demand schedule of another, the goods are said to be "independent."

SUGGESTIVE LABELS

Is "personal worth" just a fancy label? Note the distinction between labels or names as a) "identifiers" versus b) "descriptor-definers." A movie labeled "Gone with the Wind" has nothing to do with a past hurricane. A "hot-dog" is not a dog in heat.

The word "worth" in "personal worth" is dangerous, because it suggests some inherent "worth" in the good being demanded. Economists have used the word "utility," which suggested a reason the good was demanded. But what is "utility" to one person is often "disutility" to another. Smoking, alcohol, pornographic literature, golfing, and playing games on computers have disputable "utility." By using the more neutral expression "personal worth," we can avoid disputable opinions about "good" and "bad." If someone is willing to pay for something, it has "worth" to that person, whether other people approve or disapprove.

QUESTIONS AND MEDITATIONS

1) Figures 5.3A and 5.3B illustrated the difference between a change in demand and a change in quantity demanded. This distinction is crucial. In figure 5.3Alt, identify which movement indicates a change in demand and concomitant change in quantity demanded and which indicates a change in quantity demanded with no change in demand.

2) The following is characteristic of Mr. A's market demand for pencils. Each price is associated with the number of pencils he would buy each year.

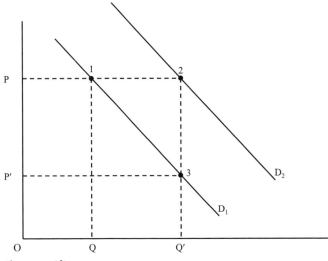

Figure 5.3Alt

At price OP and demand D1, we are at point 1. If price falls to OP', quantity demanded increases from OQ to OQ', but demand (D1) has not changed. Alternatively, starting at point 1, demand increases from D1 to D2. If price doesn't change, quantity demanded increases from OQ to OQ'—so both demand and quantity demanded increase.

Price	Quantity	Total Revenue
$1.00	1	$1.00
.90	2	$1.80
.80	3	$2.40
.70	4	$2.80
.60	5	$3.00
.50	6	$3.00
.40	7	$2.80
.30	8	$2.40
.20	9	$1.80
.10	10	$1.00

At a price of $.60 Mr. A would own five. At a price of $.50 he would own six. At each of these two prices, he would have a total of $3.00 in pencils. Does this mean that he attaches no value to a sixth? What value does he attach to the sixth?

Answer:

He values the sixth at $.50.

3) The demand schedule of the preceding question shows that at a price of $1, the annual consumption is 1 unit. At a price of $.90, the annual consumption is 2 units.

Can it be said that this person wants each one of those 2 units more than he wants 90 cents' worth of annual expenditures on any other goods? Note that at the price of $1, he spent annually $1.00 on this good, whereas at a price of 90 cents he spent $1.80 or $.80 more than previously. Do you still say he values the extra unit at approximately 90 cents, even though he spends only $.80 more? In explaining your previous answer, what is meant by "value"?

Answer:

No. Only a second unit.

Yes — 90 cents.

He can choose to buy one or two or more at the price of $.90. He chooses to buy two, so the second must be worth the extra $.90 he pays for it. Value is the amount of some other good one is willing to give up to get this good whose value is being defined.

4) Can the table in question (2) be read as follows: "A person sees a price of $1, and he therefore buys one egg. The next hour he sees the price has fallen to 80 cents; so he dashes out and buys three. A couple of hours

later, the price rises to 90 cents; so he buys two"? If it can't be interpreted that way — and it can't — how is it to be interpreted?

Answer:

A person's demand schedule relates his quantities demanded at alternative possible prices at a given time; if a purchase is then made, circumstances affecting his preferences are thereby altered, and he will have a new schedule.

5) Consumption is a rate concept, even though the good being consumed may be held as a stock of goods. True or false?

Answer:

True.

6) Mr. A currently uses water at a rate of 3,650 gallons per year at the present price. Suppose that his demand doubles, so that his rate increases to 7,300 gallons per year. How many more gallons of water will he consume during the first week of higher demand?

Answer:

If Mr. A spreads his purchases out evenly over each week of the year, he will consume an additional 70 gallons for a total of 140 gallons during the first week. However, consumption is a rate concept, hence we do not know the pattern of purchases — we do not know how many he will consume during the first week. He may consume nothing during the first 51 weeks and then in the 52nd week consume the initial 3,650 gallons as well as the additional 3,650 gallons (maybe to refill his now new and larger swimming pool).

7) "According to the law of demand, the lower the price of vacations, the more vacations I should take. Yet I take only one per year. Obviously the law of demand must be wrong." Is it?

Answer:

No. I may take longer vacations. Or, the length of my vacations does not change, but they will be more elaborate or exotic.

8) There are three conceptions of the amount demanded: (1) the rate of consumption; (2) the quantity a person wants to buy in order to increase his current stock; (3) the quantity a person wants to own. As an example of each: (1) a person may consume eggs at the rate of 6/7 per day (which does not necessarily mean he buys and eats a fraction of an egg each day); (2) on Saturday he buys a half dozen eggs; (3) he may own an average of

three eggs in his refrigerator. Which of these three measures is a rate of activity and which is a "stock"?

Answer:

First is rate; second and third are stocks.

9) Using the demand-schedule data in question 2, suppose that these refer to the number of diamond rings a person would want to own at each price. He now owns four rings.
   a. How many more would he buy or sell at each possible price?
   b. If the equilibrium price in the market turned out to be $.30, how many would he want to buy or sell and how many would he then own — remembering that he has four initially?

Answer:

   a. Sell 3 at $1, for he presently holds 4 but wishes to hold only 1 at a price of $1; 2 at $.90; 1 at $.80; and so on. Buy 1 at $.60; 2 at $.50; and so on.
   b. He would buy 4 more to have a total of 8.

10) Why is it nonsense to talk about urgent, critical, crying, vital, basic, minimum, social, or private needs?

Answer:

No such thing as basic, vital need — except that we "need" more of everything that is not free. It's a matter of what price we are willing to pay and a matter of more or less, not all or none.

11) A book was entitled *Social Needs and Private Wants*. Would the title have suggested something different if it had been *Social Wants and Private Needs*?

Answer:

Whatever might be suggested to innocent readers, each title displays sloppy use of analytic language.

12) An increase in demand (the demand schedule) is shown graphically by a demand curve above (to the right of) or below (to the left of) the old demand curve. Which is it?

Answer:

To the right or above.

13) Which of the following would increase the demand for wigs?
   a. A raise in one's salary
   b. Higher price of hats

    c. Having a swimming pool

    d. Rise in cost of hair care

    e. Getting divorced

    f. Number of other people who wear wigs

    g. Lower price of wigs

Answer:

    All, except the last one. Why? (Lower price induces a movement along the demand schedule, not a shift in the schedule.)

14) Explain how what is often called "impulse" buying is consistent with the laws of demand. Explain why habitual buying is also consistent. Suggest some behavior that would not be consistent.

Answer:

    Whatever provides the impulse, the lower the price of the item, the greater is the probability the impulse to buy will result in a purchase, and the higher the price, the less likely the impulse will be effective. Habitual buying is consistent with knowing the price from prior purchases and having settled on a consumption plan which is generally repeated over time. However, let the price of the consumption goods change, and the habit will be revised. Only with inconsistent behavior would less be purchased at lower prices and more at higher prices.

15) Does the demand to have children obey the fundamental theorem of demand? The demand by immigrants for entry to the United States? The demand for divorces? The demand for pianos? The demand for a winning college football team? The demand for "As" in this course? The demand for appendectomies?

Answer:

    Yes, to all.

16) A governor of California once asserted that the reduction of Mexican labor in California (as a result of the end of the guest worker program) did no harm, because the total value of the crop harvested was larger than before. Evaluate the relevance of that criterion.

Answer:

    Welfare change is not measured by total market value of the entire crop. If demand elasticity is less than one, bigger supply will lower total market value (total market revenue) while total personal worth increases because of larger supply (larger total worth measured by total area under the relevant portion of the demand curve). Do not confuse total personal worth with total market-exchange value (market sales revenue). Total personal worth is closer to a welfare criterion.

17) If one pair of shoes can be exchanged for four shirts, and one shirt trades for two pairs of socks, and if one pair of shoes trades for six pairs of socks, what series of trades could you make to get steadily richer? (This is known as "arbitraging" among markets for different goods.)

Answer:

Borrow one pair of shoes; sell the pair for four shirts; sell the four shirts for eight pairs of socks; then sell the six pairs of socks for one pair of shoes — leaving you with two pairs of socks. Repeat the operation, each time picking up a net gain of two pairs of socks.

18) What are prices? Can there be prices without money?

Answer:

Exchange rates among goods are prices, whether or not money is one of the goods exchanged.

CHAPTER 6
THE EXTENT OF EXCHANGE

With the concept of the demand function, we can answer the question asked at the end of the refugee camp story, "What determines the *extent* of mutually preferred exchanges?"

EXCHANGE

We start with two-person exchange and later explain the advantages of intermediaries in facilitating trade. Figure 6.1 shows two demand curves, one for Rae and one for Ted. Each person initially has 20 eggs. Rae places a higher marginal worth, $.12, on one more egg, when she has 20, than does Ted, whose marginal worth of eggs at 20 eggs is only $.04.

Mutually advantageous trade opportunities exist when the marginal worths of a good differ among people. Both Ted and Rae would gain by trading, wherein Ted offers to sell some eggs at a price over $.04, and Rae will buy at a price below $.12. When their marginal worths are *equalized*, with Ted then having 8 fewer for a total of 12 eggs and Rae having 8 more at 28, there can be no further mutually beneficial trade.

The Gain to Rae: Consumer Surplus

Because their marginal personal worths differed initially ($.12 and $.04), both will gain by trade at some price between $.12 and $.04 per egg. When Rae has 28 eggs per month, her marginal personal worth of eggs is down to $.08, the price. Her total gain in personal worth is represented by the area under her marginal worth line, her demand curve, and above the $.08 price paid to Ted. That gain is "buyer's surplus," or "consumer surplus," obtained by trade.

The Gain to Ted: Seller Surplus

Ted was willing to sell 8 eggs to Rae at a price of $.08 each, because his marginal worth of the 8 eggs sold was less than $.08. His gain, "seller's surplus," is represented by the shaded area above his demand curve and below the price received for what is sold.

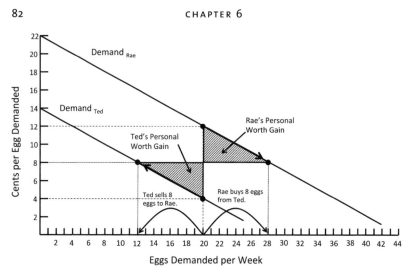

Figure 6.1 *Demands and Exchange*

Rae will buy some eggs at prices below $0.12, and Ted will sell at prices above $.04. Buying eggs at $.08 gives Rae the gain indicated by the shaded area under her marginal worth line and above the price line at $.08. Rae's purchase of 8 eggs brings her total amount to 28 and reduces her marginal worth of eggs to the price. As the seller, Ted's gain is shown by the area under his price line ($.08) and above his marginal worth line for 8 units sold.

The Extent of Gains to Both: Exchange Brings the Marginal Worths of Both Parties to Equality

The total personal worth of Ted plus that of Rae was maximized. Of course, neither Ted nor Rae cared about that combined total personal worth; they each traded only because what they got was "worth" more than what they gave up. Whenever marginal personal worths are not equal, there is an exchange that both will be willing to make.

The exchange benefits the trading parties *as if* there had been a costless increase in goods to both of them. Each achieves a situation of greater personal worth even though the total *amount* of goods has not increased. The *reallocation* of various goods in the trade benefited both. It is as if we each had bread and butter, but I had a lot of butter and only a little bread, and you had a lot of bread and only a little bit of butter. A trade of some butter for bread would improve each of our situations.

BASIS OF NATIONAL POLICY ON MARKET COMPETITION

Demand versus Demand, Instead of Demand versus Supply

The two traders are viewed as "cooperative rivals," "cooperative" in being willing to trade, and "rivals" in trying to buy at a lower, or sell at a higher, price. Cooperative rivalry is a fundamental trait of a civilized and productive society.

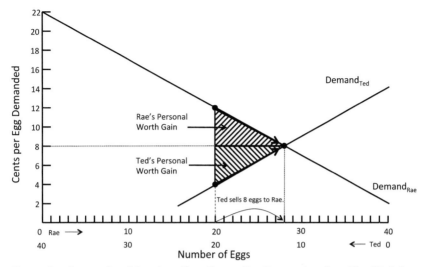

Figure 6.2 *Demand and Supply as Two Competing Demanders for a Fixed Total Supply (Stock) of a Good*

Reversing and then superimposing one of the marginal worth lines of figure 6.1 interprets exchange in terms of a demander and a supplier—with the lower marginal worth demander becoming a supplier to the higher marginal worth demander. One person's demand confronts demands of other people. The supply to a person is represented by the amounts not demanded by other people at various prices. The supply facing you is what is released, at the price offered, from the demand by the rest of the world. Fundamentally, it's not demand and supply—it's your demand curve against the rest of the world's demand curve, which is perceived as the supply curve to you.

In figure 6.2, the total supply of 40 eggs is measured by the entire width of the base of the diagram. Both Ted and Rae initially have 20 eggs. Ted's demand is measured to the left from the right edge. We start with the case in which there are no costs of trading—that is, no search, information, or transactions costs are incurred by either Rae or Ted.

We wish to see not only why trade is mutually beneficial, but also why intermediaries, despite their costs, can reduce the total costs of trade and enable everyone to obtain more total personal worth.

In the initial allocation, each party has 20 eggs. Rae's marginal personal worth exceeds Ted's. That difference in heights (marginal personal worths) of the two demand curves implies that both would gain by trade, by sales of eggs from the lower marginal worth person (Ted) to the higher marginal worth person (Rae). The feasible gains to each are marked as shaded areas.

Supply to "Me" Depends upon "Your" Demand

The supply of more eggs to Rae depends on the demand by Ted. And the supply of eggs to Ted depends on Rae's demand for eggs. The supply conditions facing you depend on the demands of other people. The higher their demands, the smaller is the supply to you from the existing supply of eggs.

Convergence to "Equilibrium"

We can expect a series of transactions in moving to the final revised distribution. The agreeable prices will be between the two different initial marginal valuations of the traders.

With 20 eggs held by each, Rae would offer up to $.12 for an egg, and Ted would be willing to sell at any price above $.04. As they trade, Ted's marginal worth of eggs rises, and Rae's decreases. The price to which they converge is 8 cents, indicated by the height at which the two demand curves intersect.

Trade slides people along their demand curves toward equalization of their marginal personal worths. Each puts a higher worth on what is obtained than on what is given up. The resulting price is the "equilibrium" price, and the final marginal worth equalizing allocation is the same no matter what the initial allocation. A good from other people is obtained by pushing up the price so as to induce others to demand less (offer more) to you, when you are willing to pay a price higher than their marginal worth of those units.

We have dealt with the prerequisite conditions, the direction, the gains, and the extent of trade. But there are, for both parties, costs of searching for someone who wants to sell or to buy eggs.

INTERMEDIARIES AND TRANSACTION COSTS

The extent to which the full potential of trade can be realized depends on costs of discovering the differences in marginal worths and of arranging for purchases and sales. A vast array of auxiliary devices, procedures, activities, and arrangements has evolved to reduce transaction costs.

"Transaction costs" is a name for costs of shopping among potential traders, discovering goods and qualities being offered, finding and canvassing alternate possible suppliers, assembling, transporting, and making the goods available at the time desired, providing inventories to enable inspection and prompt delivery, record keeping, advertising, insurance, warranty service, replacing defects, negotiating and recording the terms of trade, and enforcing the exchange and contractual agreements — to name some aspects of exchange.

Rarely is trade conducted directly between the ultimate parties. "Do-it-yourself" transaction costs are not small. They are usually larger than the observed spreads between the retail and wholesale prices of goods. Otherwise, people usually would buy direct from producers rather than retailers. At the retail level for most household consumption goods, the spread between buying and selling price ranges from about 15 percent to 50 percent of the price to the consumer. Some discount houses provide a smaller spread by asking the consumer to bear some of those costs by self-service. The customer receives less retail service, less credit, less delivery and location convenience. To customers whose time is less valuable, that may be worthwhile. To others it is not. So the degree of intermediation varies to suit various customers.

Intermediaries, as in the refugee camp, reduce the costs of finding trade possibilities, of assessing the characteristics or qualities of goods, and of negotiating exchanges and arranging for such legal protection as warranties. The cost reductions permit more of the potential trade to be realized.

How much would you buy if you had to buy your food directly from the farmer, your shoes from the manufacturer or the wholesaler, your gasoline from the refinery, and your milk from the dairy farmer? And how would you feel about being *denied* the opportunity to sell your used car through a dealer, and being required to find a willing buyer completely on your own? Successful intermediaries make their livings by performing their services at lower costs than feasible for the consumers and producers of the purchased goods.

INTERMEDIARIES' REDUCTION OF FULL PRICE BY REDUCING TRANSACTION PREPARATION COSTS

Both the buyer and seller can benefit by intermediaries' reductions in transaction costs.

Benefits to the Buyer — Lower Full Price

In table 6.1, consider the buyer of the eggs. *Without* helpful intermediaries, the cash price is $.08, along with self-service transaction costs of $.01, the full price being $.09. The cash price *with* intermediaries is 8.5 cents, a greater money charge but less than the full price in the do-it-yourself transaction.

Benefits to the Seller — Higher Net Price

Without intermediaries, he receives a price of $.08, but bears costs of 0.5 cents, yielding a net return of 7.5 cents. *With* intermediaries, his receipts are 7.75 cents.

Total transaction costs for the buyer and seller are 1.0 + 0.5 = 1.5 cents in a do-it-yourself arrangement; they are only .75 cents with intermediaries.

Table 6.1 *Money and Full Prices without and with Intermediaries*

Without Intermediaries

	Money	Nonmoney	Full Price
Buyer	8	1.0	9.0 (paid)
Seller	8	0.5	7.5 (received)
Do-it-yourself costs		1.5¢	1.5¢

With Intermediaries

	Money	Nonmoney	Full Price	Gain Cost Reduction
Buyer Pays	8.5	0	8.50 (paid)	0.50 (= 9 − 8.5)
Seller Gets	7.75	0	−7.75 (received)	0.25 (= 7.75 − 7.50)
Cost Reduction with Intermediary			.75	+.75 Gain to Buyer and Seller

Reduction in Transaction Costs	
Do-it-yourself Cost	1.50
Intermediary Cost	0.75
Intermediary Cost Reduction	.75

The intermediary has *earned* .75 cents per egg for his services — he saved the buyer .5 cents and saved the seller .25 cents for a total saving of one-half the transactions costs the buyer and seller would have incurred without his services.

DIAGRAM OF REDUCED COSTS OF ARRANGING EXCHANGES

Figure 6.3 shows a buyer and seller trade without an intermediary. Both buyer and seller are at X_1 before trading. (Remember that Ted's demand curve is reversed, so for him a move to the right is a reduction.) As trading occurs, both — buyer and seller — move toward X_2, the point at which their respective personal worths equal the full price. If the buyer's (Rae's) "do-it-yourself" prepurchase search and product inspection costs are the equivalent of $.01 per unit of the good purchased, the buyer's full price is $.09 ($.08 paid to the seller, Ted, plus the $.01 of Rae's prepurchase costs).

The seller also has prepurchase search, negotiation, and exchange enforcement costs equal to, say, $.05 per unit of egg. So the seller's *net* realized price is only $.075, not $.08. Of the total potential gain from trade, part is dissipated by the prepurchase search and negotiation costs, and part is unrealized because of

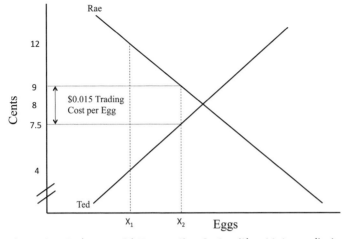

Figure 6.3 *Exchange with Transaction Costs without Intermediaries*

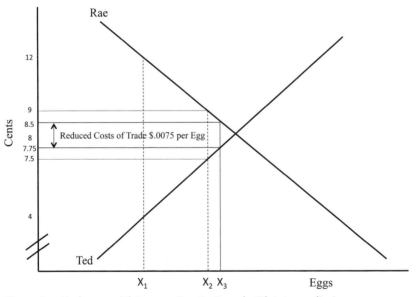

Figure 6.4 *Exchange with Transaction Costs and with Intermediaries*

the reduced extent of trade — trading stops before reaching the intersection of the two demand curves because of the existence of transactions costs.

Figure 6.4 shows a situation with intermediaries doing some of the transaction preparation actions. Both the consumer-buyer and the producer-seller gain from trade when intermediaries reduce the "shopping" costs. The *full* price paid by the buyer is reduced to $.085 and the net amount received by the seller rises to $.0775. Importantly, the quantity of eggs traded increases to X_3—closer to the equilibrium that would have resulted in a world without transactions costs.

Full Price Is the Pertinent Price

Intermediaries reduce the seller's money receipts (from 8¢ to only 7.75¢) and raise the buyer's money payments (from 8¢ to 8.5¢). However, both the buyer and the seller are made better off in light of the distinction between the "money price" and the "full price." The costs of the trading have been reduced and the extent of trade is greater because of the specialized services of an intermediary.

"Buy direct from the manufacturer and eliminate the middleman's cost." In fact, it is incorrect to regard intermediaries as interposing extra costs and raising the price for the buyer and lowering the price paid the seller. Successful intermediaries reduce the costs of exchange, permitting benefits to both the ultimate buyer and seller.

MARKETS: OPEN OR CONSTRAINED ACCESS?

The narrowed spread (resulting from competition among middlemen) between the buying and selling prices of intermediaries is a consequence of free-entry market competition, or "open markets." "Open markets" mean that access to markets is open to all people without arbitrary, contrived barriers—not that there are no costs involved in providing exchange-facilitating services.

Constrained Access to Markets; "Closed Markets"

Open markets are not universal. Constraints are interposed—often at the urging of those already in the business. Existing intermediaries would prefer to restrain newcomers and tend to complain of the new "unnecessary, inexperienced, low-cost, cutthroat, excessive, unfair" competitors. Existing intermediaries or suppliers may be able to protect themselves by closing newcomers' access to markets. Several possibilities are available, some crude, some refined, but all in use.

Threats of Violence

An intermediary contends to a prospective intermediary, "It was my idea to develop the trade. Why should you be allowed to copy and benefit from my innovative actions?" The initial dealer may warn impending new dealers about a few lost teeth and possibly a broken leg.

Collusion

As a desperate tactic, a current intermediary approaches a newcomer and offers to merge, agreeing to maintain the old price spread and divide the profits, which is better than seeing the profits eliminated. But if new entrants joined the collusion, the profits of collusion would be spread among more suppliers until the gain to each was virtually zero.

Compulsory Licensing as a Restraint on Entry

The colluders ask for political help. They offer to contribute to the election campaigns of legislators. They lobby for restrictions on entry, or higher costs of entry by newcomers. Normally, licenses and permits to do business require that performance meet certain standards of safety and reliability. Applicants for entry are often required to have taken costly prior training or education. And incumbents argue there are already enough people in that business. Or consumers should be protected from "fly-by-night, quack, unreliable" dealers — or from imports from foreigners in order to protect local suppliers. Or newcomers could be screened and refused admission under the pretense that the newcomers would not maintain the "highest standard of quality." However, newcomers may offer the politicians rewards greater than those from incumbents. The cost of the competition between incumbents who are trying to defend restrictions and newcomers seeking to remove or bypass them can exhaust the potential gains to restricting competition. But this tactic is widely used.

Reducing the Pie to Get a Larger Share

Competition for favorable legislation or regulation is often called "political rent-seeking." "Rent" refers to the "gains," which are called "rents" because they are obtained not by production of more value, but instead by transferring wealth from one person to another — either directly or indirectly — by altering competitive conditions. Competition for the politically obtained favors differs from market competition for purchase and production of goods and services. In the market, you buy as many units as have marginal worths exceeding the price of a unit, and you compete by superior production, not by attempts to prevent other sellers from producing or selling.

In contrast, when you compete in politics or in nonexchange form, you are using productive resources to increase your prospects of getting protection from competitive market forces. Although market competition among sellers redounds to the benefit of consumers, political competition tends to result in transfers of wealth. Consultants, lobbyists, and lawyers are hired, and contributions are made to political campaigns. Those resources are diverted from producing more goods and services. The politically imposed restrictions on potential competition are equivalent to changing the share of the total pie (national income) going to competitors, while reducing the size of the total pie.

MARKETS — EVERYWHERE

Markets are arrangements and means for facilitating exchanges. To say that the "market" does something is a shorthand way of saying that people, in the process of arranging for and completing *mutually preferred* exchanges, bring about certain consequences. Don't think of the "market" as a *place*, but rather it is people who are doing something — usually seeking, negotiating, and conducting mutually preferred exchanges. In that sense, the "market" is a *process* by which people's beliefs, values, and demands are compared, with resultant exchanges of rights at mutually agreeable prices or terms that enable mutually preferred exchanges.

Members of Congress trade votes on issues in the "political market." Professors trade offices, furniture, and course assignments in an "academic market." In a family, children trade duties and obligations. Favors are exchanged, and exchanges occur in markets. It is impossible to conceive of a society without exchanges or trades, or of any society without markets — whether they are for personal favors, ideas, private property rights, political favors, family obligations, and so forth. This text focuses primarily on markets for exchanges of goods with private property rights, where money is involved in the exchange. However, we will see also that exchanges still occur in "markets" in which money prices are controlled or are not permitted.

IMPLICATIONS OF MARKET EXCHANGES, NOT JUDGMENTS

As stated in chapter 1, economic principles are silent on normative issues and questions. The implications of economic analysis are not judgments about whether something is good or bad, desirable or undesirable — no more than are those of physics, chemistry, or biology. Economics deduces only what happens in response to some change in specified circumstances. It says that if you think in terms of preferences of individuals, you can interpret exchanges as mutually preferred exchanges. Each person is seeking a preferred situation, as judged by each. If you believe individual judgments and choices are desirable actions, then you could deduce that markets are "good."

There is a strong temptation to conclude that economic analysis proves that exchange improves a person's situation. But some critics of the "desirability" of personal choice attach more weight to the consequences for those who make unfortunate choices, than the weight they place on the "right to make one's own choices." Neither the critic nor the defender of the right to make choices is necessarily the more humanitarian.

Everything in life involves a trade-off between alternative amounts of goods and degrees of achievement of goals. The question then arises of who might make better judgments for others. Can you expect other people to act entirely on your behalf? Or could you plausibly argue that people, as a matter of moral duty or propriety, should have to make their own decisions? It is universally the case that some people are not regarded as being capable of properly understanding the consequences of their decisions and therefore should be restricted or controlled "for their own good," much as with children.

Indeed, in many instances — for example, for medicines, health care, and food — even "mature" adults are prohibited from entering into some mutually agreeable exchanges with whomever they please. Furthermore, it has been contended that people do not always have the appropriate tastes: the contention is that people would place a higher value on classical music, museums, or education if properly exposed to those things, and they would spend less on flashy cars, television, or sports. If these critics had their way they would try to tax more heavily "improper pleasures." Where and how is the line to be drawn — and by whom?

Warning: Don't jump to the inference that economic analysis therefore assumes that people do not care about ethics. Quite the contrary: we'll show later that the analysis includes issues of ethical behavior. The point here is that economic analysis doesn't tell you what is "good" or "bad"—just what "is" or "is not."

CONTRACTS AND RELIABLE PROMISES: THE BINDING FORCES OF SOCIETY

We have been examining the fundamental forces and features of exchanges enabling people to gain by market activity. We assumed that once a deal is struck, the goods are exchanged as promised. But it's pertinent to know what tangential features we have been ignoring. One thing, which we'll explore later, is the *reliability* of the promised performances by the parties in an exchange. There's often a temptation to renege and get a quick gain. For example, an employer may promise payment to you after you have worked two weeks, or a retirement pension if you work a specified number of years with that firm. You want assurance the promise will be fulfilled.

Explicit contracts involving binding written or verbal commitments are usually enforced in a court of law. But that can be too expensive. No one can foresee all the possible future events and pertinent details. To help ease that enormous task, the contract is taken to include well-established side conditions, sometimes called "commercial codes," as completions of the contract by the law. Nevertheless, explicit contracts are difficult to adjust to unforeseen contingencies.

An unexpected change in the availability of a resource may prevent delivery of a product as scheduled. Even before entering into negotiations, you may incur costs preparatory for business with that person. You drive to a distant grocery to get some bargains, only to find out upon arrival the price has changed or the items are sold out. The person you expected to deal with may refuse to deal or may ask prohibitively higher prices.

Most of the time, however, the promises and expectations will be made reliably without enforcement by a legal proceeding. An astounding variety of noncontractual methods exists for increasing the assurance of promised performance — such as publicly preannounced fixed prices, reputations, goodwill, social pressures, ostracism, and the force of "ethics." We'll be examining these commonplace, though much misunderstood, "noncontractual" procedures that rely on "natural" consequences of the market. An "exchange," or "trade," is more complicated than merely paying money and receiving the good.

QUESTIONS AND MEDITATIONS

1) Which of the following are compatible with open (or free) markets?
   a. A lawyer must get permission of present lawyers before he can engage in that profession.
   b. Medical doctors must pass a state examination before being allowed to sell medical services.
   c. Selling is prohibited on Sunday.
   d. Pure food and drug laws restrict the sale of "impure" foods and drugs.
   e. Consumption, manufacture, or sale of alcoholic beverages is restricted.
   f. Securities dealers and brokers must be certified by the US Securities and Exchange Commission before they can act as middlemen in buying and selling stocks and bonds — that is, before they give advice or execute transactions.

Answer:
All are denials of open markets.

2) You are campaigning for mayor or councilman in your hometown, in which the taxi service (or garage service, trash pickup, electric power, water, gas, etc.) is provided by anyone who wants to operate a taxi business or drive his own cab. In other words, the taxi service is provided by an open market. You campaign for more government control on taxi drivers in order to ensure better quality of service.

    a. If elected, would you initiate a system of giving just one company the right to perform the service? Why?

    b. If so, how would you decide which company?

    c. Would that company be one of your campaign contributors?

    d. In some states, the right to sell liquor is restricted by the state government to far fewer stores than would prevail otherwise. Would you be surprised to learn that the liquor dealers are a political "lobby" and source of "power" in state politics? Why?

    e. What generalization does this suggest about use of political power once obtained?

Answer:

    a. Yes, unless all consumers could agree to pay me more than the one seller to whom I gave the monopoly right. (In principle, they could always pay more than a monopolist would gain.)

    b. The one who helped me most to get elected.

    c. Answered in b.

    d. No surprise. Their monopoly rents are partly used to aid (pay?) politicians, and are also dependent on political favors and support.

    e. Once in office, create favored monopoly privileges by prohibiting entry of competitors to those who support you. As we shall learn later, consumers lose more than the monopolies gain. But the ability of monopolists to pay politicians exceeds that of consumers, who have more difficulty in arranging payment because there are so many consumers, each with only a small amount involved.

3) A piece of history: "It is well to remind ourselves from time to time of the benefits we derive from a free market system. The system rests on freedom of consumer choice, the profit motive, and vigorous competition for the buyer's dollar. By relying on these spontaneous economic forces, we secure these benefits: a) Our system tends automatically to produce the kinds of goods that consumers want in the relative quantities in which people want them. b) The system tends automatically to minimize

waste. If one producer is making a product inefficiently, another will see an opportunity for profit by making the product at a lower cost. c) The system encourages innovation and technological change. . . . I regard the preservation and strengthening of the free market as a cardinal objective of this or any Administration's policies" (President John F. Kennedy, September 1962). It is discouraging that while extolling the virtues of an open, competitive economic system, businessmen and politicians restrict markets — for example, by controlling allowable imports of sugar to maintain sugar prices in the United States above the open-market level — in order to maintain larger wealth for incumbent businessmen and their employees. Confusion between freedom *of* competition and freedom *from* competition is suggested. What explains this praise of the virtues of a system of private property and open markets with simultaneous attempts to suppress it?

Answer:

Restrictions on entry by new competitors are denials of open or free markets. Those in the restricted industry gain at the time the restrictions are imposed, although their gain is less than the loss imposed on others.

4) Some discount stores advertise that they can sell for less because they buy directly from the manufacturer and sell to the consumer, thus eliminating many middlemen. What is the inadequacy in this reasoning?

Answer:

It assumes that the middleman performs no service to consumers or producers in facilitating exchange, and therefore he can be eliminated without someone else having to perform the service in which he specialized. Eliminating the middleman is a form of the do-it-yourself principle, and is not necessarily more economical.

5) A history textbook might tell you that trade in the Mediterranean Sea developed after the Greeks began to produce a surplus of olive oil and found that the Spaniards were producing a surplus of silver. What would economics have to say about the development of trade of olive oil for silver?

Answer:

There was not a surplus of either olive oil or silver. But the worth of additional amounts of olive oil to the Greeks and silver to the Spanish declined as production increased. Greeks became increasingly willing to trade olive oil for a quantity of silver, while Spaniards became increasingly willing to trade silver for a quantity of olive oil. It became economical to pay for boats and crews to transport the olive oil and silver, while still leaving both the Greek olive growers and Spanish silver miners better off than if trade had not developed.

6) For most of the items you find in the produce department of your grocery store, the packaging, transportation, and distribution costs are a much larger share of the price you pay than the share of the price that goes to the farmer. Is that a fair distribution?

Answer:

Economics does not help in making judgments about what is fair. The farmer cares most immediately about how much he is paid — relative to his costs — not about what share he received of the final selling price. The same is true of all others who participate in bringing food from the farm to the grocery store. Of course, some people enjoy "cutting out all the middlemen" and incurring the personal costs of traveling to "farmers markets" to purchase fruit and vegetables and transport them home. However, personally incurring such middleman costs does not deny that they exist and must be borne by someone.

7) It is easy to see how we all can gain by increasing aggregate output — the social pie gets bigger. It is not so apparent that everyone engaged in a trade is made better off — that seems to be just reapportioning the pie. And if there are middlemen involved in the trade, they siphon off some of the pie, leaving less to divide between the traders. What can be "the gains from trade"?

Answer:

Preferences — marginal valuations — differ among people, and they change for a given person as his holdings of goods are altered. A has cheese and would like some crackers; B has crackers and wants some cheese. Each would like to get his desired good as manna from heaven, but he is willing in this hard world to give up some of his initial holdings of the one good in exchange for some of the other. Each puts a greater personal valuation on what he gets than on what he gives, so each gains from the transaction. And some of that gain can be paid, if need be, to a middleman who conducts the trade.

8) The text speaks of "money" price and "full" price in trade, with
   and without intermediaries (middlemen) involved in carrying out a
   transaction. Distinguish between these price measures.

Answer:

The money price is the equilibrium price paid by the buyer and received
by the seller when there are no costs of making the transaction. But there
can hardly be a costless transaction, and those costs are reflected in a full-
demand price greater than the money price and a supply price less than
the money price — and there is a reduced volume of trade. Often, intermediaries can arrange and carry out the exchange at a cost smaller than
that incurred when buyer and seller deal directly with each other — and
which results in trade greater than the volume would be on a transactions
do-it-yourself basis.

CHAPTER 7

KEEP YOUR EYE ON THE MARGINALS

The principles of economic analysis require a persistent focusing on *marginals* rather than on just *averages*. This chapter illustrates the principle of *maximizing a total by equalized marginals.*

TOTALS, MARGINALS, AND AVERAGES

Suppose you have taken two tests in a class, receiving scores of 80 and 86, for a current total of 166 as listed in table 7.1. Your average score is 83 (= 166/2). You take a third test and score 89, raising your total score to 255. That addition to your total score is your *marginal* score. Because that marginal score of 89 on the third test is higher than your average (83) of the first two scores, your new average rises from 83 to 85 (= 255/3). The average is a historical measure of the past, whereas the "marginal" is more identifiable with the present. And the present or future is the basis of a current decision.

Table 7.1 *Marginal, Total, and Average Test Scores*

Tests	Marginals	Total	Averages
1	80	80	80
2	86	166	83
3	89	255	85

Table 7.2 *Marginal, Total, and Average Costs*

Chairs Made Daily	Marginal Cost	Total Cost	Average Cost
1	100	100	100
2	80	180	90
3	105	285	95

Table 7.3 *Prices and Total, Marginal, and Average Revenues*

Chairs Sold Daily	Price	Total Revenue	Marginal Revenue	Average Revenue
1	110	110	110	110
2	100	200	90	100
3	90	270	70	90

COST

In table 7.2, a firm producing chairs can make one chair a day, at a total cost of $100. If it makes two chairs a day, the total cost rises to $180. This $80 *increase* in the *total* cost when making one more chair is the "marginal" cost of chairs.

Producing three chairs daily raises the total cost to $285. That increase of $105 is the marginal cost at a rate of three chairs daily. The average cost at three chairs is now $95 (= $285/3). Adding a $105 marginal cost that exceeds the former average cost ($90) will pull up the average, from $90 to $95. Looking back at the change from one chair to two chairs daily, the average cost fell from $100 to $90, because the $80 marginal cost at two chairs was less than the preceding average ($100) at one chair.

REVENUE

Suppose you are selling chairs. The sales revenue data are in table 7.3.

You set your price at $150, but you don't sell any. So you cut your price to $110, and you sell one chair a day. To sell more chairs each day, you cut the price to $100 and sell two. Your total revenue rises to $200. The marginal revenue is $90, the increase in the total revenue. The marginal revenue, $90, is less than the $100 price received for that second chair, because, to sell two chairs per day, you have to cut the price from $110 to $100 on *both* units. You give up $10 on the one chair you could have sold alone if you hadn't cut the price to sell the second chair. The $90 *marginal* revenue is the increase in *total* revenue when selling two chairs at $100 each, rather than selling just one for $110. The *average* revenue *per chair* at two chairs daily is $100.

You could sell three chairs if you cut the price to $90. Your total sales revenue would be $270. The marginal revenue, that is, the increase in total revenue, would be only $70. The marginal revenue is the *change* in the *total* revenue consequent to cutting the price on *all* units enough to sell *one* more per day. The $10 cut in price in order to sell three chairs at a price of $90 each means the price is cut on two chairs that could have been sold at $100 each. That $20 reduction ($10 on each of the two chairs) offsets part of the $90 price received on

Table 7.4 *Total, Marginal, and Average Sale by Clerks*

Clerks	Total Sales	Marginal Sales	Average Sales
1	$1,000	$1,000	$1,000
2	$1,800	$800	$900

the third chair, bringing the total revenue increase to $70. The marginal is the change in the total, not just the amount obtained on the additional marginal unit sold.

Who Did It?

In a retail store, more clerks enable better service and more sales revenue as illustrated in table 7.4.

One clerk alone generates sales revenue of $1,000. With a second clerk, the revenue rises to $1,800. The marginal is $800 and the average is $900. In fact, the second clerk registered zero sales, while the first one's sales rose to $1,800, because the second clerk assisted customers, and the first clerk recorded the sales. The marginal revenue is $800 *with* a second clerk. The two clerks *as a team* added $800 to total revenue. The *marginal* is the change in the total consequent to including one more unit.

USE THE MARGINAL OR THE AVERAGE?

Suppose you were told that the *average* cost per life saved by expenditures on automobile airbags was $1,000,000 while the *average* cost of saving a life with seat belts was only $500,000. Should greater safety be sought by spending more for airbags or for seat belts? You shouldn't answer without knowing the *marginal* costs for saving lives by airbags and the *marginal* costs for saving lives by seat belts. That might be $2,000,000 if seat belts are used to save an extra life, while it's only $1,100,000 with airbags. That comparison of the marginal costs reverses the ranking by the average costs. The average does not tell what the *additional* effects or *additional* costs will be. It summarizes only the past— the accumulated—effects, not the next effects. When considering where to put more resources, the marginal effect is pertinent, not the average per unit of input to date.

RELATIONS AMONG TOTALS, MARGINALS, AND AVERAGES

The total, the marginal, and the average are related to each other. In table 7.5, the first column lists the number of inputs of labor in some productive act. The second column lists the total product at each amount of labor. The third

Table 7.5 *Production and Inputs*

Labor (1)	Total Product (2)	Marginal Product (3)	Average Product Per Unit of Labor (4)
First	6	6	6
Second	16	10 (= 16 – 6)	8 (= 16/2)
Third	24	8 (= 24 – 16)	8 (= 24/3)
Fourth	30	6 (= 30 – 24)	7.5 (= 30/4)
Fifth	34	4 (= 34 – 30)	6.8 (= 34/5)
Sixth	36	2 (= 36 – 34)	6 (= 36/6)
Seventh	36	0 (= 36 – 36)	5.14 (= 36/7)
Eighth	35	–1 (= 35 – 36)	4.375 (= 35/8)

column lists the marginal products, the change in the total amount with an additional unit of labor. The fourth column lists the average product per unit of labor.

The following relationships are: (1) The total products increase by the amounts of the successive marginal products. The total product is the sum of the marginal products up to that level of activity, because the marginal product is defined to be the *change* in the "total product" with each added input. (2) In this table, a *special* feature is that successive *positive* marginal products get larger at first, but then later, beyond the second unit of input, begin to decrease in size. The amount of an input at which the total product begins to increase by diminishing marginals is the "point of diminishing marginal products from that kind of input." (3) When the "marginal" is *negative*, the total decreases. (4) If the marginal is less than the prior average, the new average is lowered. Saying the same thing, when an added input lowers the average product per unit of that kind of input, the marginal product must be less than the average product.

In table 7.5, the marginal products first increase, from six to ten. Then they decrease, even becoming negative values. When the marginals are negative the total decreases, because the marginal is, by definition, the change in the total. Where the total is *maximized* (and then starts to fall), the marginal is zero (changing from positive to negative).

Marginal products rise initially, but at larger amounts of input marginal products begin to decrease. Average products rise initially when marginal products exceed average products, but when marginal products decrease to below the average product, the average products are pulled down.

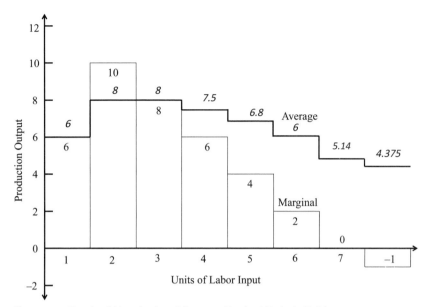

Figure 7.1 *Graph of Marginal and Average Product Data in Table 7.5*

Marginal products rise initially from six to ten. But at amounts of labor input in excess of 2 units, marginal products begin to decrease. Total output is increasing throughout this range up to 6 units of input, but by decreasing amounts after 2 units of input. Average products rise initially, when marginal products exceed average products; but when marginal products decrease to below the average product, the average products also decrease. The total output is greatest (maximized) where the marginal product is zero at 7 units of labor input. The total output is falling where the marginal product is negative, at 8 units of labor.

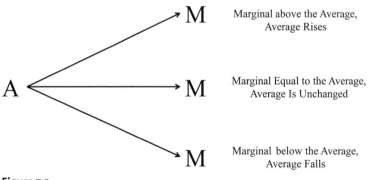

Figure 7.2

A BASIC PRINCIPLE: "THE EQUALIZATION OF MARGINALS AT THE MAXIMUM AGGREGATED RETURN"

We can now state a principle that pervades much of Economics. "Allocate resources among alternative uses so as to keep the marginal returns equal, or as near equal as possible." Or, "if marginal products aren't equal, there's a gain to be had by reallocating some resources from the use with the lower marginal product and assigning them to where the marginal product is higher."

A General Task: The Assignment of Limited Supply among Alternative Uses
In this vale of scarcity and frustration, we are incessantly confronted with problems of how best to assign limited supplies among alternative uses. We have only twenty-four hours each day for working, playing, eating, and sleeping. We have incomes too small to buy all of everything we want, so spending choices are unavoidable.

Imagine you have ten coin-like tokens which you can insert into two "money machines," A and B, from which dollars will be obtained. Your goal is to maximize the total number of dollars you get. The amounts that can be obtained from machine A and machine B are listed in tables 7.6 and 7.7.

A marginal return is the dollar output from a machine with *an added token*. The marginal returns decrease with additional tokens. The "average per token" is the total output, the sum of the marginals to that point, divided by the number of inserted tokens. For machine A, the marginal returns decrease from the

Table 7.6 *Marginal, Total, and Average Dollar Returns from Machine A*

Tokens	Marginal	Total	Average
1	20	20	20
2	18	38	19
3	16	54	18
4	14	68	17
5	12	80	16
6	10	90	15
7	8	98	14
8	6	104	13
9	4	108	12
10	2	110	11

Table 7.7 *Marginal, Total, and Average Dollar Returns from Machine B*

Tokens	Marginal	Total	Average
1	15	15	15
2	14.5	29.5	14.75
3	14	43.5	14.5
4	13.5	57	14.25
5	13	70	14
6	12.5	82.5	13.75
7	12	94.5	13.5
8	11.5	106	13.25
9	11	117	13
10	10.5	127.5	12.75

Table 7.8 *Aggregated Marginal and Average Dollar Returns from Two Machines*

Tokens	Machines and Tokens Used in Machine	Marginal Returns	Total Returns	Average Returns
1	1st in A	20	20	20
2	2nd in A	18	38	19
3	3rd in A	16	54	18
4	4th is 1st in B	15	69	17.25
5	5th is 2nd in B	14.5	83.5	16.7
6	5th is 3rd in B	14	97.5	16.25
7	7th is 4th in A	14	111.5	15.93
8	8th is 4th in B	13.5	125	15.63
9	9th is 5th in B	13	138	15.33
10	10th is 6th in B	12.5	150.5	15.05

initial maximum of $20 at the first token. For B, the marginal returns start at a lower value, $15, but the marginals of machine B decrease less rapidly.

In trying to get as much money as possible, you won't put all ten tokens into machine A. You'd get $110.00. Nor would you put all 10 into machine B, even though its total payoff of $127.50 is greater. Instead, you'd rationally allocate the 10 tokens between the two machines, and get as much as $150.50, ending with essentially "*equalized marginals*" of the two machines. Table 7.8 shows the sequence of allocation to maximize the total return from the two machines.

You would put the first token in the machine that yielded the highest marginal return, machine A, which pays $20. The second and third tokens also

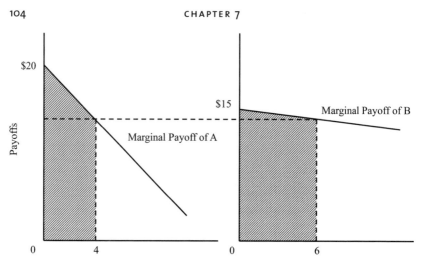

Figure 7.3 *Allocating Successive Tokens between Two Machines to Maximize Total Payoff*

The marginal products from machine A start higher but decline faster than those from machine B. With ten tokens, the largest reward can be obtained with four tokens in A and six in B. To maximize total return, the rule is to allocate the next token to the machine with the highest marginal product with that additional token. With continuous inputs, the amounts going to each should be such as to equate their marginal products to each other.

would go into A, for their marginal returns ($18 and $16) are greater than the return of B's first token ($15). The fourth token in machine A has a marginal yield of $14, but that's less than the marginal return for the first token in machine B, so the fourth token becomes the first in B.

See how the averages can mislead. The average return with a fourth token in machine A would be $17, and the average with one token in machine B is $15. Nevertheless, we put that fourth token in B, because the marginals, not the averages, are pertinent. If we mistakenly used the average to direct where we put the fourth token, and put it in A, our total return would be only $68, rather than the $69 we'd get by using the marginals to direct our tokens. The next token, the fifth, would get $14.5 from machine B, compared to the marginal return of only $14 as a fourth token in machine A. That fifth token does not go into the machine (A) with the highest available average.

The ten tokens would go four into A and six into B. The four tokens in machine A obtained $20 + $18 + $16 + $14 = $68. The six tokens in B obtained $15 + $14.50 + $14 + $13.50 + $13 + $12.50 = $82.50. The aggregate total is $150.50. No allocation other than four in A and six in B will get as much.

If we think of the inputs as perfectly divisible and continuous (like rates of hours of labor input, instead of tokens), the marginal returns of added inputs would be measured by continuous lines, as in figure 7.3. There, the *area of all the marginal returns* represents the *total return from a machine*. With two machines, total return is represented by the areas under the *combined* marginal return lines in the graph. For a maximum total product from the two machines, the amount of inputs to each machine, A and B, should be such as to equalize their achieved marginal returns.

COST MINIMIZING

Let's apply the principle — equalize the marginals — to a production situation. If two plants under common ownership are producing the same goods, we will want each to operate at a rate of production that will minimize the costs of *total* production. We won't produce goods in one plant at higher marginal costs than are possible in the other. The idea can be stated as "assigning rates of production to each so as to *equalize the marginal costs of the two*." Whether plants are maximizing the total returns from two producers or minimizing the total costs, the rule is to have each produce at rates at which their marginal returns (or marginal costs) are equalized. At any point, adopt the best of the remaining options — the highest remaining marginal return, or the lowest remaining marginal cost.

QUESTIONS AND MEDITATIONS

1) Explain or criticize the following statements and questions about the substitution postulate:

   "Every student substitutes some romance for grades when he dates rather than studies as much as he otherwise could have."

   "The substitution postulate says that a student does not seek the highest possible grades." Does the substitution postulate deny that water, food, and clothing are more basic or more needed than music, art, and travel? "There is no hierarchy of wants." What does that mean? Can you disprove it? Is travel in Europe a substitute for formal academic education? For some food? For a bigger house or new clothes or medical care? For what would it not be a substitute?

   "I'd like to play poker with you again tomorrow night, but I don't think my wife would like it." Is this consistent with the substitution principle? Is the wife's utility being compared with the husband's? Explain.

   Answer:

   Substitution means there are trade-offs. A person gives up some (not necessarily all) of one good or service for some more of another. This applies to all desired things — goods, services, goals, objectives, ideals, morals.

People give up some of one ideal for some more of another ideal. All goals and ideals are competitive and substitutable in *degrees* of achievement or fulfillment. The emphasis is on more versus less — not on all or nothing.

2) Suppose that I am indifferent if given a choice among the following three combinations:

Table 7.9

	(pounds per year)		
	Steaks		Artichokes
Options A:	100	and	30
B:	105	and	29
C:	111	and	28

   a. What is my marginal personal worth of steak (between options A and B)?

   b. What is my marginal personal worth of artichokes (between B and C)?

   c. If the amount of steak in A were doubled to 200, what can be deduced about the amount of steak required in B to make personal value equal to A?

Answer:

   a. One artichoke is worth 5 steaks, or 1 steak has a marginal personal worth of .2 artichokes, given options A or B.

   b. Between B and C, my marginal personal worth of artichokes is 6 steaks, greater than between A and B, because I have fewer artichokes at B or C than at A.

   c. Increases the amount of meat that expresses the marginal personal worth of artichokes, because I have fewer artichokes (and more meat).

3) Principles of economics are used to characterize some aspects of human nature and behavior.

   a. Do you think any of them are also applicable to nonhuman animal life? For example, which of the principles would validly apply to the behavior of monkeys, ants, bees, tigers, and birds?

   b. Which principles, if any, do you think serve to distinguish human from nonhuman behavior?

   c. What evidence can you cite to support your answers?

   d. Do you think the human race would survive if it lost the attribute described by the principle "each person is willing to forsake some of an economic good to get more of other economic goods" while some animals retained it?

Answers:

a. Yes.

b. We don't know that any of them do.

c. Behavior of bees, ants, and baboons.

d. No.

4) A parent gives each of his two children some milk and meat. The two children then exchange with each other, one drinking most of the milk and the other eating most of the meat. If the parent does not permit them to make that exchange, which of the principles (if any) is he denying? Or does the explanation rest on some new principle not made explicit in the text?

Answer:

Denies none in the text. The implied new principle is that power over other people is a good or a goal.

5) If I regard each of the following combinations as equally preferable, which principle is denied?

Table 7.10

	Goods		
	X		Y
Options A:	100	and	70
B:	105	and	69
C:	110	and	68
D:	115	and	67

Answer:

The principle "the more one has of any good, the lower its marginal personal worth" is denied because in the table the marginal substitution rate between X and Y is constant between all the options.

6) Explain the difference between the statements, "People act in accord with certain fundamental principles" and "People consult or refer to such principles for guidance in choosing their behavior." Does either

interpretation assume "free will" or independence for other people's behavior or tastes?

Answer:

The first statement contains no implication about any necessary thought process. It would also apply to rocks and water obeying the law of gravity. The second statement suggests some common or necessary mental calculation and choice making. Economics does not have to assume the second statement as a basis for its theory, despite common arguments that it does.

7) In testing a person's preference between two known options, it has been suggested that if a person agrees to let some unknown party choose for him, then he is indifferent between the two options. Do you think that is consistent with the principles listed in the text?

Answer:

It is.

8) It is a good rule to avoid costs which exceed benefits and to seek benefits greater than costs. But with interactions of two parties, costs and benefits to whom? The longer the stay in a hospital, the greater may be the benefit to a patient, but the higher is the total hospital cost he must pay. If the total bill is $15,000 for five days, the cost of a day to the patient (and the revenue to the hospital) might be said to be $3,000. So is an extra day in the hospital worth the additional $3,000 to be paid by the patient?

Answer:

Consider also the *marginal* cost to the hospital along with the *average* cost to be paid by the patient. Perhaps the major costs occur in the first several days of care; in the later days, the care, though important, is much less costly — less than the $3,000 average cost. Should the patient be kept in the hospital for an extra day? Yes, says the hospital: It receives $3,000, equal to its *average* cost, but its *marginal* cost is less than $3,000. Maybe no, suspects the patient, for whom the *marginal* benefit may be deemed to be less than the *average* (daily) expenditure.

CHAPTER 8
MORE FEATURES OF DEMAND

The First Law of Demand is critical: A sufficiently higher price will decrease the quantity demanded, and a sufficiently lower price will increase the quantity demanded. But price is not the only thing that can affect the quantity demanded. With greater income, the quantity demanded at each price is larger for most products. Also age, gender, education, and health, to name a few things, affect the quantity demanded at each price. When so many other factors affect the quantity demanded, why concentrate on price? After answering that question, this chapter explains some measures of the degree of response in amount demanded when the price changes, and why the degree of response is important.

WHY SO MUCH ATTENTION TO PRICE?

The first question really should be, "Why so much attention to price *adjustments?*" A major reason is that price adjustments make the aggregate quantity demanded of a good equal the aggregate available supply. Unhappily, our tastes, preferences, or total personal worths don't change to make us desire to have only as much of a good as our income allows. Prices change so as to reconcile personal conflicts for available goods, they direct *production* from the less-highly to the more-highly demanded goods, and they affect your *earnings* and the kind of work you will be doing.

CHANGES IN MONEY PRICES AND
CHANGES IN RELATIVE PRICES

College tuitions have increased in recent decades far more than the average of other goods, while prices of televisions, computers, and travel have fallen. These changes in *relative* prices are results of events that changed the demand for or supply of one good relative to the demand for or supply of other goods.

WHICH DEMAND?

We distinguish three demands. (1) There is the demand by *one person* for a good. (2) Another is the aggregated demand by all people for a good, from all suppliers — the *market demand*. (3) A third is the demand seen by *one* seller when offering that good to the market—to people in general. This is the "demand facing a seller."

<h2>ELASTICITIES OF DEMAND: RESPONSIVENESS
OF QUANTITY DEMANDED TO THE PRICE</h2>

A measure of the *responsiveness* of the quantity demanded of a good to a change in its price is the "elasticity of demand with respect to price," or "price elasticity of demand." A seller who contemplates the effect of cutting price expects an increase in the amount demanded by customers. The *additional* units sold will bring more sales revenue. But, at the same time, the cut in price will reduce the sales revenue on the units salable at the former higher price. Which dominates, a) the *added sales revenue of the additional units sold* at the lower price or b) the *lost revenue on former sales at the higher price?*

Elasticity of Demand

"Elasticity of demand" for a good is the ratio of a) the *percentage change* in the quantity demanded in response to b) a *percentage change* in the price of the good.

$$\text{Elasticity of demand} = \frac{\text{percent change in quantity}}{\text{percent change in price}}$$

A $1 cut in price from $10 is more important than a $1 price cut on a good from $100. The first is a 10 percent change, whereas the second is a 1 percent change. If quantity demanded increased by 5 units, from 20 units to 25 (a 25 percent increase), that would be more significant than a 5 unit change from 100 to 105 units, only a 5 percent increase.

If a price cut of 10 percent results in a 20 percent increase in the quantity demanded, the ratio of the 20 percent change in quantity to the 10 percent change in the price is 2 (= 20 percent/10 percent).

$$\text{Elasticity} = \frac{20 \text{ percent change in quantity}}{10 \text{ percent change in price}} = 2$$

The increase in quantity demanded is in the *opposite* direction to the change in price in the denominator, a decrease in price. Therefore, the ratio, the elasticity, is algebraically "negative." Typically, that's ignored, and is called 2 rather than −2.

Table 8.1 gives data on selected points (combinations of price per unit and number of units demanded) of a demand schedule. The percentage changes in price in moving down the schedule and in corresponding quantities are indi-

Table 8.1 *Elasticities of Demand*

Price	Price Cut %	Quantity	% Change of Quantity	Elasticity	Market Value
$10		1			$10
	10		100	10 = 100/10	
9		2			18
	11.1		50	4.5 = 50/11.1	
8		3			24
	12.5		33	2.6 = 33/12.5	
7		4			28
	14.3		25	1.7 = 25/14.3	
6		5			30
	16.7		20	1.2 = 20/16.7	
5		6			30
	20		17	0.85 = 17/20	
4		7			28
	25		14	0.56 = 14/25	
3		8			24
	33		12.5	0.38 = 12.5/33	
2		9			18
	50		11.1	0.22 = 11.1/50	
1		10			10

cated, along with calculated elasticities between successive positions. Finally, market values (seller receipts, buyer expenditures) are provided as products of price multiplied by quantity.

A minor point in table 8.1: The measure of elasticity for a price cut from $6 to $5 is not $1.00, as it should be when the total sales revenue is the same at the two prices. This discrepancy arises because the data represent discrete changes in prices, so that the measures depend upon the prices and quantities used as the basis for computing the percentages. This slight ambiguity could be removed if we had a smooth continuous demand curve rather than widely separated points.

Elasticity Review

Elasticity of demand is a measurement of movements *along* a demand schedule, not a result of a *shift* in the schedule. Figure 8.1 presents a straight-line demand schedule. The initial price is indicated by OP on the vertical axis, and

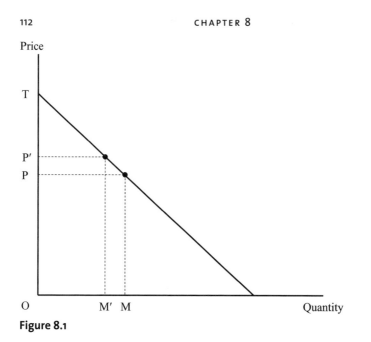

Figure 8.1

the initial quantity by OM on the horizontal. We want to measure how "elastic" the demand is at, or near, price P. Consider the small segment of the demand schedule between OP and OP'. That is, for an increase of price from P to P', is the *relative* decline in quantity from M to M' larger, smaller, or the same?

Since elasticity is measured by the proportionate change in quantity divided by the proportionate change in price:

$$\text{Elasticity} = \frac{\Delta Q/Q}{\Delta P/P} = \frac{MM'/OM}{PP'/OP} = \frac{MM'}{OM} \times \frac{OP}{PP'} = \frac{MM'}{PP'} \times \frac{OP}{OM}$$

$$= \frac{OM}{PT} \times \frac{OP}{OM} = \frac{OP}{PT}$$

If we are at the midpoint of the curve, then OP = PT, and elasticity at that point is equal to one (unity). At higher prices, OP > PT, that is, elasticity is greater than one; at lower prices, it is less than one. If we are in the upper half of the curve, where OP > PT, elasticity is greater than one; a decrease in price will cause a greater proportionate increase in quantity, so total revenue rises. Caution: Do not confuse elasticity of the demand curve with its slope. In particular, do not presume that a relatively flat curve is more elastic.

It has been noted that elasticity determines whether market value increases,

Table 8.2 *Elasticity, Price, and Total Revenue (Expenditure) Change*

	e > 1	e = 1	e < 1
P↑	↓	—	↑
P↓	↑	—	↓

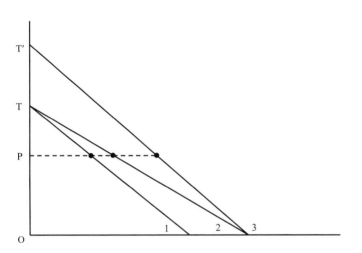

Figure 8.2

decreases, or remains unchanged as price rises or falls as we move along the demand schedule. Table 8.2 provides a summary of the relationships:

For any combination of price changes and elasticity conditions, the table indicates whether market value is increased, decreased, or is unchanged.

Compare the three demand curves of figure 8.2. Curves 1 and 2 have a common price-axis intercept; curves 1 and 3 are parallel, that is, they have a common slope. Since elasticity = OP/PT, curves 1 and 2 have the same elasticity at price OP. Demand 1 is more elastic than demand 3 at price OP, although their slopes are the same: OP/PT > OP/PT′.

Few, if any, actual demand curves are straight through their entire length. A special exception to a linear curve is a rectangular hyperbola. In figure. 8.3, any price multiplied by its corresponding quantity demand, for example, OP × OM, equals any other price times quantity indicated by the curve, for example, OP′ × OM′— market value is constant as we slide along the curve — for OP/PT = OP′/P′T′ . . . = 1, unitary elasticity.

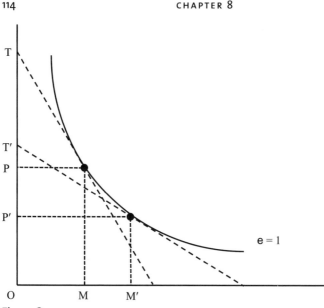

Figure 8.3

Elasticity of the curve at price OP = OP/PT, when T is the vertical axis intercept of a straight line tangent to the curve at that price. Similarly, T′ is located by a tangent line at the lower price.

WHY BOTHER WITH ELASTICITY OF DEMAND WITH RESPECT TO PRICES? THE CHANGE IN TOTAL REVENUE

"Elasticity of demand with respect to prices" is a way to refer to effects on *a seller's total market revenue,* if a seller changes the price.

With elasticity greater than one, a rise in price of, say, 10 percent will reduce the amount demanded by more than 10 percent. Total revenue will fall, because the quantity was reduced more than proportionally to the increases in price on each unit. And with an elasticity of greater than one, if a seller reduced the price, the total sales proceeds would increase. The percentage increase in the amount demanded would be greater than the price cut.

Suppose, instead, the elasticity were less than one: the price effect dominates the quantity effect. A higher price will increase total sales revenue, and a lowered price will reduce total sales revenue. Look at the drop in price from $4 to $3 in table 8.1. The quantity demanded increases from 7 units to 8. The percentage increase in quantity demanded (14 percent) is less than the percentage fall in price (25 percent). The elasticity is less than one. Total sales revenue is lower. It was $28 (= 7 units at $4 each); now it's $24 (= 8 units at $3 each). If *elasticity is less than one,* the *total market* value of quantity sold *decreases* at a lower price, and increases at a higher price.

Meanings of "Inelastic"

"Inelastic" demand is in the range of prices where the elasticity is *less* than one—where the percentage change in amount demanded is *less* than the percentage change in price along that demand schedule. "Inelastic" does *not* mean the *change in quantity is zero*! That would be "complete or perfect INelasticity" or, more commonly, "zero elasticity." Because the elasticity is generally not the same at all parts of the demand schedule, the expression "elastic" demand refers to the region of prices at which the elasticity is greater than one. And inelastic means it's less than one.

REMEMBER: ELASTICITY OF DEMAND IS A MEASURE OF MOVEMENTS *ALONG* A DEMAND SCHEDULE, NOT A RESULT OF A SHIFT IN THE DEMAND SCHEDULE.

The price changes referred to here are changes along a given unchanged demand schedule. If, instead, the price change were a result of a shift in the whole schedule, we couldn't use a measure of elasticity to indicate the resulting change in total market value. The difference is indicated in figures 8.4A and 8.4B. In figure

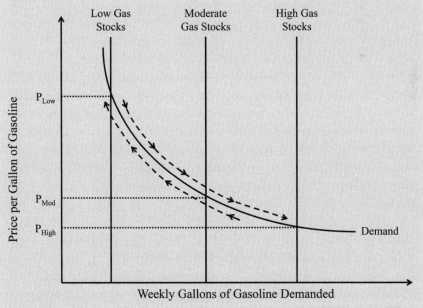

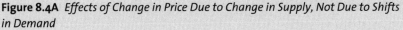

Figure 8.4A *Effects of Change in Price Due to Change in Supply, Not Due to Shifts in Demand*

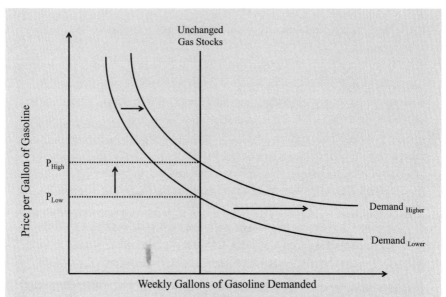

Figure 8.4B *Change in Price Due to Change in Demand, with Unchanged Supply*

8.4A, the quantity demanded changes as the buyer slides along an unchanged demand curve in response to changes in available supply. In figure 8.4B, it is supply that is unchanged, and the price changes as a result of a shift to a higher demand curve.

Why Use the Concept of Elasticity When Its Measures Are Unknown for Almost All Goods?

No one can know the required actual data well enough to compute exact elasticity. But the concept explains several commonly used pricing and selling tactics, identifying situations that are "monopolistic" and "monopolizing," which are usually, though not always, regarded as "undesirable" and prohibited by law. The concept of elasticity helps in the analysis of effects of government taxes and subsidies. But here we can use it to express the *second law of demand*.

THE SECOND LAW OF DEMAND

The fact that adjustments are less expensive — and therefore more fully accomplished — with the passage of time is the basis of the Second Law of Demand: *Elasticities of demand with respect to price are greater the longer the time after a price change.*

When the price of gasoline first rose significantly after a war in the Middle

East, the quantity demanded in the United States fell very little at first, but after a few months the reduction was more noticeable, and after a few years the quantity demanded was reduced drastically. Hastier adjustments are more expensive. Substitution by new types of cars and other forms of, and arrangements for, transportation, such as car pooling, consolidating errands, using buses and scooters, airplanes and railroads, become more economical as older cars wear out. Existing equipment appropriate at the older prices will be replaced in time with equipment designed to use the higher-priced inputs more effectively. Because the immediate effect is often quite small, observers tend to ignore the later extensive and major consequent adjustments.

When wages of labor are raised — say, by a legislated increase in the minimum wage — the first law of demand indicates that less labor will be demanded. But often the reductions in employment occur only many months later after the producer has been able to substitute equipment that uses less labor. By that time, observers forget that the reduction is a response to higher labor costs. With the passage of time, these changes become more difficult to measure because so many other things also change.

A quicker, more complete adjustment is preferred to a delayed adjustment, but the costs of faster adjustments are greater than slower ones. The Second Law of Demand says that in the "longer-run" more adjustments are completed.

Short and Long Runs

The terms "short run" and "long run" roughly separate the more immediate from later adjustments. Not all responses to every event occur immediately. The timing depends on a) the costs of determining the appropriate changes and in making the changes earlier rather than later and on b) the benefits of doing so earlier rather than later.

Sometimes, "short run" is taken to mean the length of time before all desired adjustments are completed. This is often summarized by saying that the "short run" is that period in which some things are "fixed" but which are "variable" with the passage of time. Saying they are "fixed" is a way to recognize that faster adjustments are too costly to be worth doing immediately. Categorizing the adjustments in just two stages, the more immediate "short run" and the delayed "long run," is convenient and usually adequate.

We could think of long-run adjustment to mean the "completed" adjustment, which will persist only until there is another change in events that affect the demand or the supply. Considering the effects during both the initial adjustment actions and the subsequent adjustment, it would be tempting to think that the long run means "later and ultimate," while the short run means

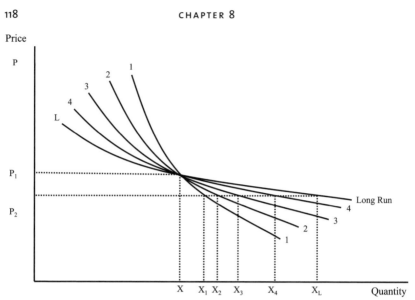

Figure 8.5 *Effect of Time on Price Elasticity of Demand*
The longer the time after a price change, the greater the effect on the rate of demand — shown by the flatter, more elastic curves for more elapsed time after a price change.

"sooner and temporary." However, there's no basis for presuming later adjustments will long persist, as if there were no more shocks to which to adjust.

A FAN OF DEMAND CURVES

One demand curve alone, representing the adjustment to a change in price after some interval, is not capable of completely representing "demand." For every succeeding moment, the demand becomes more elastic or less inelastic. A single demand curve is one of a set of demand curves, like a fan, radiating from the initial price. Figure 8.5 illustrates the idea.

The fan of demand curves shows the general pattern of the various quantities demanded at successive moments after the price falls from P_1 to P_2. The price effect on quantity demanded increases over time until it reaches its ultimate full "long-run" adjustment shown by the flattest curve.

INCOME, WEALTH, AND DEMAND

Many and possibly most goods are "normal," as defined in chapter 5: a higher income raises demand, as represented by an upward (rightward) shift of the demand curve, roughly proportionally to the increase in income. For "superior" goods, increases in income or wealth result in shifts in demand that are more than proportional. For "inferior" goods, increases in income result in proportionally smaller increases in demand. A good may be "superior" for someone in the low-income range and "inferior" for someone in a richer range. Cheap wine may be a superior good at low incomes, but with greater wealth people may consume more expensive wines. We usually will be investigating situations in which the goods are believed to be normal.

Income Elasticity

Analogous to "price elasticity of demand," "income elasticity" is the percentage change of the quantity demanded divided by the percentage change of income. But which income? — transient momentary income or expected longer-run "permanent" level of income? A 20 percent increase in quantity demanded in response to a 10 percent increase in "permanent" income at an unchanged price means the income elasticity of demand is two at that income range. A momentary rise in income probably will have little effect.

Definition: *Income elasticity of demand for a good is the ratio of the percentage change in quantity demanded to the percentage change in income that caused the change in the demand schedule.*

WEALTH AND INCOME EFFECTS OF A CHANGE OF PRICE

The quantity demanded depends on price, as reflected by a movement along the demand curve. However, a change in the price of a good can shift the demand curve for that good — in addition to causing a movement along the demand schedule. This can happen when the demander already owns a very large amount of the good. The rise in its price makes that person wealthier. The increased wealth can shift the demand curve upward to larger amounts demanded at each price.

This is a situation in which the price change affected both the position of the demand curve and the position on the demand curve. (1) One effect is the slide along a demand curve. This "substitution" effect is the movement to a smaller amount of a good at a higher price, and to more of other goods the prices of which have not increased. (2) The other effect on amount demanded is through the effect on a person's wealth when the price of a good changes. This is the "wealth" effect of a change in the price of some good of which a person owns a substantial amount. That resulting increase in wealth tends to shift the demand curve upward. The two effects of a price change — substitution and wealth — are in opposite directions.

When the price of oil first rose sharply in response to a smaller supply available from Middle East oil producers, the owners of oil wells in the United States became enormously wealthier, and that increase in wealth increased their demand for bigger cars and for oil products, such as gasoline. The effect of that increase in wealth shifted up their demand curves for gasoline more than enough to offset the substitution effect of a higher price *along* the higher demand curve. But there seem to be few instances in which this wealth effect is important enough to be noticeable in individuals' responses to price changes.[1]

PRECISELY WHAT IS MEANT BY THE DEMANDED AMOUNT?

For most things, we purchase bulk *amounts* at convenient shopping times, while consuming more smoothly at some rate per unit of time. Usually, the "demanded amount" refers to the *average rate* associated with a price, and around which there are momentary random deviations.

At any given price, for each person the quantity purchased (and consumed) by that person would vary around the average amount associated with that price. The transient fluctuations in sales from day to day usually don't call for adjustments in prices or production. However, they cause difficulties when the seller can't reliably distinguish between the temporary deviations and a change in the underlying rate around which deviations occur, and the fluctuations around the mean are important in explaining some pricing policies, which we'll be exploring later.

RATE OF DEMAND VERSUS AGGREGATE VOLUME DEMANDED

The difference between the "rate" and the "volume" demanded is parallel to a distinction between speed of travel and distance traveled. "Rate" is a "speed" while "volume" is like a distance. For demand and for supply, there's a rate (speed) of purchase and of production, such as 5 units per hour. That is the same as "40 per 8-hour day" or "200 per 5-day week." Each of these expressions denotes the same rate, or speed, of "amounts" or "quantity" demanded (or supplied). But they do not tell how many (the volume) are demanded.

A grocer may have a customer who buys at a low rate, but who continues as a nearby resident to buy for a long time at that low rate. Another customer may buy at a very high rate but for only a couple of days and then disappear. From

---

1. The "substitution" effect of a price change always is associated with the price of a good and the quantity of the good demanded changing in opposite directions. This is the effect we emphasize and appropriately presume to prevail, yielding negatively sloped demand curves. The "income" effect can be of such nature and so large as to overbalance the substitution effect, resulting, over a limited range, in a price change inducing a change in quantity demanded in the same direction. This uncommon phenomenon characterizes a so-called Giffen good.

the point of view of the seller, which buyer reveals the greater demand? Is it the total anticipated *volume* of purchases over time, or is it the *current rate* of quantity demanded that determines how a seller will respond, or is it some weighted combination? Later, we'll return to this question.

This distinction between the rate of activity and the total aggregated volume over time is important both in analyzing demand and also in considering production. If production at the rate of 5 an hour continued for only 2 hours, the volume would be 10. If production continued for 8 hours at that same rate of 5 per hour, the volume would be 40 units. When referring to "quantity" or "amount" of production or "amount" of demand, we must know whether we are referring a) to the rate, without specifying how long that rate continues, or b) to a volume, which won't tell us at what rate or speed that volume is produced over some period.

How Can We Compare Demands Differing in Rates and Timing?

Consider some different patterns of amounts demanded over time at a given price. One buyer purchases 10 per week for 2 weeks (a visitor at a vacation site). A local resident buys an average of 1 per week every week of the year. From the point of view of the seller, which is the "bigger" demand? Which is more important in its economic effects on production and price?

This kind of problem about the "temporal length of demand" by a customer faces every producer, whose planned or possible production, cost, and revenue patterns vary over time.

Some variables are at higher rates for shorter spans of time, and slower for longer spans. Which is bigger or more important in the effects on prices, production, and income? In choosing among them, the producer has to convert the varying and varied *streams* of costs of production and the *streams* of revenues from customers to comparable single-valued measures.

Miraculously, there is a way. It's being done all the time, with "capital values," one of the most important procedures and principles in all economics. Later we'll devote several chapters to it. In the meantime, we'll set aside the potential volume- and time-related effects, because they're not pertinent for the illustrations of the simple but realistic demand and supply analysis in the next chapter.

QUESTIONS AND MEDITATIONS

1) Are the following statements correct or incorrect? Explain your answers.
   a. "A 1 percent rise in price that induces a 3 percent decrease in amount taken indicates elasticity greater than one."

b. "A 1 percent fall in price that induces a 3 percent increase in amount purchased indicates an elasticity of greater than one."

c. What is wrong with asking whether a 1 percent rise in price induces a 3 percent decrease in demand?

Answer:

a. Correct.

b. Correct.

c. It is conventional to call this a decrease in amount demanded, not a decrease in demand—which would refer to a shift in the whole demand relationship.

2) "Elasticity is a measure of the percentage increase in demand for a one-cent change in price." There are two errors in that statement. What are they?

Answer:

Elasticity is the *ratio* of *percentage* change in quantity in response to a *small percentage* change in price. It is "percent," not one-cent. And it is "quantity demanded," not demand.

3) In the graph below, which of the three demand curves has the greatest elasticity at price P1? At price P2? Does the elasticity change as the price changes along each curve? Is the "slope" of a demand curve equal to the "elasticity" of the curve?

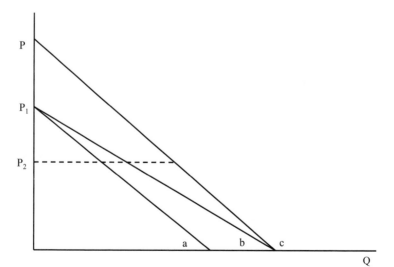

Figure 8.6

Answer:

> Demands *a* and *b* have the same elasticity at any common price. But the elasticities of *a* and *b* decrease at lower prices. Remember: With O as the origin, P as the price, and T as the vertical-axis intercept of the demand curve, elasticity = OP/PT. Demand *c* has lower elasticity at any price than demands *a* or *b*, and its elasticity decreases at lower prices. Demand *c* has the same slope as *a*, but its quantities are larger at any price. Hence, for any small price cut, the absolute change in the amount demanded on line *c* and *a* is the same, but for *c* the increase is a smaller percentage of the amount demanded (at that price). Elasticity = $\Delta Q/Q \times P/\Delta P = \Delta Q/\Delta P \times P/Q = 1/slope \times P/Q$.

4) Price and demand:
   a. If the price of gasoline rose 100 percent, automobile manufacturers would make changes in the designs or operating characteristics of automobiles. True or false?
   b. What effect would that price rise have on gasoline consumption?
   c. Would the effect be more extensive at the end of one year or at the end of three years?

Answer:

   a. True. Economic theory says they would. Compare cars in countries with higher gasoline prices with those in countries with relatively low gas prices.
   b. Reduced gasoline usage.
   c. Effects would be more extensive in three years than in one year.

5) Price and amount demanded:
   a. Because we represent a demand curve with precise numbers, does that mean that people have these numerical schedules in their minds?
   b. What essential property illustrated by the demand-schedule data does characterize their behavior?

Answer:

   a. No.
   b. The negative functional relationship between price and amount demanded — at a higher price a smaller amount is demanded and in the reverse direction, at a lower price a larger amount is demanded.

5) If the price of candy rises from $4 to $5 per pound while the price of ice cream rises from $2 to $3 a quart, in what sense is that a *fall* in the price of candy?

Answer:

>   It is a fall in the price of candy in ice-cream units. Candy is cheaper relative to ice cream than formerly. The percentage increase in the price of candy is less than the percentage increase in the price of ice cream.

6) "If the price of gasoline rose by only 10 percent, many people would not immediately change their consumption." Explain why this does not refute the law of demand.

Answer:

>   The law of demand does not say that every person will instantly respond, and respond fully, to every price change no matter how slight. It says a sufficiently high price will induce a response now, and it also says the response will be greater the longer the time allowed. In the case at hand, some people will respond quickly though some will not. Even for a small price rise the aggregate amount demanded over all people will respond because some will respond. In time, all will respond to a sufficiently large price rise.

7) Income and demand:
    a. As your wealth or income increases, what happens to your demand (schedule) for gasoline?
    b. If you owned a dairy farm and the price of milk went up, would you consume more or less milk?

Answer:

>   a. Demand increases. Schedule shifts upward (to the right).
>   b. Can't tell. Milk production may be so important a source of your income that you consume more when its price rises (despite the higher price, because you are wealthier). But you consume less than if your wealth had increased for other reasons and without a rise in milk prices.

CHAPTER 9

SOME IMPLICATIONS OF LAWS OF DEMAND

The universal principles of demand apply to most human activity—
much more than merely the prices of goods sold in markets.

"NEEDED" OR "DEMANDED" AMOUNTS?

Many speak of "needs," calling them "vital," "basic," "urgent," "critical," "crying," "minimal." Such words are appropriate in a letter to Santa Claus, not in economics. They are challenged by the concept of the demand function. There is scarcity. Command over more is better, and less is worse. We all want more of every good. The price of "more" is what must be given up to get more of the "needed" thing. If we "need" more police protection, more schools, or more housing — then what is it that we need less of, which we will give up?

Potential production is limited. Choices must be made. Poor people are poor not because they "need" or are "satisfied with" or are "accustomed to having" less. Some shamefully contend that the cost of labor is low in poor foreign countries because the people there "don't need as much as we do." But they haven't been fortunate enough to be born in an economy where they can earn as much as others do. We'll look at the reasons a person's labors are worth more in one place than another.

Direct Implications of the Laws of Demand

Because greater amounts can be sold at a lower price, prices of fruits and vegetables are lower at harvest time when the supply is larger. Merchants have clearance sales at lower prices, not higher prices. Still, public opinion polls report that many say they would not reduce their use of gasoline just because the price went up — they bought no more than they needed and would not buy less than they needed. In fact, when gas prices rose there was a reduction in the amount demanded — apparently the amount they "needed" fell when the price went up! That was in accord with the first law of demand. Further, the reduction has been greater in the long run, in accord with the second law of demand.

Demand for Beef

If beef prices rise in response to a reduced supply, people buy less beef and more of other types of meat or sources of protein — eggs, cheese, poultry, fish, tofu — which are now less expensive relative to beef. In time, they adjust still more as they learn new ways to use the cheaper product.

Demand for Wood

If wood prices rise, less wood will be demanded. We substitute some plaster, plastics, steel, aluminum, copper, glass, paper, coal, oil. You and I may not consciously respond to a 10 percent rise in the price of wood, but industrial product designers shift in varying degrees to substitutes.

Demand for Water

Although we cannot live without water, we reduce (not eliminate) water usage when prices are higher. In arid regions, the very high price of water induces people to demand less; it is not that they don't "want" or "need" less water. At that high price for water, they reduce the amount of water they use, and spend more on other things.

Per capita daily water usage has varied from 230 gallons in Chicago to 150 in New York and Los Angeles, down to 120 in San Diego and 110 in Boston. Among the reasons are differences in industrial uses. Chicago has steel and oil refining industries that use a great deal of water; New York City businesses — finance, retail, apparel — are light water users. And the cost of water had something to do with determining the locations of those industries! In many cities, industrial users take about half the water. Their demands are probably more elastic with respect to price than the demand for domestic uses. Further, there can be enormous differences in water use within the same industry. The amount of water used in production varies with the local price, as it does in consumption.

In Arizona or Nevada — with high prices of water — people have smaller gardens and lawns or just rock gardens. Sidewalks and autos will be swept or dusted, rather than washed. Softened water will be used because soft water washes cleaner with less water in flow-restricting shower heads. More houses will have circulating hot-water systems so as not to waste cold water waiting for hot water to reach the faucet.

In New York City, about 10 percent of the total water consumption has been estimated to be leakages; at higher prices, it would pay the water supplier to install meters as an incentive to reduce waste. Agriculture in California uses 70 percent of the water in the state — at prices of water to farmers that are far lower than prices to city users, even after adjustment for purification and distribution costs. If prices to farmers were as high as for water in the cities, farmers would more accurately bear the costs of farming. The extent of farming in California would be reduced. Water to grow watermelons, lettuce, rice, grapes, and alfalfa would be diverted to more valuable city uses, and more of the farm products would be produced in other states or countries where water is cheaper.

The growing population pressing on the available supply of water will require some strong means of allocating water use. Will it be similar to the method for controlling use of land, food, oil, and electricity—by market prices—or will it be political control?

Learning How to Adapt

When the price of water rises, people may not initially know how or to what extent to adjust. One way they learn is by being informed by sellers of substitutes or devices that economize on water. They sell water recycling equipment, water softeners, automatic faucets, fertilizers, irrigation and sprinkling equipment, air conditioning machinery, hardtop patios, chemicals that reduce evaporation from reservoirs, washing machines that use less water, and so forth. More expensive water creates market prospects for their production, and they will eagerly provide guidance to those trying to adapt.

INDIRECT IMPLICATIONS OF THE LAWS OF DEMAND

The power of the laws of demand can be demonstrated by indirect, less obvious implications.

Good and bad grapes: larger proportions of relatively good quality California oranges and grapes are shipped to New York than the proportions that remain in California. Are New Yorkers richer or more discriminating? Possibly—but the quality ratio is higher also in the poor districts of New York and the whole East Coast. The question can be posed for other goods: Why are disproportionately more expensive foreign cars and other "luxuries" exported than are purchased in the home country? Why do young parents go to expensive plays rather than movies on a higher percentage of their evenings out than do young childless couples? Why are "seconds" (slightly defective products) more heavily consumed at the site of manufacture? Why do more of the better, rather than the mediocre, students attend more distant colleges? Why should a tourist be more careful buying leather goods in Italy than when buying Italian exports in other countries? Why is most meat shipped to Alaska "deboned"?

The answers to these questions are based on an implication of the first law

Table 9.1 *Better Quality Is Shipped Away*

Prices of Grapes in New York = Transport Costs + Prices of Grapes in California

Choice $1.50	= $.50	+ $1.00
Standard $1.00	= .50	+ .50

Relative Prices in New York   Relative Prices in California
1.5 Standard for 1 Choice   2 Standard for 1 Choice

---

of demand. In table 9.1, suppose California grapes a) cost 50¢ a pound to ship to New York, regardless of quality, and b) in California the choice grapes sell for $1 a pound and the standard grapes for 50¢ a pound. Since the cost is the same per unit of shipping either quality to New York, the price in New York is 50¢ higher than in California for both types. But in New York, a consumer of choice grapes sacrifices only 1.5 pounds of standard, whereas in California, one pound of choice costs two pounds of standard.

New Yorkers have a lower cost of choice grapes *relative to* standard grapes, and, therefore, in accordance with the first law of demand, they will demand a larger fraction of choice grapes than do Californians. In California, where standard grapes are cheaper than in New York *relative to* choice grapes, a larger fraction of standard grapes will be consumed. We don't need to resort to conjectures about differences in "consumer tastes and preferences" to understand this phenomenon.

A general effect of an added cost to related products: an *addition of a constant value* to a *high* and to a *low* value will reduce the resulting ratio of the new values. The prices of high- and low-quality meat might be $10 and $5. Now, add $10 to each, which become $20 and $15. Though both absolute prices are increased equally, the high-quality meat becomes cheaper *relative to* the low-quality; or, in reverse, the low-quality becomes more expensive relative to the high-quality. Formerly, a purchase of high-quality meat was equivalent to giving up twice as much low-quality meat. But, with $10 added to both prices, the new price of the high-quality is lower *relative to* the low-quality—being only 1.33 rather than two times as expensive.

So the amount of high-quality meat demanded increases *relative to* the demanded amount of low-quality meat, when the price of each is increased by the same absolute amounts. The percentage reduction in demanded amount of low-quality meat is greater than for the higher-quality. Of the total demanded amount of meat, a larger proportion is now the higher-quality meat.

ALLEGED EXCEPTIONS TO THE LAWS OF DEMAND

Some say you could conceivably be wholly insensitive to price or that you buy just as much of a good when its price rises because you "need" that amount. Really? We have already illustrated how the "need" for such life-supporting goods as water conforms to the first law of demand. Evidence indicates also that goods like insulin are not exceptions. Diabetics can stretch intervals between injections, use lower dosages, and modify food intake. These are hazardous, unpleasant, and risky actions. But at high enough prices for insulin, that's what happens. Again, this does not mean the substitution leaves one equally well off. But the ability to substitute makes one better off than if no adjustment were possible or utilized. Another alleged exception to the laws of demand is a prestige or "conspicuous consumption" good like Mumm champagne, Chanel purses, Cross pens, Mercedes Benz cars, Waterford crystal, or whatever the products for which the "elite" competes. Desire for prestige goods shifts upward the demand schedule, resulting in a higher price. But this says merely that a higher demand curve leads to a higher price, not that the demand curve is sloped upward. The pursuit of prestige is perfectly consistent with the laws of demand. Let the price of the prestige good be even higher, and less will be bought; else what prevents its price from going infinitely high?

Also alleged as contradictions to the laws of demand are occasions when a low price makes a potential buyer hesitate because of doubt that it could be the genuine article at that low a price. That is a sensible doubt given the fact that price commonly reflects quality. (Expensive, genuine Rolex watches sell better than curbside knockoffs.) But for a given degree of belief about the quality of a good, a lower price will induce more purchases, not less. Higher-quality goods sell at higher prices to restrict the greater amount demanded of those better goods to the available supply.

The nearest thing to a real exception is the previously explained "change in wealth" effect when a person holds a large amount of the good whose price has changed, for which the oil price change was given as an example. This effect is a shift in the demand curve, not a change in the sign of its slope. Though a person's wealth may have increased substantially when the price of some good rises, it's still true that the amount demanded, though larger than before, is smaller than it would have been if that person's wealth had increased by the same amount without a rise in the price.

Some people may act contrarily, giving no heed to the price of an action, no matter how costly. Such a person may well be declared "incompetent." In fact, one basis for determining competency, according to legal standards, is the extent to which the person's behavior is consistent with the laws of demand. If someone pays no attention to price and buys regardless of price, or throws away valuable things, these actions are inconsistent with the laws of demand, and such a person is likely to be regarded as basically confused.

QUESTIONS AND MEDITATIONS

1) Why is it when a couple goes out, the probability is greater that they will attend an expensive theater if they have infants than if they are childless?

Answer:

Hiring babysitters at, say, $10 an hour and staying out for four hours will cost $40. Add the cost of two movie tickets at $10 each. Theater seats are priced at $40. So the theater costs $120 (= $80 + $40), and movies cost $60 (= $20 + $40). Taking all costs into account, the $40 theater tickets cost only twice as much as the $10 movie tickets for parents who must pay babysitters. But if a couple has no babysitter fee, the theater will cost $80 and the movie $20 — a ratio of 4 to 1: theater going is relatively more expensive in real terms, that is, in terms of other goods given up for childless people.

2) Let P_1 be the price of a higher-quality version of a good, and P_2 be the price of a lower-quality version. Both prices are the prices in the United States. Let T_1 and T_2 be the transport costs of these goods to a "foreign" market. Show that if $T_1/T_2 < P_1/P_2$, then *relatively* more of good "1" will be shipped; if the inequality is reversed, relatively more of good "2" will be shipped. "Relative" to what?

Answer:

If T_1/T_2 is less than P_1/P_2, $(P_1 + T_1)/(P_2 + T_2)$ will be less than P_1/P_2. Therefore, the price (including transport) of good 1 in the more distant market will be lower relative to the price of good 2 in the more distant market. More of good 1 will be demanded than of 2 relative to that in the domestic market, because the relative price of good 1 is lower in the distant market.

3) Explain how each of these is a denial of the law of demand and the basic postulates of economics:
   a. "The budget of the Department of Defense covers only our basic needs and nothing more."
   b. "Our children need better schools."
   c. "Nothing is too good when it comes to education."
   d. "America needs more energy."

Answers:

    a. There is no such thing as a basic need. We could use more security, and we could also get by with less. It's a matter of what price we are willing to pay, and a matter of more or less, not all or none.

    b. We "need" more of everything that is not free. The amount of any economic good we choose to have is a function of its price. To say our children need more schools ignores what we propose to give up to get more schools.

    c. It depends upon the price, whether it is good enough to have at that price. If this says simply that more is better than less, OK. Otherwise, it seems to deny relevance of alternatives.

    d. Same as comment to b.

4) Diagnose and evaluate the following news report: "Our city needs more golf courses, according to a report submitted to the City Recreation and Park Department by the National Golf Foundation. The survey discovered that many people do not play as often as they would like because of the lack of courses." Does this differ from the situation of filet mignon, champagne, and autos?

Answer:

The difference is that price is ignored in determining how many golf courses would be demanded (needed?).

5) A competitor of the authors of this text claims his text is "invaluable." Does that sound consistent with economic analysis?

Answer:

What does "invaluable" mean? We are reminded of a news item. "This priceless necklace is now in the possession of Mrs. Lovely, who bought it for $85,000." Rarely do we find such an incongruous juxtaposition of obvious inconsistencies. However, in fairness to those who often use the term "priceless," we suspect they usually mean that it is not reproducible or replaceable. Thus, a Grecian urn or an original Dufy cannot be replaced at any price if destroyed. At the same time, one should be careful not to think it can't be bought at a finite price, or that a nonreproducible item is necessarily valuable.

6) Economics asserts that people prefer more to less. Yet there are waiting lists of people seeking small apartments in slum areas while bigger, better apartments do not have a list of applicants. How can people want smaller, less luxurious apartments rather than bigger apartments

without violating our postulates about people's preferring more economic goods?

Answer:

If this happened with *equal* prices for slums and for high-quality spacious apartments, we would be stumped. In fact, however, we find that the prices of the high-quality dwellings are higher, which reduces the amount of the high-quality apartments demanded. Given the law of demand, with a sufficiently higher price of higher-quality apartments, the amount people want or demand is reduced so that it does not exceed the amount available.

CHAPTER 10

MARKETS AND PRICES AS SOCIAL COORDINATORS

When the supplied amount of a good is less than the demanded amount, that's usually called a "shortage." The suppliers seem to be blamed for not supplying enough, or other demanders are accused of having too much. It is more appropriate to wonder why the price of the good failed to rise enough to clear the market and eliminate the "shortage." "Shortages" and "surpluses" are results of a failure of an adjustment in the market price.

A "MARKET-CLEARING" PRICE?

The "market-clearing price" is a price at which the amount demanded equals the amount supplied. All mutually desired exchanges at that price will be accomplished. It's also called an "equilibrium" price. That is an idealized — but exceedingly useful — concept.

For the real world, market prices are pushed toward the market-clearing price — that at which all mutually preferred exchanges can be "cleared," that is, accomplished. This presumes that people who propose exchanges are reliable and do what they say they will. (We defer analysis of less reliable behavior to later chapters.) In saying that "price depends on demand and supply," the analysis pertains to what changes in price are induced by changes in supply and demand.

MARKET-CLEARING PRICE FOR ALLOCATION
OF A FIXED SUPPLY OF A GOOD

How do changes in price help people adjust to new mutually preferred situations? This can be most easily illustrated first in situations where the supplied amount is a fixed total despite a change in the market price, as it is for houses, at least for a few weeks. Any increase in the amount available is so small, relative to the existing total, that we can treat the supply amount as given. A fixed supply situation applies to many goods, even if only for a very short interval. For some things, such as land or Michelangelo statues, it's constant for a very long time, at least for increases. Land can be considered as fixed in amount, though level land can be created from hilly land by hard work. Setting aside those refinements, we'll look first at fixed supply situations — meaning the amount supplied does not respond to changes in price. More might be produced, but we'll confine our initial analysis to effects of price adjustments in the interval before the total supply is affected. That interval is the "market period."

"THE MARKET" SETS THE PRICE

It can be misleading to say "the market sets the price." The market is an arrangement and process for comparing people's demands and offerings and for conducting exchanges of private property rights. People search for and compare options prior to agreeing to an exchange, and that *competition* drives the prices of all the exchanges toward the same price — the market price. Saying the "market" sets the price is a superficial way of recognizing that all who buy and sell in markets have an influence in the determination of prices.

THE MARKET DEMAND: THE SUMS OF THE INDIVIDUAL DEMANDS AT EACH POSSIBLE PRICE

Table 10.1 describes a society of four persons, A, B, C, and D, and seven automobiles. The number of cars *initially* owned by each person is in the top row. The demanded amounts for each person at various possible prices are listed in

Table 10.1 *Auto Ownership Demands of A, B, C, and D*

Price	A has 4 cars	B has 3 cars	C has none	D has none	"Market Demand"
$10,000	1	0	1	1	3
9,000	1	1	1	2	5
9,000	2	1	1	2	6
7,000	2	1	2	2	7
					Equilibrium
6,000	2	2	2	2	8
5,000	2	2	2	2	8
4,000	2	2	2	3	9
3,000	3	2	2	3	10
2,000	3	3	2	3	11
1,000	4	4	2	4	14

A initially owns 4 cars. At price $2,000, he will be satisfied with only 3, that is, he is willing to sell 1 car for $2,000. B starts with 3 cars, and is willing to reduce his holdings to 2 by selling a car for $3,000. C would pay as much as $10,000, but he can bargain to buy from A for $2,000. And D also values a car at $10,000, but he may find that B will sell for $3,000. As trading goes on, the price in the uncleared market approaches $7,000. At $7,000, each of the four people has the number of cars he wants at that price, the total demanded being 7 cars, equal to the total number available, and the market is cleared.

the columns for A, B, C, and D. The extreme right-hand column lists the total amounts demanded by the community at the alternative prices. It's the "market demand," the sum of all the individual demands. We presume that no person's wealth, and hence demand schedule for cars, is changed significantly by the sequence of trades.

The market price is established by competition in the market although no one acts as if the market price could be affected by that person's demand or amounts offered of the good. What's the final "equilibrating" distribution and market price if the cars can be sold among the members of this community?

IRRELEVANCE OF INITIAL ALLOCATION OF GOODS FOR THEIR FINAL ALLOCATION TO HIGHEST-VALUING USERS

Many different sequences of purchases are possible from the initial allocation, when A has 4, B has 3, and C and D each have none.

C and D are each willing to offer up to $10,000 for a car, but they discover, after some shopping, that they can for only $2,000 buy a car from A and one from B at $3,000. A would then have 3 cars, B would have 2 cars, and C and D would each have 1 car. C could buy another car by offering $4,000 to A, leaving him with 2 cars. C then has 2 cars, with the second car being worth $7,000 to C, though it was bought for $4,000. D would offer up to $9,000 for a second car, but can buy it from B for $7,000. After that transaction, A has 2 cars, B has 1, and C and D have 2 each, for a total of 7 cars.

No one could buy another car at any price less than $7,000, and no one would demand another at $7,000, which is therefore the clearing price. The amount *each* person has equals the amount each demands at that price, and the *total* amount demanded equals the total supply of cars. At every step in the sequence of trades, each party was moved to a personally higher-valued, "more preferred," situation.

No matter what the initial allocation of cars among the public, the cars will end up in the same allocation among the demanders. We assumed this reallocation does not affect anyone's wealth enough to alter his demand. If it did, some market-clearing price still would be achieved, with everyone having as many cars as demanded.

If a car were destroyed, the resulting series of exchanges would depend on whose car was destroyed. But the resulting pattern of ownership of cars would not depend on who suffered the initial loss of a car, assuming that the loss does not affect that person's demand. In every circumstance, competition in the market for cars results in a distribution and market price at which each person owns the number each demands at the resulting market-clearing price.

Resources will be pushed toward their highest market-valued uses, no matter who initially owns the income-producing resources as private property. That's a consequence of everyone's desire for more wealth.

SHORTAGES ARE NOT RESULTS OF REDUCTIONS IN SUPPLY

"Shortages" are not results of too little being supplied to the market. They are results of restrictions on prices. And a shortage should not be confused with universal, inescapable, pervasive "scarcity." As we'll explain later, "ceilings" on higher rents as part of a rent control program create "shortages" and wasteful forms of competition. These shortages often provoke a surplus of complaints that "needs" aren't being satisfied. And surpluses of goods are the result of legislation or regulation prohibiting transactions at prices *below* the free-market price.

Neither a shift in the supply curve nor in the demand curve is required to eliminate a shortage or a surplus. Instead, they are results of laws that restrict prices. And yet, there is persistent agitation by "housing consumers" to impose "rent controls" with too-low rent ceilings for apartments. In the opposite direction, farmer "food producers"—in almost every nation—have successfully lobbied for governments to prohibit sales of agricultural goods below a price "floor." The result has been a "surplus" of production in excess of the amount demanded at the legislated higher price.

MARKETS AND "RIGHTS"

The operation of a market depends critically on the kind of rights that can be traded. What's traded are titles, or rights—not the goods themselves which may be located someplace else and immovable, such as land and buildings. We have been concentrating on exchanges of private property rights in a "capitalistic" market. A "political market" would refer to trades of government actions.

Young people—usually defined as less than eighteen years old—are considered by the law as "legally incompetent" to know the implications of the rights being transferred. "Minors" don't have rights to buy or sell many specified rights—for example, tobacco, alcohol, guns, specific movies, marriage licenses. On the day after age eighteen or twenty-one, the legal system presumes that individuals become fully competent and aware of the rights being transferred. But "rights" in exchanges are not always clear-cut.

Does the "seller" really confer the rights you think you will be getting? Why are you asked to sign some papers? You don't have to sign papers when paying cash—but do not throw away the "bill of sale" receipt handed you by the seller, because you might have to establish your ownership rights to the goods when you walk out of the store.

When paying tuition to attend college, did you sign a contract specifying what rights you and the college have with respect to each other? Probably not. Are the rights you got as simple as those for "attending" a movie by paying the ticket price (tuition)? It's astounding how often we buy a "pig in a poke," not knowing what rights are specified, or what rights the seller obtained with respect to your future actions.

CREATION OF MARKETS

Some markets are created and organized as business ventures. The range of "formal markets" extends from stock, bond, and commodity "exchanges" to shopping malls and weekend flea markets and garage sales. While not all are equally reliable, the owners of the market institutions provide more than a convenient place or means of exchanging information. They also provide assurance that what you get is really what you were told you would get. And the seller is guaranteed that the money you agree to pay is actually paid.

The buyer or the seller may not care who are the intermediaries in an exchange. The owners of the major stock exchanges are highly reliable intermediaries who pay money to the seller and deliver to the buyer ownership rights of the purchased stocks and bonds. That reliability is strengthened by surveillance of federal regulatory commissions.

In a well-functioning market, the prices of a good asked by sellers and offered by buyers are sufficiently close together that there's no way remaining for anyone to make a profit by purchasing from a lower-price seller and selling to a higher-priced buyer. In other words, "arbitrage" assures that there are no certain opportunities to profit remaining in a well-functioning market.

RESERVATION DEMAND TO OWN

For durable resalable goods, such as land, houses, and corporation stocks and bonds, it's helpful to think of a "demand" schedule that measures the amounts a person demands to *own*, or have, depending on its market price. The amounts to *purchase* would depend on the amount already owned and the amount a person wants to own at alternative prices. If at the existing market price of the good, you own 3 units, but you want to own 5 units at that price, the purchase amount demanded is 2. Your total "reservation" demand amount at that price is 5 units, and your additional purchase demand amount is 2 units. For price behavior of a durable good of which there is a large amount in existence, the reservation demand for amounts to own can be more important than the rate of production and purchase of additional or new items.

Stocks and bonds, existing houses, used cars, and land are common examples of items being bought and sold without any change in demand or supply or in production and consumption of the good. You buy some when the amount you demand exceeds the amount you have. The law of demand still is operative in that the higher the market price of a good, the less of that good a person will want to *own*.

Variations in extent of market transactions may reflect merely some adjustments to shuffling individual demands, increasing for some people and decreasing for others, while the *aggregate* "market" demand for ownership may be unchanged. If Jack's demand to own rises by an amount that exactly offsets Jill's decline in demand to own, that will create *sales* from Jill to Jack, but not necessarily a change in price, because aggregate *demand to own* has not changed. The extent of market transactions of durable goods reflects adjustments to changes among people in their demands for that kind of good, not necessarily a *general* rise or decline in aggregate market demand.

When referring to a "demand," be clear whether you mean 1) the amounts a person wants to *own* at different prices or 2) the *rates of purchase and consumption* at alternative prices or 3) the amount to be bought or sold at a moment in time. More often, we'll be using the *rate of purchase* demand, such as when thinking of goods that are consumed or used in production at a fairly stable rate.

RENTS

Finally, consider some meanings of the word "rent." Fortunately, the context of use usually will reveal the meaning. Often, "rent" means the "value of services of a durable resource." It can mean the user's payment made to the resource owner, such as the "rent paid" to the owner of a rented apartment. It can mean also the service value from some resource you own and use yourself, though you don't pay yourself.

LAND RENT—A PURE SURPLUS?

Rent often means the *excess of the value of services* over the *current costs* of using existing durable goods. The service of land is almost universally called "rent," because land tends to be "permanent," or very long lasting, and with little damage to the value of the land when it's used. With "insignificant" costs of wear and tear and replacement, all the payment could be called a "rent"—an excess of what is obtained over the costs of maintaining the existing resource.

A physician who starts practice will receive an income that contains some rent, because once educated as a doctor, some of the doctor's services would be provided even at an income lower than that which would cover the sunk cost of the education. A person contemplating becoming a doctor would not view that large *anticipated* future reward as a "rent." The *anticipation* of that reward is necessary to induce the investment in becoming a doctor. However, once educated, those costs are sunk and irrelevant for the existing doctor to provide the services.

This is the same for paintings, books, and for every good that has some durability. The concept "rents" is necessary for avoiding confusion when considering the otherwise mysterious relation between "costs" of the current service and the effects of price changes on future supply.

A price change of an existing good or asset does two things: 1) it influences the allocation of goods or assets to their most valued uses and 2) it affects the future supply of those goods or assets that can be created.

QUASI-RENT

When the value of services of an existing resource has no effect now or in the future on the services supplied by that resource, the service (or the price received by the owner if used by someone else) is called "*pure* rent." The supply curve of the land services is vertical at the existing rate of service. If the land is considered "permanent," the service value is called "rent." If the amount supplied in the future responded, though not soon enough to affect its current rental or use value, the rent for its current services is a "*quasi-rent*," to indicate it won't last long.

More generally, "rent" for an existing house or a building is a "quasi-rent," because the resource yielding the service is not permanently durable. The earnings to Tiger Woods for playing golf contain "quasi-rent," being more than necessary to induce him to compete, but perishable in time. Almost everyone has obtained some "quasi-rents" or hope they will. Though not altering the immediate amount supplied, reallocating the presently existing supply toward higher-valued uses maximizes the "rent" component of earnings. The effect of an increased prospective quasi-rent is to speed revision toward prospective higher-valued uses, though not in the immediate amount of the good yielding the quasi-rent.

"POLITICAL RENT-SEEKING"

A modified use of the word "rent" is the phrase "political rent-seeking," often shortened to "rent-seeking." It means attempts to obtain political influence for special government benefits that cost society more than the worth of the benefits obtained by the "rent-seeker."

Tariffs on imports of automobiles reduce consumer worth more than the gains to the political rent-seekers — the *domestic* automakers. Contributions made to political parties to obtain legislation or regulations that handicap competitors are a form of "political rent-seeking." Government administrators inevitably are targets of "political rent-seekers."

REVIEW OF CONCEPTS TO KNOW

Market: An arrangement, place, or device where or by which offers and bids for goods can be communicated and sales-purchases are being made.

Market Price: The price agreed to by both the seller and the buyer in actual market transactions.

Market-Clearing Price: Price at which amounts demanded equal amounts offered. Same as "equilibrium" price.

Shortage: Excess of amount demanded over the amount supplied at the existing, *non-market-clearing price*. Always a result of price controls.

Surplus: Reverse of shortage. An amount supplied that exceeds amount demanded at the existing non-market-clearing price is always a result of too high a price.

Demand: The *schedule* of *amounts* demanded for purchase at *various possible market prices*.

Demanded Amount: The amount demanded at a *specified* price.

Market Demand: Schedule of amounts demanded by *all demanders* from all suppliers in a market at possible market prices.

Reservation Demand: Schedule of amounts already owned and which, depending on the market price, would be retained rather than offered for sale.

Rent: The value of the services of a durable resource.

Economic Rent: A rent that does *not affect either the present or the future amount of that good*.

Quasi-Rent: A payment or service value that does not affect the amount currently available, but affects the *future* amount.

Political Rent-Seeking: Attempts to obtain political influence for special government benefits that cost society more than the worth of benefits obtained by the "rent-seeker."

Communal Government Ownership: Every person in the society bears some of the consequences of changes in values of *all* durable goods, whereas in a private property society people can each choose which goods they own and which risks to bear as a consequence of changes in market values. This is discussed at greater length in later chapters.

QUESTIONS AND MEDITATIONS

1) The demands to own by A and by B for good X are:

Table 10.2

Price	A's Demand	B's Demand	Market Demand
$10	0	0	_____
9	1	0	_____
8	2	0	_____
7	3	1	_____
6	4	2	_____
5	5	3	_____
4	6	3	_____
3	7	4	_____
2	8	5	_____
1	9	6	_____

a. What is the market demand by A and B?

b. If six units of X are available, what will be the resulting allocation between A and B if open-market exchange is used?

c. With six units available, if price were legally imposed at $4, would there be a shortage, a surplus, or exchange equilibrium?

d. If the price were legally imposed at $9, would there be a shortage, a surplus, or exchange equilibrium?

e. How can there be a change from a shortage to a surplus without any change in supply or demand?

Answer:

a. 0, 1, 2, 4, 6, 8, 9, 11, 13, 15 for prices from 10 through 1.

b. 4 to A and 2 to B.

c. Shortage.

d. Surplus.

e. There is a change in the stipulated or imposed (disequilibrium) price.

2) In the previous question, increase the amounts demanded by B uniformly by two more units at each price.

a. What will be the new open-market price?

b. What will be the allocation between A and B?

c. If the price is held at the old level by law, will there be a surplus or a shortage?

d. How can that surplus or shortage be eliminated?

Answer:
  a. $7.
  b. 3 to each.
  c. Shortage.
  d. Remove the price control.

3) Distinguish between the law of demand and the law of market
   price (which says price equates the amount supplied to the amount
   demanded). Which holds more generally?
Answer:
   The law of demand relates purchase rate to price. The law of demand and
   supply states price is at the intersection of supply and demand. The law
   of demand holds generally; the law of supply and demand at market price
   may be made ineffective by governmental suspension of the open market.

4) A Petroleum Crisis? Occasionally, charts are published plotting quantities
   of so-called demand and supply of something against future time. If the
   anticipated demand is greater than the supply (perhaps for petroleum),
   we supposedly will be facing an oil crisis; if supply is greater (maybe
   for engineers), we are to expect a glut of such specialists. Why are such
   diagrams fallacious and just plain wrong?
Answer:
   The price is ignored in its effect on amounts demanded and supplied. Past
   balance or equality reflects the simple fact that the *price* was allowed to adjust up or down so as to equate *amounts* demanded with amounts supplied.
   Any particular forecast path of amount demanded must presume some
   particular price in each year. A higher projected price would reduce the
   amount demanded and raise the amount supplied, keeping them equal. An
   appropriate path of price over the future will affect the amounts demanded
   and the amounts supplied so as to keep the two equated. Every such projected future imbalance of amounts demanded (probably labeled "needs,"
   "requirements," or "demand") with amounts supplied of any good (probably labeled "supply," "availabilities," or "stocks") is merely a prediction
   that price will not be allowed to move to equate amounts demanded with
   amounts supplied.

5) When prices on the stock market fall, the financial pages report heavy
   selling; yet every share sold is bought by someone. Why don't they refer
   to heavy buying?

Answer:

They probably use the phrase "heavy selling" to mean increased supply — or so we hope.

6) Which tactic would be more likely to get you a lower price on a new car: going to just one dealer and acting like a tough and aggressive bargainer or going to several dealers and mildly asking for their selling price while letting it be known that you really intend to buy a car and are shopping around? Explain why.

Answer:

Shopping several sellers is better because alternatives are what sellers must beat. It's sellers who compete against other sellers, not buyers who compete against sellers.

7) Are the words "scarcity," "reduced supply," and "shortage" synonyms? If not, what is the difference?

Answer:

Scarcity is pervasive, for we have available less than is desired, but what people call shortages are simply the result of prices that are kept too low. A reduced supply is not a shortage. A reduced supply is a reduction in the amount available — pictured as a shift to the left of the supply curve.

8) "Under open-market, private property pricing, a person is allowed to make any kind of appeal to a seller to get some of the good. Under price controls, the buyer is told that there is one appeal he cannot use — that is, offer a larger amount of other goods." True or false?

Answer:

True. "A larger amount of other goods" is an increased price offer, which is precluded by the price control.

9) You are collecting data for a cost-of-living survey. For each of the cases below, which "price" would you report as the price? Why?
   a. "List price $125. Special discount to $90!"
   b. "Get a $1 box of Kleenex for only 29 cents."
   c. "One cent sale. First for $1. Second for 1 cent."

Answer:

Sales price, if goods were available at that price at the time of sale. Price means actual exchange prices.

10) "Allowing the prices of goods to rise when more of the good cannot be produced is immoral, because the higher prices do not induce a larger output. They merely give unwarranted profits to those who are lucky enough to own the goods. Either prices should be prevented from rising, or the government should take over ownership in order to prevent unjust enrichment." Do you agree with this analysis?

Answer:

You should disagree. A higher price permits a reallocation of existing goods — a reallocation that would not occur in the absence of higher prices. The higher price serves a rationing function even if the amount of the good is fixed and more of the good cannot be produced. Higher prices do have a consequence — reallocation — moving resources from one use or user to another.

11) "The community's demand to own houses may remain unchanged; yet the market demand to *purchase* and to sell houses may change enormously." Explain how the demand to hold houses (in a two-person community) could be unchanged while the demand to *purchase* and sell houses increased.

Answer:

When the demand of some people to purchase houses is exactly offset by other people's supply of houses for sale, overall demand and supply remain unchanged. Exactly offsetting shifts in the demand to purchase the supply for sale are rare, so the market price moves to adjust the mismatched demands and supplies.

12) "It is wrong to profit from someone else's misfortune."
   a. Explain why, if that were taken literally, we would all be poorer.
   b. Does the doctor profit from your illness? The farmer from your hunger? The shoemaker from your tender feet? The teacher from your ignorance?

Answer:
   a. All voluntary exchange benefits both parties.
   b. Yes.

13) An open-market system presumes enforcement of certain institutions or rules. What are they?

Answer:

> 1) Open access to markets with rights to trade or exchange; 2) private property rights in goods and services; it's also presumed that 3) each person has a desire to achieve a more preferred situation — in this case through increased profits and lower costs of getting the products.

14) When you hear, "Everyone is selling, and driving down the price," you should respond, "For each sale, there is a buyer! Why aren't the buyers driving up the price?"

Answer:

> Of course, what is sold is bought. But in an open market, each trader ends with the amount he demands at the resulting market-clearing (equilibrium) price.

CHAPTER 11

ILLUSTRATIVE APPLICATIONS OF
DEMAND PRINCIPLES

Prices commonly adjust rapidly to clear the market. However, several marketing arrangements and processes that help make markets work better also *slow* the pace of price adjustments, and that tends to mask how markets work. In this chapter, we first explore how two of these arrangements — inventories and productive capacity — delay price changes and obscure the source of these changes. Then, we'll use demand and supply analysis to deduce land price adjustments to a tax on land, and who actually pays the tax and who benefits. Last, we extend the analysis of land values to some consequences of pollution reduction and see a reason landowners play so strong a role in governments.

MARKETING ARRANGEMENTS: BUFFER STOCKS,
RESERVE CAPACITY, STABLE PRICES, WAITING TIMES,
AND PRICE RESPONSE TO DEMAND UNCERTAINTY

Stable and Predictable Prices

Imagine a restaurant in which the price of food and service is adjusted instantly to avoid any waiting. With uncertain prices, planning by diners would be more difficult. Willingness to wait a bit for a table can permit more convenient planning and action on the basis of predictable prices and costs.

Some degree of price stability — as a means of producing price *predictability* — is desired, despite the resulting transient imbalances between amounts demanded and supplied. The extent of price stability depends, in part, on the cost of holding inventories and on the value of timing of delivery of the product. It depends also on the value to customers of reliably predictable prices, when potential customers are making investments preparatory to purchases.

Because the costs and benefits of predictable or stable prices vary among customers and types of services, some sellers hold prices steady despite increased general demand and ration in favor of certain customers. Others let the price vary to clear the market to the highest demanders at the moment, without any favoritism. We'll see why each of these occur for "sensible" reasons appropriate to particular circumstances.

Inventories

Why do sellers hold inventories of goods? One reason is that shoppers can then inspect and compare goods before deciding whether or not to buy. A second is that customers' purchases fluctuate daily. Neither consumers nor suppliers know exactly who will want to buy how much of what in any given hour, day, or week. Inventories act as buffers to accommodate the variations in transient, unpredictable fluctuations in amount demanded.

Consider the options of a newsstand selling a daily average of 100 copies — but not exactly 100 each day. The seller could: (1) require buyers to place advance orders; (2) buy fewer than 100 copies and rarely have unsold copies; (3) buy more than 100 and usually have copies left over; (4) buy 1 copy at a time, replenishing a stock by special delivery service when the copy is sold.

While each of these alternatives has been used for various goods, in the case of newspaper sales, the third option, inventories, is common. Customers are willing to pay a slightly higher price, which covers the cost of unsold copies, in order to have immediate availability at a predictable price. The cost of inventories may result in a smaller paper or fewer retail outlets, but this will result also in a lower *full* cost/price to consumers than will the other options. Thus, a third reason for inventories is that they help a seller maintain stable, reliably predictable prices despite minor fluctuations in demand and supply, thereby helping customers plan their shopping.

Reserve Capacity

Capacity is a form of inventories — of productive resources. It's sometimes called "excess" because it is almost never fully used. But Palm Springs, Sun Valley, and Orlando do not have "too many" hotel rooms for rent just because some are unused at almost any given time.

Nor are empty apartments necessarily wasteful if demand is not perfectly predictable. Though rents may be higher to cover costs of buffer vacancies to accommodate shifting demands, vacancies permit lower search costs and enable people to move without committing themselves long in advance. Housing costs seemingly could be reduced by building fewer houses with fewer vacancies, but that would increase the inconvenience of advance planning and commitments, and thus increase the *full* cost of housing.

Imagine what it would be like to try to move into a community with no current vacancies and have to wait until someone moved. The inventory of vacant housing serves a useful purpose. It has been estimated (we don't know how reliably) that something like 5 percent of the rent paid by apartment dwellers covers the cost of providing vacancies to accommodate the unpredictability of amount and timing of demand. Neither second bathrooms and toilets, nor extra dining room chairs, nor fire extinguishers are wasteful just because they aren't always in use.

We turn to examining how some markets work in various situations. Often cause and effect are easily reversed. The next chapter will derive some (probably surprising) implied effects of price controls.

SPEED OF DETECTING CHANGES IN DEMAND OR SUPPLY: THE ILLUSION THAT COST DETERMINES PRICE

Buffer stocks, inventories, and reserve capacity help make it appear as if prices are sluggish or inflexible and are determined by costs, instead of by competition among consumer-demanders. Suppose that for some reason (possibly higher incomes) demand for meat increases. As sales and consumption increase, butchers' inventories are unexpectedly depleted. Normally, as with any retailer, inventories are large enough to accommodate transiently increased sales without producers having to raise prices. Inventories larger than an average day's sales help assure that supplies are immediately available to demanders at predictable prices.

One day's above-average sales is not regarded instantly as a persistent increase at that price; nor is it viewed as a long-term sales increase that requires a higher price to keep inventories from being further depleted. When the increase in sales reflects a higher average demand, no seller will be able to detect the increase in demand immediately. A high transient deviation may induce retailers to purchase more for replacement of normal inventories, but they would buy even more if they knew the long-term demand had increased.

If the public's aggregate demand really had increased (not just toward this one butcher and away from other butchers), the demand by all butchers to restore inventories would increase the demand facing the meat packer-suppliers. Packers will see their inventories declining as they supply more meat to retailers.

To replenish their extraordinarily depleted inventories, packers will compete with each other for more cattle than before. But with an unchanged supply of cattle, some packers must get less than the increased amount they demand at the old price. They bid up the price of cattle. The packers are, in this scenario, the first to see a price (cattle cost) rise consequent to the increased consumer demand, and they will correctly interpret that as a rise in their costs.

The existence of inventories in the chain of suppliers from producer to consumer can cause a delay during which the increased consumer demand is communicated from retailers to initial producers. That delays the price increase until the cattle-producer stage.

WHO IS RESPONSIBLE FOR HIGHER
PRICES? LOOK IN THE MIRROR

Packers raise their prices to retailers, saying their prices are higher because their costs are higher. But we know that costs are higher because it was the increased consumer demand that prompted a higher price of cattle at the feedlot. Because of the increased consumer demand, a higher price is obtained and maintained in the consumer market. When consumers complain about the higher price of meat, butchers say it isn't their fault. Their costs have gone up. And the packers can say the same. To see who really was responsible for the higher prices, the consumers can look in the mirror behind the butcher's counter and see themselves.

Not all prices adjust instantly to the new equilibrium price to clear the market, as they do in the organized stock and commodity markets. In fact, a lag occurs between the time some demand or supply situation has changed and the time people detect and distinguish that from a random, transient, reversible change in the current purchase rates or in supply conditions.

As emphasized earlier, the amount demanded may refer to the underlying average amount demanded in an interval, with momentary random offsetting deviations taking place around that average value. Because of the transient variations around the average, a shift in that average may be hard to detect quickly. An increase in sales may be interpreted as only a randomly high sales rate, rather than as a new higher normal sales rate. And once a seller begins to suspect that demand has shifted, difficulties exist in knowing what are the best adjustments to make in supply response.

If the demand is believed to have fallen, should a supplier shift to some other production activity or should the price be lowered and work continued at a lower rate? Should an employer attempt to reduce wages of employees immediately when sales fall?

So-called delays and lags in adjusting price or output are the result of inability to foresee the future perfectly and to understand what really is happening. They are not results of some inherent inflexibility in, or inability to change, prices. It takes time to decide that an underlying change, rather than a random, transient deviation has occurred. And the time it takes to discover what is the most appropriate adjustment misleads outside observers into thinking that prices are "rigid." Prices actually are instantly flexible—as instantly as it is discovered that a change is appropriate.

WHAT MADE THE PRICE CHANGE?
ALWAYS, THE INITIAL QUESTION

A *universal rule* of economic analysis is: Without a shift in the demand (curve) or the supply (curve), the price won't change. So when price changes, or when asking what is the effect of a price change, first ask what made the price change. Did that initiating event shift the demand curve or did it shift the supply curve (or possibly both)?

Did a price rise because of a reduction in supply, or was the cause an increase in demand? And why did that initiating event occur? Then, investigate the effect of a change in price. Don't confuse a) the many effects of the change that caused the price movement with b) the effect of the price change.

A second rule of analysis is that if both supply and demand shifted, you must know in what directions they shifted. Thus, before you assert that a rise in the price of wheat will reduce the amount of wheat demanded, be sure the event that raised the price of wheat didn't also shift the supply of wheat.

WHO BEARS THE TAX ON LAND DEVELOPMENTS —
DEVELOPERS OR LANDOWNERS?

A developer proposes to buy some land and construct apartment buildings. As a condition of granting the building permit, the local government requires amenities (like parking spaces and green areas) to a greater extent than the developer would find it profitable based on how much the occupants would be willing to pay for those amenities.

If the rental value of those required additions had exceeded their costs, they would have been voluntarily provided without the law. When they don't, who bears the excess of added costs over the value of the added amenities to the occupants? Neither the developer nor the occupant. These mandated costs are borne by the original owner of the land from whom the developer proposes to buy the land.

Being aware of the requirement for a building permit, potential developers would offer less for the land because of the costs of added amenities that exceed their worth to renters. But suppose there are benefits to other people who will not become renters. The increased parking spaces may reduce congestion on the streets and thereby make local travel safer and faster. Would that added "public benefit" imply that the "excess" cost of "excessive" parking space may not have been a waste? If not a waste but a net gain to the community, the question would then be: Is it "desirable" that the original land owner should be the one who bears the costs for better travel on streets, or should it be the users of the streets? Later chapters on property rights will discuss such questions.

TAX ON ECONOMIC RENT?

Sometimes it is contended that land should be taxed, because land rent value is a social surplus in the sense that its receipt by the landowner has no effect on the supply or use of the land. This used to be called a "single tax" by people who believed that that tax alone would be sufficient to finance all governmental actions. It has been argued that the supply of land is fixed and won't be diminished whether a "landowner" or the government collects the rent. The land will still be used in its most valuable ways. The only difference is in who gets the rent. That's correct analysis — so far.

Of course, not all land is really costless to maintain or protect from erosion. In addition, filling in bays and swamps can create more land, and no one would do that if the resultant rental value were all taxed away. Nevertheless, compared to a tax on anything else, a land tax has relatively small diversionary effects in the sense of affecting the supply. The immobility of land is a reason it's heavily taxed. The fact that it's fixed in amount is less relevant, as can be seen in comparing land to Picasso paintings. His paintings are in fixed supply, but they can be moved to areas where taxes are lower.

POLLUTION AND LAND VALUES

As another application of demand and supply analysis with fixed supply, imagine that the authors of this text possessed a magic capsule, which, if crushed, would permanently and costlessly cleanse the air of smog over the city of their residence, Los Angeles. The improved air would lead current residents to place a higher personal worth on land in the area. That would increase the demand for land and raise the price of the land.

Those people who were repelled by the smog and refused to move to Los Angeles will now do so and add to the demand for Los Angeles land. The increase in demand would result in a higher rent to occupy land and a higher price to purchase it.

Better Air versus More Other Goods

Renters would be paying higher rent for the land, sacrificing other goods with the equivalent market value of the better air. (As a result, they would not necessarily achieve improvements in their overall situation.) However, the original landowners unambiguously gain wealth (equaling the value of the improved air captured in the increased rents paid by the renters). There has been a transfer of wealth or income from one group to another. Is it worth removing the smog, even if costlessly, for that result? If we were major landowners the answer would be, "Yes." If we had been renters, the answer might be, "No."

Existing Resident Renters versus Newcomers

Consider the newcomers. They had not moved to Los Angeles earlier because the old air quality was not worth the land rent they would have to pay. The existing residents in Los Angeles did not consider the former smog level so bad as to prevent their living in that area. The potential newcomers placed a higher personal worth on cleaner air than did the existing residents.

After we crush the capsule, the newcomers will bid up the rents for the now smog-free land to reflect their higher marginal worth of the cleaner air — higher than the marginal worth obtained by the prior existing residents. The newcomers, from the Midwest and East, attracted by the now better air, will certainly be beneficiaries, as will be the landowners. Some of the prior resident renters, faced with higher rents, will lose. No one knows whether the prior renters will gain or lose on net.

Which Land Values Increase?

The authors own land near the Pacific Ocean in the fringe area where there is no smog. Removing all smog in the region would lower our ocean-area land values, because people would tend to move closer to the center of Los Angeles that used to be smoggy. We are like landowners of the Midwest, who would suffer a land value loss as people migrated toward the now less-smoggy west coast.

We, therefore, would not crush the magic capsule to remove the smog. We would lose, despite the gains to others. Or so it would seem, at first sight. However, if we possessed such a capsule, we would be induced to crush it and improve the air, regardless of the loss of value of our land. Why? The landowners in the area now heavily infested with smog would offer us a large part of the potential increase in their land values that would occur if the capsule were crushed. They could "bribe" us with part of their gains and still be better off than before. That's an offer we couldn't refuse, and so the capsule would be crushed.

Actually, only costly methods are available for reducing smog. Considering the implications of the preceding analysis, who should bear the costs of reducing the smog? That question is more complicated than most suppose.

Improved Air over Entire Nation

Let's now extend our example of improved air from an improvement of the air in one locality to an improvement of the national area. If the crushed capsule removed smog from the entire nation, landowners in some regions would benefit more than those in other areas. People living in the Great Heartland are living there now partly because there is less smog in that area. With all smog eliminated everywhere, Los Angeles would gain relatively in attractiveness. There is less smog everywhere, but land values rise more in places that formerly had more smog. And they rise because the smog-disliking residents of the Great Heartland prefer Los Angeles without smog to the Midwest without smog.

QUESTIONS AND MEDITATIONS

1) "The rent for land in New York City is not a payment necessary to produce the land. It is a necessary payment to obtain use of the land. From the first point of view, it is an economic rent; from the latter point of view, it is a cost." Do you agree?

Answer:

Yes.

2) It has been estimated that carrying a spare tire on automobiles costs the public millions of dollars every year. Is this a waste of idle resources? What would be the cost if that figure were cut to zero by not carrying any spare tires?

Answer:

A spare tire — idle resources — is a way of adjusting to uncertainty and unanticipated future changes or "emergencies." If no spare tires were carried, other more expensive adjustments would be made at the time the flat occurred. For example, a taxi or emergency road service could be called — both of which could involve not only the price of the service but additional costs of delay (such as missed or late meetings, appointments, and deliveries). Uncertainty is a fact of life, and information and adjusting to unanticipated changes is costly. Costs are higher for more rapidly acquiring information and adjusting to physical changes.

3) You are constructing an apartment building. You can build one with many units and have vacancies sometimes, or you can build a smaller unit and have a no-vacancy sign virtually all the time. If the latter behavior

is profitable, can the procedure of having vacancies sometimes be even more profitable?

Answer:

Yes. It pays to have some vacancies in order to satisfy unpredictable fluctuations in demand rather than instantaneously changing rents and keeping the apartments fully occupied. In maintaining some vacancies, the apartment owner is accommodating renters desiring to be able to move when they want to rather than having to make costly advance preparations, such as matching a departing tenant's move-out date with the incoming tenant's move-in date. Maintaining some vacancies economizes on the high costs of predicting the future and of immediately producing whatever a person wants. Alternatively, we could reduce housing costs by more advance planning of people's activities and by refusing to allow them to change their minds; to do this would reduce housing services and convenience and raise other adjustment costs. And it would reduce liberty.

4) Idle resources buffer against uncertainty. Consider the amount of money you hold; items in the medicine cabinet; food kept in the refrigerator, freezer, and in canned goods; fire extinguishers; general education. Are these idle, unemployed — and thus wasted — resources?

Answer:

It is efficient to hold some resources in inventory for ready access when wanted for use; some inventory — for example, fire extinguishers — you hope never to have occasion to use.

5) Economics suggests that if cheap enough methods are invented for metering the extent to which each motorist uses a street, streets are rationed more with a price system. Do you know of any such cases now in use?

Answer:

Tolls on bridges; parking meters; tollways; "turnpikes" with usage charges. In some countries, cars using highways must be equipped with transponders and the motorist is charged for distance driven, based on day of week and time of day.

6) Shopping centers often provide free parking spaces, some of which are used by nonshoppers. Perhaps the free spaces provided are more than would be required to clear the market if a charge is levied to cover the construction and maintenance costs. However, policing "pay"

parking space involves costs of estimating charges, collecting fees, and prosecuting violators. With such costs, might it be better to provide "too much" parking space than to provide the "right" amount with a price-rationing system?

Answer:

While it is not possible to know what is necessarily better, the total cost of providing parking space could be cheaper if it were not policed as carefully as a park-for-pay lot. A free lot would impose the costs on those who purchase from the persons who provide the free parking lot, but not on those who use the lot without doing any business with the providers of the space.

7) The Council of Economic Advisers (to the president of the United States) once argued that keeping down the price of cattle could keep down the price of meat to the consumer. The Federal Energy Agency once asserted that holding down crude oil prices reduces the price of gasoline (made from crude oil). Explain why economic analysis rejects these contentions.

Answer:

Holding down the wholesale price of cattle to the meat processors increases the spread between purchase price and selling price for processors. The price to consumers would rise anyway if there is increased demand for meat. The wealth that would have been available to cattle growers is instead given to the cattle processors. The reasoning is analogous for oil.

8) "Higher prices cause higher costs." Explain.

Answer:

Price increases often appear to be set by rising costs rather than by competition for consumer goods. This occurs because the way prices rise in response to increased demand is often hidden by inventories in the distribution process from manufacturer to wholesaler to retailer. When demand increases, sales at the existing price rise. Retailers often hold inventories to accommodate uncertainty about consumers' purchases (rather than by requiring advance orders, prepayment, or instantly raising prices). When their inventories are depleted faster than expected, the result is passed along to their wholesalers, then to manufacturers who turn to suppliers for additional raw materials. Prices of raw materials are bid up, which manufacturers see as higher costs. Those higher costs are reflected in the higher prices manufacturers charge wholesalers and that wholesalers charge retailers and are ultimately reflected in higher prices to consumers. Hence, although it appears to be higher costs that cause higher prices, it's the increase in demand that causes the higher costs and subsequent higher prices. Earlier in this chapter, we considered how increased meat demand raises the price of cattle, which appears as higher costs to meat packers, butchers, and ultimately higher meat prices for consumers.

9) "Demand-and-supply is not simply a classification that is applicable only to private property market exchange. It is applicable to any problem of allocating scarce resources among competing uses. In any given possible use, the usefulness of the resource in that use is what is meant by its demand, while its usefulness in all alternative uses (against which this particular use must compete) is the supply." Do you agree?

Answer:

Yes, demand reflects the worth or value of a resource in a specific use while supply reflects the value of the resource in all other uses. All systems for determining who gets what resources are discriminatory through some process or mechanism. Under private property and open markets, competition for resources is heavily influenced by money — the amount of other goods offered. Under a non-private-property system — such as the socialist system — nonmoney criteria such as persuasion, personal connections, personality, appearance, and cultural features become more dominant.

CHAPTER 12

SHORTAGES, SURPLUSES, AND PRICES

In chapter 10, we noted that shortages and surpluses are not caused by changes in the supply of a good. They are caused by failure of the market price to adjust to changes in demand or in supply. Sometimes the adjustment is prevented by a law or regulation that restricts market prices. And sometimes the seller refuses to change the price. Those restraints on price adjustments increase the weight of nonmoney forms of competition, including such things as personal characteristics and the social and political status of the buyers.

SHORTAGES AND PRICE CEILINGS

To compare holdings of housing space before and after a demand change for housing, we start with an increased demand for housing space. Perhaps some people have become wealthier. Their increased demands for housing shifts their original housing demand curve, D_b in figure 12.1, to D_b'. The demand by people whose incomes have not increased, D_a, is unaffected.

The aggregated line $D_a + D_b$ is the community's initial demand. The associated initial market-clearing rental price, P_1, is indicated by the intersection of the total demand, $D_a + D_b$, with supply S, the existing amount of housing space. The increased total demand curve, $D_a + D_b'$, intersects supply S at price P_2.

If rents were not allowed to rise as group B people seek more housing, the amount demanded would exceed the amount available at all rentals below P_2. When cities have restrained rents below the market-clearing price, the resulting excess amount demanded, FG, is perversely called a "housing shortage" rather than an "excess demand at the restrained price." There is not enough housing to satisfy the amount demanded, or as it is misleadingly called, "housing needs."

If there are no rent controls, price is bid up to P_2. As the price rises, both the A people and the B people move up their respective demands, and thereby reduce the total quantity demanded by the amount of the original "shortage," and the housing market is cleared.

Almost everyone would blame the owners for raising rents, but in fact the B group's increased demands caused the higher rent. Housing owners are merely intermediaries, like auctioneers, letting the demanding tenants compete for

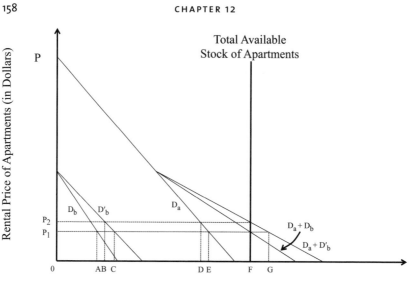

Figure 12.1

Demand of group B increases from D_b to D'_b, with aggregate demand rising from $D_a + D_b$ to D_a $+ D'_b$, creating a shortage of FG at price P_1. The amount demanded would be equated with the amount available by allowing rent to rise to the market-clearing level, P_2. The B people's quantity demanded initially increased by AC (= FG) at the original price, P_1; it then fell by BC as the price rose to the new equilibrium, with a net increase of AC − BC = AB. A people reduced their quantity demanded by DE (= AB) with the price increase. These reductions—BC + DE—eliminated the shortage of FG.

space. The market for housing would be called "tight" or "strong" or a "seller's market." However, the owners gain by a wealth transfer in the form of higher rents, and those renters whose demands have increased also gain from the right to compete for more space by offering higher rents, while the displaced renters are worse off. The gains to the owners and to the increased demanders may exceed losses to the displaced. That is small consolation to the displaced, but it is a reason for permitting people to compete by offering higher prices in the market.

SHIFTS TO NONPRICE COMPETITION

When any prices are legally restrained so as not to exceed some value (less than what the new market-clearing price would be following an increase in demand), the amount demanded exceeds the amount available, and people shift to *nonmoney* forms of competition as they seek the price-controlled goods.

People then complain both about a "housing shortage" and about "capricious, discriminatory behavior" by housing owners, who in selecting renters discriminate more by gender, marital status, age, creed, color, pet ownership, eating and drinking habits, personalities, and so forth. The *full rent* now is more heavily loaded with nonmoney features. Laws passed with the intention of preventing the resulting discrimination are impossible to enforce. "Shortages" require selective allocation, and however conducted, whether by income, willingness to pay, or color of eyes, the selection is "discriminatory," meaning that it ignores money competition.

Rent controls are popular with people already in a rented unit who expect not to be moving. But newcomers will compete in any permissible ways to get more space from the present occupants. No frustrated demander or newcomer will idly let others get or keep something worth more than the restricted money price. Their marginal personal worth of space in excess of the permissible market price is how much cost—beyond payment of that money price—they are willing to incur in *other forms of competition* to curry the supplier's favor and to displace or reduce the space for existing occupants. New demanders will drive up the *full rent* paid for the higher worth of housing space. At the same time, the landlords will, if they are restricted from accepting more money, begin to solicit or accept more of the other forms of value or rewards offered by competing demanders.

Formerly, with unrestrained money competition, the people who are less well endowed with personal and cultural attributes could offset their disadvantages by offering more money. With price controls, nonmoney features necessarily have greater weight. Price controls don't hold down the full price; they change the *form* in which the competitive price is paid.

WEALTH TRANSFERS VERSUS COSTLY COMPETITIVE ACTIVITY

The supplier would prefer to be paid with a transfer of money, rather than have the demanders compete in costly ways—such as going on waiting lists or standing in lines—worth less to suppliers.

That's a reason the increase in nonprice competition caused by price controls is usually considered wasteful. But people whose time is of lower value may be benefited by price controls. (Warning: don't jump to the conclusion that what is wasteful is necessarily "wrong" by all criteria.)

RATIONING BY COUPONS

Rationing with coupons entitling a person to buy a specified amount of the good can avoid some of the wastes of nonprice competition under price controls, if the coupons can be traded. The sale would benefit the person selling the coupon (who values what could be obtained with the money more than what could be had with the coupon) and would also benefit the purchaser of the coupon. The worth of the ration coupon is the excess of the worth of the good obtained with the coupon above the restricted price of the good. Therefore, the full price for every consumer (money price plus coupon value) equals what the free-market price would be. The rationing does not lower the full price of the good; instead the form of the payment of the price is changed, from all money to some money plus the value of the coupon if sold to someone else.

Changes in Supply over Time

Typically, price controls have been placed on housing when the cost of maintaining and producing housing has increased, as in times of inflation. The controlled rent is almost always less than the cost of maintaining the existing supply and quality of housing. In general, rent controls would lead not only to an immediate "shortage," but also an eventual reduced growth in the stock of housing, and therefore an even greater shortage. Ultimately, the quality of housing may deteriorate to where it's worth only the lower rent-controlled value, as in a slum. That would eliminate the "shortage."

The Energy "Crisis"

A few decades ago, the amount of oil supplied to the United States and other oil-importing countries was suddenly reduced by major crude oil–producing countries. (The same kind of situation can occur on a smaller scale when there is sudden news of a crop failure, such as for coffee.)

A leftward shift of the vertical supply line in figure 12.2 portrays the reduction in the supply of oil. A vertical supply line indicates the amount supplied will not respond to the price—for the interval we'll be examining. As the market price of oil began to rise, the permissible legal price was restricted at P_3 by governmental price controls. The highest permitted price—the ceiling price—was below the new equilibrium price, P. The result was a "shortage" of oil.

It was the price control, not the reduced supply of oil, that caused this "shortage." If the price had been allowed to rise, it would have reduced the amount demanded to where the amount demanded matched the reduced amount supplied. As with every other good, people could then buy as much as they demanded at that new (higher) price.

The initial supply, S, with demand D, determines a market-clearing price of P_1 at the quantity Q_1. If supply falls to S_1, market activity would generate a price of P_2 at quantity Q_2. However, if price is governmentally restrained at OP_3,

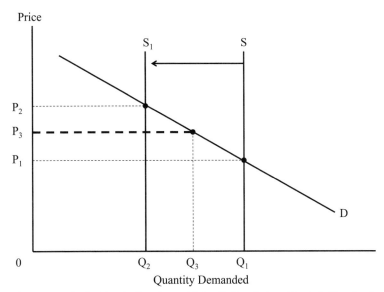

Figure 12.2 *Reduction in Supply and Price Ceiling below Market-Clearing Level*

the quantity demanded will be Q_3, greater than the Q_2 available. The excess of quantity demanded over quantity supplied at the controlled price, Q_3Q_2, is a "shortage."

Price ceilings often have been placed on gasoline in domestic markets. When the money price of gasoline has been kept down by controls, everyone has a marginal worth of another gallon higher than the legal price. So people begin to compete more by nonmonetary methods. Some in the United States hire students (whose cost of time is low) to take their cars to the service station and wait in the lines. Tie-ins of overpriced car washes with every fill-up become more common. Everyone has to engage in additional nonmonetary forms of competition for the gasoline — just as they do for price-controlled housing. They wait in line meekly and longer, tolerating shorter hours, poorer service, and paying the seller more for other things (e.g., an oil change or tire rotation) — up to where the full price (money plus these other costs) equals the higher marginal personal worth of the reduced amount of gasoline.

To repeat, price controls — not a reduced supply — create a shortage and change the form of the competition and the full price. People incur costs of engaging in more of the distasteful, less preferred competitive activity. People who can engage more cheaply in those nonmoney forms of competition tend to benefit. Almost all the nonmoney competition to get favored status will be of trivial value to sellers relative to a payment of money, and the time customers waste in lines could be used for production. Competition is not eliminated; its form and components are changed, and they become part of the higher full price.

PRICE CONTROLS ON INPUTS (PETROLEUM) DO NOT REDUCE THE PRICE OF OUTPUTS (GASOLINE)

The president, Congress, and news media sometimes argue, incorrectly, that the price of gasoline could be lowered by restricting the price of petroleum, the major input in gasoline-producing refineries. But a low, controlled price of petroleum couldn't reduce the price of the product (gasoline) unless it increased the supply curve of gasoline relative to the demand curve for gasoline. Holding down the input price won't increase, and may reduce, the amount of that input, thereby *raising* its full price.

STATEMENT OF A BASIC PRINCIPLE

The value of a productive input is *derived from the sales value of its final products.* The cost or value of inputs does not determine the final product price. Paying a star athlete an enormous salary does not require the team's owner to raise ticket prices. That has the causation in reverse. There is great demand to watch the athlete in competition. In anticipation of being able to sell tickets at a high price, the team owners compete for the athlete's services, pushing the price to the public's high value placed on seeing that athlete's service.

This is the same as star actors who attract a large audience and therefore get a higher income. The higher demand for their performances raises the price of admission, and the larger box office receipts influence what the actors get. The higher costs of actors and athletes are the response to the higher demand for their performances. The costs which consumers deem worth incurring for a good reflect — rather than determine — its value.

Similarly, you hear that housing developers force up the price of land when bidding for land on which to build houses. In fact, the high demand for houses on that land induces higher values of the land on which to build the houses. The resulting price of housing then depends on the supplied amount of housing on that land. The effect of the developers supplying more houses makes the prices lower than they otherwise would be.

Suppose that the products derived from a barrel of crude oil (gasoline, diesel, jet fuel, kerosene, fuel oil, plastics, asphalt, chemicals, drugs, rubber, etc.) have a free-market value of $65. Assume the producers of nongasoline products derived from a barrel of oil are willing to pay $20 for their share of the oil. If gasoline is selling to the consumer at $2.60/gallon and 25 gallons of gasoline can be obtained from each barrel, that's $65 in revenue for the companies selling the gasoline. However, if the average cost of refining gasoline from oil and distributing the gasoline to retailers, including taxes, is $35 per barrel, the part of the oil in a barrel that is used to make gasoline is worth only $30/barrel to the refinery. Given the $20/barrel value for the crude oil used to produce nongasoline products, the derived market price of crude oil will be $50/barrel.

The demands for both gasoline and nongasoline petroleum products will be subject to both short- and longer-run shifts, like any other consumer products. The consequence will be that the derived demands for oil to make those products also will shift. A further consideration in the market for crude oil is that it is a worldwide market. The supply comes from many places, while the demand for final products is everywhere. Past political responses to consumer complaints about "high gas prices" have resulted in ceilings being placed on *domestic* crude oil prices. But that only reduces domestic production of crude oil and increases the derived demand for imported oil that is not subject to the ceiling.

Holding down the price of any input cannot *increase* the supply of consumer products derived from the supply of that input. Indeed, the input supplier is being induced to produce less! Because curtailing the price of petroleum does not increase the supply of petroleum, the supply of refined products — gasoline, heating oil, plastics — does not increase, and thus it does not hold down the price of the refined products. The final product's price will still rise to the market-clearing price.

THE OIL INDUSTRY DIVIDED — SOME ATTACKING AND OTHERS DEFENDING PETROLEUM PRICE CONTROLS

When the question of whether to remove price controls on petroleum was raised, it was fallacious to argue that removing the controls on petroleum (an input) would result in a *rise* in the price of gasoline (a product). First, not even the money price of gasoline had been kept down by price controls on petroleum. Second, price controls on petroleum had tended to reduce the amount of petroleum extracted from domestic oil wells. When price controls were removed on domestic petroleum, more was produced, so the price of gasoline, instead of rising, actually fell.

The so-called oil industry fought both for and against price controls on crude oil. The "oil industry" is not a monolithic group. The crude oil producers (e.g., drilling companies and "wildcat" exploration companies) fought against price controls on crude oil. The users of crude, the refiners (who were allotted crude oil at that low price and refined gasoline from it) loved the price controls—except that they, too, suffered from the "shortage" of crude. They demanded more than was available at the controlled price. So they, like consumers of gasoline, competed in new ways to get a larger share of the supplied petroleum. Some refiners, arguing they were small and therefore more deserving of help, were allotted quotas (some of which were promptly sold to other refiners at the higher worth of the crude).

Refiners began to compete more intensively in the *political market* for allocations by the federal government agencies that were assigning the supply. Since there was a shortage (caused by the price controls), someone had to allocate the oil among the refiners who were demanding more than was available. The refiners funded politicians' election campaigns in order to maintain price controls and get larger quotas. The crude producers contributed to the same politicians, trying to eliminate the controls. Politicians knew that with price controls they would acquire valuable authority to determine who gets the price-controlled goods.

Why Are Water Prices Kept So Low?

As population increases and rainfall does not, in some areas water supplies don't match the amounts demanded at the existing price of water. At a higher price, people will demand less water, eliminating lower-valued uses of the water according to each person's worth of water for various purposes. It does that more effectively than if the price of water were held down and water rationed by decree, used according to politically derived opinions about the best uses of water.

From time to time, California suffers from a reduced supply of water as a result of lower than normal rainfall. But the price of water is not raised whenever there is a drought, so a "shortage" develops. Immediately, political authorities impose "rationing" on quantities and permissible uses by governmental edicts, such as prohibiting watering of gardens, washing cars, using fountains, and so forth. However, in Arizona, where the supply of water is far less, no shortage exists, and no rationing rules are imposed. Instead, the price of water in Arizona has been allowed to rise to a market-clearing level at which the public can use however much water for whatever purpose it wishes. The higher price fosters conservation.

SURPLUSES AND PRICE FLOORS

What is typically called a "surplus" is a situation in which the price is not allowed to be as low as the market-clearing price. A limit on how low the price may be is often called a "price floor," in contrast to a "price ceiling," which

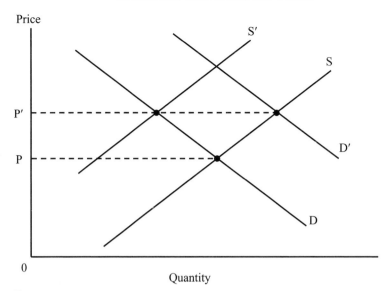

Figure 12.3

The specified price P′ (higher than the market equilibrium price, P) is attained either by reducing supply to S′ (tax "excessive" production or subsidize producers to reduce output) or by bloating demand to D′ (government buys "excessive" output and holds it or uses it in welfare programs and foreign aid).

is an upper limit on legally allowable prices. A minimum or floor price may result from government policies to curtail supply or cause a bloated demand, as illustrated in figure 12.3.

As illustrated in figure 12.4, a surplus is the result of the price control, not of some physically "excessive" supply. The disequilibrium in the case of a surplus stems from the *controlled price* below which transactions are not allowed. Yet, commonly, a "surplus" will be interpreted as if the supply were "too large," greater than the "demand" — as if price didn't matter. It's even been contended that the producers are so "efficient" that they're producing "too much," hence the surplus! It's then contended that *production controls* have to be placed on the producers to eliminate the "excessive" production (rather than letting the price fall).

Perhaps the most common price floors are for agricultural products. In almost every nation, farmers have induced legislation controlling some farm product prices at a high level — above the market-clearing level. The resulting surplus is then commonly solved by limiting the permissible amount of production.

There are three options in a surplus situation: 1) a lower permissible price or 2) the output and the amount that is offered for sale must be restrained

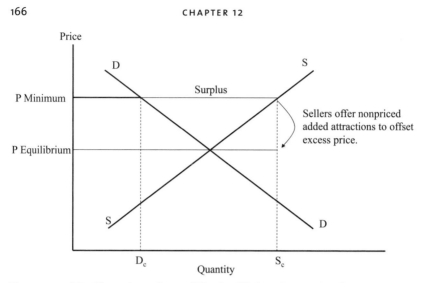

Figure 12.4 *Price Floor above Competitive Equilibrium Creates Surplus*

or 3) the excess of the amount supplied over the amount demanded must be destroyed or disposed of "elsewhere." Since the first alternative is contrary to the purpose of the policy — a high market price — the other two are the pertinent alternatives. The surplus at that controlled price (often called the "support price") — $S_0 - D_0$ — is usually purchased by the government.

One response is to force the producers to reduce production, commonly by putting a tax on "excess production" or paying producers to curtail production. The permissible production is restricted in an attempt to have a sufficiently small supply to maintain the desired high price in the otherwise free market (at the cost of higher prices to consumers).

In the case of milk, the surplus is stored as cheese or powdered milk or distributed as "aid" to poor countries or as "free" cheese to senior citizens and school lunch programs. The cost is borne by the purchasers of the higher-priced milk products sold in the markets and by the taxpayers who finance the purchase of the "excess" milk products.

COMPETITIVE BEHAVIOR DURING A "SURPLUS"

With the price-induced surplus, suppliers compete in ways other than the dollar price alone. The price restriction is usually on just the money amount paid, but the "product" being sold can be improved. The sellers offer more side benefits and amenities, thereby increasing the "full product" worth to match the high price the buyer must pay. Free delivery, free credit, stronger guarantees, and free supplementary goods and services are examples.

When the airlines colluded with the federal government to control airfares at a high level, almost every flight had "surplus" capacity — empty seats. Each airline competed in other than explicit dollar fares. They increased services, size of planes, frequency of flights, free companion flights, better dinners, and free drinks. Once the airfares were freed from lower limits, the surplus capacity disappeared, and the "free" amenities were reduced.

With too high a fixed price, if amount produced is not limited, suppliers will compete by offering "better" goods, or by concealed or camouflaged price reductions. The price-controlled products can be bundled with other non-price-controlled goods and services — as a "tie-in" in which the added goods are offered at less than their competitive price. The whole package then has a competitive price.

IMPLICATIONS

The implications of all the preceding examples are that imposed price restrictions: 1) make the amount demanded at the money price exceed or fall short of the amount available; 2) restrain exchange from lower- to higher-valuing users; 3) reduce the quality and quantity of goods; 4) induce wealth-wasting forms of competition by altering the full-price components; and 5) increase nonmonetary discrimination in competing for goods. Finally, 6) imposed price ceilings do not keep the full price low — they change the composition of the full price, increasing the nonmoney costs until the full price is an equilibrium price more heavily weighted with nonmoney types of discrimination.

We may note situations in which it *seems* markets do not work as heretofore explained. However, it's not that markets cannot work. Instead, they aren't *allowed* to work. That happens when private property rights to some goods are not well specified or enforced and therefore can't be bought or sold. That's not a "defect" of markets. It's an *absence* of markets for those goods.

It is sometimes impossible or prohibitively costly to define and enforce private property rights over some goods, such as the air, and for land with respect to noise and views. So, in the next chapter, after exploring markets for goods controlled by private property rights, we'll examine some of the consequences for the uses of resources that are not controlled by private property rights.

QUESTIONS AND MEDITATIONS

1) Do you think the rent controls that have existed in many cities were good or bad for each of the following: a) middle-aged couple who do not contemplate moving, b) young married couple with two children moving

to a new town, c) black person or other minority moving to a new town,
d) young person receiving a raise in salary, e) old person in retirement,
f) person who likes to drink and smoke, g) beautiful young woman,
h) homely immigrant, i) Muslim in a Jewish community, j) Jewish person
in a Muslim community, k) woman who likes to work around the house
and care for gardens, l) old couple who have saved wealth and invested in
an apartment house.

Answer:

Rent controls establish a maximum rent, a ceiling above which rent cannot
be legally raised. When the market-clearing rental price rises above the
legal maximum, forms of competition other than money prices become
more important — such as cultural, ethnic features, political connections.
People who have more of the "desirable" features will acquire housing
more easily than those that don't. Meditate on how well each of the groups
listed above might fare in nonmoney competition for rental property.

2) It has been argued that politicians tend to gain from price controls, and
hence they advocate them. What line of reasoning would support that
argument?

Answer:

Price-controlled goods are distributed with more political and government
influence and authority: government officials set the prices and enforce the
program — and take credit for supposedly keeping down the living costs
of constituents.

3) The military draft of the US government involved a form of price
control — in which the maximum price (compensation) that could be
paid by the military services was set by law. As a result, the number of
personnel demanded exceeded the supply *at that price*, but the buyers (the
army), instead of accepting the amount sellers (young men) were willing
to provide at that proffered price, resorted to a compulsory draft to satisfy
their "excess" of demand. Who gains and loses what by this system of
price controls?

Answer:

The military draft was collusion by employers against employees, with
the draftee obliged to work at tasks and at wages stipulated by the government. A limited segment of the population received less than market
wages, which minimized budgetary government expenditures, but with
draftees paying a great tax in-kind. Monetary taxation required to finance a

volunteer (free-market) military is less than the real, unevenly borne costs
of a drafted military.

4) News item from the past: "Seoul, Korea (AP). The city government
   ordered the capital's 1500 restaurants not to sell any meal containing rice
   during lunch hours. The measure is designed to encourage the customers
   to take other food. South Korea is experiencing a serious food shortage
   because of a poor rice crop." Would open-market prices achieve the same
   result? How effective would this measure be?

Answer:

The poor rice crop is not corrected by the price control. The temporary
reduced supply has to be dealt with by curtailing consumption. The
curtailment can be accomplished by permitting the market price to rise,
thereby conducing to individual decisions which in the aggregate will restrain amount demanded to the amount available.

5) "With open-market pricing, housing units are scarce or expensive,
   whereas with rent control the housing market is characterized by
   shortages." Explain.

Answer:

All economic goods are scarce; shortages result from prices below the
market-clearing level. Possession of nonpecuniary attributes will now play
a greater weight in allocative decisions. Over time, housing quality and
quantity will deteriorate.

6) At the same price for each, you choose an internet-ready television over
   a standard flat-screen television, but when the standard flat-screen
   television costs 50 percent less than the internet-ready television,
   you choose the standard flat-screen television. In which case are you
   "discriminating"?

Answer:

Both. Choice is an act of discrimination.

7) A distinguished professor of law has said: "Some people believe that
   every resource which is scarce should be controlled by the market.
   And since, in their view, all resources except free goods are scarce, all
   resources — even rights to radiate signals — should be so controlled.
   But surely some resources are 'scarcer' than others, and thereby possibly
   merit different treatment. It doesn't advance the argument very much to

place a label of 'scarcity' on everything." Do you think economics should be studied by professors of law?

Answer:

Yes. The problem of economics — scarcity — involves how to determine who gets how much of which goods. What forms of competition are used to resolve these questions? It does advance the argument (analysis?) to grasp the meaning of scarcity and to understand that economics says nothing about which scarce goods *ought* to be allocated through the exchange-market form of competition and which scarce goods *should* be allocated by other forms of competition, such as physical force (violence), first come first served, waiting in line, who you know, appearances, personality, personal favors, cultural features. We leave it to you to try to figure out why the "degree of scarcity" should affect the form of competition that *should* determine how a scarce resource is allocated among alternative uses and users. In any case, scarcity implies competition to resolve who gets how much of which goods. If money competition is suppressed, other forms of competition must occur.

CHAPTER 13

MARKETS AND PROPERTY RIGHTS

*"It is sufficiently obvious, that persons and property are the
two great subjects on which Governments are to act; and that the rights
of persons, and the rights of property, are the objects, for the protection of
which Government was instituted. These rights cannot well be separated."*
JAMES MADISON, *Speech at the Virginia Convention*, 1829

Apples on a tree in a public park are picked before ripe. Public beaches are littered. Garbage is dumped in rivers. Pollution of the air is prevalent. Mistakenly called "market failures," such phenomena reflect absence of private property rights. Markets are places or methods whereby demanders and suppliers can communicate to buy and sell private property rights. This chapter identifies key features of private property rights and how they determine the uses of resources. And we will see why no matter who owns a resource, private property rights help deter "waste," "pollution," and "abuse."

You propose to construct a building that would block the view from my neighboring apartment building. A "market transaction" between you and me can settle that dispute without a lawsuit — if we *first* know *who* has what rights. A judge could toss a coin to determine that. But that decision would affect only who is made richer, *not* whether the proposed building would be built. To explain, we'll run through the two alternatives, where I initially have the rights to the view, and then where you have the rights to block my view.

If initially ownership of my building includes the rights to the view, I could prevent your construction of a building without my permission. However, *if* your profit on the proposed new building would exceed the value to me of the view, you could buy from me the rights to the view. You would then construct your building, and the view would be lost to renters in my building. You would have an added expense, and I would be richer in money (but poorer in view), because you had to pay me to give up my rights. While I'd lose some rental value of my apartments (the occupants of my apartments would enjoy less view, but they'd have a compensating lower rent), the amount you pay leaves me financially better off. So, you'd pay me and construct your building. Both of us gain from the transaction.

In the alternative situation, you have the right to build. You could proceed with your construction without compensating me. But there is again a possible (initially beneficial) transaction. If my valuation of the view is greater than your anticipated profit, I could bribe you to forgo building. You thereby gain, and I minimize my loss.

HOW RELATIVE PREFERENCES ARE IMPRESSED ON THE OWNER

The choice of ingredients used in the preparation of food in a restaurant shows how an indirect force channels resources to the highest market-valued use. For example, the restaurant owner can decide whether or not to use a cooking ingredient such as MSG (monosodium glutamate), or in Europe whether GMF (genetically modified foods) are allowed. However, it is the customers, through revealing their preferences, who determine whether restaurants advertising that MSG or GMF is not used will be successful.

Without ordinances or regulations prohibiting smoking in bars or restaurants, the preferences of nonsmoking customers versus those of smokers will determine whether the restaurant owner will find it more profitable to restrain smoking. These are the same market forces that determine whether or not a restaurant offers alcoholic beverages, or how long it is open, or whether it is quiet or has loud music, or has tablecloths, or air-conditioning, or quicker service.

While smoking is permitted in most casinos in Las Vegas, some attract patrons by advertising that they offer a "smoke-free environment." Instead of competing by direct payments to have or not have smoking, the patrons merely choose among restaurants, bars, and casinos that do or do not restrain smoking. Owners are umpires between customers who have different preferences. The owner collects a reward in the greater revenue from patrons for a more highly valued environment. That's true for every business.

GOVERNMENT AGENCIES AND PRIVATE PROPERTY RIGHTS

Both preceding examples illustrate how the ability to *buy and sell enforceable private property rights* pushes resources toward highest market-valued uses no matter who owns them initially. The result is independent of how wealthy is the owner. A deep pocket does not increase the willingness to invest in unprofitable ventures.

Imagine an investor in a proposed oil refinery or a wood processing facility, which would spread odors for miles around. Negotiation for purchase and sale of many individual rights to satisfy the whole surrounding population would be much too expensive. As the population has increased with more interdependence in larger cities, problems formerly individually or privately handled, such as for water, sewage, personal protection, and roads, have become duties of a government, often by new regulatory agencies. If they alter private property rights in scope or value, the US Constitution, Amendment V, states *"nor shall private property be taken for public use without just compensation."*

The scope of that stricture on government power over private property has been the subject of much dispute and different interpretations in the courts of law. Were the rights that have been taken truly private property rights, or were they public property rights that had been used privately? Were the uses proposed really for "public use" or for private benefit? Was the amount of compensation "just" or too little?

Market Exchanges of Rights to Use Air Can
Measure a Worth of Pollution Rights

When anyone mentions buying rights to pollute the air, the typical immediate response is, "You can't place a price on the environment. You economists assert everything can be reduced to money — as if market values could be placed on aesthetics and the environment." Look at what economic analysis actually says.

Purchase and Sale (Alienability) of Rights to Pollute the Air

"Alienable" is the legal word for "salable." In major metropolitan areas, air quality control agencies of the local government monitor the amount of pollutants, such as sulfides and oxides, emitted from commercial firms in an area defined by a "bubble" of airspace within which not more than a specified amount of pollutants is permitted.

Some years ago, the City of Los Angeles established a limit on the total amount of pollutants emitted by all commercial firms. The limit to be allowed ten years later was set at 25 percent of the total amount emitted in the first year. Either production of goods had to be reduced or more expensive methods of production with less pollution were necessary.

Each firm's permissible amount ("rights") of emitted pollutants was determined (usually set at the amount it had been emitting previously, establishing an initial cap on emissions). Each was allowed to sell to other firms its rights to emit pollutants. A market for pollution rights immediately developed. Incidentally, anyone could buy rights even for the purpose of reselling at what they hoped would be a higher price.

Our interest here is less in what the prices were or how much they fluctuated than in what *alienability* of property rights permits. Owners of some firms

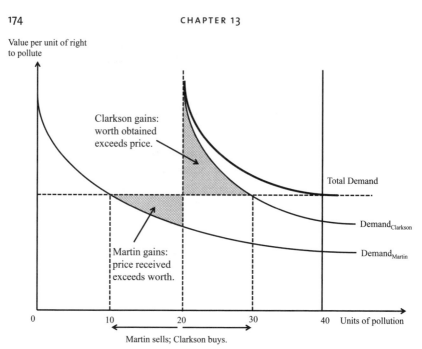

Value per unit of right
to pollute

Clarkson gains:
worth obtained
exceeds price.

Total Demand

Demand$_{Clarkson}$

Demand$_{Martin}$

Martin gains:
price received
exceeds worth.

0   10   20   30   40   Units of pollution

Martin sells; Clarkson buys.

Figure 13.1 *Mutual Gains from Trading Pollution Rights*

Clarkson and Martin differ in their marginal values of production. Clarkson's additional value from expansion of output is greater than the cost of buying the marginal pollution rights. He will wish to buy rights from Martin, for whom the price of rights is greater than the value of his reduced output.

found it profitable to replace older equipment with less-polluting types of facilities, because their unused pollution rights could be sold to other firms where the rights to emit pollutants were more valuable.

The effects *of alienable pollution rights* are the same as for tradable eggs between Ted and Rae (chapter 6), with "pollution rights" here replacing "eggs." The polluters can be the Martin Refining Co. and Clarkson Paint Co. Instead of "personal worths" of Ted and Rae, we compare the "marginal market values" of products.

In figure 13.1, both Clarkson and Martin initially emit 20 units of pollution. But the marginal value of further output for Clarkson is greater than the cost of buying pollution rights to generate the greater production, and the cost of buying pollution rights is greater than the value of more output to Martin. So both gain by Clarkson buying 10 pollution units from Martin, with each equating his marginal worth of output with the price of polluting. Salable, privately owned pollution rights result in maximum product value for a given total permissible amount of pollution. The rights to emit pollutants are attracted to their highest market-valued uses. As with Ted and Rae, the initial holdings of rights do not determine the final allocation, if the rights are salable.

Altering Production Techniques or Volume to Reduce Pollution

There can be reduction of pollution by a reduction in production with the initial technologies. But the price of polluting can affect the choice of methods of production, possibly encouraging less-polluting techniques.

The sites of production and pollution will be affected by choices of residence as well as by moving production. People may choose to live in places where pollution is less even when that is more expensive. Lower-income people tolerate more pollution and lower-quality living space in order to have more food, furniture, and health care. Poorer people buy cheaper used cars. They cause more pollution. But they prefer that to having better cars and less of other goods. All behavior involves and reflects choice among trade-offs.

TWO FALSE ISSUES

1. Fairness and Amount of Wealth?

Opponents of allowing sales and purchases of pollution rights have argued that the richer firms will get pollution rights from the poorer ones, and that is unfair. However, the wealth of a firm has nothing to do with the marginal value of pollution rights. Greater wealth does not mean a person will, nor should, be foolish. Some believe (or argue as if) trade yields a benefit to only one party at the loss of another. Selling, as well as buying, can benefit a trader.

2. The Myth of "Economics versus the Environment"

There is no conflict between economics and the environment. Everyone prefers a cleaner, safer environment. Everyone prefers more income. Some regard visits to the mountains, wilderness, and communing with nature more highly than do others. What economics emphasizes is that more of "this" means less of "that."

Arguments persist about *whose* benefits should dominate. But it's not a question of dominance. It's a question of trade-offs. Members of the Sierra Club and Audubon Society would prefer to have more natural resources preserved. Others, less interested in "nature in the raw" relative to other things, would like to have more development of public lands for homes and easier access (roads rather than hiking trails) to mountains. Economic analysis is not biased for or against either, nor does it indicate what the relative preferences should be. Instead, economics recognizes the necessity of choices among the alternatives.

THE RULE OF PRIVATE PROPERTY RIGHTS

Alienability of private *property rights* rests on (1) *control* of the resource and its services and (2) clear *specification* of the rights and the object.

1. Control: The Cost and the Worth

What's the value of a private property right to the North Star? You couldn't control its condition or its services as a directional guide. If you were declared to have a "private property right" to a tagged whale last seen in the Alaskan region of the Pacific Ocean — good luck.

You may perform beautifully at the piano. You can say the music is your private property, but you'd have to control the sound as private property. Once the music is created, anyone in the room can hear it. But you can arrange to play the piano in an auditorium and sell rights to people *to be in* that room. You "tie" two rights: to be in a room, and then to hear the music at no extra cost. You could advertise that there will be "free music" to anyone who rents a seat in the auditorium from you.

You pay for the right to sit in the theater at the time a specified movie is shown. A sporting event, unlike one in a public park where anyone can watch, often is played in an *enclosed* arena. Spectators must pay to enter; control is effective.

Private enforcement of control abounds. Locks, fences, burglar alarms, safes, barred windows, home and office security devices, and security service firms protect control of the object. The private enforcement depends, as you would expect, on the costs relative to the benefits. Hardly anyone bothers to enforce limits on parking time on low-valued land (in suburban shopping areas). For midtown parking, a price is charged, and times are monitored. Some formerly almost free and unowned resources can become more valuable as populations increase.

Lakes, rivers, oceans, and the air are being subjected to more extensive control either by establishing private property rights or by direct controls by governments. The higher the potential worth of use of a resource, the greater is the cost that's worth incurring to control it. Airport landing rights and moving cocoons of airspace for commercial flights are bought and sold among airlines.

As the cost of effective surveillance over the ocean decreases, or as the worth of the control increases, greater distances from shore (200 miles instead of the old 3-mile or 12-mile limits) are being claimed by nations as their "property."

Whether currently disputed areas (for example, deep-sea floor minerals and Antarctica) will be established as private or government property of one or more nations remains to be seen. Even the western states in the

United States have sued each other in federal courts for Colorado River water rights, and surely would consider military action if they were separate nations.

2. Specification of Rights

No matter how well controlled are the objects, the rights to the good must be *verifiable*. The more complete, unambiguous, and reliable is the specification of the good and of the rights to the good, the more cheaply will the private property right be alienable.

As a buyer, you'll want assurance the seller does own the rights and that they are alienable, without unknown encumbrances and claims by other people, such as creditors or other partners. Verifying that is a major part of the "costs of transactions," especially for land and durable resources. Ownership of property rights to houses, land, and automobiles are recorded in government files. They are usually the most authoritative, reliable records. In almost all parts of the United States, private firms also record the information, the reliability of which is usually guaranteed by "title insurance" companies.

PROTECTION AND PRESERVATION OF ALIENABILITY

English courts have for centuries crafted and preserved alienable (marketable, salable) private property rights to resources. You may be told that with private property rights no one else can affect what you do with what you own. But others can and do affect the market *value* of what you own — an owner's wealth, as will be explained in following chapters, reflects its "capital value." The values (prices) of resources you own (except for money) depend on what other people think about your uses of resources you own. If they don't like what you are doing, they punish you. They do that in ways and to an extent to be explained. Nor are you are allowed to dictate all the *future* uses of the resources you leave to future generations. No "dead hand of the past" is allowed exclusive control.

So great is the value of alienability, the law has preserved it at the cost of other potential benefits. For example, shared private property rights among several people decreases the ready salability of shared resources. The law has generally been framed and interpreted so as to reduce the costs and difficulties of reaching decisions to sell or buy property "of the sharing group," as we'll show later.

SHARED OWNERSHIP

Sharing of private property rights is prevalent, even though it tends to weaken control, definiteness, and alienability of the shared rights. A form of sharing is marriage and the family. Methods of sharing have been devised that tend to protect the objectives of sharing ownership against diverse interests of the sharing owners.

A family may own a newspaper publishing company. Negotiation for sale of the rights to publish the paper can be hindered by disputes within the family about the wisdom, price, and sharing of the proceeds. There is also the uncertainty of who is a member. For a family, are all people born into the family sharing owners? Do descendants of members inherit rights of members? Does marriage into the family make the newcomer a member?

Unless these questions are answered appropriately, buyers will not be sure of what rights are being purchased or whether a sale is really a completed sale, or is challengeable by people claiming to be members.

HOW TO BECOME A MEMBER-OWNER?

A predominant feature affecting the rights and behavior in shared groups is how membership is obtained. May you enter at will with no payment or contribution to the group and without requiring permission from the existing members? If so, that could be called an "open" group. If a payment or contribution must be made to another member or to the whole group, that group would be a "closed" group. Entry into a political party is "open," as it is in most religions and cities. You do not have any salable rights of shared membership. Being a member (citizen) of the United States does not require a purchase from an existing member, although the government controls entry.

The meaning and worth to a member of what the "group owns" depends on how entry and membership are determined and on the behavior of members. If entry is open, congestion awaits. For "closed" groups, wherein membership must first be purchased from the group or another member, the members are guided by other members.

Stockholders own the modern corporation. Admission to that class is by purchase only. Anyone can enter the membership by purchasing a share (membership) from an existing owner. No one can object, or even know who are the other stockholders. It's called an anonymous society by the French. It's a limited liability corporation in the United States.

Many Swiss corporations have two classes of stockholders. In one class, any shareholder can sell to whomever that shareholder chooses. The other class of members must first obtain approval by the administrators of the corporation. A share of each type of stock typically has the same claim to dividends and assets of the corporation, so they differ primarily in confidentiality of who are the owners.

The incentives for the members to maintain the benefits of membership in open groups are less strong than when members own salable rights to membership. Market sales of membership rights in closed groups increase incentives of members to help maintain the advantages of membership. This is evident in different types of "country clubs." The members own some clubs as a closed group with entry only by purchase. Some grant only daily rental rights.

Courts have tended to judge and decide issues of ownership so as to preserve and facilitate reliable alienability of well-identified property rights. The general belief is that this tendency to maintain alienability reflects a social consensus to maintain the influence of market values as guides of future actions — by limiting who in the future will be recognized as a member.

Corporations can have thousands of members — stock or "share" holders. But how does that group sell or buy property rights to what the group shares in ownership? At one extreme, unanimous agreement of the members might be required. More commonly, the sharing members of a corporation are allowed to delegate to some one person or small group the authority to sell what the whole group owns, or to buy for the group and also to direct the use of those resources. An obvious difficulty with this method is the "principal-agent moral hazard," in which the agent may act more in accord with self-interest than the promised interest in the group, as will be explained later.

The other extreme way permits each member alone to sell or buy for the group. That's close to a family in which the husband or the wife can decide to sell what the family owns or to buy for the family. It's similar to some forms of business partnership. We'll explore later why in a business corporation the alienability of rights is among the shareholders and not among the employees.

WHY DELIBERATELY SUPPRESS PRIVATE PROPERTY RIGHTS OF A COLLEGE?

Although a member of a college student body, you can't sell that membership "right" to anyone else. It's nonalienable.

Your attention to what happens at your college might be more serious if you had an "alienable" (resalable) right of membership whenever you dropped out or graduated. If you are inclined to believe a system of salable rights would ruin the college's reputation, recall that similar rights are used for membership in the group of "owners" of Hewlett Packard, Ford, AT&T, and Apple, but they aren't "ruined." What, if anything, is different about a college? Most likely, none of its resources are held under private property rights.

What is meant by the "*college's* resources"? No one owns them; no one can treat the resources as private property. Instead, the college has an administrator with authority to control and to buy and sell the college's resources. Why are private property rights and responses to market values suppressed, when almost everywhere else efforts are made to strengthen responses to market values?

What can a person or a group do if a board of trustees administers the college? The board can use gifts of money donated to the college to buy things that then become "owned" by the college. The board of trustees can buy private property rights to goods, as when they buy automobiles or labor or building materials. But no one can legally let anyone use the college's resources as if they were private property. The college bought the private property rights to goods, but the board is bound by laws saying that not all the components of private property rights to those goods would be exercisable by the board.

Why would anyone ever establish a college that had to give up those features of private property rights? For two reasons: first, the government gives favors — the school is exempted from some taxes that would have to be paid when using private property, and people who donate to the college avoid taxes; second, and more important, the incentives of the trustees are directed away from profit and wealth maximizing. And it's considered good when the purpose is to help students obtain an education *without paying the full costs*.

A college is somewhat like a charitable organization. You might wonder why successful privately owned, profit-seeking schools exist at the elementary level. And private, for-profit schools exist for engineering, foreign languages, electricians, computer programmers, hairstylists, golfers, driving autos, and flying.

EXTERNALITIES

Although consequences to the owner dominate decisions about the use of privately owned goods, we are allowed to act in ways that affect other people. These effects are called "externalities." When you wear clean, pleasant-appearing clothes, or cultivate a pretty garden, which other people enjoy, that's a "positive externality." Living in a nation where everyone has at least a high school education is a positive externality benefit for everyone.

Many actions you take benefit other people, even though you are not paid to do so, in contrast to explicit exchange. If permissible actions are disliked or harmful to other people, the actions create "negative externalities." If other people are slovenly garbed and dirty, and speak in a rude fashion, we suffer negative externalities. Informal rules of social etiquette and social customs motivate positive, and suppress negative, social behavior externalities. This is sometimes labeled "internalizing external effects."

We typically don't offer to pay neighbors or friends to behave in some way, yet methods of compulsion exist. Probably the major forces are social ostracism and governmental force. Social ostracism is a subtle and powerful force. Etiquette in social conformity with custom helps internalize externalities. If you behave otherwise, friends begin to snub you, your reputation falls, and life becomes more lonely and confined. The line between "innovative leadership" and "disgusting nonconformity" is not bright and clear, but it does exist.

A society of generally educated people who read and write and speak the same language is generally advantageous to everyone. This "externality" effect is so important that compulsion by law to acquire those features is commonplace. Every child must attend school, whether governmentally provided and financed or a private school. Adults are not compelled by law to know the common language, but the economic and social penalty often is persuasive.

Physical externalities, if harmful, are usually declared illegal. However, pecuniary (financial) losses on competitors (negative pecuniary externalities) do not necessarily make an action illegal. Our better textbook reduces a competitor's earnings. That's not illegal, and is regarded as benign, in that more preferred goods are allowed to displace less favored goods. The analysis of the preceding chapters is consistent with, and not upset by, externalities or public goods.

PUBLIC GOODS

So far we have dealt primarily with goods that are useful for only one person at a time. If I eat an apple, I alone get the benefit. Goods are "private" goods if one person is the consumer or user. But for "public" goods, the amount of worth to one person does not reduce the amount of the good or its worth to other people. More for me does not mean less for you, *once the good is produced.*

Examples of goods almost exclusively composed of public-good attributes are mathematical theorems, TV and radio programs, melodies, poems, vaccinations, basic education, technology, ideas, and some public parks and wilderness. One person's access to, or knowledge of, an idea does not reduce the worth anyone else could also get with it. One viewer of a TV program does not displace another. Mosquito control districts, air pollution controls, flood controls, garbage and sewage disposal, streets, and police patrols are, or have some characteristics of, public goods. The same holds for some forms of national defense: if there is more for me, there is also more for you, unless it is a local antimissile defense for your town rather than mine.

What are called "commons" often are areas to which everyone in a community has a right of access. Some goods have mixtures of private and public-good attributes. The space around a musical band concert is limited, and a better space for me means a poorer space for others. The only *worldwide* public goods we can think of are the sun, moon, and stars.

Why are public goods specified and treated as different from ordinary goods? What are the economic aspects and problems posed by public goods, other than those posed by private goods? One major feature is that the creation of public goods is hindered because a reward for creating and maintaining them is difficult and expensive to provide. Two common procedures for such provision are (a) by governments with financing by taxation and (b) formation of private voluntary clubs for services to the members (its public). One widely applied process relies on the community of users voluntarily agreeing to rules of use and care. The control of abuse is both informal and formal. The community may establish a voluntary patrol or may rely on ostracism of abusers. Later, we'll explore a few of the means of controlling behavior.

GOVERNMENT CONTROL

Governments can apply force to obtain payment and to restrain free riding. Governments can use force that cannot be employed privately (such as jailing or imposing a fine on a detected nonpayer). Sometimes, if the government charges a fee for access to the public good, a complaint is voiced against charging an admission price. But the price can be used as a *rationing* device, to prevent the public good from being so over used as to be destructive of benefits.

What has been a public good now can become a nonpublic good. A public good (more for me does not mean less for you) can become a shared good. We share in having equal rights to access, and in having equal shares, but the shares can diminish with open entry. Public goods yesterday become congested goods tomorrow, and methods of control of entry or access will change. The oceans are ruled by the doctrine of freedom of the seas — except that what are called "seas" is being reduced as nations claim that more of the oceans are within their expanded national boundaries.

PUBLIC, OR GROUP, GOODS: CLUBS

Whatever the group, large or small, the prospect of free riding by someone in that "public" is likely to shrink the investment in production and maintenance of the public good. This initial free riding on the original investment could be reduced if the potential beneficiaries had to bear the cost of creating the public good. The investors would then be the subsequent beneficiaries.

A private yacht club facility, a privately owned golf course with owner-members only, or a fraternal organization used and owned exclusively by members, provide public-good services to members who pay the cost of both the investment and the subsequent service to the members.

A "club" can be defined as a "firm" in which both the investors and customers are the members. The public-good aspect of associating with those who are allowed to be members, not monetary profit, is the objective. For that, excludability is critical.

Even with entire nations, the residents have a club-like relationship and tend to object to newcomers who are "strange in behavior" and haven't paid for entry to obtain the privately supplied public goods.

PRIVATELY SUPPLIED PUBLIC GOODS
FINANCED BY TIE-INS

Several ways have been devised to supply services privately and profitably despite, or because of, free riding. Private provision of some public goods occurs for which exclusion of nonpayers is "impossible." Paradoxically, in some cases, the more free riders, the better it is for the private supplier.

Examples are typical television and radio programs. You pay "nothing" to watch or listen, but it's not free. You pay a price—the time during which advertising is displayed. No charge is made, and no one is excluded. As a concert pianist does not force the listener to sit in a specified room for which an entry fee is charged, television and radio broadcasters and the suppliers of the internet services cannot compel you to devote some of your time watching advertising. However, when you want to obtain their services, this tie-in is the price of admission.

Forcing the viewer to see advertisements uses some of the viewer's time, which has alternative use values. To hold the viewers' attentions, the advertising is made attractive rather than only informative of the advertiser's brand name. The same method (advertising) of paying for underpriced (or "free") services is true for almost all newspapers and magazines, which are grossly underpriced relative to the costs of creating and supplying them. The payments for advertising in the magazine and newspaper serve the same purpose as advertising on "free" television for covering the costs. In several European nations, each television set is taxed to prevent free riding. In the United States, advertising provides funding and sidesteps free riding—that is, getting the benefit without paying any cost. In some nations, both advertising and government taxes on owning TV sets are common.

CHARITY

Another form of allocation of existing goods is by gift or charity. You may be at a college founded by charity of the founder. At some time you have used a library built and maintained by the charity of the Andrew Carnegie Foundation or by government use of tax money to create a "free library." Some television stations are financed by charity. Hospitals are probably the most prominent example of charity-supported organizations. Why is charity devoted primarily for schools, hospitals, and churches? Who gains what? Are the intended effects also the achieved effects? We'll see that some, but only some, of the principles and consequences of market exchanges apply to charity.

Who Gains What from a Gift?

Whatever the motive and intent, gifts (not in cash that can be spent, however much that is preferred) usually have some "waste" from the giver's point of view.

The US government grants aid to foreign governments, ostensibly for specific purposes. If a foreign government is given $100 million to build a dam *which it would have built or bought even without the gift*, what has it gained? The recipient's resources are released for other purposes. So the gift gives the recipient government some wealth with which to do more of whatever it wants.

To operate a television station in the United States, a license is required from the Federal Communications Commission (FCC). The law forbids assigning licenses on a first applier, first served basis. The winner is the applicant deemed most fit (based on responsibility, dedication to public service and education, etc.). Competition in establishing and comparing fitness is expensive; the combined costs incurred by all competitors in that competition can even exceed the value of the license. Much is expended in competing for the award — using lawyers, lobbyists, and political donations — because once obtained, the license is transferable at the market value. The cost of competing for the license is high because there's much to be gained by winning.

Governments have moved toward selling rather than "awarding" licenses or valuable rights, such as rights for oil exploration, use of a portion of the radio spectrum, or for "monopoly" rights to operate liquor stores, taxis, dairy herds, and tobacco farms. All these rights are salable once they have been awarded.

Nontransferable Aid and "Earmark" Financing

Some other gifts cannot be legally reallocated or resold. Examples are rights to enroll in a college or medical school, to move to the United States from another country or join some unions, adopt a child, camp in a national park, or be bused to school. Nevertheless, gifts received for what you would have done or received even without a gift release more of the gift for other purposes.

One dollar, no matter from where, is the same as any other. Money is fungible. So when children are bused to school "free of charge to the parents," who gets what benefit? Once relieved of buying transportation they otherwise would have provided, the parents are able to divert their expenditure from transportation to something else. The children whose parents would have had them walk get a gain in the form of a ride. The principle is simple: to the extent that recipients would have purchased the services now provided by a gift, they can use an equivalent amount of wealth for other purposes.

Governments levy a special tax for a specific purpose. Though the tax receipts are earmarked for that purpose, city officials can release equivalent amounts from other tax sources formerly allocated to that purpose. The net increase in the activity will be less than the earmarked tax receipts. Proceeds from the California lottery are assigned to public schools, but some of the money formerly assigned to schools is diverted to other uses. The net addition of the lottery to schools is smaller than the funds from the lottery by an amount equal to the reallocated funds.

QUESTIONS AND MEDITATIONS

1) M owns and lives in a home near an area where a series of 20-story apartment buildings are to be built. M sues to prevent the construction on the contention that it will create extra traffic hazards and congestion. In court, M proves to the judge's satisfaction that his allegation is correct. How should the judge rule?

Answer:

M is suing for property rights to uncongested streets. Under current law, this kind of right seems not be recognized, and presumably the judge would rule against him. Who owns the streets, with authority to determine how heavily they can be used?

2) A California city prohibits construction of any building whose shadow will fall on some other person's land between 9 a.m. and 3 p.m. Is that a restriction of private property or a strengthening of it?

Answer:

If you define access to sunlight as an aspect of landownership, then it is a strengthening of private property rights. But other property rights of building construction are being curtailed.

3) A city passed a zoning ordinance prohibiting the owner of a large parcel of land from constructing homes on it because of a fear that the noise of a nearby airport owned by the city would be so disturbing to the new tenants that airport operations would have to be curtailed.

  a. Whose rights were being curtailed by the zoning ordinance?
  b. Under the definition of private property rights, were the landowner's rights being taken from him?
  c. Can you suggest some other solution to the problem?
  d. If you were a taxpayer in that town and did not live near the airport, what solution would you have voted for?

Answer:

  a. If the zoning at the time the owner purchased the land included the right to build the homes, then his rights are violated by a subsequent change in zoning that forbids the building of homes. If there was no zoning at the time the current owner purchased the land, the new zoning or ordinance clarified, defined, and allocated the rights for the first time.
  b. If there was a question of what rights were included with the land, a potential buyer of the land could ask for a clarification of those rights before purchasing the land.
  c. Possibly require that the contract of sale of land to intended home builders provide acknowledgment of the proximity of the airport; this would reduce the value imputed to the land to a level which informed buyers are willing to pay.
  d. Taxpayers in the town would probably want the homes built so that there would be more homeowners paying property taxes to help pay for schools and other city services. Best for taxpayers would be if the new homes near the airport were restricted to seniors only so they would be paying property taxes but not have children to send to the schools.

4) Ralph Nader, a well-known exposer of product defects, complained that a person who relieves himself in a river is fined, but industries that pollute the same river are not. Muggers are punished, but smoggers are not. These he cited as illustrating the inequities and irrationalities of our society and economy in its attitude toward big corporations. What has Nader overlooked?

Answer:

He ignores the social gains provided by activities that produce smog and pollution as a by-product. As automobiles and airplanes produce "risk of death"; as travel takes up land for roads; as making sheet-steel involves less of other desirable things like leisure, quiet, and rest; as oil wells create an offensive odor in the neighborhood — so all productive activity involves some undesirable by-products. All of these pollutions of our environment are part of the costs of production and could be avoided if we were willing to have a less convenient, more Spartan life. We should not look only at costs and think that something is wrong with those economic activities that involve the largest costs, for they may also yield the greatest benefits. Relieving oneself in the river may be less valuable than the value of output from a factory that creates equivalent pollution and may be avoidable at lower cost. Similarly, smoggers are producing other services in the process, whereas muggers produce no social service.

The complaint that Nader should have developed is that governments and courts had not introduced a system of making people pay for the *right to pollute*, thereby bearing the full costs of their actions. Such a system would induce people to pollute *less if* the gains obtained from activities that yield pollution are worth less than the pollution damage. As we could produce less oil or less paper by having less pollution, there is a trade-off between more or less clean air or cleaner water and more or less other desirable goods output. Efforts to expose that trade-off rate and to induce the pollution costs to be taken into account by a system of prices for the right to pollute (by fines) rather than with zero prices or absolute prohibitions (infinitely high prices) are what Nader might more usefully have recommended.

5) Camping fees in almost all state and national parks are so low that people want more space than is available, at certain times of the year.
   a. Why is the price for camping not at a market-clearing level?
   b. How much space would people want at a market-clearing price?

Answer:
   a. Camping sites are not privately owned.
   b. Less space per person.

6) In Los Angeles, two closely situated golf courses, one privately owned and one publicly owned, are both open to the public.
   a. Which do you think charges the higher price, and which do you think requires less or no advance reservation?
   b. Who is benefited in what respects by each course's policy?
   c. As land values rise around the course, which one do you think will be converted to housing or business first?

Answer:
   a. Privately owned courses charge more and require less or no advance reservation. More amenities are provided to those who are willing to pay for them.
   b. More proceeds go to identifiable owners of the private course.

c. Owners of the privately owned course will compare the return they could get from selling the land and investing the proceeds in alternatives — versus the fees they can charge from continuing to operate the course. Because individuals cannot benefit financially from selling the public-owned course, the political authorities may compare the property and other tax revenue that might be gained by selling the land, versus the fees generated by the golf course. Probably the privately owned course will be sold first.

7) "Californians are crazy. Near a beautiful California beach, there is a luxurious motel and a state-owned camping area. Despite the greater luxury of the motel facilities, scores of cars are lined up for hours each morning seeking camping sites, whereas at the motel there is hardly a day that the rooms are all taken. This shows that Californians prefer outdoor, dusty camps to the luxuries of a motel with pool, TV, room service, and private bath." Do you agree?

Answer:

Tendency to price public parks and services at less than a market-clearing price is the explanation. Motels, priced higher than facilities in parks, rely on the law of demand to keep the amount demanded in line with facilities available.

8) Churches are typically nonprofit institutions. Can you think of a problem in allocation of church facilities that is solved without use of the price system?

Answer:

Seats are allocated first come, first served rather than sold to worshipers — except in some churches, where a person donates a large sum and is given a special pew as a token of appreciation.

9) The college you now attend is most likely a not-for-profit institution. Are any of its resources allocated at less than market-clearing prices? (Library facilities? Athletic facilities? Counseling? Course admission? Campus space?) Who gains by the power to select admissible students?

Answer:

Administrators have little incentive to maximize profits in a not-for-profit institution. On the other hand, they can gain personal and institutional popularity (with enhanced donations and charging of higher tuition) by providing attractive amenities and admitting children of the right sorts of families.

10) Tickets to sporting events:

Why do college athletic conferences chronically have an enormously larger number of people wanting tickets than are available for the playoffs and important games?

Why are admission tickets for the Masters Golf Tournament (a prestigious golf tournament) fewer than the number demanded by the public?

Answer:

Receipts and returns are not wholly in the form of money revenue from selling tickets. And maximizing the money revenue does not enhance salaries of the administrators. The administrators and their organization can gain social and community stature by pricing tickets below the market-clearing level.

11) "The imbalance between governmentally and privately provided services is evidenced by the fact that the family that vacations in its air-conditioned, power-braked, power-steered car passes through cities over dirty, badly paved, congested streets, not to mention the billboards. When the family picnics with excellent food provided by private business, they must sit by a polluted stream and then spend the night in a public park that is a menace to health and morals and littered with decaying refuse. Private abundance and public poverty are facts that assail every observant person. A plentiful supply of privately produced goods, and a shortage of publicly provided services, is inescapable testimony to the lack of a social balance between private and governmentally provided services."

Why are these arguments — taken from a popular book advocating more governmentally provided services — faulty and do not indicate anything about whether there is too little of such services? (Hint: Note the use of the term "shortage." How are governmentally provided services rationed?)

Answer:

Ignores *prices* at which government goods are distributed. Price of such goods is so low as to create a shortage and appearance of insufficient amount.

12) You are running a university, and the faculty is asking for higher salaries, some of which you would be able to grant only by reducing funds available for buildings and activities such as sports. Now, the foundation of a rich alumnus gives your university a grant of millions of dollars, with

the condition that the donated funds be allocated exclusively to faculty salaries. Who gains what?

Answer:

Building and nonfaculty purposes gain, and faculty also gains to the extent faculty salaries are raised more than they otherwise would have been raised. Money from other sources that would have been spent for faculty salaries now can be spent for other purposes.

13) The faculty of many colleges are given free parking space.
   a. Who gains what?
   b. What would be the effect if the faculty could sell their space to students?

Answer:

   a. Those professors who obtain a desired space receive a gift (nonsalary compensation) in kind. But the university is giving away something of value, and it is forgoing money revenue it could have collected through renting the spaces.
   b. If the faculty is permitted to rent spaces to students, the spaces would be allocated more fully in accord with revealed preferences of the academic community, with proceeds going to the teachers rather than to the institution. An alternative would be for the school to leave the space vacant as scenic lawn.

14) Immigration-quota rights to the United States are priced at "zero" instead of being sold at a market-clearing price to "acceptable" types of people. Who gains what? Why are these rights not sold at the highest price to acceptable people?

Answer:

The immigration administrators are salaried and do not receive money beyond their salary. Their motivation on the job is not to maximize profit, leaving them open to seek fulfillment of other personal and policy goals.

15) "More of a public good can be produced without the production of other goods being curtailed." Evaluate.

Answer:

False; it is the *consumption* of the good that is referred to in the definition of a public good. Once the good is produced, any person can have as much as he or she wants without reducing the amount to anyone else.

16) Public goods are those for which (choose the correct statement):
   a. several people can simultaneously enjoy the good;
   b. it is impossible to exclude some customers;
   c. no consumer reduces the amount of the good available to others by his act of consuming the good;
   d. prices should not be charged;
   e. the government should provide the goods.

Answer:

Answer c is best.

17) A theater performance with a group of viewers is not a public good. Why?

Answer:

Each spectator displaces someone on the outside who might wish to enter — and the theater presumably cannot seat everyone who wishes to attend.

18) "Economic theory is applicable only to a capitalistic society." Evaluate.

Answer:

The market-exchange system characteristic of private property (capitalism) has been the dominant institutional context of the preceding chapters. But the economic theory used there is applicable to any system of competition — resolving conflicts of interest among people arising from the fact of scarcity. In fact, the analysis of allocation with prices at less than the market-clearing prices is an application of economics to a socialist society in which free-market prices are not used. If the money price is below the free-market price, how will goods be allocated among the competing claimants? The use of nonpecuniary "discrimination" should come as no surprise.

Many Communist systems have relied on money prices and private property to ration existing stocks of *some* consumer goods. In Russia under communism, many goods were sold for money, and individuals got money income from wages and salaries — but *not* from ownership of productive physical capital goods and land. Given a person's money income, he was allowed to choose among a variety of consumption patterns by voluntary exchanges with other people via controlled (as distinct from open) market prices.

The principles are not idiosyncratic to capitalist systems. They hold for all known societies. The laws of demand and production hold also, whether or not exchange of resources via a private property exchange system is used.

Keep in mind the distinction between economic theory and analysis, on the one hand, versus, on the other, the institutional (legal and political) circumstances or conditions to which they are applied.

19) In a public park an apple tree yields excellent apples, which may be picked by the public. When will the apples be picked? If the American bison had been owned by someone, do you think the animals would have been so nearly exterminated? Do you think seals and whales would be faced with extinction if some person or group were able to buy, as private property, the right to catch whales and seals?

Answer:

The apples would be picked and the bison slaughtered prematurely, for, with no designated and enforced ownership rights, the taking would be first come, first served. If you do not take now, some other greedy person is likely to beat you to the prize. If assets are privately owned, the owners have much incentive to protect and preserve them until optimum harvest time and then to harvest them at the optimal rate for the long run.

20) Contrast socialism and private property as means of distributing risks of profits and losses.

Answer:

Socialism does not permit discretionary (optional) selection of wealth holdings by each individual. Gains and losses are borne in accord with taxes, rights to use government resources, and powers of political office. In a system of private property with open access to trade, consequences — value-change of resources, profits, and losses — are borne by the owner. By selectively purchasing and selling goods, people can adjust the combination of risks they bear. The right to buy and sell facilitates or permits profits and losses to be revised in accord with consumers' personal preferences.

21) A wealthy industrialist has a stable of race horses and a breeding farm. The two, although operated as a business, lose over $500,000 annually. Yet that continues year after year because the owner enjoys the activity more than spending a similar sum for travel or conventional types of consumption activities.

   a. Is the owner maximizing wealth in that business?
   b. Is that behavior maximizing personal worth?
   c. Would an increase in the losses induce a decrease in that kind of activity? What does economic theory say about that?

Answers:
   a. Probably not.
   b. Probably yes.
   c. Yes. The higher the price, the less will be demanded.

22) A large lake is stocked with excellent fish, but no one owns the fish or the
    lake. Only by catching the fish can you acquire ownership in the fish.
    a. What do you think will be the average age of fish caught as compared
       to the age of the fish in a privately owned lake?
    b. Which system will induce overfishing in the sense that more resources
       will be devoted to catching fish than the extra fish caught are worth?
       Why?
Answers:
   a. Fish will be younger and smaller, for the same reason that apples don't
      ripen in a public park. No one owns the fish (or trees in a public park),
      and the only way to capture the value of the fish is to catch the fish (or to
      cut a tree on public lands and take the wood).
   b. When no one *owns* all fish in the lake, the extra value of the fish taken
      will be judged by each separate fisherman according to *his* catch rather
      than by the *total* catch in the lake. Absence of property rights in the *lake*
      causes competition to acquire property rights in the *fish* by catching
      them first.

23) Someone invents a new type of sail for a boat to capture the force of the
    wind. The inventor makes some sails and offers to rent them to a boat's
    owner. Instead of accepting this offer to rent sails, the boat's owner
    estimates that by taking a year off from fishing and investing one year
    of his crew's time in making their own sails, he and his crew could then
    catch more cod. He also estimates that the value of the additional cod
    caught in the subsequent three years of fishing will be greater than the
    cod sacrificed while making the sails plus the cost of renting sails. The
    boat's owner puts the decision whether to rent sails now or take a year off
    from fishing while they make their own sails to a vote by all the people
    on the boat. The decision is against the proposal to take the year off and
    make their own sails. Why is that result not surprising?
Answer:
   Nonowners are less interested in the future effects than are owners, who
   are interested in the present *value* of the longer-run gains from current
   investment, as explained in chapter 30 on capital values. Ownership of a
   resource forces attention to *capital values,* which reflect the full long-run

effects, and the owners bear the effect in the *salable* capital value. Employees bear less significant effects. "Employee ownership" does not give an employee any rights to sell a portion of that "ownership," as can be done with one's ownership in a stock corporation. What an employee "owns" is a right to vote on a decision about who will manage the "employee-owned" enterprise, but not the right to sell shares "owned" by the employee. Management is under less extensive policing by shareholders, who can sell their shares.

PART TWO

SPECIALIZATION, PRODUCTION, TEAMS, AND FIRMS

CHAPTER 14

PRODUCTIVITY AND COSTS OF PRODUCTION

The pricing and allocation of *existing* goods was the primary topic of earlier chapters. But what determines *who* produces *which* goods, and *how much of* each? You will not produce everything you consume, as a Robinson Crusoe would have to do. Somehow, we are persuaded to produce and sell goods demanded by other people, and in doing so we become richer than if we were *self-sufficient*. We start by explaining (a) the difference between productive ability and cost and (b) the meaning and typical pattern of marginal costs.

PRODUCTIVE ABILITY VS. COSTS OF PRODUCTION, OR ABSOLUTE ADVANTAGE VS. COMPARATIVE ADVANTAGE

Bill and Susan each can produce cake and jam. Table 14.1 lists a) their productive *abilities* and b) their *costs* of producing cake and jam. Superior productive ability does not mean lower costs.

MEASURE OF COST

Costs, by definition, reflect the *relative* productive abilities — for making cakes *relative* to making jam, or making jams relative to cakes. Bill's *productive ability* is such that he could produce up to ten cakes or five jams in a ten-hour day. His *cost* of making one jam is 2 cakes (= 10 cakes/5 jams), which is the amount of cake forsaken if 1 jam is produced. Each jam not produced releases time and resources to make 2 cakes. Bill's cost of making a cake is half (.5) a jar of jam (= 5 jams/10 cakes), the amount of jam not produced in order to make one cake.

Susan's cost of making a cake is .67 jam (= 10 jams/15 cakes). Each cake forgoes .67 jam she could have made that day. She is twice as productive as Bill in making jams (10 jams/5 jams), and she is 50 percent (1.5 times) more productive in making cakes than is Bill. It's tempting to conclude that Susan therefore is a lower-cost producer overall. But she does not have lower *costs* in *both* jam and cake: she cannot produce cakes as *cheaply* as Bill can.

Table 14.1 *Production and Costs*

Producers	Daily Productive Ability			Daily Costs	
	Jam		Cake	Jam	Cake
Bill	5 jams	or	10 cakes	2.0 cakes	.50 jam
Susan	10 jams	or	15 cakes	1.5 cakes	.67 jam

COSTS VERSUS PRODUCTIVE ABILITY

Absolute productivity abilities do not tell us anything about the costs of producing goods. Suppose some miracle causes an increase of Bill's productivity
in both goods by 10 times — to 50 jams and to 100 cakes daily. Bill's marginal
and average costs of making one jam would be unchanged, 2 cakes (= 100
cakes/50 jams), and the marginal and average cost of cake would still be .5 jam
(50 jams/100 cakes). The *cost* of jam is the *trade-off* in the amount of other goods
forgone when producing a jam; that is, the amount of other goods *necessarily*
forgone. Superior absolute physical productive ability in every good does not
mean lower costs in everything.

NO ONE CAN BE THE LOWEST, OR THE HIGHEST, COST PRODUCER OF *EVERY* GOOD

No one can have a lowest cost in every good. No matter what numbers you put
into table 14.1, Susan cannot have lower costs in both activities, though she
could be capable of producing more of each than Bill. This is true no matter
how many different goods a person could produce, or how many people are
involved. A greater absolute productive ability will result in greater production
and earnings or in greater wages per day of work. But differences in costs reflect differences in *comparative* production ability between goods.

ABSOLUTE PRODUCTIVE ABILITY VERSUS LOWER COSTS

Absolute advantage refers to greater absolute productive abilities such as Susan's
in both cake and jam. But Susan's *relative* ability in cake *compared* to her ability
to make jam is *inferior* to Bill's. Susan is a lower-cost producer of jam. She has
a *comparative advantage* in making jam; similarly, compared to Susan's abilities,
Bill has a comparative advantage in making cakes. So, even if Bill is inferior in
his absolute ability to make cakes, he is *superior* to Susan in his *relative* ability to
make cakes.

MARGINAL AND AVERAGE COSTS

There are measures of cost which should be separated. One is the *average* cost of cakes (no matter how many), and another is the *marginal* cost of a cake. The average daily cost of making cakes is the *total* cost of the cakes divided by the number of cakes. For Bill, that average is .50 jam per cake (= 5 jams/10 cakes), no matter how many cakes he makes daily. Similarly, Susan's average cost of cakes is constant at .67 jam daily.

MARGINAL COSTS

Bill's marginal costs of cake are .50 jam at every possible rate of daily output of cake, because each added cake *raises* costs by .5 jam. That increase in cost— the marginal cost—happens here to be numerically the same as the average cost. No matter how many cakes Bill produces, the added cost for one more is .5 jam. And when the added cost equals the previous average, that is, when marginal cost equals average, the average remains unchanged.

Susan's daily marginal cost is .67 jam. Each added cake diverts her productive effort from jam, resulting in a reduction of .67 jam. That's the increase in total daily cost of making one more cake.

TEMPORARY SIMPLIFYING ASSUMPTIONS

Three arithmetic simplifying assumptions have been made which we'll remove later. The first is that there is no initial set-up investment, for example, an oven or dough-making equipment. Second, there are only two goods of interest, cake and jam. Third, the marginal and average costs of cakes and of jams are constant—the same at every possible rate of daily production.

RICARDIAN SUPERIORITY AND RICARDIAN RENT

If superiority is a result of a natural superior productive ability (achievable neither by investment nor training), it is often labeled *Ricardian superiority*. (The name is for David Ricardo, the eminent economist of the early nineteenth century who formulated the conception, and who undoubtedly had some.) That natural superior ability can be distinguished from ability obtained by (a) investment and training in enhancing one's productivity or by (b) restricting or prohibiting other people from competing (a *contrived* monopoly rent). Muhammad Ali, Milton Friedman, and Whitney Houston undoubtedly had Ricardian superiority and became rich and famous because of Ricardian rents; they did not benefit from monopoly rents.

RATES VERSUS VOLUME OF PRODUCTION:
AN IMPORTANT DISTINCTION

It is important to distinguish between (1) the *rate*, or speed, of production and (2) the total amount, or *volume*, to be produced when referring to costs. Cost of production depends on the rate and volume of production in ways similar to the way cost of travel depends on speed and distance. These are guides about relations between costs and rates and volumes of production of a good:

1) The larger the volume, the higher will be total cost.
2) The faster the rate of production of a *specified* volume, the higher will be the total cost of producing that volume.

Usually, the marginal cost of volume is lower at a larger volume. (But if some exhaustible resource is being produced, such as iron ore, oil, or coal, the cheapest is extracted first.) And that means the average cost per unit of volume falls. And marginal cost may fall as a result of learning by doing or experience.

There are two different amounts of production to consider. One is the *rate* per time period; the other is the *total number* to be produced, whatever the speed at which that volume is produced. When Ford prepares to make a new model, the process selected will depend on estimates of *how many* it will make and also upon *how fast* it plans to make them. Certainly, the volume will make a difference in the method of production to be used and in the average cost. Typically, the faster the cars are produced with any given method of production, the more each will cost. But with larger total numbers to be produced, mass production techniques will permit lower cost per unit produced.

In traveling, you don't confuse miles per hour with total distance. So, when referring to more, or greater, or higher production, distinguish between (1) a greater speed at which some fixed volume is produced, and (2) a greater volume at some fixed speed. In this chapter, we're concentrating initially on how costs are affected by the speed of production — rate per day — of some given total planned volume. That's similar to concentrating on how the cost of driving an assigned distance depends on the speed and how the amount of gasoline required increases at higher speed.

MARGINAL AND AVERAGE COSTS AND THEIR
REALISTIC RELATION TO RATES OF PRODUCTION

Realistically, marginal costs (increases in total cost) tend to be higher the faster the rate of production. Adam is producing cakes, but we don't know what he might be able to produce instead. In the Bill and Susan example, there were

Table 14.2 *Adam's Daily Production Costs (in Units of Y)*

Daily Output of Cakes	Total Cost	Marginal Cost	Average Cost	Alternate Product, Y (Dollars)	Marginal Worths of Cake
1	2	3	4	5	6
0	—	—	—	13.50	—
1	.90	.90	.90	12.60	1.15
2	1.90	1.00	.95	11.60	1.05
3	3.00	1.10	1.00	10.50	.95
4	4.20	1.20	1.05	9.30	.85
5	5.50	1.30	1.10	8.00	.75
6	6.90	1.40	1.15	6.60	.65
7	8.40	1.50	1.20	5.10	.55
8	10.00	1.60	1.25	3.50	.45
9	11.70	1.70	1.30	1.80	.35
10	13.50	1.80	1.35	0.00	.25

just two possible products, jam and cake. In the world of Adam, cost means the highest forgone value of many alternative possibilities. We'll call that highest-valued production alternative Y, and measure it in dollar values, as $Y. The dollar value measure of the cost is a measure of the value of forgone real goods or services, without having to know which particular goods are forgone. We need only note its dollar value measure, $Y. All the data are in table 14.2.

The first column lists the number of cakes Adam could produce daily. The next to last column lists the dollar value of the bundles that Adam could produce instead of producing the indicated amounts of cakes. If *no* cakes were produced, Adam could produce 13.5Y; if he produced one cake, 12.60Y could still be produced; he could produce two cakes and 11.60Y.

The second column, Total Cost, lists the largest daily value that must be forgone. If 1 cake is produced, .9Y cannot be produced; so the total cost of one cake is .9Y. If 2 cakes are produced daily, 1.9Y are forgone. That's the total daily cost of 2 cakes; the addition to total costs at 2 cakes rather than just 1 is 1Y (= 1.9Y − .9Y). That's the marginal cost at 2 cakes, listed in the third column. The fourth column lists the average cost. For 2 cakes, it's .95Y per cake (= 1.90Y/2 cakes). Finally, the last column on the right lists marginal worths of cakes for Adam's own consumption. As explained in chapter 5, a person's worth of something is defined as the *amount of other goods* that person would be willing to give up to get it.

ARITHMETIC OF MARGINAL COST

Marginal daily rate of cost is the increase in the cost of a one unit greater daily rate of production. *Marginal* pertains to a double margin—the added unit of production and the added cost. At three cakes daily, the total cost is 3Y—the most of other products that could otherwise have been produced. If a unit of Y has a market value of $1, then we can refer to dollars, rather than units of Y, as the measure of the cost. The 3Y total cost of the 3 cakes would be $3. That's $1.10 more than the 1.90Y ($1.90) total cost of two ($1.10 = $3 − $1.90). Therefore, the marginal cost of the third cake is $1.10.

THE SUM OF THE MARGINAL COSTS IS THE TOTAL COST

Since we have assumed there is no initial set-up investment cost, the marginal cost for one cake per day added to the marginal cost of the second will give the total daily cost of two cakes per day. If the marginal cost at three cakes is added in, the sum will be the total cost of three cakes per day. In dollar equivalents, that's $3 (= $.90 + $1 + $1.10).

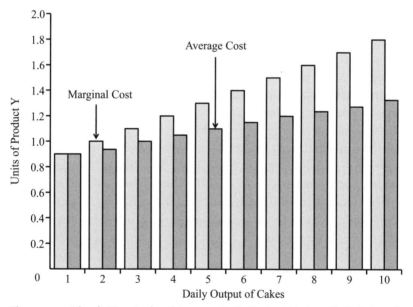

Figure 14.1 *Adam's Marginal and Average Daily Costs at Various Daily Rates of Production*

The total cost of producing at the rate of six cakes daily is the sum of the successive marginal costs—0.90Y + 1.00Y + 1.10Y + 1.20Y + 1.30Y + 1.40Y = 6.90Y. That's represented by the sum of the marginal cost bars out to six cakes. The total daily cost at six units per day is 1.4Y more than at five units per day.

THE MARGINAL-AVERAGE RELATIONSHIP

The relationship between the marginal and average costs is not immediately obvious. Notice that the marginal cost for seven exceeds the average cost at six. The average cost for seven cakes is pulled up above the average cost at six, because marginal cost—the added cost—in making seven ($1.50) is higher than the average at six ($1.15).

Bruiser Bill, the star fullback on the football team, has an average of five yards per carry coming into today's game. On the first carry today, he plows ahead for six. His marginal yardage being greater than the initial five-yard average, the average rises a bit, though not to six yards. Then he is stopped after a two-yard gain, which pulls down his average.

The marginal-average relationship can be summarized: *A marginal that is lower than the average will decrease the average; a marginal greater than the average raises the average; if the marginal equals the average, the average will be unchanged.*

RATE AND VOLUMES OF PRODUCTION

Rising cost is tied to the faster *speed*, or *rate*, of production, not to an increased quantity produced. But there is learning by accumulated experience. Production of a larger fixed volume, whether at a slow or fast speed, permits and motivates learning by doing. Discovered lower-cost methods will be adopted. And larger volumes can be produced with a larger variety of methods than are optimal for small volumes. A hand hammer is more economical than a power hammer for a few nails, but not for thousands of nails.

The marginal costs of added units decline with larger volumes, whatever may be the rate of production. And marginal costs of increased speed rise with faster rates of production of whatever may be the volume. In the example of Adam's activities, we looked at the speed, or rate, of production, not the total quantity or volume of cake or Y that Adam could produce. The amount of the planned total volume will strongly affect the chosen method of production, which we'll consider later.

CHOICE OF PRODUCTION AND CONSUMPTION
BY SELF-SUFFICIENT ADAM

Now, we can identify a principle characterizing Adam's choices of how many cakes to make daily and consume as a self-sufficient person. The principle is *personal worth maximizing.* Adam produces as many cakes as have marginal personal worths in excess of his marginal costs of cakes. The *cost* is the most worthy thing that could *otherwise* have been produced. Adam's marginal worths of

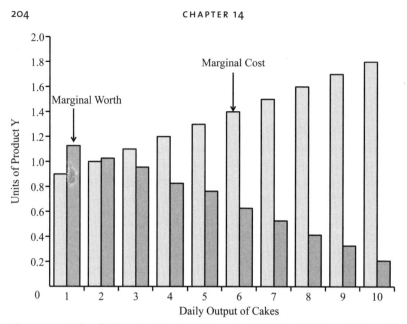

Figure 14.2 *Adam's Marginal Costs and Marginal Worths at Various Rates of Daily Production*

cakes, expressed in units of Y, are listed in column 6 of table 14.2. We don't have to know the numbers. It's sufficient for our purposes to know that Adam's (a) marginal worths of cakes diminish at more cakes per day, and (b) the marginal costs in column 3 increase at higher rates of production of cakes.

As shown in table 14.2 and figure 14.2, Adam's marginal *worths* for cakes start at 1.15Y for 1 cake per day, diminish to 1.05Y at two cakes per day, and fall to .95Y for a third cake. Adam's marginal *costs* start at .90Y at 1 cake per day, and increase to 1.0Y at 2 cakes and 1.1Y at three. For 3 cakes per day, the marginal cost of 1.10Y exceeds the marginal worth of .95Y. Therefore, Adam will produce and consume only 2 cakes daily and 11.6 units of Y (the other goods). The marginal worth of the good falls to, but not below, its marginal cost.

MARGINAL COSTS ARE HIGHER AT
FASTER RATES OF PRODUCTION

Why are marginal costs higher at faster (greater) rates of production? Basically, there are two reasons. One is that to produce more per day, more equipment is used, usually of the less productive, reserve equipment used only for the extremely high rates. But there's a far more prevalent universal force—the *law of diminishing marginal returns.*

THE LAW OF DIMINISHING MARGINAL RETURNS

The law: *"As more units of one of the resources being used are added to a fixed amount of other inputs, the marginal returns with the additional units will, beyond some amount of that kind of resource, begin to decrease."* No exceptions.

The data in table 14.3 illustrate the law.

With none of the variable input being used, the output is zero. With one unit of the variable input, the total output is 6. With 2 units, the total product increases to 16, giving a marginal product of 10 units ($10 = 16 - 6$). The average output per unit of input is 8 per unit of the variable input ($8 = 16/2$) — but the average is irrelevant so far as the law of diminishing marginal returns is concerned.

The point of diminishing marginal returns is where the marginal products thereafter decrease — at 2 units of the variable input. Beyond that amount of variable input, the marginal product of an additional unit diminishes, even to becoming negative and reducing the total product.

If there were no diminishing returns to additions of one kind of input, we could grow the entire world's wheat from one flowerpot of soil. We'd add seeds to that one pot and get as much wheat as desired from a small, fixed amount of soil. Or instead of seeds, we could add fertilizer and grow as much as desired.

The law of diminishing marginal returns doesn't deny that at the initial

Table 14.3 *Law of Diminishing Marginal Returns*
(Marginal Products)

Uniform Inputs (1)	Total Products (2)	Marginal Products (3)	Average Products (4)
0	0	0	0
1	6	6	6
2	16	10	8
3	24	8	8
4	30	6	7.5
5	34	4	6.8
6	36	2	6
7	36	0	5.14
8	32	−4	4
9	27	−5	3
10	21	−6	2.1

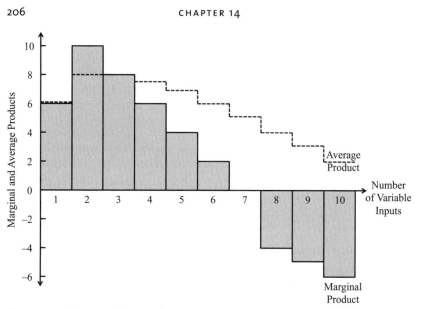

Figure 14.3 *The Law of Diminishing Marginal Returns*

In producing some product, when more units of one input employed in making that product are added, while all other inputs are fixed, beyond some point — here at input number 2 — the addition to the output produced, the "marginal product" of that output, will decrease. The relationship between marginal and average continues to hold. As the marginal product decreases, it pulls down the average product.

amounts of the variable input, the marginal products may increase. But beyond some amount of that kind of input — holding the other inputs constant — the marginal returns (marginal products) will decrease, and continue to decrease, at all larger amounts of that input.

PRICE OF LABOR VERSUS LABOR COST OF OUTPUT

It is often said that foreign labor gets lower wages per hour — thereby yielding lower costs per unit of output than the cost of producing with higher-wage labor in the United States. But this is a difference between the *price* of labor (wages) and the labor *cost* per unit of product.

The relationship is:

(1) Labor cost per unit of output = (2) Wages per hour / (3) Product per hour.

High wage rates per hour for one worker can reflect higher productivity, which can more than offset a less productive worker paid a lower wage. A higher-wage worker can be a lower-cost input per unit of product, as illustrated in table 14.4.

Table 14.4 *Wages per Hour and Labor Cost per Unit of Output*

Nation	Wages per Hour	Units of Output per Hour	Labor Cost per Unit of Output
US Labor	$20	10	$2
Foreign Labor	$10	3	$3.33

With a US labor wage rate of $20 per hour and a productivity of ten units per hour, the labor cost per unit of product is $2. If wages in another nation were the equivalent of $10 per hour, but the hourly output were only 3, the foreign labor cost per product would be higher. Within the United States, a $100 per hour computer programmer is lower cost per program produced than is a $20 per hour programmer producing less than one-fifth as much per hour. High wages per hour can be low-cost labor per unit of output.

QUESTIONS AND MEDITATIONS

1) "A businessperson's costs for material, labor, and equipment are measures of the other most valuable output the businessperson could produce with the resources he buys or hires." Evaluate.

Answer:

True.

2) Why are costs not measured in terms of labor hours?

Answer:

Hours of labor have different uses with different values for different quality of labor as well as for different uses of labor. How would you value one labor hour of a skilled surgeon in comparison to one labor hour of a supermarket stocker? Which one would you use as a basis for measuring cost? Hours cannot be used. The best *forsaken* use *value* of an hour is the cost of any hour of use of labor.

3) What is meant by efficient production?

Answer:

Production is efficient if the output of one of the possible products is maximized for stated amounts of the other products. Or production is efficient if an increase in output of one of the products can be achieved only by reducing the output of some other product. Roughly, it means no waste of potential output.

4) What is meant by a subsistence, self-sufficient, economy as contrasted to a specialized interdependent economy?

Answer:

> A subsistence economy is one in which people consume only what they produce. Specialization means people produce more of a good than they consume, and consume more of a good than they produce. Specialization also generally means that producers do not produce complete consumer goods, but instead concentrate on components or portions of assembly tasks.

5) A premier of a new emerging country bragged that he was going to make his country self-sufficient and independent of foreigners. Do the principles of this chapter suggest anything about how you, as a native of that country, might be affected?

Answer:

> The boast suggests that you will be poorer and engage more in "do-it-yourself" activity. Reduced opportunity to trade limits the extent to which gains from trade can be achieved.

6) Some years ago, India proposed to build a steel mill, and asked the United States government to finance the project. In defense of the request, an economist serving as American ambassador to India wrote: "There is no doubt that the steel is needed. While the plant would be costly, it would soon pay for itself in the imports that it would save. To import a million tons of steel products would cost the Indians about $200 million. The proposed mill with an annual capacity of 1 million tons would cost $513 million to build. Three years of operations would thus recover the dollar cost of the mill and more. Since India combines her pressing need for steel with an equally acute shortage of dollars, the economic attraction is obvious. She could not, in fact, afford to import the steel that the mill could supply." Explain what is wrong with every sentence of that quotation except the third and fourth.

Answer:

> First consider the costs and benefits of steel relative to other products that could be produced. How much steel is "needed" depends on costs as well as the relative benefits. India "needs" more of many things. Cost measures the value of other products that could be produced with the resources used to produce the steel mill. Are those other products more valuable relative to costs? Would you produce the steel mill that's less valuable relative to costs? Next, consider whether it's more economical (cheaper) for India to acquire steel by importing or building a steel mill. If it's cheaper to import

the steel, India can have the steel as well as more of other valuable products (such as more housing, schools, roads) that could be produced with re-leased resources that would otherwise be used to build the more expensive steel mill. Imports are not costs.

Present values (which we consider later) are ignored in the three-year calculation. "Need for steel" and "shortage" of dollars are rhetoric. In-dia also has a "pressing need" for and an "acute shortage" of many other products, as do other countries. The issue is for which of those "pressing needs" and "acute shortages" the resources will be used. And what forms of competition will be utilized in determining what to produce and how to produce it.

7) A lower-cost producer can produce more than a higher-cost producer. Do you agree?

Answer:

Can't tell. Cost — marginal cost — reflects the cost of producing an addi-tional unit of the product. But the total amount which might be produced by the lower (marginal) cost producer could be either more or less than the total amount which might be produced by the higher (marginal) cost producer.

8) "Someone always has a comparative advantage in the production of some good." Explain.

Answer:

Comparative advantage pertains to relative production-efficiency (output/ input) ratios of different producers of more than one good. With two pro-ducers, unless one is absolutely superior by the *same degree* in two goods, each will be relatively superior in one good and inferior in the other.

9) To incur a cost is equivalent to saying that one has sacrificed an opportunity. Do you agree?

Answer:

True by definition. Cost is what's given up to get something. In produc-tion, cost measures the most valuable of the other products that could be produced with the resources.

10) "Unfettered world trade would tend powerfully to reduce all workers (and other resource owners) to the world's lowest level. For a nation with lower wages — and all nations do have wages lower than those in the

United States — could then undersell us, not only in third markets, but in our own country. Thus, American producers would be ruined; or, in order for us to be able to sell and thus to survive, our wages would have to be cut to the lowest level of our competitors. It would be ridiculous to expose our high standard of living to the ruinous competition of the poorer rest of the world." How could you dispute this?

Answer:

Confuses the price of labor (wages) with the cost of producing per unit of product. Cost is the value of output given up per unit of product. American wages of $20 per hour reflect the productivity of labor; they do not measure cost, which involves labor productivity per unit output. At 10 units of output per hour, cost is $2.00 per unit of output. Foreign labor with wages of $5 per hour may produce only 1 unit of output per hour. In this case, higher-wage, more productive American labor is a lower-cost producer than the low-wage, less productive foreign labor.

11) Different dimensions such as rate and volume can be used to describe the amount of a product that's produced. Although in the text we usually refer to both rate of output and the volume of output, in any actual problem different dimensions of output are relevant. If you are analyzing costs of operating an airline, for example, what measure or measures of output could you use?

Answer:

You could use rate and volume as we did in the text. Costs will be affected by, among other things, the size of the operation (type of planes, terminal accommodations, maintenance facilities and personnel, routes served) and the daily frequency of flights.

12) Rates and volumes:
   a. If every mile you travel at 40 miles per hour costs you 32 cents, while at a higher speed of 45 miles per hour each mile of travel costs you 34 cents, what's the marginal cost of one more mile per hour increase in speed?
   b. Does it mean that if you travel for one hour at the steady speed of 41 miles per hour, your costs will be higher than if you had traveled an hour at 40 miles per hour? Why not?
   c. "If all the inputs could be increased as if by clones, they'd be available for use here only by attracting them from productive activities elsewhere. The more resources that are attracted away from producing

other goods, the higher will be the resulting prices of those goods
because less of them will be produced. That means the prices of
the inputs demanded here will be increased, resulting in increasing
marginal costs." Right or wrong?

Answers:

    a. It's a cost accruing at the rate of 2 cents *per hour*—no matter how far or
    how long your travel. If your time is worth $10 an hour, which speed is
    more economical for you?

    b. That's an increase in both speed and distance traveled, 41 miles com-
    pared to 40 miles and 41 miles per hour compared to 40 miles per hour.

    c. Wrong. Diminishing marginal returns are not results of higher prices of
    the inputs, which may or may not be happening. Diminishing marginal
    returns are *physical* effects of not increasing all the inputs appropriately.

Note: In chapter 2 we introduced the concept of the production possibility
boundary; the following several questions build further on that concept.

13) Smith's daily production possibilities are indicated by the following
table:

Table 14QA.13

Oats		Soybeans
10	and	0
9	and	.2
8	and	.4
7	and	____
6	and	____
5	and	____
4	and	____
3	and	____
2	and	____
1	and	____
0	and	2

    a. Compute the missing data, assuming linear interpolation.

    b. For each increment of oats, he incurs a uniform sacrifice of an amount
    of soybeans. The ratio between these two changes is the marginal rate
    of transformation between oats and soybeans. This rate also yields his
    marginal cost of oats (in terms of soybeans). What is the marginal cost
    of a bushel of oats?

c. Of a bushel of soybeans?

d. If that marginal cost is constant at all combinations, the production is said to involve constant costs. Does this example reveal constant costs?

e. Graph Smith's production possibility, with oats on the horizontal scale.

f. On the graph, label, as point I, the output that has an equal number of bushels of oats and soybeans.

g. What is the number of bushels of each?

h. Which is the larger output—1.67 bushels of each, or 5 bushels of oats and 1 of soybeans?

Answers:

b. 2 soybeans for 1 oats

c. 5 oats per 1 soybeans

d. Yes

g. 1.67 of each

h. Question is ambiguous. Are we to measure in units of number, weight, value?

14) On the graph of the preceding question, plot the production possibility of Baker.

Table 14QA.14

Oats		Soybeans
3	and	0
2.5	and	.5
2	and	1
1.5	and	1.5
1	and	2
.5	and	2.5
0	and	3

Label this line BB and mark the point of equal numbers of bushels of oats and soybeans (that is, 1.5 of each).

a. What is the maximum amount of oats that Mr. Smith and Mr. Baker jointly can produce if they produce only oats?

b. Only soybeans?

c. What is the maximum amount of soybeans and oats they can produce if each person produces as many bushels of oats as he does of soybeans?

d. What is the total output of each if they divide their time and resources equally between oats and soybeans?

e. Which output is larger — where (i) each divides his time equally among the two products or (ii) where each produces as many bushels of oats as of soybeans?

Answers:

a. 13

b. 5

c. 1.67 of each good for Smith; 1.5 of each for Baker

d. 5 oats and 1 soybeans for Smith; 1.5 of each for Baker

e. Meaningless question, comparing (i) 6.5 oats and 2.5 soybeans with (ii) 3.17 of each

15) Introducing prices of the commodities with the tables given above:

a. If the price of a bushel of soybeans is $1 and the price of a bushel of oats is 50 cents, which good should Smith produce if he wants to maximize his wealth? Which should Baker produce?

b. If the price of a bushel of oats rises above $1 while soybeans stay at $1, what should Baker do if he wants to maximize his wealth?

c. At what ratio of prices would Smith be induced to produce soybeans?

Answer:

a. Smith grows oats and Baker grows soybeans.

b. Switch to oats.

c. If the price of oats is less than one-fifth the price of a bushel of soybeans, Smith should switch to soybeans.

16) What is meant by efficient production? Try two different versions of the definition.

Answer:

a. Production is efficient if the output of one of the possible products is maximized for stated amounts of the other products.

b. Production is efficient if an increase in output of one of the products can be achieved only by reducing the amount of some other product.

CHAPTER 15

SPECIALIZATION AND EXCHANGE

Unlike Adam, you'll not be self-sufficient. You'll provide some service to earn income, and you'll be dependent on others to produce and sell to you many goods to consume. You'll be richer as a result. This "specialization" avoids unnecessarily higher marginal costs of production. It's an efficient allocation of production among producers. Specialization also permits concentration on one task, which can increase individual productive skills and the technology used.

We start with a two-person economy to indicate, first, the gains from specializing in production of a good for trade. In our imaginary economy, we find Adam of our preceding chapter joined by Baker. We'll focus production on cakes and Y, as before. Baker's productive abilities, marginal costs, and personal marginal worths of cakes are given in table 15.1. Baker's personal worths of cakes are measured as the most of Y that would be given for a cake. Our attention will be on differences in *marginal costs*, which are the source of gains in production by specialization and exchange.

While self-sufficient, Baker produces and consumes 2 cakes (and 7.80Y) daily, with the marginal worth (.80Y) greater than the marginal cost (.60Y). At 3 cakes, Baker's marginal worth of cakes would be .70Y, less than its marginal cost, .80. This is illustrated graphically in figure 15.1.

ADAM'S AND BAKER'S PRODUCTION
AND COSTS COMPARED

Table 15.2 reproduces table 14.2, which shows Adam's self-sufficient costs of production and his (demand) personal worths of cakes.

Graphically, Adam's marginal costs and personal worths are shown in figure 15.2. Like Baker, he will not produce a third cake for his own consumption, because the marginal cost would be greater than the personal worth.

Baker is less productive "absolutely" in both goods — cakes and Y. He can make only eight cakes daily (compared to ten cakes by Adam) or only 8.80 of other goods, Y (compared to 13.50Y by Adam). Adam has an "absolute advantage" in production of *both* goods. But that does not mean Adam is a lower marginal and total cost producer of both goods — as we discovered in the Su-

Table 15.1 *Baker's Daily Potential Output and Costs of Cakes*

Daily Output of Cakes	Total Cost	Marginal Cost	Average Cost	Alternate Product, Y (Bundles)	Marginal Worths of Cakes
1	2	3	4	5	6
0	—	—	—	8.80	—
1	.40	.40	.40	8.40	.90Y
2	1.00	.60	.50	7.80	.80Y
3	1.80	.80	.60	7.00	.70Y
4	2.80	1.00	.70	6.00	.60Y
5	4.00	1.20	.80	4.80	.50Y
6	5.40	1.40	.90	3.40	.40Y
7	7.00	1.60	1.00	1.80	.30Y
8	8.80	1.80	1.10	0	.20Y

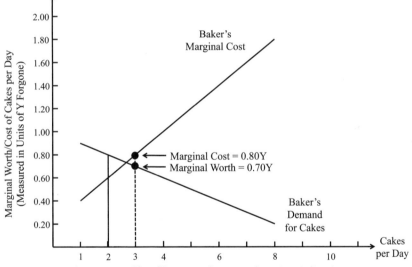

Figure 15.1 *Baker Being Self-Sufficient with No Trade or Specialization*

san and Bill example. Absolute productive abilities indicate how wealthy a person will be — not a person's costs of production. It's the *differential* abilities in one good relative to other goods that defines costs of production of the good.

Despite having less absolute productivity in every good, Baker has lower marginal, average, and total costs of cake in the range of production of 1 through 5 cakes daily. Above that range, Baker's marginal costs of cakes (forgone other potential product, Y) exceed Adam's marginal costs.

Table 15.2 *Adam's Daily Production Costs (in Units of Y)*

Daily Output of Cakes	Total Cost	Marginal Cost	Average Cost	Alternate Product, Y (Bundles)	Marginal Worths of Cakes
1	2	3	4	5	6
0	—	—	—	13.50	—
1	.90	.90	.90	12.60	1.15
2	1.90	1.00	.95	11.60	1.05
3	3.00	1.10	1.00	10.50	.95
4	4.20	1.20	1.05	9.30	.85
5	5.50	1.30	1.10	8.00	.75
6	6.90	1.40	1.15	6.60	.65
7	8.40	1.50	1.20	5.10	.55
8	10.00	1.60	1.25	3.50	.45
9	11.70	1.70	1.30	1.80	.35
10	13.50	1.80	1.35	0.00	.25

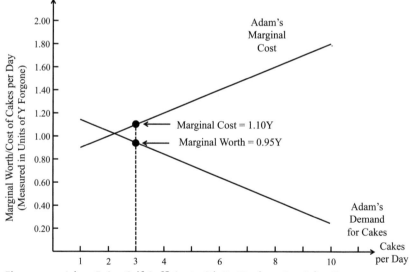

Figure 15.2 *Adam Being Self-Sufficient with No Trade or Specialization*

In figure 15.3, Baker's marginal costs at the lower rates of producing cakes are less than Adam's, but Baker's marginal costs rise more rapidly at the faster rates of production to an equality with Adam's at a daily rate of 6 cakes. Above that rate of production, Baker's costs of producing are greater than Adam's. When thinking of costs, think of "at what rate of production"?

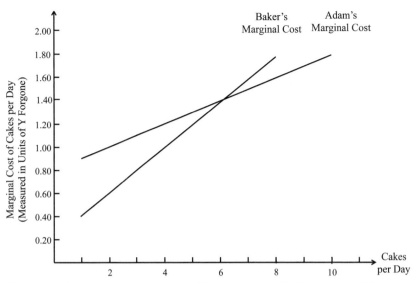

Figure 15.3 *Adam and Baker's Marginal Cost Curves for the Production of Cakes per Day*

DIFFERENCES IN COSTS AND MARGINAL WORTHS
CREATE OPPORTUNITIES FOR TRADE

Both being self-sufficient, Adam and Baker each produces and consumes two cakes per day (they do not produce partial cakes/day). However, they can do better. The difference in their marginal worths at the amounts of cake they can produce implies there can be gain to both by trade. Baker will not produce a third cake for his own consumption, for the marginal cost of .8Y is greater than the marginal worth to him of only .7Y. But Baker making a third cake and selling it to Adam is beneficial to both so long as the price is less than Adam's marginal worth of a cake and higher than Baker's marginal cost of making the cake.

As the data in tables 15.1 and 15.2 show, it would cost Adam 1.10Y to produce a third cake, but it is worth to him only .95Y, so he won't make it. But Baker offers to sell him a cake for only .90Y—less than it is worth to Adam—and they both gain.

Adam ends with 3 cakes and 10.7Y (= 11.6 − .9 expenditure), instead of the original 2 cakes and 11.6Y. After selling his produced third cake, Baker still has 2 cakes with 7.9Y (= 7.8 − .8 marginal cost + .9 receipts from the sale), instead of 2 cakes and 7.8Y. Under self-sufficient production, Adam and Baker produced and consumed a total of four cakes. By cooperating and engaging in

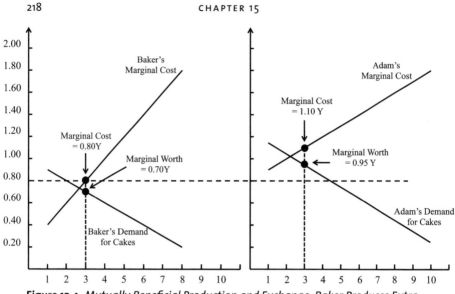

Figure 15.4 *Mutually Beneficial Production and Exchange: Baker Produces Extra Unit to be Sold to Adam*

exchange, they are able to consume a total of five cakes. Side-by-side, the data from tables 15.1 and 15.2 are shown in figure 15.4.

TWO'S COMPANY, THREE'S EVEN BETTER: EFFECTS AND OBJECTIONS TO NEW ENTRANTS

Though the preceding exposition relied on a two-person economy producing two kinds of goods — X and everything else, represented by Y — the analysis applies to the real economy with many goods and millions of people concentrated in cities with both small and giant firms engaged in international trade.

In a two-island economy, the lower-cost island can catch more fish than is demanded by its own population, and sell the extra fish to those on the higher-cost island. The individual and combined wealths of the islands will be increased. It will be profitable for the first island to expand production beyond its own demand as long as the marginal cost of production is less than the demand for, or marginal worth of, additional fish to those in the second island. The equilibrium price is where total quantity demanded is equal to total quantity supplied.

Where just two people are involved in a trade, the trade that occurs must be mutually desired, else it wouldn't take place. But when more than two people are concerned, as with international trading, some people in each nation are likely to be adversely affected. There are appeals such as, "Keep the money at home," "Buy American," "Be self-sufficient." And, of course, "Don't buy products from greedy corporations selling goods made by exploited, low-wage foreign workers."

Are the opponents to trade confused? Possibly some are. But is there a valid basis for some of their objections?

AN ECONOMICALLY COMPLETE ANALYSIS

Two substantial objections are voiced to admitting more people to buy and sell in an economy. One pertains to national defense. An import may be a military item which would make the country's defense dependent on another nation. This objection is obvious, but deciding when a component part — such as for a computer — might have a military application is not always obvious.

Another objection is the reason for most of the raucous demonstrations in favor of maintaining barriers to international trade. Domestic incomes are threatened! The imports, whether shipped in or produced by an immigrant worker, would compete as substitutes for goods made by those already in the market. Into the Adam and Baker economy we introduce Carter, a foreigner who proposes to be allowed to enter (either as a person or as products from Carter living abroad). Carter's production data are in table 15.3 and shown in figure 15.5.

Like Adam and Baker, Carter produces in isolation only two cakes for his own consumption. He does not produce a third cake because the marginal cost is .60Y while the marginal worth to him is only .30Y. Carter then learns about the Adam/Baker economy in which Baker is selling a cake to Adam for .90Y. Carter realizes that he can produce a third cake more cheaply than can Baker, so he offers to sell a cake to Adam for .65Y, less than Baker's marginal cost of producing a third cake.

Table 15.3 *Carter's Daily Production Costs (in Units of Y)*

Daily Output of Cakes	Total Cost	Marginal Cost	Average Cost	Alternate Product, Y (Bundles)	Marginal Worths of Cakes
1	2	3	4	5	6
0	—	—	—	3.00	—
1	.20	.20	.20	2.80	.50
2	.60	.40	.30	2.40	.40
3	1.20	.60	.40	1.80	.30
4	2.00	.80	.50	1.00	.20
5	3.00	1.00	.60	0	.10

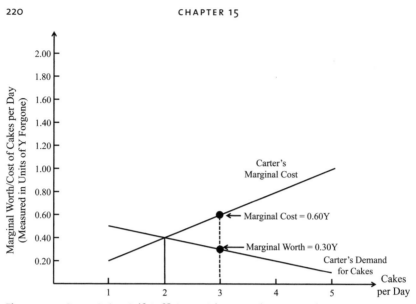

Figure 15.5 *Carter Being Self-Sufficient with No Trade or Specialization*

Adam, the major consumer of cakes, gains by buying cakes at the new lower price from Carter. Baker must reduce his production back to only two cakes, forgoing the extra income he had earned by producing and selling a third cake to Adam. The reduction in price of a third cake to Adam reflects part of what Baker lost as income when Carter entered and supplied more cake. The gain to Adam is partly a transfer from Baker, not part of the increase in social income. Some resources formerly used by Baker to make the third cake will have to move to make more of other goods, Y. This increased production by the released resources is the *social net benefit* consequent to Carter's entry, and is shared by everyone to the extent they buy goods produced by Baker's resources in their new activity.

The effects of Carter's entry are a lowered price of cakes with a benefit to Adam, a loss to Baker, and a higher income to Carter. If Baker's released resources were people, rather than physical resources, they would object to having to find new jobs, possibly with a lower wage, but with some chance of a higher wage. It is the *owners* of the displaced human or nonhuman resources, as competitors to the new entrant, who object to Carter's entry.

The opportunities for improved economic well-being of Adam, Baker, and Carter are the same as for Atlanta, Boston, and Chicago and also the same as for Argentina, Brazil, and Chile. Specialization and trade allow productive resources to be employed in their most cost effective uses, and neither the size of the trading partners nor political boundaries alter these basic economic principles.

In considering disputes about enlarging access to any market, economic principles say there's always a total *net* economic gain, though there are likely to be some who lose, but less than the others gain. There is a net gain in worth of aggregate national production by the *release of resources to their next best production alternatives*. That is what is meant when it is said that freer, more open trade is beneficial.

REDUCED COST, PROFIT, AND DISPERSION OF THE PROFIT

Suppose an existing investor produces a product at a cost of $10 a unit. The selling price is $12, generating a profit of $2 per unit. You see an opportunity for you to copy his technique and start production at the same cost of $10 a unit. You can cut the price to almost $10 and still make a small profit. The prior investor-producer responds by matching your price, rather than losing everything. The price is competed down to the $10 cost, leaving you with no profits. The profit stream was competed away to consumers through lower prices when the new competitor's output increased the total supply. There was gain in social output, and *transfer* of that increase in social output to consumers as a result of *entry by a competitor*.

IMPROVED QUALITY AND THE
DISPERSION OF THE BENEFIT

Innovations might be quality improvements instead of cost reductions of existing products. The same general consequences occur. Suppose you had improved the quality of the product, making it worth $1 more than the existing product, but you can still make it at the same $10 cost. You might try initially to sell your improved product for a price $1 higher — $13 instead of the prevailing $12 price. However, your competitors could respond by cutting their price below $12 to retain sales.

You might then counter by lowering your price to $11 — reflecting the worth of your products' $1 greater quality to consumers. You'd still receive $1 profit (your cost is $10). Competitors would receive only $10, matching their costs. To recap: consumers used to pay $12, leaving the producers with a $2 profit. Consumers would have been willing to pay $13 for your improved product, but your entry into the market increased total supply and competition drives down the prices of both the older product and the improved version to $10 and $11, respectively.

All profits the prior producers would have obtained in the future are transferred to the consumers by the lower prices. Your profits of $1 ($11 price minus $10 cost) reflect and constitute your contribution to the increased worth and value of output.

National Development

These examples outline the basic elements of actual economic development in a nation. If there were any additional investments that would be profitable, whether by foreigners or domestics, competition in the production and sale of the product would increase the supply and lower the product price. That permits everyone to have more at unchanged money earnings. And competition to hire people would drive up wages.

These are the two fundamental ways in which societies develop: (1) initial saver-investors get all of the first investment gain; (2) subsequent competing entrants (a) lower the cost of living, and (b) drive up (real) wages. In each step, competition from newcomers is essential. Competition from foreign or local investors increases output, lowers product prices and the cost of living, and thereby raises standards of living. The initial investor's prospects of profits attract and motivate these two forces of gain to the entire population.

The gains from foreigners' investment are as real and large to the rest of the public as are gains from investments by local investors, although it is often complained that foreigners invest and "take all the profits" away. Note the similarity of this analysis to how, in the refugee camp (of chapter 4), the second intermediary reduced costs and further benefited the refugees.

Development of a nation into a richer society requires profitable investment. Competition in investments distributes the gains over the society through higher (real) incomes and lower product prices. Natural resources like land, rain, and sunshine are desirable, but they don't produce income without labor and investment.

Without labor and investment, there is no way for more to be produced, and without competition, the gains are distributed less rapidly and extensively. The large benefits popularly attributed to greater internationalization are the effects of increased competition involving other nations, where security of property and rule of law prevail.

To object to domestic corporations investing abroad on the grounds that they are exploiting foreign employees (who are less educated people working at lower wages) is to condemn those poorer people to continued poverty. Those who might benefit from curtailment of foreign investment and trade are domestic higher-income workers whose productivity is not great enough to offset the competitive pressures of lower foreign wages.

The losers from limiting foreign investment and/or trade include a) the domestic consumers who would lose the benefits of lower prices on products made by foreign workers and b) the domestic workers who would have made products that could be exported and sold to the foreign consumers who are now enjoying rising standards of living.

Local Residents instead of Foreigners as the New Entrants into Production

Existing domestic competitors incur a loss as a result of new investment (as did Baker in the preceding example) while consumers of that product (Adam) get a benefit. If Carter — the owner of the new firm — is a resident of the nation, there's rarely any protection or compensation for the already existing producers. But if he is a foreign producer, there may be a call for protection from competition. But no matter who is the new investor, the profit stream to the new firm will later be eroded as it's passed to consumers by competition from other producers.

To be fully effective as a competitor, Carter doesn't have to migrate *personally* into the Adam-Baker economy. Instead, Carter could have been a foreign investor who installed manufacturing equipment and hired local laborers to work in the new bakery. The effect is not different when the new investors bake cakes abroad and ship them to Adam-Baker, rather than produce down the street from them. The only difference would be that Baker would object to the imports, claiming the investors were exploiting low-paid foreign workers — who should be protected by not buying the products they make.

You can't blame the Bakers for espousing those self-protective, illogical contentions. But you can blame people who believe these faulty contentions. The foreign laborers would prefer that even more of them should be "exploited" by foreign investors. The surest way to aid foreign workers is to encourage purchase of more, not less, of the foreign supplied goods, and also to advocate more internationalization of investment for more products from the less-developed nations.

TWO MEANINGS OF SPECIALIZATION IN PRODUCTION AND SEVERAL SOURCES OF BENEFITS

1. Avoiding Unnecessarily Higher Marginal Costs

There is specialization in production of just one or a few kinds of goods for *sale* while consuming a variety of purchased goods. In a modern market economy, everyone specializes in production, because we can buy most goods at less cost than producing them ourselves. Think of this as an avoidance of unnecessarily higher marginal costs for what one consumes.

A society that permits markets to direct the production of various goods to their lower-cost producers will become increasingly richer. Economists in

the eighteenth century — such as David Hume and Adam Smith — first emphasized this higher-cost avoidance when analyzing the reasons for promoting
international trade.

2. Increased Absolute Productive Ability, or "Learning By Doing"

A different form, or meaning, of specialization is producing one good or doing
one task more efficiently, regardless of whether the product will be sold in a
market. "Practice makes perfect" and "learning by doing" are ways of expressing it, increasing facility in that specific task. It often results in discovery of new
ideas and new methods.

Individual productive skills are increased by practice and repetition. Since
we cannot concentrate on everything, we are bound to specialize to some extent and to develop superiority in some tasks relative to others. This effect increases our dependence on other people to produce more of what we consume.
Graphically, this is represented as a *downward shift* of the marginal, total, and
average curves of costs of production.

This gain in absolute productive ability and technology is expected by almost every producer. It's been quantified into something called a "learning
curve" or "progress curve" representing declining costs per unit of product —
perhaps as large as 20 percent with every doubling of the amount produced.

But of course you also would learn to be better at each of many tasks if you
don't specialize. So what's the benefit of learning to be a *lot* better in one,
rather than *somewhat* better in many tasks? Why specialize in being better in
just one task?

3. Avoiding Wasteful Investments

A reason people specialize in learning certain skills — rather than learning
many things less intensively — is that they avoid wasteful investments in learning tasks they might later use only rarely, if at all. Not all attainable skills would
prove to be very valuable.

4. Greater Specialization and More Productivity
the Larger the Population in a City

The larger the city in which you work, the more you are likely to be able to
use your specialty all the time. Your investment and learning in one specialization will be more profitable. With only one doctor to supply a town, that
doctor would be supplying a variety of health care services as a generalist. If
the population is large enough for several doctors, each could concentrate on a
narrower specialty that would result in greater knowledge and skills.

Specialists know a lot about one thing, rather than a little about many things. Similarly, a restaurant chef in a small town couldn't concentrate on one kind of food — a specialty restaurant — as a chef could in a big city. Teachers in the little red schoolhouse in the smaller towns taught every subject. The same is true of repair shops, hairstylists, and antique stores. Average income and wealth of residents of the larger cities tend to be greater than in smaller towns, though on the margin the benefits of big and small cities tend to be the same.

In recent decades, electronic communications have reduced the costs of communicating among dispersed people. This effect reduces the value of being physically closer together in cities, and tends therefore to permit more specialization among the physically dispersed.

5. Larger Volumes in Larger Markets Reduce Total Costs of Production

An additional gain associated with a larger population is the lowered cost of mass production of a larger volume of a good. The technological procedures for larger volumes of output are cheaper per unit. Larger volume of the same product can be produced at both lower average and marginal costs. Imagine what clothing would cost if every garment were unique, with a very small volume of each type, or if every automobile were specially handmade.

NO FREE BENEFITS: INCREASED DEPENDENCE

Industries tend to concentrate (specialize) in regions. Obvious cases are agricultural products that grow best in certain climates and terrains. Historical cases have been Detroit for automobiles, Los Angeles for movies, San Jose, California, for electronics, and of course, major seaports for international shipping. In recent decades, new auto assembly plants have been in southern right-to-work states with more flexible labor laws.

Concentrations of production can depend upon the site of some raw material — coal, iron ore, timber, weather, a confluence of rivers, or oil deposits. But if demand for a product falls, many of the jobs in that area fall in value. Cities that are more specialized in particular industries have a higher risk of swings in employment, but wages are higher as a compensating adjustment.

QUESTIONS AND MEDITATIONS

1) Increased output resulting from more efficient specialization is distributed via what means in a capitalist open-market system?

Answer:

> Open access to exchange of the products, property rights to products and services. Also assumed is the desire of each person to obtain a more preferred situation through additional profits or lower costs of obtaining the product.

2) "It is better to buy from a firm that is losing money than from one that is making a profit, because the former firm is charging too low a price while the latter is charging more than costs." Evaluate.

Answer:

Not necessarily correct. Losing firm may have higher costs than the profitable firm.

3) In the discussion on pages 214–18, let Mr. C be a resident of Japan, while the others are residents of the United States. Mr. A is a tuna-boat owner and fisherman; B are American workers in other American industries. Let Y be "tuna" and X be "other products." Mr. A persuades his congressman to induce other congressmen to join him in passing a law prohibiting the importing of Japanese tuna — product Y produced by Mr. C. Who gains and who loses by a tariff or embargo on Japanese tuna? (This example captures the essence of the purposes and effects of tariffs and embargoes.)

Answer:

B loses compared to what he would have been able to purchase with his income had C been able to produce Y and sell to A. A keeps wealth compared to what he would have had with open access to markets by C. That C lives on an island across the Pacific rather than on the American continent does not change effects.

4) The three-person problem can also be interpreted as a case in which admission to the market for sale of one's production of Y requires a license from the state, and this license is given only if the current output from those now in the production of Y is deemed "inadequate to meet current demands." Who gains and who loses? Can you give some real examples of this situation?

Answer:

There are literally hundreds of products and services that require licenses, certificates, or permits in order to produce and offer for sale. In some states, even home decorating advice and braiding hair a certain way can require a license that might require hundreds or even thousands of hours and dollars to obtain.

5) Would the three-person, new entrant problem also serve as an example of the effect of apprenticeship laws that prohibit a person from acting as a "qualified" carpenter, meat cutter, and so forth, until he has served a specified number of years as an apprentice? Explain.

Answer:

Yes. Such requirements delay entry.

6) "The increased output of specialization is distributed as profits and as a lower price to consumers." What determines the portion of each?

Answer:

Speed of entry of new resources and their similarity to existing resources.

7) Does efficient production assume that perfect knowledge exists? Explain.

Answer:

No. It assumes that existing knowledge can be used and subjected to performance tests. It assumes no restrictions on rights to purchase or exchange knowledge. Knowledge is a valuable (economic) resource. To assume it is free is, for example, to deny that teachers perform a useful and desired service. A substantial fraction of our wealth is devoted to gathering information of one kind or another. Do not suppose that ignorance is always irrational, ridiculous, or the result of inefficiency or wastefulness or lying.

8) Do you think specialization will be carried to a greater extent in a large city or a small one? Why? Give examples of what you mean by greater specialization.

Answer:

Large. Greater variety of relative talents and training so that differences between people's relative abilities are more common. Further, the larger market enables a person to sell more of his special output at profitable prices.

Greater concentration of time on same repeated subtasks. For example, hair shearing for poodles only; architects specializing only in certain types of buildings; greater number of specialty shops such as medical specialties — foot specialist, ankle specialist, knee specialist.

9) Evidence of the great, but not always helpful, extent of specialization of knowledge is provided by Albert Einstein's assertion (*Socialist International Information*): "The economic anarchy of capitalist society as it exists today is in my view the main cause of our evils. Production is carried on for profit not for uses." Expose his error in economic analysis.

Answer:

Capitalist society does not restrain production. Production for profit is production for higher-*valued* uses — not just anything for any *use*. Einstein didn't seem to understand what value and costs meant or how they affected profitability.

10) A steals from B successfully. Is that "production"? Why? If you say "No, because someone is hurt," what would you say about the case in which a new invention displaces some other producers? Are there some kinds of production that you think should not be allowed?

Answer:

Usually "production" refers only to activity that is not illegal. We wish we knew a better answer. The question helps to reveal the hidden normative content of concepts that at first seem to be objective and free of ethical presuppositions.

11) If it were illegal to sell automobiles outside the state in which they were made, would cars be cheaper or more expensive in the United States? Give two reasons for your answer.

Answer:

More expensive since we would lose the gains of a) volume and b) greater specialization.

12) Why do manufacturers produce a few standardized models rather than a much larger variety of custom-made, custom-designed models?

Answer:

Public prefers lower-cost standardized models rather than greater variety of higher-cost custom models.

13) When a group of Soviet officials touring American farms asked, "Who tells the farmers how much to produce in order to supply the appropriate amounts of goods?" the host farmers said that no one told them. But the Soviet visitors were convinced the American farmers were concealing something. What would you have told the Soviet visitors?

Answer:

Private property rights plus knowledge of the market prices of various alternative crops make rational individual decision making feasible.

14) A former president of the Rockefeller Foundation said after a trip to China, "China is now able to meet all of its energy needs and is even in a position to export energy." Is that a meaningful statement? If so, does it mean China is better off than if it imported sources of energy? Why?

Answer:

How much energy does China "need"? China also "needs" schools, roads, hospitals, and teachers. At what price? Which sources of energy and how much—coal, gas, electricity, nuclear—and what is the cost relative to value of each? Would China be better off (wealthier) producing energy domestically if it were cheaper to import energy? Why? If it imported cheaper foreign energy, China could produce products using fewer resources than if it used more expensive domestic energy sources. With the released resources (from using cheaper imported energy) China could produce more of other valuable products.

15) Evaluate and compare the following statements on the immediate source of the "gain from trade" by an eighteenth-century economist and a nineteenth-century economist:

"Foreign trade . . . carries out that surplus part of the produce of their land and labor for which there is no demand among them, and brings back in return for it something else for which there is a demand. It gives a value to their superfluities, by exchanging them for something else, which may satisfy a part of their wants, and increase their enjoyments."[1]

"The only direct advantage of foreign commerce consists in the imports. A country obtains things which it either could not have produced at all, or which it must have produced at a greater expense. . . . Adam Smith's theory . . . was that it afforded an outlet for the surplus produce of a country. . . . The expression, surplus produce, seems to imply that a country is under some kind of necessity of producing the corn or cloth which it exports; so that the portion which it does not itself consume, if not wanted and consumed elsewhere, would either be produced in sheer waste, or if it were not produced, the corresponding portion of capital would remain idle."[2]

Answer:

The nineteenth century wins. We gain from what we get, not from what we give up. We gain from imports embodying foreign resources; exports are

1. Adam Smith, *An Inquiry into the Nature and Causes of the Wealth of Nations* (1776), ed. E. Cannan (New York: Random House, Inc., 1937), p. 415.

2. John Stuart Mill, *Principles of Political Economy* (1848), ed. W. J. Ashley (London and New York: Longmans, Green & Co., 1929), p. 578.

a cost, a drain, for our economy, with American production utilized by the rest of the world.

16) Why are plans to reduce restrictions to foreign trade commonly protested?

Answer:

Proposals to open a nation's market to producers of just one kind of product provoke intense opposition by the few projected losers. The many projected beneficiaries, though gaining more in total, individually gain too little to induce united dominating pressure for approval. That appears to be a reason why attempts to reduce world trade barriers are often in the form of general agreements covering many commodities and many nations.

CHAPTER 16

MARKET SUPPLY AND PRICE WITH PRICE-TAKERS

We've seen how negotiation among demanders and suppliers in a market determines a market price that allocates the existing supply among consumers (chapter 10). And we identified (in the preceding chapter) gains from specializations and exchanges. Now, we look at how market prices influence production decisions and market activities, along with the role of profit-seeking and how profits are surprisingly converted to costs.

SUNK INVESTMENT OR SET-UP COST

When making investment decisions, wise investors distinguish between the initial amount spent and the portion that will be sunk — not recoverable. If you buy a $100,000 machine that you could quickly resell for $95,000, your sunk investment would be only $5,000. That is not recoverable, so it's irrelevant for any future decisions.

Sunk cost does not determine whether you stay or leave if the movie you attend starts poorly. If you have paid a nonrefundable $1,000 in advance for a vacation at what turns out to be a miserable place, your sunk cost should play no part in deciding whether or not to leave. It's not the total initial expenditure that can be a barrier or obstacle to entry. It's only the nonrecoverable, sunk amount that is a cost of entry.

WHAT RATE OF PRODUCTION?

After completing an investment, the price and the rate of production must be chosen so as to maximize profits. Why assume maximum profit is the objective? No matter what the personal objective may be, competition ensures that firms that fail to make profits will not survive.

For the Ford Motor Company, competitors are more than other automakers. The resources employed by Ford are purchased in competition against manufacturers of all other products. Competition appears in the prices paid for inputs on the production cost side as well as on the product sales side — where Ford competes for customers against sellers of everything else. Competition is everywhere even though we tend to think of our competitors as only those who are selling the same goods.

PRICE-TAKER/SELLERS

It's useful to separate sellers into two categories, price-takers and price-searchers. The distinguishing feature is the difference in the nature of the demand facing the producer/seller. In this chapter, we'll deal only with price-takers, who face a *market price that is not affected by the amount of product that any one seller offers to sell.*

A certain price is observed to prevail in a market for some good or service. If any *one price-taker* (seller) were to try to sell in that market at a higher price, all customers would choose other suppliers. But at the prevailing market price, every seller can sell as much as would maximize profits. Each of the suppliers in such a market accepts the price and chooses how much to supply. We want to see how the price influences production and coordinates production among the producers.

Examples of price-taker's markets are plentiful. No one grower of crops such as corn, wheat, or soybeans can affect the prices of those crops. The same is true of cattle ranchers and chicken farmers. Prices of gold, silver, coal, oil, and natural gas are all determined in international markets, and often change minute to minute.

For most corporation stocks and bonds, the financial markets determine the prices; share prices are not posted by the corporation. The rates of interest on instruments such as commercial paper and money market funds are not set by any one borrower (or lender). No one bank dealing in foreign exchange perceptibly affects the prices of foreign currency.

In brief, the features of a price-taker are: (1) there is a market price that is unaffected by any one of the suppliers of that product, and (2) a price-taker/seller can sell as much as the seller desires to sell at that given market price. Very few wage earners can affect the prevailing wage rate by altering the amount of services offered; most income-earners are price-takers.

What would make a seller a price-taker? Customers regard what is offered by other sellers as essentially identical, and don't care who is the seller. For products easily standardized or classified into similar grades of quality — wheat, cotton, soybeans, shares of common stock of Apple or Chevron, labor to pick strawberries, units of foreign money — all that matters is the price. Any seller charging more will lose all sales; anyone charging less will be swamped with orders.

Contrast that with a different situation (examined in chapter 19) such as buying a dinner in a restaurant, or an automobile, or a movie, or shoes. For these items, the price alone is not all that counts. Lowering the price below that of a rival won't attract every buyer, because there are competitive differences in the qualities of offerings. Competition occurs in prices, qualities, and varieties for customer preferences. A price higher than a competitor's won't lose all customers, nor will a lower price attract all customers.

For homogeneous goods supplied by several sellers, the *price is set in a market*, and each producer has no alternative but to accept that price, and then decide how much to produce and sell. Also, customers choose only on the basis of price, without brand names or knowledge of who is the producer-seller.

If customers don't care who is the supplier of some good, no seller can charge more than any other. This doesn't mean many suppliers must exist at every moment. Imagine a village with only one seamstress, who raises the price. Within a few days, several other people who know how to sew could enter the market. The price would fall back.

Both conditions are necessary: (a) *homogeneity* of services from the suppliers and (b) *sufficiently quick entry* to dissuade existing suppliers from raising the price. The speed and cost of entry or departure of new equipment or sellers is what matters, not the number of sellers now.

PRICE-TAKER/SELLER SEES A HORIZONTAL DEMAND CURVE AT THE MARKET PRICE

Two market characteristics of a price-taker/seller situation are: (1) each seller can sell as much as that seller wants to sell, and (2) the market price will remain the same whether he decides to sell none or a great amount.

Although both the aggregate market demand and an individual consumer's demand for the product are negatively sloped, the demand seen by a price-taker looks like a horizontal line at the existing market price. Because any amount a seller offers to sell can be sold without any effect on the market price, the demand appears to him to be infinite at that price. However, if a price-taker tried to sell at even a slightly higher price, all customers would switch to other sellers who already exist or would quickly enter into production with an off-setting supply. And an individual price-taker could not cause the market price to fall by offering more, because that seller is too small a supplier of the total market supply. In terms of the elasticity of the demand facing a price-taker, that demand is infinitely elastic. (Review pages 109–17.)

NO RIVALRY AMONG PRICE-TAKERS

Price-takers do not regard other producers of the same product as rivals. A wheat farmer doesn't regard a neighboring farmer as a competitor whose ac-tions will affect the price of wheat or the amount that can be sold at the market price. They are more like colleagues subjected to market forces that none of them affect individually. They see prices for wheat that fluctuate daily or even hourly, and no one of them has any effect on it. They are not like a grocer, gasoline station operator, hairstylist, or antique storeowner who regards a neighboring seller as a rival, a competitor.

AGGREGATED DEMAND AND AGGREGATED
SUPPLY IN THE MARKET

A *market* is a place or arrangement wherein potential buyers and sellers can exchange information about offer prices and qualities of goods. It's sometimes called an exchange — thus, the New York Stock Exchange.

Organized markets exist for many agricultural products and basic industrial goods. The Chicago Mercantile Wheat Market is a highly organized arrangement, owned by the members, who are the traders. They are responsible for reliability that transactions are completed as agreed. The members buy and sell in that market in behalf of other people. When acting as agents for others, the members are brokers. Members also can act directly for themselves as dealers.

Competition among members in that marketplace (as agents for others or as dealers for themselves) — seeking low asking prices by potential sellers and seeking high bid prices by potential buyers — tends to bring the prices of each of the competing dealers together. Sellers flock to buyers who are offering more, and buyers flock to where some sellers are asking less. The prices of all the trades tend to be clustered together, depending upon how rapidly and cheaply the potential offers of other people can be observed.

The major forces in a price-taker's market can be summarized by the market demand curve and the market supply curve, as in figure 16.1. At the market-clearing price, the amount demanded and the amount supplied are equalized. It is an equilibrating price. Each buyer and each seller decide how much to buy and how much to produce at that given market price. They don't haggle over the price, because they can't affect it.

What every individual seller sees as the demand for that seller's products can be described as a horizontal line at that market price, not the downward-sloping market demand curve. If the market price changes, the demand line as seen by each seller shifts up or down with the market price. A price-taker/ buyer sees only the prevailing price. At any moment, there is only one price. At a higher price asked by a seller, none will be sold. And offering to sell at a lower price is pointless, since a seller can sell all that a producer would care to produce at the market price.

The consumer/buyer chooses to buy the amount of a good that brings the consumer's marginal worth of that good down to match the price. More would be worth less to the consumer than the cost. On the supply side, the presump-

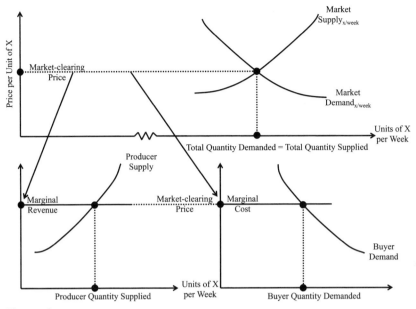

Figure 16.1

Though the market demand for every good is negatively sloped, the demand facing a given producer/seller of some good is characterized as a horizontal line at the prevailing market price. The demand is horizontal at that price (rather than downward sloping), because if a seller tries to raise its price above that market price, all buyers will switch to other sellers of the same kind of good. A price-taker/seller can, at the market price, sell all that he desires to sell without having any noticeable effect on the market price. Similarly, a price-taker/buyer sees only the market price and can buy as much as desired at the prevailing price.

tion is that maximizing profits is a key objective determining each producer's behavior.

MARGINAL COSTS, PROFITS, AND A PRICE-TAKER'S SUPPLY RESPONSE TO THE MARKET PRICE: A PRICE-TAKER'S MARGINAL REVENUE IS EQUAL TO THE MARKET PRICE

Every seller's marginal revenue is the change in total revenue when one more unit of the product is sold at the best price available for that unit. But a price-taker doesn't have to cut price to sell more. Therefore, the price-taker/seller's marginal revenue is always the same as the market price. This is merely a different way of expressing the fact that at the given market price, a price-taker/seller can sell as many units of the product as the seller chooses, without having to lower the price. If the market price is \$25, an additional unit can be sold at that price, bringing in \$25 more revenue, so marginal (and average) revenue is \$25. We will see later that for most producer/sellers, price is not equal to marginal revenue.

Table 16.1 *Costs at Various Daily Rates of Production*

Rate of Production 1	Constant Costs 2	Variable Costs 3	Total Costs 4	Marginal Costs 5	Average of Constant Costs 6	Averages of Variable Costs 7	Averages of Total Costs 8
0	10	0	10	—	—	—	—
1	10	9	19	9	10.0	9	19.0
2	10	17	27	8	5.0	8.5	13.5
3	10	23	33	6	3.3	7.7	11.0
4	10	28	38	5	2.5	7.0	9.5
5	10	35	45	7	2.0	7.0	9.0
6	10	48	58	13	1.7	8.0	9.7
7	10	70	80	22	1.4	10.0	11.4
8	10	100	110	30	1.25	12.5	13.8
9	10	140	150	40	1.11	15.5	16.7
10	10	191	201	51	1.0	19.1	20.1
11	10	256	266	65	0.91	23.3	24.2
12	10	336	346	80	0.83	28.0	28.8

DETERMINING THE RATE OF PRODUCTION AND SUPPLY

Marginal cost, not average cost, is the key cost to consider when determining the rate of production. In the following examples, we are concentrating only on the *rate* at which some product is being produced, rather than on the *volume* that will eventually be produced.

Increasing Marginal Costs at Faster Rates of Production

Marginal costs ultimately become higher at greater (faster) rates of production. This was shown in the cost data for Adam, Baker, and Carter; we show it again in table 16.1.

TWO TYPES OF CONSTANT COSTS:
1) CONSTANT TOTAL DAILY COSTS REGARDLESS OF DAILY RATE OF PRODUCTION (EVEN IF ZERO);
2) CONSTANT COSTS PER UNIT OF PRODUCTION

Constant Daily Costs

The costs listed in column 2 are the constant total daily cost, regardless of the daily rate of production. Examples are rent paid for land or a building, insurance, custodial and security services, and administration (back-office or other contractual costs that cannot easily be reduced or eliminated).

Constant cost doesn't enter into marginal cost. If the constant cost were $50, instead of $10, the marginal costs would be unaffected. All that counts in marginal costs are the variable costs, those that change with changes in the rate of output. Warning: the constant costs listed here are not sunk costs, which are costs incurred in the past.

Total Daily Cost

The total daily costs are listed in column 4. They are the sums of the costs in columns 2 and 3, the constant and the variable daily costs.

A second kind of constant cost, not listed in table 16.1, would accrue at a constant rate per unit of output. A cost of emblems on shirts, at $1 for each emblem, would be a constant $1 per shirt. The total cost of a shirt would be $1 greater than if no emblem were attached to the shirt.

Marginal Costs

Marginal costs — the additions to total cost — are greater at the higher rates of production. Marginal costs (column 5) are changes in total costs (column 4). As already noted, constant costs (column 2) don't change with a change in the rate of output, and therefore don't affect the marginal costs. The remaining columns of data (6, 7, 8) are the averages of constant, total, and variable costs, but they don't affect production decisions.

THE PLANNED OUTPUT RATE FOR PROFIT MAXIMIZING

The firm's owner, the investor, estimates the product's anticipated market price will be about $25. So he invested in a building and machinery for a designed rate of daily output that would be most profitable at a price of $25. Upon starting production, happily the price happens to be $25.

THE SHORT RUN

What is the profit-maximizing rate of output at the $25 market price? From the data in table 16.1, seven units is the profit-maximizing (daily) output. Producing eight would bring in $25 more revenue daily, but the marginal cost for the eighth unit is greater, $30. Daily profits would be reduced by $5 (= $30 marginal cost − $25 marginal revenue). At a smaller output of six units, increasing production by one unit would add more to revenue (MR), $25, than to cost (MC), $22.

All output rates other than seven units daily would yield smaller profits or bigger losses. For a price-taker, maximizing profits is the same as producing at a rate where the marginal cost matches the market price, because the market

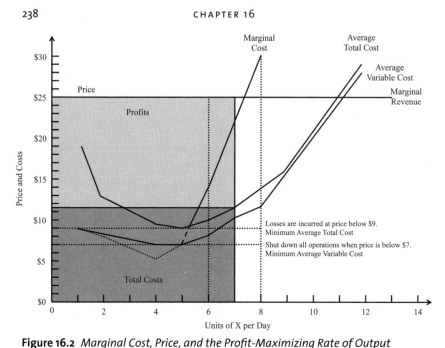

Figure 16.2 *Marginal Cost, Price, and the Profit-Maximizing Rate of Output*

Total costs are indicated by a rectangle over the base of seven units of output and an average total cost of $11.40. The total cost of 7 units is $79.80 (= 7 × $11.40). The profit, $95.20, (= [25 × 7] – [11.4 × 7]), which is total revenue minus total cost, is represented by the rectangle above the cost rectangle and with a vertical height of $13.60 (= $25 − $11.40). So long as price exceeds $7 (the lowest average variable cost), production with the existing facility would continue until time for replacement. At the time equipment renewal is contemplated, operations would cease unless the expected price were then at least $9, the full cost of production with a new facility.

price is the marginal revenue — each added unit sells at that price and therefore brings in that much more revenue.

A GRAPH SHOWING PRICE-TAKERS'
RESPONSE TO THE MARKET PRICE

Figure 16.2 is based on the cost data for our firm, with the market price, $25, represented by a horizontal line. At that price, the firm can sell all it finds worth producing, the rate at which the marginal cost equals the price — which for a price-taker is also the marginal revenue.

PROFIT-MAXIMIZING RATES OF OUTPUT
AT OTHER MARKET PRICES

For any firm in any market, the profit-maximizing output rate is that at which marginal cost equals marginal revenue. If the market price were only $13, the profit-maximizing rate or production would be 6, rather than 7 units, with profits of just $20, the excess of total revenue of $78 (= 6 × $13) over total cost of $58.20 (= 6 × 9.7).

WHY ANALYZE PROFIT-MAXIMIZING RATE OF PRODUCTION THROUGH MARGINAL REVENUES AND MARGINAL COSTS?

When circumstances change (a change in aggregate market demand or supply), it's the effect on marginal costs that enables us to deduce the direction of the resulting change in production. A rise in rent paid by the firm (column 2, constant costs) won't change the marginal costs, but it will increase average cost. That will not affect the rate of production in the short run, although it will affect the long-run (later) production when replacement of equipment is considered.

Changes and adjustments that are maintainable under the new circumstances are dependent on their effects on the marginal costs. If we know in what directions the initiating changes will affect the marginal costs (and the marginal revenues), we can deduce the direction of change to the most appropriate — most survivable — rate of output. Anything that raises the schedule of marginal costs will reduce the firm's profit-maximizing rate of output. If the marginal costs for a large number of firms rises (perhaps because of rising fuel costs), the result would be reduced aggregate market supply and raised market price.

Producers don't have to understand consciously these economic principles. Those firms that happen, whether willy-nilly or by superior management, to be best suited for the new conditions will prosper more. That differential survival in business and production, as in all other life, is a result of competitive winnowing of the less appropriately adjusted firms — regardless of how some firms came to be those that are more appropriate for the new circumstances.

A ROLE FOR AVERAGE COST

We have said that the sum of all the producer's marginal cost curves indicate the amount supplied to the market at each price, but we have to be more precise. In the long run, a producer will continue to produce only if the price is above the producer's minimum average cost. But there are two minimum average costs: one for long-run production, and a lower one for short runs with an existing production facility. In the short run, production will continue as long as price is above the variable cost.

THE LONG-RUN AVERAGE COST

For initial investment decisions, the anticipated market price must be at least as high as the minimum average of total costs of production. In table 16.1, that is $9. If that price were to prevail for a long time, the investment and subsequent production would break even: no profit, no loss. It is the lowest price at which the firm could survive.

THE SHORT-RUN AVERAGE COST

Suppose, however, that the investment on special machinery, factory, or building has been made, and the firm now exists. We're in the short run — lasting until new replacement investments would be made. If the price falls below $9, the initial investment would have been unprofitable. But once the investment has been made, it would pay to continue producing so long as the price is above $7 — the minimum average variable cost — until the equipment wears out.

By producing five per day, and getting $8 for each ($40 total), it will more than cover its short-run average variable cost of $7 ($35 for all 5 units). The extra dollar ($8 price minus the $7 cost) for five a day will be more than the nothing the firm would earn if it stopped production. While there is still a loss, at a price over $7 production will lose less than not producing and shutting down.

MARKET SUPPLY CURVE OF PRICE-TAKER/SUPPLIERS IS
THE HORIZONTAL SUM OF THE MARGINAL COST CURVES

We've assumed the existence of a market price to which a price-taker/supplier responds. What determined it? Supply and demand, of course. The aggregate supply — the market supply — is the sum of the supply curves of all the producers. Each producer has a supply curve representing its rates of supply at various prices. Adding (horizontally) the supply curve of each of the suppliers gives the aggregate (or industry) supply curve.

Each supplier offers more at a higher market price, as indicated by the marginal cost curve. A supplier tends to produce at a rate at which that supplier's marginal cost equals the market price. Since for each producer a higher market price increases that firm's profit-maximizing rate of production, for the aggregate of all producers a higher market price prompts a larger output.

Thus, a price-taker chooses the amount to produce and sell, without individually affecting that price. A price-taker's guiding signal of a change in demand is a change in the given market price. Price-takers do not watch other producers of the same goods as competitors or rivals. Each is facing the same (given) market price regardless of what any of them does.

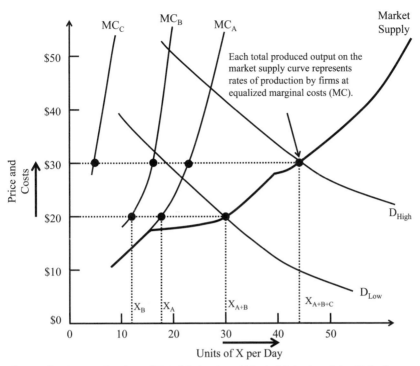

Figure 16.3 *Determination of Total Output and Market Price in a Price-Taker's Market*

The market supply is the horizontal sum of the individual marginal cost curves, here labeled as MC_A, MC_B, and MC_C. The rise in the market-clearing price from $20 to $30 is the result of an increased market demand, from D_{Low} to D_{High}. Its intersection with the market supply sets a higher market-clearing price, which induces a larger output by each producer. The graph indicates B entering the market at price $18, and C begins production when the price rises to $28.

AN UPWARD-SLOPING MARKET SUPPLY CURVE

As indicated in figure 16.3, for the industry, or market as a whole, the horizontal sums of the outputs of all producers at the respective prices form the market supply curve. The higher the market price, the larger the profit-maximizing rate of production by each producer in the industry. Each firm's marginal cost curve (above its lowest average variable cost) is the firm's supply curve to the market.

INDUSTRY-WIDE COST MINIMIZATION OF THE PROFIT-MAXIMIZING OUTPUT

Wealth-seeking producers are guided to an unintended beneficial effect — the minimization of cost for the industry-wide output. Maximizing profits for an individual firm means that the firm would be producing at a rate at which its own marginal cost is equated to the market price. To say that the marginal cost is equated to the market price is to say that profits are maximized.

Since every price-taker in the industry sees the same market price, every firm produces at a rate of output that brings its marginal costs toward equality with that same price. An equality of marginal costs of each of the several producers is a necessary condition for minimizing the total cost of the aggregated output of all firms in an industry. Competition for profits drives each firm toward that situation.

With individual producers at their profit-maximizing rates, the aggregated amount will be produced at the minimized aggregated cost of the entire market supply. The equalization of marginal costs across all the producers of the product (and the consequent cost minimization) is achieved without anyone intending or controlling that effect. This process is part of what Adam Smith called the economy's *invisible hand*.

Achieving profits is a condition of survival. Consumers leave no alternatives for producers. If the products don't satisfy consumers, producers won't cover costs and won't survive. The drive for profits is compelled by consumer preferences for better or more economically produced goods. Over time, competition displaces less satisfactorily performing producers — those who don't earn profits.

IS THE PROFIT TEST OF SURVIVAL "SOCIALLY DESIRABLE"?

Economic analysis implies only what happens and why it happens, not its desirability. Suppliers can continue to produce only if they create at least as much value to consumers as could otherwise be produced. They will not continue if they fail to make profits or avoid losses. Competition in the market is competition to create goods worth more than the costs.

An argument has been advanced that the profit-maximizing rate of output in open markets is a socially optimal rate for each good. The argument is simple.

a. If the market price exceeds the marginal cost, producing more of the good would increase both profits and personal worth. The marginal personal worth of some good supplied to the market is at least as great as the price paid for it — else it wouldn't be demanded at that price.

b. Producing more than the profit-maximizing rate would increase total personal worth (measured by the price) by less than the personal worth of other goods given up (measured by the marginal cost).

c. Producing less than the profit-maximizing amount would mean producers are failing to produce goods that have a marginal personal worth (market price) greater than the marginal personal worth of goods that are being made instead.

d. Therefore, the rate of production that maximizes profits — marginal cost equals price — maximizes the aggregate consumer personal worth.

A conclusion that maximizing total personal worth is good rests on the criterion that what a person is willing to pay for something is a more appropriate standard for what is good than is the judgment of some other person. But since how much a person is willing to pay (personal worth) depends in part on that person's wealth, this rationale accepts the current relative earnings and wealth as a given.

This rationale about the desirability of maximizing profits by equalizing marginal costs to prices was initially developed by socialist economists, who were trying to decide what "should" be — in some socially desirable sense — the criterion to determine the appropriate amounts to produce of various goods. When trying to determine such amounts, the desirability of profit maximization by the equality of marginal cost to market price was implied. The socialists were embarrassed, because the rationale proved to be a rationale for private property and markets.

Maximizing Profits: A Result, Not Necessarily a Goal or a Guide

No manager knows enough about conditions of demand and of production to know what will maximize profits. Even if managers could know, it is not necessary to assume that they strive for the last possible additional cent of profit. When earnings and profit streams are high, they might relax and still survive, like members of a team who might relax with a big lead.

But it's each person and each firm against all the others. Losses will be suffered by those who can't put resources to uses of equal or higher value than if used elsewhere. And profits will be earned by those who can. Newcomers are always entering. When one firm changes members or tactics, others respond lest they lose their profitability.

COMPETITION FOR PROFITABLE RESOURCES CONVERTS PROFIT INTO COST

Rivals compete for the resources and managers who can earn profits. That competition raises the prices of the resources earning that profit. What had been profits are converted into normal future earnings of more valuable resources. What are profits one day become costs of future use of the resources.

When people see a profitable firm, they look for the secret of its success. They search for the responsible resource, and their offer to buy it capitalizes the future profit into a higher present capital value of the resource. The profits are converted into someone's wealth. That person is not necessarily the owner of the firm.

If the source of the profit were an idea that had been patented, competition for the right to use it would drive up its market value to absorb the profit. If the profits were due to a manager with talents greater than formerly foreseen, competition for that person's services would drive the salary to match the profits, transferring the profits to that responsible person. The competition capitalizes that profit into the responsible person's higher salary.

The profits disappear, or more accurately, the profits are now converted to costs of use of the resource. For every firm, competition for ownership of its profit-creating resources — or avoidance of those yielding losses — brings resource values and costs to a level matching their contribution to the product's value.

Consider a firm that became worth $600,000 because of its novel equipment. Without that special equipment, the firm would make no profits. If the equipment could provide 100,000 units of service before replacement, the present capital value cost of its use per unit of output would be $6 (= $600,000/100,000 units). That would raise the total costs enough to reduce the profits to zero.

All the profits will be computed into the value of that equipment and the cost of its use. That's imputing the current market value of its services into its current cost. That now higher value is the correct base of depreciation (cost) when that equipment is used. The owner of the equipment is richer, but the profits are now zero — just the normal rate of interest on the $600,000 equipment.

A PERSON, RATHER THAN EQUIPMENT, AS THE RESPONSIBLE RESOURCE

Many a winery is successful only because of the superior talent of its vintner. That person's value is the basis of the profits of the winery. Any other winery owner who wants to hire that vintner would have to pay wages that match the profits; that is, competition for that person's services will force up the wages to match the previous profits. By this process, what had been viewed as profits has become part of the costs of doing business.

Changes in relative values of jobs and kinds of products mean people will begin to shift away from now lower-paying to better jobs. International trade has grown tremendously as trade barriers have been lowered. As the workers of other countries become more affluent as a result of manufacturing goods for export to US consumers, they can afford to buy more US products such as grains.

The result has been that the production of wheat and corn for export has become more profitable, so the quantities produced have grown. Some laborers who would otherwise work in nontradable services or skills, such as barbers, carpenters, or gasoline station attendants, shift to planting, harvesting, and transporting wheat and corn. Their former jobs may be filled by people drawn from still other jobs, but it is unlikely that a connection will be drawn between job openings for barbers and corn exports to China.

PROFITS ARE INCREASES IN WEALTH — NOT TRANSFERS OF WEALTH FROM ONE PERSON TO ANOTHER

The profits of producers are not transfers of wealth from consumers, and the losses of producers are not transfers from producers to consumers. The profits are the economy-wide increases in wealth as a result of more valuable uses of resources.

Profits are the unpredictable, but now discovered, increases in values of the responsible resources. The former lower values underestimated the future use values. No one knew earlier what the value of the resources would prove to be, else their market value would already have been that high. The earlier value, or cost of use, was the highest value that anyone *formerly* was willing to bet it would yield. The fortunate buyer of the resource at that earlier price was able to get the resource's more valuable services before others (or possibly even that buyer) knew what it would ultimately be worth.

A profit is obtained by the innovator who creates value. But the initially lower cost of utilizing those resources for any purpose will not continue to be low once final products are revealed to be worth more to consumers. Resource values and costs of use are derived from the demands for final goods and services, so they will be revised upward when new or more valuable uses are discovered. The owner will then receive only a normal rate of return on that greater wealth. Whether profit was a result of luck, better foresight, quicker perceptions, or whatever, is irrelevant.

These *profits by competition* in the market should not be confused with gains in wealth obtained by imposing restrictions on competitors' access to markets. Those gains are *contrived-monopoly rents* — obtained by restricting other people's access to the market. A monopolist may get rich, but not from profits.

The conversion of profits into costs is not merely a matter of definitions. Because the concept of costs in economics refers to the highest valued alternative use of resources, discovery of a new, better, or more valuable use for a resource raises the *cost* of continuing to use it in the former way. The "profit" that is observed when the resource is revalued to a higher capital value becomes greater wealth to the resource owner.

Prior to the revaluation, an investor who had acquired ownership of land or equipment, or had contracted for a person's services, at a price that was less than its later revealed market value, is certainly richer. However, the competition for that resource raises its value to where the rate of return on that higher value is brought down to the rate of interest—with no subsequent profits. At the end of the process, what can be observed is the greater wealth on which only the competitive rate of return will be received.

Any manager or owner who failed to respond to the higher costs of continuing to utilize in the former way the now-discovered-to-be-more-valuable resource would lose in competition with those who offer to pay that higher value to get the person, equipment, or service that is creating more value to consumers.

The stock market helps business managers know how valuable the firm is, and it also warns them that their equipment costs are not depreciation based on an initial purchase price. A new, higher value is what is depreciated by continued *use* of the equipment. Or if it were some person, the higher wage bid for that person's now-perceived-more-valuable services becomes the cost of his services.

EXAMPLE OF RESOURCE REVALUATION, PROFITS, AND ACCOUNTING MEASURES OF DEPRECIATION
To Invest or Not to Invest?

We start with an initial decision to spend $10,000 for purchase and installation of a machine in a business. Once this machine is installed, it's worthless for any other use, and it has no salvage value. We assume the machine can produce 5,000 units before it loses all productive ability. Costs of all other required material and labor are $1 per unit. Added to that would be the $2 per unit depreciation of the machine (= $10,000/5,000 units). The total cost of production would be $3 per unit (= $2 depreciation plus $1 cost of other inputs). At any market price less than $3, the investment would not be profitable. Suppose that the anticipated product price is $4.

Table 16.2 *Summary of Costs, Values, and Depreciation*

(A)

Purchase Price	$10,000.00	
Sunk Cost of Investment	10,000.00	
Product Price of $4		$4.00
Unit Cost of Associated Inputs		1.00
Net Unit Earnings		$3.00
Machine Use Value	$15,000.00 = 3 × 5,000	
Cost of Machine Use	$3.00 per unit = $15,000/5,000	
Decision: Invest	Profit = $5,000.00 (= $15,000 – $10,000)	

Possibilities after Investment

(B) If Product Price Were $3.50		$3.50
Unit Cost of Associated Inputs		1.00
Net Unit Earnings		$2.50
Machine Use Value	$12,500.00 = $2.5 × 5,000 units	
Cost of Machine Use (Depreciation)	$2.50 = $12,500/5,000	
Decision: Produce	Profit = $2,500 (= $12,500 – $10,000)	

(C) If Product Price Were $2.00		$2.00
Unit Cost of Associated Inputs		1.00
Net Unit Earnings		$1.00
Machine Use Value	$5,000.00 = $1.00 × 5,000 units	
Cost of Machine Use (Depreciation)	$1.00 = $5,000/5,000	
Decision: Continue to Produce	Profit = $0 (= $10,000 – $10,000)	

(D)

If Product Price Is Below $1.

Value of Machine Is Zero.

Decision: Terminate.

Rule: If a resource's value falls to zero, terminate its use.

A. If Market Price = $4

The product price proves to be $4. That permits $20,000 total revenue (ignoring, for arithmetic convenience, interest over the time the units are produced and sold). A $4 price gives an excess of $3 per unit over the $1 unit cost of other inputs. That makes the machine's value in use $15,000 (= $3 × 5,000 units). The business could be sold for that price, now that it is seen what it will earn. The excess of $15,000 over the purchase price of $10,000 is a profit of $5,000. At the product price of $4, the machine is worth $15,000. When it is used, depreciation cost is $3 per unit of use (= $15,000/5,000 units), not the former anticipated $2 per unit ($10,000/5,000 units).

You might contend that since you could replace the machine for only $10,000, its purchase cost, the cost of using up this machine is really only $2 per unit (= $10,000/5,000 units). But don't forget the meaning of "cost"—the highest sacrificed alternative value—and the presence of competition. The cost of using that particular machine is now the erosion of its $15,000 value. That's how much the machine's value falls with each unit of output. Depreciation is the reduction in value (not of the purchase cost) when something is used.

Further, if you think you'll be able to buy a replacement at the earlier $10,000, you'll be disappointed when others bid the price up to $15,000 for the machine to duplicate what you are doing. If it happens that they can't duplicate what you do with the machine, then it's not the machine that is worth more, it's *you*. The cost of using *you* will be $5,000 higher as people compete for your demonstrated ability to take $10,000 and turn it into something worth $15,000—assuming you really had that talent, and weren't just lucky.

B. What If the Product Price Falls?

In Part B of table 16.2, as the investment is completed and production is started, the product price is $3.50, not $4, and is expected to stay at $3.50. The yield is $2.50 per unit above the $1 per unit costs of other inputs (= $3.50 − $1) for each of the 5,000 possible units of service. The machine's market value would be $12,500 (= $2.50 × 5,000 units). The investment would yield a profit of $2,500. Use of the machine now costs $2.50 per unit (= $12,500/5,000 units)—the depreciation.

C. What If the Price Happens to Be Below the Anticipated Long-Run Average Cost of $2?

In Part C, the market price proves to be only $2 as our product hits the market. With the $1 cost of other inputs, that price leaves only $1 for each unit of the machine's services, or $5,000 (= $1.00 × 5,000). Costs and revenue both are $10,000, so profit is zero.

D. At What Initial Price Would Production Be Abandoned?

Part D shows that at any price below $1, it would be better to abandon production, because $1 is the minimum average cost of all the other associated inputs.

PRODUCTIVE RESOURCES THAT ENTER AFTER A NEW TAX

Investments in new equipment, *after* a tax change or a new tax on production, will be made only if they are expected to be profitable under the new circumstances in which the price is sufficiently high to cover the tax.

The losers are 1) the owners of existing equipment that becomes less valuable and also 2) any employees whose available wages elsewhere are lower than the wages they were getting before the change.

Whether the costs that later potential investors know they must cover are higher because of taxes, or higher wages, or higher material costs, makes no difference. New investments will be made only if they are expected to yield at least the competitive rate of return available elsewhere. But the higher costs reduce the probability and expectation of getting a significant yield.

DEPRECIATION VERSUS CAPITAL VALUE CHANGES

A reduction in the value of a machine (or any productive resource) caused by its use is *depreciation*. That cost must be distinguished from a *fall in the market value* of the machine caused by an unexpected decline in its service value, which is a *loss* — pure and simple. In reports issued by corporations about their financial situations, the two are commonly confused. And changes in values of resources — because of changes in values of their services — are not mentioned.

Every business firm calculates depreciation of a resource on the basis of the original purchase price — not its current value. Firms report the wrong data — the historical record — but usually harmlessly. The accountant's task is to record expenditures, receipts, and accumulating debits and credits to monitor the behavior of managers. Accountants do not try to estimate or explain current values of equipment or of the business. They let the rest of the world do that in markets for capital goods and in stock markets, where the stock prices reveal the new values and implicit value based on revised information and anticipations.

OBSOLESCENCE VERSUS DEPRECIATION

Depreciation is the reduction in the machine's value because of use. Depreciation is not dependent upon the purchase price of the equipment. It's dependent on the *current* value of the resource. Obsolescence is the change in value of a resource when its product value falls for reasons unrelated to its use. Better resources or a reduced demand for its services caused possibly by higher costs of associated inputs are sources of obsolescence. In our example, the price of the product fell. That product price decline immediately resulted in a change in the resource's value, an obsolescence, not depreciation. In the other direction, a rise in resource value is *appreciation* — a windfall profit.

WHY DO ACCOUNTING RECORDS SHOW DEPRECIATION AS EROSION OF INITIAL COST OF RESOURCE, RATHER THAN OF CURRENT VALUE?

In financial reports of business firms, the purchase cost, not the current market value, of the equipment is listed. Why? The accountants don't know the values of resources in the firm. The resources aren't sold, so there's no objective market value.

Accounting records are not maintained as a basis for making decisions about output and inputs. Instead, such data reveal what the firm spent and received as money. Included are data on liabilities to, and claims on, other people. Accounting data help owners monitor financial actions of the firm. Accountants do not record current values of resources, nor costs of their use.

Trying to estimate the current market values of the firm's resources would introduce subjective personal opinions. To avoid such judgments, accountants record only past known outlays and receipts and initial purchase costs. Calculations of depreciation or other costs are done in accord with tax rules, which often have no relation to the market values of the resources.

PROFITS IN TERMS OF CAPITAL VALUES

Look forward over a span of one year, with daily output of 7 and 200 days of production per year, at a product price of $25. That would bring a total revenue of $35,000 (= $25 per unit × 7 units per day x 200 days). Assume annual total cost would be $16,000 (= $80 per day × 200 days). The annual profit rate would be $19,000 (= $35,000 − $16,000), or $95 daily (= $19,000/200). Capitalize that annual profit of $19,000 to a present value, assuming that the profit rate would persist for, say, ten years. At 10 percent per year interest, that's $116,660 (= $19,000 × 6.14), as verified in the present value tables in chapter 30. If this firm were a corporation with 10,000 shares of common stock, each share would have a market value of $11.67 (= $116,660/10,000).

QUESTIONS AND MEDITATIONS

1) The current market price of wheat is $2 per bushel.
    a. You have 1,000 bushels. If the rest of the suppliers provide 9,999,000 bushels, could you detectably affect the market price by withholding any of your supply from the market?

b. If you offered to sell at $2.25, while the market price was $2, would anyone buy wheat from you? Would you be tempted to sell at $1.75?

c. From your perspective, what does the demand curve for your wheat look like?

Answer:

    a. No.

    b. No. No.

    c. Horizontal line.

2) In a price-taker's market, does the marginal revenue of each seller virtually equal the average revenue (price)? Why?

Answer:

Yes. Trivial effect on price by offering more by any one seller, and if the average is not affected, the average equals the marginal.

3) Explain why the marginal-cost schedule above the lowest average variable cost is the supply schedule of the firm in a price-taker's market? How low a permanent price would make the firm stop production permanently? How low could price be in the short run without the firm suspending production?

Answer:

The portion of the marginal cost curve above the minimum point on the average variable cost curve is the supply of the price-taker. (Remember the marginal/average relationship.) When price is above the minimum variable cost, but below total per unit cost, the producer is losing money but will continue to produce since he is covering more than the current operating costs. However, when equipment wears out, the producer faces new acquisition and repair costs. He will shut down, since the projected receipts will not cover the new costs.

4) "Marginal costs serve as a guide to how much of a good to produce, while average costs help indicate whether to produce the good at all." Explain.

Answer:

Marginal costs along with marginal revenue indicate maximum wealth output, while average costs in relation to price indicate whether the profits are positive or negative.

5) Is there a short-run cost and long-run cost for a given output program, or are there two different contemplated output programs, each with its own cost?

Answer:

Two different programs, each with a different cost.

6) Suppose the marginal cost of the resources in producing an X is $5, where cost is interpreted as the highest sacrificed use value. If these same resources had been used elsewhere, their sacrificed value of output Y would have been $6. What would make these two different "costs" of the same resources converge to the same value?

Answer:

Resources would be withdrawn from the production of Y, moving back down its marginal cost curve; the cost of an extra value of output of Y falls. Some resources withdrawn from Y can be added to the production of X, where marginal cost of production was lower, but rising. The cost of producing an additional Y and an additional X converge at the margin to the same value — between $5 and $6.

7) "The free-enterprise, capitalist system is a system of consumer sovereignty. Consumer preferences determine what shall be produced and how much shall be produced." Evaluate.

Answer:

"Individual sovereignty" is more accurate than "consumer sovereignty." Individuals make choices both as consumers (buyers) and as producers (sellers). An individual expresses choices about working conditions as well as about consumption goods. If mining is unpleasant compared to cutting timber, so that individuals are more willing to work at the latter, the amount of lumber relative to coal will be larger than if individual preferences as producers were reversed.

With so many other people, each of us is usually powerless to affect output or market demand significantly. This does not mean we cannot choose among available alternative purchases or products to produce. Nevertheless, because we can hardly change the range of offers made to us, each open-market producer thinks the consumer (a personification of the market) is sovereign, while the consumer believes that producers (personification of supply) decide what consumers can have.

8) What constitutes or determines the market supply curve of a price-taker industry?

Answer:

Each of the numerous firms maximizes profit by equating marginal revenue and marginal cost, producing at the output where the upward-sloping

MC curve intercepts the horizontal MR curve. At each feasible price, the amount supplied by the industry is the sum of the individual firm outputs at that price.

9) If a business firm finds its selling price and output so related that larger output is associated with lower selling price, is this an indication that it has lower costs with larger volume or that the demand is such that more can be sold only if the price is lower?

Answer:

The latter, regardless of the relationship between output and cost.

10) "New business firms can underprice older firms, because the newer firms can buy the latest equipment and are not burdened with the older, less economical equipment which older firms must retire before they can economically adopt the new. This is why continued technological progress contributes to maintaining a competitive economic system." Explain the errors in both sentences.

Answer:

Old firms are not burdened by old equipment. That they don't simply shut down or switch to producing other goods means they can compete by using old equipment, whose value is recapitalized to whatever level will enable it to continue to be used — unless its value drops to zero, in which case it will certainly be retired. The first sentence is typical of a very common error — an error that ignores the market's revaluation process of existing productive resources. What is relevant for production decisions is current *market* value of equipment and resources, not the historical value or initial purchase price.

11) Evaluate this assertion: "Suppose that at an additional cost of 3 cents per bottle, Coke is made better than Pepsi. And suppose that improvement is worth 5 cents to a consumer. A consumer switches from Pepsi to Coke when each is priced at $1/bottle. Therefore, the customer who gets only 5 cents more value imposes a one dollar cost on Pepsi in a lost sale. That's wasteful, for the loss to Pepsi is far greater than the gain to the consumer." Is that correct?

Answer:

No. The loss to Pepsi is not the lost $1 of sales revenue. The lost profit is what is lost to Pepsi. That's a lot less than $1 per bottle. The resources not used by Pepsi, when making less product, worth $1, are transferred to making other products. A loss to Pepsi would be the reduced value of resources that are not transferable to other uses without some drop in their value, which is something we will explore later. The moral here is that a transfer from one person to another (loss to one person and gain to another) — if not a loss of resource values — is not a social loss.

CHAPTER 17

TIMING OF ADJUSTMENTS

Most adjustments to new events take time. It took a few years to make automobiles smaller and more fuel efficient after the price of gasoline jumped during an early "oil shock." Later, when the price of oil fell, it took several years to return to bigger cars. Some responses are so long delayed that it's hard to remember the cause.

Economists usually categorize the timing of completed adjustments: the immediate, the short run, and the long run. The immediate responses tend to be in prices before production is altered. The short run includes adjustments in the rate of production, but before altering the amount of durable productive resources. The long run refers to the completed final adjustments, including reductions or increases in the stock of productive facilities.

TAX IT: DEMAND AND SUPPLY

When analyzing the effect of a tax or arbitrary change in cost, first identify the effects on the *supply curve* and the *demand curve*. Price and quantity are not affected by an extraneous event without an effect on demand or supply — or both.

Suppose there's a new 10 cents a gallon tax on gasoline. Whose wealth is reduced by the tax? And what adjustments are made in the price, production, and consumption of gasoline and related products? In any case, it makes no difference whether it's the consumer or the seller who hands the tax to the government, except possibly emotionally and politically.

One way to interpret the tax on gasoline is that it leaves less revenue for the suppliers, so we deduce the effects on supply. Alternatively, we can interpret the tax as a rise in costs to the buyers, and then deduce the effects on demand. These alternative views of the situation imply the same results in the prices and amount of gasoline consumed, because the same event is being interpreted with the same principles. Figures 17.1A and 17.1B guide the analysis with each point of view.

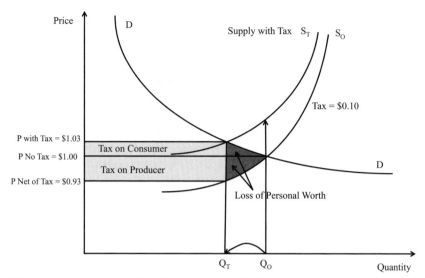

Figure 17.1A *Tax on Gasoline: Tax Shown as a Rise in Supply Cost*

In figure 17.1A, the tax is interpreted as a 10¢ rise in the cost of each gallon supplied to the market. That shifts up the marginal cost curve, including the tax, by 10¢. The intersection of the demand curve with the new market supply curve (based on the new marginal cost curve including the 10¢ tax) indicates the new short-run price, $1.03. The consumer price inclusive of the tax is higher by 3¢, and the cost to the producers is higher by 7¢. The area above the initial price line and below the new price represents the total tax collected from consumers. The total tax collected from the suppliers is the area below the initial price and above the net-of-tax price received by the suppliers.

The actual division of the tax will depend on the slopes of the demand and market supply lines.

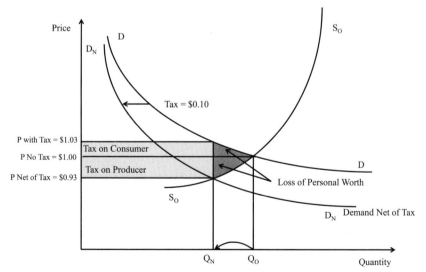

Figure 17.1B *Tax on Gasoline: Tax Shown as a Reduction of Demand*

The tax is interpreted as a 10¢ reduction in gasoline demand facing the sellers. The lower net of tax demand curve results in a lower after-tax price to the seller. The resulting price and quantity of gasoline is the same as in figure 17.1A using a shifted supply curve.

a) Tax Viewed as an Increase in Producers' Costs

Interpreting the tax as a rise in the cost of supplying gasoline, marginal cost is raised 10¢ a gallon, because 10¢ must be paid to the government for each gallon produced. The aggregated market supply curve also rises by 10¢. How much will be supplied? A smaller amount—an amount at which the marginal consumer worth on the demand curve will be high enough to equal the 10¢ higher marginal cost, which includes the tax. With less gasoline being produced, and an unchanged demand curve, the market price will rise to where the amount demanded equals the reduced production.

Suppose the resulting price including tax is $1.03. The consumers pay 3¢ more per gallon, and the producers receive, after paying the tax, 7¢ less per gallon. That is, the consumer has paid 3¢ and the seller 7¢ of the tax. The amount of gasoline being produced is reduced to where its marginal cost is 7¢ less than before the tax, that is, to 93¢.

The approximate triangular area between the demand and supply curves for the range of reduced amounts consumed represents a *social welfare loss*. That's the reduction in consumers' personal worth when resources are transferred to other goods yielding lower personal consumer worth. That reduction is the *burden* of the tax.

b) Tax Viewed Alternatively as Reduction in Demand Seen by the Seller

In figure 17.1B, the lower net-of-tax curve is pertinent to the seller. Of the basic demand price, $1.03, 10¢ goes to the government. The net-of-tax portion is smaller by the unit tax of 10¢ a gallon. The cost of producing gasoline and the supply curve are unchanged. The *net-of-tax demand curve* intersects the supply curve at the price of 93¢—7¢ less than before the 10¢ tax. The consumer pays the additional 3¢. At that lower net-of-tax receipt of 93¢ a gallon to the supplier, less gasoline will be produced. This is the same result as implied by raising the marginal cost curve in figure 17.1A. The short-run effects on prices and supply are: a) a reduction in amount supplied and consumed, b) a higher price to consumers, and c) a lower net price (price minus the tax) to the suppliers.

DEADWEIGHT WELFARE LOSS

Some resources that would otherwise be used to make the taxed good are shifted to make goods worth less to consumers than the gasoline no longer produced. The forgone gasoline was worth between $1.00 and $1.03 for each gallon. What's produced instead is worth less than that, else it would already have been in production.

That loss of (a) the worth of the forgone gasoline in excess of (b) the worth of the goods now being produced instead is (c) a *deadweight social loss*, a burden of the tax. There is forgone personal worth borne by everyone using less of the taxed good. Those who buy the other goods now being produced (instead of gasoline) get a gain that is worth less than the lost worth of the forgone gasoline.

MOBILE VERSUS LESS-MOBILE RESOURCES

Resources that are perfectly mobile — able to shift elsewhere and earn as much as before — move and suffer only the cost of moving. The crude oil formerly used for refining gasoline can almost instantly be used to make other equally valuable products or gasoline for other less taxed areas. The refinery equipment is less valuable elsewhere, so its value falls (capital value of the reduction in its earnings). The past costs for building the refinery's immobile items are sunk and irrelevant for future decisions about use of the refinery or for its value.

You'd be regarded as *perfectly mobile* if your best alternative job were as good as your present one. You'd be very immobile if your next best option were worth a lot less. A resource would be completely immobile if its best alternative use value were zero. This can happen when the moving cost to an alternative job is too high to make the move worth the cost.

The taxes reduce the earnings to the less mobile resources, which thereby bear some of the tax. With passage of time, more resources will move away or be eroded and retired and not replaced. The supply of gasoline will fall toward a quantity at which the market price of the gasoline will cover the entire refinery and refining costs plus the tax. From that time, consumers will pay all the tax. But in the interim (the short run) before the full long-run adjustment in refineries, the reduction in wealth will be borne in part by the owners of the productive resources and by some of the employees who are laid off.

The $.10 per gallon tax collected by the government can be categorized into two parts: (a) the rise in price to consumers (from $1.00 to $1.03) and (b) the 7¢ per gallon loss imposed on the owners of immobile refinery resources that are less valuable in alternative uses. These two losses, as well as taxes collected, should be measured in *capital values* (discussed in part 3), which would take account of the various lengths of time for the adjustments to be completed. The loss in capital values when some of the resources are transferred to next highest uses is a measure of productive loss, as distinct from the wealth being transferred to the government by the tax. The loss of value pushes resources away from refining to next best options.

COMPARISON OF SHORT-RUN AND LONG-RUN EFFECTS

To derive and compare the temporal sequence of the price and quantity responses to the tax, look at figures 17.2A and 17.2B, which portray the short-run and long-run demand and supply conditions, respectively.

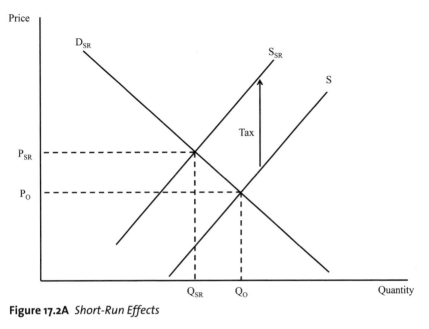

Figure 17.2A *Short-Run Effects*

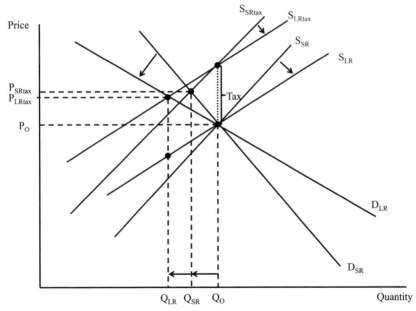

Figure 17.2B *Short- and Long-Run Effects of Tax*

The tax is here viewed as an increase in the costs to the refiner, though it could as well be viewed as a reduction in demand net of the tax. The crucial differences are in comparisons between the elasticities of short- and long-run demands and of short- and long-run supplies. The elasticities of demand and of supply in the short run are smaller, because faster adjustments (short run) are more expensive than if made less rapidly (long run). The greater elasticities in the long run make the quantity effects greater than in the short run. More of the tax is borne by consumers, rather than by suppliers, the longer the tax has been in effect, except for taxes on constant, fixed-supply resources, such as land sites.

Figure 17.2B shows the long-run effects with the more elastic demand and supply curves. The tax's long-run negative effect on the quantity is larger than the short-run effect. This graph shows how the tax affects the price, no matter what the pattern or size of the costs and the tax. But the resulting changes in the price and quantity depend on how much the costs change.

Longer-run adjustments in productive facilities are more extensive, easing pressure to produce gasoline in more costly fashion with existing equipment. That investment in new facilities or retirement of worn facilities makes the long-run supply curve of gasoline more elastic than the short-run curve. The long-run effect of a tax per gallon of gasoline is a larger reduction in quantity and a smaller rise in price than in the short run, as indicated in figure 17.2B.

In the longer run, some refining capacity would wear out and not be replaced. That would reduce the supply curve (shifting it leftward) and result in a higher price. That's why a tax on a product seems at first to be paid by the producer with little effect on production, but later, as the greater supply and demand elasticities take effect, the price to consumers rises and the quantity demanded and produced falls. But by the time that happens, who remembers it was caused by the tax?

AFTER THE LONG-RUN ADJUSTMENTS, CONSUMERS PAY ALL THE TAX; NEW INVESTORS PAY NONE

Ultimately, as the immobile resources for refining gasoline from oil wear out, it won't pay—with that tax (and price that has risen by less than the tax)—to replace all the refining capacity as it deteriorates. Gasoline production will fall further and its price will rise further, up to where it covers long-run costs and taxes of producing. (We ignore growth of demand over time to concentrate on the tax effect.)

At that long-run higher price, consumers of gasoline will be paying all the tax, which leaves enough after-tax profits of refining to make it worthwhile to build new refineries, once the existing refinery wears out and needs to be replaced. The investors in *new* refineries, with a smaller total capacity than before, will be bearing none of the taxes.

The portion of the tax initially borne by the owners of existing immobile refinery resources has been shifted fully to consumers, because the price will have been pushed up enough to cover the long-run average cost of creating and operating refineries. That's why owners of *new* refineries will bear none, and consumers will bear all, of the tax thereafter.

New investments in refineries will be made only if they are expected to yield the same rate of return as any other new investment. Competition tends to equate the rates of return, as explained in later chapters on capital values. The long-run higher price paid by the consumers to producers will cover the tax, as it covers all other costs.

ONLY PRESENT AND FUTURE COSTS ARE REALLY COSTS

Subsequent to a reduction of the supply and the higher price of gasoline, if the price more than covers the *future* costs of production, the refinery appears to be earning a profit. Actually, it's earning a profit on only the *continuing* costs of production, which do not include replacement costs once it wears out.

Consider a common analogous situation. You own a car you decide to use as a taxi, but the revenue from operating it doesn't have to cover the prior purchase price of the car. You already own the car. To continue to use it, the revenue must cover (a) subsequent remaining operating costs or (b) what you could get from an alternative use of the car. However, when the car wears out, your taxi service will end if you have not created a reserve sufficient to purchase a new car.

Since the refinery is immobile and has no use for anything but refining, it will continue to operate so long as the revenues cover its *operating* costs. The earnings may be too small for the initial investment to have been profitable. But once the investment has been made, any earnings in excess of the operating costs are a surplus — until the equipment wears out. Economists apply the label *quasi-rent* to that temporary excess. *Quasi* emphasizes that it's a surplus over its current operating costs, for continued, but temporary, operation (until replacement or transfer to other uses).

QUASI-RENT: A TEMPORARY SURPLUS

An existing house will be used even if the stream of monthly rents in the future would not be large enough to cover the costs of repairing it or building a new one. Quasi-rent indicates that the current rate of service value will not maintain that resource permanently. The asset will render current services, but not into the indefinitely long future. It's only a temporary surplus. The initial cost is sunk and therefore irrelevant for future decisions about use of the resource — except, of course, it might be a predictor of future costs if a replacement were contemplated.

The concept of quasi-rent can be applied also to earnings of people. You invest in professional education as an electrical engineer, which would be profitable if you then earn $60,000 a year. But after your education is obtained, the sunk cost of your education is irrelevant. Suppose you are earning $60,000 a year, and your next best job is only $40,000. The $20,000 difference is unnecessary to keep you at your present job, because that's the amount your current earnings could be cut before you'd shift to the $40,000 job. That $20,000 is a quasi-rent in your earnings at your present work.

Later we extend the analysis of a tax on gasoline into the future by using the more inclusive capital value concept of wealth — the present value of all the future tax payments — rather than just the current rate of tax payments. Thinking and measuring in terms of wealth rather than current flows is more complete and informative — though less common!

INFINITE ELASTICITY OF SUPPLY

Consider a long period in which the long-run supply is represented by a horizontal straight line, a schedule of infinite elasticity. This could be valid if the productive resources are sufficiently similar so that all the refineries have the same average cost. The tax is shown as an addition to the costs, shifting up the supply line in figure 17.3.

The quantity of gasoline will be reduced. The price would rise in the short run until some refineries were shut down, leaving the reduced rate of production at the initial average cost. At the lower rate of production, the higher price would cover the unchanged average cost plus the tax. Production falls more when the supply is perfectly elastic than when it is less elastic.

As an exercise, repeat the analysis by lowering the demand curve by the amount of the tax, rather than raising the supply line. (The implications are the same.)

THE LONGER-RUN RESPONSES AND EFFECTS

If the supply in the long run were perfectly elastic, it would, in our preceding example, be horizontal at $1.10, that is, the long-run price would be $1.10. All the tax would then appear to be borne by consumers. But there is a loss of

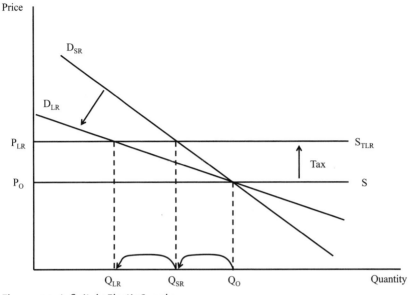

Figure 17.3 *Infinitely Elastic Supply*

wealth to owners of refinery equipment, which fell in value and was therefore removed from production. That hits them as a one-time loss of wealth. The consumers suffer a series of purchases of gasoline at higher prices. That series of future higher payments has a present capital value, which measures how much of their wealth is taxed, even though the payments are strung out over time.

The reduced rate of production is achieved at lower average and marginal costs. That reduction in costs at a lower rate of production offsets part of the tax. As a result, the net effect is a long-run price that is not raised as much as in the short run, with a horizontal long-run supply curve. Also, the long-run equilibrium output rate would be smaller, since production is reduced more in the long run than in the short run.

FOR WHAT IS THE TAX USED?

We are not to ignore what is done with the collected tax. It might finance more and better streets. You might say that the worth of the streets is greater than the worth of what's not produced. That would mean a social gain — greater total personal worth, not less. That is the public policy basis for taxes — to finance worthwhile activities that would not otherwise have been possible.

REDUCING NEGATIVE-WORTH EXTERNALITIES

Some gasoline is converted to noxious fumes with *negative worth* to the rest of society—a negative worth that is generally ignored by the user. That's a *negative externality*. The market price of the gasoline overstates the worth of the gasoline use.

The tax, by raising the price of gasoline, would make the traveler bear at least some of the cost of the negative worth of the pollution. The reduced amount of gasoline used would be closer to where its marginal worth for travel matched the marginal cost (the worths of the forsaken alternative products and cleaner air).

Unfortunately, no one knows whether the present gasoline tax (or any tax) is too high or too low. That is, no one knows whether the cost of further reductions in air pollution is worth the higher cost of travel. But economic analysis helps to deduce some effects of a market for rights to pollute—to use the air—similar to the way we buy rights to dump garbage in a garbage disposal site.

ADJUSTMENTS BEFORE *PREDICTED* EVENT OCCURS

Consider the timing and persistence of some responses to an *anticipated* change in demand.

a. Demand for transport to skiing resorts predictably increases spectacularly during the winter. Response: special (seasonal) airline flights are quickly supplied.
b. In Washington, DC; Hong Kong; Manila; and many other cities, hundreds of people with full-time jobs become taxi drivers during rush hours.
c. Steel mills use their higher-cost furnaces during peak demands, as do electrical power suppliers; employees work overtime at higher wages.
d. Barber-shop and hair-salon chairs that are idle most of the time are maintained for use when demand is transiently high.

None of these involve *excess* capacity. These so-called higher-cost resources are the *cheapest* ways to meet predictable peak demands quickly. The temporarily high demands make such extra (not *excess*) capacity profitable. That available extra capacity, like a second car in a family, is idle most, but not all, of the time. Resources for temporarily high demands are often called marginal resources or marginal firms. Every firm is always on the fringe (margin) in terms of its rate of production, because it generally could produce more, and it certainly could produce less.

GASOLINE AND OIL PRICES

Prices sometimes seem to change before or without any change in demand or supply conditions. At other times, they seem not to change when demand and supply have changed. The price of gasoline, for example, is said to rise *too soon* when supply falls, and to fall *too slowly* when supply increases. Some existing producers are said to restrain new competitors by premature price-cutting, sometimes labeled *predatory* pricing. But competitive pricing and supply situations commonly are misinterpreted.

Gasoline prices rise quickly when crude oil prices rise, but they do not fall as quickly when crude oil prices fall. The same asymmetry occurs for frozen orange juice, coffee, cotton, and meat. Why?

a. Gasoline, along with several other refined products like plastics and fuel oil, is made from crude oil.
b. Gasoline is expensive to store, compared to the cost of storing crude oil; gasoline stocks at refiners are very small, about a couple of weeks' worth of consumption.
c. Most critical for the present question about the speed of responses is the fact that future goods can't be brought backward to the present, while existing goods can be carried forward to the future by storing them. The fall crop of apples cannot be brought backward to the previous spring, but they can be stored for the winter by canning or drying.

These facts — especially item c — help explain the asymmetric timing of response of product prices to changes in supplies of inputs. News that an oil-producing country in the Middle East has been invaded by a neighbor creates an expectation of a reduced future supply of oil. It would be foolish to sell current inventories of petroleum at a price far below what is expected in the near future. Crude oil available now above ground in storage tanks can be withheld for use in the future at the expected higher price. The current price rises immediately. But the reverse is not the case. Expected larger future supplies of oil (or any other good) cannot be brought to the present — although current producers who have excess capacity can produce now at a higher rate in order to sell more at today's higher price, before the new supply comes on stream and results in a lower price.

The adjustment process is eased by spreading it over time. Some oil that would be consumed today if prices were kept low by price controls is held for the future when supplies of oil will be scarcer and more valuable. The higher present prices reduce consumption now. More is withheld for future refining, when it will be worth more. Prices of oil in the future will then be lower than if more oil had not been withheld from the present.

This immediate price rise does not reflect or presume monopoly or collusion of refiners. Indeed, conserving more of the present inventory for future use helps to offset the future reduction in supply.

The same thing happens with the price and consumption of wheat, cotton, oats, soybeans, and so forth. When the future crop begins to appear smaller than formerly expected, the newly expected higher future price is instantly reflected in a higher price of present supplies. (Of course, if it were some non-storable good, the future higher price would not be reflected in a big jump now: current strawberries cannot be held as fresh strawberries for a future higher price.)

Yet members of Congress sometimes complain that oil refiners are acting improperly when the price of gasoline immediately increases in response to news of a new war in the Middle East. Regardless of the motives of oil refiners, the conservation and the higher price ease the task of adjusting to a smaller supply. The immediately higher price is a messenger. Punishing the messenger doesn't change the message or aid in adjustment to the decreased supply.

Changed present anticipations and forecasts of prices or supplies of future goods affect current prices if present stocks can be saved and carried to the future. If they can't be saved, the present price of the existing supply would not rise significantly when a future decrease is expected.

Some years ago, the federal government, in response to environmental concerns, mandated that gasoline had to emit fewer pollutants. One state, California, went further and enacted relatively severe requirements for refiners of oil to invest in expensive technology. The air would be cleaner for each gallon of gas burned, but each gallon of that cleaner-burning gasoline yielded fewer miles per gallon.

The California price of gasoline did rise as expected. Nevertheless, the public bought more gallons of gasoline to obtain their desired miles traveled, and the refineries profited. Does this go against the law of demand that says that less is demanded at higher prices? No, because the supply of gas also shifted.

The persisting higher price was the result of government-imposed conditions on the refiners, equivalent to results of an effective conspiracy by the

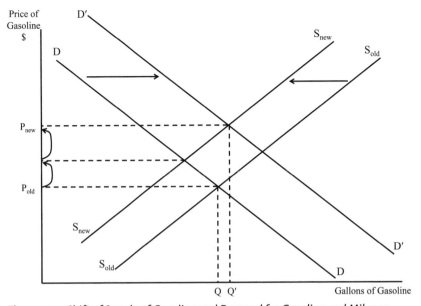

Figure 17.4 *Shift of Supply of Gasoline and Demand for Gasoline and Mileage*

The cleaner-burning gasoline is more expensive, indicated by the leftward shift of the supply curve in figure 17.4 from S_{old} to S_{new}. People demanded more gallons of the new gasoline to help offset reduced mileage per gallon. Both the shift of supply because of higher costs of production of cleaner-burning gasoline and the upward shift in demand for gallons of the new gasoline resulted in a higher market-clearing price of gasoline and increased profits for the refiners.

refiners. In a *privately* attempted conspiracy, the refiners would have to agree to reduce production or require each to raise its price. But each would then try to gain by secretly lowering price or increasing quality, or both. Here, the government helped enforce both requirements. No refiner could ignore the official mandate and sell the old kind of gasoline that cost less.

COMPETITIVE PRICING RESPONSE TO NEW ENTRANTS: IS IT PREDATORY?

Predatory pricing suggests that the intent of price-cutting is to impose losses on competitors in order to drive them out of business and also to dissuade potential entrants. Then, it is alleged, the price is raised above this predatory level. It is uncertain that this has ever been effective in competitive markets. The initial price cut would cause losses to the predator, and it would be costly to repeat that behavior to deter all future entrants. More to the issue here, what looks like predatory pricing can be something that is economically efficient, and not motivated by predation.

Table 17.1 *Existing System's Long-Run and Short-Run Costs*

Annual Depreciation per Channel	=	$1,000

($1,000,000/50 channels equals
$20,000, which for a 20-year life is
$1,000 annually.)

Operating cost [Short-Run Cost]		$200
Annual Long-Run Cost per Channel		$1,200

Suppose Old owns a telephone service capable of carrying 50 simultaneous calls — we will call these channels of service. When the copper-wire line, expected to last 20 years, was purchased and installed at a cost of $1 million, all the initial investment cost became sunk, with no salvage value in any other use. The cost of operations is $200 per year per channel. When the initial investment of $1 million was made, say, 15 years ago, it was expected that enough revenue would be earned to provide at least $1,200 per channel, which is the annual 20-year equivalent of the $20,000 initial investment per channel (ignoring interest rate discounting) plus $200 per year for operating costs. The expenses are summarized in table 17.1.

Once the initial investment had been made, revenue exceeding the $200 per channel annual operating costs is enough to warrant continued operation for the short run — though not enough to recover the initial investment cost, nor warrant reinvestment in the future. We suppose that the present price of service is $1,200 for a year's service per channel, which is just enough to recover the entire initial investment cost plus the continuing operating cost. (We could have supposed demand was high enough to yield $1,500, which would have made the original investment very profitable, but, as we'll see, that wouldn't change the issue involved here.)

New, a potential entrant into the business, announces the intention to invest $1.5 million in a fiber-optic system that can handle 50 telephone channels, lasting 50 years. Once built, the entire investment would be sunk. The pertinent data are summarized in table 17.2.

New must expect minimum revenue of $675 annually for 50 years for each of the 50 new channels; otherwise the investment would not be profitable. Because of new, low-maintenance technology, annual operating cost per channel is estimated at $75, which would cover the continuing costs of operation, and

Table 17.2 *New Proposed Investment*
(We conveniently assume a zero interest rate.)

Investment = $1.5 million for 50 channels, which is $30,000 ($1.5million/50 channels) per channel for 50 years, or $600 annually per channel ($30,000/50 years)

This results in:

$600 annually (= $1.5 million/50 channels/50 years = $30,000/50 at zero interest rate)
+$75 = annual short-run operating cost
$675 = annual long-run cost per channel

---

anything above $75 would be left to go toward the initial investment of $600 per channel. Therefore, $675 will be the long-run costs, with $75 of that covering the short run — if the investment were made.

Upon hearing about the proposed investment by New, Old warns New: "If you invest in new equipment, the price will be cut below your cost." While the new system, at an anticipated revenue of $675, would be considered economical, once the investment is made (and therefore sunk), revenue could fall to as low as $75 without forcing the newcomer to cease operations.

Suppose that before the New investment, revenue is $1,000 per channel per year. That might look as if the new investment would be profitable. However, if the new fiber-optic system were installed, which would double the total market supply to 100 channels, all those channels would be demanded only at a lower per channel price. Perhaps the price would fall from its present $1,000 down to $500 as the two systems compete for customers.

At that lower price, the old system would continue to operate (so long as the price didn't fall below $200). But New would have regrets, because the revenue would be less than the $675 needed to cover long-run cost per channel. New would suffer a loss, the actual amount depending on how long Old continued to operate and what the revenues would be after Old ceases operation. New would continue to operate, because its continuing costs are only $75 annually per channel, and although losing money — not recovering its sunk investment — New would be minimizing its losses by operating at any price over $75.

So the investment by New would have been premature and therefore wasteful. The resources needed to invest in creating and operating more channels so soon are worth more elsewhere (which is what the cost measures) than they are worth here (which is what the revenue measures).

If Old's earlier warning to New were taken as a threat, New might allege *predatory intent.* But if New foresees the competitive effects of a larger supply on the price and the irrelevance of sunk, initial investment costs for existing operators, New will refrain from, or postpone, the investment. New will wait until the demand for services is large enough to support 50 additional channels (for a total of 100) at a price of at least $675 per channel, or until the old copper-wire system is closer to wearing out.

QUESTIONS AND MEDITATIONS

1) A tax of 1 cent is levied on each pound of peanuts grown by farmers.
   a. What effect will this have on the output of peanuts?
   b. How will it induce that effect?
   c. What will happen to the price of peanuts?
   d. Will the land on which peanuts are grown fall in value — in view of the facts (i) that peanuts are grown from plants that must be seeded every year, and (ii) that the land can be used for other crops?
   e. What will happen to the value of *existing* machines used for harvesting, shelling, roasting, packaging, and crushing peanuts? Why?
   f. Explain why these changes in value will not be permanent even though the tax is permanent.
   g. Does the temporary drop in value (of land and equipment) mean that the wealth-reduction effect of the tax is only temporary? Why or why not?
   h. The proceeds of the peanuts tax are used to finance purchases of this book for free distribution to college students. Who is paying for the books so distributed? (The answer is *not* that those who lost wealth from the revised valuation of existing resources are paying for books. That loss of wealth is not offset as a gain to anyone else.)
   i. Who gains what as a result of the tax and expenditure of the proceeds?

Answer:
   a. Reduce the output.
   b. At first, if output is not reduced but taxes are paid, the wealth of peanut growers will fall. Higher marginal costs indicate a lower output as the new wealth-maximizing output. Or some who formerly made a profit or broke even will now have a loss and be induced to abandon or reduce peanut production.
   c. Reduced supply, shown by shift of the supply curve to the left, implies higher price.
   d. Land will fall in value only to the extent it was worth more for peanut growing than for next best use.

e. A tax imposed on the output — peanuts — will reduce the value of specialized equipment used to produce the product.

f. As marginal peanut farmers cease production in favor of some alternative crop, remaining peanut farmers will be able to restore profitability by charging higher prices; total market supply will be less and the value of resources that continue to be used to produce peanuts — land and equipment — will be restored.

g. The wealth loss to peanut farmers that exited the business in favor of the next best alternative is real and permanent.

h. Peanut consumers.

i. We would have to know how the government uses the proceeds of the tax on peanuts to know who may be gaining.

2) Suppose that the tax in the preceding question is levied against only *one* producer of peanuts.
   a. What will happen to the price of peanuts?
   b. To the output?
   c. To the wealth of the various peanut producers?
   d. Whose wealth will be affected by this tax?

Answer:
   a. Nothing noticeable.
   b. Nothing noticeable, since the one producer yields a trivial part of industry supply.
   c. This taxed producer will lose wealth of resources specialized to growing peanuts on his farm. Other peanut producers are unaffected.
   d. See answer to c.

3) In question (1) above, after full adjustment to the new tax on peanuts, has there been a "deadweight loss"? What does that mean?

Answer:
   Yes, a deadweight loss occurs as a result of the eventual decline in the total production of peanuts. The difference in the lower value of alternative crops that are produced instead of peanuts versus the value of peanuts is a social loss and a measure of the burden of the tax. Nothing in this answer helps to know whether the society is worse off or even better off because the uses of the proceeds of the tax are not known.

4) Long after the tax on peanuts has been put into effect, the demand for peanuts has increased and existing peanut farmers have become more

profitable. An investor is considering whether to acquire some land and enter the business of growing peanuts. If he does, how much of the burden of taxes on peanut production will he incur?

Answer:

A new entrant into the business of growing peanuts will not incur any of the tax burden imposed on the production of peanuts. The prices he will have to pay for land and equipment to grow peanuts will already reflect the existence of the tax.

5) Pittsburgh put a 20 percent tax on gross receipts of private commercial parking-lot operators while exempting competing publicly operated lots. The US Supreme Court held the tax constitutional even though its enforcement may destroy particular businesses. The Court also concluded that, in any event, a shortage of parking spaces in Pittsburgh would enable private lot operators to pass the 20 percent gross receipts tax on to their customers. The burden of the tax thus will fall upon customers. Is the Court's economic analysis correct? Explain.

Answer:

Ability to "pass tax along" to consumers will depend upon relative elasticities — slopes of demand and supply curves. The Court's ruling assumes the price of parking in the privately operated lots will rise by the full amount of the tax because of a "shortage" of parking spaces. Such an opinion implies that the private parking lot operators were charging less than a market-clearing price prior to the tax. It also implies that even in the longer run, visitors to the city will not choose to switch from driving to use of buses or trolleys as a result of the higher cost of parking.

6) It is learned that there has been very bad weather in regions that are major coffee growers, so supplies of coffee will be smaller. The result is an almost immediate increase in the price of coffee. Alternatively, it is learned that there are expected to be bumper crops in coffee-growing regions next year, but the current price of coffee does not decline in spite of the expected increase in supply. Explain the asymmetry.

Answer:

In the case of expected future smaller supply, current stocks of coffee beans can be stored (at some cost) in expectation of even higher prices of coffee in the future. That adjustment causes the current supply for sale to be less than otherwise — hence the higher current price. However, future coffee beans cannot be brought forth for current consumption, so the only effect on current prices will be if current coffee bean holders decide to carry smaller inventories forward and thereby increase current supply for sale.

7) "The government decides to levy a tax on a commodity. It could tax the sellers of the good and thereby induce a reduction in supply, or it could tax consumers and thereby reduce demand. It is better — fairer and less disruptive — to tax businesses rather than individuals and households." Is this sound public finance?

Answer:

As illustrated in figures 17.1A and 17.1B, it does not matter how the analysis is couched. It can be stated in terms of reducing supply or of reducing demand. In either case, the effects on quantity bought and sold and price are the same, with quantity reduced and the price paid by the consumer rising (by less than the unit tax) and price received net of tax received by the seller falling (by less than the unit tax) — with a deadweight loss to society, because the resources released from reduced production of the good will be less valuable in an alternative use.

CHAPTER 18

FACTS OF LIFE

An experienced business manager's opinion about the analysis and presumptions in the preceding chapters is likely to be:

"First, you've overlooked the entrepreneur, the risk-taking experimenter, innovator of new and improved products, techniques, and lower costs of production.

"Second, hardly any producer makes a complete product and gets the entire price paid by the consumer. Receipts are divided among producers of components of the final product. That division has been ignored.

"Third, business managers don't know or record costs in terms of marginal costs. Indeed, they don't calculate marginal costs and marginal revenues and then select some price. They can only try to make some profits, not *fine-tune* to *maximize profits*.

"Fourth, in almost every firm some equipment helps produce several products at the same time. An airplane carries both passengers and freight. It's impossible to know what part of the cost of the crew, airplane, and fuel is caused by freight and which part by passengers. This is the pervasive problem of allocating costs of several jointly produced products.

"Fifth, there's a big difference between *rate* and *volume* produced. The volume effect on cost was ignored. The marginal cost of additional units of volume falls when larger amounts are produced, in contrast to higher marginal costs at higher rates of production. Producing things at a faster rate is not the same as producing more of the goods. A higher speed of a car is not the same thing as more distance traveled. One can drive slowly for a long distance or rapidly for a short distance, and similarly for rates of output and aggregate volume.

"Sixth, on the demand side, too, the aggregate volume and the rate per day are important differences. One customer buys three today; another buys only one today but will do so every day. The volume that will be demanded is as important as the rate demanded now.

"Seventh, almost all business firms, big and small, are not price-takers who must choose how much to produce and sell at the given market price. Instead, they each set some price and advertise for customers who choose how much to buy.

"Eighth, some goods are more highly demanded the more widely they are used by others. The more people using that kind of good, the more valuable it is to a user, such as telephones, internet, fax machines, credit cards, and computer operating systems and application programs. This is a *network* effect. It traps, or locks in, all the users into that one network, and restrains successful entry of improved networks.

"Ninth, repeated transactions take place in markets with other *specific persons* — not with *people in general*. If a person who is relied on doesn't do what was expected, the results could be far different from *mutual benefit of exchange*. These dependencies on another specific person and the actions taken to ensure reliability of the dependency to avoid losses by disappointments have been ignored.

"Tenth, often when demand increases, sellers prefer to not raise prices and instead tolerate a shortage in supplying some customers. The supply is then rationed among more dependent customers. Your analysis is not consistent with this fact.

"Eleventh, firms are far more complicated than pictured here. They usually are corporations with owners, most of whom hardly ever do anything except invest and hope for dividends and higher stock prices. They have long-time employees, working in teams, directed and supervised by a boss, and paid wages, rather than by some market prices and daily negotiations about wages.

"Finally, unlike a fishing boat, where only the number of people on board is important and all employees receive the same wage, in many if not most firms wages differ because the employees are not identical. Differences in personal abilities and traits upset the law of diminishing returns, which applies only if the added inputs are identical in every respect. Not just numbers of workers, but also who they are, affects production and wages."

We'll attend to the first six objections in this chapter, and we will deal with the others in later chapters.

THE MISSING ENTREPRENEUR

Fortune does not hand down information and guidance to discover improved techniques of production and distribution of better products. It's obtained by investing in risky exploration and experimentation with one's own wealth. Some experiments, perhaps most, fail. The failures disappear with little publicity.

An entrepreneur is more than an investor. Entrepreneurs think of new ideas and make investments in research with trial and error in the hope of finding profitable products or methods of production and distribution. Entrepreneurs, though trying to augment their personal wealth, have improved the well-being of the populace, and not merely by competing in prices of goods. They have invested in attempts to discover better goods and methods of production and distribution.

Innovators can't rely on *rules*. But it seems clear that entrepreneurship is stimulated and enabled in a private property capitalistic society, where each person can experiment without prior approval or permission and where the rewards and failures are more concentrated on the experimenter.

The successful ideas or products of entrepreneurs typically displace inferior products and procedures. Entrepreneurship is both creative and destructive. But it creates more worth than it destroys if the entrepreneur is profitable. The successful entrepreneur captures some of the net gain in the profits obtained. If the creative worth is less than the destruction, the entrepreneur suffers a loss.

EXAMPLE OF EFFECT OF CREATIVE DESTRUCTION

As we saw earlier, if at an additional cost of 3 cents per bottle Coke is made better than Pepsi, and that improvement is worth 5 cents, a consumer will switch from Pepsi to Coke when each is priced at one dollar. Pepsi loses a whole dollar of sales. Therefore, the customer, who gets only 5 cents more of worth, seems to impose a one-dollar cost on Pepsi.

But the loss to Pepsi is not the lost $1 of sales revenue. Instead, it's Pepsi's *profits* that Pepsi loses, and that's a lot less than $1 per bottle. And the loss to Pepsi is not a social loss; it is a transfer from Pepsi to consumers.

The resources not used by Pepsi, when making less Pepsi, are worth up to $1 in other uses. The loss to Pepsi could include reduced value of resources that are not transferable to other uses without some drop in their value. The gain to Coke consumers exceeds the reduced value of resources specialized to Pepsi production, since Pepsi producers could otherwise have offset that gain through lower Pepsi prices or better quality.

A transfer from one person to another (*loss* to one person and *gain* to another) is a loss of resource values, not a reduction of consumer worth. Creative destruction is that which results in a creation of wealth exceeding any destroyed wealth. *Accompanying* creative destruction is a reallocation of wealth, but the gains exceed the losses.

MANY PRODUCERS OF A CONSUMER PRODUCT

The second objection was that several people are involved in the process as a series of links in a sequence of production from raw materials to finished products. For wheat to be converted to pasta on the table, a farmer grows wheat; a miller mills it into flour; a pasta maker makes it into pasta; and a grocer sells it to the consumer.

From the final consumer price, the grocer takes some, the pasta maker takes some, and then the miller takes a portion, with the farmer getting what's left. Or maybe it's the other way around. Initially, the miller — when buying the wheat — pays the farmer. After the wheat is milled into flour, the pasta maker pays the miller, the grocer pays the pasta maker, and finally the consumer pays the grocer. The grocer keeps any excess of the price of the pasta over the cost of the pasta. The risks are borne differently in the two approaches, but the basic process is the same.

The pasta was sold for $1, its market value. The grocer competitively obtains $.05, leaving $.95. *Competitively obtained* does not mean the grocer competed against the pasta maker, the miller, and the farmer for some of the $1 final product value. The grocer competed against other grocers. The grocer willing to pay the largest amount, $.95 out of the $1, to all the other producers in the successive stages, was the winner — the surviving grocer, who settled for $.05, with $.95 going to the other stages.

The winning baker, who paid the miller $.35 for flour, was able to obtain, or derive, only $.60. The miller was left with $.35 from which he competitively derived $.20, while the winning farmer competitively derived the remaining $.15. This competitive derivation is also called competitive imputation of values. They are typically called added values, though they are also subtracted values — subtracted (derived, imputed) from the final product value.

If the cost in each firm is greater than the competitively derived added value, the firm will not survive. If some firms obtain more than enough to maintain their services, others will begin to enter, competitively reducing the amount taken at each stage. That will result in larger outputs at each stage, which increases the supply and reduces the market prices of the intermediaries' services and of the pasta.

MANAGERS DON'T KNOW THEIR COSTS AS ACCURATELY AS THOSE SHOWN IN THE EXAMPLES

The third objection was that hardly any manager knows the cost data or future market price sufficiently precisely to move to the profit-maximizing rate. That's true, but it does not falsify the economic analysis or make it uninteresting.

Managers are not totally ignorant. They know enough to curtail use of inputs whose prices have increased and to shift to lower-priced ones. They know that increased sales of products suggest that increasing output would be better than reducing it. They know that higher prices of inputs raise costs — which we represent as an upward shift in marginal costs. That means the profit-maximizing output is smaller. They may not know the amount of the best change, but they usually know the direction. And they experiment through trial and error. If adjustments aren't made after rational calculation, they are confronted by inescapable force and incentive — survival of the fittest.

Even if managers were totally passive and acted randomly or just stayed put, those that happened by chance to make a change, or had already been doing what is now most appropriate to the new circumstances, might cover costs and reap profits. They'll be the lucky survivors and grow. Those that don't make the right adjustments, or didn't happen to be in the right situation, are less likely to survive.

Whether the successes are those who deliberately and consciously knew the correct adjustment, or were closest by chance, is irrelevant. The managers who, for whatever reasons, were nearer the marginal-cost-equals-marginal-revenue situation will be the competition survivors. All that economic analysis can do is help us deduce whether a larger or a smaller output, or a smaller or larger amount of some inputs, will be more profitable when circumstances, such as demands or prices, change.

Of course, some producers, by compiling data with which to estimate costs, may increase their probability of being nearer the wealth-maximizing output rate. They know that when demand rises and sustains a higher price, an expanded output becomes more profitable, even if they may not know how much larger the output should be.

We all notice successes — the survivors — rather than the failures. The magazine *Fortune* is popular, but there is none called *Misfortune*. Some people are relatively successful because of better information, better ability, or better luck — or a combination of all three. Economic analysis does not depend on the basis of their decisions, or methods of calculation and reasoning, or whether they think in terms of marginal costs and adjusting output accordingly. What finally matters is who is in, or nearest, the profit-maximizing situation — not how they got there. Both informed rational calculation and good luck can play a role.

ALLOCATING COMMON COSTS TO JOINT PRODUCTS

The fourth complaint of the practical business owner was that some costs can't be allocated among products that are produced together, such as the cost of feed for meat and hides of cattle, or fuel costs for passengers and freight on an airplane.

This objection is correct but not significant. It is not necessary to distribute common costs accurately among the jointly produced products. To know how much feed to give the cattle, all that's necessary is knowing whether the marginal value of an extra dollar spent for feed brings in more than a dollar of revenue, no matter whether from hides or meat.

With airliners, it's the marginal costs of a passenger or a pound of freight that is pertinent. That decision doesn't involve accurately distributed common cost. Just ask how much the total cost of all inputs is increased when carrying more passengers or freight in the cheapest way—total costs, without regard to whether the costs are more for common inputs, or for costs of services used only by passengers, or only by freight customers.

Getting data to estimate the marginal costs will be hard, but what is to be estimated is unambiguous and pertinent. In contrast, attempts to distribute the common costs accurately among the joint outputs must be arbitrary. For purposes of efficiently managing a business, there's no point in trying—hopelessly—to find the correct allocation of those costs that are common to many products.

Consider a situation in which the event for which the cost to be estimated is ambiguously identified. A baker supplies cookies to a retail grocery chain, called A. Later, along comes retailer B, desiring a small number of cookies from the baker. Data in table 18.1 show how confusion can arise—and be avoided.

Ovens and other equipment will have to be used to produce the cookies for A, whether or not cookies are baked for B. Producing cookies only for A has a cost of $90. The baker can bake the extra cookies for buyer B, and the total cost for both A and B will be $140.

The cost of baking cookies for B on the condition that some are going to be baked for A in any event is $50 ($140 − $90). However, if baking for B alone

Table 18.1 *Costs of Joint Products?*

Production only for Customer A	$90
Production only for Customer B	$60
Production for Customers A and B	$140
Production for B, on condition that cookies are being produced for A	$50 ($140 − $90)
Production for A, on condition that cookies are being produced for B	$80 ($140 − $60)

were already under contract at cost of $60, then the extra cookies for A would have cost $80 more ($140 – $60). On one basis, we get a cost of $50 for B (with cookies also being baked for A), but on another we get $60 (without cookies for A). Similarly, we get two different costs for A: one with B and one without B. Which is correct? They both are.

Finally, maybe the situation is, "Cookies are going to be baked for both A and B, with no cookies being baked otherwise. What is the cost of baking for both?" The answer is $140, and there is no implied unique allocation of that cost between the two.

The more pertinent question is what price could be charged to each. The answer is a price of $90 to A, for that is the price formerly being charged to A. And $60 is what B is willing to pay. But the answer is *at least* $90 and $60. The best prices depend on factors we investigate in the next chapter. At present, the moral is: Do not confuse the question of what price to charge with the question of what the costs are. And be sure the act whose cost is being measured is precisely identified.

SUPPLY IN TERMS OF MASS PRODUCTION AND THE VOLUME PRODUCED

Larger amounts, or volumes, of output cost less per unit of output. The marginal and average costs of volume decrease at greater outputs. That's true for virtually all goods produced.

There is an important distinction between (a) the rate, or speed, of production, and (b) the volume, or amount, of output. Until now, we have measured output almost always with respect to the rate of production. But producing beer at the rate of 60 barrels per day doesn't tell how many barrels are brewed, unless you know how long that rate is maintained. And knowing only the total volume doesn't tell how many per day are being produced.

When referring to greater output, we must specify at least two of the following three dimensions of amount of output: (a) the rate of production; (b) the planned volume; and (c) the length of the time production will continue. Any two of those will imply the third.

It's probably true also that the larger the *volume* to be produced, the lower will be the marginal costs at various possible *speeds* of production. Stepping up the rate of production from 30 to 31 units per day — when the total volume to be produced is 5,000 units — is probably less expensive per bottle than if the total volume to be produced were only 100 units. The techniques of production for larger volumes are usually also techniques appropriate for speedier — higher rates of — production.

Learning, Progress, Experience Curves

For at least two reasons, average and marginal costs are lower for larger volumes. One is that people learn from the experience of production, of trial and error. As more units are produced, people discover better component designs and production methods. Producing a larger volume, at any given rate, takes longer, so general knowledge-enabling imitation of discoveries elsewhere is more likely, the longer the time. So the larger the volume — and the longer the time over which to acquire new knowledge — the lower will be the unit and average cost.

Divisibility

Another reason for lower unit costs with mass production is that a wider choice of techniques is available for larger planned volumes. Larger volumes could be produced using the best of small-volume techniques and repeating the process, but not all large-volume techniques are economical for small volumes. To paint automobiles, you could use large, paint-dipping vats and heating ovens to dry the paint. That technique could be used for just one car at a very high cost, but it would be much cheaper per car in painting a thousand cars.

Learning during production is so pervasive and reliable that cost engineers in many large firms refer to a learning or experience or progress or 20 percent learning curve, indicating (with exaggerated precision) the percentage reduction in marginal unit cost with each doubling of the volume of production. It's also called an 80 percent curve, meaning a doubling of volume reduces marginal costs to 80 percent of what they were at the smaller volume.

SUMMARY OF COST AND VOLUME OUTPUT RELATIONS

Subsequently, we'll be relying on the following propositions about how costs are related to rates and volume of production.

a. Total costs are higher at faster rates of outputs, for a specified volume, in both short- and long-run operations.
b. Marginal costs and average costs of rates of output may fall at very low rates of production, but they will rise at higher rates of production. This is true for short-run and for long-run production. For virtually any specified volume of production, faster rates of production will have higher total, average, and marginal costs.
c. The average and the marginal costs are lower for production of larger volumes.
d. When both the rate and the volume are increased, the net effects on the

average and the marginal costs are impossible to generalize, except that the rate effect will ultimately dominate.

WARNING

These propositions about cost and production are quite reliable, but they are not all based on some known physical law of nature. It is possible that in some situations, the product and its rate, or its volume, of production will exhibit patterns of costs different from these standard relations between costs and rate and volume of output.

DEMAND IN TERMS OF VOLUME DEMANDED

Once the importance of volume and the rate of production is recognized, it's easy to see that a seller or producer must be influenced by how long a buyer/demander is expected to purchase at that rate. The longer the duration of that rate of purchase, the greater is the volume. A buyer demanding ten a day for just today can be far less important to a supplier than a buyer demanding one a day for a year.

The Two-Dimension Demand for a Good:

a. the *stock* demand, as the amount to have on hand or owned; and
b. the *flow* rate of demand, for the rate of current consumption

The demand for computers can be thought of as: (a) the quantity of computers the public wants to have on hand — a stock, and (b) the rate of demand for more computers — a flow — measured as the number per day purchased for current use as well as for building or maintaining the stock on hand. As discussed in earlier chapters, economists sometimes distinguish between a good's value-in-use and its value-in-exchange. The price for which a person might be willing to sell something already possessed and in use is likely to be different than the price that same person would be willing to pay for something desired and not already possessed.

THE HISTORICAL PATTERN OF PRICES OF A PRODUCT

The relatively wealthy are the first demanders of a new product. We often observe that the initial market prices of new products are viewed as quite high to the average consumer. Quartz watches, cell phones, and high-definition televisions are recent examples. Then, as the rate of purchase declines when demands of high-worth buyers are satisfied, prices will decline to cater to demanders with lower marginal worths. Prices will be lowered also because of a larger output at lower costs of production resulting from learning and production by new firms — competition from new entrants.

QUESTIONS AND MEDITATIONS

1) Heat and light are joint products of an electric light bulb that uses electric power at the rate of 1,000 watts. In one hour the cost of the power is 5 cents.

   a. How much does the light cost? How much does the heat cost? How much do the light and the heat together cost?

   b. If you were selling the heat to someone, how much would you charge him? And if, at the same time, you were selling the light to someone else, how much would you charge him?

Answer:

   a. Can tell only that both together cost 5 cents an hour.

   b. No way to distinguish the buyers with cost data only. With open markets, the price of the package will be competitively lowered to a level where receipts from the joint products are just sufficient to cover the costs of production.

2) Meat, wool, and hides are joint products of sheep.

   a. What assurance do you have that the prices paid for meat, for wool, and for sheepskin are just adequate to cover their cost of production?

   b. What assurance do you have that meat users are not paying a disproportionate share of the common costs?

Answer:

   a. None. That they will not far exceed it for long is a result of open markets.

   b. None.

3) A filmmaking company once advertised, "The price of a new organic chemical depends on how badly it is wanted — precisely as conceived by classical economic theory, except for reversal of direction. The bigger the demand, the lower the price. A 1,000-pound-per-day process operates more efficiently than a 1,000-pound-per-month process — which is obvious to you but wasn't to Adam Smith. Old Adam set down the rules for our game in ignorance of elementary chemical engineering and advanced advertising." Explain wherein the ad writers for the company are doubly confused — on both the demand and the supply side.

Answer:

> The ad writers have mixed up rate and volume effects on costs. A greater supply—volume—implies a lower unit cost and also a lower price. Bigger volume demand yields lower price because it evokes a greater supply (in volume sense). But in the *rate* (or speed of production) sense, higher demand yields a higher price. When demand increases in both the volume demanded and the speed at which that volume is demanded, price may fall (in response to volume effect), but it will be higher than otherwise in order to increase the rate of production. What advertising can do is to affect the volume demanded, but if it also increases the rate at which the good is demanded, it leads to higher prices.

4) A firm plans to produce 2 million cameras in the next six months. What is the volume and what is the rate of output?

Answer:

> 2 million is volume. Rate is 4 million per year.

5) If that rate in the question above is continued for one year, what will be the volume?

Answer:

> 4 million units produced in the year, with rate of production unchanged.

6) What happens to marginal and average cost per unit for larger rates of output with constant volume?

Answer:

> They begin to increase.

7) What happens to marginal and average cost for larger planned volumes with unchanged rates of output?

Answer:

> They decrease.

CHAPTER 19

PRICE-SEARCHERS

Hardly any business firm is a pure price-taker, although the price-taker model explains important features and operations of the economy. The next step up the analytic chain is explanation of *price-searchers*, often called sellers with *market power* or *monopoly power*.

PRICE-TAKERS AND PRICE-SEARCHERS

Price-takers can sell as much of their good as they choose without having to cut the prevailing market price. But price-searchers cannot sell as much as they want at their announced selling price. Even if each price-searcher is offering the same physical product, the convenience, service, and personality of the sellers may result in some customers preferring one seller over all others. Sellers are not perfect replicas of each other.

Customers' preferences may be sufficiently strong that at a slightly higher price many customers continue to buy. Some rivals offer better services, or are more reliable than others, at least in the opinion of some buyers. Some are located closer to the consumers; some are more pleasant. Neither the seller nor the offered goods are identical among competing sellers. A slightly higher price will not push all customers to a rival seller. Nor will a slightly lower price attract all customers from a close competitor.

For a seller lowering the price to attract an additional buyer, marginal revenue is less than the price. Unlike a price-taker who can sell more without having to cut the price, the price-searcher knows that he cannot, and as a result, he concentrates on the marginal revenue — the added sales value when the price is lowered. The lower price on all the units sold offsets some of the sales value of the added units sold. Marginal revenue is the net effect of: (1) the additional revenue from the added units that are sold minus (2) the revenue lost by the lower price on the units that could be sold without the price cut.

Though we call them *price-searchers*, these sellers search all aspects of the goods and services and conveniences provided to their buyers. Price-searchers endeavor to sell more, not merely by price reductions, but also by marketing tactics, such as discount coupons for groceries, senior citizen discounts, special sales, free parking, free delivery, return privileges, rebates, quantity discounts, and college tuition scholarships. Price-searchers advertise and have brand names, which enable buyers more readily to identify preferred sellers, but price-takers don't.

DIFFERENCES FOR CUSTOMERS BECAUSE OF
DIFFERENCES AMONG COMPETING SELLERS

There are differences in customer behavior because price-searchers sell products that customers do not regard as virtually equivalent among the competing sellers. And the prices and products of rivals affect the demand facing a price-searcher seller. This contrasts with price-takers, who sell identical products at the same price.

Price-searcher/sellers respond to *changes in the amount demanded* by customers at the existing offer price. This imposes an additional problem for the price-searcher — distinguishing between: (1) random daily changes around an unchanged average amount and (2) a change in the average amount around which the daily sales vary randomly.

No price for a seller's goods is announced in a central market, so a price-searcher has to set his own price, at which potential customers choose how much, if any, to buy. The first law of demand is effective: at a lower price determined by a price-searcher, more will be sold. And marginal revenue is the change in total revenue when the seller reduces the price on all units, reducing it enough to sell one more unit.

PRICE-SEARCHERS SEARCH FOR THE BEST
PRICE TO MAXIMIZE PROFITS

A price announced by a price-searcher reflects that seller's estimate of the demand for its goods. Some customers would buy from a higher-priced seller who provides more service, or is easier to find, or are sellers in whom many buyers have more confidence of getting what they want. They would not depart at the slightest increase in the price, but would demand less because of the higher price. This persistence of some, but not all, customers is why the demand curve facing the seller is a negatively sloped line, rather than horizontal at the market price.

The negative slope of the demand facing a price-searcher causes the marginal revenue to be less than the *price* — which explains almost all differences between the selling tactics of price-searchers and those of price-takers. One effect is that the price charged by a price-searcher will not be the same to all customers, because the customers of a price-searcher differ in the amount demanded and differ in their elasticities of demand for that seller's goods.

Even if sellers offered identical goods and services, not all potential customers would know the items were identical, because getting information is costly. To reduce customers' cost of getting information about various sellers, price-searchers advertise and have brand names (while price-taker/sellers don't).

A difference in *only* the price is not always decisive in buyers' choices among price-searcher/sellers. Automobiles are the same in that they transport you. But not everyone buys automobiles from the lowest-priced seller. Buyers are choosy about competing sellers, and they differ with respect to which features of the seller are more important. Some customers will buy from their favored seller despite that seller's higher prices. This behavior is consistent with a price-searcher facing a negatively sloped demand for its products.

A price-searcher must also engage in *market search* to determine the best price to set while weighing the effects of (a) a *higher price* on each unit sold against the (b) *reduced number* sold at that higher price. The change in total revenue resulting from these two conflicting effects is the marginal revenue.

PRICE-SEARCHERS MUST SET THE PRICES FOR THEIR PRODUCTS

Price-takers, such as farmers, face a price at which they each decide how much to produce and sell. However, for a price-searcher, customers choose how much to *buy* at the price set by the price-searcher.

Presumably, the price a price-searcher should announce is the price that maximizes the seller's profit. But determining that price is not easy. Competing producers offer similar products and advertise their offerings to help customers search the market. Though the products of different sellers are the *same* in a rough sense, they are not entirely the same.

A difference in the prices is not the only thing that counts in a customer's choice among sellers. But potential buyers do not know the differences in qualities of goods and services of competing sellers before shopping, nor are they known with certainty even at the time of purchase.

Shoppers squeeze bread, smell cheeses, heft oranges, sniff perfumes, shake walnuts, choose among shoes, slam car doors, bounce on mattresses, and test the fit and appearance of clothes. Shoppers are attracted by warranties and special services. They rely on a seller's reputation and brand name. There's no *given* market price facing each price-searcher/seller.

Though the attributes of a product may not be tailored to each customer, the price can be tailored, so not all buyers of the same product pay the same price. Negotiations, bargaining, dickering, and bluffing are part of the business for many price-searchers.

SIGNALS TO PRICE-SEARCHERS

Unlike price-takers—who do not regard other producers of similar goods
as rivals—price-searchers recognize other sellers as competitors. A price-
searcher is affected by, and takes account of, the prices of rivals. Since there
is no given market price for the price-searcher, evidence pertaining to demand
conditions includes *changes* in the *amount demanded* at that seller's *current offering
price*. But changes in amount demanded can vary from day to day at random,
complicating assessment of the market and the activities of the other sellers.

PRICING AT A UNIFORM PRICE TO THE ENTIRE PUBLIC

The negative slope of the entire public's demand facing a seller (1) permits
certain pricing and selling tactics, and (2) leads price-searchers to adjust price
as well as production in response to changes in amounts demanded. Whereas
price-takers adjust only production in response to a change in the given market price, price-searchers are responsive to changes in amounts demanded at
whatever price is posted.

An important effect of a negatively sloped demand is that the marginal revenue is less than the associated price, as in table 19.1.

PRICE VERSUS MARGINAL REVENUE

Though the amounts demanded and sold are greater at lower prices, that's not
invariably the case for the total sales revenues (the total market value of the
purchase), as illustrated in column 5. Marginal revenue is the change in the

Table 19.1 *The Demand Function and the Associated Marginal Revenue*

Price (1)	Daily Quantity (2)	Personal Worth (3)	Marginal Personal Worth (4)	Total Revenue (5)	Marginal Revenue (6)
$1.00	1	$1.00	$1.00	$1.00	$1.00
.90	2	1.90	.90	1.80	0.80
.80	3	2.70	.80	2.40	0.60
.70	4	3.40	.70	2.80	0.40
.60	5	4.00	.60	3.00	0.20
.50	6	4.50	.50	3.00	.00
.40	7	4.90	.40	2.80	−0.20
.30	8	5.20	.30	2.40	−0.40
.20	9	5.40	.20	1.80	−0.60
.10	10	5.50	.10	1.00	−0.80

total sales revenue when the price on all units is lowered enough to sell one bottle more each day.

Note the change in total revenue when the price is lowered to $.80 (from $.90) in order to sell 3 rather than just 2 bottles. Total revenue increases by only $.60, not the $.80 price at which the third bottle is sold, because the price was lowered on all bottles sold. So long as an additional unit is sold by lowering the price on all units, marginal revenue will be less than the price at which the additional unit is sold.

If the price is lowered enough to sell 4, rather than just 3, the price would have to be reduced to $.70. The total revenue at that price would be $2.80 (= 4 × $.70), only $.40 higher than the $2.40 (= 3 × $.80) when three were sold at a price of $.80 each.

If 5 per day were being sold at $.60 each, lowering the price to $.50 to sell six leaves total revenue ($.50 × 6 = $3.00) unchanged. This price, $.50, is the revenue-maximizing price, at which marginal revenue falls to zero. Going to a still lower price, $.40, to sell seven, reduces total revenue by $.20, from $3 to $2.80, which means marginal revenue is negative. The $.10 reduction in price on each of the six inframarginal units more than offsets the $.40 price received on the marginal unit.

The relationship between average revenue (demand) and marginal revenue is illustrated graphically in figure 19.1.

THE PROFIT-MAXIMIZING PRICE AND QUANTITY: MARGINAL REVENUE EQUALITY TO MARGINAL COST

Next, we identify the price and the associated demanded amount that maximizes a price-searcher's profits, not the total sales revenue. Surviving firms are more likely to be those that somehow had prices and outputs that were closer to the profit-maximizing price and output, no matter what may have been the owners' objectives and tactics. Profit is increased by expanding output and sales as long as expansion increases revenue (MR) more than cost (MC). The profit-maximizing quantity and the price for the product are determined by where marginal revenue is brought to equality with the marginal cost. This is illustrated in general in figure 19.2, where marginal cost is shown as a straight line.

PRICE-SEARCHER WITH *INCREASING* MARGINAL COSTS

For most producers, marginal costs of additional units produced rise while marginal revenue for additional units sold is falling. In table 19.2, assume a fixed cost of $.20 at any level of production. The best profit-making output and associated price are revealed by comparing marginal revenue and marginal cost: expand output as long as that adds more to revenue than to cost.

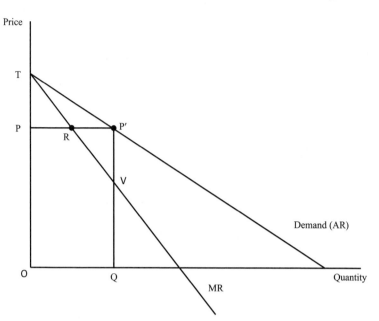

Figure 19.1 *Marginal Revenue and Demand*

Total revenue (price x quantity) is the area OPP′Q. It is measureable also as the area under the MR curve to quantity OQ. OPP′Q = OTVQ, so triangles PTR and RP′V are equal, with equal area and equal corresponding angles. Therefore, PR = RP′: the MR curve bisects any horizontal line from the vertical axis to the AR curve.

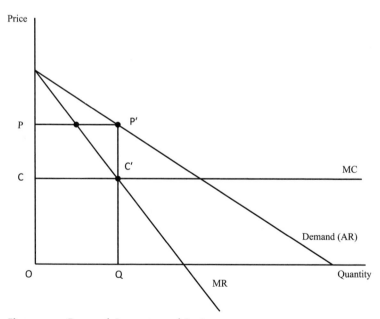

Figure 19.2 *Demand, Revenue, and Cost*

The quantity sold, OQ, is determined where the marginal revenue intersects the marginal cost line, point C′. Going up from that quantity to the average revenue (demand) curve gives the profit-maximizing price, P. Total revenue at that price and quantity is the rectangle OPP′Q; total cost is the rectangle OCC′Q. The difference, profit, is the smaller rectangle CPP′C′.

Table 19.2 *Demand, Revenue, and Costs for Water Sellers*

Price	Daily Quantity	Personal Worth	Marginal Personal Worth	Total Market Revenue	Marginal Revenue	Marginal Cost	Total Cost	Total Profit
$1.00	1	$1.00	$1.00	$1.00	$1.00	$0.10	$0.30	$0.70
.90	2	1.90	.90	1.80	.80	.20	.50	1.30
.80	3	2.70	.80	2.40	.60	.30	.80	1.60
.70	4	3.40	.70	2.80	.40	.40	1.20	1.60
.60	5	4.00	.60	3.00	.20	.50	1.70	1.30
.50	6	4.50	.50	3.00	.00	.60	2.30	.70
.40	7	4.90	.40	2.80	−.20	.70	3.00	−.20
.30	8	5.20	.30	2.40	−.40	.80	3.80	−1.40
.20	9	5.40	.20	1.80	−.60	.90	4.70	−2.90
.10	10	5.50	.10	1.00	−.80	1.00	5.70	−4.70

The optimal output is 3 bottles, with price of $.80. Total revenue is then $2.40, and total cost is $.80, so profit is $1.60. Adding a fourth unit of output would pointlessly increase both cost and revenue by $.40, leaving profit unchanged. And output of five would actually reduce profit. The average cost plays no role here. It does not tell what price to charge, nor whether you are making profits or incurring a loss. (Notice that the sum of the successive marginal costs for each of the rates of output gives the total cost of that output. And the rise in marginal cost means that the average costs increase at the higher rates of production.)

INCREASING MARGINAL COSTS AND THE PROFIT-MAXIMIZING OUTPUT

Marginal costs are higher at faster rates of output. At the maximum profit output and price, the marginal cost matches the marginal revenue and exceeds it at faster rates of production. In figure 19.3, the profit-maximizing rate of output is indicated by the intersection of the marginal revenue curve and the upward-sloping marginal cost curve.

KNOWING PATTERNS OF MARGINAL COSTS AND MARGINAL REVENUES

Rarely, if ever, does the seller know the data required to state the exact profit-maximizing price. Instead, some price, usually close to some competitor's price, is set in the hope it's optimal. The nearer the chosen price to the profit-maximizing price, the greater the probability of profits and survival.

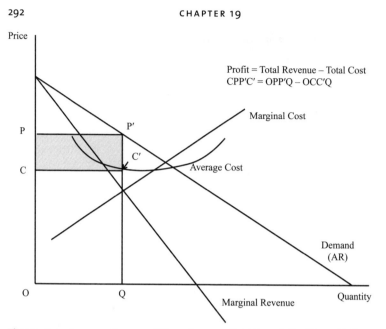

Figure 19.3 shows total costs, total revenue, and total profits as three rectangles. The smooth lines of the graph, in contrast to the lumpy data of table 19.2, reflect continuous function of infinitely small variations in output. Total revenue is the rectangle with a base measuring the output rate and a height equal to the price at the profit-maximizing output, OPP'Q, the equivalent of price multiplied by output. Total cost is the rectangle with the same base, a height given by the average cost curve at that output, OCC'Q. Profit is the excess of the total revenue rectangle over the total cost rectangle, CPP'C'. The profit per unit is indicated by the distance of the price above the average cost at the profit-maximizing rate.

SELLERS AREN'T NAIVE

We said that the profit-maximizing rate of production for price-searchers is the rate at which marginal cost matches marginal revenue. But another kind of pricing strategy can get higher marginal revenue than would be obtained by cutting the price on all units. A greater marginal revenue and greater profit possibility exists if the seller can lower the price on only the additional units sold.

An airline advertises, "Take along your spouse at half fare," which lowers the price on just the second unit. Lower prices to children avoid a cut in price to parents. Discounts to seniors in barbershops and theaters lower the price for only some customers. An offer such as "$5 each, or 3 for $10" lowers the price on only the second and third units, not on the first, because the price is $5 for one, while the prices for the next two are $2.50 each.

Discount coupons give reduced prices on some, but not all, units to a customer, and also to some, but not all, customers. A "free" shuttle ride from an airport to a hotel is a method of lowering hotel prices to some, but not all, customers of the hotel. For movies, ticket prices are not constant over time, starting high when the new movie is released, then lower a few months later. With such price offers on some additional units, total revenue is greater than it would be if the price were cut on all units. The customer achieves more of the *consumer surplus worth*, though in all these pricing tactics the seller's interest is in his profit.

It's tempting to judge that such pricing must be nefarious. In the next two chapters, we'll explore some examples that are especially pertinent when considering national antitrust laws affecting what business firms can or cannot do legally.

CLOSED, RESTRICTED, AND OPEN MARKETS

In addition to the distinction between price-takers and price-searchers, we categorize markets according to the extent to which they are open to everyone without restrictions. *Restrictions* mean contrived, nonnatural, and costly obstacles limiting (or raising costs of) access to customers. They may be minor business taxes and cleanliness standards, not always to be regarded as *undesirable* or *inefficient* in the sense of unnecessarily reducing achievable aggregated personal consumer worth.

The contrived restrictions can be mild or severe. A restriction can be as complete as permitting only specified sellers to have exclusive right to sell. Markets are closed to those who don't pay added costs or meet more expensive conditions of entry. All taxes on goods and tariffs on imports from foreign nations are examples, if we define restrictions to be any imposed cost or physical barrier to trade.

Patents, copyrights, exclusive public utilities, and the one cable TV company in your neighborhood are examples of restrictions on potential rivals. Similarly, there are acreage limits for growing tobacco, on sizes of dairy herds, and in local bus transportation. Not all are necessarily undesirable, but they are contrived restrictions.

Monopoly Rents

Classic early examples of closed markets were the English Crown's grants of exclusive rights to favored persons to import and sell wine in England, or to manufacture playing cards, or to print books, or for whatever the Crown decided to grant an exclusive privilege, with resulting higher prices to consumers. Economists call these gains to the protected sellers *monopoly rents*.

Monopoly emphasizes that the seller is the only permitted seller, and rent suggests that it's a price higher than necessary for the service to be rendered. The combination means a payment in excess of cost and obtained as a result of government closure or restriction of access to the market by competitors. Even where more than one seller is permitted, contrived barriers such as tariffs, quotas, and other restrictions of imports result in some monopoly rents to benefited parties.

WHO IS RESTRICTED BY A RESTRICTION ON THE SELLER?

Usually, market limitations are expressed as restrictions or fees or higher costs on sellers. However, there are instances where the objective of the restrictions is intended to limit potential buyers of a product or service. The difference usually is whether the buyer or the seller will be punished if a sale is made. If you are underage and buy beer, who is punished by the law? If you buy a concert ticket from a scalper, who is punished by a law against reselling tickets? While the intent is to prevent a purchase from being made, it will be the seller who will be punished by the transaction.

CATEGORIES OF SELLERS

We have seen that whether sellers are classified as price-taker or price-searcher is based on the extent to which the marginal revenue is less than the associated price. If they are equal, the seller is a price-taker. If marginal revenue is less than the associated price, the seller is a price-searcher.

In a large market economy, business organizations are found in vastly variegated forms and appearances. They differ enormously in size, from street vendors to massive institutions. They produce both personal services and physical goods, some specializing narrowly and others offering much variety. Some sell to final consumers, others to other firms and to government. Traditionally, most firms are privately owned, but there are significant government enterprises, some joint arrangements of private and government control, and much government regulation throughout the economy. And, of course, some prosper some of the time while others fail and disappear.

How can we usefully categorize and generalize in analyzing this business world of such complexity? One approach is to specify a continuum of market structures:

Monopoly Duopoly Oligopoly Monopolistic competition Competition

Price-Searcher   Price-Taker

By usual definition, a "monopolist" is a single seller of a good, while "competition" requires so many sellers that no one of them can perceptibly affect the market. "Duopoly" refers to a market of two sellers. "Oligopoly" involves more than two, but only a "few," sellers. But the respective classifications are not functions only of the number of sellers. Especially in contrasting "monopolistic competition" from "competition," there is the consideration of product differentiation: we have monopolistic competition with many sellers offering products which are deemed by consumers to be somewhat differentiated.

There are still further complications. Duopoly is designated as a two-firm industry. But there is much substitutability among most products. Might we consider a third firm sufficiently similar to the first two to constitute a three-firm "industry"?

And how few are a "few" in an oligopoly? Is there an oligopoly when only three firms dominate the product group—or should we include four or five dominators? And what constitutes "domination"? Twenty percent or 30 or 40 or 50 percent of something? Percent of what—sales revenue, profit, assets, customers, employees?

Interdependence and concern for strategies and tactics of other firms bulk large in most segments of the market. A price cut that would be profitable if other sellers did not also reduce their prices could be a disaster if competitors do cut their prices. Even the monopolist takes note of advertising and innovating and investing and government taxing and regulating and subsidizing elsewhere—or he may not long remain a monopolist.

All is not hopeless in trying to comprehend the essence of things. Economic concepts and techniques of analysis provide much system and order in our thought. But we cannot realistically expect complex classifications always to be perfectly clear-cut and unambiguous.

WHO IS A MONOPOLIST?

One widely used pair of labels is *seller with market power* and *seller with monopoly power*. A seller with market power may be simply a price-searcher, someone who must select a price. A seller with monopoly power might mean a seller whose products are so widely and so strongly demanded (say, Apple iPads) that this seller's price and offering significantly affect the demand and hence prices of other sellers.

Congress has been unable to specify what it meant when legislating that, "It is illegal to monopolize or attempt to monopolize or be a monopoly." The resulting confusion among lawyers, legislators, judges, and the general public is almost sure to be found in any lawsuit alleging monopolistic behavior. Probe beyond emotive names and look, for example, at such things as whether contrived restrictions (like patents or copyrights) are affecting competitors' access to markets, and whether a seller can affect only its price, or also the demand and price of other sellers.

For price-takers, we could choose the label competitor. Similarly, instead of price-searchers, we can say monopolists, sellers with monopoly power, monopolistic competitors, imperfect competitors, price-setters, or sellers with market power. At any rate, the seller must try to find the best price, whether that seller is your local grocer, gas station, clothier, plumber, shoe-repairer, restaurant, or college.

CARTELS

A cartel is a group of sellers who manage to act jointly, as if they were one big firm, by arranging for the many sellers to act as one price-searcher. In some nations, the government permits or promotes otherwise independent competing firms to coordinate their actions. ("Collude" would be the word, if the action were secret and illegal.)

In the United States, cartels are common. Producers of milk, tobacco, raisins, wheat, cotton, and peanuts are some who are allowed and encouraged by the government to determine aggregate production jointly as if they were a single firm as part of the farm support program.

The entry of one more supplier imposes a very small and unnoticed downward pressure on the market price and profits to all the others. The federal government suppresses "excessive" production. Everyone must be prevented from privately and secretly expanding. The group wants to concentrate attention on the group's marginal revenue rather than on just the price.

PERSONAL SERVICES?

The pertinence of the price-taker/price-searcher distinction is unclear for *personal services* of an individual. Almost anyone can get some work at different earnings. Everyone is unique, even twins. We have to choose between thinking of people as price-searchers with a choice of jobs producing different earnings (thus selecting a price for one's services) or of individuals as price-takers with no influence on earnings. We'll use this classification exclusively for business firms although it is applicable to unions, some of which are *closed* while some are *open*.

OBJECTIVES OF THE LANGUAGE OF ECONOMICS
AND THE LANGUAGE OF LITIGATION

The procedures and objectives in litigation have spawned a language adapted to dispute, emotional appeal, and confusion. In the sciences, language is oriented toward explaining and testing evidence objectively with no regard to a preferred goal, result, or beneficiary.

In a notorious antitrust litigation against Microsoft, when Bill Gates was asked, "Is Microsoft a monopoly?" a useful answer would have been: "Yes, in the sense that Microsoft faces a negatively sloped demand curve for its products. And so are almost all the other merchants in the economy. If you mean that Microsoft is protected from some competitors, it is, because it holds patents and copyrights, both of which are legal. If you mean something else by monopoly, tell me what you mean."

Federal law says only that it is illegal to monopolize or attempt to monopolize, but the law doesn't say what *monopolize* means. Presumably, it didn't mean negatively sloped demand curve. One meaning would be: "You compete in ways that don't maximize total consumer worth though your fine products have increased consumer worth. It's illegal to compete in a manner that reduces total consumer worth below what you otherwise could have created." But the law has never used this last test, because every seller and buyer would be acting illegally, unless they were acting as price-takers with no bargaining about the price.

We now look at the objection to price-searcher behavior and the praise for price-takers — usually and misleadingly characterized as objection to monopoly and praise of competition. We start with the simplest, strongest case, the closed-market monopolist.

OBJECTIONS TO (1) CLOSED MARKETS AND (2) PRICE-SEARCHERS IN OPEN MARKETS

We note three reasons why closed markets are considered to be bad. First, they restrain potential competitors from exploiting their production abilities. That reduces the potential total productivity, as illustrated by the gain in total output when the Adam-Baker economy was opened to Carter (in chapter 15).

Second, resources and effort are diverted from productive uses to attempts to obtain and maintain political support for constraints on competitors' access to markets. Competition, being inescapable, moves from markets and price competition toward political arenas, and that altered and restricted competition is a waste.

Sellers who are protected by contrived restrictions devote much attention and effort to maintaining the restriction. Once obtained, closure must be maintained with continued costly political pleadings for continued protection. Competition for government favors is *political rent-seeking*. Such rent-seeking is regarded as a subversion of the democratic process with resultant corruption of the government.

Third, the discipline of market competition is reduced. A competitor spurs your ingenuity — in wooing a mate or playing on a team or competing for grades. Similarly, producers are more alert to discern and seize opportunities to reduce costs, improve products, and better serve customers.

NORMATIVE STANDARD FOR THE LAWS: OPEN MARKETS AND FORGONE CONSUMER WORTH?

Consider a (*normative*) proposition about what is *good* or *bad* about price-searchers and restrictions on access to markets. To guide the policy of what are acceptable (i.e., not illegal) competitive actions, there must be a criterion of what are good and what are bad effects. The criterion is fairly well identified by the consistency of actions of government agencies responsible for surveillance of marketing and organizational actions. The two agencies are the Antitrust Division of the US Department of Justice and the Federal Trade Commission (both examined later). The goal appears to be that of maximized consumer worth, expressed also as consumer sovereignty or open markets. But the real problem is to know which actions have undesired effects.

The culprit is that price-searchers pay attention to marginal revenue, not to price. The price-searchers' profit-maximizing rate of production is that at which marginal cost is brought to equality with marginal revenue. Because marginal revenue is less than the price, the profit-maximizing rate of production is a rate at which marginal cost is less than the marginal worth of the product to consumers. That is, the rate of production that maximizes profit to the seller is smaller than the rate at which marginal cost would equal the price, which measures the consumer's marginal worth.

"MONOPOLY" DISTORTION: INEFFICIENT OUTPUT RATIO

The reduction in personal worth resulting from producing an amount at which marginal cost is lower than the price (marginal worth to the buyer) is occasionally referred to as monopoly waste. Avoiding that loss is regarded as one of the major objectives of national antimonopoly policy embodied in federal and state laws, especially the federal Sherman Act of 1890 (considered later in chapter 26).

So price-searchers are said to produce too little. And because the label monopolist has been attached to every seller facing a negatively sloped demand, this is commonly called monopoly inefficiency.

In figure 19.4, the profit-maximizing price-searcher's output has a marginal cost equal to marginal revenue, and marginal revenue is less than price. The value of an additional unit to consumers is the price, not the lower marginal revenue to the seller. But the seller heeds the smaller marginal revenue, be-

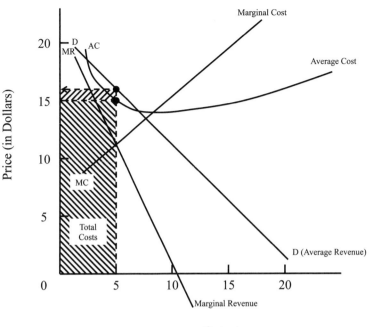

Figure 19.4 *Price-Searcher's Profit-Maximizing Output and Price*

A price-searcher, whose marginal revenue is less than price, has a profit-maximizing output where marginal revenue equals marginal cost, at five units of output. The price is $16, which yields a one-dollar net above the costs of $15 per unit.

cause that is what he would get if he sold an additional unit (and all his output) at that new price.

An additional unit would be worth $16 to consumers; the resources required to produce it are elsewhere producing products whose value to consumers is only about $12, the marginal cost at six units. That is what marginal costs measure. Resources are then used elsewhere to produce products worth only $12 when they could have produced here a product worth $16 to consumers — a sacrifice of a potential social gain. This lost value is often misleadingly called the result of monopoly distortion, although it is not a result of "closed" or restricted markets. The distortion arises because the seller rationally heeds the marginal revenue rather than price of the last unit produced and sold. Since the extra receipts to the producer would not equal the price, but instead would equal the lower marginal revenue (because he must cut the price on all the units sold in order to sell more), he declines to produce more. If he could somehow sell more for what they are worth to consumers — the prices at those outputs — without at the same time having to cut prices on all the former rates of output, the extra revenue would then be equal to the price of those extra units rather than to the lower marginal revenue when prices are cut on all the units sold.

By the maximum-consumer-worth criterion, the rate of output should be that at which the marginal cost rises to equal the price, rather than equality with the lower marginal revenue at the smaller rate of production. But a price-searcher/producer who wants to survive must maximize profits, not consumer worth.

IS IT REALLY WASTEFUL OR INEFFICIENT?

Though the preceding misdirection of some resources is called "wasteful," think a bit further. Waste or inefficiency is only what can be avoided at a cost less than the waste. If the cost of avoiding some seeming waste is greater than the waste, it's not really a waste.

In a supposedly ideal world, would we eliminate the price-searcher situation? We then would eliminate variety and everything that made one seller's goods and services different from those of other sellers. All automobiles, clothes, shoes, and restaurants would have to be uniform. But price-searchers are ingenious, and use pricing tactics that actually do tend to increase output toward the consumer-worth-maximizing output, as we'll see in the next chapter. Some of these actions are challenged as *anticompetitive*, because they are not normally seen in price-taker markets. Another reason they are challenged seems to be some confusion and ambiguity about the meaning of consumer worth.

LONG-RUN RESPONSE: CAPACITY AND COST
RESPONSE TO DEMAND CHANGES

So far the analysis has concentrated on the response of existing firms to changed demand: existing firms expand with higher demand. But increased wealth of existing firms cannot be long concealed. Firm salesmen know who is doing well. In various ways, the word gets around. Other firms imitate this firm. Employees organize their own company, taking with them part of the company's know-how. Hundreds of firms have been created by former employees of older electronic-computer companies. If the production of electronic organs, pianos, Cokes, or Arrow shirts becomes more profitable, others will produce close substitutes and dissipate the profit of the first producer as some customers switch to the substitutes.

Profit streams of innovators and lucky firms are reduced as competing producers enter this market and bid up prices of resources: assemblers, su-

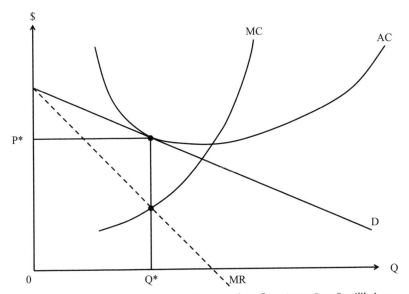

Figure 19.5 *Price-Searcher's Output, Price, and Profit at Long-Run Equilibrium*
No other price than P* and its output Q* would avoid losses. Imitative competition, making similar products available, pushes demand toward this situation. Innovative activity can push the situation away from this result, then initiating forces tending to restore it.

pervisors, designers, production engineers, salesmen, managers, and research staff. As these employees respond to competitors' offers, their wages rise, and hence their current employers' costs of keeping them rise. Formerly undervalued inputs are paid more, absorbing the profits into costs and terminating the undervaluation of resources. Their owners are richer. This is as true for land, buildings, and labor—whether the labor be plumbers, managers, or teachers—as it is for resources owned by a business. Even the cost of an owner's own services in his business must be valued at a higher figure; the more he can earn in his own business, the more others are willing to offer for his superior managerial skills. Those sacrificed options in other jobs with higher pay are *costs* of continuing in his own business. Figure 19.5 is a sample of a zero-profit long-run equilibrium, with price equal to average total costs.

If demand falls, the events are reversed. Values imputed to currently used resources fall. Those resources will be shifted to other activities where the values of their services are not so low. Business owners and all other resources whose values are affected will be poorer because consumers' demands for their prior services are lower. To keep them at their old jobs at the former income would require compelling consumers to continue to buy things they no longer value so highly. And that can't be done in a free-enterprise open-market system. But it can be done if sufficient government authority can be exerted by special taxes to subsidize those producers — a topic we explore later.

The zero-profit solution shown by figure 19.5 assumes that no special services are given to some customers to achieve the output at which marginal cost equals price.

THE MEANING OF CONSUMER WORTH
AND TO WHOM IT BELONGS

Consumer worth is the *most* a buyer would be *willing to* pay for a good. If the consumer gets a good for less, the consumer gets a gain, a consumer surplus. "Consumer surplus" may suggest that it *belongs* to the consumer. If you place a personal consumer worth of $100 on something I offer to you at my cost of only $60, should that $40 differential have been obtained by you? Is there reason for believing that if I had charged $75, instead of only $60, I'd be inappropriately taking some of *your* consumer surplus?

You might contend it's *your* consumer worth. You insist that the market price should just cover costs because consumer worth *belongs* to the consumer. A seller could respond, "I produced that good. I created that consumer worth, which you verified by being willing to offer its full worth in order to get it. If I were the only producer, the price could be high enough that I would reap the full gain.

"Nowhere in Economic principles is there any implication as to who should get how much of the worth of the product. You want more of what I created, and you think I deserve no benefit or only enough to keep me working with all the benefit going to consumers. Consumers are merely passive opportunists. Producers are the real contributors to welfare."

Whatever your opinion, economic analysis has nothing to say about the best or most appropriate or fair division of the total personal worth of a good.

This chapter introduced several distinctions, categories, and concepts. The first was in the demand facing the seller. In chapter 16 we saw that for price-takers, the marginal revenue to each seller always is the same as the given market price. But when a seller does not face a given market price, we must focus on the associated marginal revenues.

The second distinctive feature between price-takers and -searchers is in the market signal that guides production decisions. (a) For price-takers, prices are determined by all demanders in the organized commodities spot and futures markets. For each price-taker, a change in the market price of the good guides that producer's production decisions. A price rise motivates a larger output. (b) There are no such markets for price-searchers, except possibly producers who specialize in commodities that do have central markets, such as copper, gas, and petroleum products (heating oil and gasoline).

For a price-searcher, the guide to a change in the rate of production is not a price change. Instead, it's a change in *rate of demand* for the product. An unexpected rise in quantity demanded at an unchanged price motivates a larger output, because that will be profitable. The price tends to be changed only later when the increase in demand appears to be longer lasting than just a transient increase.

QUESTIONS AND MEDITATIONS

1) Product differences:
   a. Can you suggest some goods for which the differences among various brands are insignificant? (Hint: sugar, flour, aspirin, white bread, milk, soap, corn flakes, canned peaches.)
   b. What do you mean by an insignificant difference?
   c. What makes you prefer one brand over another at the same price?
   d. Can you name any good and two of its brands for which you believe "no one in his right mind" would have a good reason for preferring one over the other?

2) Answer the questions concerning the following demand schedule. Complete the total revenue, marginal revenue, and average revenue data.

Table 19 Q&A

Price	Quantity	Total Revenue	Marginal Revenue	Average Revenue
$20	2			
19	3			
18	4			
17	5			
16	6			
15	7			
14	8			
13	9			
12	10			
11	11			
10	12			

a. What happens to the difference between the selling price and marginal revenue?
b. How many units would you want to produce and sell if you could produce as many as you wanted at an average cost of $8 per unit and if you wanted to maximize your net receipts (revenue minus costs)?
c. What price would you charge?
d. Could you charge $18 if you wanted to? What would be the consequences?

Answer:

a. It goes to inframarginal purchasers at a lower price. For example, between a price of $18 and $19 with sales of 4 and 3 units, respectively, the marginal revenue, $15, is less than the average revenue, $18, by $3. This amount is distributed to buyers of the three units by a price that is $1 lower than formerly.
b. Seven units.
c. $15.
d. Yes. But profits are less than if the price were set at $15.

3) Searching for price:
   a. How can a price-searcher be searching for a price, when in fact there is available an infinite range of prices — any of which he can charge?
   b. What happens if he is not good at finding what he is searching for?

Answer:

a. He is searching for the wealth-maximizing price.
b. He is likely to find himself losing money as others enter the business and reduce the price-cost spread.

4) A theatrical producer expressed delight that tickets for his play had been sold out for the next four months. Explain why he might have cause to be sad, rather than happy.

Answer:

A higher price would have induced a smaller quantity demanded. If the price was below the market-clearing level, some increase in price would simply reduce the "shortage" of seats, and all the seats of the theater could still be sold. If the price were raised enough, some seats would remain empty, but if demand were inelastic, total revenue from ticket sales would increase.

5) What is the wealth-maximizing output for a producer with zero costs? At the price to be charged for that output, what is the elasticity of demand (average revenue)?

Answer:

> If costs are zero, then marginal cost is zero, and marginal revenue will equal marginal cost at the output where the marginal revenue curve intercepts the horizontal axis. At that output, revenue is maximized, so elasticity of demand equals unity.

6) The difference (for pricing and output behavior) between price-taker's and price-searcher's markets can be characterized by a difference in the demand curve facing each seller. Describe the difference in the demand curves.

Answer:

> Price-taker's demand curve is horizontal at highest price at which seller can sell any of his product, while in price-searcher's market his demand curve is a negatively sloped function.

7) For some products, you prefer one brand over the other if both have the same price, but if there is any price difference between them, you will take the lower-priced one.
   a. Would you say that you discriminate among brands?
   b. Is that justifiable, rational discrimination?

Answer:

> a. Yes, although the strength of your preference may sometimes be very small.
>
> b. It is, when I do it.

8) Compare and evaluate the following two assertions:
   a. "Advertising and brand names create impressions of differences among competing brands where no significant difference really exists. As a result, because of consumer ignorance, sellers face a less elastic demand and can raise price without losing all sales to competitors. Creation of impressions of significant product differentiation by advertising is a social waste."
   b. "Advertising and brand names identify rather than create differences among products. They permit customers to know more surely, cheaply, and fully the differences among various products. Otherwise, customers would select blindly, letting the price difference be their only reason for choosing one over the other, much as people would choose purely on the basis of price among superficially identical goods. By identifying products and their makers more fully prior to purchase, brand names and advertising permit customers to be more,

and not less, discriminating about qualities with less costly other investigation into product details. Hence advertising and brand names make demands less elastic because they identify more fully differences in product and quality assurance as a social benefit."

Answer:

Doubtless, there is truth in each statement. Advertising can consist largely of fiction and exaggeration. But where there is virtually no overt advertising, consumers are denied much useful information.

9) "Sony announces a new 55-inch flat-screen television for $1,000." "Apple iPads are sold at an announced price of $495." "Sunbeam appliances are sold at retail prices set by the manufacturer." If prices are pronounced by sellers, why aren't these prices set perhaps three times as high?

Answer:

Price that maximizes sellers' wealth depends on demand, not simply on their desire for more wealth. Prices three times as high would, in the judgments of sellers, yield smaller wealth or profits.

10) Suppose a $5 tax is levied on your business — an annual license tax of a flat $5 regardless of how much you produce.
    a. What will this do to your price and output?
    b. What does it do to profits?

Answer:

    a. Nothing. While the flat tax doesn't affect current output and price, it does affect profits. If the tax raises total costs (by raising average fixed costs) above marginal revenue, the price-searcher will not reinvest and will go out of business.
    b. Reduced by $5.

11) As a superior student, you provide a tutoring service to other students. The higher the price you decide to charge, the fewer the hours of work you get.
    a. Are you a price-taker or a price-searcher?
    b. The daily demand for your tutor services varies at "random" around a mean rate of daily demand which depends on the price you charge. If, at the price you currently charge, you find that all your available time is always used, and there are occasional applicants whom you must reject because you are fully booked up, do you think you are charging the wealth-maximizing price? Explain.

  c. If you are charging a price at which you occasionally have idle time, are you charging too low a price?

  d. Given a fluctuating demand, how can you be sure that you have charged the right price?

Answer:

  a. Price-searcher.

  b. If you could serve as many, or virtually as many, customers at a higher price, you have not been charging enough.

  c. If raising the price appreciably reduces the number of customers, we have a question involving elasticity of demand. If demand is inelastic, raising the price will increase the revenue.

  d. You can't be sure. You appeal to observation, experimentation, estimation, and tea leaves.

12) In what sense can the marginal cost curve of a price-searcher be considered a supply curve?

Answer:

In the sense that it indicates the amounts of the good that the productive resources would be willing to provide through the intermediary of the businessman. But it does not present the supply schedule of the amounts actually forthcoming at each potential selling price of the good, because the intermediary businessman is heeding marginal revenue rather than price (average revenue). Only if marginal revenue is essentially equal to price, or very close to price, will the marginal-cost schedule approximate the supply schedule, and no significant difference will exist between price and marginal costs.

13) Suppose you could live in a society in which trademarks were not protected by law and anyone could imitate the trademark.

  a. As a consumer, would you prefer to live in that world or in one where trademarks were exclusively reserved for a particular manufacturer as a part of his property? Why?

  b. As a producer, which would you prefer?

Answer:

  a. As a consumer, I welcome aids in identifying and remembering producers I have found attractively reliable—and those I wish to avoid in the future.

  b. If you worked to develop and produce a reliable product, would you want to have some way customers could distinguish your product from those of competing producers? If the consumer cannot readily identify which product you produced, how would that affect your incentive to produce a product of a high quality?

14) Tentatively classify the following, on the basis of your present information, as a) price-takers, b) closed monopolists, or c) open monopolists. (Remember, market closure does not necessarily convert a price-taker's to a price-searcher's market.)
Electric company
City bus line
Airline
General Motors Corp.
Corner drugstore
Prescription pharmacist
Microsoft
Lettuce grower
Electrician
Pop star

Answer:

Distinguish between open-market price-searchers and closed or restricted market access. That is, how difficult/costly is it for potential competitors to enter a market if the incumbents are either unusually profitable or operate with high-cost inefficiency. Closed markets imply higher price. Also, government-sanctioned monopolies have less incentive to operate at lowest-cost efficiency.

15) "Retail grocery stores are monopolies." In what sense is that correct and in what sense is it false? "The medical profession is a monopoly." In what sense is that true and in what sense false? Which kind of monopoly implies a higher price?

Answer:

If a grocery store raises prices, it will sell less; at lower prices it will sell more. At a given location, a grocery store has an exclusive right to offer products to customers, but there is not restricted entry, and so potential competitors will enter the market if they can do so profitably. The medical profession restricts entry through licensing, which implies higher prices than if there were no barriers to entry.

16) Higher costs have induced a firm to reduce output and raise price.
   a. Is this to be interpreted as an example of the power of the price-searcher to raise price?
   b. If your answer is no, how do you reconcile your answer with the President's Council of Economic Advisers, who, some years ago, regarded the attempt of Alcoa to raise the price of aluminum as an "unjustified" use of the power to set prices?

Answer:

Greater final demand for a product causes greater demand for the resources to produce the product. Any one producer will see his own costs of production rise, and will justify his "need to raise prices" as a reflection of his higher costs of production. If Alcoa justified its higher prices as reflecting the higher costs of bauxite or natural gas to produce aluminum, it may be that the demand for those inputs had risen.

17) "Every profit represents the gain from moving resources to higher-valued uses." Do you agree?

Answer:

No. Fortunately, this is commonly the case, but the statement ignores cases of monopoly rent and government-imposed restrictions of entry.

CHAPTER 20

PRICE-SEARCHER PRICING

Noting the difference between price and marginal revenue, several common but often misunderstood pricing tactics can be explained. The effects of some of the tactics are criticized as undesirable, while others, which do exactly the same thing, are praised.

Basically, some of the tactics attempt to equate marginal revenues to marginal costs to maximize normal profits. But a few do more—transfer more of the value of the consumer surplus to the seller, even though the output may not be increased. Underlying this entire search is the presumption that the demand for the seller's goods will be high enough to result in a price that covers the cost—but most firms starting in business don't last more than three years.

CHARGING DIFFERENT PRICES AMONG CUSTOMERS TO EQUALIZE MARGINAL REVENUES

Though all customers of some seller's goods may be charged the same price, the marginal revenues from each customer will almost certainly be different. There can be two customers with different demand schedules for the product. Differences in received marginal revenues from selling to them result, though both pay the same price.

Differences in marginal revenues mean the seller isn't maximizing the revenue from the amount being sold. Less should be sold to the lower marginal revenue customer and more to the higher marginal revenue customer—even though that may require different prices. The kind of situation shown in table 20.1 illustrates the demands for two customers and the resulting prices and quantities to each.

Suppose a seller has 8 units available for sale. What's the maximum total revenue the seller could get? (We here ignore the cost of producing them.) At $7, customer A would demand 6 units, and customer B would buy 2, selling all 8. That would bring a total of $56 (= $7 × 8) to the seller, $42 from A and $14 from B.

At that price of $7, marginal revenues are different. Marginal revenue at the sixth unit demanded by A is $2, while it's $6 at the second unit bought by B. That suggests that more revenue might be obtained by shifting some of the units from the lower to the higher marginal revenue customer.

Table 20.1 *Equalization of Marginal Revenues among Customers by Different Price to Each Customer: "Price Discrimination"*

		Customer A			Customer B	
Price	QA	Total Revenue from A	Marginal Revenue	QB	Total Revenue from B	Marginal Revenue
$12	1	12	$12	0	0	0
11	2	22	10	0	0	0
10	3	30	8	0	0	0
9	4	36	6	0	0	0
8	5	40	4	1	8	8
7	6	42	2	2	14	6
6	7	42	0	3	18	4
5	8	40	−2	4	20	2
4	9	36	−4	5	20	0
3	10	30	−6	6	18	−2
2	11	22	−8	7	14	−4
1	12	12	−10	8	8	−6

If the price to customer A were raised to $8, at which only 5 units would be bought, the revenue from A would change from $42 (= $7 × 6) to $40 (= $8 × 5), a reduction of $2. That unit could instead be sold to B by lowering B's price from $7 to $6, at which B would buy 3 units. The revenue from B will rise from $14 (= $7 × 2) to $18 (= $6 × 3), a marginal revenue of $4. The $4 marginal revenue for B more than offsets the loss of the $2 marginal revenue from A, and the two marginal revenues are equated. The total revenue is now $58 (= $40 + $18), a gain of $2 (= $58 − $56). To maximize total revenue from a given number of available units to sell, the prices have to be such that the marginal revenues are equal.

This marginal revenue equalization, in order to maximize revenue, is called price discrimination because the prices are different. If it's to be successful, the lower-priced buyers must not be able to resell to the higher-priced customers by undercutting the higher price.

WHAT RATE OF PRODUCTION?

Moving beyond a predetermined number of units to be sold, what determines the amount produced? Suppose marginal cost is a constant $2 per unit. Equating MC and MR for each customer, data in table 20.1 show that output will be 10 units, with 6 sold to A at $7 and 4 to B at $5.

At a price of $7 to A, marginal revenue is $2, and total revenue from this customer is $42. That's the profit-maximizing price for A. At a price of $5 to B, marginal revenue would be $2, and total revenue is $20.

Two conditions are satisfied: the marginal revenues are (a) equalized for both customers and (b) equal to marginal cost. Total profit is maximized at 10 units. Producing more units would incur marginal costs exceeding the possible marginal revenue.

MARGINAL REVENUE EQUALIZATION:
PRICE DISCRIMINATION?

This kind of differential pricing is *price discrimination* because the prices are not the same to all customers. Discrimination suggests something bad, so we'll call it marginal revenue equalization. The applicability of this principle of equalizing marginal revenues is easily illustrated. In figure 20.1, an equal price, P_0, charged to both buyers A and B would result in amounts sold of Q_a and Q_b. However, by raising the price to A to P_A, and lowering the price to B to P_B, more will be sold to B at greater revenue over cost, and less will be sold to A.

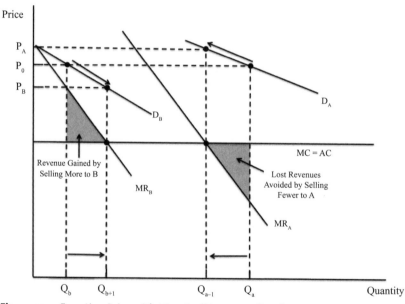

Figure 20.1 *Equating Price with Marginal Revenue of Each Customer*

Any seller whose prices to different buyers result in unequal marginal revenues among buyers would increase his profits by changing prices so as to equate marginal revenues. This is shown in the diagram with the gains to seller (or avoidance of losses) being shaded. This price differentiation is called price discrimination. If it is to be successful, lower-priced buyers must not be able to resell to higher-priced buyers.

The data in table 20.1 could represent customer A as Japan and the United States as customer B. The goods being sold are automobiles made in China. The price to buyers in Japan is $8 — higher than the $6 price of the same cars sold to buyers in the United States. That pair of prices equalizes marginal revenues of both markets. A transport cost of any amount up to $2 would be worth incurring in the process. This is the situation in which goods are shipped, at some cost, to distant markets and sold at a lower price than at home or nearby markets. It pays, because the carmakers can get a higher marginal revenue by more sales in the distant markets than from local customers, despite a lower price in the distant markets. The price to the US customers covers the marginal costs incurred by the Chinese manufacturer.

DUMPING IS NOT SELLING BELOW COST.
IT'S SIMPLY MARGINAL REVENUE

Foreign countries are sometimes said to be *dumping* their products in the United States when the price of the exported goods is lower in the United States than in the home country. It is asserted also that the foreign producers are subsidizing US customers by selling at prices below cost. But the producers are not being charitable. Every unit is covering the cost of production, with marginal revenues that exceed their associated marginal costs. The prices are different, but the marginal revenues are equalized.

American consumers are delighted. Within the United States, the objectors are those who own resources and sources of income specialized to the manufacture and sale of domestic products competing with imports. Some members of Congress request federal agencies to announce that "dumping" is occurring and hurting US producers and therefore is to be prohibited by denying or taxing imports. But restricting such imports is counterproductive. It's analogous to Baker's restricting the entry of Carter in chapter 15.

COLLEGE TUITION SCHOLARSHIPS?

What does a college do when it gives tuition scholarships to talented, less-wealthy applicants? Applicants with higher demand (wealthier parents) are not given discounts. The discounts to lower-income applicants are sometimes called "charging only what you can afford to pay."

A wealthy student might be willing to pay $30,000 tuition, whereas a less-wealthy one would be willing to pay only $8,000. Setting a tuition rate of $8,000 to attract both would get the college $16,000. But the college could charge more, say $30,000 to each — and at the same time award a $22,000 tui-

tion fellowship to the low-income student. In that way, the college would collect $38,000.

DISCOUNT COUPONS

A discount coupon is a device to cut the price to some, but not all, customers. Prices may be raised a bit when first issuing coupons for purchases of specified products. People who use the coupons get a price a bit lower than the original price, though they incur some cost of collecting, assembling, and carrying the coupons with them to the store.

The store divides its customers into two classes: 1) those who were sensitive to a price change and 2) those who were less sensitive. Any loss of sales to the less-elastic customers resulting from the higher prices is more than offset by the gain in increased sales to the high-elasticity customers.

FREE AND SPECIAL SERVICES: A FREE TIE-IN

Free and special services to only some customers can be a means to cut prices to get more customers, without cutting prices on all units to all customers. Free parking, free delivery, free return privileges are often provided by retailers. Those services are costly to produce.

A hotel charges $100 for a room, but it transports some — not all — customers from an airport to the hotel at no charge. The transport costs $15, which the hotel pays, for the shuttle service. The customer pays the hotel $100, of which $15 is spent for the transportation, leaving $85 received for the room. The hotel has cut its room price to this occupant (who takes the airport transport), but it does not cut the price to other occupants who drive there in their own car. That makes the marginal revenue from the subsidized customer $85, which is higher than if the room rate were cut to all customers.

There are many ways sellers try to produce as many units as are worth more to each customer than the marginal cost of producing those units. Each price-searcher is aware of the effect on marginal revenue of cutting prices to all customers on all units. Sellers try various methods of cutting prices on only extra units or only to certain customers who wouldn't buy at the higher price, which is paid by others.

IS MARGINAL REVENUE EQUALIZATION
REALLY PRICE DISCRIMINATION?

If a doctor charges two patients different prices for delivery of a baby, or if a lawyer charges a wealthy person more for preparing a will than he charges a poorer person, is that price discrimination? Probably not. A higher medical fee to a rich patient may be charged because of better, more expensive service to the richer patient. We use the expression *price discrimination* to refer only to those situations in which the product or service is identical in every respect — but different prices are charged to different customers.

Night telephone charges are lower than for daytime, although the costs of providing the service are the same — or are they? Because the demand is greater during the day, the phone company must acquire and maintain greater capacity — bandwidth for cell phones — to satisfy this larger daytime demand. This makes the daytime calls more costly to provide. The fact that night calls are cheaper than day calls for the same service is not an indicator of price discrimination.

The airfare per mile is usually less between mass passenger cities, such as between New York City and Los Angeles, than the shorter distance between New York City and Buffalo. One reason is that it costs less per person per mile in large planes, which can be used if there are many passengers. Mass production is cheaper per unit, and should not be thought of as price discrimination.

It used to be that airfares and other things about air travel were highly regulated. Fares between long-distance, mass-service markets were maintained at higher-than-competitive prices. Competition on such routes resulted in *nonprice* attempts to attract passengers from other airlines — greater frequency of flights, more space between seats, more and better food and beverages, low hotel fares at the destination.

But with deregulation, those "frills" in nonprice competition disappeared as prices fell. To the customers, the frills weren't worth the cost — or else they would have been continued. Airlines have unbundled travel services by separating the basic price of an ordinary seat from the amount charged for other associated services, such as checked baggage, food, more leg room, and entertainment. Customers pay different amounts to get from one city to another, because they value these unbundled services differently.

PRICE-SEARCHER BUYER — MONOPSONIST

A *buyer*, as well as a seller, can be a price-searcher. That is, an individual buyer may be facing a *positively sloped supply curve*, which means that buyers' purchases affect the price. When a buyer's purchases push up the price, such buyers are *monopsonists*, analogous to price-searcher sellers, who are *monopolists*.

You are a price-*taker*/buyer when you shop for food and clothes, because the prices are not affected by how much you demand. In contrast, a price-searcher/ buyer, a monopsonist, could be an employer with many employees in a relatively small town. The more employees he tries to hire, the higher may be the wage that must paid to all workers. The additional employees might have had better alternatives than to work at the lower wages. Some live farther away and will earn less after transport costs. Some have children or elderly parents requiring care.

A higher wage to additional workers can result in two different situations. If only the new employee is paid a higher wage, say $90 a day, while all other employee wages continue unaffected at $80 day, the marginal cost of the added employee is just $90. But there's a reason the wages of all the employees may have to be raised.

WHY HIGHER WAGE RATES TO ALL EMPLOYEES?

Equal wages for all the employees doing the same kind of work isn't a result only of a desire for equality or "fairness." Instead, competitive forces push wages toward that equality. A monopsonistic employer, with 30 employees being paid $80/day, hires a thirty-first at a wage of $81 per day. Any of the other 30 employees receiving the lower wage could then quit. A monopsonist employer faces an upward-sloping (positively sloped) supply curve for labor. Table 20.2 shows an example.

The initial wage rate is $80 a day for each of 30 workers, for a total labor cost of $2,400. If an added worker is available only at $81 a day, the employer's cost of hiring the additional worker will be more than $81 if that higher wage must be paid to all the employees. One dollar more for each of the 30 employees, plus the $81 paid the new employee, is $111. The employer would hire an added worker only if that added worker were expected to result in an increase in total product value ("marginal value product") by at least $111. Though the *marginal value product* of an added employee exceeds the $81 wage for one worker, that person will not be hired unless the marginal value product exceeds the $111 marginal cost of an added employee.

The employer and the potential employee can seek ways to arrange employment without raising the wage to all 30 existing employees. One way is by benefits.

Table 20.2 *Marginal Wage Cost*

Before: Wage Rate with 30 Employees, @ $80/day: Total Wages $2,400
After: Wage Rate with 31 Employees, @ $81/day: Total Wages $2,511

Added Total Wage Cost: The Marginal Wage Cost $111

DIFFERENTIATING BENEFITS

Suppose the potential added worker had a preschool-age child. The employer could offer childcare at a cost of $10 paid by the employer as a benefit. The existing employees would probably object to the inequality if the wage paid to the new employee were $90, while they would more easily tolerate a wage of $80 plus company-provided childcare worth $10.

Similarly, if some employees drive to work and get free parking, while others walk or take the bus, there seems to be little disagreement. And there are some who drink a lot of coffee provided by the employer, while others do not. Even among the coffee drinkers, some like it black while others use cream and sugar.

These real forms of *discrimination* appear almost always to be accepted as reasonable and not nefarious. Perhaps it's not regarded as nefarious because it's not tied to ethnicity, race, or religion (though it can be correlated with gender and age — as with discounts for seniors or ladies day at the baseball game or the local tavern).

Why are benefits that discriminate among employees acceptable and often praised? Why are *senior discounts* for golf or theaters generally regarded as unobjectionable when the situation could as accurately be called a "premium charge for youth"—which likely would raise a fuss?

This divergence between the $81 wage paid to all employees and the marginal wage of $111 is analogous to our price-searcher/seller, whose marginal revenue is less than the price of the goods being sold. The marginal revenue for a price-searcher/seller is below the price because the price of every unit sold would have to be lowered to sell one more. These are the marginals that are compared — the marginal cost and the marginal product value of an added (marginal) input.

Summary of Three Features

1) The profit-maximizing price of a price-searcher is not given by some market price. A search must be made for that price by a trial-and-error process.
2) What that best price is and whether it's profitable depends on the demand for the product and the costs of producing it.
3) When analyzing some pricing structure or output decision, keep in mind the marginal revenue and marginal cost, not just the price or average cost.

QUESTIONS AND MEDITATIONS

1) "Suppose some firms producing X have unsold output potential that they would like to use to produce more X at current selling prices, if only the market demand were great enough. In this situation, the good X is being sold in a price-searcher's market." Explain why that conclusion can be drawn.

Answer:

When a price-searcher changes the output rate, that change affects the sales price. To maximize wealth, price-searchers produce at the output rate at which marginal revenue (which is less than price) just covers marginal cost. When the price-searcher has unsold output potential and produces more output, that larger output results in a price decrease so that the additional cost exceeds additional revenue. Profits are lower. In contrast, in a price-taker's market, the producer can sell all the producer wants to sell at the existing price. The price just covers production costs.

2) The difference (for pricing and output behavior) between price-taker's and price-searcher's markets can be characterized by a difference in the demand curve facing each seller. Describe the difference.

Answer:

Price-taker's demand curve is horizontal at highest price at which the seller can sell any of his product, while in a price-searcher's market the demand curve is negatively sloped so that price must be lowered for the seller to make additional sales.

3) Market closures need not result in price-searchers' markets, especially if the existing number of sellers is very large. Can you identify or suggest cases where market entry is restricted and yet a price-taker's market exists? (Hint: How about agriculture — wheat, tobacco, milk producers? Teachers?)

Answer:

If the government limits acreage allowed of existing wheat farmers and prohibits new entrants into wheat farming, it still is a price-taker's market for individual wheat farmers. The same would be true of other markets which have a very large number of present producers, output of each is limited, and new entrants are not permitted. The Common Agricultural Market policies in Europe produce that result for many products.

4) You are buying trees to landscape your new home. The following demand schedule characterizes your behavior as a buyer:

Table 20 Q&A1

Price	Quantity Demanded
$10	1
9	2
8	3
7	4
6	5
5	6
4	7
3	8
2	9
1	10

The price is quoted at $6. Accordingly, you buy five trees. Then *after* you buy the five trees, the seller offers to sell you one more for only $5.

a. Do you take it?

b. Suppose, strange as it may seem, he then offers you an opportunity to buy more trees (*after* you have already agreed to purchase five at $6 each and one more for $5) at the price of $3. How many more do you buy?

c. If the price had been $3 initially, would you have bought more than eight trees?

d. Suppose you had to pay a membership fee of $5 to buy at this nursery, after which you could buy all the trees you wanted for your own garden at $3 each. How many would you buy? (Assume price at other nurseries is $4, with no membership fee.)

e. If you could buy trees at $3 each from some other store without a membership fee, would you still buy only eight trees — saving the $5 for use on *all* your consumption activities?

f. Now explain why, according to the demand schedule, your purchase of eight trees at $3 each, at a total cost of $24, is a consistent alternative to your purchase of eight trees under the former sequential offers, in which you pay a total of $41 (five at $6, one at $5, and two at $3). (In this example we assume we can slide down an unmodified demand curve, because the required modification by the change in wealth is slight.)

Answers:

    a. Yes.

    b. Two more, for a total of eight trees.

    c. No. An eighth tree is worth at most $3. What you paid for "earlier" trees is irrelevant except insofar as it affects your remaining income and thus your demand for everything else. But this effect is spread over all your purchases, and we assume it is a trivial amount compared to your total income.

    d. Eight.

    e. Yes.

    f. Marginal price is the same under each circumstance, and we adjust to the price of the extra units. What's different is who gets how much of the consumer surplus. Does the producer get more of the consumer surplus when you purchase eight trees at $3 each or when he sells to you using sequential pricing? (The latter.)

5) Price discrimination between two markets consists of selling in one market at a price below that of another. This is also called "dumping" into the low-priced market—a very misleading term. The actual purpose is simply to equate marginal revenues. Yet some allege the reason is that the seller is trying to drive some other competitor in the "class B" market out of existence so he can later raise prices. No such objective need be involved. Finally, it is argued that the seller must be selling below cost in the class B market, else how could he sell at a lower price and still cover transport costs?

    a. Show how he can.

    b. Show that even if it cost 25 cents to ship a unit of the good from the factory—located where all the class A customers are—to class B customers, profits for the producer would increase despite the fact that the selling price is $2 less for class B customers than for class A.

    c. Would he ever sell at a price below costs—marginal costs?

Answers:

    a. He need only cover marginal costs with marginal revenue, but marginal revenues are not the same as price.

    b. As long as the initial difference in marginal revenue (at equal prices) exceeds transport cost, it will pay to ship to the lower-priced market.

    c. No.

6) Some colleges charge high tuitions, but at the same time they give a large number of tuition fellowships ranging from full tuition payment down to practically nothing. Can you show that tuition grants are a form of discriminatory pricing of education? Does that make them undesirable?

Answer:

Yes, they are discriminatory. Tuition scholarships lower the price to some students (who would otherwise not be able to attend) without lowering it to all students. Instead of price discrimination, we could call this marginal revenue equalization — since the additional revenue the college collects is not reflected by price (full tuition) for the price-searcher (the college) but by marginal revenue.

7) An attempt to impose losses on competitors in order to achieve a monopoly position with subsequent "above-competitive" prices would be a predatory action. A case frequently alleged to be a predatory action involved Rockefeller's Standard Oil Company in the nineteenth century, when Standard's low prices in selected local markets were interpreted as devices to bankrupt smaller refiners. Would this be an intelligent tactic — that is, wealth-maximizing — even if no law prohibited it?

Answer:

Both predator and prey lose wealth, and the bigger firm will take a bigger absolute loss. The smaller firms may shut down production of that item and wait out the return to higher prices. If a firm were to gain by driving a competitor to bankruptcy, the prey's productive assets must be retired. Bankruptcy does not destroy productive resources; they go to someone else, who probably acquired them at a sufficiently low cost to make their continued use profitable. The aggressor, who has been suffering losses to impose losses, would have to continue his predatory tactics as long as required to wear out or absorb the other resources, and this would mean still larger losses. There is substantial evidence that Standard Oil Company bought rivals at a handsome price and retired the productive capacity.

8) Suppose you, the seller, have six units of a good available. At any price you ask of buyer A you must let him buy all he wants, and you must permit buyer B to have all he wants at the price you ask of B; but the prices asked of A and B can be different.

Table 20 Q&A2

	Units Demanded		Marginal Revenue	
Price	A	B	A	B
$10	1	0	$10	0
9	2	0	8	0
8	3	0	6	0
7	4	0	4	0
6	5	1	2	6
5	6	2	0	4
4	7	3	-2	2
3	8	4	-4	0
2	9	5	-6	-2
1	10	6	-8	-4

a. What price should you charge A, and what should you charge B, if you want to maximize your revenue?

b. If you charge the same price to both buyers, what is your best price and revenue?

c. Suppose you can produce this good at a cost of $2 for each unit you make. How many should you make, and what price should you charge to A and what to B in order to maximize your net earnings? How many will A buy, and how many will B buy?

d. What will be your net earnings?

Answer:

a. Equalize marginal revenues: 4 units to A at price $7; 2 units to B at $5; total receipts $38.

b. Price $6; total revenue $36.

c. Sell five to A at $6; three to B at $4.

d. Net earnings are $26 (= $42 − $16).

9) "Suppose some firms producing X have unsold output potential that they would like to use to produce more X at current selling prices, if only the market demand were great enough. In this situation, the good X is being sold in a price-searcher's market." Explain why that conclusion can be drawn.

Answer:

When a price-searcher changes the output rate, that change affects the sales price. To maximize wealth, price-searchers produce at the output rate at which marginal revenue (which is less than price) just covers marginal cost. When the price-searcher has unsold output potential and produces more output, that larger output results in a price decrease so that the additional cost exceeds additional revenue. Profits are lower. In contrast, in a price-taker's market, the producer can sell all the producer wants to sell at the existing price. The price just covers production costs.

CHAPTER 21

PRICING AND MARKETING TACTICS

Some pricing and marketing tactics aren't quite what they are popularly thought to be, including tie-ins, basing-point pricing, predatory pricing, dominant firms with market power, price-leaders, oligopoly pricing, network lock-ins, patents, and copyrights.

TIE-INS

When examining rent controls on housing in chapter 12, we found that tie-ins can circumvent the controls. The house owner wants to charge more than the legal limit, and therefore ties *nonmoney* requirements or restrictions to the renter's behavior.

Examples of Successful Discriminatory Tie-Ins

One type of discriminatory tie-in occurs when buying one item requires purchase of another specified item — at a price higher than it could be obtained at other stores. If you want to buy a certain printer/copier, you might have to buy only a specified type of paper from the seller of the copier, and pay a higher price for that paper than if it were bought elsewhere. The purpose of the tie-in is price discrimination, to charge in accord with differing worths of the item to different customers. The seller would collect more revenue from selling copiers if he could charge different prices in accord with how much the different customers value the copier. The difficulties are in discovering who would pay more and finding a way to collect the different amounts from the different customers for the same copier.

Imagine you are the only producer and seller of a copy machine. You can raise your price without losing all your customers, and at a lower price you will have more customers. You have two customers (enough to explain the idea) who differ in their demand. Suppose a copier lasts one year. The pertinent data for your two customers, Big and Small, are in table 21.1, Big being the buyer with the higher worth for a copier.

Big's worth of copies is $430. The cost of labor to operate the copier is $100. The cost of the paper, which Big buys for 1¢ per sheet, is $30 for 3,000 sheets. Subtracting the $100 cost of labor and $30 for paper from the $430 worth of

Table 21.1 *Worths and Costs Associated with Copier*

Activity	Big	Small
Worth of Copies	$430	$250
Cost of Labor	$100	$90
Cost of Paper	$30 = 3,000 @ 1 cent	$10 = 1,000 @ 1 cent
Worth of the Copier	$300	$150

the copies leaves $300 as the maximum worth of the copier to Big. For Small, a copier is worth at most $150 (= $250 value of copies – $90 labor – $10 paper cost).

What Price Do You Charge?

1) Highest Same Price to Each Customer to Sell One to Each Customer
   When faced by those different demands of the two customers, you could charge the highest same price to each at which each would buy a copier. That's $150, for total revenue of $300. Your cost of making a copier is $30. Your profit would be $240 (= $300 – [2 × $30]).
2) Highest Possible Price to Sell One Copier to the Highest Valuing Customer
   Alternatively, you could charge a price of $300 and sell only one copier, to Big. Your profit would be $270 (= $ 300 – $30). That is a larger profit, though Small would have been willing to pay up to $150, which is $120 more than your $30 cost.
3) Different Prices to Each Customer

A still better pricing tactic would be a price of $300 to Big, to capture all of Big's personal worth, while the price to Small would be $150, to capture Small's entire $150 worth of the copier. Your profit would be $390 (= $300 + $150 – $30 – $30). This kind of pricing captures the entire consumer worths of Big and of Small for copiers — and leaves them no consumer surplus. However, Small would be tempted to arbitrage for a profit by undercutting your price and reselling the copier to Big. Also, charging different prices is likely to be considered illegal discrimination, and gets you involved in a lawsuit. But a tie-in can be a way to charge more to Big than to Small, so that you could capture more of Big's worth, $430, and also more of Small's $250 worth of copies.

We've assumed you, the copier manufacturer/seller, knew that Big has a bigger demand (higher personal worth for copies) than does Small, and that

Table 21.2 *Worths and Costs Associated with Copier*

Activity	Big	Small
Worth of Copier's Product	$410	$240
Cost of Labor	$100	$90
Cost of Paper	$250 = 2,500 @ 10¢ each	$95 = 950 @ 10¢ each
Cost of Copier	$30	$30
Worth of the Copier	$60	$55

you knew what those worths were. In reality you don't know them. What you do know is that their worths differ. Sometimes there's a way a tie-in can detect differences, and charge a higher price to Big. You offer to sell a copier to each for $55 (your cost is $30), and you insist that all the paper used must be purchased from only you at 10 cents per sheet, higher by 9 cents per sheet than from other paper suppliers.

A tangential effect of the higher price of paper is that Big and Small will each use less paper. That will reduce the worth of a copy machine.

In table 21.2, the slightly reduced worths of a copier reflect the higher price of paper and the fewer copies. For Big, the amount of paper demanded at 10 cents falls to 2,500 sheets, with a larger total paper cost of $250. The worth of a copier to Big falls from $300 to $60 (= $410 − $100 labor − $250 paper). For Small, the worth of a copier falls to $55 (= $240 service value − $90 labor − $95 cost of paper). You receive $110 for the two copiers, earning a profit of only $50 (= $110 − $60). But look at your profit on the paper.

Your Paper Profit

From Big, you will receive $250 for the paper, which costs you $25 (= 2,500 sheets at 1 cent each) to get it from the initial paper supplier, leaving a profit of $225. From Small, you will receive $95 for the 950 sheets of paper, for which you pay $9.50, net revenue of $85.50 ($95 − $9.50). Your profit from Small is $85.50 (paper) + $25 (= $55 − $30 on the machine). Your profit from Big is $225 (paper) and $30 (= $60 − $30 on the machine). Total profit from Big and Small on the copiers plus paper is $365.50 (= $225 + $30 + $85.50 + $25).

The Fallacy of the Idea of Leveraging or Extending
Monopoly Power from Copier to Paper

You, as copy-machine producer and seller, have not used this tie-in to monopolize and profit from the sale of paper — which is the argument generally presented in lawsuits challenging this tie-in. Your purpose has been to collect more of the consumer surplus provided by the manufacture and sale of copiers, represented by more of the area under the demand curve for copiers. And the tie-in helps ensure that all potential buyers who value the copier at more than its marginal cost of production will buy one.

If you could have charged different prices to Big and Small for the copiers, you'd have done that explicitly. You would have collected $450 (= $300 + $150) for a profit of $390, after the $60 cost of the two copiers. You didn't really want to raise the price you charge for paper, because a higher paper price reduces the worth of the copiers. It's the worth of the copiers that's the original source of your profits.

Sources of Confusion

There can be various purposes of tie-ins. A *convenience tie-in* is a combination of two items into one package in conformity with the preference of most customers. A radio or an automatic transmission, or both, in an automobile were once options. Today, they often are not; you'd probably have to pay extra to buy a new car without a radio. It's too expensive to leave them as options when most people prefer the combination. Shoes and shoelaces are tied together — you'll get no discount if you try to buy just the shoes without the laces.

A common tie-in was imposed by sellers when gasoline prices were controlled at too low a level. Some gasoline stations would sell only on the condition you bought a car wash or an oil change — usually at an elevated price. Some motorists bought special high-price lube jobs to get a fill-up of "free" gasoline.

When airline fares were governmentally controlled at higher than market-clearing prices, airlines competed for customers by offering additional services, tie-ins of fancy food or travel lounges or transport to and from the airport — free of charge. With rent controls restricting the legal price, you could rent an apartment only if you bought the rugs in the apartment, at a high price. Those tie-ins were ways to conveniently avoid price controls. If the controlled price is too high, the sellers will offer freebees. If it's too low, the buyers will offer extra forms of nonmoney compensation.

Are Tie-Ins Anticompetitive? A Wrong Question

In the example of the copier manufacturer/seller, tie-ins are not *anticompetitive* in the sense that they alter any other person's right or ability to make offers. It does not affect any other supplier's costs of producing. It's a way for the seller to get more of the worth of the tying product — the area under the demand curve. The relevant but unanswerable question is, "Who has a right to the area under the demand curve — the producer of the good that yields that worth, or the consumer to whom it is worth that much?"

Examples of Automatic Tie-Ins

If you are thinking of buying a mobile phone, you may discover the price of the phone to be very low, far under its cost of manufacture — maybe even free. Why? The use of the device at the stipulated user fee is tied to the purchase of the telephone — you have to sign a contract and pay more for greater usage. In our preceding example, the price of the copier could have been even less than the $30 cost of manufacture. It could have been zero and still been profitable to produce and give away, so long as there was a tie-in of the purchase of the paper.

There can be other reasons for tie-ins. The seller, as a condition of warranty of satisfactory performance or repairs, may specify (tie in) a specific brand of the associated (genuine) repair parts, or who is the authorized repairer. These arrangements may be to protect reputation, but they also may be structured to meter usage, and therefore differences in demand.

Apparently Irrelevant Tie-Ins — That Are Relevant

Big and Small are construction companies. You might sell copying machines to the two construction companies (at an equal price) only on the condition that the buyers agree to buy from you, at a premium price, all the hard hats used by the companies' employees. That may seem like a ridiculous tie-in. But suppose you know that Big, having more employees and needing to communicate with more printed messages, will place a greater worth on having a copier than will a small firm. So the number of hard hats purchased will be correlated with the greater worth of a copier to Big. (The tying item must be one for which there are not cheap substitute safety devices.)

Alternatively, you might insist that the buyer of your copier purchase from you all the coffee for the coffee breaks provided "free" to employees. If the worth of a copier is correlated to the number of employees, for example, then selling something else at a premium price can actually be a way of metering demand for use of a copier.

It's all a way to collect *different* prices from customers in accord with the buyer's *willingness* to pay. It's basically no different from movies charging young people more than senior citizens, or charging richer parents more than poorer parents for college tuition (net of scholarships). Some of these devices for differential (discriminatory) pricing are considered bad, and some are commended.

Renting Machines

There are alternative ways a tie-in can serve as a metering and collection device. Instead of selling copiers, you could have rented a copier to each user and charged 9 cents per copy made, letting the users buy paper wherever they like. With the tie-in of paper, you gained from the higher price for *each sheet*; with a fee for use, you collect with *each use* of the machine. If allowed and technologically feasible, the fee system probably is better in that it avoids substitute sources for the metered item, the paper. With a meter on the machine's use, the user can't cheat, whereas with paper you've got to keep monitoring the source of the paper used by the copier owner.

Instead of paper usage, copier/printer manufacturers have found that demand of different buyers can also be metered by requiring that replacement ink cartridges be bought only from the manufacturer of the machine. This can be effective where it is possible to block generic alternatives from entering the cartridge market.

BASING-POINT PRICING

Basing-point pricing is a method of competitively quoting market prices. The basing-point for plywood once was the price in Seattle, the site from which almost all producers of plywood shipped to the entire country. No matter where a customer was located, the price was quoted in terms of two components: (a) the price of plywood in Seattle (the basing-point price) plus (b) transport costs from Seattle to that customer. (Most automobiles used to be made near Detroit, and automobile prices were "Detroit price plus transport cost.")

In the lumber basing-point system of pricing, prices of lumber shipped to other areas were connected by the differences in transport costs from Seattle. A price change as a result of a change in demand for plywood in one city will be matched immediately in all other cities. Similarly, an increase in supply in Seattle will reduce prices in all parts of the United States.

Where Is the Price Determined? Everywhere.

Price in each locality, given demand and supply in each city, is determined, and this price minus transport cost is the basis of how much is bid for plywood from Seattle. Thus, the Seattle price is *derived from* the demands from the entire United States, with competition on the supply side among the several Seattle plywood producers. It's the *local city price minus transport cost*. Or it's the Seattle price (reflecting national demand and local supply) plus transport.

The supply to each city appears as a *horizontal line* at the Seattle price plus freight. Because the Seattle price must reflect demand in the entire United

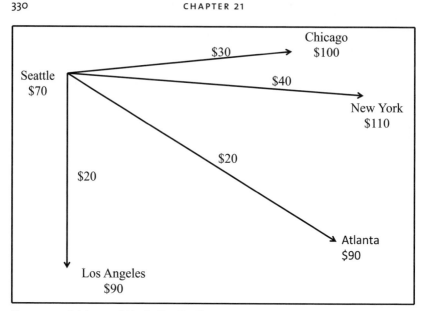

Figure 21.1 *Pricing and Marketing Tactics*

The prices to consumers in the several geographic market areas are different but are tied together by the differences in transport costs from the production site. If transport costs from Seattle to New York are $40 per unit of lumber, the New York price will be $40 higher than the Seattle price.

States, in each city the supply at that price is as large as that city demands. In each city, sellers and buyers are price-takers.

Someone in the Atlanta area discovered how to convert local timber into plywood. That would permit the local producer to sell in Atlanta and avoid the transport costs. But the price in Atlanta would still be — Seattle plus transport cost. The fact that no transport was involved made no difference. The market price in Atlanta was virtually unaffected, because the new producers initially supplied only a trivial part of the supply of plywood sold there. The Atlanta producer charged the competitive price, which was determined by national demand and national supply — which now included the small amount produced in Atlanta.

Some Atlanta buyers of plywood produced in Atlanta accused the local producers of charging too much, alleging that the prices included transport costs the producer did not incur. That transport cost was labeled *phantom freight*. This is similar to when local egg producers with lower transport costs keep a larger part of the market price than does a more distant supplier. This larger amount is not phantom freight, but instead is the higher rent of a superior location.

Phantom Freight and Phantom Amounts of Surgical Services

The error in claiming overcharges via phantom freight is equivalent to failure to notice that surgeons, or auto mechanics, are not all equal in ability. The better ones do more and earn more. Gas stations with superior locations charge more.

Suppose you are a surgeon who can remove an appendix as well as any other surgeon, but you can do it in one-third the time others take. If the competitive fee for the operation is $500, and you can perform six per day while others perform only two, you will earn more per day, but not more per appendectomy. How should your fee be stated? As $500 per appendectomy? Or as $3,000 per day?

The patient noting you had done the surgery in much less time might complain that you are charging for phantom time — the extra amount of time that other surgeons need. You would respond, "Yes, I charged the same price for the same procedure that other surgeons took more time to do. I didn't raise the price of the appendectomy. My earnings reflect my superior ability, not a higher price than the competitive price. Whether the bill is expressed per day or per surgery, the cost to you is still $500."

That's what the Atlanta plywood producer should have said, replacing appendectomy with plywood and superior talent with superior land site for growing timber nearer Atlanta than in Seattle. In fact, the productive land near Atlanta jumped in value, and the higher land rent captured the difference in transport costs. The full costs of timber produced in Atlanta rose to match the profits. (Recall the analysis of derived resource value in chapter 16, how profits are converted into *costs* by competitive revaluation of responsible resources.)

EFFICIENT, COMPETITIVE PRICING RESPONSE TO NEW ENTRANTS, MISCONSTRUED AS PREDATORY PRICING

In chapter 15 we saw that when a lower cost producer (Carter) enters a market, there is a net social benefit. Total supply of cakes increased, prices were lower, and resources were released to the production of other goods. Nevertheless, Baker lost sales of cakes to Adam and might find sympathy for his claim that Carter had engaged in "predatory pricing" by offering to sell cakes to Adam at a price lower than Baker could afford to do. However, that is not the relevant criterion. Carter's cost of production was lower than Baker's; the lower price he offered to sell to Adam was not predatory. If, however, Carter had offered to sell to Adam at a price lower than his (Carter's) own cost of production in order to impose losses on Baker and force him out of business, that would have been viewed as predatory and thus illegal. Similarly, if Baker had foreseen the potential loss of sales as a result of Carter's entry into the market and had then offered to sell cakes to Adam at below his (Baker's) own costs of production in order to discourage Carter from entering the market, that also would have been construed as predatory and thus illegal.

But how likely is either of these pricing strategies? For it to be worthwhile for Carter to incur losses temporarily by offering to sell cakes to Adam at prices lower than his own costs in order to drive Baker out of the market, Carter would have to expect to charge premium prices subsequently in order to recoup previous losses. Of course, that would be possible only if Baker or other potential producers did not then enter the market and drive the prices back down.

Similarly, for Baker to discourage Carter from entering the market by offering to sell to Adam cakes at below his (Baker's) costs of production, he also would have to expect to charge premium prices to Adam later in order to recoup previous losses — without inducing Carter or other potential producers to enter and drive down prices.

Ultimately, the accusation of predatory pricing depends on a producer's ability to recoup losses without attracting new competitors. Without barriers to entry to a market — such as government-imposed licensing requirements — lower-cost producers will always have an incentive to add to aggregate supply and drive down prices.

In the adjustments to the long-run result, the price will *temporarily* fall below the ultimate new level, because the total output will be temporarily larger than what it will be at the new, fully adjusted equilibrium output. These *transitional* deviations are not the result of mistakes; they occur because some inputs are *specific* to their *current* tasks. They are not instantly mobile and capable of shifting or being converted to other equally, or next best, paying tasks without costs of moving and *learning*. Almost all resources have some degree of specificity to what they are doing. Grapevines cannot be converted to apple trees, or wine presses into chicken coops.

Examples of these transitional adjustment prices, outputs, and values of *specific-use* resources are common. The entry of jet engines to compete with existing propeller-driven airplanes caused a drastic drop in the value of those planes. The microwave transmission system increased the supply of communication channels and reduced the value of wire-based systems. The successively faster and greater capacity microprocessors lowered the values of existing microprocessors.

In each case, the temporarily larger supply from new resources depressed the prices below the level that would persist after the older, less economical items were no longer worth using. But the new entrant is likely to call the temporary fall in price "predatory" or "cutthroat" pricing by existing producers, though there were no actions with intent to affect survival of competitors.

As a final note, it is useful to distinguish between how economists and lawyers think about the issue. Existing producers/suppliers will always view a new entrant into a competitive market to be a predator — even when the new entrant is clearly a lower-cost provider. New Mexico had a statute that said a new entrant into a market area (such as a second dealer of a certain brand of automobile) could not enter unless they could demonstrate that there would be no loss of business to existing vendors.

DOMINANT FIRM, WITH MARKET POWER

What is called a dominant firm, or a firm with market power or monopoly power, is one that supplies a sufficiently large portion of a good's total supply to affect the market price of all suppliers. That's quite different from dominating.

More fully, a dominant firm can profitably raise its price as well as the sustainable market prices of all other suppliers. To do so, it must restrict its own output, and it does not eliminate competitors. Instead, it helps them survive by letting them sell more at that higher price, while the dominant firm restricts its rate of production.

The dominant firm announces its most profitable selling price, and then the other firms supply as much as they choose. None of the others could profitably expand production enough, at least in the relevant immediate future, to offset the effect of the dominant supplier's reduction in output. No agreement with other suppliers is required. They continue to seek to maximize their profits by supplying amounts at which their marginal costs match the market price determined by the restrained output of the dominant firm.

How does this raise the dominant firm's profits? What would be the market price that maximized its profits, while allowing all the other smaller firms to sell the amounts they would at increased profits for themselves? We know that in a price-taker's market with many small firms, the prevailing price will be where the sum of supply curves equals market demand. Suppose a large number of these small firms merge into one large dominant firm, or cooperative. The total supply schedule is the same, but the price will be higher and amount actually supplied will be less than in the price-taker's market.

The now dominant firm will look at how much it would sell at each price,

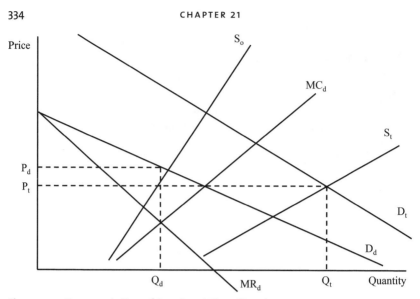

Figure 21.2 *Representation of Dominant Firm Situation*

Assume a price-taker's market for a generic commodity, maybe crude oil, coffee, or wheat. As we saw earlier, in such markets the price is determined by total market demand, D_t, and total market supply, S_t. Now suppose a large number of firms merge into a single large firm, or form a marketing "cooperative" or co-op. The sum of the supply curves of this combined firm or co-op is its supply, or marginal cost, schedule, MC_d. The demand seen by this dominant large firm or co-op is derived from the market demand less the amounts supplied by all the other, still-small firms, S_o. Subtracting S_o from D_t will give the derived demand faced by the dominant firm, D_d. At a price where S_o intersects D_t, the other small firms would be supplying all of market demand, so demand as seen by the dominant firm would be zero; however, other firms supply less in the aggregate at lower prices, so the quantities on D_d are greater at lower prices. Profit of the dominant firm is maximized at a price and quantity where its marginal cost, MC_d, is equal to its marginal revenue, MR_d.

This profit-maximizing price for the dominant firm, P_d, is above the price that would have prevailed in a price-taker's market, P_t. The small other firms can still sell all they want to produce at this higher price, but the total amount produced and sold by all firms will be less than it would have been in the price-taker's market before the dominant firm or co-op was formed.

after estimating how much all the other firms would supply at alternative possible prices. That schedule of remaining demanded amounts facing the dominant firm is the *residual demand* facing the dominant firm. That dominant firm then sets the price, which (in view of the residual demand facing it) will maximize its own profits — where its marginal revenue (of that residual demand curve) matches the dominant firm's marginal cost (the sum of the supply curves of the now merged firms).

Figure 21.2 shows the pertinent relations among the market demand, the aggregate supply curves of the other firms, and the residual demand, marginal revenues, and marginal costs of the dominant firm.

Dominant Firm Limitations

Two features limit the power of a dominant firm (or a collusion).

1) In the longer run, more new suppliers — or investments and expansions by existing firms — will be attracted, causing supply increases that can more than offset the initial reduction in output by the dominant firm.

2) Customers will discover ways to substitute or to economize on the product, so that after some interval and initial higher profits to the producers, income will fall to below what it otherwise would have been.

In accord with the second law of demand, the longer-run elasticity of demand may be so great that a price rise would be partially offset (or possibly more than offset) by losses of sales. The transformation of the Soviet nations toward capitalist economies opened world access to the great oil reserves of the Caspian Sea. Argentina and Brazil went from oil importers to exporters, and Mexico and Canada greatly expanded their production and exports. Saudi Arabia then largely lost its dominant firm status. Since the Caspian Sea reserves are divided among several independent nations (Azerbaijan, Iran, and Kazakhstan), and other new sources of oil and natural gas have been developed (especially the United States), there is not now a dominant firm in the world supply of petroleum.

Other Dominant Firms?

Is Coca-Cola a dominant firm? Could it announce a higher price for its cola syrup and get more profits despite the consequent expansion of Pepsi and other soft drink suppliers? Would the others so extensively displace Cokes, by not raising their prices as high — and thereby selling more — that Coke would lose too many sales and suffer losses or reduced profits? We don't know.

To be a dominant firm, the supply from other firms must be small and unresponsive enough to the higher profitable price as not to result in an expansion of production that displaces the dominant firm. It's easy to explain what a dominant firm means, but not which, if any, actually is a dominant firm (for reasons other than patent and copyright protection, or other government-protected, closed monopoly situations, such as some labor unions and airlines and local telephone and television services once were).

PRICE LEADERS?

Often the largest firm, or one of the largest firms, in an industry is the first to adjust price when market conditions change — and others appear merely to follow. Imagine an aluminum producer who has just received a sequence of larger orders. Is it just a transitional happenstance of a bunching of orders? Or has demand for aluminum really increased? If demand has increased, will it persist, and will sustainable higher prices be possible? Or would other producers immediately capture more of the increased demand if this firm's prices were raised? How can one firm know that circumstances have changed so that a higher market price will be required to clear the market?

Whether a higher price is sustainable is a question facing all firms. Usually, a larger firm has greater rewards for more reliably finding the new price earlier, and a greater loss by hastily adjusting to false signals. When a larger firm does change its price, that change provides some evidence to the others that market conditions really have changed. What mistakenly appears to be a price leader dictating what all the firms should charge — in some imagined process dubbed a tacit collusion or shared monopoly — is instead independent competition among incompletely informed people, as is always the case.

OLIGOPOLY

Oligopoly denotes a small group of price-searcher firms that are interdependent in their pricing and output decisions. Each knows or believes its price affects its competitors' demand and hence their chosen prices, which in turn affects the price each will choose. United Airlines knows that the price it charges will affect the demand faced by Delta Airlines and the price Delta will then charge — the anticipation of which affects what United would choose initially. The demand facing one firm may change if its competitor decides to change its price for any reason.

This interdependence can prompt conjectures about all sorts of potential feedback chains of actions and reactions. But economists have been unable to specify a reliably valid model for analysis of oligopolies. It's unknown whether, in such an industry, price will tend to fluctuate more or be more rigid, or whether output and earnings will fluctuate more or less, than if the firms acted without regard to conjectures of what a competitor would do.

NETWORKS, MONOPOLY LOCK-INS?

An essential demand feature of what's called a *network* is that with more members, the greater is the worth of the network to each participant. Residents of the United Kingdom, much of North America, and the former British colonies all use the English language. The more widely English is used, the better for each user. In the early days of the telephone, the demand curve for telephone service by each user shifted upward as more people used the service.

Such networking is seen in the internet, the formats of recording devices and compatible computer software, a uniform standard gasoline, a uniform money, a system of measurement, rules of etiquette, and every standard of weight, speed, and law.

Though a new system may be better technology and more economical — once it has become widely accepted — its initial worth to users is small if there are few other people willing to use it. What can a new aspiring entrant do? There are two problems. One is to induce potential customers to learn about the new item. The other is to overcome the networking feature which makes the value of some item to one person depend on how many other people are using it.

Microsoft successfully entered the business of word processing despite an existing and widely used alternative, WordPerfect. Microsoft Word was better at adapting to improvements in computer technological capabilities, and ultimately succeeded despite the costs of learning a new system and the wide user base of the then dominant word-processing system.

For many years, Microsoft's word-processing and spreadsheet applications software was compatible only with their Windows operating system — which was used by most computer manufacturers. Some of the early resistance among consumers to the purchase of Apple computers was that their proprietary word-processing and spreadsheet applications software was not compatible with that of the great majority of Windows computer users. That is, the network effects of large numbers of Microsoft Windows users served as a hurdle to persuading customers to buy Apple computers — until Microsoft provided compatible applications software for Apple brands.

Strong networking effects can be barriers to entry of potential competitors, but that is not a natural monopoly. A firm whose product or service becomes the *industry standard* — such as a computer operating system — definitely has an advantage. Employees who learn it can shift among employers without having to learn new systems. Employers will prefer methods most commonly used by others. The pool of available employees will be larger at lower cost. This is the reason there is a standard keyboard on computers.

The learning costs and the personal ease of using *any* typewriter (before computers) was an inducement for the producers to offer the same *user interface*. That's a reason why customers prefer the competitors to offer products operated the same way. Competition among alternatives is heightened the more they have the same or very similar user controls. That does restrain some advances, but life is full of trade-offs.

PATENTS AND COPYRIGHTS: CONFLICTING OBJECTIVES AND AMBIGUOUS POLICIES OF REWARD TO INVENTORS

The Constitution of the United States, Article 1, Section 8, states Congress shall have "power to promote the Progress of Science and useful Arts, by securing for limited Times to Authors and Inventors the exclusive Right to their respective Writing and Discoveries." These exclusive rights are *patents* and *copyrights*.

That grant of power contains a conflict with a general policy of open access to markets. Some of the benefits of open markets are forgone for the benefit of enhancing incentives for discoveries of better products and procedures. Actions of patent holders are often challenged as being too restrictive, for not achieving maximum consumer worth, and not promoting innovative marketing tactics. The resolution of such challenges depends upon courts of law.

Patents on Newly Discovered Medicines and Drugs

Successful developers of new medicines (prescription pills) are accused of: 1) setting prices of drugs far above the cost of making the pills and 2) charging lower prices to foreigners than to home-country residents. In what sense are the charges both pertinent and correct? What actions have been declared improper and therefore illegal?

Some drug companies spend many millions of dollars searching for new drugs hoping for profit with the patent right, which is the constitutionally granted reward. In many, probably in most, cases of success, once a discovery is made, the average cost of manufacturing and distributing the medicine is low, say $1 per pill. (Big pharmaceutical companies like to say, "The first pill costs a billion dollars, the second costs 50 cents.")

Suppose the price of a pill is set at $20—a per unit profit of $19 ($20 price minus $1 average cost of production). This can happen because the demand is so great and the initial rate of production is so small. As the rate of production is increased, the price might fall to $15, but the profits per pill are still very large.

Then, suppose the US drug company offers to sell the drug in, say, Mexico for only $2 per pill. This pricing causes two complaints: profits are "exorbitant" in the home-country market, and it is "unfair" that the drugs are sold for much less abroad. Nothing in economics will tell you if these complaints are "justified," but it can help explain why this pricing occurs.

The first problem is deciding what is meant by the *cost* of the pills. That is, we have to specify the relevant *action* resulting in the availability of the pill. The question can mean, "What were the research and testing costs of *discovering* the drug?" Or simply, "What is the cost of *manufacturing* each pill" after it was discovered?

The drug research firm spent millions (or billions) of dollars in research in several areas (some of which were failures), culminating in discovery of the new drug. In economics, those costs are *sunk*, but that does not mean those *actions* should not be priced. *After discovery*, subsequent costs of *making* a pill do not include these initial costs of the research. However, when looking at the $20 selling price, what's the action being priced? Since the only reward for all those actions — first research and testing, then manufacture — comes from the price charged, it's the cost of *all* the actions that should be compared with the price of the pill.

It's neither useful nor consistent to compare the cost of only one action that resulted in the availability of the pill. Much was spent in the discovery and development of the drug. Those were the costs of the *actions* the patent policy was intended to reward, not merely that of producing a pill once the drug is discovered.

With several firms competing, and with most research resulting in failure, the anticipated profits to the winner would have to be very large to induce the research and development attempts. As in all contests with several contestants, the reward to the winner will be big profits, while the others get nothing. The patent system gives a prize, the size of which is related to the worth of the discovery, judged by the worth to the consumer. How much of the worth to consumers will the winner be allowed? The answer to that is often settled in a court of law or by government regulators.

Price Discrimination Again

Consumers in foreign nations are often charged less, depending on the relative elasticities (and marginal revenues) of demands in the several nations. That's similar to the pricing of movie admission prices, with discounts to the elderly (or premium prices to the nonelderly). Such pricing differences reflect differences in customer demand.

Prestigious colleges charge higher tuition to students with richer parents. Why object to offering lower prices to foreigners who are poorer? Economics cannot answer that. Economics does tell us that in some situations price discrimination (different prices to different consumers) increases aggregate consumer worth, and in others that worth is decreased.

Consider a situation without patents. *After* a large initial investment, the price that would cover the costs of production *plus* recover the investment costs is, say, $10 per unit—of which $8 is for recovery of the initial (now sunk) investment. The firm could produce at a price as low as $2 (= $10 – $8) and still cover its subsequent production costs—at least until the durable equipment wore out. With no patent protection where competitors can easily duplicate the product, the price is likely to be competed down toward the $2 manufacturing cost. However, the price could be higher than $10 if entry is expensive (secret ingredients, special machines?) or if it would take more time for competitors to offer a product than the transiently higher demand is likely to last.

Some patents offer protection in countries other than the home country, as a result of treaties. However, enforcement of patented rights can be costly and vary greatly in effectiveness in different countries. A manufacturer may have effective patent protection in one country but not another. Differential pricing of the same product in different countries may reflect both differences in customer demands and differences in legal and other costs of protecting patent rights.

If a major part of the resources are durable and not quickly adjustable, the selling prices of the products can fall far—as well as rise high—with swings of demand, because the supply curve of the product would be less elastic, like land. But if the firm relies more on adjustable inputs, like labor, prices will vary less, and production will vary more. For production relying mostly on only one fixed, durable—not cheaply adjustable—resource, production will continue, and prices will vary with demand. Resource values will vary more. In contrast, if all resources are mobile and can be used for other kinds of output (as most labor can), supply will be elastic, and prices will not change as much, but output of the whole industry will.

QUESTIONS AND MEDITATIONS

1) Is Microsoft's browser (Internet Explorer, now Edge) with its operating system a tie-in? Apparently the European Union thinks so. What are its purpose and effects?

Answer:

A computer operating system that includes a bundle of applications can be thought of as involving tie-ins. For example, Apple includes its proprietary browser, Safari, with its operating system, even though some Apple users may choose to install other browsers such as Firefox. Presumably, the producer believes demand for the operating system will be greater — and revenue and profitability greater — than if all applications were sold separately.

2) You arrive at a hotel very late at night. A room rate is quoted at $100. You say, "It's late, you have several vacancies. You know you won't rent them all tonight at this hour. Your only cost of renting one to me is for cleaning and caring for a room, which is perhaps $20. I'll offer you $50." You'll rarely get the room. Why is the hotel operator willing to throw away a gain of $30?

Answer:

The hotel is forgoing this particular gain. But predictability of price is valuable information to customers. Advertising and posting prices reduces search and information costs and unhappy surprises to potential buyers, thereby promoting long-term, wide demand. Imagine if a restaurant's menu did not show prices and your bill at checkout time were determined by the spin of a large wheel with lots of different numbers on it.

3) The spread among gasoline prices of Regular, Intermediate, and Premium is larger for full-service than for self-service. For self-service, the difference in prices may range from about 15 to 20 cents; for full service, the spread would be from about 20 to 30 cents. You get the same gasoline whether it's self-service or full service. What makes it more costly for the attendant to fill the gas tank with the premium than filling it with regular?

Answer:

It is not more costly; the gas station judges that the demand is more inelastic for full service.

4) Is a car rental fee that includes a charge per mile driven the same as overpriced gasoline with no fee per mile? If you rent a copy machine and pay a fee per unit of use, is that different?

Answer:

Charges for per-mile-driven and per-copy-made are ways of metering the demands of different customers. Overpriced gasoline causes a customer who drives the rental car a long distance and returns the car with an almost empty tank to pay more than another who drives only a short distance before returning the car with an almost full tank. That is, the rental price per mile driven will be different for each customer.

5) Why are rebates offered rather than direct price reductions?
Answer:

> Rebates lower the prices to those customers who receive them, versus other customers who do not take the time to send for the rebate. The proffered rebate is a selling point — but not all buyers will cash in on it.

6) The following is a quotation from a science magazine: "Recently a number of steel-making organizations in Western Europe and the USSR have eliminated several costly steps in the manufacture of steel by advancing the technique known as continuous casting. US steel firms, which account for about a third of the world output, were for the most part content to observe these developments. They were inhibited by a paradox of industrial supremacy: the huge sums already invested in established methods made experimentation with the new technique seem impractical. The smaller producers, whose competitive position might have been enhanced by continuous casting, could least afford to build the pilot plants."
Assume that the facts stated in the first sentence are correct. The second sentence describes the alleged behavior of large US steel firms in response to these facts. Do you agree that the last two sentences present an economically acceptable explanation of the events in the second sentence?
Answer:

> Industrial supremacy has nothing to do with reluctance to buy new equipment now. Existing equipment was more economical to continue using. When new technologies emerge, older technologies become less valuable. If a firm utilizing older technologies fails to write down the value of such equipment as it depreciates or its market value falls because of technological obsolescence, managers perceive their costs to be higher than is economically correct. Smaller producers can spend as much as bigger ones when profit prospects appear, for investors will be ready to provide funds, and small will become big.

7) Why are tickets to sporting events typically declared not legally transferable at higher prices at the scene of the event (i.e., no "scalping")? Yet the buyer and the seller would both prefer to be able to do so. Who, if anyone, would lose?
Answer:

> Sometimes tickets are deliberately underpriced — such as those made available to college students by their university — and the administrators

don't want the students to buy the cheap tickets solely for the purpose of reselling to nonstudents. At other sporting events, organizers may fear that large blocks of tickets will be purchased by potential scalpers for re-sale (with the embarrassing revelation that the organizers had underpriced their product), and if the tickets are not successfully resold, there will be a lot of empty seats.

8) Drug research companies invest heavily in search of drugs or devices for better health. Once success is achieved, the item itself (we'll call it a "pill") can be produced at very low cost, say 1 cent. Any ordinary chemist could then make the pill, at a cost of 1 cent. However, the incentive for research and development would be suppressed if anyone can produce the pill. That's the general rationale for granting patents — "a closed monopoly" right. The pill's price will then appear to be higher than its seeming cost. Suppose ten drug companies each had separately invested in a different research project. One of the projects does succeed. All the other research firms fail. The successful one reaps big revenue, far bigger than its costs. What would you regard as the correct measure of costs of the success? Are the profits excessive for the successful firm, in light of the risks and costs of the ill-fated unsuccessful research? If so, excessive relative to what and for what actions?

Answer:

There is substantial risk involved in long-term medical research projects. Investors may have to wait years to know whether they have lost everything or stand to make large gains. Any venture capital undertaking also requires significant up-front investment of capital that may be lost if the project is not successful. Competition and unrestricted entry will mean the profits are not "excessive."

CHAPTER 22

TEAMWORK AND FIRMS

From the most primitive and ancient times, hunters — people or wolves — have worked as *teams* to catch more prey than by hunting alone. Two people lifting beams, or two researchers sharing ideas, can achieve more than if each worked independently. A surgeon and nurses working as a team perform surgeries they could not otherwise achieve.

The design and production of practically everything is done by some teamwork. Successful teamwork requires coordination. What one person does depends on what the others do, even when separated by great distance.

We'll concentrate on the organization, direction, and control of the team's members, or associates, in business firms.

What is a firm? It's not a club. Except for one-person enterprises, it has one or more owners and some employees specializing in tasks and making components of products and services to be sold. Unlike market transactions with different customers from day to day, members (employees and owners) of a firm are the same people day after day, working as a team.

Teamwork helps explain distinctive features of business *firms*, such as: 1) how the jointly produced product value is shared; 2) who hires whom; 3) how the team's size and the membership is determined; 4) who manages or directs the teamwork; 5) who bears losses if the firm fails to cover costs; 6) the property rights of the participants; 7) what is meant by the *owner* of the firm; and 8) what part of the firm the *owner* owns.

NO DEFINABLE, SEPARABLE, INDIVIDUAL
PRODUCTS FOR EACH TEAM MEMBER

Teamwork means the *product* is not divisible into components attributable to each worker. The actions of each person can be identified, but that is not to identify what part of the team's final product each person produced. On a football team, some members never make touchdowns, yet each contributes to scoring. A law firm has a team of lawyers working on a case, but many never go to a courtroom. How is the total product value of the team distributed among the members, when it's impossible to define the part of the total value each produced? And therefore, when you work in a team, what is meant by the assertion you are paid according to the market value of what *you* produce?

The increased productivity by teamwork was not available for Adam, Baker, and Carter of chapter 15 in their single-person firms. There weren't the tasks of direction, coordination, cooperation, and control within a team of workers. Production could be expanded by adding more units of homogeneous inputs, such as electric power and raw materials. But for effective continued teamwork among several people, contractual relations, informal agreements, customs, and controls of members appear to be necessary.

INTRATEAM DEPENDENCIES

Successful teamwork requires coordination. Each member knows the idiosyncratic traits of others. These distinctive features are reasons the members tend to be the same persons day after day. Imagine finding every day a different clerk in charge of filing or new employees with whom to work, or working in a restaurant with different chefs and waiters each day, or a surgeon working with different nurses and anesthesiologists in each operation, or having a different instructor every day in a college course. Finding and assembling new compatible working groups every day is prohibitively expensive. Long-term membership and interdependencies among the members are hallmarks of successful firms.

Determination of rewards for services was simpler centuries ago in the *putting-out* system of production. An entrepreneur supplied raw materials to be processed by the workers at their homes. The finished products were then delivered to the entrepreneur-investor. With development of steam power and manufacturing equipment too large and expensive for workers to own, the workers began to work outside the home, where the machinery was located. A *firm* consisted of several people, employees, working in a joint effort with owners of the expensive equipment.

What objectives, constraints, cooperative actions, and conflicts occur within firms that are absent in single-person independent enterprises? In our exploration of price-*taker* firms, they were *independent economically*, though possibly dependent technologically. In the case of price-*searcher* firms, they were *dependent* economically on the production and supply actions of other sellers. The production decisions of Adam, Baker, and Carter were independent technologically, though those three people were economically dependent, where what one did affected the decisions of other sellers.

With teamwork, the members of the team are interdependent technologically as well as economically. Each affects the output and the rewards of other members.

Teamwork in firms is managed by a director or coordinator, more familiarly called the boss. The boss gives general directions, specifies who is to do what, and monitors performances. Later, we'll discover that recognition as a boss depends on which of the resources involved in the activities in the firm are owned by that person. Here, we ask how the team's product value is apportioned among the members of the team.

ARE YOU PAID WHAT YOU ADD TO THE TOTAL VALUE? A FUTILE QUESTION

It's tempting to say that you will be paid an amount up to the increase in the value of the team when you join — what you add to the total value of the team's product value. That addition is usually called your marginal product. But is it really yours? The other members of the team could say they contributed to the addition.

How much *you* added and how much *they* added isn't determinable. Further, nothing indicates how much each should be compensated. Instead, with competition from other groups you might have joined, you must be paid at least the best detected alternative to entice you to join this team. Jack and Jill, in table 22.1, when each is alone, and alternatively when they work as a team, illustrate this.

When alone, Jack's product value is $5, and Jill's is $7. When Jack and Jill work as a team, they produce $15 — $3 more than their $12 total when sepa-

---

Table 22.1 *Jack and Jill Production*

Jack, Working Alone $5
Jill, Working Alone $7
Total $12
Jack and Jill, Working Together = $15

Marginal Product of Each, Working in a Team
Jack's = $15 − $5 = $10 (Increase above Jack's Alone)
Jill's = $15 − $7 = $8 (Increase above Jill's Alone)
Total $18

The $18 sum of the marginal products of Jack and of Jill exceeds the $15 total product value.

rate. How is the total of $15 to be divided between them? If each claims the individual marginal product as being the increase when working with the other, that would be $15 − $5 = $10 for Jack, while for Jill it's $15 − $7 = $8. The total claimed is $18, but that's impossible since the total to be divided is only $15.

The conflict is not resolved by each claiming the increase of $3, with none of the value of working as a team going to the other. Team members cannot claim that they alone caused the increase in value resulting from teamwork.

In a private property economy, the amount obtained by each member in one team depends on what that person could have received by working with competitors. Competition pushes earnings toward the value of the best opportunity elsewhere — the cost of working *here*, rather than *there*. If the team total is less than the sum of what the members could earn elsewhere, that team won't be formed, or if formed, won't survive.

HAZARDS TO EFFECTIVE, VIABLE TEAMS: DEPENDENCIES, MORAL HAZARD, UNCERTAINTY OF TEAM VALUE, AND A RISK-ACCEPTING OWNER

The team we'll consider is an organized group intending to persist with the same members for a significant time. But coordination is not always automatic with full effort by everyone. Success of the team is affected by:

1) How well each member's skills are matched to their tasks and each other.
2) There is *moral hazard* in that members are tempted to shirk unless free riding is readily detected. Effective teamwork involves reliable dependency on the behavior of the other members.
3) The team's worth is uncertain; there must be some agreement about who will bear the results of the uncertainty.

How are the difficulties overcome? Usually, someone agrees to be a risk-taker — who guarantees amounts to be paid the other members. That person will also want, and be allowed, to take charge as the *boss* by assigning duties and monitoring the members.

In the earlier Adam, Baker, and Carter story of single-person firms, teamwork was not involved. The additional inputs were *identical homogeneous* units of inanimate inputs, not persons. There, the law of diminishing returns was dominant, whereas in teamwork people are interdependent. An explanation of some effects of teamwork on dependencies and determinants of personal earnings will be elaborated after exploring a hypothetical economy called Codlandia.

THE SAGA OF CODLANDIA

Codlandia has 1,000 adults, all fishing from the shore for cod. Each catches 8 codfish daily, the total social catch of 8,000 being their national income. One day a boat is found. The discoverer takes control of the vessel and begins to catch 12 codfish daily on the boat, 4 more than he could have caught on the shore. The relevant data are listed in table 22.2.

The principal features to be explained are: 1) meaning of the marginal product; 2) dependency of the amount of product on the team's size; 3) how the product value is divided among the team's members; 4) the determinants of the size of the team on the boat; and 5) the amount of social income.

The Marginal Return of an Input

To our assemblage of marginals — marginal personal worth, marginal revenue, and marginal cost — we now have the marginal product of a kind of input, listed in the third column, "Marginal Products on Boat." As successive units of a given kind of resource are added, the resulting marginal products form the marginal product schedule, where all units are assumed to be alike or interchangeable so far as their effectiveness on the boat is concerned.

The discoverer of the boat will soon learn that with a second person on board the catch more than doubles, from 12 to 30 codfish. This does not mean the second person caught those 18 additional codfish. The group with their

Table 22.2 *Codlandia Fishing Product Data*

Persons on Boat	Total Product on Boat	Marginal Products on Boat	Average Product (per Person on Boat)	Social Total: Shore plus Boat (Always 8 per Person on Shore)	Social Marginal Products
0	0	0	0	8,000 + 0 = 8,000	0
1	12	12	12.0	7,992 + 12 = 8,004	+4
2	30	18	15.0	7,984 + 30 = 8,014	+10
3	46	16	15.3	7,976 + 46 = 8,022	+8
4	58	12	14.5	7,968 + 58 = 8,026	+4
5	66	8	13.2	7,960 + 66 = 8,026	+0
6	70	4	11.7	7,952 + 70 = 8,022	−4
7	72	2	10.3	7,944 + 72 = 8,016	−6
8	64	−8	8.0	7,936 + 64 = 8,000	−16
9	52	−12	5.8	7,928 + 52 = 7,980	−20
10	30	−18	3.0	7,920 + 30 = 7,950	−30

resources caught them. The marginal product with an added person is the increase in the catch consequent to one more person on board. That person could have been looking for schools of codfish, helping to cast and pull in a heavy net, or tending the boat's engine. The marginal product is the difference in total amounts between 1) the former combination of inputs and 2) the combination with one more unit of a specified kind of productive input — here a person.

The increase of marginal product to 18 codfish with the second person can be considered a result of teamwork. However, as the team is enlarged, at some size the marginal products will begin to fall, according to the law of diminishing marginal returns. In Codlandia's boat, that starts at the third person.

Consistency with the Law of Diminishing Marginal Returns?

This magic of teamwork is not contrary to the law of diminishing marginal returns, although the law must be used with care. First, the law of diminishing marginal returns doesn't deny increasing marginal returns at the initial low ratios of that input where the fixed resource is so large as to have been underutilized.

Second, the law of diminishing marginal returns is not reliably applicable to a situation in which people are the added units, because people aren't all the same in temperament, reasoning, compatibility, judgment, experience, personalities, leadership, age, vigor, or risk-taking. Further, an added person alters the behavior of the existing members. With added people, no laws about patterns of returns have been formulated, except: "It depends on who, as well as on how many."

A Social Marginal Product

In Codlandia, with 1 person on board, the marginal product on the boat would be 12 cod. But with 8 less codfish caught on the shore, that's a gain of only 4 codfish (= 12 on board − 8 on the shore). The social marginal product, 4 codfish (= 8,004 − 8,000), is the increase in the amount of codfish in the entire economy.

With a second person on board, the marginal product of labor on the boat would be 18 codfish, with a total catch of 30 codfish on board (30 = 12 + 18). These 2 people would have caught 16 on the shore; therefore the social marginal total is 14 codfish (= 30 on board − 16 forgone from the shore). The social total national product increases by 14 cod to 8,014 (= 8,000 + 14). The marginal products on the boat begin to decrease with the third person on board.

With 7 people on the boat, the marginal product is only 2 codfish — 6 less than the forgone alternative of 8 codfish on the shore, a *social loss of 6*. At the eighth person on board, the marginal catch becomes negative, −8, for a marginal social catch of −16 codfish.

The total social catch of the whole community would decrease when 6 or more people are on the boat. The amounts of cod forgone from shore fishing would begin to exceed the marginal catches on the boat.

Episode 1: Economic Democracy: Share and Share Alike

The boat's discoverer and possessor initially believed that everyone who is allowed on the boat should share equally in the total catch. And he permitted those who are on the boat to decide on admission of more people. With 2 people, the total catch, 30 cod, is divided 15 to each, 7 more than the 8 cod each could have caught from the shore.

With 3 on board, the marginal catch is 16 cod, raising the total to 46, or 15.3 per person. Three people now have about twice as much as those on shore. Yet no one is poorer. You could say the society is richer.

Compensatory Entry Payments: The 3 incumbent members would not consent to having 4 on board. The share of that new total of 58 cod would fall from 15.3 to 14.5 (= 58/4) for each person on the boat, though the daily social total would have increased by 4 cod, from 8,022 to 8,026.

Those already on board refused to admit more people than the number that maximizes the average product per existing member. This incentive to maximize the average per person in the group is present in organizations in which everyone can a) share equally in the total product value and also b) vote on the size of the membership. Fraternities and sororities and labor unions of longshoremen, electricians, and musicians determine membership size by this process. Under majority voting and equal sharing, the average product per existing member dominates — a result sometimes called "inefficient" in that the social total is not maximized. Society is poorer than it need be, though some individuals are better off.

A rebuffed applicant could solicit access by offering, for the right of membership in the crew, 1 fish daily to each of the existing three members, who then would have 15.5 (= 14.5 + 1). The applicant, if admitted and paying 1 cod to each of the existing crew of 3, would be left with 11.5 cod (= 14.5 − 3), which is 3.5 more than the 8 that would have been caught on the shore.

That prevents dilution of benefits to existing members while enabling admission of new members to obtain a benefit. This side-payment is very common, called an up-front payment or membership fee in country clubs. Some unions require a substantial entry fee. Any applicant who would gain by admission could offer to compensate the incumbents for a dilution of incumbents' benefits, if the gross benefit to the applicant exceeds the total of the negative effects on incumbent members.

Episode 2: Private Property: Owner and Employees

The discoverer of the boat decides to take full command. In hiring people, he knows that employees must be paid at least 8 cod daily, because they could catch that amount on the shore. What pushes the wage down to 8 cod is competition among *those seeking work on the boat*. (We are presuming that working on the boat is no worse than working on the shore. If it were worse, a higher wage — a compensating wage difference — would have to be paid.)

The boat owner, seeking to maximize his income and wealth, would hire as many as have marginal products equal to the 8 codfish wage. This results in five people on the boat, of whom four are employees. The total catch with 5 people on board is 66 cod. The owner, after paying each employee 8 codfish, for total wages of 32, keeps the 34 excess of the 66 (34 = 66 − 32). Since the owner could have caught 8 cod on the shore, the owner's *net* daily income is 26 cod (34 − 8 opportunity cost of the employer).

No other number of people on the boat would yield a greater daily income to the owner. With 6 people on board, the total onboard catch of 70 cod would result in a daily reduction of 4 cod to the owner.

Effect on Social Total: The social total is maximized at 8,026 cod, when the owner's profits are maximized. But it was not the intention of the owner to maximize the social total income. And this coincidence is not caused by any special, unusual relationship between output and inputs in this example. It happens because competition by other people to be on the boat drives their boat incomes to match the best that could be earned elsewhere — 8 cod on the shore. This gain in income to the boat owner can be called a profit.

Wage of 3 cod: How many people would be hired if the competitive wage were 3 — as it would be if only 3 cod could be caught daily *on the shore?* The boat owner would hire at most 5 people for a total of 6 on board, with marginal product of 4 cod. Hiring 6 would reduce marginal product to less than the wage. Total wages would be 15 cod (= 5 × 3), while the total catch of 70 cod would leave 55 (= 70 − 15) for the boat owner. Owner's income from the boat is increased when income from the shore is decreased, and more people shift from the shore to the boat.

Wage of 15 cod: If everyone could catch 15 cod on the shore, the wage on the boat would have to be at least 15. Three people, the owner and two employees, would catch 46 cod. Marginal product with 3 people on board is 16 cod (= 46

– 30), close to, but not less than, the wage of 15. Paying the two employees 15 cod each (= 2 × 15) for a total of 30 would leave 16 as the reward to the owner, which is one more than the 15 the owner could have caught on the shore. The general principles of demand for productive inputs are:

1) The amount of a resource (productive input) demanded is that at which its *marginal product* is brought to *equality* with the *market price* of the resource. Or, the resource will be employed so long as its price of use does not exceed its marginal product value to the buyer of the services.
2) At a higher cost of a resource, fewer units are hired, and more at a lower cost.

Hardly anyone thinks and decides in conscious awareness and recognition of these concepts. You didn't have to know the law of gravity and falling bodies when you learned to walk, run, and ride a bicycle. Still, it's possible to understand, theorize, and discover its principles. Economics can identify some reliable propositions about viable responses to changes in the economic environment.

Episode 3: Renting the Boat

The owner decides to return to work on the shore and rents the boat to a team of five members. The "team of five" would pay him a daily rent of 26, equal to his old net income on the boat. The renters catch 66 cod; after paying the rent of 26, they have 40 (or 8 per person), equal to what they could have acquired on shore. With respect to crew wages, owner profit, and social income, it does not matter whether the boat is owner-operated with hired employees or is rented to a team.

Episode 4: Dependent Investment

A visitor — Sailor — comes to Codlandia. He invents sails to increase the boat's speed to more distant fishing areas. The boat's owner agrees to lease a sail from Sailor and make monthly payments, because the boat owner can't pay the full cost at the time of installation of the special mast and sail. Both the sail and mast are carefully matched to this boat's size and structure. As predicted, the boat's catch now increases, but so does *opportunistic behavior.*

Specific Dependency: The wily boat owner conjectures that upon refusal to pay all the promised rent, or failure to pay on time, Sailor could not effectively respond by threatening to take the sail and mast off the boat, for they wouldn't be worth much elsewhere. Sailor's wealth has become dependent on the boat owner. The mast and sail have low salvage value. They are specialized, to a specific boat, because removing and transferring them would cost more than their best alternative use.

With hindsight, Sailor realizes that the threat of nonpayment should have been avoided by obtaining a reliable commitment from the boat owner *before* making and installing the sail and mast that would be valuable only on that boat. Or Sailor and the owner could have formed a *partnership*, with specified shares in the value of the boat with the new mast and sail. That eliminates a unilateral right to remove the mast and sail.

A key feature of private property rights is that the rights to several goods can be dispersed or integrated among several people in whatever way they find mutually acceptable. The combining of the rights to the mast, sail, and boat into one package of rights is integrated ownership of the several resources. The ownership of that package of rights can be shared, as is done with shares of the common stock of a corporation. A share of common stock is a share of property rights to a collection of resources.

If ownership is integrated so each owner has some share in each item, opportunistic behavior that would make one of the items more valuable at the expense of other items would be pointless. Opportunism to affect the relative values of the items would merely transfer wealth from one item to another, all of which are owned by the same person. But some opportunities for opportunism among the members of the group would remain.

Examples of Risks of Opportunistic Behavior: A Pittsburgh steel mill owner relied upon a promise of the sole local gas supplier to supply gas at a price warranting construction of a gas-fired steel furnace to convert iron to steel. As soon as the gas-fired furnace was created and operational, the gas company raised the price of gas. The steel mill owner should have anticipated this possibility and obtained an enforceable commitment for price and delivery of the gas. Or, as suggested above, the owner of the gas company could have made the investment in the steel furnace. Or they might have integrated into one firm, so that the interdependent resources would be owned in common.

Imagine that you build an oil refinery and plan to buy your crude oil from the only and separately owned crude-oil pipeline. After you invest in constructing the refinery, the pipeline owner might raise the price of pipeline services. You would have to build another pipeline or shut down or relocate the refinery — an expensive action. How much could the owner of the existing pipeline threaten to extract from you? That would be an amount up to the costs of building a new pipeline or an amount equal to the excess in the refinery's value over its next best use.

But you, the refiner, could threaten not to pay, and if the pipeline owner had no alternative customers, its owner would be in a similar standoff situation. Because both parties know these possibilities prior to building either the refinery or pipeline, they could form one *integrated* company to build and operate both — a joint venture.

An employee may develop abilities or knowledge specific to the current employer. That skill becomes worthless if the employee is terminated. Therefore, might the employer cut wages by threatening to terminate the employee? Seniority and tenure rights help protect specifically dependent employees against an employer's expropriative action.

Specific Reciprocal Dependencies: Specific dependencies can be in both directions between the dependent entities, as reciprocal dependencies. Each of two people or two firms becomes dependent on the other. Marriage is probably the most common and strongest instance of *reciprocal* dependency. In contrast, children initially are completely and *specifically* dependent on parents.

One method of ensuring reliability of dependencies in proposed investments is to increase the required initial sunk cost involved in creating the interdependencies, and which would be lost if the interdependency failed. That higher vulnerable cost of the initial investment induces greater care in creating and entering into the dependent status. Later, we'll explore means of reducing the risk of this opportunistic behavior.

The Opposite Extreme: General, Mobile Resources: In Codlandia, the people and their fishing equipment are perfectly mobile between shore and fishing on the boat. But some items, such as the ropes and nets, are useful almost exclusively for fishing from the boat. Those boat-specific resources will be owned by the person who owns the boat. In contrast, resources that can be used elsewhere with nearly the same value are more likely to be owned independently of the boat. Generalized resources can more cheaply transfer. Their value is less dependent on their current employer.

Episode 5: Sale of the Boat

The boat's owner is to retire, and the boat is for sale. The best offer is to buy ownership of the boat by paying in installments, 8 cod per day for five years. The seller agrees, and the new owner starts to fish with 3 employees, each paid 8 codfish per day. On the first day, the catch is a disappointing 16 codfish, not 58 as expected from the data in table 22.2, which was shown to the new buyer before the purchase. The former owner consoles the buyer, and the buyer continues to pay the seller, and continues to fish. The average catch for the next few weeks is still less than expected.

Did the former owner cheat by exaggerating how many codfish had been caught? But the new buyer had been wary, and had verified the catches by the former owner, who had not lied.

The former owner accompanied the new owner the next day and found the trouble—weak management. The best fishing spots were being missed. And the crew wasn't being monitored as carefully as by the former owner. The crew malingered below deck, didn't rebait the lines carefully and quickly, and let too many cod escape.

The former owner explained that people who are paid a fixed amount per day have incentives to relax excessively and be less careful. Effective teamwork leadership requires management, direction, and an appropriate structure of rewards and penalties as incentives. Moral hazard is present when people depend on others. The new owner either learns how to manage the crew or sells the boat to someone who can.

Episode 6: Nationalization to Public Communal Property

Social disquiet was brewing, because all the increased wealth has been going to the owner of the boat. Some campaigned politically, under the slogan of "fishing reform," to nationalize the boat. And government officials thought that was desirable for their own interests.

What would determine who gets on board and who consumes the catch? Does any government official have as strong an incentive as a private owner to avoid managerial opportunism or shirking and negligence? Use will certainly be less directed by and tied to market values if the boat is owned or managed collectively—that is, by the government—and is more influenced by political processes.

One procedure could view the boat as publicly owned—like public parks, rivers, lakes, beaches, and highways—and would permit anyone to board the boat. So long as everyone onboard shares alike in the total, and the shared average return exceeds 8 codfish, up to eight people will board the boat.

However, with eight people on board the total catch *falls* from 72 cod with private ownership to 64 cod—8 per person—no more than they would have caught on the shore. A communal boat with open access and equal sharing will have become so congested that everyone's reward is reduced, so that a person might as well not be on the boat. There's no social gain. Think of the greater congestion when there is open access to public beaches, highways, and city streets, versus beaches where fee permits are required or toll roads.

There is excessive congestion because no one would have incentive to heed the effect on total output. That incentive (reward) does exist under private property rights. Where private property rights are absent or deemed too ex-

pensive to establish and enforce, government agents often are instructed
to administer the resource, as with, for example, air, river water, interstate
freeways, wild salmon, deer, ducks, the radio spectrum, and landing rights
at some airports, to name a few. This phenomenon of overuse of nonowned
resources — *overcatching* fish from a not-owned lake, or picking apples before
they are ripe from the nonowned tree in the public park — is the *Tragedy of the
Commons.*

People are not passive bystanders who persist in tolerating wasteful
overcrowding of valuable commons. They typically form rules and conven-
tions about use of the commons. In Switzerland, milk cows are driven in
late spring to high mountain pastures for summer grazing and feeding in a
commons — an area shared by all the cattle. That is easier than having a defined, fenced area for each herd. The pastures are a common area controlled by
the community, enforcing its customs and traditions. Each person is allotted
the right to pasture a certain number of cows, based on the number that can
be maintained during the winters — which tends to be a limiting constraint
preventing overcrowding during the summer.

Similarly, in the western United States, water usage is often communally
controlled with allocations based on the number of acres of adjoining land.
Lobster-harvesting areas off the coast of Maine are not owned by anyone under formal law, but each area is marked with lines and buoys, and enforced by
the group against poachers. The areas are inherited or transferred voluntarily
among the present group-recognized possessors. Newcomers who poach are
not brought to court; there is no formal law about the lobster areas. However,
newcomer poachers find their lives suddenly become intolerably uncomfort-
able. These examples illustrate the value of customs and how people make
efforts to create and enforce customs and *privileges* over valuable resources,
especially those that are sources of income.

Episode 7: Government Control

A government agent might be assigned to control access to the boat in the
public interest. What would the agent do? Control the boat for maximum public
use, maximum total cod caught, for maximum profit, or for personal political advantage? It seems unlikely the agent would maximize profitability, even
if told to do so, for he couldn't keep the profit. Lacking a validated theory or
model of government agencies' behavior, we offer some conjectures.

If instructed to maximize public welfare or the public interest, what should
(or would) the agent do? Would he lose (or gain) by not trying to charge the fee

that would maximize government revenue? A political authority suffers less loss (or gains less) of the potential wealth than a private owner.

The agent could permit more people on board—to make the demand for the resource appear larger. The agent would then request more such resources, enlarging the agency and the administrator's salary or political standing. Or the agent might allow uses of the boat only on weekends to ease the agent's tasks (closing on every minor holiday). We don't know. But that is the point. While their personal goals are the same as anyone else's, the constraints, strictures, and consequences that guide and control government employees in control of governmental resources are different from those that guide them in their use of privately owned resources.

Episode 8: Increased Inequality: Good or Bad? When and How Will Everyone Be Benefited? New Competitors

The pattern of wealth in Codlandia became very unequal. The initial quantity of 8 cod for everyone before the boat was found had changed to 26 cod for the boat owner, but still only 8 for everyone else. Increased inequality can mean greater gains to some people, with no losses to any others. More often, increased inequality is consistent with almost everyone being richer, the wealth of some increasing more than others.

Someone figures out how to build another boat. With two or more boats competing for crew members, and with more cod being caught, the price of cod (in terms of other goods) will fall.

Suppose coconuts are also harvested in Codlandia. As more cod are obtained, the number of cod exchanged for coconuts would rise—that is, the cod price of a coconut would rise (and, of course, the coconut price of a cod would fall). The community of Codlandia is richer—more cod and the same number of coconuts. However, part of the gain in wealth to the boat owners is dissipated to the rest of the community through the lower (coconut) price of cod. It is 1) competition *among owners* of more boats that distributes the gains to the public at large, and 2) their competition to get *crew members* that pushes up wages as people leave shore fishing. There is redistribution of increased wealth and income by competition.

Trickle Down or Ripple Out: In our example of Adam, Baker, and Carter, we saw that Carter (the low-cost and low-income entrant) gained wealth when allowed to enter the economy. With continuation of the story, that stream of gains to Carter will be dispersed into gains for the rest of society by the competitive entry of later entrants.

In Codlandia, the first boat acquirer became wealthy. Did the rest of the community gain? We saw that Adam had gained by a lower cost and greater amount of the good called Y as a result of the entry of Carter. In Codlandia, the first boat acquirer's wealth increased without reduction to any other people. But when other people invested in boats and increased the supply of cod, the price of cod fell to the benefit of everyone — except the first boat acquirer. Entry of more boat owners would also push up the wages to the employees on the boats. Boat owners compete against each other for labor, raising their costs and dissipating their profits to the rest of society. As more people are attracted away from fishing on the beaches, the wage rates would start to rise and the employees — the rest of the population — would begin to share in the larger product.

Redistribution of Profits: Suppose an investor started to produce a product at a cost of $10 a unit while selling it for $12, generating a profit of $2 per unit. You copy the technique and start production at the same $10 unit cost. You can cut the price below $12 and still make profits. The initial investor/producer responds by matching your price, rather than losing everything. You respond again, and the price is competed down to your $10 cost, leaving you with no profits. Also, the original producer's stream of profits ends. That profit stream is competed away to consumers through lower prices when the new competitor's output increases the total supply. We should distinguish between a) the gain in social output by the new entrant and b) the transfer of the increase (the gain in social output) to consumers as a result of entry by competitors.

NATIONAL DEVELOPMENT

Some of this discussion suggests the basic elements of a process of development in a nation, assuming that nation has reliable private property rights and a reliable, noncorrupt government administration. If there are any investments that would be profitable, analogous to building boats, the initial investor would get a big gain — all the increased output — for a while. When others, whether foreigners or domestics, also save (or borrow) and invest, competition in production and sale of the product would increase the supply and lower the product price, thereby permitting everyone to have more at unchanged money earnings. And competition to hire people at the more valuable work would pull up wages.

These are the two fundamental ways in which societies develop: 1) Initial saver/investors get the first investment gains. 2) Subsequent competing entrants a) produce more and lower the cost of living and b) drive up wages. It's competition from newcomers that is essential. Allowing only one investor would increase the total product, but with all going to that investor. Without barriers to entry, the initial investor's profits attract and motivate the forces that spread the gain, by the ripple out effect, to the entire population.

It makes no difference whether the investor is a foreigner or a local resident. It is often complained that foreigners invest and take all the profits. But the benefit is prevented from being spread over the general public only if just the one investor is allowed. That one investor may become very rich (by the exclusion of competitors) and pay large taxes, and then later give some of that wealth to the public as a great benefactor. But competitors — foreigners or domestic — could have provided more benefits earlier. (Notice the similarity of this analysis to that in the refugee camp [chapter 4], where competition with the second intermediary reduced costs and benefited the refugees more than with just one intermediary.)

It's worth repeating that development of a nation into a richer society requires profitable investment. Competition in investments distributes the gains over the society through higher incomes and lower product prices. Natural resources are desirable, but they don't produce income without labor and investment. And without competitive investments, the gains are distributed less rapidly and extensively. The large benefits often attributed to greater internationalization are the effects of that kind of increased competition into other nations. To object on the ground that the foreign investors are "exploiting" the beneficiary employees who are less educated, poor people working at low wages, is to condemn those people to continued poverty.

QUESTIONS AND MEDITATIONS

1) Our laws and customs reflect the assignments of risk bearing. Would you advocate that people bear wealth losses to their private property regardless of cause (aside from legal recourse to violators of property rights)? Would you want a homeowner to bear the consequences of a meteorite's falling on his house? From fire caused by careless use of gasoline in the house? Flood damage to houses near rivers? Income loss from cancer?
Who should bear the loss if the individual does not?

Answer:

We cannot outlaw risk. The pains and costs of bad events can be minimized by prudent behavior. But unfortunate things happen, and somehow consequences inevitably are borne by someone. In a community which values and generally relies on a high degree of personal independence and decision making, much of the unhappy consequences of life tend to be borne by the victims. However, individuals can pool resources and share costs in schemes of insurance against more or less predictable misfortunes. And some social and governmental efforts can comfort the weaker members of the community from slings and arrows of outrageous fortune. Usually a distinction is made between misfortunes that result from negligence rather than from "acts of God."

2) Contrast socialism and private property as means of distributing risks of profits and losses.

Answer:

Socialism does not permit selective, discretionary optional selection of wealth holdings by each individual. Profits and losses are borne in accord with taxes, rights to use government resources, and powers of political office. In a system of private property with open access to trade, consequences — value change of resources, profits and losses — are borne by the owner. By selectively purchasing and selling goods, people can adjust the combination of risk they bear under private property.

3) What is the relationship between the right to buy and sell and the distribution of profits and losses?

Answer:

The right to buy and sell facilitates or permits the distribution of profits and losses to be revised in accord with consumers' personal preferences.

4) "Private property permits selective, discretionary risk bearing." Comment.

Answer:

Sentence is correct. By selective purchase of assets of personal wealth holdings, people can vary their mixtures to suit their risk-bearing preferences.

5) A wealthy industrialist has a stable of race horses and a breeding farm. The two, although operated as a business, lose him over $50,000 annually. Yet he continues year after year because he enjoys the activity more than if he spent a similar sum for travel or conventional types of consumption activities.
   a. Would it be correct to say that he is maximizing his wealth in that business?
   b. Would it be correct to say he is maximizing his personal worth?

    c. Do you think an increase in the losses would induce an increase in that kind of activity? What does economic theory say about that?

Answer:

    a. Probably not.

    b. Probably yes.

    c. No. The higher the price of the activity, the less of it he will do.

6) If the boat owner, in the example in the text, were to employ the fishermen at a promised wage of 4 fish per day, the owner would bear the risk of the day's catch. But suppose the fishermen rented the boat from the boat owner for a fixed daily fee of, say, 14 fish. If the day's catch on board is less than enough to pay the rent and still leave at least 4 fish per fisherman, the renters will have lost. The risk is borne by the renters, not by the boat owner, who was promised 14 fish no matter what the catch. Is that correct?

Answer:

Assuming that today's rental contract is honored by the fishermen, they bear today's loss. But future rental value may be affected.

7) A large lake is stocked with excellent fish, but no one owns the fish or the lake. Only by catching the fish can you acquire ownership in the fish.

    a. What do you think will be the average age of fish caught as compared to the age of the fish in a privately owned lake?

    b. Which system — privately owned or "open to the public" — will induce overfishing in the sense that more resources will be devoted to catching fish than the extra fish caught are worth? Why?

Answer:

    a. Fish will be younger and smaller in a lake is not owned or fishing otherwise restricted, for the same reason that apples don't ripen in a public park. No one owns the fish (or trees in a public park), and the only way to capture the value of the fish is to catch them (or to cut the tree and take the wood). No one will have the wealth incentive — or legal power — to save or conserve the fish from those who prematurely catch and take them (or preserve the tree from those who cut it now for lumber).

    b. When no one *owns* all fish in the lake, the extra value of the fish taken will be judged by each separate fisherman according to his catch rather than by the total catch in the lake. Absence of property rights in the *lake* causes competition to acquire property rights in the *fish*.

8) Congestion:
    a. Why may zero congestion be wasteful?
    b. What social institutions prevent too much congestion and
       approximate optimal congestion?
    c. What is "optimal" congestion?

Answer:
    a. Because marginal product value of the activity in question, though de-
       creasing, still may exceed marginal cost.
    b. Private property rights that are enforceable and transferable; also polit-
       ical controls where private rights are not enforceable.
    c. That at which marginal product value equals marginal cost.

CHAPTER 23

THE FIRM'S CONTROL AND REWARD STRUCTURE

A GLANCE BEHIND, A LOOK AHEAD

Virtually everything we obtain carries some kind of cost and requires payment of some kind of price. Trade, we have seen, is an activity of simultaneous cooperation and coordination while there is also conflict and competition. Both parties gain from the exchange, but in trading each tries to gain the largest possible advantage over the other.

Production is as socially complex as exchange. People are more productive when associated with others. So we live in families and communities, and we work in teams while we trade locally and globally. But interrelations and webs and dependencies necessarily entail costs and inconveniences and frustrations along with increased efficiencies. Hence we try to protect ourselves from and minimize such burdensome and frustrating aspects of living together.

Chapter 22 dealt with the efficiency benefits of teams operating in a variety of circumstances and challenges. But not all teams are highly efficient or successful, and further complications and difficulties of control and direction are considered in chapter 23. In particular, issues of mutual dependency in production and commerce are examined in chapter 24. And chapter 25 is directed largely to modes of at least partial protection against the inevitable perils of such dependency.

In a firm, you work with the same persons, day after day, relying on predictable actions and reliable information from other members. When changes in the membership occur, they can be disruptive. Without a boss (manager/supervisor), everyone would have to negotiate continually with other members about what to do and who could become a member and how the rewards are shared. With a boss, team members can be more effectively selected, organized, directed, and rewarded.

However, even in the best of teams there's usually some disagreement about sharing the team's values and about the behavior of some members. A reason is that though the total output of the team can often be objectively measured, the contributions of each member to the final team output is difficult, if not impossible, to measure. We'll examine some resulting conflicts and the methods for inducing and maintaining reliable performance by the members of a firm.

Coordination in teamwork is not always automatic, and "full effort" by everyone, all the time, is never assured. Success depends on:

1) How well each member's skills are matched to their tasks and each other.
2) Effectively addressing "moral hazard": each member will be tempted to relax or shirk if that is not readily detected by the others.
3) Achieving and maintaining reliable dependency on the behavior of the other members, recognizing that the team's worth is uncertain.
4) Reaching some agreement about who will bear the uncertainty.

Despite substantial obstacles, many firms are successful and persist. How are the difficulties overcome?

THE BOSS

Who will be most interested in good monitoring of the team? Who would pay the most to have those rights? The owner of those resources most dependent on the success of the firm will have the greatest incentive to monitor the members. Therefore, the owner of such resources (which vary the most in value with the team's performance) would obtain rights to direct the team. In making automobiles, the person owning the design will find it worthless if the team fails to make the car profitably. The dies for stamping the metal parts that are unique to that firm's car will lose value. The value of the *brand name* will lose value. We'll call such resources "firm specific." The owner of those firm-specific assets tends to be the boss.

WHAT IS THE MEANING OF "OWNING A FIRM"?

Literally, the firm — consisting of all the resources and *people* — can't be owned. What "owner of the firm" means is the person who owns the salable resources, the values of which are most dependent on the firm's success. The owner acquires the authority to:

a. determine who is on the team,
b. direct team effort,
c. monitor performances of team members,
d. bear the changes in the market value of the team-specific resources and the marketed products, all in return for

e. bearing the obligation to pay the promised amounts to suppliers of services sold to the firm.

That obligation motivates the boss/owner to hire a good manager as an agent of the owner.

Ownership may be vested in several people as joint owners, as in a partnership or a corporation. Ownership and control ties responsibility to authority — the responsibility to bear the results of one's actions, a critical condition of a private property economy.

The resources now serving Ford Motors, the removal of which would cause a serious loss of value, are said to be dependent specifically on Ford. Resources with values heavily dependent on the firm's activities and not readily replaced will be owned by the corporation, not rented, lest the outside owner threaten to withdraw those resources unless paid more than initially agreed. As protection against expropriation actions, or failures of a single supplier, Ford manufactures some of the items itself, or relies on several suppliers, called multiple outsourcing.

If profits of a firm should fall and production were to be reduced, owners of economically mobile resources and mobile employees — a janitor, secretary, or assembly worker — would move elsewhere for virtually the same earnings. Because owners of the less mobile resources have fewer or less desirable alternatives, they have greater interest in what happens in the firm and in maintaining its profitability.

Increased specialization in ownership and in management over the past century does not mean *separation* of managers from control by the firm's owners. That belief is fostered by the expression "separation of ownership and control." A more accurate expression is "specialization in ownership and in management."

MANAGEMENT REWARDS

To encourage employee-managers to be more effective in maintaining or increasing the value of the enterprise, owners often give them rights to share in the "residual" gains — the profits after stipulated payments to other members. Then the managers also become risk bearers, as well as adapters to unpredictable future circumstances. An additional compulsion is competition among present or potential managers. Within a firm, employees eagerly compete to displace those who don't perform well in the employer's interests.

SHIRKING AS MORAL HAZARD OR
OPPORTUNISTIC HOLD-UPS

Self-interest tends to thwart full interest to the group goal. Everyone, no matter how helpful to other people, has a personal interest. Whether a form of laziness, carelessness, duplicity, or moral hazard, it's a problem in all group activity, sometimes called the "principal-agent" problem. An "agent" agrees to act for the benefit (interest) of someone else, the "principal." From this agreement arises the task of controlling and monitoring the performance of the agent. The problem is probably present in every relationship among people. Every group that shares some goal must control each member's laziness and abuse of prerogatives.

An employer (the principal) usually regards some personal interest behavior by the employee (the agent) as acceptable, because it's anticipated and not worth trying to avoid. It is tolerable moral hazard. But money wages paid to the employee will be lower, the greater the moral hazard. Only the employee's *undetected* excess above the acceptable level is a loss to the employer and a gain to the employee. A deliberate attempt to get more than was anticipated by the employer could be described as a form of stealing. *Shirking* is the reduction of performance to levels expected by the employer, who will penalize excessive shirking.

MONITORING AND DETERRING SHIRKING

The members of the team must be monitored to ensure promised performance. We'll look at monitoring done directly by the employer (boss). Then we'll examine indirect monitoring by nonowners, after which we'll look at protecting employees from an *employer's* opportunistic, excessive shirking or inferiority in management.

LOYALTY AND SHIRKING

Employees have a legal duty and moral obligation to work in the interests of their employer rather than of other firms. Trade secrets or techniques should not be disclosed to other firms. Employers often require certain employees to agree not to work for a competitor until a number of years after leaving the current employer.

In many situations, excessive shirking is reduced by self-enforcing incentives such as personal ethics. In others, monitoring and the prospect of subsequent punishment deter it. There are some more subtle and effective methods, "direct" by the boss and "indirect" by customers and competitors.

CUSTOMERS, RATHER THAN THE EMPLOYER, MAY MONITOR AND RESTRAIN EMPLOYEE SHIRKING: "TIPS"

Paid for Expected Service

The owner of the restaurant you visit could carefully watch your waiter to see that you receive the promised degree of service. But that would be more expensive than letting the customers monitor the waiter and then pay the waiter an amount appropriate to the quality of service.

As we have seen, the tip is not entirely a premium paid for extra-good service. The customer is better at monitoring the services given the customer than is the restaurant owner. It's more economical to let the customer do that in places where employees provide services directly to the customer and service quality can vary widely. Tips are methods of monitoring to avoid excessive shirking.

Premium Wages to Restrain Employee Shirking

Another way to restrain excessive shirking is to pay a wage exceeding a competitive wage and inform the employee that if caught cheating he will be terminated, with the future large stream of anticipated premiums lost. To be effective, the expected present capital value of the stream of premium payments must exceed the expected current gain by shirking. The longer the expected tenure of the job, the greater is the present capital value of the loss to an employee who is caught shirking.

Temporary employees won't be around long enough to be influenced by threat of loss of future premium streams. They will tend to be paid less than will workers who are expected to be long-term employees.

Efficiency Wages for Better Services

A similar way to compensate is efficiency wage rates to induce better services. "Pay me more per hour, and you'll get higher-quality services from me each hour." Decisions about which employees are salary and which are hourly often reflect the incentives to shirk and the costs of monitoring performance.

Often Mistaken Perception of Reason for, and Effects of, Employee Commitments to Long-Term Employment with the Employer

Some employment includes on-the-job training in skills that are useful for work also with *other* employers — "general" job training. Training to arrive on time, not to disturb other employees, how to serve customers, how to use a computer, to type, to operate a "machine tool," or to be a waiter — all would help that employee get higher wages elsewhere. The value of that training, financed by the employer's investment, would be lost to that employer, if the employee quits after only a short time.

To protect the employer making the investment, employees either (a) initially accept a lowered wage to compensate for that "general value" training or (b) agree to stay with that employer for some specified length of time at wages less than could be earned elsewhere.

That's what the military accurately advertises when recruiting by combining a long-term employment contract, a "tour of duty," with the promise of training. These commitments are commonplace in motion picture and sports contracts. The commitment is explicitly stated in the contract, or it's enforced by custom among alternative employers.

Employer Dependency and the Strike

A drastic example of exploitation of the employer's dependency on employees would be a farm labor union striking at harvest time for an increase in wages. With a short harvest season, a fear of opportunistic behavior by workers is the principal reason farmers are so strongly opposed to unions, especially those with no reputation of forgoing that opportunistic tactic.

Restraining Employer Opportunism: "Firm Dependent" Employee Investments

There are opposite risks that the employer will opportunistically confiscate an employee's "employer-specific" (firm-specific) investments.

As an employee, you may have invested, at your own expense, in learning and developing skills the value of which depends primarily on your continued membership in your current firm. Or you may have incurred a large cost to move to the site of the work. That firm-specific investment helps you earn more in this firm than you could earn elsewhere.

The greater amount you can earn here rather than elsewhere, or would lose if you were to relocate, is now dependent on your current employer. Protections include long-term contracts for employees and the custom of not changing wages or prices frequently with every variation in business.

"Up-or-Out" — Promotion or Dismissal within Specified Number of Years

Tenure for college professors or partnership status for lawyers, accountants, and investment bankers are methods of protecting firm-specific employees. "Up-or-out" agreements protect the aspirant employee from an employer's potential opportunistic cheating. In a law firm, after a specified number of years of employment, the employee-lawyer must either be promoted to partnership or terminated. Usually after a few years, a college instructor is either terminated or promoted to tenure status. Without this time limit in the up-or-out decision an employer could delay in the hope of getting additional years of work from the underpaid employee before finally terminating the employment or belatedly granting full-tenured employment.

Delayed Measurement and Compensation for Earlier Underpaid Performance
Abilities of college professors, especially in research, will be demonstrated only over several years. It takes time to do research, publish, and have the work evaluated. Compensation for superior earlier performance will be paid as higher wages years later. This may appear to be overpayment relative to the value of later performance, but the later high wages are compensation for the then-verified high value of earlier productivity.

Paying for work after the work is completed is quite common: you pay after your dinner in a restaurant; you pay after receiving medical and legal services; you pay for a house after it is built. Payment after services is more common where what's purchased cannot be reliably identified and evaluated before purchase.

This method of full payment after the service is evaluated creates the reverse risk that the college might later refuse to pay higher wages as compensation for earlier superior performance. The professor could not get an equally high wage from other colleges which would be willing to pay only wages reflecting current productivity. Faculty protection can be gained by the tenured professors who can't be fired.

The Boundaries of a Firm: Who Are the Members? What about Customers?
The "boundary" of a firm refers to all the contractual relations in which the firm is involved. You have bought a car, the worth of which is dependent on specified continuing responsibilities of the manufacturer. A warranty specifies generally what kinds of maintenance and repairs will be made without additional charge. (The initial price of the car must cover the costs of expected repairs covered by the warranty.) The warranty indicates also the customer's general maintenance responsibilities. The owner of the car therefore has a contract or understanding with the producer. Maintenance services are thus part of the package of ownership rights that accompany the car.

FIRMS NOT OWNED BY FULL PRIVATE PROPERTY RIGHTS

Not-for-Profit, Nonprivate "Firms"

Some "firms" or "enterprises"—like most universities—are not owned. Whether operated by the state or by a foundation, they have no "owners" in the same sense as a private business—only administrators. The administrators don't hold private property rights in the enterprise, so they neither gain nor lose as a consequence of the value of the enterprise. While there would be some value placed on the resources utilized by the not-for-profit enterprise if offered for sale, such values cannot be readily ascertained. The administrators are therefore relatively unresponsive to effects on the market value of the resources they administer (as in our Codlandia saga in episodes 6 and 7 on nationalization and government control, chapter 22). Historical events—such as the transition of "socially owned" enterprises in the former Soviet Union to private ownership—provide clear evidence of the altered incentives of owners versus the former administrators.

A Labor-Owned Firm: An Oxymoron? No

The same principles hold for human capital as for nonhuman physical resources. Often enterprises are voluntarily formed where labor is the primary team-reliant resource, such as groups of physicians, architects, and lawyers, who are owners of their own firms. Although the individuals who work at such a firm are employees, this is not what is generally meant by employee owned.

More accurately, such firms are labor owned. In a law firm, new young members enter as employees, with a stated salary. Their human capital is not "firm specific," that is, they could do as well at other law firms. But over many years they will develop a specific knowledge of the firm's clients that allows them to serve those clients better than would other lawyers. Eventually, some will be offered partnerships (a share of ownership of the firm) to prevent them from leaving and taking clients with them.

"Union Owned" or "Employee Owned": An Oxymoron? Yes

Some enterprises, called employee owned, grew from desperation, as a means of restructuring costs—usually by revision of the contracts between the employees and the employers. Both agreed to reduce their direct rewards (wages and salaries) as a condition of continuing to work in the enterprise. The trade-off is usually that the employees gain shares of ownership entitling them to any future dividends if the firm returns to profitability.

There have been a good many such cost-cutting reorganizations to emerge from bankruptcy or avoid termination of the enterprise. Such experiences suggest that employee ownership may be a sort of rescue from impending disaster, rather than a means of prolonged success.

In these rearrangements of rights, no employee owns *salable* shares of the common stock of the firm. Instead, the employee union holds the shares on their behalf. If an employee quits, none of the shares of ownership will be retained by that individual. They reside with the union. The union agents determine how much of the firm's revenue is allocated to wages and how much to reinvestment for new equipment.

Inevitably, the employees want the firm to pay out more of the revenue as higher wages now, instead of investing in equipment for future income—when the employee is less likely to still be an employee. This pressure to concentrate more on present payout and less on investment won't help the enterprise survive long in competition with investor-owned firms that are making longer-lived investments.

Mutuals and Clubs: Integrated Ownership by the "Customers"

When many parties are reliant on a single asset, the solution is often joint ownership by all, rather than integrated ownership by one. If two or more firms desire to share the use of a resource upon which they will become reliant, there is an incentive for the firms to merge.

Two chemical firms separated by a river decided that it would be mutually advantageous to build a pipeline to supply chemicals from one to the other. However, neither wanted the pipeline to be controlled by the other. They ultimately agreed to form a jointly owned firm to build and own the pipeline on which each firm would be reliant.

Jointly owned enterprises are common where two otherwise independent companies want legal arrangements to protect their rights and bind the other to predetermined performance standards.

In the Swiss Alps, dairy farmers brought milk to a processing plant, the only one accessible to them. Rather than becoming reliant on an independently owned processor, all the farmers in that region constructed and owned the processing plant as their common property—a mutual enterprise. Similarly, the fishermen in an area typically form a mutually owned co-op for the packing and shipping of the fish to customers.

A mutual enterprise is a way to protect the group from opportunistic exploitation by one independent supplier of a necessary service. Small retail grocers may form a mutual organization for the purpose of owning their wholesale distribution network. There are mutually owned savings banks that are chartered by state or local governments, but not owned by the members. A credit union is a form of mutual enterprise to provide financial services to members — who are not owners.

Most social and golfing country clubs are mutuals. The dependence on the other members explains why social clubs like the Kiwanis, Rotary, or local country club are said to be owned by all the members. If membership in a social group were determined by an independent owner, the value of the benefits of the social matching of the members could be extracted by high membership fees paid to that owner, rather than being retained by the members.

A recent development is in the provision of education services by way of "charter schools" that compete for students with both the "public schools" (usually owned and operated by local governments) and "private schools" (owned and operated by investors). These charter schools are typically organized as nonprofit corporations, without stockholders or other investors. Parents of the students attending charter schools have more influence in the operation of such schools, but still are not owners. If the school ceases to operate, there is no residual value that can be retained by anyone, nor can the rights to operate the school be sold to other individuals.

QUESTIONS AND MEDITATIONS

1) "The employer is called the boss because he is able to tell people what to do." Evaluate.

Answer:

> The boss is able to tell people what to do because he pays them. Turning it around, the employee tells the boss what to do — that is, to pay the employee some money. Neither finally tells the other what to do. Each agrees to do something if the other will do something. If it is said, "an employer can fire an employee," so can an employee fire his boss by changing jobs.

2) What is the measurement problem in joint teamwork that is not present in specialization of the type where each person produces by himself and then trades some of his output for products of other independent producers?

Answer:

> It is more difficult to assess the performance of each member of a team. More than one person contributes to an outcome, and it is generally im-

possible to impute the portions of the total to the individual contributors, who meld their efforts and rely upon each other.

3) In a business firm — essentially a team of employees and employers — all members have a legal obligation of loyalty to the firm, lest the team's performance be subverted. Employees cannot sell their jobs or firm-related information to whomever will pay an adequate price — unlike some renters who can sublet to new tenants without the owner's prior approval. Only the boss can authorize substitutions or additions to the group — by hiring and firing. In contrast, the stockholders of a limited-liability corporation can sell their ownership rights. Why?

Answer:

Stockholders don't form a team in which changes in membership can change obligations or rights of the other stockholders. If such changes were likely, the firm would not be organized as a corporation with freely alienable shares of common stock (ownership) of the firm.

4) The players of familiar team sports — hockey, basketball, football, baseball — all have assigned responsibilities. The success of the team depends on the performance of each player. But the team coaches and managers are never in the game, so what is their unique contribution to the performance of the team?

Answer:

Team activity requires monitoring of the performance of each individual member of the team. No player on the field/rink/court of play is in a good position to monitor the performance of other players, while also executing his assigned responsibilities to the best of his abilities. The coach or manager of a team is expected to maximize team performance by making judgments about individual performance — and making substitutions as appropriate to enhance overall results. Similarly, the conductor of an orchestra has no instrument and makes no sounds, but contributes to the quality of the music by monitoring and evaluating the performance of each member of the orchestra.

5) During the final years of the former Soviet Union, top government officials decided they must introduce "private property rights" that they saw were common in the more successful market economies. After only one year, they boasted, "Moscow has the highest incidence of home

ownership in the world." However, selling and buying houses was still prohibited. What were the Soviet leaders not understanding about home ownership?

Answer:

Exclusive use of something—whether living in a home or using the desk and computer provided by your employer—is not ownership. Property rights include *both* exclusive right to use *and* the right to transfer exclusive right to use to another party. Where open markets are not permitted, possessing a "certificate of ownership" has little meaning.

6) Over the past two decades, many states in the United States have permitted the opening of charter schools to offer educational services to children as an alternative to the traditional public schools. Most of these charter schools are funded by appropriations from the state legislatures—taxpayers' money—and are not "private schools." Since these new types of schools are not "owned" by investors and are not profit-oriented, why would there be any difference in quality of education services provided?

Answer:

Traditional public schools do not compete with each other for customers—students and their parents. Children are assigned to a school and cannot choose to attend another school across town that may be getting better results. The consequence has been that public schools are primarily "producer driven"—teachers and administrators do not have to be concerned that customers—students—will take their business elsewhere if they are not satisfied. It is rather like being in an isolated town with only one restaurant and you are required to eat out five times a week; the cook will not be so concerned about how much you like the food. In contrast, charter schools do not have students assigned to them—they must attract them by offering higher-quality education services. This customer orientation of such schools causes the teachers and administrators to be sensitive to changes in demand—the students and their parents can always go to another school they believe is offering better services.

7) The B-17 was a World War II bomber that had a highly coordinated team of specialists, including a pilot, a copilot, a bombardier, a navigator, an engineer/gunner, a radioman, two waist gunners, a ball-turret gunner, and a tail gunner. Which of these ten was most important?

Answer:

It is a misdirected question: any of them might make the most critical contribution on a given mission. The plane will not leave the ground without the work of the pilots; it may not find the target or return to home base without the navigator; the bombs are not likely to come close to the target without the input of the bombardier; the plane and its crew may not survive the flight or even reach the target if the gunners fail to keep enemy fighters at bay. All on the team must contribute as circumstances require, but it is an empty exercise to try to measure individual productivities, designating one vital contribution as more vital than another vital contribution — the crew live, fight, and sometimes die together, and there is little temptation to shirk at 20,000 feet in enemy territory.

8) In the former Yugoslavia, most firms were said to be "employee owned." The top managers of these enterprises tended to be the most senior employees — those who had worked there the longest and worked their way to the top. The government discovered that these firms spent very little on maintenance, experienced frequent equipment breakdowns, and were reluctant to acquire and install new equipment. The consequence was that the government mandated minimum expenditures on maintenance and investment in new equipment. Why was neglect of maintenance and purchase of new equipment predictable?

Answer:

Employees were not allowed to sell their share of ownership — either to someone else in the firm or to someone outside the company. Senior managers could not transfer their position to another — even their own children. There was no way for present employees to capture the value of future earnings of the firm after they had retired. True ownership includes a "residual claim" on the future earnings streams that result from new investments — and maintenance of the present equipment. Skimping on maintenance and underinvesting in timely equipment upgrades reflected the incentives of decision makers to focus only on short-term performance, to the neglect of longer-term results.

CHAPTER 24
PROTECTING YOUR DEPENDENCIES

On a two-lane road, cars approaching you on the left have drivers on whom you suddenly become extremely dependent, expecting them to stay on their side of the road. What assures reliable performance by other drivers? One is "hostage" dependency: if that driver doesn't behave as predicted, both you and that driver lose. Many on whom you will become dependent will not be as reliable.

A member on a basketball team may try to be the star, to the detriment of the team. A business partner might behave in ways to your disadvantage and to that person's benefit. You go on a first date without much initial dependency on the other person, but — not always fortunately — after repeated dating there may develop a specific dependency on that specific person.

To avoid disappointment, you may take advance precautions. Consider some techniques for increasing predictability and reliability of actions of other people. Before you buy, you inspect the goods, especially those that are easily and cheaply examined before purchase, and for which no future repairs or related services by the seller are expected.

You can easily inspect a head of lettuce, and if, after purchase, it surprisingly proves defective, the loss is minor. But when buying a computer or income tax services, you can't cheaply and reliably assess the product or services. You often must rely on a promise of future performance. You rely on the seller's reputation for reliably supplying the expected service.

Once you make the purchase or do business, you become dependent on that specific seller. How can you be assured you'll get what you were promised? You could take legal action afterward, but that's expensive, and you may lose. The usual alternative is to obtain protection before you become dependent on a specific person/vendor. Each of the competing suppliers — among whom you will choose one on which to be dependent — wants to assure you of their future reliability. Assurances can be strengthened by contracts and by reputation.

DEPENDENT INVESTMENTS

You can't protect yourself by refusing to become dependent. You make yourself dependent upon someone simply by driving to a store for a purchase at a special price. You use gasoline and your time, and you risk an automobile accident. At the store, you discover the advertised price was incorrect, and the actual price is higher. After indignantly berating the seller, you disappointedly consider your alternatives. Either you go home empty-handed or you pay the higher price. And after making a purchase, there are risks. Deliveries can be late; the product may be defective; repairs and upkeep may be unexpectedly expensive. These risks are universal.

A student may have chosen a certain college because of its distinguished professor of biology, or its football coach, after which the relied-upon person moves to another college. You buy software for your computer, and when it doesn't work as advertised, the software developer and the computer maker blame each other.

On the seller's side, some customers are unattractively unpredictable. They falsely claim products are defective and seek a refund. Whether it's a result of chicanery or negligence, or of factors beyond control (earthquakes, hurricanes, war, strikes, riots), there's always some uncertainty about price and performance.

INTEGRATED OWNERSHIP

Consider some hypothetical examples of specific dependencies. Airline-West is the only airline carrier of passengers between San Francisco and Chicago. Airline-East is the sole carrier between Chicago and New York. Suppose the fare for the whole route from San Francisco to New York (connecting in Chicago) is $500. How would it be divided between the two airlines? If West charged $400, only $100 would be left for East to charge for its portion. If, instead, East charged $300, there'd be only $200 left for West.

This mutually destructive conflict between the two interdependent firms would be avoided if one company owned the two segments. This is a reason trunk lines (end-to-end lines) for railroads, airlines, and telephone and cable lines tend to be owned as one system.

To provide reliable predictability of fares to customers, the two independent airlines may agree to joint scheduling or joint setting of fares of the two segments, which does not mean they agreed to collude to get more revenues. However, that agreement might give the impression of nefarious conspiratorial actions.

An analogous example is a hotel owner and an independently owned restaurant in that hotel. The hotel owner would want prices in the restaurant to be low (for a given quality) to help attract people to stay at the hotel. However, the restaurant owner has the opposite desire — low hotel rates and correspondingly higher prices in the restaurant that services the hotel guests. These situations of dependency on a specific other person are laden with potential for serious dispute and disruptions.

RECIPROCAL DEPENDENCY

Two interdependent firms can have *reciprocal dependency*, with each dependent on the reliable predictability of the behavior of the other. If one threatens the other, the other can match the threat in the reverse direction, which will restrain incentive for the initial threat.

To reduce transport costs of gasoline from refineries to retail service stations, a Shell refinery in Houston could supply gasoline to stations of a competitor — say, Exxon's stations in the South and West regions — as well as to its own Shell service stations in the Southwest. At the same time, Exxon's refinery in New Jersey would supply gasoline to Shell stations in the New York area.

A reciprocal service agreement helps assure that each will reliably supply the other. This reciprocity can be viewed as an exchange of hostages. "I have what you want, and you have what I want. If you take or destroy mine, I'll do the same to yours." Such reciprocity might appear to be a method for Exxon and Shell to collude to control the price of gasoline, when in reality it would be a method of reducing costs to consumers.

EXCLUSIVE SERVICE CONTRACTS TO PROTECT RELIABILITY OF INVESTMENTS IN A PERSON

An arrangement designed to create reliability of predicted services is an exclusive service contract. Consider young aspiring actors who believe that if they have a chance, they'll skyrocket to fame and fortune.

Only a few will be a great success. TV studios and producers take a big risk when they invest in making a test (pilot) episode for a TV series with a new aspirant. The hope for large earnings on the rare successes is expected to offset, on average, the losses of the several inevitably failed investments. The studio-investor offers to make the investment in training or exploration, and he will have the exclusive rights to share in the future earnings of the discovered star. Or the aspirant might persuade someone to make the investment in return for a share of future earnings. The few successes grab public attention. The many more failures walk into obscurity, leaving the investor with the loss of the investment.

When the investment in training and exploration is successful, another future risk exists for the investor. The new star is now in strong demand with the prospect of very large salaries. The potential to command those big salaries —

derived from the demand for programs featuring that star—motivated the willingness to invest in the aspirant. But the star, who can now command a high salary from rival producers, might walk away, keeping all the high salary. Or the newly famous actor could threaten to refuse to act in any future episodes of that series unless given a bigger share than agreed to initially. To the initial investor, the success then could become a matter of, "Tails, I lose; heads, you get everything." Facing that risk, investors would refuse to make the initial investments, and the potential stars would remain undiscovered. That's why investors wouldn't invest in a pilot or series unless they obtained exclusive rights, for perhaps several years, to the acting services of the discovered star. The few successful stars look in dismay at how much of their new salary is reserved for the investor (or withheld by the producer of the shows if the producer had been the initial investor). The stars sometimes claim they are being cheated by an unconscionable earlier contract with the initial investor. But the exclusive service contract actually benefits both the investor and the aspiring newcomer.

EXAMPLE: THE CONTROVERSIAL
BASEBALL RESERVE CLAUSE

When a young baseball player signs an initial contract, he has to agree not to negotiate thereafter with other teams. This is called a *reserve clause*. Only about one in ten actually plays in the major leagues for as long as one season, and about one in one hundred stays for two years, hardly enough to make the team owner's investment worthwhile.

If Ford and GM tried to impose a reserve clause on their new employees, it would be declared illegal. How could the reserve clause be defended in baseball? The defense rests on the necessity of expensive training and testing of athletes during their early careers. A team owner makes exploratory, developmental investments in many rookies, hoping that a few players will ultimately be worth the expense. The reserve clause restriction protects the team owner's investments. Absent the initial investments by the team owners, the aspiring players would have had to bear more of their own investment costs during their early careers, possibly playing with no salary in the minor leagues or not trying at all.

VOLUNTARY MAXIMUM RETAIL PRICE

Most things are produced and distributed through a succession of business firms from manufacturer to wholesaler to retailers. They depend on each other—reciprocal dependency. A gasoline station that is dirty and gives poor service will reduce the sales of the *refiner* of the gasoline. A car dealer who poorly displays and demonstrates cars and fails to provide good warranty service hurts the *manufacturer*.

A newspaper or magazine publisher depends on distributors (retailers) to help sell the publication. The retail price charged by the distributor-retailer will affect sales, so manufacturers may want retail prices to be set lower than the retailers would like. (We'll examine cases where manufacturers *prevent* retail prices from being reduced.)

PUBLISHER VERSUS DISTRIBUTOR CONFLICT ABOUT RETAIL PRICE

The primary source of revenue for a newspaper or magazine publisher is from advertisers, not from sales. Similarly, advertising is the basis of revenue to a network TV station. Advertisers will pay more for advertising in a newspaper that has more readers, or in a TV show that has more viewers.

The publisher of a newspaper or a magazine wants the retail or subscription price to be as low as possible so as to increase the copies sold and therefore the advertising revenue. The price is sometimes zero, as with neighborhood "throwaway" newspapers. This difference in strategy (advertising revenue versus revenue from sales) creates a conflict of interest between the publisher and the independent distributor-vendors who want a higher price, because all they get is the sales revenue.

One solution is to impose a ceiling on the retail price charged by the distributors of the publication. The price can be printed on the publication, which makes it difficult for the independent distributor-retailer to charge more. Since the distributor gets only the sales revenue and none of the advertising revenue, the distributor would want to charge more than the low price preferred by the publisher. At one time, imposing a *maximum* price at which the distributor could sell was declared by some federal judges to be illegal *price fixing*. Later, other federal judges declared it legal, because it served consumer interests. Finally, in 1997, the US Supreme Court, in reversing its earlier prohibition of price fixing, ruled that a manufacturer can legally set a ceiling on the retailer's price.

Price fixing has been declared illegal only if it tends to monopolize or create a monopoly. But we have seen (chapter 19) that monopoly and price fixing have no uniform accepted meaning in the courts.

INTEGRATION?

The ultimate solution to the price-fixing conundrum is integration. The publisher could own the distribution system and use his own employees to distribute the paper or magazine. He then sets the price and gets all the revenue from both sales and advertising. In this case, there's no price fixing as the law sees it.

MORE EXAMPLES OF PRICE CEILINGS
IMPOSED ON RETAIL DISTRIBUTORS

The same kind of conflict between publishers and their distributors is found between manufacturers of personal mobile telephones and telephone companies. The manufacturers of phones want a lower price for the phone *service* than the telephone companies would prefer, so as to have more phones using more services. And telephone companies offer portable phones at a low price for the phone, sometimes giving them away if the customer will sign a multiyear service contract.

This same kind of pricing occurred long ago when disposable razor blades were invented. The razor-blade *holders* (analogous to mobile phones) were given away, the blades (analogous to phone calls or text messages) were not. Similarly, at one time cameras were given away, to promote revenue derived from the sales and processing of the film.

MINIMUM PERMISSIBLE RETAILER PRICES,
KNOWN AS RETAIL PRICE MAINTENANCE (RPM),
TO AVOID FREE RIDING OF DISCOUNTERS

At the other extreme, there can be a setting of minimum retailer prices. Why would the manufacturer want to prevent a retailer from cutting the retail price in order to sell more units? The retailer still would pay the same wholesale price to the manufacturer. You'd think the wholesaler would be pleased to have more units sold, even if the retailer must be content to have a smaller margin.

However, there's a dependency. The manufacturer depends on the independently owned retailers to help generate sales by informing potential customers of the merits of the item. Retailers give personal services to customers in displaying, demonstrating, fitting, and finishing the item.

Cosmetics are demonstrated at the retail counter, at the expense of the retailer. Such information and specific customer service is typically and more effectively provided by the retailer when dealing personally with a potential customer. When you propose to buy clothes, shoes, appliances, or an automobile, typically you talk to the retailer, not the manufacturer, about the good. And the retailer displays, holds inventories for immediate availability, and will provide delivery of bulky items to the customers' homes.

In turn, a retailer relies on the manufacturer to provide goods that are reliable and of the promised quality. To increase the reliability of that *mutual dependence*, the manufacturer and retailer often agree on the minimum price the retailer will charge customers, confident that other retailers cannot undercut them. Look at an example of what otherwise would happen.

A customer shopping for a hearing aid wants a demonstration and information on fitting and acoustical properties of the device. The supplying of these presale services at a retailer's own expense opens an opportunity for a competing retailer to profit by reducing the price and the service by selling hearing aids straight from the box with no demonstration or fitting. Customers could browse, getting information at the *full-service* retailer's expense, and then buy the appropriate model from a non-full-service price-cutter.

The manufacturer and the full-service retailer want to stop the free riding of the price-cutter. The reduction of those services would reduce the demand for that supplier's hearing aids by raising the costs to potential customers for getting well-fitted reliable hearing aids.

If the manufacturer refuses to sell to price-cutters, from where do unauthorized, discount sellers get their supply of that manufacturer's products? One source is some *authorized* dealer, who covertly, at a small margin over the wholesale price, sells to discounters who resell at a price below the *authorized price*. That illicit supply could be prevented if the rogue retailer were to be severely punished with a large financial loss. The manufacturer must ensure that the loss to the cheating retailer be greater than the potential gain to the cheater.

A *retail-price-agreement* setting a minimum retail price is a contractual arrangement that assures the retailer of a predetermined profit margin at the agreed-upon wholesale price to a retailer. That margin — the difference between the set retail price and agreed wholesale price — must be sufficient to compensate the full-service retailer for the services involved in selling the product, plus a return on investment.

Then, if a cheating retailer is caught, the termination of the unusually large margin containing larger profits results in a large loss to the retailer. That loss is equal to the present value of the future profits contained in the *premium* stream enabled by the negotiated profit margin. The present capital value of that loss in the future stream of profits must be larger than a gain by short-lived cheating.

SELF-ENFORCING HOSTAGE VALUE THAT
DEPENDS ON PERFORMANCE

There's still another way the retailer could be made to suffer a loss if caught cheating. The retailer may be required to make a large initial investment in this activity. If the retailer is caught cheating, the right to sell that product is lost, and with it the value of the investment is lost.

However, this creates a reverse hazard. Once the retailer has made the investment which makes him dependent on that supplier, the supplier could threaten to terminate the relationship unless the retailer accepts a smaller reward than had been promised initially. The retail price maintenance agreement protects the retailer.

So long as each party would lose more than they would expect to gain by cheating, the incentive for reliable performance by each is maintained. This arrangement is an example of a *self-enforcing* contract. It pays for each party to enforce (maintain) the contract to avoid a loss greater than the gain from cheating. (In the next chapter, we'll explore *brand names* and reputations, the loss of which would reduce future business prospects of that manufacturer.)

THE CASE OF COORS BEER: HOW A MANUFACTURER
ENHANCES THE RELIABILITY OF DISTRIBUTORS

Several decades ago, Coors Brewing Company introduced a beer that was not pasteurized and therefore had to be refrigerated during delivery from the brewery to the ultimate customers to maintain high quality. The distributors to whom Coors initially sold the beer had to store and refrigerate the beer reliably and properly, delivering it in refrigerated trucks to retailers who also were required to store the beer in coolers. The beer was not distributed in states farther from the brewery than permitted adequate refrigeration from brewer to consumer. But even if kept refrigerated, the beer lost its quality in about three months, so the distributors were forbidden from selling beer over ninety days old.

Clearly, Coors was more expensive to distribute than conventional pasteurized beer, and the cult-like preference for Coors depended crucially on maintaining its reputation. That meant the brewery was dependent on the distributors and retailers to assure the quality of the product.

A potential problem for Coors was that a distributor and the retailers could seize a gain — *though short-lived* — by cutting costs with inadequate refrigeration (or selling old beer) until caught and denied any more Coors beer. Customers would attribute the low quality to Coors, not knowing why the beer was not good. The brewer and all the reliable retailers selling Coors products would suffer as sales of Coors declined because of loss of reputation.

To persuade distributors and retailers to perform quality-maintaining services as promised, Coors set both the wholesale price it sold to distributors and the retail prices that could be charged to customers so as to assure higher profit margins than on other beer. That gave larger than normal competitive profits, so long as the distributors and retailers fulfilled their obligations.

This large margin became a hostage that a cheater would lose if caught cheating on services necessary to maintain the quality of the product. Coors also insisted the retail price not be cut, lest that reduce the profit margin and destroy the potential larger profits — the loss of which helped prevent retailers from cheating.

EXCLUSIVE TERRITORIES PROTECTED BY
RESALE PRICE MAINTENANCE

A wholesaler-distributor of Coors was given the *exclusive* right to supply all the retailers in a specified area and *only* in that area, called an *exclusive territory*. Sometimes there was only a single distributor in an entire state. This gave a distributor an incentive to cultivate the demand for Coors beer in its region without fear of poaching by *free-rider* distributors. This exclusive territory restriction also made that distributor a closed monopolist in that region. To prevent higher (monopoly) prices in that exclusive territory, Coors also placed a maximum on the price at which the protected wholesaler-distributor could sell to retailers.

Coors was then not alone in responsibility for the quality of the beer. There was *dependence* by Coors on the distributor and retailers for special services paid for directly by the distributor and retailers, for which the larger profit stream on sales was their reward for reliable performance. Coors, in this way, tended to avoid being *held up* by distributors and retailers who would otherwise be in a position to get a gain by short-lived cheating — or in polite terms, not fulfilling their servicing contract.

END OF COORS DOMINANCE — NEW TECHNOLOGY

Later, when the *aseptic brewing process* was developed, beer of almost equal quality could be brewed and distributed without continued refrigeration. When Coors and competitors adopted this technique of production, the value of refrigeration was eliminated, and resale price maintenance with the premium stream and monitoring to assure refrigeration were abandoned. Because other larger brewers adopted the new process, Coors's market share declined.

GOVERNMENT REGULATION TO PROTECT DEPENDENT
CUSTOMERS OF CLOSED MONOPOLY SUPPLIER

The role of regulation of public utility services is commonly understood as merely that of setting prices that are not too high. The basic purpose is prevention of exploitation of customers who are dependent on the public utility.

PUBLIC UTILITIES AND NATURAL MONOPOLIES

Some products — gas, electricity, water, land telephones — are often provided by public utilities. These are typically called *natural monopolies* because the standardized service is more cheaply supplied by one firm rather than by several duplicative systems. This is one explanation of why local governments create a public utility monopoly — a closed-market monopoly — by giving a single firm the exclusive right to sell the service in a given geographic area.

The government then also controls the prices, but not just to prevent high monopoly prices. A more powerful reason is assurance of the promised delivery at the promised price. Consumers are dependent on the natural monopoly supplier for reliable services at predictable prices. A government regulatory agency limits the right of the utility to alter services or prices without prior approval. This assures that the monopoly supplier will not expropriate the values of substantial investments in homes and businesses.

OWNING A FIRM OR LENDING TO IT

Holders of common stock and bondholders have a conflict of interests. Bondholders have prior claims to a specific amount of the firm's value, while stockholders claim the residual. Stockholders would prefer investments that are more risky than those preferred by bondholders, who are choosing a high probability of normal gains and small probability of loss of the investment.

In general, the more costly, or the less effective, is the monitoring of members of the firm, the less likely is the investor to accept a bond rather than shares of stock. Stockholders accept a higher chance of no gain with a greater chance of a big gain in the common stock value.

An investor in a research firm would rarely be a bondholder, because the researchers' mental activity must be monitored to be sure they are not daydreaming. Monitoring of physical and routine actions, probably more common in power-generating utility firms than in innovative business firms, increases the incentive to lend, rather than to invest, as an owner.

So most internet and computer design firms are financed by common stock, not bonds. Similarly, a law firm, in which monitoring of people's mental activity is difficult, will be financed by stock — shares of ownership — not by borrowing from bondholders.

We have looked at some explicit contractual precautionary protections taken before becoming dependent on a specific other person. The next chapter examines some subtle and implicit assurances to potential customers.

QUESTIONS AND MEDITATIONS

1. Why would actors, superstar athletes, and pop musicians be more prone to resort to "opportunistic renegotiation" than are doctors, lawyers, engineers, and architects? There is a sensible reason, which you may detect by pondering a bit on the principles of capital values and how those values depend on the length of popularity of such careers. (Hint: sudden

stardom changes negotiating leverage and creates incentives to "cash in" while still hot.)

Answer:

Actors, superstar athletes, and pop musicians usually can expect high earnings only for a relatively short number of years. The earnings of doctors, lawyers, engineers, and architects may not be as spectacular, but are received over decades of working. Even if the lifetime consumption of each group were the same, the former group would have many years of consuming from the proceeds of investments made during their few high-earnings years, while the latter group would more evenly match current earnings and current consumption.

2. Shopping is costly, even when there is entertainment value in browsing through malls and shops. It may often be true that the shopper is truthful when they tell the clerk that they are "just looking." It may mean also that they are acquiring valuable information about products, models, features, and performance characteristics, as well as prices. Providing the inventory of floor models for the perusal of shoppers is costly to retailers.

   a. As a consumer, do you show your appreciation to retailers who display merchandise for you to inspect by paying more than the same item would cost if bought on the internet?

   b. How might big-box retailers compete with online retailers who don't incur the costs of displaying floor models?

   c. Can you name some modes of retailing that were once common but have become rare or nonexistent as a result of ecommerce?

Answers:

   a. Paying more for appliances and furniture in a store than the same item might be available on the internet is probably not a reflection of the shopper's appreciation but is, for the convenience of purchase, ease of return or service if necessary, and reliability of warrantees.

   b. Some retailers require a "membership" for the privilege of shopping. Early in 2013, a retailer of electronic goods began imposing a $5 charge to enter the store to shop — refundable if a purchase is made.

   c. Recorded music and books were sold only in stores a couple of decades ago. Some of the retailers were giant national — and even international — companies. Such retailers have now almost entirely disappeared as the convenience of buying on the internet became common. Of course, those who enjoyed the entertainment value of browsing through a bookstore must find alternative ways to use their leisure time.

3.   "Not even independent people like Daniel Boone can avoid some
     dependency on others. But there is a degree of protection against weak
     performance of an associated entity in reputation — history of past
     performance is an indicator of reliability of future performance." Might
     reputation either reduce or increase confidence in reliability? And does
     a dubious reputation invariably eliminate a server? How do the Postal
     Service and the department of motor vehicles continue operations?

Answer:

     Few of us live in splendid isolation, and there is much effort — both prod-
     uct production and propaganda — to foster sterling reputations. A repu-
     tation of poor performance can ruin an enterprise that is active in market
     competition. The US Postal Service has lost business and profit to private
     competitors, but it holds a legal monopoly on some types of service. The
     DMV has no competition in serving those who insist on owning automo-
     biles.

4.   One person owns a baseball team and the stadium; another owns the
     adjoining parking lot. Might there be a conflict of pricing strategies —
     admission to the game and parking — of the independent owners? Can't
     each of them seek his own profit-maximizing price?

Answer:

     Each can seek, but perhaps neither will find. Each hopes to set his price
     optimally, given the price selected by the other. But each could wish that
     the other would lower his price, preferably to zero. And any change in the
     other's price, up or down, will affect the circumstances in which his own
     price is determined.

5.   Many products are produced and then distributed to consumers by
     separate firms in differentiated but interdependent activity. Each of the
     firms is looking for profit. But they can disagree significantly on pricing
     and distribution policies and performances. Why?

Answer:

     Firms at different stages of an activity can have different primary sources
     of revenue and different concerns about the reliability and effectiveness
     of their associates in the overall enterprise. Recall illustrations in the text.
     The newspaper publisher obtains most of his revenue from advertisers,
     so he likes to keep the price of the paper low (even zero), with large cir-
     culation attracting ads; the newspaper vendor gets all of his revenue from
     sales, so he wants an appropriately high price of the product. Telephone
     manufacturers want very low prices of telephone services in order to have

large sales; telephone service providers seek profit-maximizing prices for usage — and want the manufacturer to make and sell the phone as cheaply as possible. Note the difference in price for a new model smartphone when purchased without a service contract versus the much lower price (or "free") when purchased with a contract. Wholesalers have little love for inept, inefficient retailers who alienate potential customers; retailers have little love for suppliers who alienate potential customers by failing to maintain product quality.

6. "Everyone knows that monopolies are inefficient and exploit customers, generally managed by greedy and ruthless Robber Baron types. One of the generally enunciated functions of government is to protect the community from anticompetitive activity." And yet government establishes some conspicuous monopolization. Is such government action invariably misdirected?

Answer:

Whether or not government is typically sophisticated and efficient in its establishment of selected monopolies, the purpose can be defensible. Patents and copyrights are devices of monopoly, and they surely encourage much invention and creation. "Public utilities"—gas, water, sewage disposal, public transportation—can preclude wasteful duplicative services. And firefighting, police protection, and national defense are quite universally accepted as appropriate government monopolies. However, few people today would say the same for primary and secondary schooling or space exploration.

CHAPTER 25

DEPENDENCY ASSURANCE BY REPUTATION AND PREDICTABLE PRICE

Your reputation is the public's belief about your expected future behavior. A firm's good reputation can be a powerful enforcer of its own reliable behavior, lest it lose future earnings. A seller's good reputation is valuable also to potential customers because it reduces shoppers' costs of identifying reliable sellers. This chapter explores how brand names and reputation, as well as reliable predictability of prices, increase the reliability of dependencies.

BRAND NAMES: REDUCING COSTS OF PREPURCHASE INFORMATION AND SHOPPING

The worth of a good brand name is greater for contemplated purchases of items that are (a) harder to evaluate before purchase and for which (b) subsequent surprising defects would cause more severe damage to the buyer. The reduction in costs to shoppers for estimating predictability of various suppliers is why a reputable brand name is valuable to the seller. That value is often called *goodwill*.

Firms supplying products with brand names are more likely to supply the expected quality than are those with no brand name. That doesn't mean their products or services are better. But the expected quality and price (whether expected to be very high as in Beverly Hills Hotel or lower as in Days Inn) is what you will get. Imagine the problems and costs of shopping in the former Communist Soviet nations, where no brand names were allowed. And, conversely, without brand names, the incentives for producers and retailers to act reliably are much weaker.

COST OF MAINTAINING BRAND-NAME VALUE

The cost to maintain high reliability, and therefore a high reputation and brand-name value, is not zero. Behaving well, rather than less well, is costly. The seller must more carefully serve customers. Complaints must more likely be resolved in favor of the customer, even when there is doubt. The higher costs of higher reliability may be recovered in a higher price that contains a premium paid by customers for the more reliable assurance of getting what they expected. Better things usually cost more, and higher probability of getting what is expected at the expected price is valuable to buyers.

REPUTATION AS SELF-ENFORCER OF RELIABILITY

If actual service is worse than expected, the brand name worth to customers falls. The brand value to the seller also falls as customers withdraw their future business. Any seller who contemplates a short-lived gain, either by selling a lower-quality product than expected or by surprisingly raising price, must reckon the prospective loss of the present value of the lost profits on future sales. Sellers can maintain a reputation for honest dealing if they continue to behave honestly. But for that goodwill to be effective, the seller's expected gain from short-lived cheating must be more than offset by the consequent loss in value of the goodwill.

FRANCHISES RELY ON REPUTATION OF BRAND NAMES

An extreme reliance on brand names and predictability of quality is the *franchisee* of a franchise system, such as Domino's Pizza, McDonald's, KFC, Wendy's, Comfort Inn, Holiday Inn, Baskin-Robbins, H&R Block, and Coca-Cola. The franchisees (typically retailers to the consumer) sell products under only one brand name. The identifying brand provides prepurchase assurance of a predictable product, so buyers can confidently shop at different outlets and get the same product. Some franchisees also produce the product or substantial parts of it, and the parent company provides only formulas and standards, usually including a uniform price.

The franchisees pay a fee or royalty to invest in and own and operate outlets selling products under the franchiser's brand name, which is an indicator and identifier of a known degree of product quality and characteristics. Franchisees rely on the franchiser to maintain product quality and protect the brand name. But each franchisee has the potential to take a *free ride* on the brand name by reducing product quality and earning profits at the expense of the parent company and other franchisees. If the parent company fails to prevent free riding, the franchise system will collapse, which would reduce the gains to exchange for the producer, other franchisees, and the buyers of the product.

HOSTAGES TO THE FRANCHISER TO ASSURE
RELIABLE PERFORMANCE BY THE FRANCHISEE

As with other control situations, performance-assuring devices are agreed to in the contract. A franchisee is required to make an initial specific investment. Expensive signs advertising the franchiser's product name are often paid for by the franchisee. When the franchisee pays, the value of the sign depends on continuation as a franchisee, and becomes a hostage held by the franchiser. If the franchisee misbehaves, the sign is lost.

Courts have often judged these arrangements to be unfair. So the franchisee and franchiser accomplished the same thing with a different form of *hostage* payment from franchisees to franchisers. The franchisee initially pays for the right to be the franchisee. Thereafter, so long as the franchisee performs as promised and maintains the worth of the franchise brand name, the franchiser pays supranormal income. The supranormal return is interest paid to the franchisee on the initial franchise fee for the right to do business under the brand name. In effect, the franchisee pays first, and then gets interest on the initial investment, losing everything if terminated for abusing the brand name's worth to customers.

ADVERTISING — REDUCING SEARCH COSTS

Advertising is valuable for both the price-searcher/sellers and their potential customers. It reduces a customer's costs of searching for information about sellers and their offerings. One may think there is too much advertising. Advertisements about automobile tires in the local newspaper will be worthless to you most of the time. But on the infrequent occasions when you want to buy tires, advertisements become valuable.

For employers seeking employees, or a person seeking a job, search costs can be significant. Access to information is not "free" to those who seek it, and it certainly is not free to those who provide it. The economics of information costs and search costs play a significant role in our understanding of unemployment and of the costs of inflation, as discussed in later chapters.

GOOD SAMARITAN: AM I MY BROTHER'S KEEPER?

Ethical behavior enhances the welfare of the social group but imposes a personal cost. If you, a stranger to me, were to trip and be injured, I might ask, "What are you willing to pay for me to rush you to a doctor?" You would be astonished by such a question, and society would be scornful. Such insensitive behavior is restrained by my own compassion and sense of responsibility. So I offer to help even though the delay causes me to miss the class I was on my way to teach. The students (presumably) bear a loss.

If the benefit to the victim is deemed by others to be less than the costs to me and to the students who missed a lecture, is this sensible economically? Does ethical behavior thereby reduce aggregate welfare?

Consider the consequences if opportunistic, unethical behavior were commonplace. People would be more hesitant to take desirable actions that expose them to some risk of being caught in emergencies. And they would take more expensive safety precautions. The costs of precautionary activities and the values of forsaken risky activities would exceed the costs to people who provide emergency services in Good Samaritan fashion. Trusting that strangers will help in emergencies is beneficial, meaning it's less costly than the benefits. Society — all of us — would be worse off without ethical behavior.

PERSONAL SHAME

A purely economic analysis is too narrow an interpretation for a full understanding of Good Samaritan behavior. For most of us most of the time, there is punishment — shame — for failure to help a person in distress, and there is reward — emotional gratification — for solicitous and ethical behavior. Though an analysis of shame is beyond economics, shame does restrain reneging, even when there's no threat of other effective retaliation. We tend to honor our commitments and promises because of shame if we do not, even if no one else knows we have behaved dishonorably.

THE VALUE OF PREDICTABILITY OF PRICE

A potential investment or transaction can depend upon a price not yet agreed upon. Mistaken estimates of prices to be paid lead to less effective allocations of wealth and actions. If you contemplate building a house, the expected prices of the components affect the overall planned structure. A later, unexpected change in one of the prices would affect substitutions of components, and could affect the whole structure. Similarly, unexpected costs incurred in a long-anticipated vacation will affect your enjoyment and memories. Surprises are often not welcome when it comes to prices.

PREDICTABILITY AND ASSURANCE OF FUTURE PRICES

Usually, the predictability of a price is indicated by the stable, nearly constant price in the past despite momentary shifts in demand and supply. This suggests that the analysis of market prices in the earlier part of this text is incomplete. That analysis had prices being pushed quickly to the *market-clearing* price, with no queues of buyers or surplus inventories. Why, in actuality, are *inflexible* prices so common? How can stability of price help both buyers and sellers even though demand or supply has shifted?

Initially, we explained the importance of thinking of the demand curve and the supply curve in understanding market exchanges and prices. We were focusing on the gains to exchange participants and the competitive forces that shifted price to allow mutually preferred exchanges. We were able to see why various pricing tactics are common. We are now taking account of the costs of preparing for contemplated *future* transactions, and for protection of subsequent dependence.

When getting into a cab, you become dependent on that driver. You rarely know the total fare before hailing a cab. Even if you agree to a fare, you can't be sure the driver won't later demand a higher fare for completing the trip. How reliable is the driver? The driver's lack of prospects of repeat business with you weakens his incentive to supply reliable service to you.

To help protect you, regulation of taxis is widely adopted. But that regulation also is convertible into a taxi-owner protection device. In New York City, when cabs were initially regulated, each cab owner obtained a *medallion* to place on the car as a sign of authorized *reliable* service. As demand grew, the value of a right to operate a taxi (possession of a medallion) grew. But if more cabs were allowed, the incumbent taxis would fall in value. This desire to maintain the medallion value resulted in fewer cabs being authorized. As always, regulations can be turned into double-edged swords — to protect consumers by assuring safe, reliable service, *and* at the same time protecting the existing supplier by excluding new entrants as demand increases.

There are other ways to increase probability of reliable services. Many cab drivers organize themselves into one large company, and by providing good service they establish a reliable identifying brand name. If a member is discovered to be cheating, the whole group suffers a reduced prospect of future business, and the sinning member is ejected.

In another example, suppose you plan to build a house. When selecting a location, you look at the neighborhood facilities, traffic conditions, businesses, schools, and shopping centers. The value of your home will become dependent on the prices and qualities of goods and services from those neighborhood enterprises and conditions. The more predictable (not necessarily the less variable) the future pattern of prices and quality of service in those enterprises, the more secure is the value of your investment.

In the event of a local disaster (flood, hurricane, earthquake), will those stores boost prices to clear the immediate market — while trying to extract from you some of the suddenly high value of the emergency equipment demanded? If that opportunistic behavior were expected, fewer people would live in that area, and those who did would engage in more self-protection — in advance. Instead of jacking up the price of portable generators, the local hardware store may see the value in future sales of maintaining prices — and in the reputation of being a good neighbor.

One readily sees how awkward and costly shopping would be in every day nonemergency situations if you had to shop where the prices were fluctuating from moment to moment—or if you had to haggle in every purchase. Price predictability permits less costly shopping and haggling, and it also avoids emergency-induced exploitation. An announced fixed price can be lower than the average of the haggled prices—reflecting the reduced costs of making transactions.

The benefit of predictability of prices is found in seemingly esoteric financial and commodity futures markets. You can get an assured future price (not to be confused with a *futures* price) by paying someone to guarantee such a price. That's done in markets for futures contracts, financial derivatives, and options. Some may use them for gambling, but those markets couldn't survive if they were only for gambling, as is explained in chapter 37.

ANNOUNCING RELIABLE PRICES

Sellers announce prices at which they will offer to sell during an indefinite future. When demand or supply conditions change significantly and then are expected to persist, the sellers often give notice of their intention to raise prices in the near future. *Sale* prices are announced for a limited time—which is a way of advertising when the price will rise. Frequently, guarantees of price are assured in cases of inventory depletion by providing *rain checks*. All such methods of achieving price predictability are valuable to customers—and therefore affect demand.

VOLUNTARILY TOLERATED QUEUES: INVENTORIES AND RATIONING

In the interests of predictable prices, sellers often voluntarily keep price constant and voluntarily tolerate shortages or surpluses, rather than clear the market at every moment. The full costs of exchanges are thus reduced, and the extent of exchange is increased, even when it may appear that the market-pricing process is failing.

The costs would be great if sellers always had inventories and employees sufficient immediately to service extraordinarily high demand. And if the costs of inventories were to be minimized, there would emerge highly costly forms of competition to augment the inadequate currently available supply. Both idle clerks and inventories can serve an economic function.

In maintaining predictable prices, the seller faces two questions. 1) Should prices be maintained generally, but not invariably, at a level that is characteristically predictable and stable, in a market which is rarely in perfect equilibrium? 2) If prices are maintained, in the face of periodic disequilibrium, what method should be used for discriminating among customers when demand is excessive at that price?

The dominant choice appears to be (a) relatively fixed and predictable prices, (b) with rationing among customers according to who are expected to be customers in the future. Those who are known by the seller to have made themselves heavily dependent on that seller's supply are more likely to be the repeat, long-term customers.

PREFERRED CUSTOMERS AMONG THOSE WHO DIFFER IN VOLUME AND RATE OF DEMAND

As customers have preferences for sellers, sellers prefer some customers to others. Though two customers may be buying at the same rate today, one may be a steady customer representing a greater volume of demand over time. A seller anticipates the demand by a customer as the whole volume of expected sequence of future purchases, not just today's rate of purchase. The effect of anticipated large volume is especially evident during transient peak rates of demand, or during transient reductions in available supply, as during local emergencies following earthquakes or hurricanes.

In a temporary shift of demand for emergency supplies, prices to local, long-time customers will not be raised, while sales to outsiders will be refused in order to accommodate customary and dependent customers. Rather than risk the loss of future business of a loyal customer, 1) prices are sometimes held constant at below the momentary market-clearing levels when the current rate of demand exceeds the available supply, and 2) loyal customers are favored above the others in rationing the available supply during that self-imposed shortage.

NO SURPRISE AND NO HAGGLING: SAME ANNOUNCED PRICE TO ALL CUSTOMERS

Announced prices tend to be the same to all customers. They aren't adjusted to match randomly varying different amounts of services. In a clothing store, one shopper uses a great deal of the clerk's time in finding a suitable garment, or not buying anything. Another shopper picks an item immediately. Both pay the same price regardless of the amount of clerk's time occupied. That's cheaper for the store owner than itemizing separate prices for each of the services and amounts of time.

In automobile repair shops, though the price may be formally quoted as so much per hour of labor, the customer is often quoted a prestated, fixed price for the repair — leaving the repair shop with the uncertainty of higher or lower actual costs. This model restrains the shop's ability to raise the price, claiming the repairs took longer than expected. The same-price-to-all is a feature of competition among several sellers.

If a firm were to go to several banks during a year to get new loans to meet seasonal demands, a substantial cost to provide and obtain information for each bank would be required. Instead of repeating the borrowing procedure for each loan at a different bank, a loan arrangement with one bank can protect the borrower. The bank and its customer agree that the interest rate on the loan will be tied to the bank's prime rate, which is offered to all its customers — adjusted for the risk of a loan to that borrower.

This kind of arrangement assures the borrower that the rate to all subsequent new or renewed loans is calculated on the basis of an observable market-determined rate — independent of who is the borrower or lender. This pricing of loans (tied to the prime rate) allows necessary flexibility during the continuing relationship, assuring reliant buyers that changes in the interest rate reflect changes in the market rate, and match rates charged other borrowers.

BLIND BLOCKS TO ECONOMIZE ON
DUPLICATIVE INSPECTION AND SORTING

Units of goods are not always uniform in quality or size. When fruit is sold at a fixed price per pound in an open bin, earlier customers select the higher-quality units. Each subsequent customer is left with lower quality and at some point will refuse to buy unless the price is reduced on all.

Alternatively, the grocer would have relatively high costs of sorting the fruit into finer and finer grades and posting a separate price for each grade. If each customer is allowed a random selection, at a price appropriate to the *average* quality, the full price (with less sorting cost) would be lower.

Buyers may be offered bags (*bundles* or *blocks*) of *randomly selected* items from the initial supply. Each bag has the same price. This is a method of preventing excessive (overall wasteful) sorting and inspection and frequent price adjustments. The bag will tend to be of average quality. The costs of sorting by each buyer are avoided, with each buyer getting essentially the same quality.

However, if the variation among bags is substantial, buyers will begin to inspect each bag, searching for those of relatively high-average quality. One common technique for preventing the search among bags is to make the bags opaque so that buyers are buying blind. But this blind bundling would have the undesired effect of increasing the potential for sellers to hold up buyers by a disguised quality reduction. Sellers with good brand names would lose more by loss of the brand name's value.

You may have shopped where the grocer selected the items, telling you "Please don't touch the fruit!" In an open air central market, you perhaps found that the vendor insisted on selecting for you the requested number of items. However, familiar, repeat customers may be granted the privilege of choosing for themselves. This is a form of *price discrimination* that is quite common.

DE BEERS DIAMONDS

Consider an extreme case — where the sorting costs are high and each bundle is prepared for a specific buyer — and a buyer who doesn't take that bundle will not thereafter be supplied by that seller.

The De Beers Consolidated Selling Organization is the world's dominant seller of uncut diamonds. Uncut diamonds are heterogeneous: they vary by shape, quality, color, and weight. De Beers sorts diamonds very carefully — into two thousand or more categories. But the exact quality of an uncut diamond is difficult to judge, and probably won't be fully revealed until after the cutting and polishing is done. So there is still a great deal of variation in the quality of the uncut stones in each of the categories.

To avoid presale extensive examination for sorting into fine and finer categories, each year De Beers sells diamonds to only a few hundred selected diamond dealers and cutters. These buyers periodically inform De Beers of the number and type of diamonds they want, based on the two thousand categories. De Beers assembles a box — a *sight* — of diamonds approximating the dealer's request. Each sight contains envelopes filled with diamonds requested from each category. The buyer may examine the individual diamonds, but that buyer must buy the entire box. If a box is rejected, De Beers will not do business with that buyer.

And, like the sacks of fruit, some sights will have a below-average quality of diamonds, and thus be overpriced, while some prove to be underpriced. This method of selling reduces the costs of transactions and assures customers of some quality control. So long as the present value of the profits due to the reduced price outweighs the one-time gain in profits from rejecting an overpriced sight, buyers continue their relationship with De Beers.

PROFESSIONAL CODES OF ETHICS

High-trust professions rely heavily on codes of ethical behavior. For some services, customers are in a position of necessarily trusting the supplier with a substantial part of their wealth or welfare. The customers cannot detect the quality of service at the time it is rendered, and they are unlikely to know, until it is too late, what was really done.

Where risks are high, the suppliers of the service have an incentive to provide some assurance of the reliability of service. Physicians, engineers, dentists, architects, and lawyers, among others, are considered to be in high-trust professions. One way to increase trust and reliability is to have competing members of the profession act as monitors and enforcers of reliable services. The members of a profession will castigate or disavow those who are known to have violated the code of ethics.

Though they have a strong interest in eliminating competitors (deficient or not), they also have an interest in assuring the public that they themselves will serve as promised. Governments permit and help enforce codes of ethics, even though the code might be used (also) for collusive purposes to control competition and prices, such as by mandatory *certification* or licensing. A society could not well persist without a dominating sense of ethics, honesty, and proper respect for others.

All the marketing and pricing tactics explained in this and the preceding two chapters are legal. They are competitive, and do not constrain permissible feasible actions or restrain other persons' access to markets to sell or buy goods and services.

QUESTIONS AND MEDITATIONS

1) "Brand names are simply a superficial element in advertising propaganda. Having the name of a brand pounded into your consciousness does not mean that you have thereby gained useful information." Right?

Answer:

The statement is incomplete. The brand name by itself may be considered an uninformative word, but it is a device of identification and thus communication, distinguishing one version of a good from competing versions. The identification of this particular product may warn the shopper to avoid it, for he has learned that it is of poor quality or is too expensive — or the shopper may be attracted because of the fine reputation he has learned to associate with the article. The brand name gives to the potential buyer a basis for evaluating the appropriateness of the price, accepting a relatively high price tag with expected relatively high qualities of the product.

2) Some products — including fast food restaurants and sleeping quarters for travelers — are provided by franchise chains. A parent company (franchiser) sells to retail distributors (franchisees) the right to operate under the home name. Is this a one-way street, with the working retailer paying tribute to the unproductive headquarters simply to be able to use the corporate name?

Answer:

Franchise arrangements take various forms. But in all cases, there is interdependence of the franchiser and its franchisees. Some franchisers participate in production of the product or service; they advertise and promote the product; they have incentives to maintain a stellar reputation for professional reliability and product quality, which is critical to the well-being of the franchisees. In most cases, predictability of product or service is critical to franchise businesses. Customers come to expect "no surprises" from such establishments, regardless of location. Either the franchiser or a franchisee could perform poorly or in such a costly manner as to subvert the other — there is truly a codependency.

3) A television mogul sees potential in an attractive but young, inexperienced, and generally unknown performer. The novice performer is signed to a five-year contract, and is expensively groomed and promoted to be featured in a new TV series. After a couple of successful years, the young star becomes discontented with a salary that seemed initially attractive but now supposedly does not befit a star. A contract is a contract, but might a proponent of free enterprise and the open market agree that the performer is being exploited?

Answer:

Many investment prospects do not pay off well. Actors are contracted, but do not blossom as glamorous and successful performers; wells are drilled into dry holes; enormous research expenses yield no miracle drugs; books are published and promoted but sell only ten copies; baseball players are cultivated in the minor leagues for years without becoming big leaguers.

Potential investors seek some degree of protection against ultimate disappointment, lest the speculative investment not be made. The young performer in the question above was overpaid for a time, but then under-paid, the later underpayment being an offset to the initial high probability of a failed nontrivial investment.

4) Simple demand-and-supply analysis suggests very frequent, almost continuous price fluctuations as demand and/or supply fluctuate. But a high degree of anticipated price stability, or price movement within a very narrow range, is commonly observed — and can be advantageous to both sellers and buyers. How can it be that substantial price stability can be a good thing in generally found circumstances, but price flexibility in response to market pressures is useful in other cases?

Answer:

Constant price movements can be distracting and upsetting to buyers. It would be difficult to act systematically and confidently if each day, as you leave home, you could not well anticipate the prices you will be paying for bus fare, a cup of coffee, a newspaper, lunch at the deli, or groceries to bring back in the evening. Sellers don't want nervous and frustrated haggling customers, so they promote prices which will prevail for some while, advertising and managing inventories to maintain prices which are steadier than the ever-shifting demand and supply forces might indicate, and to build and maintain a reputation of predictability and reliability.

Still, prices are not to be set permanently in the face of evolving and sometimes volatile markets. If prices are stubbornly maintained (perhaps by government decree) in the face of sudden, large movements in the equilibrium level, allocation of factors and goods have to be made by non-market devices. Such devices are arbitrary and invidious, although adopted in the name of fairness. If a hurricane suddenly wipes out much of the regional availability of gasoline and a maximum price is imposed below the new, higher market-clearing level to prevent "gouging," (a) there will be vexing problems in rationing the "short" supply, and (b) the artificially low price will discourage movement of outside resources into the blighted area.

5) "Society — all of us — would be worse off without ethical behavior." "A purely economic analysis is too narrow an interpretation for a full understanding of Good Samaritan behavior." "A society could not well persist without a dominating sense of ethics, honesty, and proper respect for others." Such observations may be expected in philosophy, sociology, psychology, and poetry, but do they belong in economic analysis?

Answer:

Economics is concerned with pervasive and fundamental aspects of individual and social behavior in a hard, competitive world of scarcity. Economic analysis is more than a dispassionate "logic machine." The basic nature of a society is largely determined and represented by the nature of its economy—and the manner and functioning of an economy is heavily shaped by the character of the society.

The world has seen many autocratic, repressive governments that hide behind elegantly written constitutions of proclaimed democracy—yet the people enjoy few liberties. There have been purportedly open-market, free-enterprise economies which are basket cases of business and governmental corruption and underhanded ineptitude. We have extensively discussed the necessity and the perils of estimating various economic variables, of anticipations of future actions and responses, of interdependences and required confidence in the reliability of others to fulfill obligations. Thousands of years of recorded history present a persistent story of poverty and tyranny, with an occasional experiment in personal freedom and opportunity being fulfillingly productive. If we are to foster the good society and its responsive, efficient economy, intellectual competence must be married to high character. Otherwise, we will defeat ourselves by generating increasingly efficient gulags.

CHAPTER 26

PROHIBITED MARKETING TACTICS

The framers of the US Constitution sought a government that enforced private property rights. Except in cases of "eminent domain," they did not contemplate imposing restrictions on private property rights. Any actions that would interfere with the private property of other people would be expropriation and violation of their private property rights.

But a century later, Congress legislated restrictions on acceptable use and contracts for use of private property. People, self-interested, found ways to benefit themselves while imposing greater losses on the rest of the public, without violating private property rights. What about malicious disparaging of a competitor's products? Or colluding with competitors to restrict output and obtain higher prices and profits? May two independently owned firms agree not to place their competing retail outlets near each other? May a producer insist that retailers of its products not sell similar products of other manufacturers? May a seller charge different prices to different customers for the same good? May a manufacturer set the retail price that retailers must charge customers?

Some actions that would be legal under a strict interpretation of private property rights were observed to have effects sufficiently harmful to others to provoke prohibitory or restrictive legislation. This chapter explores the basis on which legislation has declared what may be done legally in marketing and competition. But first, why are those laws and regulations called *antitrust* legislation?

WHAT IS ANTITRUST?

The term *antitrust* comes from one of the first of the actions that were restrained by an act of Congress. A trust is an arrangement whereby someone, a trustor, grants control of assets to a trustee who is to direct uses of the assets for a beneficiary (who may be the trustor himself). A mentally handicapped person may become a beneficiary of a trust set up in his behalf.

In the last couple of decades of the 1800s, stockholders in oil, steel, railroads, sugar, and cotton, among others, placed their stocks in a trust and received rights to a share of the profits in the companies managed by the trust. Several of the trusts engaged in what was later called *monopolization*. Standard Oil Company, founded by John D. Rockefeller, was one example. In response to the tactics of the trust, Congress legislated the Sherman Act in 1890 — the initial antitrust legal act — on marketing and organizational actions in interstate commerce. Since then, legislation and actions related to inter-firm competition and marketing commonly have been called antitrust law. It's really not against trusts, but instead against any agreements that are viewed as having undesirable, rather than benign, market effects. Most of the subsequent antitrust actions and policies have been based on the Sherman Antitrust Act and supporting legislation.

That Act stated in section 1: "Every contract, combination in the form of trust or otherwise, or conspiracy, in restraint of trade or commerce among the several States, or with foreign nations, is hereby declared to be illegal" and punishable as a felony (prison sentence and fine). Section 2 declared: "Every person who shall monopolize, or attempt to monopolize, or combine or conspire with any other persons, to monopolize any part of the trade or commerce among the several States, or with foreign nations, shall be deemed guilty of a felony."

Section 1 criminalized *restraint of trade*, and section 2 made it a crime to *monopolize interstate commerce*. Unfortunately, restraint of trade and monopolizing were not defined in that legislation, and still have not been defined. As seen in preceding chapters, those words cover a variety of actions and situations, not all necessarily regarded as undesirable, and some indeed may be deemed desirable.

Immeasurable amounts of argument, discussion, analysis, and lawsuits have been directed at trying to specify what actions were covered. If two or more lawyers form a partnership and thereby restrain competition among them, is that restraint of trade? Not as the law is actually interpreted. Indeed, they are now better able to compete against other lawyers. Judging from the general implementation of the antitrust laws and regulations, the objection is not to restraint of trade, but to restraining benefits to the consuming public.

THE CLAYTON ANTITRUST ACT OF 1914

The Clayton Act, twenty-four years after the Sherman Act, removed some of the ambiguities, identifying practices that would be definitely illegal under the meaning of the Sherman Act. Subsequent amendments prohibited 1) price discrimination, 2) exclusive-dealing contracts and tying arrangements, 3) certain types of mergers, and 4) interlocking corporate directorships. However, these actions are prohibited only if they *substantially reduce competition* or *foster a monopoly* — again leaving much room for debate and interpretation.

THE FEDERAL TRADE COMMISSION ACT OF 1914

The Federal Trade Commission Act of 1914 created the Federal Trade Commission (FTC) to detect violations and to issue cease and desist orders. The FTC is a regulatory, or administrative, agency of the government with authority to interpret the law and enforce it. The Act states that "unfair methods of competition in commerce are hereby declared unlawful." This was broadened by a 1938 amendment forbidding "unfair or deceptive acts in commerce" regardless of any competitive effects. Again, there is the difficulty of specifying the meaning of terms such as deceptive and unfair in particular cases.

REMEDIES AND ENFORCEMENT AGENCIES

In addition to private suits in the courts, anyone who feels injured by what he contends is a noncompetitive business practice can sue the offender for damages, and, if successful, the offender can be fined three times the damage, payable to the victim. A complaint could be directed to the Antitrust Division of the US Department of Justice, which has jurisdiction over enforcement of the Sherman Act. Or an appeal can be made directly to the FTC. The FTC and the Justice Department each specializes in the industries they oversee. Both agencies can enforce the Clayton Act. Violations of these laws and regulations can result in imprisonment, substantial fines (such as triple damages), or injunctive relief imposed and enforceable by courts.

SPECIALIZATION AND DEPENDENCY

A major source of confusion has been failure of some courts to recognize the necessary dependency among firms for production and distribution. Most antitrust laws and regulations appear to be based on the idea that production occurs only with *specialization* by technologically independent firms. Therefore, any contracts or agreements made among firms, for whatever reason, are looked at with great suspicion, as if there could be no purpose other than trying to control competition and prices by restrictive agreements. But that incomplete understanding ignores technological interdependence and problems of ensuring reliability among the technologically interdependent firms and team members in their production activities.

To assure reliability of promised performance, agreements are made among the otherwise independent parties. *Agreements*, like all contracts, are *restrictive*. Investments relying on the promised performance of specific other persons are made more secure. Without these restrictive contracts, is that investment unlikely to be made? This was one of the ideas emphasized in the earlier Codlandia fishing boat, sail, and mast episode (chapter 22). Fortunately, some courts early recognized that some contracts and agreements among firms serve a legitimate, desirable purpose.

MEANING OF A BENIGN AND A MALIGN EFFECT?

What is the criterion for deciding whether some effects of an agreement are beneficial or are harmful, and therefore illegal? What is the ultimate objective of the antitrust laws? When some marketing tactics affect the sharing of the total gain from trade, is that good or bad? If a single firm reduces its own rate of output and raises prices and then finds that it enjoys greater profits, in what sense would that be viewed as bad?

If two firms voluntarily agree to reduce combined output to raise their joint profit, why is that viewed as bad? If two young lawyers form a law firm to earn more and get higher fees than if each worked alone, is that joint action bad? Apparently not, because in reality most lawyers work for law firms, so it's legal. However, if two big law firms merge, that might be viewed as too much concentration and therefore bad and illegal. Why? The fundamental question should be what is the basic criterion for permissible actions?

THE BASIC CRITERION: MAXIMIZING CONSUMER WORTH

Economists, during the past century of legislation and court actions addressing issues of competition and concentration, proposed a criterion. The economists' criterion is the total personal worth of aggregate national output. For each specific good, the area under the combined individual demand curves for all persons demanding that good represent the aggregated personal worth. When Ted and Rae (in chapter 6) traded to where their marginal worths of the traded goods were equated and also equated to the market price, that was interpreted as resulting in a maximized total personal worth for the two consumers.

Even if no one had consciously made this the explicit criterion, the actions taken by courts and regulators might all be consistent with that result. It may be partly a consciously recognized criterion, and it's the one most commonly implied in the guidelines and enforcement actions of the Antitrust Division of the Department of Justice and the FTC. No other unambiguous goal could be found that is consistent with their enforcement actions.

However, some members of Congress have advocated other goals. They assert a desire to preserve "mom-and-pop" family businesses by restraining the growth of the lower-price, lower-cost, larger stores to which customers are attracted. Such protection of small business has been advocated despite the higher costs and reduced consumer worth to the rest of the public.

Which is the better objective, aggregate consumer welfare or mom-and-pop survival? That depends upon the kind of world in which you want to live; it is not an economic criterion. At any rate, the total benefits of the system of larger chain stores have been so great that the smaller, independently owned retailers have tended to lose the public's patronage.

Almost every socially benign advance in technology or production has harmed someone. The development of electricity harmed the whaling industry, which provided oil for lamps. The telegraph harmed the Pony Express owners and riders, but the worth of the benefits to the public far exceeded those costs. Supermarkets forced most small retailers to switch to employment as managers or clerks in big stores, and the public benefited by lower prices and more convenience. Electric refrigerators displaced ice deliverymen. The zipper hurt button producers. The automobile, radio, television, and computers all displaced producers of other goods and services, but the public at large gained. If an agreement among two or more competitive firms would have such net benefit to the public at large, then it would tend to be called a *coalition* rather than an anticompetitive *collusion* or *conspiracy*.

Of course, anyone — politician, business entrepreneur, or academic — can assert that objectives other than consumer worth should count, such as protecting small businesses or family farms. But such objectives appear not to be part of the national policy, though they have been pursued and partially achieved by political competition in special-interest legislation. As with almost all competing objectives and goals, we engage in trade-offs among public goals as well as private goals. Indeed, that's recognized in the first principles of economics — substitution at the margins among *goals* (*goods*) in our preferences.

EFFECTS ON COMPETITORS

A complementary test of legality would be: "Does the agreement restrain the right of any other person to offer services or buy goods from other people?" If it does, it's not legally permissible, and commonly is called "anticompetitive." If other peoples' rights to enter the market to offer to sell or buy are not restrained, that agreement is usually considered legal.

Authoring and offering this book for sale to the public is the result of an agreement (collusion?) among the authors and the publisher. Competitor authors and publishers may be harmed when buyers shift to this text, but the agreement to write and publish this book does not restrain the right of others to compose and offer to sell texts they may write. But if this text is so successful that others withdraw and this book's price is then raised, what would the antitrust authorities do when the harmed competitors complain?

SURROGATE CRITERIA FOR PERMISSIBLE ACTIONS: RULE OF REASON

One basis on which courts decide cases is *the rule of reason*. This refers to the analysis and assessment of the effects of a challenged action. It was gradually adopted several centuries ago in Britain. Now it's the generally prevailing standard for judicial decisions in antitrust litigation. The rule of reason is not easy or cheap to apply. An obstacle is the difficulty of reliably identifying the actual consequences of challenged activities. And even when the consequences seem to be well understood, the courts have differed as to whether they are desirable and, hence, legal.

PER SE ILLEGALITY

For situations where a sufficiently thorough analysis would be too expensive, and where the results of some action were believed to be clearly destructive of consumer worth, the courts have declared the action to be *per se* illegal. The act itself was deemed illegal no matter why the action occurred. No further evidence or mitigating considerations would be admitted as a possible defense, because they surely wouldn't alter the predictable effects. Some practices commonly found illegal under this *per se* standard included those called *price-fixing* and *collusion* in submitting bids for, say, purchases or construction contracts.

A difficulty in the application of per se illegality arises from the ambiguity of the names used to identify the actual actions. The term "price-fixing" was soon discovered to be so general in scope that it covered many pricing actions that were socially and economically helpful for consumers. In some instances, the courts have regarded the particular challenged pricing actions as desirable, or at least not repressive of competitors in the particular circumstances that prevailed. The court then simply declared the pricing action really was not price-fixing, and was legal. "Price-fixing" may sound bad, but it is not a useful label for an allegation of *per se* illegal actions.

Other commonly used *labels* are terminologically suggestive, but sufficiently ambiguous to obfuscate reality. For example, the phrase *leveraging monopoly and market power by tie-ins* has only two unambiguous words — and and by. The other words are too ambiguous to permit accurate understanding, communication, or agreement. Nevertheless, they are widely used by lawyers to generate lawsuits and fees for themselves, and inadvertently for economists called as experts to expose the confusions.

VERTICAL OR HORIZONTAL AGREEMENTS

One quick but indirect and unreliable method to judge business practices relies on distinguishing between *vertical* and *horizontal* agreements. If the agreement is among producers and distributors of similar competing products at the *same stage* in the sequence of production, it is a horizontal agreement. However, if an agreement is among firms participating in the *several stages* of the sequence of production to final consumers, it is a vertical agreement.

An agreement between Ford Motors and its retail car dealers, for example, could be called a vertical agreement — a set of vertical contracts among co-operators, not competitors. But when Ford Motors establishes agreements with each of its franchised retail dealers, the competing dealers have agreed with each other (horizontal agreement via all agreeing with Ford Motors) in addition to each agreeing — vertically — with the supplier, Ford Motors. It's apparent that a vertical/horizontal distinction can be ambiguous.

Several *vertical* agreements (resale price maintenance agreements between producers and dealers), tying agreements, restrictions on a retailer's territory, and exclusive dealing agreements, have been declared to be per se illegal.

A horizontal agreement is more likely to be challenged in court, though in some cases they have been declared legal. Horizontal agreements among otherwise competing computer firms and competing auto firms, to share in research and agree on standards of performance — which ultimately will reduce costs and innovate better products to consumers — have been declared legal.

CONCENTRATION RATIOS

Federal law, as stated earlier (pages 402–4), declares that actions which may substantially lessen competition or tend to create a monopoly are illegal. This pertains especially for mergers of two firms or *takeovers* of one by another. The presumption was that the merger would result in higher prices or reduced quality.

As a potential predictor of the likelihood that a merger of two firms, or even the growth of one firm, would tend to monopolize or restrict competition, a measure called the *concentration ratio* has become popular. It's the ratio of the total sales of the largest four (or sometimes three) firms in the industry to either sales of all the firms in the industry or to total assets, or sales of a specific product of the leading firms to the industry total. This approach raises a number of questions.

1) Many firms produce a variety of products, so the industry to which they belong is ambiguous. And because some products are used for a variety of purposes, they could be included in more than one industry. The question then becomes what is the relevant product? What does a garment manufacturer produce? What is a hospital? What is a drug research firm?

2) Which firms are in the industry? There are only two tailors in the United States regularly making plus fours (the knee pants golfers once wore). If those two tailors merged and raised their prices, would that attract new entrants?

3) What number of firms must make agreements with each other for it to be illegal joint action? One solution asserted that if the group of firms, consciously acting together, could profitably sustain a price rise of 5 percent for at least one year, the group action would be challenged. When evaluating a proposed merger, regardless of the current degree of concentration, there must also be the presumption that new firms and resources (or existing firms in other industries) would not be likely to enter in a short time to prevent higher prices. As the Department of Justice and the FTC recognize, it is not sufficient to look at the number of current firms without regard to potential entry by new competitors.

Aside from classification problems, and looking at the significance of the numerical value of the concentration ratio, what would be a high concentration, and what would it imply? A large measured ratio doesn't imply either industry control or lack of competition. The biggest firms now existing in concentrated industries do not own all, or even most, of the resources capable of producing those products by potential new firms.

One income tax preparation franchise system, H&R Block, used to account for about 40 percent of commercially prepared tax returns. Yet it had an insignificant fraction of the resources capable of offering income-tax preparation services. Its larger earnings did not come from exclusive access to special resources, or from restricting entry, or from colluding with other tax preparation firms. Having a large fraction of current sales is not the same as possessing a large fraction of the relevant resource capability.

General Motors, Ford, and Chrysler never did "control" a large share of the resources that could be used or converted to making automobiles. Nor have they been colluding to keep prices high—except in the different, but important, sense of asking Congress to pass legislation, such as preventing consumers from buying foreign cars (discussed later), or setting *fleet standards* for emissions or fuel consumption. Clearly, collusive behavior has been deemed legal when authorized by legislation.

There is also the question of the direction of cause and effect between size and profitability. Superior productivity implies higher profits and more rapid growth to become larger-sized firms and result in more concentration. That's the opposite of saying that a larger share of total sales results in higher prices and profits. Apple is profitable and big because it produces superior products — not that it's profitable because it's big. General Motors, Chrysler, and Ford were giant firms, but that's not why they were profitable. Each has suffered in recent decades because international competitors better satisfied the public. Size does not mean greater profitability or success.

Production of some expensive types of products is probably most economically organized in large firms, for example, autos, steel, electricity-generating turbines, airplanes, and telephone service. If we compare the same industries in different countries and find that they have similar structures, this is a quick indicator that these structures are determined by cost and production considerations.

Evidence rejects the presumption that greater concentration results in higher prices to consumers or in inferior output. Still, a concentration ratio is explicitly included in the antitrust guidelines of the Department of Justice, and is therefore widely used in assessing the appropriateness of proposed mergers. However, the Department of Justice has undermined the concentration ratio with a hedge stated in the official guidelines. The hedge is that, regardless of the measured concentration ratio, if within two years after a 5 percent increase in prices, sufficient new resources were expected to enter and restore the initial prices, the proposed merger would not be challenged.

COALITION VERSUS COLLUSION

A *coalition* is an agreement among individuals or firms that does no net harm to society. Two lawyers forming a partnership can be said to have entered a coalition. That may harm competition in the sense that they don't compete with each other, but they offer better services of more worth to consumers. That's a net benefit to society.

An agreement among a group of firms which benefits the members, but which will reduce the achieved consumer worth, is usually called *collusion*, or a *cartel* if enforced by the government. Here, we examine some collusions and cartels, looking at some of the conditions that are reputed to make them effective.

PURPOSE OF COLLUSION

A group of competitors — say, dairy farmers or makers of computer chips — want to restrain their market actions in order to increase their revenue and profits. They might want to raise their prices because the aggregate demand facing the group has a smaller elasticity than the demand each seller sees when others are competing for sales.

Competitors will profitably grab the customers of a competitor who alone raises its price. An effective collusion would require each one to abide by an agreement to restrict output. Otherwise, *cheaters* will gain as customers switch from the colluders' higher price. But that reduced output would reduce *total consumer worth*. Even if that were legally permitted, forming an effective collusion that binds enough of the total supply is not easy, because profits to a price-cutter would be large.

OBSTACLES TO EFFECTIVE COLLUSION

The chances of a successful collusion are greater, the more fully the following conditions are fulfilled. First, every existing and *potential* producer has to be identified and involved. Second, all existing producers must be persuaded to agree to raise price, while potential producers are dissuaded from entering the market. Third, individual colluders must not raise the quality of the product or associated ancillary services to offset the price rise. Competition in *all features* that appeal to customers must be restrained. The sellers must be monitored to avoid their cheating by secretly cutting the collusive price. Fourth, cheaters must be punished by more than their potential gain. These are not necessarily all the conditions, but they appear to be the principal ones.

1) Who are the significant actual or potential suppliers? Are other goods or services so similar that buyers may easily substitute? If you were trying to organize doctors to set prices, what would be done about interns, chiropractors, registered nurses, midwives, paramedics, technological equipment, druggists, and drug companies?

   If you were a major steel producer and attempted to collude with other large producers to restrict output, what would you do about the hundreds of small steel foundries? And worse, what about plastics, aluminum, and concrete, all of which are to some extent substitutes? Also, firms that make steel for their own use could expand production. Steel producers who are not in the agreement will prosper under the umbrella of higher prices enabled by the output restriction of the colluding firms.

Actual and potential suppliers both in and out of the collusion have private incentives to expand and to undermine the agreement to restrict output or raise price. Even OPEC, the Organization of Petroleum Exporting Countries — often referred to as a highly effective cartel — has had these problems.

2) Not all participants will agree on the amount of output restriction by each firm or on the appropriate price. Those things will depend on each firm's cost conditions and equipment and its prospects for future growth relative to other firms. Specifying all features of the product and associated services is difficult. Collusions, insofar as they are effective, change the nature of the competition, diverting it into something other than price competition.

If firms produce slightly different varieties of the product, a common price or agreement on quality control becomes virtually impossible to enforce. When there are many detailed aspects of a product to be policed by the colluders, successful cheating is less difficult. Grades of steel, special services such as precutting to specified size, storage facilities, delivery dates, payment and credit terms, and return privileges are only a few of the avenues of differentiation and cheating that must be controlled.

When governments controlled airline fares, competition took the form of better planes, frequency of flights, in-flight services, special hotel accommodations tied to the airfare, in-flight prizes, and so forth. These were ways to attract customers in lieu of cutting money prices. Profits will be dissipated into higher costs of ancillary competitive services. Moreover, the cost of producing these competitive services will exceed their worth to the customers, else the services would already have been provided. Anticompetitive agreements really restrict only certain forms of competition — such as price — while they increase other forms of competition among the colluders.

3) Violations of collective agreements must be detected. One technique that helps curtail cheating is for all suppliers of a relatively standardized product to sell the entire output through a central selling agency, often called a "sales pool," which controls how much will be sold. Raisins, almonds, lemons, peanuts, and milk are sold through central pools that decide how much to sell. Each member then competes for a larger share of the total permissible sales.

4) The penalties must be sufficiently severe to be deterrents. What kind of punishment does the NCAA impose on colleges caught cheating

on the athletic collusion? Colleges are willing to pay substantial fines to remain in the collusion. The sharing of gate and TV receipts is important enough to offset that fine.

The inherent internal conflicts of interests and hazards to an effective collusion explain why so few appear to succeed. But there is something that facilitates effective collusions: governments facilitate and help enforce cartels — as in local public transport, labor, and for products like raisins, almonds, lemons, peanuts, milk, and college educations, to name a few.

VULNERABILITY OF GOVERNMENT
AGENCIES AS LESS-CAREFUL BUYERS

Governments not only help enforce some cartels, government purchasing agencies are "sitting ducks" as customers of colluders. Effective collusions have been found among sellers of cement, flour, water, steel and concrete pipes, furniture, milk, asphalt, and meat — for sales to government agencies (including elementary schools and colleges) or to profit-regulated utilities. The buyers obtain bids on projected purchases; however, they are restrained from forcing rebidding by sellers and from seeking price cuts on the contracts (for fear of being accused of helping friends by informing them of the lowest bid).

Managers of government agencies have weak incentives, and are more constrained in their authority, to be aggressive in shopping and getting the best prices. The incentives for effective control of purchasing agents is stronger in firms dependent on earned profits for survival than in government agencies, which rely on taxes. The expression, "I will always be more careful in spending my money than I will be in spending your money," explains the difference between private owners and public-sector administrators.

GOVERNMENT-ENFORCED CARTELS: FOR WHOSE BENEFIT?

Despite all the opposition to *voluntary* collusion, restraint of trade, and monopolizing among businesses, some cartels are created and enforced by explicit government legislation.

Often the legality and support of restrictions depends upon how much political power a group can muster, rather than upon economic analysis of their effects. In some industries in some nations, the government tolerates, encourages, or even insists on collusions.

In the United States, it is legal for firms to collude when selling to foreign nations, which supposedly hurts only the foreign customers. However, when firms in other nations are allowed to do that for sales to the United States, our politicians often complain. Nevertheless, coffee-, cocoa-, and sugar-producing nations are *encouraged* to collude to restrict supplies to the rest of the world — including the US. That's a form of covert foreign aid — consumers pay higher prices to the benefit of the producing countries.

FARM SUPPORT PROGRAMS

Farmers have been especially powerful politically in virtually every nation. Japan has long restricted the importation of rice as a way of maintaining higher incomes of rice farmers — and expensive rice to consumers. Europe's *Common Agricultural Policy* is notorious for causing food prices to be much higher than would prevail with open competition. In the United States, restrictions are placed on the importation from foreign producers of sugar, peanuts, raisins, figs, meat, tomatoes, and many more products as a way of supporting higher prices of domestic producers. This means that US consumers face a smaller supply and pay higher prices.

The government sets a price higher on dairy products than would prevail otherwise. Farmers may not sell below that price. As a result of the higher price, the amount demanded is less, creating a surplus. Naturally, at that higher price farmers would want to raise more milk cows. But that would create an even larger surplus. The government must either restrict the size of dairy herds or buy the surplus. Historically, some of both have happened.

If the government buys the surplus milk and cheese, what happens to it? Some may be donated to charities or used for school lunch programs, some has been stored until it spoils, and some has been given away in foreign aid programs. However, when given to foreign nations, some leaders in the recipient nations have complained that that constitutes unfair competition with their domestic producers.

If the US dairy farmers could agree among themselves to reduce output and prevent other farmers from switching to dairy cows, they could monopolize and get the higher monopoly rents. (It is monopoly rents, rather than monopoly profits — distinguishing between gains from restrictions on production and earned profits.)

This kind of involvement of government in agriculture is worldwide. Sometimes it is defended as necessary in order to be independent in production of food, although it leaves the country poorer. Whatever the original justification, after many decades of agricultural subsidies and *price-support programs*, the continuation of such policies at consumer/taxpayer expense rests on little more than the contributions the recipients make to political campaigns of elected officials.

In addition to agriculture, governments often put restrictions on actual and potential competitors in other industries — such as the retail distribution of liquor in some states. Sometimes services such as cutting or braiding hair require an expensive license as a way of limiting competition. In a few places, even advising on home decorating is illegal without a proper license. The main point is that preventing potential competitors from increasing output and lowering prices to consumers is legal when the government is a member of the collusion; otherwise, it's illegal.

LABOR UNIONS

Labor unions, the topic of a later chapter, are notable in that they involve significant collusion, and yet they are legal. Decades ago, the federal government agreed (Wagner Act of 1934) that labor unions are effective only if they can restrain competition from nonunion labor. The Wagner Act gave unions the legal right to strike — and in the process restrain nonunion labor from replacing the strikers.

Some years later, Congress enacted other legislation granting unions the exclusive authority to represent all employees in a firm, even those who are not members of the union. This authority includes the collection of dues from all employees, whether or not they want to be represented by the union. The general rationale for the right to restrain competition from nonunion labor has been the proposition that otherwise original employees would be at a disadvantage in negotiating terms of employment.

This government-backed power of a simple majority to set the conditions under which the minority can offer their services for employment has been controversial for decades. Adding to the controversies has been the use of union-collected dues to support politicians with whom individual union members may disagree. The result of these controversies has been that now over one half of the state legislatures in the United States have enacted their own legislation — called *right to work* — which prohibits agreements between employers and unions that would require an individual employee either to join the union or to pay dues to a union.

POLITICIANS: AGENTS OF THE PUBLIC IN THE COMPETITION FOR GOVERNMENT AID

Government is essential to modern civilization. Sometimes it is useful to think of government as it — documents setting forth rights, powers, and limits, such as the *Magna Carta*, constitutions, and articles of incorporation. Other times it is useful to think of government as *they* — officials who hold the elected and appointed offices of government. These individuals are often competitors in the economic arena because they control productive resources—such as uses of land—and their permission is often required in order to engage in some enterprise.

Similar to the competition in markets for privately produced economic goods and services, people compete against each other for government-supplied goods and favors. Elected politicians are intermediaries competing against other politicians, all working on behalf of their respective supporters. Political entrepreneurs often seek to control and direct the uses of resources—sometimes vying with private entrepreneurs for uses of the same resources.

The political arena is a *marketplace* as much as the open-air fruit and vegetable stands or the commodity exchanges. Just because there is not a negotiated money price for services rendered does not mean that the Economic Principles of competition for scarce resources do not apply. Incentives matter in politics no less than in business.

Sometimes one hears of something being "anticompetitive"—meaning it is bad—or something being "procompetitive"—meaning it is good. These are not useful expressions. Because scarcity exists, competition is inevitable; some allocation must be made. If *price* competition is restricted or suppressed, *political* competition of one form or another will occur. When prices are arrived at by the free interaction of producers and consumers, it is possible to ascertain worth to consumers. When distribution of scarce goods and services is made by nonprice political criteria, worth to consumers remains unknowable.

CONTENDING ECONOMISTS

When professional economists face each other as *expert witnesses* in an antitrust lawsuit, no dispute between them should arise about the economic analysis of the situation. They are using the same validated principles of economic analysis. Instead, the dispute is about the facts or circumstances. Two good economists could readily agree about which set of observed facts would warrant one inference and which set the other. Or they could agree that the existing economic analysis isn't sufficient to settle the issue. Unfortunately, many lawyers and litigants think there are conflicting economic *theories*. Instead, there are many contested issues of factual conditions, weighing of criteria, and appropriate market procedures.

PROBLEMS WITH SUCCESSFUL COLLUSION

If just one of the sellers raised price, some customers would switch to other sellers. The elasticity of demand facing one seller is high, meaning that a rise in price would result in a much larger percentage decrease in quantity sold. The total revenue to the seller would fall. But if all raise their prices together, the buyers won't have any sellers to whom to switch. They'll buy less, but the total market value of what they buy will be higher if the market demand elasticity is less than 1, called inelastic. So long as the elasticity of the market demand is less than 1, an arbitrary increase in the price will result in larger total revenue and lower costs, with bigger profits.

To raise the price and keep it there, the competing sellers must agree not to cut the announced higher price. And each seller will on average have to produce and sell fewer units, otherwise not all the produced amount will be sold. But each seller wants some other producer to reduce output. The problem then is to get an agreement to cut output and amount offered for sale, otherwise the higher price won't be sustained. There is therefore an incentive to organize all sellers to raise prices. At the same time, that would increase the incentive to be the *lone* holdout who does not raise prices and captures a large increase in quantity demanded. For an effective collusion, the sellers of all or most of the amount supplied must raise their prices together, but getting that agreement to be observed is extremely difficult, as the leaders in the oil-exporting nations know. As consumers, we try to prevent collusions of suppliers, though as consumers we also have incentive to collude against sellers — as in rental price controls enforced by governments against the sellers as well as against any consumers who privately would try to offer more.

QUESTIONS AND MEDITATIONS

1) Ten concrete-block companies in a certain community were accused by the city attorney of colluding to restrain output and fix the prices of concrete blocks. The accusation stated that the ten producers accounted for 85 percent of the output of concrete blocks in the community. What might be meant by "colluding"?

Answer:

Who knows? Meeting or otherwise communicating in an effort to reach a nefarious agreement? Actually reaching an agreement? A phenomenon

of intellectual spontaneous combustion in which all simultaneously concluded that it would be shrewd to diddle with output and prices? Or perhaps a common reestimation of current market conditions?

2) Assume that all existing firms producing a commodity were successfully
   and effectively to collude to restrict output and raise prices. What open-
   market forces would operate to obstruct the effectiveness of the collusion?

Answer:

At higher prices new prospective producers could enter and underprice
the collusion. Use of lower-priced substitutes will become more attractive. Some members of the collusion have an incentive to cheat by price-
cutting since they have different cost-output relationships. (Lower prices
are more advantageous to lower-cost firms with more growth prospects.)
The collusion must have a way to detect price-cutting by cheaters, and punish violators sufficiently to deter further cheating. Other forms of nonprice
competition must also be controlled among members, such as quality
changes, delivery charges, warrantee and repair services, credit, and trial
and refund policies.

3) The first case prosecuted under the federal laws against collusion to raise
   prices involved steel pipe sold to the US government. What explanations
   are there for the fact that many prosecuted cases have involved collusion
   against the government?

Answer:

Government agencies enforcing laws against collusion predictably concentrate on collusion against government. Appropriately, government
often uses a system of sealed bids which are publicly opened. This is intended to prevent secret price-cutting and for detecting collusion.

4) What are the differences among collusion, cooperation, and
   competition? What distinguishes desirable coalitions from cartels?

Answer:

Collusion connotes elements of deception in seeking to negotiate exchanges in the pretense that the sellers are acting as independent competitors. Buyers are misled into presuming sellers are acting independently.
With open collusion, such as mergers, there is no pretense of "inter-seller"
competition, as with two salespersons of the same firm, and buyers are not
deceived. Partnerships, being open, are not deceptive.

Competition connotes interpersonal striving about who will get what of existing resources, while cooperation connotes joint action to increase the total stock of wealth to be distributed. Some actions do both at the same time. Exchange with specialization is both competitive and cooperative in increasing wealth as well as in allocating it. Sometimes speakers/writers use the term "cooperation" to suggest that the parties involved know each other and some sort of mutual agreement is arrived at. They intend to distinguish this situation from that where many independent parties contribute to the joint production of, say, a wooden pencil. However, there is much cooperation involved in making and selling component parts of a product in a competitive market even if the producers are total strangers.

5) European coal producers once pooled their sales through a central agency.
   a. Why was that essential for an effective policing of the collusion agreement among the producers?
   b. Why didn't some coal producers stay out of the agreement and take advantage of the opportunity to sell more coal at the price maintained by the "cartel," as it was called?

Answer:
   a. To control secret violations of sales of a homogeneous product.
   b. The law compelled them to join.

6) Almost every team in the two baseball major leagues is subsidized by city governments, which provide stadium facilities. If new leagues cannot be assured of access to these facilities, will this have any effect on the income of the existing teams?

Answer:
   Yes. Enhances prospect of monopoly rents.

7) Is a "tacit agreement" in business the same as a contract?

Answer:
   In legal cases, "tacit agreement" is often used to suggest that every form of interdependent or related actions between firms or businesses is at least a result of some tacit agreement akin to a contract. For example, when I recognize that if I cut my firm's price, you will cut your price in response, that's sometimes called a tacit agreement. It may be a tacit understanding of what people probably will do in response to competitive forces, but it doesn't impose any obligatory restraint or behavioral responses on the parties, whereas contracts do, by definition.

CHAPTER 27

THE CORPORATE FIRM

The corporate form of a firm, developed by our forebears, is one of the great inventions during at least the past five centuries. It's the dominant method of organizing and financing durable teams of people and resources for increased production of marketable goods — real income and wealth. Without it, aggregate national income would be far smaller. It also provides a method of investing household savings in long-lived productive resources — ownership, rather than only lending and borrowing.

FORMS OF OWNERSHIP OF FIRMS

Firms commonly take one of three legal forms: individual proprietorship, partnership, or corporation. A *proprietorship* is owned by one person, who is responsible for all the firm's debts. The owner has unlimited liability for all the debts of contracts. The entire owner's wealth, whether or not in the firm, can be assessed to pay debts. A *partnership* is jointly owned by two or more persons. Each one has unlimited liability for the entire firm, and each partner can make contracts binding the other partners. A *corporation* is a form of shared, transferable ownership with *limited liability* — limited to the wealth in the firm. None of any owner's outside wealth can be claimed for future obligations of the corporation.

THE CORPORATE FORM OF BUSINESS

Government approval is necessary for establishing a corporation. Though often called a *creature of the state*, a corporation is a set of resources related and controlled through *voluntary contracts* among cooperating owners of the resources. In the United States, any of the state governments, not the federal government, is the authorizing government. Approval is usually pro forma. A corporation is not *created* by a government. It is *recognized* and authorized by the state governments as a legally enforceable contractual arrangement. Delaware has been the state where most articles of incorporation are filed, because Delaware has been least restrictive in what corporations are permitted to do.

SHARES OF OWNERSHIP

Ownership is represented by shares of the corporation's common stock. Each share entitles the share-owner to one vote. The owners of common stock are said to be the *equity owners*. In contrast to equity owners, bondholders lend wealth to the corporation, rather than *invest* as owners.

MANAGEMENT STRUCTURE

Typically, an executive manager—the president or chief executive officer—is hired or is one of the major shareholders. Also initially appointed is a board of directors to represent the shareholders' ownership authority over the management of the enterprise. Often, the major stockholders are members of the board of directors. It is commonplace to say the directors *control* the corporation. We'll see that's too narrow a view of what is meant by control and who controls the corporation.

CHARACTERISTICS OF OWNERSHIP OF CORPORATIONS — SHARING IN LARGE INVESTMENTS

Typically, the amount to be invested in the corporation is larger than any one, or a few, would be able or willing to invest. The initial investors, or promoters of a new corporation, offer shares to individuals, who will become co-owners. Eventually, the directors will use an investment-banking firm to arrange the sale of additional stock to new investors, in a sale known as an Initial Public Offering (IPO). The investment-banking firm estimates a price at which it believes all the shares can be sold, and will guarantee to sell them at that price. For its guarantee and selling services, the investment bank will charge an *underwriting fee*. If the investment bank fails to sell all the shares at the stated price, it must nevertheless pay the promised amount and bear any losses.

NONDISCRIMINATORY SALE OF SHARES OF OWNERSHIP

The initial and subsequent shareholders don't care who are the new investors and co-owners. The new shares were sold to anyone who was willing to pay the price. Anonymity of sale makes the corporation form of business highly effective. To see why, look at the history of how it appears to have developed. The history of the corporate form of ownership in Scotland and England is best known.

EVOLUTION OF THE CORPORATE OWNERSHIP STRUCTURE

1. The Corporation for Large, Shared, Long-Lived Investments

During the fifteenth and sixteenth centuries, English and Scottish investors shared in expensive investment in ships and equipment for ventures to explore and trade with foreign lands. Each investor obtained shares of common stock proportional to the investment in the joint-stock company for one venture. Each share was granted one vote in making decisions and electing managing officers.

The ocean venture might take several years before the ship returned—or it might never if pirates were successful or the ship sank in a storm. The ventures were longer-lived than the length of time some investors wanted their investable funds to be tied up. How could people be persuaded to invest in a long-lived venture if they thought they might later want to consume some of the profits or withdraw their investments for consumption or an alternative investment opportunity before the voyage was completed? A first step was to permit the initial shareholders to sell their shares. With salability of the shares, the corporation could continue, but with different (partial) owners.

2. Limited versus Extended Liability to Facilitate Transferability of Shares

Salability was not enough. Under unlimited liability, each owner-shareholder's ultimate liability would be strongly dependent on the other shareholders, in particular on how wealthy they were. If some shareholders couldn't pay their share of some future liability, the others would have to pay more. A shareholder wouldn't be allowed to resell a share to some person not approved by the rest.

That desire to assure the reliability of other shareholders made it very difficult for a shareholder to sell. The solution turned out to be that of restricting every shareholder's liability to the amount already invested. Individual investors placed at risk only what they had paid for the stock, whether they had been an initial investor or a subsequent buyer of stock. The limited liability enables easy sale to anyone, a nondiscriminatory policy of anonymous salability.

In France, this kind of corporation is a société anonyme. In Great Britain, the suffix Ltd. in the name of the corporation indicates a limited-liability corporation, as in Harrods, Ltd.

This limited liability (absence of any recourse against the stockholder's other wealth) does reduce the creditworthiness of the corporation and raises its cost of doing business and borrowing. But it increases the willingness of people to make large long-term investments in the corporation. Lenders would be less eager to lend, but investors would be more willing to invest. The increased attractiveness of investing has dominated the credit risk. This limited liability, with anonymity of sale, is an effective way to obtain (a) large investments from (b) several sharing investors in investments, which are (c) of longer life than any investor wants to be committed to the investment. Almost every modern corporation is a limited liability corporation.

3. Stock Markets

A well-functioning stock market is crucial for the corporate form of business because it provides quick, low-cost salability of shares of common stocks. It's not primarily a place where new investments are made. Investments in new businesses are more cheaply and effectively done elsewhere—with investment banks or a group of stock brokerage firms (as explained earlier) called *underwriters*. The stock market functions mostly as a *resale* market for existing shares of corporation common stock. Stockbrokers usually serve primarily as specialists for transactions in already outstanding shares of common stock.

Common stocks of thousands of corporations are traded in stock markets of all advanced nations. When you sell to or buy a share from some unknown person through the stock market, your stockbroker plays a role of *guarantor* of the sale. If the other party fails to supply the stock to your stockbroker to be delivered to you, the stockbroker is liable and must provide it. If the other party is a buyer and fails to pay, the stockbroker must pay you. Without the stock market and the stockbrokers who constitute that market, sales of shares would be almost prohibitively expensive.

The criticism of the stock market as a place where people *gamble* ignores the fact that the stock market does not create the uncertainty over which gambles occur. Every investment is a *gamble*—the outcome is uncertain. The stock market makes it *less* costly to bear that uncertainty. If *bettors* could *rig* the competition, we could complain, not about gambling, but about cheating. With respect to integrity, it is hardly possible to find any group activity that has more proven integrity than the organized stock markets.

HISTORICAL EVIDENCE OF THE EFFECTS
OF THE CORPORATE ENTITY

In contrast to the rise of the corporation in Western Europe during the past millennium, in Islamic nations a partnership among a group ended with the death of *any one* of the members. Long-term investments (and large investments) therefore were riskier and less frequent.

In Western Europe, no one could claim more from the corporation owners than they had already invested in the corporation. In Islamic nations, liability was not limited to specified resources; the borrowers' entire personal wealth was at risk. These appear to be the primary reasons the Islamic nations, which once were more advanced economically than Western Europe, have been retarded in subsequent growth. The corporation aided Western Europe's more rapid and extensive economic growth.

LEGISLATION TO CONSTRAIN CORPORATE FORM OF ORGANIZATIONS

The success of the corporate form of enterprise by the seventeenth century quickly spawned a large number of *joint-stock* ventures. Inevitably, many failed, not because the corporate form was inappropriate but because the proposed activities were not profitable. The failures perversely provoked legislation in England prohibiting the corporate form. But loopholes were found, and evasion of the law overcame the prohibition. Opposition to the corporate form of organization was weakened by the realization that it was resilient and productive and could financially serve governments by taxes.

DIFFERENCES BETWEEN LARGE AND SMALL FIRMS

The corporate structure helps finance the creation and operation of larger firms. What's a large firm? A firm can be large in dollar value of sales, or total payroll, or number of employees, or size of assets, or market value of all its common stock. There is no common criterion for saying a firm is large. Thousands of small corporations produce components that a few very big ones assemble and distribute. Over a thousand firms are associated in a network of contracts and subcontracts for making and assembling subcomponents for a Boeing airplane. Some large firms are retail distributors who contract with other firms to make items sold by and under a brand name of the distributor, like Sears, Safeway, and Walmart.

All the measures of size of a firm are sufficiently highly correlated with each other to permit almost any of them to serve as a measure of size. We'll think primarily in terms of number of employees and also capital equipment owned by the firm.

   a. Generally, the ratio of capital (nonhuman) to labor (human capital) is larger in large (more employees) firms, possibly because monitoring physical capital is easier than monitoring people.
   b. Capital equipment is more intensively used (less idle time) in large firms. This is probably because the larger ratio of capital to labor in large firms makes downtime of capital more wasteful, so employees work more shifts.

c. Larger firms buy more new equipment than do smaller firms, probably because downtime is more expensive for a large firm.
d. Larger firms have employees of higher formal educational levels, with a higher fraction of employees in supervisory work (monitoring), and they have relatively fewer part-time workers.
e. Hourly and annual earnings of employees are on average greater in large firms, probably because of higher average skills of employees.
f. Larger firms produce more standardized items, while smaller firms are more prevalent for custom-made varieties of goods.

One hears that larger firms are more profitable and last longer. That reverses cause and effect. The more profitable ones grow to larger size and last longer because they are more profitable. This is not much different from saying that healthy people tend to live longer than do less healthy people. But a larger firm, especially one with a variety of products or activities (research, manufacturing, distribution, retailing), will have losses in some of those activities. Since all activities are totaled into an aggregate, the entire firm may be profitable, though some divisions are not at a given time. If separate firms performed each of the activities, the unprofitable firms would die.

WHY VERY LARGE FIRMS?

1. Resolution of Conflicts of Interests

Very large collections of resources in making complicated items require extensive coordination, management, and information exchanges. That can be more reliably achieved among people within a firm than across independently owned firms with partial conflicts of interest.

2. Mass Production Requires Large Initial Investments

The degree to which products must satisfy differences in tastes of consumers affects the possibility of standardization and its lower unit cost of large volume. For clothes tailored to the relatively wealthy, the firms are smaller than for more mass-produced, lower-cost clothes. Small restaurants provide gourmet foods, specialized to wealthier customers, whereas hamburgers and pizzas typically are supplied by very large firms with mass production. Special automobiles, of which only a small volume will be demanded (Ferraris, racing cars, stretch limousines) are more commonly made by smaller firms.

The greater the differences in demand for some specialized items (legal representation, beauty salons, tax services), the more likely are suppliers to be small. Production processes that are less dependent on nondiscretionary, standardized, repetitive production decisions by employees are more likely to benefit from economies from mass production. For example, large-scale, *continuous-flow* brewing of beer is so effective that fewer, but larger, breweries now serve most beer drinkers, while *microbreweries* produce in smaller volumes — at higher cost. In automobile production, a few very large international suppliers coexist with several makers of custom cars along with thousands of small shops that customize automobiles.

Production techniques are only part of the story. Distribution, management, and financing skills can be applied to more than one product in large corporations. Soap, cereals, peanuts, cake mix, candy, and canned goods use the same distribution facilities and expertise in wholesale and retail distribution, even if many small units of production make the individual items.

A large bank can have many small branches, which provide common standardized banking and financial services, while the branch managers specialize in knowledge of local borrowers. An analogous situation is a large, centrally controlled franchise chain of fast food outlets compared with small, independent gourmet restaurants for foods that cannot be cheaply standardized over many chefs. McDonald's is very large with respect to a standardized product, but very small in terms of each retail outlet.

3. Markets Are Larger

The reduction in transport costs has been especially strong for communication and intellectual services (e.g., banking, insurance, and advertising). Administrative services for management, design, and accounting are heavily intellectual and far more cheaply and effectively communicated in an age of low travel and telecommunication costs. That's a reason banks and insurers have become international firms.

Until recently, domestic laws restricted US banks from expanding beyond state boundaries and from offering financial investment and management services. Foreign banks were not restricted from providing those services, so they rapidly gained market share until domestic companies gained the same authority.

4. Larger, Fewer Firms, with More Competitors and Options for Consumers

Lower transport and communication costs over wider areas permit more potential mass production economies with fewer larger producers, each serving more communities with more alternatives for each buyer. More options and opportunities are available for customers, despite fewer firms. In the last century, especially in the final decades, transportation and communication costs fell astonishingly. Foreign goods became a much larger portion of every country's economy.

Now that more people can be informed and served by a firm, economies of scale can be utilized more fully. This results in more options for a consumer. As a result of reduced costs of international trade, smaller national firms are merging with firms in other nations. A consumer has a wider range of choice among suppliers, though the number of independently owned suppliers worldwide is smaller.

Continuation of restrictions on international trade has become more expensive and damaging, because more trade opportunities with lower transport and communications costs are obstructed. Political pressures to remove the barriers by entering into trade agreements intensified in the last two decades.

NEW TAX ON EXISTING CORPORATIONS

When a new tax is imposed on existing corporations, many resources already in a corporation have virtually no opportunity to move and escape the tax. Nor can the corporate form be easily changed to a noncorporate form. Employees and owners of resources in a corporation who are not mobile or transferable at zero cost will suffer a loss of wealth. The value of common stock falls. A new tax on existing corporations affects the wealth of those who were stockholders when the tax was announced. People who later buy shares do not bear the burden of the tax, because the price they pay is the lower present value of the anticipated future net income after tax.

NEW INVESTMENTS IN CORPORATIONS AFTER THE TAX

People who later form a new corporation, knowing a tax must be paid, treat the tax like other foreseeable costs. Investors demand a return sufficient to cover all foreseen costs with an excess at least equal to that on any other available investment. Anticipated rates of returns on all investments are brought to equality by competition for investment funds. Consequently, new investors in old and in new corporations — after the tax is known — will be no worse off than investors in other untaxed activities.

The cost of corporate business will be higher because of the tax on the corporate form. That tends to divert investments toward less effective (but less taxed) noncorporate forms of firms. Because the expected returns on new investments must be high enough to cover the higher tax on corporations, fewer investments are made in corporations, the supply of corporate products will be smaller, and the price to consumers will be higher. The implication is that the corporate tax reduces national productivity and national income.

This analysis does not imply that the corporate tax is necessarily bad. Recognizing the necessity of government activity, the question is, "Which and how much taxation is appropriate?"—not "Is taxation of corporate activity appropriate?"

QUESTIONS AND MEDITATIONS

1) "Decades ago, there were scores of producers; today there are a few large firms, so consumers now have fewer sources of supply. This is one of the disadvantages of large firms." Evaluate.

Answer:

It is not true that with fewer and larger, nationwide or international corporations producing a large share of US sales, consumers have a smaller range of purchase options. Today's consumers now have more alternative suppliers. If, for example, there were 1,000 small towns, each with five sellers, every one of whom, like every buyer, did business only in that one town, there would be 5,000 different business firms, but each buyer would have only five from which to choose. Cheap, fast transportation and communication covering larger areas allow each firm and buyer to do business in a larger number of towns. The number of business firms could be cut to, say, 40, and if each firm and consumer were now able to trade in half the markets, each buyer would face, on average, 20 possible sellers. Transportation and communication have improved, so today the average consumer has more options from more suppliers.

2) "A corporation owned by one person is the same as a proprietorship." Do you agree?

Answer:

The corporate owner and the proprietor act under different sets of rules and procedures. In particular, the corporation is held to limited liability of the owner; the proprietor's wealth is not so protected.

3) "Continuity of a corporation means that if any or all of the current owners of the corporation die, the corporation continues as a unit of ownership." Right?

Answer:

Yes. Shares of stock can be passed on to heirs and beneficiaries, and generally shares of ownership (common stock) are salable without permission of other owners.

4) Why is the corporation the dominant form of ownership of very large conglomerations of wealth?

Answer:

It's a convenient way to assemble capital. No one owner has to put all his wealth in one company in order for the company to be large. Easy salability of ownership also enhances attraction of investment. In other words, it is an efficient form of property risk-bearing.

5) "Business firms exist because many people do not have enough wealth to own the capital equipment and machinery with which they can work more efficiently." Evaluate.

Answer:

The advantage of producing in a firm rather than producing alone is that business firms lower transactions costs of having to negotiate and establish payment and provide services for each interrelated transaction. The firm is also conducive to discovering better methods of organization, monitoring, and controlling incentives of the employees. The form in which the business firm is organized — such as a corporation, partnership, or proprietorship — affects the ability of the firm to accumulate wealth to acquire equipment and machinery.

APPENDIX TO CHAPTER 27:
INTERPRETING FINANCIAL STATEMENTS

Business firms periodically (commonly every three or six months and annually) report their financial activities and current status. Reproduced here is a simplified example of a balance sheet reported for the "United Mining Corporation" for June 30, 2018. A "balance sheet" is a listing and cost valuation of a company's assets, liabilities, and ownership structure. Assets are the resources owned by the stockholders of the corporation. Claims held by other people against these resources are liabilities. The net value of the assets — the value after liabilities are subtracted — is equity or net worth of the stockholders' interests.

Balance Sheet

The basic definition is: Assets – Liabilities = Equity

The balance sheet presents items classified as assets on the left side and liabilities and equity on the right.

Assets: are classified as either current or long term.

Current assets include:

- *Cash:* Money held, including checking accounts and cash equivalents.
- *Accounts receivable:* These are the past sales yet to be paid for by

Table 27.1 *United Mining Corporation Balance Sheet, June 30, 2018*
(In Thousands of Dollars)

Assets		Liabilities	
Current		**Current**	
Cash	1,929	Accounts payable	11,923
Accounts receivable	4,669	Notes payable	2,358
Reserve for bad debts	−600	Accrued liabilities, future production	10,200
Unbilled costs	13,335	Current liabilities	24,481
Inventories	7,515		
Prepaid expenses	756	**Long Term**	
Marketable securities	5,577	Long-term debt	48,623
Current assets	33,181	Minority interest	3,974
		Long-term liabilities	52,597
Long Term			
Investments	9,334	**Equity**	
Government contracts	18,244	Preferred, convertible stock, 10,000 shares (5%, $100)	1,000
Plant and equipment	69,877	Common stock ($.20 par) 5,175,000 issued	1,035
Less reserve for depreciation	−7,000	Capital surplus	26,623
Other	538	Retained earnings	18,538
Goodwill	100		47,196
Long-term assets	91,093		
Total assets	124,274	Liabilities + Equity	124,274

customers; charge accounts or credit extended to customers allowing them, usually, thirty days to pay.

- *Reserve for bad debts:* Likely some customers will fail to pay their debts. To estimate the expected amount of receivables that will become "bad," an amount called a "reserve for bad debts" or "doubtful accounts" is subtracted. This expresses a "reservation" or "qualification" about the value of the receivables. In bookkeeping, "reserve" almost never denotes a setting aside of cash or actual reserving of assets. It is almost always used to express a reservation or adjustment in the stated value of some asset or liability.
- *Unbilled costs:* The corporation is making some products to custom order; as these are gradually completed, the corporation records the incurred costs as claims accruing against the customer, for which a bill will be submitted upon completion and delivery to the customer.

- *Inventories:* This could be the value of ore removed from its mines and not yet sold, plus any other unsold products. In general, this records values of products or raw materials on hand.
- *Prepaid expenses:* The corporation has paid in advance for goods and services yet to be obtained — as when you prepay a magazine subscription, you would record the unused portion of the prepaid expenses as an asset in your personal balance sheet.
- *Marketable securities:* These are typically US government bonds or notes.

Long-Term Assets

- *Investments:* This corporation owns some stock of another company. Usually, the particular investment is identified in footnotes that accompany the balance sheet.
- *Contracts:* These may be advance orders for future services.
- *Plant and equipment:* This is commonly the original amount paid for the physical property — mines, mills, smelters, and the like — of the corporation. Sometimes this is the cost of replacing it, especially if there have been drastic changes in costs of this equipment since purchase.
- *Reserve for depreciation:* Like the reserve for bad debts, this reserve represents a method of updating the valuation of depreciable resources. The property, plant, and equipment have been used and partly worn out. An estimate of the portion of the plant so consumed, and to be subtracted from the original cost (book value), is recorded as a "reserve for depreciation." It is not a reserve of some wealth set aside to cover the depreciation. Often, it's the total of depreciation that has counted as cost of production.
- *Other assets:* These can be almost any kind of asset — mines, land, buildings, claims against others, and the like. Usually footnotes to the balance sheet will give clues.
- *Goodwill:* Patents and trademarks are often given some small or token estimate of value and called "goodwill" as a valuation of a reputation for being a reliable supplier of products. Also, this may arise with a merger of two companies when one "paid" more than the book value of the other.

Liabilities

Conventionally categorized into current and long-term liabilities, with the former usually representing claims that must be paid within a year.

- *Accounts payable:* The corporation has purchased goods and equipment for which it must yet pay.
- *Notes payable:* The corporation has borrowed, and the amount due is shown. This item may also include any long-term debt that will fall due within a year.
- *Accrued liabilities:* At the moment (the end of the month), the corporation has accrued obligations to pay taxes or wages. If wages are paid on the fifteenth of the month, then at the end of the month it will owe about half a month's wages.
- *Long-term debt:* The corporation has issued bonds to borrow money. In the present instance, these will be finally due ten years in the future. Bonds are debts of the firm to the bondholders.
- *Minority interest:* This is a relatively rare kind of entry. This corporation is the primary, but not exclusive, owner of a subsidiary company, the entire value of which has been recorded among the assets. Because this corporation is not the sole owner, it has to allow for the share belonging to other owners. A footnote in this report would tell us that the "owned" subsidiary company's recorded value is about $14,700,000. All that value has been included in this corporation's (United Mining Corporation) reported property, plant, and equipment ($69,877,000) on the asset side. However, $3,974,000 of that belongs to other people — the subsidiary company's other owners. That's the minority interest, and it's subtracted from this company's assets by entering that amount on the liability side. Instead of reporting United Mining's share of the subsidiary as being $65,903,000 (= $69,877,000 − $3,974,000) on the asset side, they report the $69,877,000 as the total value and then, in effect, subtract the $3,974,000 by putting it on the liability side.

Equity or Ownership
Many different items are recorded as having claims to the equity.

Preferred, Convertible Stock
Holders of preferred stock, in the event of bankruptcy, have a *preferred* claim for dividends and against the *equity*, prior to that of the common stockholders. The holder simply has preference to the earnings, if any, for payment of interest before any dividends can be paid to the common stockholders. Sometimes the preferred stock is *cumulative:* if any arrears of unpaid dividends accumulate, the common stockholders cannot take any dividends. And the preferred stock may

be *convertible*, giving the option to exchange (convert) it into common stock at a prescribed ratio. In the present instance, the exchange rate is 10 common for one preferred share. The preferred convertible stock has a par of $100 with 5 percent dividends; it pays $5 preferred dividends each year (if earned), and may be converted to 10 shares of common stock.

A person who buys a share of preferred, convertible stock for $100 has some hope that the common stock will rise above $10 a share; converting to 10 common shares will then give the holder more than $100. As the market price of a common share approaches $10, the price of preferred convertible stock will rise above $100, reflecting both the current value of the preferred *dividends* due and the present values of further future possible rises in the common stock price. A purchaser of convertible, preferred stock is in effect a *partial* common stockholder or owner. A purchaser of nonconvertible preferred stock is simply a creditor of the company.

Finally, some preferred stocks (and bonds) are *callable*; that is, the company has the option to prepay them prior to their due date. A $100 callable preferred stock will usually be callable at some price slightly above $100, but the premium diminishes as the due date approaches. The owner of a share of callable, convertible, cumulative, preferred stock (of $100 par value, at 5 percent, convertible into 10 shares of common stock, and callable at $105 within five years) will collect $5 a year per share in dividends, if earned. A price of $105 may be offered for the stock, which the holder must take or convert to common stock (10 shares because at $10 per share they will equal the $100 par value of the convertible preferred share).

The Ultimate Residual Claims to Equity

Equity, by definition, is the difference between assets and liabilities. In the present instance, if we subtract the liabilities (current plus long term), $77,078,000, from the assets, $124,274,000, we get the accountant's *book value* measure of the equity, $47,196,000. This is based on the values as recorded in the accounts. How was it attained? Initially, when the stock was issued, $28,658,000 was paid into the company. The figures recorded for legal and tax purposes are $1,035,000 as the initial par value plus $26,623,000 as the additional amount paid originally for the common stock, and the $1,000,000 paid for the preferred stock.

That $28,658,000 was invested and spent (along with proceeds of loans) for property, wages, equipment, and the like, and at the moment the purchases are shown as assets on one side and as incurred obligations on the other. The measure called *par value* or *book value* does not reflect any relevant economic value; it merely records values that existed in the past when the various items were acquired. The public values the firm by looking to future prospects, not at sunk costs.

Retained Earnings

The corporation has invested $18,538,000 in the purchase of equipment and facilities. It may also have paid out some dividends to common stockholders, but we can't tell from the balance sheet data. If it had losses, that would have been subtracted from the recorded earnings (if any). This is accounting data of historical value only — a record of part of what the officers and owners have done since the firm was formed.

If we divide the recorded book value of the ownership, $47,196,000 (= $28,658,000 + $18,538,000), by the 5,175,000 shares outstanding, it comes to about $9.12 a share. It is tempting to conclude that a share of common stock is worth about $9. But the figures in the balance sheet's asset column are the past outlays for the equipment (adjusted for depreciation) and do not tell us what the company will do in the future. How do we know that the mine, which cost, say, $1,000,000 to find and develop, is not going to yield as much as, say, $100,000,000 in receipts in the year, or maybe nothing? None of this is revealed by the balance-sheet asset records — unless the corporation directors decide to make a prognosis of a future receipt stream, discount it into a present value, and record it under *goodwill* or *profits*. But they don't do this, because they know that's unreliable.

The recorded book values — measuring the past costs of accumulating the assets and adjusted by a formal depreciation method — are not measures of what the assets would be worth if disposed of piecemeal. Nor is it a measure of the present value of the company's future business operations. An excess of stock price over book value is not an indication of deception of the stockholders. Nor is a stock price below the book value any evidence that it is a safe investment in the sense that if worse came to worse the company could sell off its assets and hope to collect enough to pay each stockholder the book value. Book value bears little if any relation to the future earnings prospects.

Income Statement

The company also issues an income statement of its receipts and expenditures during the year ending at the date of the balance sheet. It reported net earnings of $.08 per share of common stock for the year ending June 30, 2018. Neither the income statement nor the balance sheet reports the market value of a share

Table 27.2 *United Mining Corporation Income Statement, Year Ended June 30, 2018*

Sales		$83,261,000
Costs and Expenses		
Costs of goods sold (labor, materials, power)	$67,929,000	
Depreciation of equipment and depletion of ore	4,599,000	
Selling and administrative	6,079,000	
Interest on debt	4,105,000	
		82,712,000
Operating net income		549,000
Share belonging to minority interest		111,000
Federal Income Tax		25
Net earnings		437,975
Earnings per share		$.08

of the common stock, or preferred stock, or of its bonds. That information is available in the newspapers or internet.

The market value of the stock of a company reflects public expectations. A company with negative earnings this year, but with superb prospects of large positive earnings in the future, could be worth more than one with positive earnings this year, but no seeming prospects for future earnings growth. The ratio of the market value of a share of the stock to current earnings per share (called a price-earnings ratio) is a highly misleading basis for comparing two stocks. Current earnings are irrelevant. Estimates of future earnings are what count.

CHAPTER 28

COMPETITION FOR CONTROL OF THE CORPORATION

The ownership and control of corporations, as with other private property, is subject to competition. Ownership and control can be bought by offering a sufficiently high price to current owners. You can buy control of a corporation by buying enough of the common stock (shares of ownership). Owners of the other shares would lose effective control, but they'd still own a portion of the value and income of the corporation. Many shareholders are likely passive, inactive holders. But all holders face competition for those shares of ownership.

Salability (alienability) of shares of common stock exposes control of the corporation to competition. If outsiders believe profits could be improved, they can offer more than the current holders think the ownership is worth. If they are more successful as controlling owners, they'll gain by the subsequent rise in the price of the stock — or suffer a loss if they overestimated what they could do. Competition is intense for control of corporations to profit by correcting perceived failings.

WHO OWNS THE CORPORATION?

The majority of people in the United States are corporation stockholders — directly or through mutual, insurance, or retirement funds. Whether employed by a private company or government, if you are part of a pension plan, you probably are a stockholder in corporations. If you contribute to a 401K plan or an IRA (individual retirement account), you likely indirectly own stock.

A corporation's stockholders own, or share in the ownership of, the *firm-specific resources* in the firm and the sales revenue of the corporation's products. From that sales revenue the other resource services are to be paid. The stockholders stand last in line to share in that revenue, after all other claimants are paid. Though there's no conflict between many owners of a corporation about the desire to maximize profits, there is a conflict among the members about how that goal is likely to be approached most closely, and how the total earnings are apportioned among all the members.

The stockholders select a board of directors to oversee the management of the corporation. Bondholders, who have made large loans to the corporation, may also appoint some directors. The directors have the power to appoint, or remove, those who make the daily administrative decisions. Some directors are appointed because of their experience in *assessing* management, not making executive decisions. Some of the directors may be chief executive officers in other corporations (not competing with this one).

SEPARATION OF OWNERSHIP FROM CONTROL CAN BE A WAY TO SPECIALIZE

In a corporation with thousands of stockholders, most have neither effective ability nor incentive to control either the board of directors or the top management. This widely diffused ownership of the common stock is said to result in a separation of control (or ownership) from management. But corporations are valuable because they permit many small savers to invest in enterprises operated and managed by someone else.

We all rely on hired *specialists* as doctors, lawyers, accountants, electricians, and auto repairers. There's separation of control and management in these cases. Similarly, relying on hired, or independent, specialists to manage a giant enterprise is economically sensible, providing decisions and actions can be sufficiently aligned to the interest of their principals (the stockholders). That's a problem in all specialization, but lack of direct control doesn't necessarily lessen the gains.

Complaints about separation of ownership from control are merely ways of saying the world would be better if there were perfect control of other people who were working in our behalf. The pertinent issue is not the imperfection of some existing arrangements. Instead, is the arrangement beneficial on net to all parties? And is there a way that would be better? If there is a better way, what's preventing the improvement? Widely dispersed ownership of corporations has been a resounding success. It provides a substantial benefit, and no one has constructed a superior method of achieving what it does.

CONTROL OF BEHAVIOR OF MANAGER BY OWNERS: THE UNIVERSAL MORAL-HAZARD PHENOMENON

What are some of the ways the managers are made sufficiently responsible despite the moral hazard in the relations between *agents and principals*? Effective control does not require that every stockholder closely monitor every activity of the firm. It is adequate that some large enough blocks of shares be held by a few people or organizations to give effective voting power to that group. The common interest of major stockholders in the corporation induces coalitions, and it's rarely necessary to own half the shares to dominate the voting.

In large corporations of the United States, the five largest stockholders in a corporation (usually institutional investors such as pension funds or insurance companies) own on average 25 percent of the stock. In 15 percent of corporations, the largest five stockholders own almost half the common shares. It's commonplace to form coalitions among more than just the five largest stockholders. The interests of all stockholders are closely aligned so far as the value of that stock is concerned.

The stockholders' interests would be harmed in a corporation in which the managers gave away the corporation's wealth for personal aggrandizement or failed to manage effectively in the stockholders' interests. Such managers would likely find their salaries competed down to reflect that behavior. The issue for shareholders is whether the benefit of the corporate structure and its anticipated internal dependencies and conflicts is on net an advantageous arrangement. Historical experience has been that the corporate structure is an advantageous way of organizing ownership of productive resources — compared to alternative forms of ownership.

COMPETITION FOR ACHIEVABLE GAINS
BY SUPERIOR CONTROL

Two kinds of competition tend to protect the corporation and its owners/ stockholders from the consequences of inefficient and misdirected behavior of managers. First, outsiders can buy the stock and alter the managerial group. This is a form of competition against present stockholders to control or alter actions of the current managers. Second, there is an internal competition among existing managers at different levels, each competing for promotions and greater rewards by trying to do a better job.

Other methods receive little publicity, although it is front-page news when the CEO of a major corporation resigns at the request of the board of directors. More commonly, directors persistently and quietly alter management and corporation policies. For most corporations, resignations are not publicly noted at all; for larger companies it is simply announced that some officer has left the firm, or a major reorganization is forthcoming. These are manifestations of forces directed toward eliminating unprofitable policy or management.

OBSTACLES TO STOCKHOLDER CONTROL
OF MANAGEMENT: LEGISLATION

Some legislation hinders ability to acquire ownership in order to exert control. Beginning in the 1930s, Congress eliminated one form of strong monitoring of managers. Commercial banks and insurance companies that previously had acquired major blocks of stocks or bonds as investments in a corporation were prohibited from continuing to do so.

It naturally was in the interests of the bankers and insurers to monitor the management of the corporations in which they made investments. However, displaced or threatened managers argued that the investment firms were interested merely in short-run profits. Of course they were. Immediate changes in stock values reflect the capitalization of the changed prospects of what will happen in the future. Being interested in current stock prices is to be interested in the longer-run effects of current managerial actions. There is a very tight connection between immediately capitalized short-run gains and long-run effects.

ENTRENCHED MANAGEMENT'S RESISTANCE

Nevertheless, political forces — reflecting imagined conflict between Wall Street and Main Street — resulted in laws preventing banks from owning common stocks of corporations. That restricted a major form of monitoring and control. During the following few decades, the power of sheltered management increased to the point where other, though more costly, means of monitoring became attractive. Eventually, Congress changed the laws again to permit banks to hold bonds and stocks as part of their investment portfolio. That change increased the effectiveness of control of managerial behavior toward maximizing the net economic corporate productivity.

DISPLACEMENT OF OWNERS AND MANAGERS
BY NEW SETS OF OWNERS AND MANAGERS BY
PURCHASE OF COMPLETE OWNERSHIP

Takeovers, tender offers, and *leveraged buyouts* are means of almost complete displacement of prior owners or managers. A small group — sometimes organized as a *private equity firm* — offers to buy all, or a very large portion, of the outstanding common stock from the current, diffused stockholders at a price substantially higher than the current market price. That high offer price represents an estimate about the potential gains to be achieved by changing the corporate management or activity.

Tender offers are sometimes financed by borrowing from private investment bankers and pledging the future earnings from the revised corporation as security. Displaced managers have contemptuously labeled these debts *junk bonds.* In fact, the performance of so-called junk bonds has been as good as or better than loans made directly by banks themselves. Even more remarkable, the critics seemed not to notice that these bonds often performed as well as or better than preferred stock and many other subordinated bonds already issued. ("Subordinated" means being in line for repayment after some other bondholders.)

The newcomer investors (who make tender offers) often are asserted to be *corporate raiders* and *break-up artists* interested in only a "quick profit." Actually, any quick profits are the public's quick recognition of the prospective improvement that will be brought about by the raiders' actions. The immediate jump in stock prices does not mean that short-term interests are displacing interest in long-term effects. If long-term effects were to be harmed, the current price would reflect that and fall (or rise less). Displacements of CEOs and their ill-advised policies by new management and better policies for achieving increased future earnings have, on average, resulted in higher stock prices.

The new owners have no interest in reducing the value of the stock they have just purchased. They are displacing the influence and control of former stockholders who were less effective in exercising control of the enterprise.

Managerial buyouts are another means of seeking to improve the performance of management. Managers who see a way to increase profits, most of which will go to the stockholders, will try to convert themselves from employees to owners. The managers form a group, borrow money from an investment-banking firm, and make a tender offer to the stockholders at a premium over the current stock price. That higher price reflects the managers' confidence about how much more profitable they will make the firm if they own it. The incentive for better performance by managers is provided by paying them (as part of compensation) a part of subsequent increases in the market value of the common stock. That's done by "stock options," giving the manager the right to buy later shares from the corporation at a price that is set now. Any future rise in the stock price will be a gain to the manager when he exercises the right to buy the promised shares at the earlier lower price.

Other stockholders of the acquired or raided firms gained, while the acquirers as a whole did not get extraordinary gain from a *takeover*. Why were there no gains, on average, to the innovative buyers? As with investments in oil wells or research for better products, competition for profitable prospects will push the offered price to acquire the firm up to include the expected profit. The average rate of return over all acquirers is a normal rate of return.

Since the takeovers and tender bids have provided substantial gains for the stockholders of the acquired firms, why have some stockholders opposed tenders that offered them such handsome gains? The present stockholders who oppose an offer are trying to get a still better offer by refusing the current tender offer. But that is not the whole story.

TAKEOVERS BENEFITING STOCKHOLDERS
BY TRANSFERRING WEALTH FROM
OTHER MEMBERS OF THE FIRM

Making Riskier Investments at the Expense of Existing Bondholders

Some takeovers can be advantageous for stockholders at the expense of bondholders or other corporate creditors. This happens when the new management changes the nature of the business to a riskier one. Table 28.1 summarizes an example.

Suppose a firm had been financed with $9 of borrowing for each $1 put up by the stockholders. The security for the borrowed money is whatever assets are in the firm when the debt must be repaid. (We ignore interest, assuming the investment is very short-lived.) The firm now engages in activities that will succeed only with 50 percent probability, instead of the former much safer business.

Failure: If the new activity fails, the bondholders will have lost $9, and the stockholders will have lost $1. The firm is worthless, so there's nothing the bondholders can claim.

Success: If the new activity succeeds, the firm will be worth $20, of which $9 is repaid to the lender/bondholders, who neither gain nor lose. The stockholders who invested $1 get a profit of $11 (= $20 − $9).

The bondholders' prospective fate: the chance of success is only fifty-fifty. The bondholders will be repaid $9 if the riskier venture is successful, or will get nothing, $0, if it fails. Their *expected* payoff is $4.50 (= $9 with a probability of .5). That expected $4.50 is the new expected value of their loan of $9, giving an expected loss of $4.50 (= $9 − $4.50) — a loss engendered by the shift in activities toward greater risk.

Table 28.1 *Expected Values of Creditor and Stockholder Consequent to Increase in Riskiness of Business*

Investor	Initial Value	Value if Failure	Value if Success	New Current Expected Value	Gain or Loss in Current Value
Stockholders	$1.00	0	$11.00	$5.50	+$4.50 = $5.50 − $1.00
Lender/Creditor	$9.00	0	$9.00	−$4.50	−$4.50 = $4.50 − $9.00

The stockholders' prospective fate: If the new activity succeeds, the stock-holders repay the bondholders $9 and retain $11 of the firm's $20 total value. The .5 chance of getting $11 makes its expected value $5.50 (= $11 × .5), giv-ing an expected profit of $4.50 (= $5.50 − $1) on the stockholders' initial $1 investment.

By making the business a riskier one, the stockholders obtained $4.50 of wealth from the bondholders. It's not the initial riskiness that is pertinent but the *unanticipated change* in the riskiness, after the loan was made. Because of awareness of this possible shift in activities, bondholders (lenders) when initially lending money take precautions to avoid, or offset, a shift in the risk-iness. The interest rate on the loan contains a *risk premium* appropriate to the expected degree of risk. Loan agreements contain many restraints, conditions, and provisions about what the debtors can do.

Where it is difficult for bondholders to monitor the selection of kinds of risks the firms will take, borrowing will be more expensive. Research activi-ties are risky, and are difficult to monitor. Some prospects are very likely to be successful, and some are very unlikely—but may have a very large payoff if successful, as with a drug or computer research company, or movies or tele-vision series. Those firms are less likely to be financed by lenders rather than directly financed by investors, as stockholders/owners, who bear all the risks. At the other extreme, railroads and public utilities, which have a lower risk of loss and higher probability of normal gains, are more able to attract lenders.

This conflict of interest among classes of owners suggests that, aside from the stockholders' task of controlling their top managers, there's a conflict among different owners and between owners and lenders. These conflicts are not a result of the corporate structure of ownership. They're examples of the general conflict of interest among dependent parties—a conflict pervasive throughout every modern society.

INDIRECT TAKEOVERS

One form of takeover—gaining control of managerial decisions—is usually not perceived as an attempted takeover as such, because it's done without buy-ing shares. This occurs when advocates of "corporate social responsibility" urge a corporation's owners (stockholders) and managers to alter the oper-ation of the firm from the goal of maximizing earnings to that of some other social good.

It doesn't cost anything to suggest that other people should run their busi-ness in ways that would raise costs and reduce profit and growth and survival prospects. But by pursuing "social goals" the firm would be destroying wealth (suffering losses or reduced earnings).

CHARITY IS BETTER THAN COERCION

If there is popular and political support for some special objective, that goal can be better achieved by asking the stockholders to donate some of their wealth to these social goals. A successfully competing business firm is an enterprise that is using resources to produce goods and services of greater value than the value of the goods and services used in production. Society is being made wealthier and can better afford to fulfill desires for such political priorities. To divert the corporation from pursuing the profit-seeking goal could be socially irresponsible.

SHAREHOLDERS OR STAKEHOLDERS?
PROMISES AND AGREEMENTS?

Another prevalent misconception arises from confusion about superficially related, but fundamentally different, concepts—*shareholder* and *stakeholder*. Stakeholder denotes anyone who has some wealth or interest dependent on the corporate actions. A stakeholder could be a neighboring grocery store or gasoline station or apartments independently owned and set-up to cater to the corporation employees. The grocer's investment is certainly dependent on the corporation's success and behavior. Though a stakeholder in that sense, the grocer is not a shareholder.

The *shareholder* interest is acquired by prior contractual agreement with the owners of the corporation, whereas a *stakeholder* unilaterally has put an investment in a position of dependence without any promises or commitments, explicit or implied, from or to the corporation shareholders. It is not possible for corporate management to put the grocer's interests ahead of the shareholders' interests without violating a contractual relationship.

Legitimate stakeholders include employees who have earned *promised* future returns, such as retirement pension rights, health insurance, or deferred compensation. These are contractual obligations equal to the rights of the investors. Bankers and bondholders—who loaned money to the corporation—acquired by agreement claims against the shareholders' wealth in the corporation and therefore are contractual stakeholders.

If employees were terminated just before a deferred promised salary increase, or a few days before retirement (and therefore lost their pension rights), or if the promised pension fund had not been accumulated, such employees—

who became stakeholders with the agreement of the shareholders — have a legally and morally binding claim.

SURVIVAL OF THE CORPORATE ORGANIZATION

Adam Smith, the famous eighteenth-century economist, thought the corporate form of organizing a business would not survive because the internal conflicts of interest would be too disruptive.[1] But, severe as the conflicts are, the greater productivity of large, long-lived investments dominates. The corporation has evolved into a powerful organizer of productive activity, despite heavy taxation on that form of organization.

MANAGERS AND CONSUMERS

After all this discussion of corporations, shareholders, and managers, remember that consumers are the fundamental controllers of all firms, whether giant corporations or small firms. Managers and owners compete to satisfy customers. If consumers don't buy the product, the firm will not survive — unless an owner might manage to get government subsidies or laws prohibiting consumer purchases from competitors. Consumers control the managers, who must respond to signals and rewards supplied by consumers. Ultimately, the consumers' demands reveal which response is most appropriate.

QUESTIONS AND MEDITATIONS

1) A friend of yours, a brilliant engineer and administrator, is operating a business. You propose to bet on his success and offer him some money to expand his operations. A corporation is formed allotting you 40 and him 60 percent of the common stock. You invest $30,000. This is often described as separation of ownership from control, since he now has the majority controlling vote. Would you ever be willing to invest wealth in such a fashion — that is, give up control while retaining ownership to 40 percent of the value of this business? Why?

Answer:

Yes, because I am investing in him and his managerial talents. Few holders of corporate stock have a significant degree of corporate control.

2) Is it a disadvantage of the corporation that not every stockholder can make the controlling decisions? That the control is dispersed? That some

---

1. Adam Smith, *An Inquiry Into the Nature and Causes of the Wealth of Nations* (1776) (New York: The Modern Library, 1937), pp. 699–716.

people who own less than half of the corporation can make controlling decisions?

Answer:

Division of labor and of responsibility is everywhere. I may have happy anticipations for a corporation, but I know virtually nothing about guiding the firm, and I am engaged in other activities. It is commonly the case that ownership of far less than half of a corporation's stock is sufficient to have effective control of operations.

3) A criticism of the modern corporation is that the management or directors, by virtue of their central position, are able to collect proxies (rights to cast votes of stockholders) from the other stockholders; as a result the management cannot be easily dislodged. It has been said that "the typical small stockholder can do nothing about changing management and that under ordinary circumstances management can count on remaining in office; and often the proxy battle is fought to determine which minority group shall control." Take the assertions as being correct.

a. Does it follow that stability of management in "ordinary circumstances" is associated with substantial losses to stockholders?

b. Does it follow that a typical small stockholder "should" be able to turn out management?

c. If a minority group succeeds in getting a majority of stock votes, does this mean that a minority controls or that a majority controls through the medium of a minority group? Is this to be interpreted in the same way that political parties consisting of a group of organized politicians have elections to see which minority group shall control the government?

Answer:

a. No. In ordinary circumstances we would expect stability to be associated with acceptable current and anticipated performance.

b. Should the typical voter or minority groups be able to turn out the governor of their state? It is precisely in order to prevent every single person from making his own will count that voting systems are utilized.

c. It means majority controls — through the medium of a minority of the stockholders to whom a majority gives its votes — as the Congress is a tiny minority of the American public, being only a few hundred people representing over 325,000,000.

4) "Very few corporations lose money, and still fewer go broke." Do you agree? What evidence can you cite?

Answer:

Depends upon what the speaker means by "lose money" and "very few." Even when a corporation has positive earnings, but less than had been expected, the market value of the shares held by the owners declines — a loss is incurred. Many corporations show decreases in the value of their common stock, sometimes because of reported losses. In some years, 30 to 40 percent of all publicly held corporations report losses, although the firms reporting losses are not always the same. For a century, the percentage has always been above 20 percent, and has been over 50 percent in several years. There are also instances in which the corporation reports a loss and the stock prices rise — because the losses were less than expected. For all reporting corporations, the aggregate earnings (after taxes) normally run about five times that of the losses.

5) Regulated companies:
   a. In analyzing the behavior of corporation management and directors, why is it pertinent to distinguish among nonprofit or publicly regulated, profit-limited corporations on the one hand, and private property, for-profit business corporations on the other?
   b. Which do you think would be more marked by self-perpetuating management and stockholder lethargy? Why?
   c. Which do you think would show more discrimination in employment practices according to race and religion? Why?

Answers:

   a. Wealth constraints are different in the two cases. Private, for-profit businesses seek to maximize the value of a stream of earnings over an extended period of time, even beyond the lifetimes of the current managers and owners.
   b. Nonprofit and limited-profit organizations, because of reduced possibility of personally capturing capitalized value of improvements by new management — as can be done in private property corporations, partly via purchase and sale of common stock.
   c. If conventional personal rewards and business performance are restricted, managers can comfort themselves with discrimination by personal criteria, even though such actions lower the productive efficiency of the organization.

6) Some years ago General Electric and Xerox each sold their loss-ridden computer subsidiaries to another company because the computer subsidiaries were unable to avoid losses. Why would anyone pay for a business that is losing money? It should have a negative value. One would think that General Electric or Xerox would have to pay someone to take on a business that is losing money. Explain the behavior of these firms, including the firm that bought the loss-making subsidiaries. Can you find some explanation that doesn't make the buyer foolish? If your explanation makes the buyer look sensible, is it consistent with General Electric and Xerox selling their computer divisions rather than continuing them?

Answer:

No one would pay anything for a business that is *expected to continue* losing. However: (a) buyers are more optimistic about how they can manage the business; or (b) the business is really not a "losing business" but instead had invested more than was worthwhile, in light of subsequent returns. So a new buyer bids a price for the business sufficiently low that they will be able to cover those costs out of the future returns. In this case, there is no point in selling the business, because the loss from the prior inopportune investment is a sunk cost to the original investor, and is not avoided by the sale of the business.

7) "The federal savings and loan deposit guarantees contributed to the financial safety and security of the community by protecting the assets of the depositors." Is that the full story?

Answer:

The guarantees reduced the incentives of the depositors to heed the prospect that the managers would make risky investments — with resultant loss of the depositors' money — because the government had guaranteed the depositors against any loss. After losses were incurred, taxpayers paid for them. The problem with government guarantees — and some other forms of insurance if not properly structured — is that "moral hazard" arises wherein some decision makers who stand to capture potential gains are not at risk of incurring the losses.

8) Mergers between two firms often result in many employees of at least one of the firms losing their jobs. It is then typically alleged that the merger was designed to reduce employees, or if not designed to do so, had that wasteful result. Is that wasteful?

Answer:

It is not wasteful. It is costly — for those who lose their jobs and must then search for another. But cost is not a waste. Dismissed workers pay a price (bear a cost) while the benefits of the merger are so dispersed over the rest of the population as to seem absent. A society that refuses to tolerate that concentration of costs while achieving greater total benefits which are dispersed in small amounts would find itself becoming poorer than societies that accept that method of wealth creation. That tolerance is accepted in a private property economy and usually less accepted, or rejected, in a socialist economy.

CHAPTER 29

THE DEMAND FOR PRODUCTIVE RESOURCES

Although it is doubtful that your parents told you this, you are a productive resource. At least, that is the way your future prospective employers will view you. This chapter considers demands for services offered in order to earn income.

HOMOGENEOUS, UNIFORM UNITS OF A PRODUCTIVE RESOURCE VERSUS NONUNIFORM UNITS

For some productive inputs — coal, water, gasoline, electricity — the units of each type are sufficiently similar that just the quantity, not which particular unit of that type of resource, is important. For many other goods, especially labor, discovery of individual features is expensive.

Doctors are doctors, and teachers are teachers, but you don't choose solely on the basis of the price charged. Still, even when each unit of each type of productive input is not exactly uniform and identical, they are similar enough for the intended use that the dominant employment feature is *how many*, not *which* ones.

Assembly-line workers, sales clerks, and carpenters certainly differ among themselves, but often the differences are sufficiently trivial that the demander has no significant preference for one person over another. Only the quantity demanded is to be determined. Explanation of this demand situation rests on the law of diminishing marginal returns. That law was considered in the Adam, Baker, and Carter economy (the example from chapter 15). We will use it to explain the demanded amounts of *uniform* labor services or any other inputs to production of final goods or services.

THE DEMAND FOR PRODUCTIVE SERVICES OF UNIFORM INPUTS

The law of diminishing marginal returns is dominant for the demanded quantities of uniform or homogeneous units of a productive resource. The universal law of diminishing marginal returns states, "As more units of a homogeneous resource are added to a fixed set of other resources, the marginal products will, beyond some amount of that resource, decrease at larger amounts of that resource." Parallel to consumer demand and the marginal personal use values

449

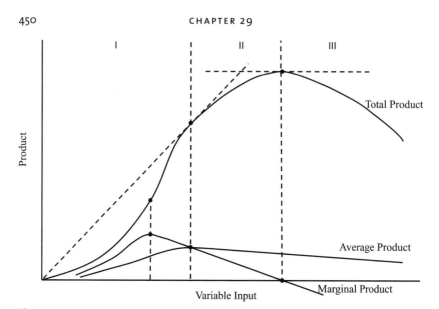

Figure 29.1

MP is positive when TP is rising with addition of variable input. MP is rising to the point of inflection, that is, where TP is rising at its greatest rate, and then it will be positive but decreasing until TP reaches a maximum (slope is zero), where MP is zero. At any given level of variable input, AP (TP divided by the amount of input) is at a maximum where a line from the origin is tangent to the TP curve. MP = AP at the input level where AP is at its maximum. The law of diminishing returns applies to all the measures of output, with MP hitting its maximum first with amounts of the variable factor added to a given amount of other inputs, then AP, and finally TP.

of a good, the schedule of the value of marginal product is the demand for inputs.

Decreasing marginal products, according to the law, are the counterparts to the diminishing marginal worths of a consumption good to a consumer. The demand curves for inputs, whether for consumption or for production by a firm, are negatively sloped with respect to price. Less is demanded at a higher price, and more is demanded at a lower price. The profit-maximizing amount of the input, say, labor, is that at which its marginal product value matches the wage rate, providing there's profit in hiring any of the input.

Figure 29.1 is a representation of a general relationship between the average and marginal products of the variable input, labor. It appears that typically additions of a variable input (labor) to a fixed amount of other inputs (land) will first increase output at an increasing rate and then at a decreasing rate up to a maximum, with still further addition finally reducing total product (TP). This yields a bell-shaped TP. When TP rises, marginal product (MP) must be positive, and MP is rising when TP rises more and more steeply. At the "point of inflection," where TP begins to flatten and to rise at decreasing rates, MP is at its maximum. When TP reaches its maximum — neither rising nor falling —

its slope and MP are zero, and the MP schedule intersects the horizontal axis. Further addition of variable inputs will cause TP to decrease (too many workers crowded onto the boat, getting in each other's way), so MP is negative. Since average product (AP) = TP/N (N being variable input), it is indicated graphically by the angle of the horizontal axis and a line from the origin to the TP curve at a given amount of variable input. That AP angle is at a maximum when the line from the origin is tangent to the TP curve. And MP = AP where AP is at a maximum.

It is seen in the figure that marginal product of the *variable* input (V) is negative in stage III. And, while not apparent in the figure, the marginal product of the *fixed* factor (F) is negative in stage I:

If 1V + 1F = 1P (product), then

2V + 2F = 2P (if there were constant returns to scale);

but since 2V + 1F > 2P (increasing APv), then 2F with 2V would *reduce* product back to 2P (because MPf is negative).

We do not rationally operate in any stage (I or III) where marginal product of either factor (F or V) is negative. There is too much variable factor relative to the fixed in stage III, so MPv is negative. There is too much fixed relative to variable in I, so MP_F is negative. Only in II are both marginal products positive.

Illustrative data from Codlandia (see chapter 22) are duplicated in table 29.1.

Table 29.1 *Product Values at Alternative Number of People at Work (Net of All Nonlabor Costs: Assumed Zero in This Example)*

People on Board Boat	Total Net Product Value	Marginal Net Product Value	Average Net Value per Unit of Labor
0	0	0	0
1	12	12	12.0
2	30	18*	15.0
3	46	16	15.3*
4	58	12	14.5
5	66	8	13.4
6	70	4	11.6
7	72*	2	9.4
8	64	−8	8.0
9	52	−12	5.8
10	30	−18	3.0

If the wage rate (in terms of the number of fish the worker could have caught on shore) is eight fish, 4 workers would be hired to join the owner, a total of 5 people on the boat, with the wage equal to the marginal value. The four hirees would be paid 32 (= 4 × 8), and total product would be 66 fish, leaving 34 for the owner. If the wage rate were 12 fish, the owner would end up with 4 people on board (3 employees) and a total product value of 58. Total wages paid the 3 employees then is 36, with 22 left for the owner.

Suppose fishing on shore becomes much more productive and 16 can be caught — that becomes the wage rate that would have to be paid to hire employees to work on the boat. However, if the owner hires 2 workers and pays them each 16 fish out of the total catch of 46, the owner is left with only 14 and would have been better off to remain on shore — boat fishing would be abandoned. The essential point is that at some sufficiently high wage no workers will be hired because the cost will result in a loss.

If there were costs of other items (in addition to labor), the boat owner would pay those costs before calculating his profit. If, after paying hired workers 8 fish each, and then paying nonlabor costs, the owner was left with less than 8, he would abandon the boat and work for someone else to earn wages of 8. At any wage lower than 8, any resulting excess of total product over the total cost of the added kind of input would be available to cover costs of other inputs. If the addition to total product is sufficient to cover both the wage and costs of other inputs, and leaves a net excess, such amount is rental value of the boat.

The demand curve for an input is the part of its marginal product below the highest average net product value (stage II). If the marginal product of labor (at which the average product is a maximum) were paid to each worker, that would exhaust the total product and leave nothing for other inputs. The profit maximizing amount of labor is that at which the marginal net product is equal to the wage. (The appendix to this chapter gives fuller consideration to input analysis of the firm in both price-taker's and price-searcher's markets for the buying of inputs and the selling of outputs and also to the mutual consistency of the input and the output rules for determining profit-maximizing rates of operations.)

This is parallel to the demand for consumption goods, elaborated earlier, with diminishing marginal personal worths. Similarly, as a consumer's demand for one good depends on its price and also on the price and amount of other goods consumed, there is dependence on the amount of other inputs.

The amount of any one kind of input demanded depends on the amounts of all the other resources being used. But the presence of complementary and substitute resources affects only the elasticity of demand for an input, not the negativity of the slope — more at a lower price and less at a higher price. And at some sufficiently high price, none will be demanded.

THE LONG-RUN ELASTICITY OF DEMAND FOR PRODUCTIVE
INPUTS EXCEEDS THE SHORT-RUN ELASTICITY

In this derivation of the demand for a kind of resource, initially more of only one kind of input, labor, was added. We started with the extreme case of no costs other than labor. This is a short-run adjustment, where we consider initially only the adjustment in the resource whose price has changed. Then, we allow for optimally timed adjustments in other resources, the longer-run adjustment. This two-stage adjustment recognizes that some adjustments are more economic if made less hastily. In the longer run, there are adjustments in all resources.

As with consumer goods, the demanded amount of a kind of input will be adjusted more in the long run. It will also pay to adjust the amounts of some of the other jointly used equipment. Less of the higher-priced resources will be demanded. If the price of gasoline rises, a trucking company will use less gasoline (by driving fewer miles), and still less gasoline will be demanded after the company has installed devices or types of trucks that get more miles per gallon. Since adjustments in inputs are less costly if done less hurriedly, the elasticity of demand for productive resources is greater in the longer run. That's the second law of demand — for all goods.

In review:

1) For an input to be hired,
   a. its price must be less than the profit-exhausting price; and
   b. the profit-maximizing amount of that kind of input is that at which its marginal product equals its price.
2) At a lower price, more is demanded, and at a higher price less is demanded.
3) The law of diminishing marginal returns to additions of homogeneous units of inputs to fixed amounts of other resources is the basis of the demand schedule for that input.

What other resources (with their costs) can affect the demand for labor? If there are costs of other resources — as when the sail was added to the boat — that affects productivity on the boat. But if the wage rate of labor is constant at 8, the only effect is on the number of people employed on the boat and the aggregate output, not on the 8-fish wage. If the boat were larger or more powerful, or the boat operator were more skilled in fishing or in organizing and administering teamwork, or if there were a dock to help unload the boat more rapidly and without damaging so many fish, or if people on board were more conscientious and more intelligent, and if people didn't shirk or steal each other's bait or hooks, the productivity of people on the boat would be higher, and more would be hired.

The wage paid depends on competition by other employers. The marginal product curves of labor in all possible uses must be summed to get the economy-wide demand curve (economy-wide production opportunities).

That demand conception is the one with which the economy-wide supply of labor is joined to determine the competitive economy-wide wage rate. In Codlandia, economy-wide demand was derived as the combination of the boat and the seashore marginal productivities.

CROSS-PRICE ELASTICITY OF DEMAND
FOR PRODUCTIVE RESOURCES

A change in the price of one kind of productive resource affects the demand schedule for other kinds, comparable to the cross-elasticity among consumer goods. If the wage rate is increased, very likely the set of other items tied to an added worker will be changed, each worker made more productive with equipment added to reduce the number of workers. At a higher price for wood, more steel, plaster, and plastic will be demanded as substitutes. There is substitution (on the margin) between electricity and gas, wood and steel, younger and older people, leather and plastic, heating oil and sweaters and insulation material, and so on. Substitution at the margin is pervasive. None of these adjustments upset the proposition that at a higher wage fewer workers will be hired. In fact, that substitution toward more of accessory equipment strengthens the principle that at a higher wage, less labor will be employed.

INPUT SUBSTITUTIONS IN PRODUCTION CAUSED BY
CONSUMER SUBSTITUTIONS AMONG CONSUMER GOODS

If the supply of lumber to an economy were reduced, its higher price would prompt consumers of wood products to shift toward more metal or plastic furniture. If carpenters increased their wages relative to other workers without being more productive, consumers would resort to fewer wood interiors in their homes. When gasoline prices have risen, consumers have demanded automobiles economizing on gasoline — even without any government-mandated restrictions on automobile fuel consumption.

SUBSTITUTES AND COMPLEMENTS

Substitutes are a pair of goods in which more of one will reduce the marginal productivity — and hence demand — for the other. Wood and bricks for building houses are substitutes for each other. Automobiles reduced the marginal productivity of horses (and the men with shovels to clean the streets). Movies reduced the demand for live stage performances. The establishment of supermarkets reduced consumer demand for small grocery stores.

The name *complement* is attached to pairs of resources wherein more of one *raises* the marginal productivity of the other. Women and men are substitutes for each other in some jobs and complements in others.

GENERALIZATION AND SIMILARITY TO DEMAND FOR CONSUMPTION GOODS

Both (a) the negatively sloped demand for *productive resources* and (b) the negatively sloped demand for *consumer goods* are forms of the same general principle. One is about diminishing marginal *products;* for the other, it's about diminishing marginal *worths.* As there are substitutions among amounts of producer goods, there is substitution among amounts of consumption goods.

SUMMARY OF PRINCIPLES OF DEMAND FOR AMOUNTS OF A KIND OF PRODUCTIVE RESOURCES

1) Marginal product values of a productive resource are the primary basis of the demand for it. The marginal product values of a particular kind of resource reflect the product's worths to consumers (net of other costs of production). A secondary factor in employing people is their personal characteristics, which we have initially ignored.
2) Demand for a resource is negatively sloped with respect to its price. More is demanded at a lower price of the input, or less is demanded at a sufficiently higher price of the input.
3) Demand for inputs is more elastic in the longer run.
4) Substitutions are marginal — not all or nothing.
5) The law of diminishing marginal returns can be applied to deduce the negative slope of the demand for the inputs, if the successive inputs are identical in production abilities.

LAGGED SUBSTITUTIONS TEND TO BE VEILED BY INTERIM EVENTS

Causes of substitutions among inputs often are not noticed, because they are so long delayed after the initiating event. Immediate adjustments are more costly, and it takes time to discern the appropriate change. That fools observers into thinking no response occurs.

Consider the prevalence of one-person-operated buses. Years ago, two persons operated and managed a bus, one as the driver and the other as fare collector and rider attendant. In response to higher wages, partially automated fare collection resulted in single-driver, but less safe and pleasant, buses. It's easy to think the changes occurred because of automation, *permitting* higher wages, rather than the reverse (wages rose, making automation more economical).

An example of unintentional adjustments is the response to the restriction of the oil supply and consequent rise in oil and gasoline prices in the 1970s. Those automobile producers who were already making smaller, higher *miles-per-gallon* cars found their product in high demand. Japanese cars had been smaller, as had some European cars, in part because there had long been a very high tax on gasoline in those nations. The switch in public demand to smaller cars left US producers in a poor competitive situation. Japanese and European producers gained an advantage by more quickly satisfying consumer demand.

THE FALLACY OF ENERGY EFFICIENCY —
OTHER INPUTS ARE NOT FREE

There can be excessive input-substitutions. Congress mandated minimum standards of energy use in cooling and heating equipment and for gasoline in automobiles. However, by arbitrarily minimizing one input — energy — others are increased as substitutes. *Energy efficiency*, that is, efficiency of any one resource, is not the same as minimizing total cost. Minimizing just one of the inputs increases the *total* cost, as more of other, more costly inputs are substituted for that input.

MORE CAPITAL INCREASES PRODUCTIVITY,
BUT WHO BENEFITS?

Better productive equipment enables a *given amount* of labor to produce more. So, for the *same* total output, less labor is sufficient, meaning the general demand for labor and some wages would tend to fall, although the workers who kept their jobs and are now working with better equipment get higher wages. However, if the demand for the product is very elastic, the lower price of that product can increase the amount demanded enough to increase the demand for labor and the amount employed as well as raise the wage rate.

Of course, labor was used in designing, building, programming, installing, and maintaining the new, more productive equipment. Generally, that labor was better compensated than the labor that was displaced by the equipment.

The net result for the firm utilizing the more productive equipment depends on (a) the extent to which the added capital displaces labor and (b) the elasticity of demand for the final product. In some industries, such as agriculture, the total number of people *directly* employed has declined as a result of greater use of equipment (employees making farm equipment are not counted as agriculture workers). In other industries, such as automobile manufacturing, the total number of people employed continued to increase long after automation occurred because the demand for cars rose as the economy became richer.

Labor's total share of the national income may rise, or may fall, with the opposite effect on income of capital. In any case, more capital increases the total national income to be divided, so even if labor's proportionate *share* declined, its total earnings could increase.

LABOR AND CAPITAL: IS THERE A REAL DIFFERENCE? IS IT CURRENT VERSUS EARLIER LABOR?

Analyzing production in terms of just two general classes of productive resources is often adequate for our purposes. It is conventional to call the two *capital* and *labor*. Labor means people. Capital refers to nonhuman durable resources, like buildings, land, and machinery, whether produced or natural.

HUMAN CAPITAL

Capital, as the word is now used, means anything already existing (even ideas) that will yield services in the future. Since people are durable and yield future services, they can be considered to be capital under this broad interpretation. Investments, by definition, are actions that create capital, as when investing in the construction of a building, or when investing in education, which creates *human capital*. Being a living entity doesn't change the fact that a person is a *capital resource* — a durable source of future valuable services, which determine wages, earnings, and income.

A musician, physician, or engineer invests more at an early age (more time in school) and earns a larger later income, called *wages*, as a result of labor — though some is profit and interest from the prior investment in creating human *capital*. You could have skipped college, worked, and invested your earnings in some machinery, the returns from which are called interest and profit. You will be a *capitalist* in either case.

Why then the distinction between capital and labor? People usually aren't bought and sold, as are ownership rights to buildings, land, and businesses. We say *usually*, because a professional athlete's future services are bought and sold under multiyear contracts. The item itself, the person in whom the investment is made, is not bought. But there is a present capital value of your future anticipated earnings. That capital value can be sold, just as the value of your share of ownership of some corporate stock can be sold. There's no *economic* difference between people and capital.

SOCIAL AND CULTURAL RESOURCES
AS PRODUCTIVE INPUTS

Productivities reflect your abilities and skills, which depend on inherited talents, education, on-the-job learning, work ethic, and personality. Their value will depend in part on 1) how many people are supplying similar services, 2) the technology and supply of resources with which you will work, and 3) the skills of the employer in estimating consumer demand for various products and in managing and selecting a well-matched team in which you work.

An individual's productivity will depend also on the "social capital." The United States is considered to be a *developed country*, because there is much more social capital — more educated people, power-generating facilities, paved streets, transport systems, banking and financial services, buildings, level land, good climate, healthy environment, civility and congeniality of the population, reliable and impartial enforcement of laws, strong private property rights, dependable accounting and auditing practices, and government stability. That social capital is the *economic infrastructure*.

IF RESOURCES ARE NOT OWNED, LESS ATTENTION
IS FOCUSED ON MARKET VALUES

The holders of productive resources held as private property will be punished more for not responding to market prices than would be holders of resources *not* held as private property. If resources are not owned (whether by one person or by shareholders of a corporation), there is less incentive for the manager to maximize profits. That's because dividends or other forms of income can't be possessed as personal wealth.

The manager/decision maker who does not answer to an owner/shareholder will be influenced more (than would be an owner) by nonprofit objectives and preferences — spending on things that don't improve the goods and services offered to customers. With any government, or not-for-profit enterprise, potential profits derived from market sales are not as strong a survival factor as for a privately owned firm. Because the administrator's rewards are less aligned with profits and bear less of the losses, attention is directed more to achievable nonmoney, non-market-evaluated objectives and criteria, such as personal characteristics of the employees or junkets to exotic places.

A MARKET FOR LABOR OR A MARKET FOR *PERSONS*

A market for labor does not imply the sale or rental of people; slavery was abolished in most of the world long ago. Instead, it means the voluntary sale by a person of some of that person's specified type of *services*. Labor services are bought and sold, as when you visit your doctor, lawyer, or music teacher. The economic forces in transactions for labor services are basically the same as for other goods. More is demanded at a lower price and less at a higher price, even though there's no central marketplace where people gather to buy and sell labor — except maybe at the corner of the local Home Depot.

But there is a *labor market*, meaning there is communication and exchange of information about people with offers and bids. If we take account of the importance of the *type of work* and *who the person is* and how *reliably* a person cooperates with other persons as part of a team, we'll understand many otherwise mysterious methods of payment and contract restrictions in labor markets.

Diversity in personal features becomes more important where people work in close physical proximity, with cooperation and exchange of information within the group, and where congeniality and responsiveness affect the group's effectiveness. Personality, appearance, age, responsibility, reliability, demeanor, cleanliness, manners, dress, religion, gender, and ethnic features of both the employer and the employee and associated other employees affect productivity of the group. All these are contained in the *services* of labor.

In teamwork, employment will probably be a relatively long-lived association with the same persons. And in teamwork, who, as well as how many, is critical. There is still a labor market, but it has a particular mixture of methods of search and contracts. Both sides demand more information about each other. It's this uniqueness that creates long-term relationships and consequent specific dependency. Specific dependencies are dangerous, even if highly productive. As we have noted, the relied-upon person might opportunistically threaten to leave unless given more of the value of the pair's value. The contractual arrangements should be tightly established before the specific dependency is established.

There is no market-revealed price of persons for that joint work. For each person, a separate market is the offers that person can obtain from competing demanders. That's illustrated by the negotiating and contract provisions for professional athletes. The personalities and interpersonal tensions and dependence are a matter of general publicity, in contrast to negotiations within customary business firms. Physically equally talented players don't have equal personalities, and the differences affect the team's performance. Within firms, the gains come from teamwork, not just specialization.

When individual personal characteristics make a substantial difference in the group's performance, the principle of diminishing marginal returns is not applicable, because that principle applies only to additions of units of the same kind of input. Where the additions or replacements are different, there's no law that says a newcomer will result in diminishing marginal products. The value of a newcomer is an amount unique to that person.

The firm is not just a place where a lot of people work in the same place to produce and assemble components. The internal relationships and dependencies can be disruptive at one extreme or exceptionally productive at the other.

INDIVIDUAL SUPPLY OF LABOR

Labor services offered by a person generally are greater at a higher wage rate per hour than at a lower hourly wage. But at some sufficiently high wage, a person may decrease the hours of work, for then income and wealth may be so great that more leisure is deemed more valuable than more earnings. At high enough wages and incomes, the effect of the increased labor income can be dominated by the substitution (of leisure for income) effect. This is reflected in a *backward-bending supply curve*.

Spouses are less likely to enter the labor force the higher are the earnings of the other spouse in the family. But unless strong evidence exists to the contrary, we will assume that higher wage rates attract more people into the market labor force.

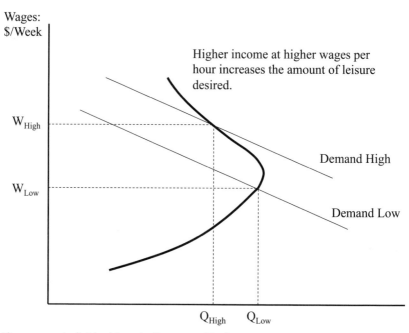

Figure 29.2 *Individual Supply: Hours per Week*

WHAT IS A UNIT OF LABOR SERVICE? THE
VALUE OF THE SERVICE IS CRITICAL

Karl Marx believed that hours of labor determine costs and prices of products and personal incomes. That is, he believed that the input of homogeneous labor units created the value of a product. But not all labor of all people is of equal value. A more fundamental flaw was his failure to recognize that values and costs are *derived from the product values as judged by consumers*. The values of labor services are deemed to differ among people, and therefore their earnings differ. The values of labor services differ because they reflect the ultimate product's personal worths to consumers. Stated more simply, the value of labor is derived from the value of the product.

QUESTIONS AND MEDITATIONS

1) A few decades ago, a federal judge blocked the firing of thousands of workers on railroads pending a final court ruling on the legality of certain drastic steps of the companies. The judge said that he felt "an interim decision affecting both jobs and capital must be resolved in favor of jobs and men." In what sense can it be contended instead that the issue is one between jobs *and* jobs, rather than between jobs and capital?

Answer:

There are jobs of workers on railroad engines and jobs the displaced workers will accept elsewhere producing other products and services, including jobs of workers making railroad equipment.

2) Who is substituted for whom when a firm uses a computer-controlled robot rather than employees to perform some repetitive task in manufacturing? This is often called a "substitution of capital for labor." Why is that misleading?

Answer:

Labor used to make the computer, the software, and the robot is substituted for the manufacturer's employees. Substitution of "capital for labor" can be misleading, because it ignores the labor used to make the capital.

3) "The advent of the one-man bus involved more capital equipment: an automatically operated coin box and a door-control device — to name two of the capital goods that replaced the conductor."
   a. Is this a case of capital replacing labor? Where?
   b. Is it a case of labor replacing labor? Where?

    c. Is it a case of no substitution of labor at all, but instead of a job
       revision with a greater total output? Where?

Answer:

    a. Yes. Equipment on the bus for a worker (the conductor) on the bus.
    b. Yes. Labor off the bus which makes the machinery (the coin box and
       door control device) for labor on the bus (the conductor).
    c. Yes. Total labor is reallocated in its tasks. No labor is released from the
       work force, since that labor is used to produce more of other goods —
       except to the extent that some workers now choose more leisure.

4) "Invention and the lower cost of power in the home have replaced the
    domestic servant by capital equipment. Without that machinery more
    people would be working in homes as servants. But the replacement of
    domestic employees by capital has not led to the replacement of labor."
    Why not?

Answer:

New opportunities for labor — including making home appliances — were
created. The laborers did not disappear. Released from their domestic
roles, they were used elsewhere.

5) The electric refrigerator replaced the iceman with capital. By eliminating
    the job of the iceman (who provided blocks of ice to keep the "icebox"
    cold), was the total number of jobs reduced?

Answer:

No. Unlimited numbers of jobs are available in this world of scarcity; only
the highest-value jobs are filled, given present knowledge and resources.
New inventions induce labor to seek and move to the best of other unfilled
jobs. The total wealth of the community is increased. The displaced person
has no assurance of realizing a net gain from the particular innovation
which displaces his previous job; but he does gain from most other innovations that do not displace his job.

6) "Automation does not mean there will be more people than jobs
    available. It also does not mean fewer jobs for unskilled people — in
    fact, a person can be less skilled if all he has to do is punch buttons, pull
    triggers, and turn steering wheels, compared to driving a team of horses,
    shooting a bow and arrow, or wielding a chisel." Do you agree?

Answer:

Yes. When people are released from some kinds of work, they can do some
other productive work — of which there is always some as long as scarcity

exists. Displaced workers search for the best (highest-valued) of the other unlimited unfilled jobs.

7) Assume that wage rates of gardeners were to double because of a reduced supply of gardeners, with an unchanged demand.
   a. What substitution would occur?
   b. Where or from whom could you learn about the available substitution techniques?

Answer:
   a. Power mowers and other equipment, smaller gardens, rocks and bark instead of grass, plants that don't require pruning, among other things, would replace some gardeners.
   b. From competitors, in this case the sellers of power equipment, cement surfaces, artificial flowers, and so forth.

8) The law of diminishing returns is a law of diminishing marginal returns. What is the difference between diminishing *total* returns and diminishing *marginal* returns?

Answer:
   With diminishing total returns, total returns are falling (negative change); marginal returns, the changes in the total, can fall even while the total is increasing. That is, a smaller increase in the total is a diminishing marginal return.

9) You operate a factory and discover that some resource used has *increasing* marginal returns.
   a. What would you do?
   b. Does this suggest that we will never find any firm using an amount of resources involving increasing marginal resources?

Answer:
   a. Increase the amount of that resource used relative to other resources; eventually the marginal returns for use of that resource will begin to fall.
   b. Yes. With a variable input being added to a fixed factor, if MP is rising, it is greater than AP. (In part of stage I of production, MP of the fixed factor is negative.) If the variable factor is paid its marginal product, total payment to it will be greater than total product.

10) "If the ratio of the price of resource A to the price of resource B exceeds the ratio of the marginal-value products of A to B, it will be efficient to decrease the employment of A relative to B." Explain.

Answer:

> To minimize the cost, increase the employment of B, the more productive resource per dollar invested.

11) "If a firm uses resources efficiently, a change in their prices will induce a change in the relative amounts employed." What will induce that change — some directive from a central planning agency, the social consequences of the employer, or what?

Answer:

> The desire for greater wealth and the competition among actual and potential employers for the resources that give greater, rather than less, wealth. This is accomplished by input and product substitution. More goods will be produced that use more of the now lower-priced inputs, and those consumer goods will become less costly.

12) "Even if only one combination of productive inputs could be used to produce some good, there would still be substitution among productive resources in response to changes in their prices." Explain what that substitution is and how it would be induced.

Answer:

> Ratios of prices of final products purchased by consumers would change, thus redirecting use of inputs toward those outputs which become relatively less expensive at the new prices. For illustration, a shovel is made with one handle and one blade; however, if the price of wood used to make handles rises sharply, fewer shovels will be made because the wood has a greater value in making other things.

13) According to the analyses developed in this chapter, resources will be employed in open markets in amounts at which marginal value product is not less than price. That also determines their earnings (price times the number of units employed).

    a. What ensures that the total earnings (payments to factors of production) will not exceed the value of the total output?

    b. Who makes up the difference if payments to factors of production exceed the value of output?

    c. If the payments to factors of production are less than the total value of output, who gets the difference (the net revenue)?

    d. In each case, what forces revise payments to factors of production toward equality with value of output?

Answer:

    a. Losses will be incurred. Producer will have to reduce production eventually or go out of business.

    b. The owner-employer — the bearer of the risk.

    c. The owner.

    d. Product and input substitution in a setting of market competition.

14) Suppose you operate a publicly owned factory in which profits cannot be retained.

    a. What would be your criterion of resource use in production?

    b. Would you have any incentive to adjust the use of resources to preserve the equality of the ratios of prices and marginal productivities — that is, to minimize the cost of the output? Explain.

Answer:

    a. Same as before: maximize personal worth. But, because no profit or net value of output can be retained or taken out by an owner, less attention will be given to earnings as a source of value. Instead, the carpets will be better, nice artwork will be enjoyed in offices, and free coffee will be available to employees.

    b. Possibly some, but not as strongly as if the enterprise were privately owned. The administrator of a nonprofit enterprise is more likely to let resource usage depart from the most efficient ratio. More personal worth is derived from other uses of resources rather than for profits or higher monetary exchange value.

15) In socialist states — in which most producers' goods (goods with which you can earn a living) are owned by the governments — targets have been assigned to factories in terms of the *total value* of the output (not profits) they were supposed to produce. Plant managers were told to accomplish and overfulfill targets as much as possible. Prices are set by law.

    a. Is it desirable to have these targets over-fulfilled?

    b. Is it more desirable to state a target for each particular good in terms of *total value* of output than in terms of maximizing profits? What are the differences in performance that will be induced?

    c. Which criterion is more likely to provide a more effective incentive for the manager?

Answer:

    a. No, not if waste is to be avoided.

    b. No, focusing only on a value of output target ignores the cost of producing products (or what is given up) and won't determine whether $1 of one output is worth $1 more of some other output. The profit criterion answers that question (it compares value of what is produced with value of what is given up).

c. It is simpler to grind out maximum physical product with dictated prices than to solve the more sophisticated problems involved in maximizing profit.

16) In Iowa, the yield of wheat is 30 bushels per acre; in Washington, it is 50 bushels per acre. Which is better?

Answer:

More is always better than less, other things equal. But the costs of growing wheat may not be equal in the two states.

17) Jet engines are given an efficiency rating according to the thrust generated per pound of engine weight. Explain why that is an inadequate measure of efficiency.

Answer:

Inadequate, because it doesn't clearly distinguish the difference between value of the total thrust and the cost of getting it. How much fuel is used and the cost of the fuel need to be known in order to say anything about efficiency.

18) Steers can be bred with such superb qualities that they will sell for about 50 percent more per pound than the standard steers raised for meat. Which type should the farmer raise? Give the answer in terms of technological versus economic efficiency.

Answer:

We can't tell. This tells us nothing about cost. We presume the new method is technologically or technically efficient, in that no more could be obtained as output for a given amount of specified input. But this doesn't tell us output is worth the input.

19) A water-storage reservoir is to be built, and engineers, asked for advice, proposed a dam and attest to its efficiency.

a. If they attest to its technical efficiency, does that still leave open the question of its economic efficiency? For example, if the value of the water stored is less than the cost of impounding and distributing it, is the dam, though it may be technically efficient, an economically efficient one?

b. This problem extends the notion of economic efficiency beyond the selection of the cheapest way of doing something. Economic efficiency is extended to include what?

Answers:

a. Technical efficiency means that the proposed dam uses the lowest-cost combination of resources and production methods. The dam may not be economically efficient, since the value of the water stored may be less than the cost of building and maintaining the reservoir.

b. To include exchange efficiency. Values of outputs are being judged by what people will pay in an exchange system. Thus, efficiency is broadened to include deciding *what* to produce, rather than merely the cheapest way to produce an arbitrary output.

20) The US Federal Communications Commission says rights to use the radio spectrum should be assigned to "permit maximum usage."

a. Explain why that statement, as it stands, is meaningless and useless.

b. Would it have been meaningful to say rights should be assigned to achieve efficient use? What would be the criterion of efficiency?

Answers:

a. Suppose you had one piece of paper and were told to maximize your use of that paper. What would you do? The expression has no meaning — or it means anything you want it to mean. Usage is not something you maximize, for usage is not measurable in a single-dimensional sense. It's like your parents telling you to maximize your time at college.

b. Economic efficiency: maximize value of product produced relative to cost.

21) Legislatures of several states started to set energy standards for electrical appliances requiring that they yield at least a specified amount of output per kilowatt hour used. A federal energy agency has stated that automobiles must yield some minimum miles per gallon (for the average of all cars sold). Why is that almost certainly wasteful of our national productive resources?

Answer:

Costs of other resources used to reduce gas consumption will exceed value of uses to which the saved gasoline will be put, because people would voluntarily prefer cars that use less gasoline if it was worth the costs. Government energy policy ignores the fact that gasoline is worth what we are willing to pay for it, and other resources used to save gasoline also would be more valuable producing other things.

22) A jet plane can fly across the United States three hours faster than a propeller plane. Which is more efficient?

Answer:

It is impossible to tell from that information. Costs are unknown.

23) Why is economic efficiency a more general test than technical efficiency?

Answer:

There are many alternative ways of doing something, all of which can be technically efficient. But, of these, only one minimizes the value of the forsaken opportunities; that is the economically efficient one. Graphically, every point on the production possibility boundary is productively efficient — but which is economically preferred?

24) There are two kinds of economic efficiency — cost minimization and profit maximization. In what sense is profit maximization a more general criterion of efficiency?

Answer:

Profit maximization compares value of what is produced with the cost, rather than merely minimizing cost of what may not be worth even that cost.

APPENDIX TO CHAPTER 29: OUTPUT AND INPUT EQUILIBRIA OF THE FIRM

We have dealt with determining the profit-maximizing (or loss-minimizing) level of *output* of a firm. Stipulating the optimal level of operations can be approached also from the standpoint of the level of variable *inputs*.

Outputs are produced with inputs. As there is an optimal level (rate) of output, there is a corresponding optimal input. The profit-maximizing output is located by equating revenue and costs at the margin: $MR = MC$. By the same logic, the accompanying best *input* is found by equating two marginal measures of revenue and cost: marginal revenue product (MRP) and marginal expenditure (ME), where $MRP = \Delta TR/dN$, and $ME = \Delta TC/dN$, with ΔTR and ΔTC being changes in total revenue and total cost, and dN being change in input.

Those inputs may be bought in price-taker's (competitive) markets or price-searcher's (monopsonistic) markets. And the product may be sold in price-taker's (competitive) markets or price-searcher's (monopolistic) markets. There are, therefore, four possible combinations of purchasing and selling situations.

DEFINITIONS

AE: Average Expenditure   N: Inputs

AR: Average Revenue   TC: Total Cost

MC: Marginal Cost   TP: Total Product

ME: Marginal Expenditure   TR: Total Revenue

MP: Marginal Product   VMP: Value of Marginal Product

MRP: Marginal Revenue Product

The first table pertains to a price-taker buyer of inputs, with average expenditure (price per unit of variable input) constant and thus equal to marginal expenditure:

Table 29.A *Price-Taker Buyer of Inputs*

Inputs	AE	TC	ME
1	$5	$5	$5
2	5	10	5
3	5	15	5
4	5	20	5

Next is a price-searcher (monopsonistic) buyer, with the price of a unit of input rising with the quantity bought:

Table 29.B *Price-Searcher Buyer of Inputs*

Inputs	AE	TC	ME
1	$5	$5	$5
2	10	20	15
3	15	45	25
4	20	80	35

The following illustrates a price-taker seller of product, noting that VMP = MP × AR (quantity times price), and MRP = ΔTR/ΔN = ΔTR/ΔTP × ΔTP/ΔN = MR × MP.

Table 29.C *Price-Taker Seller of Output*

Inputs	TP	MP	AR	TR	MR	VMP	MRP
1	$3	$3	$3	$9	$3	$9	$9
2	10	7	3	30	3	21	21
3	16	6	3	48	3	18	18
4	21	5	3	63	3	15	15

Finally, we have a price-searcher seller of product:

Table 29.D *Price-Searcher Seller of Output*

Inputs	TP	MP	AR	TR	MR	VMP	MRP
1	$3	$3	$5	$15	$5	$15	$15
2	10	7	4	40	3.57	28	25
3	16	6	3	48	1.33	18	8
4	21	5	2	42	−1.2	10	−6

The following graphs illustrate the four possible market combinations of revenue and expenditure:

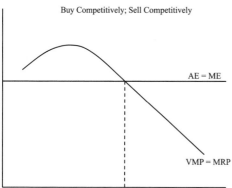

Buy Competitively; Sell Competitively

AE = ME

VMP = MRP

Figure 29A

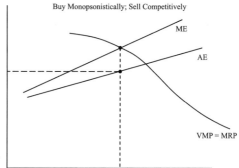

Buy Monopsonistically; Sell Competitively

ME

AE

VMP = MRP

Figure 29B

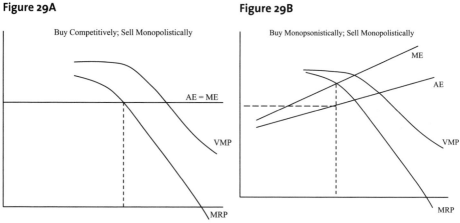

Buy Competitively; Sell Monopolistically

AE = ME

VMP

MRP

Figure 29C

Buy Monopsonistically; Sell Monopolistically

ME

AE

VMP

MRP

Figure 29D

The "output" and "input" rules are necessarily consistent with each other.

If $MC = MR$, then $ME/MP = MRP/MP$, and $ME = MRP$:

$$MC = \Delta TC/\Delta TP = \Delta TC/\Delta N \times \Delta N/\Delta TP = ME \times 1/MP = ME/MP$$

$$MR = \Delta TR/\Delta TP = \Delta TR/\Delta N \times \Delta N/\Delta TP = MRP \times 1/MP = MRP/MP$$

PART THREE

WEALTH, RATES OF RETURN, AND RISK

CHAPTER 30

ARITHMETIC OF CAPITAL VALUES

People will punish you for wasteful use of what you own. If, in the opinion of others, you make a "wasteful" decision about your resource, its market value will fall. People express their opinion through the market values they offer for your resources.

You'll be comparing salaries of job offers, or savings plans, and whether to rent or buy a house, or whether to purchase or lease a car, and you'll consider various types of insurance. If you work for a company, you'll be asked how much of your paycheck you want to have withheld and invested in a retirement plan. If you are self-employed, you'll have to think about setting aside some of your current earnings in a self-directed pension plan. Dealing with such matters involves use of "capital values."

ESSENTIAL CONCEPTS FOR YOUR FUTURE

Less Now for the Prospect of More Later

The demand for short-lived goods like candy, eggs, and milk is based on personal worth of services yielded *now*. However, many goods are durable and yield a stream of services into the future. If a TV set lasts 10 years, and in each year yields services worth $100, it's tempting, but wrong, to think the value of future services of the TV is $1,000, the sum of the future annual services. Today, they are worth *less* than that total.

Or if you win $1,000,000 in a lottery that's paid in twenty annual installments of $50,000, you haven't won a million dollars. You've won a lot less, and we're not referring to taxes that would reduce it. Getting something in the future gets you less than if you had the same thing now.

CURRENT AND FUTURE SERVICES OF DURABLE RESOURCES

Shoes, houses, automobiles, computers, and tennis rackets are durable goods. They are also "capital goods." Your demand for a capital good reflects the worth of all the anticipated future services of the good. But the value of a durable good is less than the sum of the future values of its future services. The present market value of a durable good is its "capital value." Capital values apply to a much broader range of items than bonds, common stock of a corporation, or borrowed money for a house. *Capital values apply to all durable goods.*

Capital goods have service streams, or "yields." The time pattern of these services, the yield, can be described in various ways. An apple tree may yield all its apples in one month each year, say, three hundred apples in October. Instead of saying the yield from the apple tree is zero for eleven months and three hundred in one month, it's conventional to measure the sequence as a flow per year. Here, it could be expressed as 300 apples per year, or twenty-five apples per month. For many resources and consumption goods, the yields are sold and measured in monetary terms.

Expressing the Rate of Yield

Suppose a decorative potted tree were salable at a price of $6,000 or could be rented for $50 a month. The annual rent, $600, could be *expressed* as a *percentage* yield of 10 percent per year of the $6,000 "present capital value" ("market value") of the tree (= $600/$6,000). When the yield is expressed in percentage terms, it is commonly called its "own interest rate" or "own rate of yield" or "rental rate."

Three Forms of Yields in the "Full" Yield

The "full yield" to the owner of a resource is composed of a) services or b) physical growth of the good, plus c) growth in the value of a unit of the good. To the owner, the services are usually interpreted as "income," and the expected growth is "interest," while any *unexpected* excess in the growth of value higher than the interest is "profit."

  a) *Services* — Some yields are direct consumption services, like the warmth and comfort of clothes and shoes, the shade from a tree, the safety provided by a fire extinguisher, or an eraser's services in correcting errors. Think of a $50 picture. If you choose to buy it when the interest rate you could otherwise earn by investing or lending your money is 10 percent per year, the picture's yearly services to you must be worth more than $5 a year (= .10 × $50), else why did you buy it?

  This is the resource's "rent" value. It would cost that much to rent it, adjusted for risk of payment of rent and the time at which the rent is paid. In both situations, buy or rent, you get the picture now. The difference is in when you pay and who bears the risk of changes in the market value of the resource. If you buy now, you can pay now for the services; or, if you pay later, you also pay interest for the delay in payment. Interest must be paid because, in the intervening year, the seller will lose services from what could have been obtained if the payment had been made at the time of delivery.

The most commonly recognized meaning of *rent* is certain payments in money — such as money received (or paid) for the use of a house or land. However, the rent paid for *borrowed* money is typically called "interest," though, speaking precisely, it is rent paid for the money's services. This is rent in the same sense of rent paid for services of a house. The yield on savings accounts, bonds, and other financial instruments also is called "interest" instead of "rent." This distinction is based on the difference in timing of services and payments. Payments for services of money are not paid in money ahead of the time the borrowed money is used, in contrast to payments of rent for a house, which can be paid in advance.

b) *Physical Growth* of the good — as in a tree, a field of wheat, or maturing of wine — is another form of "yield" that accumulates during the passing of time. That can happen with money if the price level is falling, so each monetary unit buys more.

c) *Growth of the Resource's Market Value* — another form in which a "yield" accrues to the owner is the accumulating rise in the market value of a resource. Suppose you have a share of common stock in some corporation, and the stock initially is worth $80 a share. You receive $5 in dividends (earnings of the corporation paid to you) during the year, while the value of the stock rises $3, to $83. That's a total return of $8 — a 10% rate of return on the $80 initial stock value. Whether the return is in the form of cash receipts or a rise in the market value of the stock makes no difference in your wealth (except for income tax considerations).

Similarly, suppose you own some vacant land now worth $1,000 and from which you receive no rent. If the land value rises by $100 to $1,100 during the year, you have received a return of $100. That's 10 percent of the initial value. And, as noted earlier, a falling price level results in a growth of the value (purchasing power) of a unit of money in your wallet.

With that background, we can concentrate on two reasons for a future item being less valuable than if it were available now. These reasons are "productivity" and "time preference and mortality."

1) *Productivity*: Successful investing can convert production for current consumption into *greater*, or *more valuable*, production of future consumption. This reason for an interest rate is "productivity" of investing.

2) *Time Preference and Mortality*: A second reason is that we commonly like things to be available sooner rather than later, and we face a probability of death before we can enjoy an anticipated future consumption. We therefore offer less for a future "enjoyment" the farther in the future is the time of its realization. This reason for placing a lower value now on more distant potential experiences is called discounting the value because of "time preference," suggesting the preference for having it *now* rather than having it later.

But it's not only the *preference* for *now* rather than later; it is the preference for *assurance* of realizing it whether now or in the future. These relationships among present and future values are summarized in the "capital value principles" which we will be considering.

PRINCIPLES OF CAPITAL VALUATIONS

We can apply the concepts of "present values" and expected "future values" to explaining the meaning of "income" and "wealth," as well as helping solve financial problems.

1. Present Value, Multiplied by "One Plus the Rate of Interest," Equals the Expected One-Year Future Value

The following expression summarizes the relation between the current value and the future value — the connection between how much you put in a bank now and how much you'll have at the end of one year as interest accumulates.

$P_0 (1 + r) = F_1$,
"P_0" denotes the present market value (price) paid or invested now, at time 0.
"r" represents the annual market rate of interest, or rate of growth of the present value to the future value.
"F_1" denotes the future value, wherein the subscript 1 indicates the number of years in the future.
When P_0 is $1.00 and r is .10, F_1 is $1.10:

$$\$1.00 (1 + .10) = \$1.10 = F_1$$

$1 today will, at a 10 percent rate of growth per year, grow by $.10 (= $1 × .10) to $1.10 at the end of the year. It makes no economic difference whether you refer to a $1 present value or to a $1.10 one-year future value, when the interest rate is

10%. They are equivalent prices. The "price" of getting $1 now is the same as the price of getting $1.10 a year later.

2. Extending Farther into the Future

What future amount in two years is equivalent to $100 now at a 10 percent annual rate of interest? In other words, to what future amount will $100 grow in two years at a constant 10% rate of interest per year? The $100 present value will grow to $110 in one year, and then that amount will grow by another 10% to $121 in the second year.

$$P_0(1+r)(1+r) = P_0(1+r)^2 = \$100(1.10)(1.10) = \$121 = F_2$$

The rate of interest in each year could be different, say .08 in the first and .10 in the second year. In that case, the two rates, .08 and .10, would replace the constant .10 in each year:

$$P_0(1 + .08)(1 + .10) = 118.80 = F_2$$

The amount three years in the future to which $100 will grow at 10% per year is:

$$P_0(1 + r)(1 + r)(1 + r) = 100(1.10)(1.10)(1.10) = \$133 = F_3$$

In more compressed symbols, we have

$$P_0(1 + r)^3 = \$100(1.10)^3 = \$133 = F_3$$

TABLES OF FUTURE VALUES OF PRESENT AMOUNTS

Table 30.1 spares us tedious computations by listing the future amounts, or future values, to which $1.00 (called the present value) will grow in the various listed number of years at alternative rates of interest. At 3 percent per year, a present value of $1 will double to $2 in 25 years — or, more accurately, slightly more than double ($2.09). How does the "doubling time" depend on the rate of interest? The answer is found by looking for the entries closest to 2 in the several columns of table 30.1. They're found at about 18 years for 4 percent and 14 years for 5 percent, at 9 years for 8 percent, at about 7 years for 10 percent, and at about 6 years for 12 percent.

Graphically, future values at alternative growth rates are illustrated in figure 30.1 below.

Table 30.1 *Compound Future Value of Present $1*

Rate of Interest

Year	3%	4%	5%	6%	7%	8%	10%	12%	15%	20%
1	1.03	1.04	1.05	1.06	1.07	1.08	1.10	1.12	1.15	1.20
2	1.06	1.08	1.10	1.12	1.15	1.17	1.21	1.25	1.32	1.44
3	1.09	1.13	1.16	1.19	1.23	1.26	1.33	1.41	1.52	1.73
4	1.13	1.17	1.22	1.26	1.31	1.36	1.46	1.57	1.75	2.07
5	1.16	1.22	1.28	1.34	1.40	1.47	1.61	1.76	2.01	2.49
6	1.19	1.27	1.34	1.42	1.50	1.59	1.77	1.97	2.31	2.99
7	1.23	1.32	1.41	1.50	1.61	1.71	1.95	2.21	2.66	3.58
8	1.27	1.37	1.48	1.59	1.72	1.85	2.14	2.48	3.06	4.30
9	1.31	1.42	1.55	1.69	1.84	2.00	2.36	2.77	3.52	5.16
10	1.34	1.48	1.63	1.79	1.97	2.16	2.59	3.11	4.05	6.19
11	1.38	1.54	1.71	1.90	2.11	2.33	2.85	3.48	4.65	7.43
12	1.43	1.60	1.80	2.01	2.25	2.52	3.14	3.90	5.35	8.92
13	1.47	1.67	1.89	2.13	2.41	2.72	3.45	4.36	6.15	10.70
14	1.51	1.73	1.98	2.26	2.58	2.94	3.80	4.89	7.08	12.84
15	1.56	1.80	2.08	2.40	2.76	3.17	4.18	5.47	8.14	15.41
16	1.61	1.87	2.18	2.54	2.95	3.43	4.60	6.13	9.36	18.49
17	1.65	1.95	2.29	2.69	3.16	3.70	5.05	6.87	10.76	22.19
18	1.70	2.03	2.41	2.85	3.38	4.00	5.56	7.69	12.38	26.62
19	1.75	2.11	2.53	3.03	3.62	4.32	6.12	8.61	14.23	31.95
20	1.81	2.19	2.65	3.21	3.87	4.66	6.73	9.65	16.37	38.34
25	2.09	2.67	3.39	4.29	5.43	6.85	10.8	17.0	32.92	95.40
30	2.43	3.24	4.32	5.74	7.61	10.0	17.4	30.0	66.21	237.4
40	3.26	4.80	7.04	10.3	15.0	21.7	45.3	93.0	267.9	1469.8
50	4.38	7.11	11.5	18.4	29.5	46.9	117.4	289.0	1083.7	9100.0

Example: *The Good Old Days, When a Dollar Was Worth a Dollar*
Suppose the price *level* were to rise at a rate of about 3 percent per year for several years. Today, a Coke costs $1 at a vending machine. If the price in dollars rises at 3 percent per year, in a little more than 24 years its price will be almost $2, twice as much.

Example: *Take It, or Leave It?*
After working several years in some firm, you decide to transfer to another. Your employer reminds you that for the past ten years, the firm has been contributing to a retirement fund for you—in addition to an equal amount subtracted from your take-home pay. The total has been invested in securities

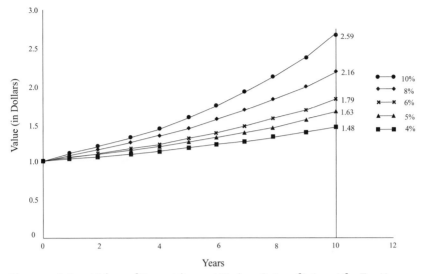

Fig. 30.1 *Future Values of Present $1.00 at Various Rates of Interest for Ten Years*

paying 4 percent per year. The total value now stands at $24,000. Two options are open: a) leave the contributions with the firm and earn 4 percent per year until retirement in 30 years or b) take out only the part withheld from your paycheck, $12,000 and give up the other half. Which shall you choose?

The answer depends, in part, on the interest rate you expect you can get on the $12,000 if you withdraw it. If you can get as high as 10 percent a year, this initial fund of $12,000 would grow in 30 years to $208,000. (See table 30.1, 10 percent for 30 years = 17.4 × $12,000.) If you leave all $24,000 in the firm's retirement fund to grow at 4 percent, the fund will grow to only $77,000. (See table 30.1, 4 percent for 30 years = 3.24 × $24,000). Only if you failed to earn at least 6.7 percent would your own fund be worth less than a fund left with the firm. Most retirement investment funds earn lower rates than are available by investing at random in the stock market. If you had only 20 years left before retirement, a rate of return of about 7.5 percent on your half would be required to match the value attained by the full fund at 4 percent in 20 years.

THE "PRESENT VALUE" OF A FUTURE AMOUNT, THE "PRINCIPAL" OR "MATURITY VALUE"

Now, we reverse our point of view and work from a future anticipated amount of $10,000 back to its equivalent present value. You will receive an amount of, say, $110 one year from today. What's its present value? That is, how much is the future $110 worth today, one year ahead of the receipt of that future amount?

What the future amount is worth *today* is its "present capital value," or just "present value." When you deposit $100 in a savings account that pays 6 percent interest per year, you buy the right to $106 to be paid you in one year. The "present value," $100, is equivalent to the "future value," $106, to be obtained one year in the future. That's another way to say the rate of interest is 6 percent per year. That's also expressed as buying the future $106 at the "discounted" present value of $100. Again, this has nothing to do with a rise in the price level.

We start with $P_0(1 + r) = F_1$. By rearranging terms, we get P_0, derived from the future value, F, and the rate of interest, r:

$$P_0 = F_1/(1 + r)$$

$$P_0 = \$110/(1.10) = \$100, \text{ the present value}$$

Dividing the $110 by 1.10 is the same as multiplying it by .909 ($= 1/1.10$). The one-year future amount of $110 is "discounted" by .909, the "discount factor" $(1/[1 + r])$, to a present value of $100 ($= .909 \times \$110$). The larger is the interest rate, r, the smaller is the discount factor, $1/(1 + r)$, and the lower is the present price (present value), P_0, of any future amount, F_1. The discount factor, $1/(1 + r)$, is simply the ratio of the present value, P_0, to the future amount one year away, F_1. A higher rate of interest, r, enables a smaller present amount, P_0, to grow to a specified future amount, F_1, and a specified future value is discounted to a smaller present value.

Though the present price (present value) of a future amount is numerically smaller than the future amount, the two are of *equivalent worth* in the sense that the buyers in the market for such claims are indifferent between having $1.10 in the future or $1 now, if the market rate of interest is 10 percent per year.

The entries in table 30.2 represent the present values of $1 due at various future dates — years to "maturity." These data are the reciprocals of those in Table 30.1, where the entries showed the *future* amounts to which $1 would grow at different rates of interest. In the 3 percent rate of interest column, the entry for year ten is .74. At a 3 percent rate of growth, $0.74 today would grow to $1 in ten years. At higher rates of interest, smaller present amounts would grow to $1 in ten years.

Table 30.2 *Present Value of Future $1 (Today's Value of a Dollar Received at the End of a Future Year)*

Rate of Interest

Year	3%	4%	5%	6%	7%	8%	9%	10%	12%	15%	20%
1	0.97	0.96	0.95	0.94	0.94	0.93	0.92	0.91	0.89	0.87	0.83
2	0.94	0.93	0.91	0.89	0.87	0.86	0.84	0.83	0.80	0.76	0.69
3	0.92	0.89	0.86	0.84	0.82	0.79	0.77	0.75	0.71	0.66	0.58
4	0.89	0.86	0.82	0.79	0.76	0.74	0.71	0.68	0.64	0.57	0.48
5	0.86	0.82	0.78	0.75	0.71	0.68	0.65	0.62	0.57	0.50	0.40
6	0.84	0.79	0.75	0.71	0.67	0.63	0.60	0.56	0.51	0.43	0.34
7	0.81	0.76	0.71	0.67	0.62	0.58	0.55	0.51	0.45	0.38	0.28
8	0.79	0.73	0.68	0.63	0.58	0.54	0.50	0.47	0.40	0.33	0.23
9	0.77	0.70	0.65	0.59	0.54	0.50	0.46	0.42	0.36	0.28	0.19
10	0.74	0.68	0.61	0.56	0.51	0.46	0.42	0.39	0.32	0.25	0.16
11	0.72	0.65	0.59	0.53	0.48	0.43	0.39	0.35	0.29	0.22	0.14
12	0.70	0.63	0.56	0.50	0.44	0.40	0.36	0.32	0.26	0.19	0.11
13	0.68	0.60	0.53	0.47	0.42	0.37	0.33	0.29	0.23	0.16	0.09
14	0.66	0.58	0.51	0.44	0.39	0.34	0.30	0.26	0.21	0.14	0.08
15	0.64	0.56	0.48	0.42	0.36	0.32	0.28	0.24	0.18	0.12	0.07
16	0.62	0.53	0.46	0.39	0.34	0.29	0.25	0.22	0.16	0.11	0.05
17	0.61	0.51	0.44	0.37	0.32	0.27	0.23	0.20	0.15	0.09	0.05
18	0.59	0.49	0.42	0.35	0.30	0.25	0.21	0.18	0.13	0.08	0.04
19	0.57	0.48	0.40	0.33	0.28	0.23	0.19	0.16	0.12	0.07	0.03
20	0.55	0.46	0.38	0.31	0.26	0.22	0.18	0.15	0.10	0.06	0.03
25	0.48	0.38	0.30	0.23	0.18	0.15	0.12	0.09	0.06	0.03	0.01
30	0.41	0.31	0.23	0.17	0.13	0.10	0.08	0.06	0.03	0.02	0.00
40	0.31	0.21	0.14	0.10	0.07	0.05	0.03	0.02	0.01	0.00	0.00
50	0.23	0.14	0.09	0.05	0.03	0.02	0.01	0.01	0.00	0.00	0.00

Table 30.2 lists the present values of $1 to be received in the future. The present values depend on the rate of interest and the number of years to the future $1.00. That future year at which the specified amount will be received is the date of "maturity." An amount to be paid to you 10 years from now is said to have a "maturity" length of ten years.

Example: A Prize to Be Paid to You in the Future

You are offered a prize of $10,000 upon graduation, four years from now. Someone offers to pay you $7,000 today if you will "sell" that $10,000 prize to be received in four years. If the rate of interest available on investments or savings accounts is 6 percent per year, is that offer one that will make you richer? You could invest the $7,000, and in four years it would grow by a factor of 1.26 (= 1.06 × 1.06 × 1.06 × 1.06) to $8,827 (1.26 × $7,000). That offer of $7,000 is not acceptable, because it will grow to less than the $10,000. Verify that if the rate of interest were as high as 10 percent, it would be acceptable.

Example: *Growth of Value and Interest Earned on a US*
Treasury Savings Bond — called Series EE bonds

You are told that you can buy from the US Treasury a bond for $75, and 10 years later you will receive one payment of $100. There's no interest paid out to you in the interim, and the bond doesn't specify any interest rate.

At what rate of interest per year will the $75 present amount paid for the bond grow to a future value of $100 in 10 years? We use table 30.2, "Present Values of Future $1." In the row for 10 years, we look for .75, because the present value ($75) is .75 of the future $100. The entry nearest to .75 is in the column for 3 percent. So the Series EE bond has an implicit rate of interest, or rate of return, of about 3 percent per year.

Suppose the bond had been initially issued for only $50, rather than $75, and still promised $100 in 10 years. The implicit rate of interest is a little larger than 7 percent.

THE RULE OF SEVENTY-TWO IS A CONVENIENT QUICK AID

Dividing the number 72 by the rate of interest (expressed as a whole number) approximates the number of years it takes for an initial amount to double. To double with a 10 percent rate of interest, dividing 72 by 10 indicates 7.2 years.

Table 30.1 shows 1.95 at 7 years, so a bit longer, about 7.2 years, would give 2, a doubling. At substantially higher rates of interest the rule becomes less accurate.

You can solve for approximately the *rate of interest* if you specify a number of years for a value to double: divide 72 by the number of years. For a doubling in 6 years, that is 12 (= 72/6), or 12 percent interest per year. To double in 4 years, you'll require 18 percent interest (= 72/4). Divide 72 by the interest rate to get the doubling time. And divide 72 by the number of years to get the interest rate required to double the amount.

QUESTIONS AND MEDITATIONS

1) You invest $350 today. At the end of one year you will get back $385. What is the implied or effective rate of interest?

Answer:

($385 − $350)/$350 = .10; so it is 10 percent.

2) How much will $250 grow to in three years at 7 percent compounded annually? How long will it take to double?

Answer:

Using table 30.1, $250 will grow to $307.50 in three years. (Using the equation $[1 + .07]^3$ it would be a bit less because of the rounding in the table.)

It would double in about 10 years (72/7 = 10.3), or from table 30.1 a factor of 1.97 at 7 percent for 10 years.

3) At the end of a year you will get $220. At a 10 percent interest rate, what present amount will grow to that amount? In other words, what is the present value of $220 deferred one year at 10 percent?

Answer:

Refer to table 30.2, present value of $1. At 10 percent, the present value of $1 deferred one year is now $.91. Therefore, the present value of $220 deferred one year is $220 × .91 = $200.20.

4) You are offered the opportunity to purchase a rare painting, and the art dealer says you can be assured that the value of the painting will rise at a 5 percent rate for as long as you care to own it. You call your banker and learn that you could invest long term at a rate of interest of 6 percent. If the painting costs $10,000 today, what will it cost you to own and enjoy the painting for twenty years before you (or your estate) sells the painting?

Answer:

Use table 30.1. If the art dealer is correct about appreciation of the value of the painting, it can be sold after twenty years for $26,500. If, instead of buying the painting, you had invested the $10,000 at 6 percent for twenty years, you would have $32,000. So the difference, $5,500, is what it will cost you to enjoy the painting.

5) If you can borrow $1,000 from your college at a 5 percent interest rate for six years, and if you can invest with a 10 percent rate of return, what is the present value of the arrangement to you? Instead of the loan that you have to pay back, you are offered an outright gift of $300. Which would you prefer, the outright gift or the loan?

Answer:

At a 5 percent interest rate, you will have to pay back $1,340 at the end of six years. If you can invest the $1,000 at 10 percent for six years, you will have $1,770. The difference, $430, is the value of the gift implied by the subsidized loan. If, as an alternative to the loan of $1,000 at 5 percent for six years, you are offered a gift of $300, at any interest rate of 8 percent or more you can invest and have more than $432 at the end of six years, so you would take the gift. (Using table 30.1, you would get: $1,771.56 − $1,340.10 = $431.46.)

6) Consider two alternative present values for a given future value, the cases differing with respect to the time period.
   a. What is the present value of $2,500 due in five years at 4 percent per year?
   b. What is the present value of $2,500 due in ten years at 4 percent per year?
   c. We have the same future value and the same rate of discount in both of these cases. Why does the difference in the time periods determine different present values?

Answer:
   a. $2,500/(1.04)^5 = $2,500/1.216653 = $2,054.82; less accurately, using table 30.2 we have $2,500 × (.82) = $2,050.
   b. $2,500(1.04)^{10} = $1,686. Check how close is the answer using table 30.2.
   c. Putting aside the detailed formula and table, look at the common sense of investing a given amount at a given rate for two periods. The initial amount invested will grow more in ten years than in five — the resulting difference between the initial amount and the ultimate amount will be larger, the longer the investment period. Here, we have the reverse problem of starting with the end amount and calculating the initial investment (present value). That initial amount will be smaller, the longer the period.

7) Consider two alternative present values for a given future value, the cases differing with respect to the discount rates.
   a. What is the present value of $2,500 due in five years at 8 percent per year?
   b. Compare the answer in (a) here with answer (a) in question 1, above. We have the same future values and the same discount periods. Why does the difference in the discount rates determine the different present values?

Answer:

    a. 2,500 (.68) = 1,700.

    b. A given future value will be attained in a given period with a smaller
        initial value, the greater is the rate of return (discount).

8) A man plants a seed for a tree. The rent for the land on which the seed
    is planted is 50 cents per year. In addition to that cost, there are other
    costs — spraying, watering, fire protection, taxes — to be paid over the
    years. In the table below, the present value of all those costs is indicated
    in column 4. The tree, if cut and converted to lumber at the end of the
    ages indicated, will yield lumber worth the amount indicated in the
    second column. The third column gives the *present* value of that future
    potential lumber, at a 10 percent rate of interest. Some of the entries are
    not presented.

Table 30QA.8

Age (1)	Lumber Value (2)	Present Capital Value of Lumber (3)	Present Value of Costs (4)	Present Value of Profit if Cut at Age Indicated (5)
0	$0	$0	$5.00	$ –5.00
5	1	0.62	5.70	–5.08
10	4	1.54	6.20	–4.66
15	11	2.63	6.50	–3.87
20	25	—	6.60	—
25	60	5.54	6.80	–1.26
30	140	—	6.82	—
35	260	9.25	6.95	+2.30
40	450	—	6.96	—
45	650	8.91	6.97	+1.94
50	800	6.80	6.98	–0.18

    a. Compute the missing values (using table 30.2, with only two-digit
        accuracy).

    b. Find the age at which the tree should be cut to provide the maximum
        present value of that tree.

    c. What is that maximum present value?

    d. Suppose that the value of the tree rises relative to current lumber
        prices. What would this imply about the rate of interest?

e. If no one owned the tree, and it could be cut by anyone who wanted to use the lumber, when would it probably be cut?

Answer:

a. $3.75, $8.40, $9.00, for column 3; −$2.85, +$1.58, +$2.04 for column 5.

b. 35 years.

c. $2.30.

d. Lower interest rate.

e. As soon as its lumber value is positive.

9) According to Uncle Louie, some whiskeys improve with age. The following table lists the consumption value of a barrel of whiskey at various ages. For example, if the whiskey is removed from its aging cask and sold now to consumers for current consumption, it will sell for $100. If sold in 10 years, it will fetch $250 for consumption.

Table 30QA.9

Consumption Date	Consumption Value	Consumption Date	Consumption Value
Now	$100	6	$205
1 year	120	7	220
2	140	8	230
3	160	9	240
4	175	10	250
5	190		

a. How much will the cask of whiskey be worth right now (at 10 percent) if it is to be held until the end of the second year before being bottled and sold?

b. For what length of time should one expect to keep the whiskey in the cask for a maximum present value? (Hint: How much is it worth paying for the whiskey now if it is to be held for five years? For ten years?)

c. If no one owned the cask of whiskey, how long would it remain unconsumed?

d. Suppose it were owned but could not be sold; how long would it be kept before consumption?

Answer:

a. $116.20 (using table 30.2, with only two-digit accuracy).

b. Three years.

   c. Not long.

   d. Cannot be determined; depends on preferences of owner — or his heirs.

10) In a certain country the only productive goods are rabbits. Either the rabbits are eaten or the rabbits increase at the rate of 20 percent per year.

   a. If there are 1 million rabbits in the country at the first of the year, what is the income of the country (measuring the income in rabbit units)?

   b. What will be the rate of interest in that country?

   c. What is the maximum possible growth?

Answer:

   a. About 200,000 rabbits.

   b. The rate of "interest" is the rate of increase in the number of rabbits.

   c. Theoretically, the growth rate would be 20 percent; however, table 30.1 gives a factor of 9,100 at 20 percent for 50 years, so the country would then be overrun by over 9 billion rabbits if they hadn't starved first. That is the power of compounding.

11) Joe bought some land 30 years ago for $5,000; it has a market value today of $85,000. Betty put $5,000 into the stock market at the same time. At what annual rate would Betty's portfolio have had to increase over those 30 years to match Joe's experience?

Answer:

   At a 10 percent rate of stock price appreciation, Betty's holdings would now be $5,000 × 17.4 = $87,000, a little better than Joe's gain.

12) If the interest rate is 6 percent, would you prefer to have $30,000 available in 10 years or $40,000 in 15 years? Alternatively, suppose the interest rate is 4 percent.

Answer:

   Using table 30.2 (only 2-digit accuracy) at 6 percent, the present value of $30,000 in 10 years: 30,000 × .56 = 16,800; the present value of $40,000 in 15 years: 40,000 × .42 = 16,680.

   At 4 percent, the present value of $30,000 in 10 years: $30,000 × .68 = $20,400; the present value of $40,000 in 15 years: $40,000 × .555 = $22,400.

CHAPTER 31

SERIES OF FUTURE VALUES AND ANNUITIES

A durable resource can yield a stream (or series) of services. An apple tree yields apples for many years. Land serves for a long time. A house yields services for decades. A painting may yield viewing pleasure for centuries. And you earn a stream of future earnings. How are the many successive future service worths converted to one present value?

ANNUITY: PRESENT CAPITAL VALUE OF
A SERIES OF FUTURE VALUES

A series of future annual amounts is called an annuity. What is the present value of four $1 receipts, one at the end of each of four years? That's a "four-year annuity" of $1 a year—with the first being received a year from now. If the rate of interest is 10 percent per year, each of the four $1 values can be discounted back to a present value.

We use the formula $P(1 + r) = F$, and rearrange terms to get:

$$F/(1 + r) = P$$

$1.00/(1.10) = $.909$, the present value of the service worth $1 when it is obtained at the end of the first year;

$1.00/(1.10)^2 = $.826$, the present value of the second year's service;

$1.00/(1.10)^3 = $.751$, the present value of the third year's service;

$1.00/(1.10)^4 = $.683$, the present value of the fourth year's service;

together, these sum to $3.169, the present capital value of the four-year annuity.

Obviously, the longer the annuity series, the greater the present value, but the present values of more distant amounts diminish. If a machine were twice as durable, it would not be twice as valuable. If it gave $1 in each of eight years of service, the additional four terms for the next four years would have the following present values:

$1.00/(1.10)^5 = \$.621 = $ present value, fifth year service;

$1.00/(1.10)^6 = \$.564 = $ present value, sixth year service;

$1.00/(1.10)^7 = \$.513 = $ present value, seventh year service;

$1.00/(1.10)^8 = \$.467 = $ present value, eighth year service;

together, these sum to $2.165 = the present capital value of the second four years of service.

The second half of the eight-year annuity adds $2.165, whereas the first half has a present capital value of $3.169. Together, $5.334 is the present value of eight years' service.

The annuity formula applies: $P = A_1/(1 + r) + A_2/(1 + r)^2 + A_3/(1 + r)^3 + A_4/(1 + r)^4 + \ldots + A_N/(1 + r)^N$ where $A_1, A_2, A_3, A_4, \ldots, A_N$ represent the future amount at the ends of the indicated years.

TABLE OF PRESENT VALUES OF ANNUITIES

Table 31.1 gives the present values of annuities of $1 each year for alternative numbers of years at alternative rates of interest—with the first amount being received at the end of the first year. An annuity of $1 a year for ten years at a rate of interest of 10 percent has a present value of $6.15. Said another way, if you know the rate of interest is 10 percent, you would have to pay now $6.15 for the right to receive $1 a year for the next 10 years, with the first receipt one year from now. A twelve-year annuity of $1 a year, with the first payment coming one year from now, would, at 8 percent, have a present value of $7.54.

If the annuity starts with the first amount being received now, rather than a year later, add the amount received now to a one-year shorter annuity. In an annuity of ten installments, the first of which is received now, there remain nine future installments. Look for the nine-year annuity present value, and add one for the initial installment. In the 10 percent column, the entry for nine years is 5.76. Add one for the initial present installment, giving 6.76 as the present value of an annuity of 10 annual installments.

Finding an Implied Rate of Interest

Reversing the approach, if you know that $8.38 is the present price to be paid for a twelve-year annuity of $1 a year, you can find the implied interest rate. In the row for 12 years, in table 31.1, find the entry nearest to 8.38: the rate of interest is 6 percent.

Table 31.1 *Present Value of $1 Received at the End of Each Year*

Rate of Interest

Year	3%	4%	5%	6%	7%	8%	10%	12%	15%	20%
1	0.97	0.96	0.95	0.94	0.94	0.93	0.91	0.89	0.87	0.83
2	1.91	1.89	1.86	1.83	1.81	1.78	1.74	1.69	1.63	1.53
3	2.83	2.78	2.72	2.67	2.62	2.58	2.49	2.40	2.28	2.11
4	3.72	3.63	3.55	3.47	3.39	3.31	3.17	3.04	2.86	2.59
5	4.58	4.45	4.33	4.21	4.10	3.99	3.79	3.61	3.35	2.99
6	5.42	5.24	5.08	4.92	4.77	4.62	4.36	4.11	3.78	3.33
7	6.23	6.00	5.79	5.58	5.39	5.21	4.87	4.56	4.16	3.61
8	7.02	6.73	6.46	6.21	5.97	5.75	5.34	4.97	4.49	3.84
9	7.79	7.44	7.11	6.80	6.52	6.25	5.76	5.33	4.77	4.03
10	8.53	8.11	7.72	7.36	7.02	6.71	6.15	5.65	5.02	4.19
11	9.25	8.76	8.31	7.89	7.50	7.14	6.50	5.94	5.23	4.33
12	9.95	9.39	8.86	8.38	7.94	7.54	6.81	6.19	5.42	4.44
13	10.64	9.99	9.39	8.85	8.36	7.90	7.10	6.42	5.58	4.53
14	11.30	10.56	9.90	9.30	8.75	8.24	7.37	6.63	5.72	4.61
15	11.94	11.12	10.38	9.71	9.11	8.56	7.61	6.81	5.85	4.68
16	12.56	11.65	10.84	10.11	9.45	8.85	7.82	6.97	5.95	4.73
17	13.17	12.17	11.27	10.48	9.76	9.12	8.02	7.12	6.05	4.78
18	13.75	12.66	11.69	10.83	10.06	9.37	8.20	7.25	6.13	4.81
19	14.32	13.13	12.09	11.16	10.34	9.60	8.37	7.37	6.20	4.84
20	14.88	13.59	12.46	11.47	10.59	9.82	8.51	7.47	6.26	4.87
25	17.41	15.62	14.09	12.78	11.65	10.68	9.08	7.84	6.46	4.95
30	19.60	17.29	15.37	13.77	12.41	11.26	9.43	8.06	6.57	4.98
40	23.12	19.79	17.16	15.05	13.33	11.93	9.78	8.24	6.64	5.00
50	25.73	21.48	18.26	15.76	13.80	12.23	9.92	8.30	6.66	5.00

THE LOW-INTEREST-RATE BIAS

If I were trying to sell you a machine that gives $100 at the end of each year for the next 30 years, would I use a high or a low rate of interest to estimate its current value? At 10 percent, it would be $943. At 3 percent, it would be $1,960. The lower the rate of interest used, the greater will be the derived present value.

Advocates of big projects (like a new "bullet train") tend to use rates that are low. This bias is pertinent also in estimates of lost values of income of people who are injured or killed. Their potential future incomes are discounted (capitalized) into a present value. The lower the interest rate applied, the higher the present capital value. Plaintiffs, seeking large awards, have incentives to use a rate lower than that preferred by defendants.

PERPETUITIES — A SPECIAL CONSTANT ANNUITY, LASTING FOREVER

Suppose you had an investment that will yield a constant annual amount of $1 in each future year, as far as you want to imagine, a hundred, or even a thousand years. At a 5 percent interest rate, what would this perpetual annuity — called a "perpetuity"— be worth now? The more distant values are discounted into much smaller present values. In fact, at 5 percent interest, the present value of an annuity of $1 a year for 1,000 years would be worth only $20.

If that seems incredibly small, note that all you have to do is invest $20 now at a 5 percent rate of interest. At the end of the first year, the interest earned would be $1 (= $20 × .05). Take out the $1 of interest and spend it, and the remaining amount is still $20. Repeat that next year, and the next, for as long as you can imagine. The present value of a perpetuity is simply the annual amount (A) divided by the rate of interest: P = A/r, a rearrangement of P × r = A. In this example, that's $1/.05, which is $20, the present value of a perpetuity of $1 a year, at a 5 percent rate of interest.

A DISTANT FUTURE SERVICE'S CONTRIBUTION TO PRESENT CAPITAL VALUE

To get a greater sense of proportion about the effects of the length of annuities and of different rates of interest, consider table 31.2.

The first 50 years of a perpetuity of $1 a year at 5 a percent rate of interest has a present value of $18.30. That's equal to 91.5 percent of the $20 present value of the perpetuity. The present value of the portion beyond the first 50 years has a value of only $1.70 (= $20 – $18.30), about 8.5 percent of the total present value of the perpetuity. At 10 percent per year, the present value of all the values after the first 50 years would be only $.09 of the $10 present value (= $10 – $9.91), less than 1 percent of the present value.

Table 31.2 *Apportioned Present Values of Perpetuities at Different Rates of Interest*

Alternative Rates of Interest	Present Value of the First 50 years	Present Value of 51st Year to Eternity	Present Value of Entire Perpetuity	% of Present Value Beyond 50th year
3%	$25.70	$7.30	$33	22%
5%	$18.30	$1.70	$20	8.5%
10%	$9.91	$0.09	$10	<1%

At 3 percent interest, the present value of the perpetuity is $33.33, with 77 percent attributable the first 50 years and 23 percent to all the remaining years forever thereafter.

HOW LARGE IS A GIFT?

Your rich uncle could buy you an annuity lasting 15 years, paying $50,000 every year, beginning a year from now. At a 10 percent market rate of interest, that would now cost $7.61 for a $1 annuity. Multiply that by $50,000 to get $380,500 (= 7.61 × $50,000). Although getting 15 receipts of $50,000 for a total of $750,000, you would be getting a gift equivalent now to $380,500.

PRESENT VALUES OF ANNUITIES OF
VARIED ANNUAL FUTURE AMOUNTS

Annuities are often not a series of constant future amounts. While we will do the tedious arithmetic, understand the logical essence of what is happening. Consider the particular six-year annuity shown in table 31.3.

We use table 31.3 to get the present value equivalent for each future term in the annuity. The first future amount, due in one year, is $1,000. Using an 8 percent rate of interest, the present value is $926 (= $1,000 × .926). The next amount, due in two years, is $2,000, with a present value of $1,714 (= $2,000 × .926 × .926) or (= $2,000 × .857). Discounting each additional payment in successive additional years and summing the present values of all the payments gives a total annuity value of $9,219.

HONOR THY FATHER AND THY MOTHER

Your parents, having reached age 70 with $500,000 on which they expect to live 15 years longer, want to exhaust the fortune at a constant rate in 15 years. After that, if either is still alive, you will shoulder your moral responsibility.

Table 31.3 *Present Value Computation of Six-Year Annuity at 8%*

Year of Yield	$ Amounts in the Future Years	Discount Factor 8% Per Year	$ Present Value
1	$1,000	.926 (= 1/1.08)	$926
2	2,000	.857 (= 1/1.08^2)	1,714
3	3,000	.794 (= 1/1.08^3)	2,382
4	3,000	.735 (= 1/1.08^4)	2,205
5	2,000	.681 (= 1/1.08^5)	1,362
6	1,000	.630 (= 1/1.08^6)	630
		Present Value of the Six-Year Annuity	= $9,219

How much can they spend each year for 15 years? Rephrased: What fifteen-year annuity has a present value of $500,000 with an interest rate of 10 percent? In table 31.1, the entry for 15 years and 10 percent interest is 7.61. Since $500,000 is in the fund, $500,000/7.61 = $65,700 is each annual amount for the next 15 years. (This is an approximation, since $65,700 is the amount that could be spent at the *end* of each of the 15 years, not *during* each year, but the difference is slight.) If they choose to exhaust the fund in ten years, they can get $81,300 (= $500,000/6.15) at the end of each year. If they plan on 15 years but invest at an interest rate of 8 percent, then the payment will be $500,000/8.56 = $58,410.

CURRENT ACTIONS, LONG-RUN EFFECTS, AND IMMEDIATE CHANGES IN PRICES

The present price of a resource changes the moment people's *anticipations* about the future value of the services of the resource change — not when the later events occur. In table 31.3, suppose some current action changed the beliefs about the future amounts to be received in the fifth and sixth years — doubling them to $4,000 and $2,000. Immediately, the present value would leap from $9,219 to $11,211, an increase of $1,992.

Do changing prices in the stock market make business managers concentrate excessively on the immediate fluctuations in current stock prices, rather than on the longer-run effects of present actions? Present changes in prices reflect not just immediate effects, but also anticipated future effects. The immediate changes in current prices force strong attention on the future long-run effects of current actions.

THE WORDS IN FINANCIAL MARKETS: LENDING IS "BUYING," AND BORROWING IS "SELLING"

In financial market terminology, it's conventional to interpret lending as buying a bond. If I lend money in exchange for your IOU, I could say I was buying your IOU. I might sell that IOU to someone else to whom you would later make payment when settling your debt. A "bond" is a document detailing the debt and conditions for repayment. Therefore, when you borrow $95 from me, I am buying your promise pay me $100 in the future, say, one year, with $5 of interest.

But the basic reason for the terminology of "buying and selling," rather than "lending and borrowing," reflects the fact of actual change of ownership. When you borrow a book or a car or a tennis racket, you are expected to return the *same item*. You acquired no legal right to sell the borrowed items. But when you "borrow" money, you are not expected to return the same physical units of money you borrowed. You may borrow $100 in coins and return $100 in different coins or paper money, because you didn't actually "borrow" the money. Instead, you bought full ownership rights to the money. That is what happens if you are a business owner borrowing from a bank. The language there is "selling your promissory note to the bank."

Every week, the US Treasury *sells* billions of dollars worth of US Treasury bills, which are promises to pay a stated amount of money in, say, ninety days.

In financial markets, lenders typically resell notes or bonds to someone else. If you buy a car "on credit" with an installment plan, the promissory note you sign is very likely resold by the retailer to another person—an investor, who collects the payments you make. And you don't get title to (ownership of) the car until you've paid the debt in full. In general, as "lenders" we don't lend money; we sell money, in exchange for promised amounts of other money to be returned to us later.

A "loan" of money is sometimes called a "purchase-repurchase" agreement. You purchase a bond now at a price of $1,000. The seller of the bond at the same time enters into an agreement to buy that bond back from you with payment of $1,050 a week later. The $1,050 includes interest of $50, even though nothing was said about "interest."

THE SIGNIFICANCE OF INTEREST AS A COST—EVEN WITHOUT DEBTS

It's tempting to think that if you don't borrow, there's no "interest cost" involved. But interest is a measure of the advantage of having something *earlier*. If a resource is not available until next year, the *delay* means you lose the advantage of having it earlier. Getting something in the future is less valuable than having it earlier. What you otherwise would have had is the "interest" yield. If you obtain something later rather than earlier, you lose the interest yield in the interval. Having a good sooner rather than later gives you the interim yield, which is why a future good is worth less than the equivalent present amount.

A common error resulting from failure to think of interest as a cost is the assertion that a lottery prize of $100,000 to be paid to you in each of the next ten years is a prize of $1,000,000. The $100,000 payments do not all come *now*. Having the money now would yield benefits to you earlier. The *earlier* you invest money or get some good, the more wealth you can have at any future time. Many goods yield a net flow of services. Any delay reduces the net growth or amount of wealth that can be accumulated at all future times. You bear a cost while waiting for the future goods.

So the interest rate enters into the profitability of production decisions, *whether or not the producer has borrowed money.* Avoid confusing true profits with an illusion of profits caused by adding future amounts to present amounts without adjusting for the timing—that is, without capitalizing the values to the same date.

A business manager invests in buildings, equipment, raw materials, wages, and inventories of finished products. Hardly ever are all these investments made after customers have placed orders. Costs are incurred first, and then receipts are sought. Even if the initial investment expenditures were paid from the owner's own wealth without borrowing, the lag of receipts after initial expenditure means it's incorrect to compare the total expenditures and the total receipts at different times to see if profits are being earned. The differences in timing must be offset by "capitalizing" the expenditures and receipts to the same date. It makes no difference to what uniform date the cash flows are adjusted. So long as they are adjusted by the rate of interest to the *same* date, the resulting capital value measures of costs and of revenues are comparable.

Suppose outlays are made at the beginning of year 1 with receipts being obtained 2 years later. The initial outlays for equipment and supplies and labor, at the beginning of year 1, were $1,000. All the $1,300 of revenue from sales of products will be obtained at the end of year 2. No assets are left at the end. Would these outlays and receipts be profitable? In answering, we must not compare the numbers $1,000 and $1,300, because they are separated by 2 years. They must first be capitalized to the same date, as shown in table 31.4. The interest rate (even with no borrowing or interest payments to be paid) affects profitability.

Table 31.4 *Interest Rate Effects on Capital Values and Profitability*

	$1,000 Outlay at Beginning of Year 1	Receipts of $1,300 at End of Year 2	Capital Values as of Beginning of Year 1	Capital Values as of End of Year 2
Values when capitalized at 7% interest rate to beginning of year 1:				
Values Capitalized Beginning Year 1	$1,000	$1,300.00	= $1,300/(1.07 × 1.07) = $1,136 (receipts) − $1,000 (costs) = $136 Profit	
Values Capitalized to End of Year 2	1.07 × 1.07 × $1,000 = $1,145	$1,300.00		$1,300 (receipts) − $1,145 (costs) = $155 Profit

IF THE INTEREST RATE IS 7 PERCENT

Capital Values at Beginning Date

The outlay at the beginning of the venture is $1,000. That $1,000 is to be compared with beginning of year 1 capital value of the final receipts of $1,300, which is $1,136 (= $1,300/[1.07] × [1.07]). The capital value of receipts is greater than the cost, valued as of that same initial date. So the capital values show a profit of $136 (= $1,136 − $1,000).

Capital Values as of End Date

The extreme right side of table 31.4 shows the capital values measured at the end date. The capital value of the receipts is $1,300, all received at that date. The corresponding time's capital value of the costs is $1,145 (= $1,000 × 1.07 × 1.07). These end date capital values also show a profit, being $155 (= $1,300 − $1,145). The profit of $136 capital value at the beginning is equivalent to the $155 capital value measured at the end date, if the interest rate is 7 percent per year. They differ absolutely only by the interest rate factor: 136 × 1.07 × 1.07 = 155.

SOME HIDDEN PRESUMPTIONS DESERVING SUSPICION

It is a common belief that the rate of interest is not the same for all people and all goods. In fact, they are equal. We'll see that mistaken belief is a result of two other confusions, between "interest" and "rent" and between two conceptions of the rate of interest—a "nominal" and a "pure" rate of interest. Before explaining the confusions, we should understand the meanings of "income" versus "wealth" and the difference between "interest" and "rent," all of which are explained in the next chapter.

Table 31.4.A

Capital Values When Capitalized at 15% Interest Rate:

Values Capitalized to Beginning of Year 1	$1,000	$1,300/(1.15 × 1.15) = $1,300/1.3225 = $983	= $17 Loss
Values Capitalized to Same Date, End of Year 2	1.15 × 1.15 × $1,000 = $1,300 $1,322.50		$1,300 (receipts) − $1,322.50 = $22.50 Loss

IF THE INTEREST RATE WERE 15 PERCENT

We repeat the calculations in table 31.4 using 15 percent instead of 7 percent. The venture has a loss. The $1,000 cost is to be compared with beginning of year 1 capital value of the final receipt of $1,300, which is $983 (= $1,300/(1.15)(1.15)). That capital value of $1,300 is less than the $1,000 cost, valued as of that same initial date. The capital values show a loss of $17 (= $1,000 − $983).

The capital value of the $1,000 in outlays, measured at the end date in year 2, is equal to 1.15 × 1.15 × $1,000, which is $1,322. The ending-date capital value of the outlays exceeds that of the $1,300 receipts by $22 (= $1,322 − $1,300), a loss.

The higher the interest rate, the smaller is the present value of *future* receipts. The costs were earlier, and if we ignore interest we will ignore part of the costs — the forgone service yield that otherwise could be obtained over the two years of venture. But when that forgone, otherwise available yield, is correctly recognized as a cost, by capitalizing all the data to the *same* date the comparable capital values show a loss *if* the interest rate is 15 percent or higher.

QUESTIONS AND MEDITATIONS

1) What present amount is equivalent to $1,000 paid at the end of each of the next three years at 8 percent interest? That is, what is the present value of a $1,000 three-year annuity at 8 percent interest?

Answer:

$2,580. Use table 31.1.

2) Two refrigerators are available for purchase. One costs more to buy but less to operate:

Table 31QA.2

		Refrigerators:
	Purchase Price	Annual Operating Cost in Each of 10 Years
A	$400	$100
B	$340	$110

Which is the cheaper source of refrigeration over a ten-year period?

Answer:

It depends on the interest rate. At 10 percent, the $10 higher operating cost of B for each of 10 years has a present value of $61.50. So machine A, which would avoid that extra cost of $61.50, but costs only $60 more to buy, would barely be cheaper. At 12 percent (or at rates above 11 percent), B would be cheaper. At lower rates A is cheaper. The extent to which it pays to economize on operating costs depends on the rate of interest and the difference in purchase price of the equipment.

3) Your grandparents say they are considering selling their house. A realtor has told them that if they sell the house now, they could get about $125,000 for it. They would then need to rent someplace to live. As an alternative, you offer to buy their house, but let them continue living in it for up to twenty years. You offer to pay your grandparents $10,000 at the end of each year for 20 years (a total of $200,000) at which time they will give you the deed to the house. Your grandparents want to know what interest rate is implied by an offer of $10,000 for 20 years.

Answer:

Essentially, the offer you make to your grandparents is to buy their house on a time-payment plan; this is similar to the way a simple "reverse mortgage" works. In table 31.1, you show them that the factor for 20 years under the column for 5 percent is 12.46. Multiplying that factor times $10,000 gives $124,600 — about the market value of the house.

4) Your business requires the long-term use of a warehouse. You find one that the owner says you can either buy now or agree to lease for 50 years, at which time it is expected to be of no value. Ignoring the value of the land and the costs of demolishing the building in 50 years, what interest rate makes a current purchase price of $250,000 about equal to annual lease payments of $20,000 for 50 years?

Answer:

In table 31.1, the factor for 50 years under the 8 percent column is 12.23. That factor times $20,000 is $244,600. So, at an interest rate of slightly under 8 percent a stream of payments of $20,000 for 50 years is today worth $250,000.

5) In deciding whether to buy or lease in the question above, your bank tells you they will lend you the $250,000 to buy the building and charge you an interest rate of 8 percent. You expect to use the building for the 50 years at which time it will be worthless. Are you indifferent between paying $20,000 per year in lease payments versus $20,000 in interest payments to the bank? What else might you consider in making your decision?

Answer:

In the United States, both lease payments and interest payments are tax deductible for a business, so the after-tax costs are the same. However, if tax laws also allow the deduction of depreciation of real property such as the warehouse against ordinary income, then tax considerations would bias your decision in favor of borrowing and buying versus leasing at the same implied interest rate. At some sufficiently high interest rate to borrow and buy, it will be cheaper to lease.

6) You are offered the choice between two annuities. One will pay you $1,000 per year for 20 years, for a total of $20,000. The other will pay you $1,500 per year for 15 years, with a first payment of $1,500 to be received at the end of year 5. The total payout in the second case will be more — $22,500 — but you have to wait five years to start receiving the money. Which will you choose?

Answer:

Your answer should depend on the rate of interest. You can see from table 31.1 that the present value of $1,000 received at the end of each of the next 20 years falls at alternative higher rates of interest. That $20,000 is worth $13,590 at 4 percent, $12,460 at 5 percent, and $11,470 at 6 percent. In order to compare with the $1,500 per year for 15 years, starting five years in the future, you will first find out from table 31.1 what the value will be five years in the future, then use table 30.2 to find today's value of the deferred, but larger payments. The $22,500 is now worth $14,345 at 4 percent, $12,140 at 5 percent, and $10,923.75 at 6 percent. Clearly, at higher interest rates the value today of the larger, but deferred, payments is less than at lower interest rates.

7) You are given alternative methods of buying some merchandise. You may pay $75 a year for 10 years with the first payment being due in 1 year. Or you can pay now a lump sum of $500. If the rate of interest is 10 percent per year, which is the cheaper way of paying?

Answer:

At a 10 percent interest rate for ten years, table 31.1 gives a factor of 6.71. So $75 at the end of each year for 10 years is now only $476 — a cheaper way to buy. However, verify that at an 8 percent interest rate, $500 now is slightly cheaper.

APPENDIX TO CHAPTER 31: APPLICATIONS
OF CAPITAL VALUE PRINCIPLES

Applications of the capital value principles can be illustrated in situations of practical affairs.

Installment Plan Payments of a Debt

You have decided to borrow $10,000 to help cover your first year's expenses for college. You can borrow at 5 percent per year, if you agree to repay in ten installments over ten years, with the first payment due in one year. Table 31.A1 shows for various interest rates the amount of each annual installment to repay a debt of $1, depending on the number of annual installment payments. For ten installments over ten years, the 5 percent column lists .130. Multiply .130 by $10,000 to get $1,300 as the annual installment.

Table 31.A1 *Uniform Annual Payments at End of Each Year to Retire $1 of Debt*

				Rate of Interest				
Year	1%	2%	3%	4%	5%	10%	15%	20%
1	1.010	1.020	1.030	1.040	1.050	1.100	1.150	1.200
2	0.508	0.515	0.523	0.530	0.538	0.576	0.615	0.655
3	0.340	0.347	0.354	0.360	0.367	0.402	0.438	0.475
4	0.256	0.263	0.269	0.275	0.282	0.315	0.350	0.386
5	0.206	0.212	0.218	0.225	0.231	0.264	0.298	0.334
6	0.173	0.179	0.185	0.191	0.197	0.230	0.264	0.301
7	0.149	0.155	0.161	0.167	0.173	0.205	0.240	0.277
8	0.131	0.137	0.142	0.149	0.155	0.187	0.223	0.261
9	0.117	0.123	0.128	0.134	0.141	0.174	0.210	0.248
10	0.106	0.111	0.117	0.123	0.130	0.163	0.199	0.239
11	0.096	0.102	0.108	0.114	0.120	0.154	0.191	0.231
12	0.089	0.095	0.100	0.107	0.113	0.147	0.184	0.225
13	0.082	0.088	0.094	0.100	0.106	0.141	0.179	0.221
14	0.077	0.083	0.089	0.095	0.101	0.136	0.175	0.217
15	0.072	0.078	0.084	0.090	0.096	0.131	0.171	0.214
16	0.068	0.074	0.080	0.086	0.092	0.128	0.168	0.211
17	0.064	0.070	0.076	0.082	0.089	0.125	0.165	0.209
18	0.061	0.067	0.073	0.079	0.086	0.122	0.163	0.208
19	0.058	0.064	0.070	0.076	0.083	0.120	0.161	0.206
20	0.055	0.061	0.067	0.074	0.080	0.117	0.160	0.205
25	0.045	0.051	0.057	0.064	0.071	0.110	0.155	0.202
30	0.039	0.045	0.051	0.058	0.065	0.106	0.152	0.201
40	0.030	0.037	0.043	0.051	0.058	0.102	0.151	0.200
50	0.026	0.032	0.039	0.047	0.055	0.101	0.150	0.200

Table 31.A2 *Ten $1,300 Annual Installments, to Repay Initial Debt of $10,000 at 5% Interest (to Nearest $10)*

Debt Year	Principal	Interest Paid	Repayments of Principal
1	$10,000	$500	800 (= $1,300 − $500)
2	9,200	460	840
3	8,360	420	880
4	7,500	380	920
5	6,580	330	970
6	5,610	280	1,020
7	4,590	230	1,070
8	3,520	180	1,120
9	2,400	120	1,180
10	1,220	80	1,220

Table 31.A2 shows how much of the annual payment goes toward reducing the principal amount owed. At the end of the first year, the $800 (= $1,300 − $500) in excess of interest due reduces the principal of the debt from $10,000 to $9,200. The second year's payment of $1,300 is apportioned about $460 for interest (= .05 × $9,200) on the $9,200 remaining debt. That leaves $840 ($1,300 − $460) to reduce the $9,200 debt to $8,360 (= $9,200 − $840).

As the indebtedness declines, the portion of the annual $1,300 payment assigned to interest is gradually reduced, leaving increasing portions of the installments to be applied toward reducing the debt.

You might want to delay all the payments for both interest and principal, so as to pay nothing until you graduate, say beginning five years from the time you borrow. To delay each payment by five years means that each will be bigger by the rate of interest compounded over five years, or 1.28 (= 1.05^5). The ten yearly installments, beginning a year after you graduate, would be $1,664 (= 1.28 × 1,300), instead of $1,300, if the rate of interest were 5 percent.

Suppression of Inventions?

You manufacture at a cost of 40¢ and sell for 50¢ a light bulb that lasts one year. You invent a bulb that lasts two years, and is as good in every other respect, and you can produce at a cost of 60¢. Should you refuse to introduce it, considering that you might sell only half as many bulbs? Details are in table 31.A3.

The present selling price of the new bulb would be the sum of 50¢ for the first year's service plus the present value of the second year's service, which is worth 50¢ in that second year. The present value of the second year's 50¢ worth of light service is, at a 10 percent annual rate of interest, 50¢/1.10 = 45.45¢.

Table 31.A3 *Value of Longer Resource Life*

One-Year Light Bulb with One Sold Each Year

Years	1st Year	2nd Year
Service Value	$.50	$.50
Price	.50	.50
Cost	.40	.40
Profit Each Year	.10	.10
Present Value of Profits of Two One-Year Bulbs Is $.195	$.10	+ .095

Two-Year Light Bulb with One Sold in Alternate Years
Cost to Make, per Bulb, $.60

Years	1st Year	2nd Year
Service Value to Consumer	$.50	$.50
Present Value of Year's Service Worth	.50	.45
Present Value of Bulb's Lifetime Services	$.95 = $.50 + .45	
Price of Two-Year Bulb	$0.95	
Cost	.60	$0
Profit from One Two-Year Bulb Is $.35		

This gives a potential present price of about 95¢ for the new bulb. The profits are larger because the bulb costs only 20¢ more (60¢ compared to 40¢) but brings in 45¢ more revenue. Formerly, you earned a profit of 10¢ each year on each bulb. Now, you sell half as many bulbs each year with present value of total profits for the one two-year bulb being 35¢ rather than 19.5¢ for two of the inferior bulbs. It pays to produce this longer-lasting bulb. The producer is interested in profits, not the number of items sold.

Though half as many items would be sold, the price could be nearly twice as high, while the costs were not. The price could, if the seller chose, be lowered to about 80¢ for the two-year bulb, only 30¢ more than for the 50¢ one-year bulb. The invention will be used whenever the increased value from the invention exceeds its cost. How the net gain is split between producer and consumer is something we'll examine later.

Interest for Credit Card Borrowing

Some credit cards grant a "grace period," typically 25 days following the end of the month in which you made purchases. If you pay the amount due before expiration of the grace period, you are not billed for interest. If you pay after the grace period, even one day later, you pay interest on the loan for the entire time from the date of purchase.

An annual interest rate of 18 percent is 1.5 percent of the outstanding balance on a monthly basis. Assume the grace period is 25 days after the close of the billing period. Suppose I make my payment a day after the close of the grace period. If I had made only one purchase of $100 on the first day of the new billing period, then the bank has extended credit to me for 55 days, on which I pay $1.50 interest. Alternatively, if I had made my $100 purchase on the last day of the billing period, then the bank has extended credit to me for only 25 days. So, the effective interest rate is very different even when it's still $1.50 interest on a balance of $100.

Personal Investments in Stocks: Dividends or Capital Gains?

Should you invest in securities mainly for capital gains or for income in the form of dividends? A corporation earns $1 a share this year, and the shares sell for $10. You have 10,000 shares for total wealth of $100,000. Compare the two extremes:

1) No dividends: If the management decided to retain all the earnings in the firm, the stock price would rise to about $11 (= $10 + $1). You have $110,000, all in the form of more valuable stock.
2) Dividends paid: If cash dividends of $1 a share were paid to you at the end of the year, you'd have $10,000 in cash and the stock price would remain at $10, for a total wealth of $110,000 (= $10,000 cash + $100,000 in stocks).

In either case, you end with the same wealth. If you want to consume but did not receive cash dividends, you can sell 909 shares of the $11 shares for $9,999. You now have about $10,000 in cash (as if dividends had been paid) and almost exactly $100,000 of stock value (9,101 shares at $11 each). But transaction costs may differ in the alternative cases. And capital gains — the rise in the price of the stock — may be taxed at a rate different from that applied to dividends paid out.

Joint and Complementary Demands

Some products are highly interdependent with other products, and serve little or no function unless used jointly. Examples of such joint products are radio receivers and radio transmitters, DVD players and DVDs, computers and computer software. Usually, these pairs of products are not produced by the same firm, yet it is often believed that independent producers won't provide interdependent products. Such fear ignores the force of capital values, the seeking of profit, and the advantages of specialization in production!

Interdependent goods don't have to be produced by the same producer, because production of any one of them opens profit opportunities for others to produce the complementary good. Production of automobiles and radio and TV signals did not wait for construction of gas stations or radio or TV receivers. Nor did FM radio transmitters also produce the receivers. Yet all these jointly dependent products were developed independently, and, in the case of FM, were developed despite laws restricting FM broadcasting. Disneyland didn't have to build hotels in the area to house tourists, without whom Disneyland would fail. Independent hotels and motels were created.

Stereo records and players, compact disk recordings and players, video players and videocassettes, frozen foods and home freezers, automobiles and gasoline service stations, to name a few, developed independently but not in isolation — they were developed in anticipation that others would seize the profit prospects of providing complementary facilities. Experience makes it clear that dependent products need not be produced together. Capitalization of future prospects into present values and specialization are high-powered forces, effective if not infallible in coordinating activities in a private property, market-oriented economy.

Developers, Speculators: Representatives of Future Consumers

An especially instructive example of anticipation, of interdependence, and of future demands is the *speculative* developer of land and housing. Future consumers rarely order far in advance for their future homes or goods. Instead, developers and producers anticipate their future demands. Suburban developers are accused of being interested in a quick dollar — correctly. But in earning that dollar now, they must predict future demands and make a timely response to have the supply of housing ready when the demand to occupy such housing occurs. Yet, though no one knew earlier who would be the future demanders, the prediction that such a demand would exist motivated anticipatory, speculative action.

Dress designers and manufacturers make clothes far in advance of coming seasons on a risky, speculative basis, rather than forcing consumers to order and pay in advance. Similarly, land developers are surrogate agents for future demanders. Competition among present anticipator-speculator-developers for all goods bids up the prices of existing land and other resources to reflect the present capitalized value of the future anticipated demand. Speculators do not increase land values. Rather, the predicted high future demand for its use drives up the price of land *now*. The speculators *reveal* that high present value; they do not *cause* it. And if the speculators are incorrect in their anticipations and the increased demand doesn't show up, the speculators lose.

Buying a Car?

Perhaps the purchase of an automobile is the most commonplace application of capital values by nonfinancial experts. Table 31.A4 illustrates that the *cost* of some act can be defined only if the act is well defined. The applicable interest rate is assumed to be 10 percent, for computational ease and probably for realism.

Table 31.A4 *Expenditures and Receipts $*

	Now	End of Year 1	End of Year 2	Present Values
Purchase Price	$16,000			
Resale If Not Used			$10,000	$8,260
Resale If Used 20,000 Miles			$8,800	$7,268
Taxes & Insurance	$800	$800		$1,528
Gas, Tires, Repairs		$2,000	$2,800	$4,132

Actions		Costs	
1a. Acquisition of title	$16,000		
Immediate resale value	−14,800		
Cost of acquiring title	$1,200	$1,200	
1b. Possess 2 years, Unused			
Resale Now	$14,800		
Resale in 2 years	$8,260		
Depreciation without use	$6,540		
Tax and Insurance	$1,528		
Possession without use	$8,068	$8,068	
Acquisition + Possession (= 1a + 1b)		$9,268	
2. Operation: 20,000 miles in 2 years			
Resale if not used	$8,260		
If used, 20,000 miles	$7,268		
Depreciation by use	$992		
Fuel, repairs, tires, etc.	$4,132		
Operations	$5,124	$5,124 (@ $0.26/mile)	
Acquisition, possess and use		$14,392 (@ $0.70/mile)	

Cost of Acquisition or Cost of the Investment

You buy a new car at a price of $16,000. If immediately resold, the car would bring back only $14,800, a sacrifice of $1,200. That $1,200 is the cost of acquiring title to the car, an *acquisition* or investment cost.

If you kept the car two years without using it, its resale price might then be $10,000. Though the assumption of nonuse is not realistic, this is a useful question. That looks like a $4,800 (= $14,800 − $10,000) reduction in the value of the car. However, the two values, $14,800 and $10,000, are at different dates. The $14,800 is a present value, whereas the $10,000 is a value two years in the future. With 10 percent as the appropriate interest rate for discounting to present value, we get $8,260 (= $10,000/1.10^2). Therefore, the reduction in present capital value by owning the car for two years is $6,540 (= $14,800 − $8,260).

We must include taxes, say $100, and insurance, perhaps $700, paid at the beginning of each year. These two payments convert to a present capital value of $1,528 (= $800 + $800/1.1), which added to $6,540 gives $8,068, as the cost of ownership for two years. The cost of acquiring title, $1,200, plus continued ownership with insurance and taxes, but with no use of the car, over a two-year span is $9,268 (= $8,068 + $1,200).

Depreciation as Part of the Cost of Use

If the car is driven 10,000 miles per year, its resale value at the end of two years will be $8,800 (compared to the $10,000 if not used). This decrease of $1,200 (= $10,000 − $8,800 two years from now) is measured as $992 (= $1,200/1.10^2) in *capital value* as of the beginning of the two-year cycle. This increased depreciation due to use is usually considered to be its user cost. For 20,000 miles of travel, that's 5¢ per mile (= $992/20,000 miles).

In addition to that "user depreciation cost," gasoline, maintenance, and repairs costs must be included. We'll assume they are all paid at the end of each year. The amounts of these expenditures and their times of payments are listed in table 31.A4. Their present value (as of the beginning of the two-year cycle) is $4,132. Cost of use is thus $5,124 (= $992 + $4,132).

The estimated total present value of the cost of purchase and of use for 20,000 miles over two years is $14,392 (= $1,200 + $8,068 + $5,124). Since no one can be perfectly accurate in such estimates, this can be called $14,000, or 70¢ per mile (= $14,000/20,000 miles). If we recognize that cost estimates within a range of plus or minus 10 percent are pretty good, then the total cost can be someplace between about 63¢ and 77¢ per mile.

Once you purchase the car, the cost will be only 26¢ (= $5,124/20,000) per mile to drive the car, including operating costs and depreciation (shown in next to last line in table 31.A4). If you believe the depreciation of the indicated amount will occur whether or not you use the car, at least for the amount of driving you do, then the cost of use, after you have purchased the car, is reduced by 5¢ (= $992/20,000) per mile, down to 21 cents per mile.

Ten-Year Replacement Cycle

Now consider the costs with a ten-year, rather than a two-year, replacement interval. Assume the car is worthless at the end of 10 years. Therefore, the depreciation over a ten-year period is $16,000, the whole purchase cost of the car. The depreciation per mile over the 100,000 miles (ten years at 10,000 miles per year) would be 16¢ per mile (= $16,000/100,000).

In comparison, the two-year cycle of $8,732[1] depreciation for 20,000 miles was 44¢ per mile (= $8,732/20,000), about 28¢ (= $.44 – $.16) per mile more. Per year, that's $2,800 (= .28 × $10,000) more. It's up to you to decide whether the two-year cycle with newer cars is worth that amount. (To avoid too much clutter of detail, we ignored the fact that the insurance and annual registration fees would be lowered as the car aged. But countering that to some extent would be the extra repair costs.) In any event, this example shows what data are required and why present values must be used.

QUESTIONS AND MEDITATIONS

1) You borrow $1,000 today and agree to pay the loan in five equal annual installments at 10 percent interest. Using table 31.A1, determine the amount of each payment, the first payment to be due in one year.

Answer:

$264.

2) You buy a house by borrowing its full price, $80,000. Your annual installments in repaying the loan are $6,400/year for 20 years at 5 percent. (Do you agree? Check with table 31.A1.)

a. At the end of the first year, how much of the house's value is yours; that is, what is your equity? (On $80,000, the interest for the first year at 5 percent is $4,000.)

b. At the end of the second year, what is the value of your equity?

---

1. The cost of acquiring the title ($1,200) plus one-year depreciation ($6,540) plus second-year depreciation ($992).

   c. At the end of twenty years, assuming the house is still worth $80,000, what is your equity?

Answer:

   a. $2,400, using $6,400 as your total payments for that year. (Note: this question and the answer assume that interest is compounded only once per year.)

   b. $4,920. Your payments will continue to be $6,400 per year for the twenty years, but the portion that is interest will decline and the portion that is principal will increase. So, in this second year, interest is 5 percent of the remaining balance ($77,600), or $3,880, so you add $2,520 to your equity.

   c. $80,000.

3) If the value of your buildings or common stock should fall, how can you tell whether there has been a rise in the rate of interest or a fall in anticipated future net receipts? (Hint: Look at the bond market.)

Answer:

   If interest yields on bonds have risen, that means the prices of such bonds have fallen. The stream of rents you get from your buildings and the dividends you get from your common stock will both have a lower present value — the prices have fallen. If, however, yields on bonds have not risen, then a fall in the price of buildings or common stock suggests that future rents or dividends are now expected to be lower.

4) Which do you think will have a bigger influence in revising your annual *consumption* rate — an unexpected gift of $4,000, or an unexpected salary increase of $20 per month? (Hint: what is the present value of each at, say, 5 percent per year?) Why did the question say "*unexpected*" gift and salary increase?

Answer:

   Depends on the rate of interest. An annual unexpected salary increase is $240/yr (= 12 × $20). The $4,000 gift is a one-time receipt. The present capital value of $240 at 5 percent (assuming it lasts 40 years) is $4,118 (use table 31.1), so the salary increase would have a larger effect on your wealth at 5 percent. But if the interest rate were 6 percent, the present capital value of the salary increase is $3,612, so the one-time gift would have a bigger effect.

   Approaching the question a different way, investing the $4,000 at 5 percent would give you an income of only $200 per year, less than the raise.

However, investing the gift at anything over 6 percent would give you a greater ability to consume each year.

5) Project your earnings until age 65. Then obtain the present value of that projection, at 6 percent interest. Are you now worth over $500,000?

Answer:

Very probably "yes" for college students. Assuming a 22-year-old makes $50,000 a year until he is 67, the present value is $772,791.60. This assumes no raises and is calculated by finding the present value of an annuity of $50,000 per year for 45 periods.

6) Inflation affects both income and asset prices:
   a. A family with income of $80,000 buys a house for $200,000. Suppose no inflation is anticipated at the time of purchase, and the family can borrow at 4 percent interest. Further, the family expects its income to rise at 3 percent per year for the next 30 years. This family borrows the entire price of a house and agrees to make an annual mortgage payment, which will extinguish the debt in 30 years. Using table 31.A1, how much will be the family's house payment?
   b. At time of purchase, the price of the house was 2.5 times family income. If income does rise at a 3 percent rate, and after 30 years the house is still worth the purchase price, what is the ratio of house price to income?
   c. Suppose instead a correctly anticipated inflation of 6 percent per year occurs. The family borrows the $200,000 at 10 percent to buy the house. How much are the house payments at this higher interest rate?
   d. If the house market value rises the same as inflation (6 percent), how much is it worth when the mortgage is paid off?
   e. The family finds that their income rises much faster than before — at an average annual rate of 8 percent — to $800,000 after 30 years. Now what is the ratio of the house value to income?

Answer:
   a. The annual house payment will be $11,600, or $966.67/month.
   b. Income will have risen to $194,400, so the ratio of house price to income is a bit over one.
   c. From table 31.A1, the factor for 30 years at 10 percent is 0.106, so the annual house payment is now $21,200, or $1,766.67/month.
   d. From table 30.1, 6% for 30 years gives us a factor of 5.74, so the house will be worth $1,148,000.

e. Now the market price of the house is 1.435 times family income. This reflects the fact that the 3 percent rise in family income without inflation was a real income gain; with inflation of 6 percent and family income rising at an 8 percent rate, real family income rises at only a 2 percent rate. Economists call it money illusion — income rising at an 8 percent rate with 6 percent inflation is not as good as 3 percent with no inflation.

7) In July, Congress passes a law reducing income taxes to take effect six months later in January. In support of the legislation to cut taxes, it was argued that, having more income left after taxes, people would begin spending more in January, increasing the demand for consumer goods. Others argued that taxpayers would increase their spending as soon as the law was passed, in July. How could the latter prediction be correct?

Answer:

Anticipated changes in future events affect consumers' behavior. In anticipation of lower future taxes (higher take-home pay), consumers could buy more in the interim and repay in or after January. They could increase credit card debt, buy on installment loans, or buy on layaway.

8) Why are capital values used as a measure of cost?

Answer:

Costs are the lost or given-up value of using the resources elsewhere — the forsaken opportunities. In measuring costs, the present and future opportunities which are given up or forsaken can be measured by reducing the value of claims to future services and goods. This can be done by discounting the values of forsaken opportunities into a present capital value change.

9) A house can be purchased for $200,000. At the end of a year it could be resold for $210,000 if you had also spent $10,000 for a new fence, $3,000 for landscaping, $8,000 for air conditioning, and $12,000 for carpeting; otherwise the house could have been resold for $190,000. Taxes of $3,000 must be paid in any event. Assume that all these expenditures — except for the taxes, which are to be paid at the end of a year — are paid at the moment you buy the house. The interest rate is 10 percent.

a. What is the cost of owning a house for one year — if you do not install fence, landscaping, air conditioning, and carpeting?

b. What is the cost of owning the house if you do install those improvements?

c. What is the year's depreciation on the house without the proposed improvements?

d. Express this cost of ownership of the improved house for one year as a constant two-year annuity.

e. Express the cost as a five-year annuity.

f. Which of these is the correct way to express the cost?

Answer:

a. $30,017 (three-figure accuracy) = $200,000 − .909 × ($190,000 − $3,000)

b. $44,820.

c. 200,000 − 190,000 = 10,000. Then dividing this by 1 year of interest at 10 percent we get 10,000/1.10 = $9,090.91 of depreciation.

d. Two-year annuity with present value of $44,820 is $25,910 per year.

e. $11,830 per year.

f. All correct.

10) You operate a cleaning establishment. A new cleaning machine has a price of $5,000. You estimate its resale value at the end of the first year to be $3,000 and $1,500 at the end of the second year. The rate of interest is 10 percent.

a. What will it cost to purchase and own the machine for one year?

b. For two years?

c. What is the present value measure of the depreciation on the machine in the first year?

d. In the second year?

e. If you use the machine, you will incur expenses during the first year of $6,000 for labor, power, and repairs; and the machine will still have a resale value of $3,000 at the end of the first year. The same expenses will be involved in the second year, and the resale value will be $1,500 at the end of the second year. Assume that all expenditures are payable at the end of the year in which they are experienced. What is the cost of having and using the machine for one year?

f. For two years?

g. What is the cost of the second year of possession and operation?

h. If, immediately after buying the machine, you should reconsider and decide to sell it, the resale value would be $4,000. What cost would

the purchase of the machine "fix" upon you? This is called "fixed,"
"sunk," or "irrecoverable" cost.

Answer:

  a. $5,000 − ($3,000 × 0.909) = $2,273.
  b. $5,000 − ($1,500 × 0.826) = $3,761.
  c. $2,273. See answer to a.
  d. $3,761 because it sells for $1,500 in 2 years, which is $1,239 in present
     value. So the remaining value is $3,761 when subtracting $1,239 from
     $5,000.
  e. ($6,000 × 0.909) plus $2,273 = $7,727.
  f. ($6,000 × 0.909) plus ($6,000 × 0.909^2) plus $3,761 = $14,171.
  g. (f − e) = $6,444.
  h. $1,000.

11) "Don't buy your business cars. Lease them from the A and A Leasing
    Company. You can lease a Chevy for $600 a month. Avoid the loss of
    depreciation and necessity of tying up capital funds in the purchase of
    capital items." This is a paraphrase of leasing advertising. What errors of
    analysis does it contain?

Answer:

The lessor of the car pays for the depreciation as part of his rental charges.
He avoids tying up capital funds only in the sense that the leasing company
is lending him the car and charging him for its rental, whereas he could
have borrowed money, bought a car, and then paid rental on the borrowed
money (as interest). The rise of leasing services is primarily a consequence
of detailed business tax laws. Renting or borrowing money or paying out
of your already accumulated wealth doesn't change the costs at all — aside
from idiosyncrasies of the business tax laws.

12) News report: "The employees of the South Bend Lathe Co. were able to
    buy the entire common stock (and hence ownership) of the company
    for $10 million in cash. The employers used a federal government
    plan known as Employee Stock Ownership Plan, or ESOP, whereby the
    ESOP employee group was able to borrow the full purchase price of $10
    million, of which $5 million was lent by the US government to the ESOP
    for 25 years at 3 percent annual interest, and the other $5 million was
    obtained from Indiana banks at 4 percentage points above the prime rate
    (then at about 9 percent)." In effect, the $5 million loan from the federal
    taxpayers at 3 percent for 25 years was a gift of how much in present

value terms? (Use 10 percent as the relevant cost of interest, even though the employees actually must pay 4 percent above the prime rate, which ranged around 7 percent to 8 percent at the time.)

Answer:

Borrowing $5 million at 3 percent annually, while market rate is 10 percent, is equivalent to an annual subsidy of 7 percent on $5 million, or $350,000. The present value of that subsidy for 25 years is $4,077,500, which is a taxpayer-financed gift of about $4,077 to each of the 1,000 employees (Note: Use table 31.1).

CHAPTER 32
WEALTH, INCOME, AND INTEREST

Wealth has several meanings. It can mean: (1) the goods and resources owned by someone; (2) the market value of a set of physical goods, sometimes called assets; (3) the market value of all resources owned minus one's liabilities, where the excess is net assets, net worth, or equity; (4) human wealth measured by the present capital value of future earnings from personal services; this often is referred to as *human capital*.

EARNINGS: PERSONAL SERVICE YIELDS

Your personal earnings can be obtained by performing services as an employee, or you may operate your own business and earn wages and profits. While you work as an employee, you are earning *claims* against your employer. The claims accumulate until payday. The money then received is not earnings. These money receipts merely alter the form of your wealth — converting your claims against your employer to *money* you now have. In economics, your wealth has increased from the moment you have *earned* your compensation, not at the time you actually get paid.

CONSUMPTION

Consumption is the chosen transformation of one's wealth into a flow of services. It can consist of drinking one's supply of water or wearing out shoes or driving your car. If the use of resources helps maintain a person's health, productivity, and pleasure, that's usually called consumption, though some of it might be considered investment by productive consumption to increase one's health and productive capabilities. Or consumption may be unintentional — an unfortunate accident that reduces one's wealth. We'll be concentrating on *intended consumption*.

No one gears current consumption solely to current earnings. The lifetime pattern of earnings of most people starts low, rising until about retirement. We all tend to smooth our consumption over the fluctuations in our earnings or income. We borrow, and we reduce inventories on hand, and we buy on credit when earnings are initially and predictably low. We expect to repay later when earnings are higher. Typically, we borrow to invest when young and starting our career — buying a house or car and paying for it over time, as our earnings exceed our consumption during the prime of our lives. After retirement, our consumption rate again exceeds earnings. Our consumption rate is related more to *expected wealth* than to fluctuations in *current earnings*. Our wealth, or more precisely, our *human wealth*, is the present value of our entire anticipated future stream of earnings. Though earnings may fluctuate widely, wealth barely changes, because it compresses all the future anticipated earnings into a present capital value.

PROFITS, LOSSES, AND UNCERTAINTY

Profit is an increase in wealth *larger than* current savings plus predicted interest on the wealth. It is *unexpected* in the sense that wealth cannot be *expected* to grow at more than the rate of interest plus any savings of income. Hence, a more rapid rise in wealth must be a surprise, not anticipated by the *valuation* of the market (the rest of the world).

If initially one's wealth is $1,000 and the interest rate is 4 percent, the *standard income*, or interest from that wealth, is $40 per year. If all of that income were to be saved (no consumption occurs), wealth would grow to $1,040 in one year. However, asset values and returns on investments can change in ways that are unanticipated. Suppose that at the end of a year, one's wealth is greater than the initial wealth plus interest. The addition is profit. (A loss occurs if the rise in wealth is less than the return of interest on the initial wealth — again ignoring consumption.)

Suppose your initial wealth is measured at $1,000, and some unexpected good news is discovered about future yields from your wealth or demands for your services. The market value of your resources jumps to, say, $1,200. You have a profit of $200 obtained at the moment the market value changes. This can be expressed by saying, "Any increase unexpected by the market is a profit."

Profits and losses occur because people do not foresee the future perfectly. Anyone with luck, superior foresight, or perception of how to invest to obtain more than the rate of interest gets a profit when the resource's market value rises more than that implied by the rate of interest (and incurs a loss when market value rises by less than the rate of interest).

SAVING

Saving means *not consuming* all of one's earnings or income. If you are given a gift or earn a paycheck and don't consume/spend it all, the remainder is *savings*.

INCOME

Wealth can serve as a basis for defining *income* from a resource. Standard income or maintainable income is the perpetually maintainable flow of the value of the services or earnings of a resource. For resources with a market value of $1,000,000, the perpetually maintainable income — presuming an interest rate of 4 percent per year — is $40,000 per year. That means consumption could be $40,000 a year with no reduction in wealth. During each year, the resources generate 4 percent more wealth or services net of replacement of depreciated resources. That net yield is the maintainable income, and could all be spent/consumed without reducing the wealth below $1,000,000.

MORE MEANINGS OF "INCOME"

Implicit Income

If you own vacant land worth $1 million, and you receive no money payments of rents from users, the courts, perhaps pressed by a hostile relative of yours, would state you have an annual *implicit* income of $40,000 (= $1 million × .04) based on the prevailing interest rate of 4 percent per year. Presumably that income is being saved and evidenced in a growing market value of the vacant land. That wouldn't count as a taxable income, because the amount is not clearly revealed by some market-valued transaction. Accountants would say that you have had a gain that has not been *realized*.

Taxable Income

The federal personal income tax collector assigns a special meaning to income. Not until the earnings (accumulation of wealth in the form of claims against others) are paid or obtained in *the form of money* does the income tax law consider you to have income — or what is *taxable* income in the tax laws. The reason for concentrating on money forms of income is that cash flows can be measured and traced quite readily. That is the *cash accrual* concept of income. Under income tax law, the accumulation of *credits* against other people (what we call earnings) is not generally regarded as taxable income.

Gross and Net Income

We distinguish: (a) gross income and (b) net income. If some of the current income is used to replace wear and tear (depreciation) of the productive resources that generate gross income, the remainder is net income. Of course, if none of the income were used to replace depreciation, in time no resources would remain to generate income. So we can think of the net income as the measure of the flow of services that could be sustained forever — after using some of the gross income to repair, replace, and maintain resources to enable them to continue yielding services.

If you have financial resources worth $100,000 (your total wealth), and if you receive $10,000 a year in interest, that is your net income. Each year you (and your heirs) could consume at the rate of $10,000 per year without reducing the $100,000 of wealth. Retired people who might decide to leave no wealth for heirs can consume more than their net income by consuming some of their wealth — until all the wealth is consumed.

Business Firms' Meanings of Incomes

Business firms have their own interpretations of words like income, earnings, and profits. *Gross income* is the name often attached to the sales value. *Net income* would be the remainder of gross income after allowance for depreciation and wear and tear of goods and costs of inputs that produce current gross sales income. Some firms use gross and net income in a different way. From their total *sales revenue*, they deduct the cost of labor and materials to arrive at what they call gross income. Then they subtract a measure of the depreciation of durable goods and also sometimes interest paid on loans to get net income. Some call this profits, and to others it is net earnings.

Investment

Investment is that portion of current income *not consumed* (saved) *and* used to create more future income. The miracle of converting some now into more later is net productivity of investment. But sometimes the chosen venture incurs losses instead of gains, called *mal-investment*. That is, projects seemed promising, but turn out to lose money for the investors.

Saving — not consuming — current income and using it instead to create goods, or the ability to produce more future income, is usually called investing whether done by the same or another person. Two stages are in that process. First, some current income must not be consumed. Second, the savings must be used (invested) to create resources, knowledge, or skills that will enable us later to produce more income. You can put some of your savings in a bank, but that would not result in investment if the bank did not lend your savings to someone to finance an increased income.

Individual versus Whole Economy-Wide Saving and Investing

I can invest by buying your house or business. But that's just a transfer of a resource from you to me. The society's aggregate investment is unchanged. Or I can save and lend to you to finance consumption that exceeds your income. That results in no societal saving. The net total of individual savings plus the total of individual *dis-savings*—consuming more than one's income—is the societal total. Only if the total of private investments exceeds the total of private disinvestments (consuming more than income) is the economy-wide investment greater than zero. For the society, saving has not occurred if investment has not occurred.

Individuals can save and invest in three ways: (1) create new productive resources; (2) buy existing resources from other people; or (3) accumulate money. Only the first is a social total investment. The other two are merely transfers from one person to another.

Interest

Interest is the *excess* of the future increased income (or wealth) over the invested amount of current income (or wealth). It's a productive, profitable investment only if the gain exceeds the market rate of interest. Otherwise, the investment was inefficient, because the invested income would have produced more in some other investment.

Whence Comes Interest?

How can more be created than is used up now? Instead of eating 100 bushels of wheat today, plant them and reap enough next year to pay the costs of all inputs used and still have more than the initial 100 bushels, say, 105 bushels, for a net productivity of 5 percent per year. The *gain* in excess of the invested amount is *interest*. Drink grape juice now—or store it for more valuable wine next year, valuable enough to cover *more* than all associated costs. Those gains are interest.

But how can a steady rate of income be *maintained* despite the fact that resources wear out? How is it possible to maintain a flow of income year after year from a given stock of resources? Surely, they must be replaced. Yielding a constant flow of income, net of depreciation and other costs, seems to be the same as having a perpetual motion machine. The laws of physics deny the ability to continue to produce and consume at a constant rate, let alone at an increasing rate.

Energy from outer space is bombarding the earth. It tans your skin and warms you on sunny days. Plants are a form of life that require and store energy in the form of wood and release it as fire. Sunshine evaporates water, clouds form, water falls on high elevations, and when running down to sea can generate electric power and nourish trees. There also are improved methods of using energy. We learn avoidance of waste, discovered usually by investment of current income. *Increases* in income are results of discovering how to capture and control new energy more effectively (less expensively) and convert it to controllable power for production.

For eons people have been discovering waste. Before discovering how electricity could be captured, people were wasteful of waterpower. All invention might have been discovered earlier. Native residents of the Americas did not discover the wheel. Without the wheel, water energy could not be used to grind grain, so a source of energy was wasted.

A business innovator who created the first supermarket revealed the waste in so many smaller markets. That saved resources for other uses. That was an invention. It could not be patented, but it conserved one use of resources, reducing cost. Even the design of an office space so that more is achieved by people working together is an "invention" that increases total consumption as surely as discovery of a better type of corn.

Improvements come in innumerable forms, many hardly noticed. The transistor and the computer chip have increased productivity immeasurably. Investment in research results in new designs or inventions, such as zippers, nylon, carbon fiber, or merely relocation of productive equipment — the list is endless. All make prior actions or previous ways of doing things *wasteful* to some degree.

The *Internet* uses materials that already existed in other forms. By diverting current income-generating power into research efforts, new possibilities were discovered. New sources of energy or additions from outer space were not required for that. Masses of trivial improvements have been effective. Velcro reduced the time it takes to dress and the expense of buttons.

Mr. Carrier invented the air conditioning machine and transformed the world. Air conditioning surely ranks close to the electric light as progress. Creativity and increased productivity are in large part a matter of learning how to avoid waste, or more correctly stated, discovering that some current actions are wasteful compared to newly conceived methods. Investment is a way of learning how to make some existing jobs obsolete! Merely "creating new jobs" is the last thing we want. There is already much scarcity and plenty of work to do. Creating more productive ways of production or better consumption goods is what's desired, and achieved by successful investment.

Two facts of history: (1) an ability to achieve an increase in future output — the productivity of investment — and (2) an unwillingness of people to trade a given amount of income *now*, unless they believe they will be rewarded by a greater amount in the future. This second fact has long been called a result of *time preference*. That doesn't necessarily mean merely a preference for having something now rather than later; it means also an unwillingness to trade $1 of income *now* for the *chance, possibility,* or *prospect* of enjoying *only* $1 of future income.

This can be expressed in terms of the amount of current consumption power (income) that would be given up in exchange for a future income (supply), interacting with the demand for current resources to invest in the effort to get a bigger future income. Investors divert the resources that would have been used to satisfy current consumption into streams of output that will satisfy demands for future consumption. A dollar of consumption now will trade for the prospect of next year's income that is larger by about the rate of interest (reflecting the public's demand for, and the supply of, current consumption power *relative* to next year's prospective consumption power).

This basic growth relationship can be expressed:

$P(1 + r) = F$, in which P represents the present amount invested now, and r represents the increased annual rate of future income. Where the interest rate is 5 percent, the standard income is $5 for each $100 of wealth. So we have, $100(1.05) = $105, of which $5 can be consumed during the year and every year thereafter, without reducing the existing wealth valued at $100.

Sometimes the interest or income is not consumed but is left (reinvested) to grow at the interest rate for an additional year or more. If a tree is capable of growing for several years at 5 percent of its size each year, the value of the lumber in the tree would grow 5 percent in one year and by the end of the second year it would grow to $110.25, 5 percent larger than $105, if none of the lumber were taken from the tree. This is expressed by:

$100(1.05)(1.05) = $110.25, or, in general, as

$$P(1 + r)(1 + r) = P(1 + r)^2 = F_2$$

The general formula giving the future amounts (F) to which P will grow is $P(1 + r)^t = F_t$ where t is the number of years into the future.

Table 30.1 (chapter 30) shows the future value, F, to which $1.00 would grow at different rates of interest over various numbers of years.

Interest, then, is the foreseeable and achieved growth in wealth. That growth can be consumed without reducing one's stock of wealth below its initial amount. That steady flow of consumption power is income or standard income.

So $100 of wealth today can be exchanged for $105 next year. You could make the investment, or you could lend to someone else who makes the investment and returns an amount up to $105 in a year. A borrower who can return more than $105 will be making a profit.

Who Cares about the Distant Future?

Investing in forests that will mature a century from now can be just as profitable as investing in growing lettuce that will mature a month from now. But how does one *cash in* on the growing value if the life of the investment is longer than the life of the investor? The tree can be sold for cash to another investor, *if it's owned as private property*, and the tree would continue to grow to its optimum life length. What is that optimum age? It's the age at which the tree's value would thereafter grow at a rate below the interest rate, that is, below a rate of growth available on other investments. Thereafter, maintaining the tree would be wasteful, because opportunities to reinvest that amount (value of the tree) in other more profitable investments would be forgone.

Does the private property, capitalist system fail to heed the values of future generations? In fact, it heeds the perceived distant future values as well as it does the near-term expectations. The value of the tree increases at a decreasing rate. At any future time, with a specified interest rate, the present discounted value can be calculated. The present value is at a maximum when the growth rate of the tree falls to equality with the market discount rate. The smaller the discount rate, the longer the tree should be allowed to mature, for the greater will be the present value.

Figure 32.1 shows the path of a gradually increasing value of a live tree that will yield lumber at future dates. Future dollar values of the lumber are measured vertically. The vertical scale is logarithmic: uniform vertical distances represent uniform percentage changes in the dollar values, not equal amounts of dollars. The straight lines show values that increase at a constant percentage each year. The curved line shows the future values of the lumber from the tree at each of the ages at which it might be cut.

The wealth-maximizing year for lumber harvest with a given rate of interest is located by the tangency of the straight interest-rate line with the curved and flattening true-growth line. The interest rate is equated with the declining growth rate.

It would be profitable to plant trees if the present value of a tree exceeds the cost of planting and caring for the tree to the time it is cut. When the value of the live tree begins to grow slower than the rate of interest, the tree would be cut into lumber. To preserve the tree solely for more lumber would be wasteful, since the revenue from selling the lumber can be used more productively for investment or for more valuable consumption than any further increase in the wood in that tree.

This "no waste" principle of terminating investments when the growth falls

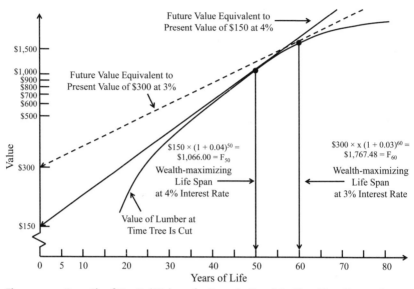

Figure 32.1 *Growth of Capital Value of a Tree: Optimal Cutting Time Depends on the Interest Rate and Pattern of Growth of Lumber Value*

The dollar values are given on a logarithmic scale. As the two interest lines tangent to the lumber-value curve show, at a 3 percent interest rate the tree should be felled in its sixtieth year and at a 4 percent interest rate in the fiftieth year. These are the wealth-maximizing life spans. Cutting the tree down any later will yield less lumber value than would cutting at these optimal times and reinvesting in new trees, which would grow faster than the interest rate.

below the available growth on alternative investments is the "replacement decision." It is applied to all investments involving durable goods.

You can expect the same rate of return—the rate of interest—whether you invest in a new or an old resource. You could get the same rate of return whether you buy a lot of young trees or an old one nearly ready to be cut. They are equally profitable. What ensures that equality? Markets for sales and purchases of durable goods! People don't give away opportunities to get more than the rate of interest. If a good were priced so low that people expected to get a higher return during the future than at the rate of interest, everyone would want to buy it. The price would rise, lowering the percentage rate of return on that higher price to match the market interest rate, that is, the rate on any other investment. At that price, no profits are realized, just the normal rate of interest.

Or a high present price would fall to raise the future expected return to equal the market interest rate. Every durable good, whether new or old, will be priced on the expectation of the same interest rate of return.

A RACE TO ACQUIRE PRIVATE
PROPERTY RIGHTS OF LUMBER

In early US history, there was a tendency toward *premature* cutting of forests. In Wisconsin and Minnesota, no one owned forests. The way to get property rights in the lumber was to cut the tree before someone else did. But if the live tree had been owned with secure rights, that devastating race to acquire rights by cutting trees would have been avoided.

In nations with political instability, property rights to land are risky. People will invest primarily in quick-yielding crops, not in longer-term ones like trees, and they will not make long-lived investments in maintaining the land's quality. These examples go far in explaining the lack of development in so-called third-world countries, where property rights are insecure and political order is tenuous.

Contrary to common belief that the private property system undervalues future goods and services, an owner of a standing tree will lose wealth if the tree is cut when its value as lumber is still growing faster than the rate of interest, which is the measure of the highest net productivity on other resource uses. Many resources — especially natural ones such as trees, buffaloes, whales, lakes, air — are resources *that no one owned as private property*. An owner would gain wealth by preventing overconsumption, as explained in chapter 13 on property rights.

QUESTIONS AND MEDITATIONS

1) A person has $100,000 to invest in stocks, and expects an income of about $5,000 annually because interest rates are about 5 percent. If you advise him to buy stocks that pay no earnings as dividends, he complains that he will have no income. How would you explain that he does have an income of 5 percent?

Answer:

Increase in value of holdings is the income. Stocks that do not pay earnings as dividends will grow in value by 5 percent, because all the earnings are reinvested in the company. If non-dividend-paying stock is bought, some of the shares which have grown in value can be sold at the end of the year, equivalent to the reinvested earnings, and the person still ends up with $100,000 in wealth. If the stocks are those on which all earnings are paid out and nothing is reinvested, the person would collect dividends and have stocks that did not grow in value. In either case, the person has $5,000 to spend while ending up with $100,000.

The gains (or income) from investment are the sum of the dividends paid and the increase in market value of the stock. Except for difference in tax treatment, it makes no difference in what form the earnings accrue.

2) You buy some stock for $100. A month later it has risen to a high of $150. Another month later it is down to $125. Have you had a profit or a loss?

Answer:

Both — you first had a profit of $50; then, by continuing to hold that wealth, you incurred a loss of $25 during the second month. Whether or not you convert your wealth to cash has nothing to do with the fact of your change in wealth — that is, of profits or losses. Only the income-tax people use the conversion-to-money principle for computing taxes on gains. Assuming you do not sell the stock at the end of the second month, you have had a net gain of $25 — and probably have a deferred tax liability that you will have to pay only when you sell the stock.

3) Suppose that rich people got rich exclusively from profits. Suppose further that those who received the profits were no smarter, no more foresighted, no nicer, no harder working, and no more physically or mentally productive than other people. Does this mean that their profits are "undeserved"? Does it mean that the rich people performed no service?

Answer:

No. The basic remaining source of their profits is risk-taking — bearing risks others chose not to bear. They perform a selective risk-bearing function, whether they know it or not. In prospecting for oil, some will lose and some may win. If we want more oil, the "lucky" investors who bear the risks relieve us risk-averse sorts of performing that function. For that contribution they are allowed, under private property rights, to obtain profits. As for taxing them away, that depends upon your desire to have risks borne voluntarily, upon your willingness to uphold a general agreement to let lucky ones keep wealth, and upon attitudes toward differences in wealth among people.

4) If your income from nonbusiness wealth is $5,000 a year, what is your nonbusiness wealth at 10 percent interest?

Answer:

$50,000.

5) If you consume all of your income for two years, what will be your wealth at the end of two years, if it is $10,000 now with 5 percent interest?

Answer:

$10,000, and it will stay at that value.

6) Distinguish between conservation of specific resources and the growth of wealth. Is conservation of specific resources an efficient way to increase the productive wealth of the community?

Answer:

Growth in wealth is an increase in the value of wealth at the market interest rate. If your initial wealth is $10,000 and the market interest rate is 6 percent, your wealth can grow by $600 per year. If you are fortunate and incur profits, it can grow at a higher rate, and if you sustain losses, your wealth grows at a slower rate or even declines.

Conservation of specific resources usually means restricting the use of resources such as forests, lumber, water, or iron ore. Conservation often means restricting or even prohibiting resources from being used in making valuable things. "Conserving the forest" by prohibiting the cutting of trees to build houses would be a choice of having less wealth in the form of homes for people to live in — and enjoying the "psychic income" of a beautiful forest.

Under transferable private property rights — by purchasing and selling resources — individuals can choose which chances of profit or loss to incur by owning the resource or to avoid risks by not owning the resource. The profits and losses are usually borne by the resource owners as value changes in their wealth. As a result, resources are likely to be used in places in which their market value is highest. In contrast, when the uses of specific resources are restricted, the resources are often overseen or administered by a board — analogous to the socialist system of allocating resources. In that case, one's ability to influence the value of the restricted resources (and incur or escape the risk of profit or loss) depends upon one's ability to affect political decisions (of the board members). Market value will not be so useful in determining resource uses nor will individuals be able to specialize in bearing various kinds of risk.

So which do you prefer? Restricted use where resource use is often determined by "a few" such as a board with little individual choice of who bears what risks of value change? Or transferable, private property rights, where owners can selectively choose which risks to bear and resource use is directed by value change?

APPENDIX TO CHAPTER 32:
BALANCE SHEETS AND BUDGETS

The economic concepts of wealth and income of an individual are often expressed by the accounting concepts of balance sheets and budgets. Your personal balance sheet lists your assets and liabilities. Any excess of your assets over your liabilities is your *net worth*. We'll assume you have cash in your wallet, money in a bank checking account, a computer, a TV, some clothes, and furniture. You have a credit card and have used it to buy clothes and furniture, and you have borrowed a couple of thousand dollars to pay tuition, so you have some debt. What is your wealth? In the physical sense, it's what you own. We will list them, and attach money values to them. The values are the amounts of money you could get if you sold the items, not what you paid for them.

Your assets are listed in the Balance Sheet in table 32.1.

Your assets have a market value of $3,125, regardless of what you paid for them. You also have some debts. Table 32.2 lists your liabilities.

The two sides will balance if we include your Equity or Net Wealth. That's defined as the excess of Assets over Liabilities. Here it's $935 = $3,125 − $2,190.

Your balance sheet is in table 32.3.

Table 32.1 *Your Balance Sheet*

Showing Only Assets — First Step

Assets	
Cash	$75
Checking Account	350
Computer	1,500
TV	600
Clothes	100
Furniture	+ 500
Total Value of Assets	$3,125

Table 32.2 *Your Balance Sheet*

Showing Only Liabilities without Equity

Liabilities	
Credit Card Debt	$90
Tuition Loan	2,000
Parking Fine Owed	+ 100
Total Value of Liabilities	$2,190

When the value of assets exceeds the value of liabilities, the excess is your wealth, or equity, or net wealth, or net worth. Here your assets exceed your liabilities; your marketable wealth is $935. The net wealth of a bankrupt person or enterprise is negative.

Your Complete Balance Sheet — Human Wealth

Ponder whether or not the balance sheet for you has left out any large items. If you were asked by the parents of your proposed spouse to show your balance sheet, how would you make your balance sheet more realistic? Surely you would add under Assets the item Me, representing you. And you would value Me at the *present value* of your entire anticipated stream of future earnings. If you owned a building, its market value would be the present value of its future stream of net rentals. Like a building, you are a durable resource, with an anticipated 40- or 50-year future stream of earnings (rents for your services). You might reasonably record $2,000,000 as the present value of your future earnings. Your balance sheet would then be the one in table 32.4.

The trouble with this representation is that the value of Me is not immedi-

Table 32.3 *Your Balance Sheet*

Assets		Liabilities and Equity	
Cash	$75	Credit Card Debt	$90
Checking Account	350	Tuition Loan	2,000
Computer	1,500	Parking Fine Owed	+ 100
TV	600	Total Liabilities	$2,190
Clothes	100	Equity	+ $935
Furniture	+ 500		
	$3,125		$3,125

Table 32.4 *Your Complete Balance Sheet*

Assets		Liabilities	
Cash	$75	Credit Card	$90
Checking Account	350	Tuition Loan	2,000
Computer	1,500	Parking Fine Owed	+ 100
TV	600	Liabilities	$2,190
Clothes	100	Equity	+ 2,000,935
Furniture	500		
Me	+ 2,000,000		
	$2,003,125		$2,003,125

Table 32.5 *Your Budget for One Day—Today*

Receipts		Expenditures	
Debt Repayment by Joe	$50	Tennis Racket	$100
Sale of 2 DVDs	+ 25	Lunch and Dinner	30
		Pair of Socks	+ 9
	$75		$139

Deficit = ($75 − $139) = −$64

ately marketable — convertible into money. But it does affect your decisions now about how much to borrow or what kind of house or car you would buy upon graduation. For such decisions, this balance sheet is pertinent. (Most business firms compute their balance sheet frequently as a running summary of their wealth position.)

A Budget: Receipts and Expenditures

A *budget* is different from a balance sheet, which is a list of assets and liabilities. A budget is a list of the expected or intended flows of receipts and expenditures of money during some interval of time that one plans. Usually a budget is created for someone or some enterprise in which some control of expenditures and receipts is believed to be feasible. There's no point in extending the time covered in a budget beyond the time of one's control. That would be merely a wish list. The simple budget shown in table 32.5 covers just one day in which a few transactions will occur.

Your expected total expenditures during the day, $139, will exceed your receipts of $75. You will therefore have a *deficit* of $64 (= $139 − $75) in your budget. A deficit does not mean something is wrong, or undesirable, nor does a surplus mean all is well. A budget tells nothing about your income, or whether you are consuming more than your income, or whether your wealth is increasing or decreasing. It's a comparison and listing of money flows in and out during some specific interval. In this example, the purchase of the tennis racket could be called an investment of $100, but the distinction between purchases for consumption versus those for investment is not pertinent nor indicated in a typical budget.

There's more to life than just the inflows and outflows of money during some short interval. Whether wealth will have increased or decreased is indicated by a balance sheet and an income statement, which were explained in the appendix to chapter 27.

The US federal government's budget is a listing and comparison of intended amounts of expenditures for various purposes during whatever period of time the current governing group expects to remain in power, or longer. It covers so many types and purposes of expenditures and of types of incomes that it is over a thousand pages long.

CHAPTER 33

A PACKAGE CALLED THE RATE OF INTEREST

Students pay a higher rate of interest on a loan from a bank than does a professor with an established reputation. Interest rates offered by savings and loan associations, credit unions, and banks differ. Actually, however, everyone pays the same rate of interest. What makes the interest rates appear to differ is that what is typically called the rate of interest is a *package* of several components, including the *pure* rate of interest. To avoid confusing the interest rate with the package, economists often use the label *nominal interest* to mean that package, while using the label *pure interest* to mean the *interest rate* in that package.

THE NOMINAL AND THE PURE RATE OF INTEREST

The pure rate means, roughly, the interest rate on a riskless investment, in the sense that the promised future amount will be paid, or received, with absolute certainty. We can think of the agreed interest rate on a loan as a package containing the pure interest rate plus *add-ons*, including those to cover costs of arranging the loan and to compensate the lender for the risk of default in paying interest and principal when due. That package of *interest rate plus the add-ons* is typically called *interest*, but we will call it the *nominal interest rate*.

PREMIUMS IN THE PACKAGE CALLED
THE NOMINAL INTEREST RATE

The noninterest *premiums*, or add-ons, could have been listed as special fees, instead of combining them into a package called the rate of interest. Some of the add-ons depend on who is the borrower, and therefore differ among people. Other add-ons depend on the type of bond, such as its length of time to maturity, or right to pay off the loan earlier. Still other add-ons are related to general market conditions at the time the loan is made, and affect all bonds. The usual use of the label *interest rate* almost always means the nominal rate package, containing the pure interest rate plus all the adjustments and add-ons for other factors.

Though a loan may be called *riskless*, no loan is perfectly secure in the sense that the value of the loan over the lifetime of the loan can be predicted with certainty. The uncertainty during the life of the loan is undesirable for lenders,

Table 33.1 *The "Pure" and the "Nominal" Rate of "Interest"*

	Borrower A (Bank Loan)	Borrower B (Credit Card and Higher Risk)
Pure Interest Rate	5%	5%
Additions for:		
Transactions and records	1	2
Enforcement contingencies	1	2
Risk of payment default	1	3
Anticipated inflation	5	5
Nominal Interest "Package"	13%	17%

who therefore are paid an *uncertainty-compensating fee*, included in what is called the interest to be paid.

ADD-ONS SPECIFIC TO INDIVIDUALS

Loan-Negotiation Costs

Transaction and negotiation costs differ among borrowers as well as among lenders. Local bankers have learned a good deal about their past borrowers. Obtaining another loan from the same lender does not require as much costly investigation and evaluation of information as for new and younger borrowers. Credit-card interest rates include a premium for a substantial risk of non-timely payments and for collection costs. More extreme are the small loans from pawnshops at, say, 40 percent per year, which are pure interest of say, 5 percent, with the remaining 35 percent for all the other costs and risks.

Default Risk

Higher-risk borrowers pay a premium to persuade lenders to bear the higher risk of lending to them. Less secure bonds pay a higher nominal rate of interest, including a premium for the risk of default.

Bonds of large firms and governments are rated for riskiness by several financial service firms. Most popular are the ratings by *Moody's* and *Fitch* and *S&P* (Standard and Poor's). The ratings of these services are very consistent with each other. The ratings run from *AAA* (*triple-A*) highest quality, down through Bs and Cs and D. Historically, US government debt was ranked the highest quality and paid about a 0.5 percentage point lower rate, a difference called 50 *basis points*. (There are 100 basis points in each 1 percent rate of interest.) Table 33.2 lists examples of interest rates for various financial instruments. Some market features make all bonds risky to some degree.

Table 33.2 *A Selection of Interest Rates on Various Financial Instruments*

	1996	2002	2012
Federal Discount Rate	5.25%	1.25%	0.15%
3-month Treasury Bill	5.20%	1.74%	0.07%
6-month Treasury Bill	5.25%	1.85%	0.12%
1-year Treasury Bill	5.39%	4.52%	0.17%
10-year Treasury Bond	5.60%	5.20%	1.47%
20-year Treasury Bond	6.03%	5.86%	2.13%
6-month Certificate of Deposit	5.28%	1.85%	0.48%
Aaa Corporate Bonds	6.81%	6.55%	3.64%
Baa Corporate Bonds	7.47%	7.87%	5.02%
Bank Prime Loan Rate	8.25%	4.25%	3.25%
30-year Mortgage	7.03%	7.00%	3.68%

THE MARKET RISK: ECONOMY-WIDE FACTORS FOR ALL PEOPLE AND FINANCIAL SECURITIES

Inflation

Every bond or resource that pays a promised future number of dollars suffers a loss when inflation erodes the market worth of a dollar. If inflation were expected over the next year, and the rate of pure interest were 3 percent, lenders must be repaid enough dollars to buy 3 percent more goods at the higher price level.

Candy selling for $1 now would be selling for $1.20 a year later if inflation is 20 percent. To buy 3 percent more candy, the lender would have to receive $1.236 (= 1.03 × 1.20). The 1.03 reflects the 3 percent rate of pure interest, and the 1.20 is the adjustment for the 20 percent higher price level. The nominal annual rate of interest package will be 23.6 percent. The lender, when repaid, will be able to buy 3 percent more candy even though the price level has risen. And the borrower will have paid the equivalent of 3 percent more candy.

If the future inflation is correctly anticipated, neither the lender nor the borrower will gain at the expense of the other. But usually inflations have not been adequately anticipated. For several decades after World War II—when the expected future rate of inflation was underanticipated—buyers who borrowed to buy homes gained from the unexpected subsequent inflation. Because the rate of inflation was not anticipated, there was not an adequate premium paid by borrowers to offset the inflation that actually occurred.

Table 33.3 *Present Values of Fixed-Coupon, $1,000 Principal Bonds, at Alternative Market Rates of Interest, Alternative Maturities*

Life of Bond	Coupon	Market Rates of Interest			
		3%	5%	7%	10%
1 Year	5%	$1,020	$1,000	$982	$954
5 Years	5%	$1,092	$1,000	$918	$810
10 Years	5%	$1,170	$1,000	$859	$692
20 Years	5%	$1,299	$1,000	$788	$573

Changes in the Market Interest Rate

When the market rate of interest changes, the market values of *existing* longer-term bonds change more than the market values of shorter-term bonds.

This is illustrated by the data in table 33.3, showing for different market rates of interest, the prices of one-year, five-year, ten-year, and twenty-year $1,000 bonds, each of which pays 5 percent interest.

The nominal rate paid on the bond is 5 percent. When the one-year bonds were issued, if the market rate of interest was 5 percent, the same as the coupon rate, the market resale value of the bond would be $1,000. But if the market rate were not the same as the promised rate on the bond, the bond's *market value* would adjust to yield the same as the market rate. Thus, if the market rate were 10 percent, the market value of the one-year bond would fall to about $954. The $50 interest (5 percent on the $1,000 stated principal) plus the subsequent rise in the market value of the bond to $1,000 when the principal of $1,000 is repaid implies an interest rate of 10 percent on the current bond value of $954. Competition in the bond market will push the bond's price to a value that will promise a yield no worse than available on other equally risky resources. The market prices of bonds adjust so that whatever their explicit promised interest rates, they all will pay a market-matching interest rate on the new market value of the bonds.

If the market rate of interest fell to 3 percent after a bond promising $1,000 in one year with 5 percent annual interest were offered, the market value of the bond would rise to $1,020. When the market rate of interest is the same as the bond's promised rate, here 5 percent, the bond will have a value of $1,000. At a 7 percent market rate, the market value of a one-year bond paying a stipulated 5 percent will fall to $982 (= $1,050/1.07), with an immediate loss of $18 from its initial $1,000 value.

Compare this one-year bond with a twenty-year bond paying that same stipulated 5 percent rate. The market values range from $1,300 down to $573, a much wider range than for the shorter-term bonds.

Long-term bonds are subject to a greater market risk than shorter-term bonds. During the time you hold a bond, you may want to sell it for cash to pay for some unexpected item. That results in a preference for shorter-term bonds. To persuade lenders to bear that "market risk" of undesirable, unpredictable swings in wealth, an add-on (based on the years-to-maturity of the bond) is in the nominal interest rate "package" for bonds.

LIQUIDITY: A SUBTRACTION IN THE NOMINAL MONEY INTEREST RATE PACKAGE

In addition to paying money interest to a bondholder (lender), some bonds yield a liquidity service to the bondholder. That nonmoney yield results in a lower money yield in the interest rate package. Liquidity reflects two features: (1) lower exchange transaction costs in preparing for and arranging and completing purchases or sales and (2) greater stability of value.

1) Business firms have receipts that don't match perfectly the obligations to pay. Firms could accumulate large amounts of money to accommodate those peaks in payments. However, instead of holding non-interest-bearing money, the firms can buy US Treasury bills (very short-lived US Treasury debt paying some interest). Then, when payments must be made, these T-bills can be sold reliably, quickly, and with low costs to bond dealers in exchange for money to make payments.

The Treasury bills are close substitutes for money, often described as being very liquid. A three-month US T-bill may pay interest of about 1 percent per year in money when 4 percent interest is paid on equally secure five-year bonds. That 3 percent difference is interpreted as a measure of the liquidity service yield.

2) Another element in liquidity is a store of value service. For short periods of time, money is the best store of value. Holding all your wealth in one non-money good, such as a basket of eggs, would be like putting all your eggs . . . you get the point. Holding some money diversifies the risks of changes in values of specific goods. Greater certainty of exchange value is part of the liquidity of a good. For both reasons — economizing on transactions costs and being a form of wealth that is secure against relative value changes — short-term T-bills pay a very low rate of interest, but more than cash.

VERY SHORT-TERM BONDS HAVE MORE LIQUIDITY AND SMALLER MARKET RISK THAN LONGER-TERM BONDS

A bill is the usual name for a loan of one year or less; a note is a loan between 1 and 10 years; and a bond is a longer-term loan. The Treasury yield curve shows the money interest yields according to length of the loan ("bond") to the US government. The lower money interest rate paid on the shorter-term loans with

virtually *no default risk* plus their greater liquidity enables these bills to (a) serve
as stores of value and (b) have lower transactions costs in their purchase and
sale. Being shorter lived, overnight loans between banks have less market risk.
They are very close to being money, and the money interest rate is almost zero.

THE "REAL" VERSUS THE REALIZED
REAL RATE OF INTEREST

A *real* rate of interest is a *purchasing-power* adjusted rate: real rate = nominal rate
– inflation. If the nominal rate of interest is 10 percent and the inflation rate
is anticipated to be 3 percent, the *anticipated real* rate of return would be about
7 percent. If actual inflation later happened to be 6 percent per year, then the
realized real rate would be only about 4 percent (= 10% – 6%). The realized real
rate could be negative if the actual rate of inflation were higher than the nominal interest rate.

Temporary reductions in the real interest rate have occurred during wars
and other worldwide disasters. During the twentieth century, the two world
wars and the oil supply reduction of the 1970s resulted in decreased productivity sufficient to reduce the real rate of interest during those episodes.

Altering Patterns of Claims to Current and Future Incomes by
Changes in Relative Prices of Shorter- and Longer-Lived Resources
Borrowing and lending are not the only ways to alter your pattern of current
and future claims to income. You can choose among shorter- and longer-lived
resources. A rise in the demand for current income (consumption) will result

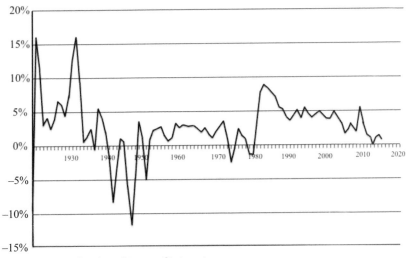

Figure 33.1 *Realized Real Rates of Interest, 1920–2015*

Table 33.4 *Interest Rates and Associated Market Values of Resources of Differing Life Lengths*

Resource	Years	Annual Return	Present Cost	Present Market Values at Each Rate of Interest				
				3%	5%	7%	10%	15%
Brick House	200	$50	$1,500	$1,662	$1,000	$714	$500	$333
Wood House	50	$50	$900	$1,286	$915	$690	$496	$333
Temp. House	10	$50	$275	$427	$386	$351	$307	$251

A market rate of interest of 5 percent would be consistent only with the prices listed in the 5 percent column: $1,000 for the brick house, $915 for the wooden house, and $386 for the temporary house. Refer to entries in table 31.1, which gives present values of annuities of $1 a year for various numbers of years and interest rates. Here, we have present values of annual streams of returns of $50 for three alternative periods.

in people trying to buy resources that yield more of their income in the near future. People will offer to sell the longer-lived resources. Table 33.4 shows an example with three resources — a temporary housing unit, a standard type of wood house, and one made with bricks. Assume (to keep the arithmetic simple) that each house yields the same annual rental value. The same analysis applies as in the examples of prices of bonds in table 33.3.

The prices listed in table 33.4 at various interest rates show that the temporary house would be worth owning or constructing only if the interest rate were a little below 10 percent, where its value ($307) would be above the $275 cost of production. The wood house would be worth owning or producing only if the interest rate were below about 5 percent; at lower rates, its value exceeds its $900 cost. The brick house would be worth owning or producing only if the interest rate were below about 3 percent, where its value ($1,662) would exceed its cost ($1,500).

CANNOT RELIABLY MEASURE THE RATE OF INTEREST BY RELATIVE PRICES OF RESOURCES

The prices and hence the interest rates on the resources in table 33.4 reflect beliefs about the future returns. But the beliefs are not known. So when the price changes, we do not know whether that reflects a change in beliefs or a change in the interest rate at which the future expectations are capitalized to a present value. Nevertheless, this example shows how and in what direction *relative prices of resources* are affected by changes in interest rates, whatever else may be affecting their prices.

INVESTMENT EFFECTS OF CHANGES IN RESOURCE
PRICES, RATHER THAN IN COST OF BORROWING

The data in table 33.4 show also why it's wrong to believe that the effect of a decline of the interest rate on the profitability of investments happens primarily through the reduced interest *payments* on loans to finance the investments. Instead, it occurs through a *valuation effect* — changes in the (a) market values of resources relative to (b) their costs of production. If you think of resources like buildings and automobiles as longer-lived, and food and current labor services as short-lived resources, then a change in the rate of interest implies a change in the prices of longer-lived resources relative to shorter-lived goods. That can alter both employment of labor and total production. That's the reason changes in the market interest rate are so important throughout the whole economy for all resources — not just for bonds.

COMPETITIVE EQUALIZING OF PURE INTEREST
RATES ON ALL BONDS AND RESOURCES

The nominal explicit interest rates paid differ from bond to bond, resource to resource, person to person, and nation to nation. To each there is an appropriate *risk-adjusted* total package called the *nominal interest*. That nominal interest rate package includes the pure rate of interest, together with adjustments for risks, liquidity, and costs in forming bonds, loans, and investments.

This implies that one cannot hope to find predictably profitable patterns of security prices. The next chapter will show that as a result of competition, market prices are adjusted so as to equate the risk-adjusted rates of returns on all the bonds and securities. Market prices clear the market, with no shortage or surplus, no queuing or rationing for buying or selling financial securities.

QUESTIONS AND MEDITATIONS

1) "I bought some stock at $70 a share. It has fallen to $55, but I'm going to hold it until it rises to $70 so I can avoid taking a loss." What is wrong with that reasoning, even assuming that the stock price does shortly thereafter rise to $75?

Answer:

Your wealth is the current market value of your assets. Whether looking at the price of shares of stock or the market value of your house, if it is less than previously, then you have suffered a loss. The question of whether to sell the stock at the lower price or continue to hold it depends on alternative investment opportunities. If some other asset will get you to $70 sooner than this stock, sell at $55 and buy the better alternative.

2) You graduate from college and apply for a loan at a local bank in order to start a new business. You are quoted an interest rate on the loan of 15 percent. You complain to the bank manager that they are engaging in age discrimination because you are young; your uncle got a loan from the same bank for his business at only 12 percent. What, other than age, might account for the difference in interest rates charged by the bank?

Answer:

Probably the risk premium on the loans is different, because your uncle has a longer and favorable credit history. Generally, the longer you have a good record of making payments on time, the lower will be the risk premium you will have to pay on new loans.

3) Your business was started with an issuance of bonds yielding a return of 7 percent to investors for ten years. A decade later, those bonds have been paid off, your business has been successful, and you want to issue new bonds for expansion. You are told that the new bonds will have to return over 9 percent to new investors. Does that mean you now are a worse credit risk? What else might explain the higher interest rate to issue new bonds?

Answer:

If your credit risk has not worsened, then look to see what has been happening to inflation. Most likely, inflation for the future is expected to be about 2 percent higher than when you issued the previous bonds.

4) You want to own a secure investment, so you decide that US Treasury bonds are the safest thing to own for the next ten years. On the Treasury's website, you see that a ten-year Treasury note is currently selling for a price that will yield 5 percent. However, you also see an inflation-indexed Treasury bond that has a coupon of only 2 percent (these bonds add the actual inflation rate of the prior twelve months to the coupon interest rate to determine how much you will be paid each year). Who, if anyone, would buy the latter bond instead of the Treasury note yielding 5 percent?

Answer:

Someone who expects inflation to average more than 3 percent per year over the ten-year period would prefer the inflation-indexed bond. They would earn the certain 2 percent plus whatever happens to be the actual rate of inflation.

5) Your investment advisor tells you that if you buy a bond (with a "face" value of $1,000) for $800 with ten years to maturity, you will earn a yield of over 12 percent even though the bond pays only $70 per year. Is the investment advisor correct?

Answer:

Yes. Your yield to maturity will always be greater than the "coupon" yield ($70 per year for each $1,000 of principal) when you pay a current price that is less than the principal—the "face value" that will be paid to you when the bond matures. In this case, the present value of ten end-of-year payments of $70, plus the present value of $1,000 paid to you at the end of ten years, is more than $800 at 12 percent.

6) You have a choice of investing in a new issue of twenty-year Treasury bonds yielding 4 percent or a new issue of Venture Corp bonds yielding 7 percent. What would be some reasons for choosing the lower-yielding Treasury bond?

Answer:

There is no default risk on the Treasury bond, but you might be wiped out if Venture Corp goes into bankruptcy before your bonds mature. Another consideration is liquidity. If you decide you want to sell the bonds before the twenty years are up, you will almost certainly get a higher price for your Treasury bonds than for the bonds of Venture Corp—assuming you can find anyone willing to offer to buy them.

7) Five years ago your company had a choice between investing in a machine that would last twenty years versus one that would need to be replaced in only five years. At that time, you chose the five-year machine, and you now need to replace it. You are considering whether to buy the machine that will last twenty years. You find that the machines are exactly the same as before—no changes in technology; but now the price of the machine that will last twenty years is much more expensive. What happened?

Answer:

Other things the same, relatively higher prices of longer-lived versus shorter-lived assets suggest that interest rates have fallen. Conversely, during periods of rising interest rates, prices of longer-lived assets fall more than prices of shorter-lived assets.

8) An increase in security of property rights in investments will increase the
demand for current resources to be invested rather than consumed now.
The demand curve will shift to the right and the market rate of interest
will be raised. Will the result be a higher pure interest rate or a lower
nominal rate with less risk premium?

Answer:

The interest rate hasn't changed. Instead, we are looking at the nominal
rate on a lower-risk class of investments and loans — where the risk premium in the nominal interest rate package is smaller. An increase in the
safety and security of property rights can induce more demand for current
income to invest for future, safer income. At the same time, increased reliability in the future of rights to the income and property at that time can
induce people now to give up more current income rights per dollar of the
more reliable future income they will have. Both the demand and supply
are larger — shifted to the right. But basically, the pure rate is unchanged.
Instead, there is a lower nominal rate — one applicable to lower-risk
investments and loans and with lower-risk premiums included in the
nominal rate.

CHAPTER 34

RISK AND INSURANCE

Life is riddled with uncertainties and surprises. Fires, illnesses, and auto collisions are uncertain and, to a degree, accidental. But their risks can be reduced — drive less often and more carefully. Yet who would stop driving to reduce that risk to zero? Risking a disastrous loss in order to achieve some desired result is not always foolish. You may even have gone skydiving from an airplane, expecting your parachute to open. Some foods are enjoyed despite an increased probability of consequent disease or earlier death.

Trade-offs among safety, wealth, and other pleasures are always present, voluntary, and adjustable. Though we can't avoid all risks, we can alter the consequences to a more acceptable form. Many methods have evolved. Two are *insurance* and *futures* markets. Futures markets and hedging are deferred to a later chapter. Here, how and why insurance can serve your interests is examined.

The motivation for insurance is to offset the possibility of very large losses. Insurance is almost always for protection against loss only of economic market value, not of friendship, reputation, connubial bliss, or emotional trauma. Parents rarely insure children, because death of a child implies relatively small economic loss, though intense psychological loss.

LOSS SPREADING FOR REDUCTION OF PRIVATE LOSS

The primary purpose of insurance is *not a reduction of the risk* of the disaster occurring. Instead, insurance divides, spreads, and diversifies the economic losses of disasters over a large number of people, reducing *each person's risk* of a large loss. The total loss by the occasional disaster is shared among the insured people, not eliminated.

If each of 1,000 people has one chance in a thousand annually of suffering a $50,000 loss from a house fire, the expected loss is measured as $50 (= .001 × $50,000) per person. The consequence to each person is changed from a small risk of a big loss ($50,000) to a sure, small annual premium payment of $50. The annual insurance premiums from all the insured people are expected to cover the insured loss when it occurs. (The premium paid is actually a bit higher, so as to cover the costs of managing and assuring the insurance arrangement.)

The insurance company can reliably promise to compensate insured losses if it has accumulated sufficient wealth. The insurance company must have accumulated that wealth (capital) with the initial investment in creating the insurance company and with the subsequent net inflow of premium payments by the insured people. The probabilities of the insured event and of sizes of losses must be adequately predictable, so that the inflow of premiums and the outflow of damage payments match (approximately), with adequate capital as a reserve to buffer large payments. That information about probabilities of the insured events is a form of *intellectual capital*, as real and valuable as physical capital or money.

In the event of catastrophic disasters, if the insurance company lacks enough wealth in the form of money or saleable assets, it might, on the basis of that intellectual capital, be able to borrow the required amount to pay the insured parties, and then to repay the debt out of future business.

How much is it worth to reduce the risk of deaths? That question is often misleadingly phrased as, "How much is it worth to save a life?" Some estimates indicate that using expensive vented gas heaters costs $100,000 per life saved. Seat belts in autos are estimated to save lives at a cost of $300,000 per life. Asbestos regulations have been estimated to cost about $100,000,000 per life saved from premature death. Safety regulations imposed on grain storage elevators (silos) are estimated to reduce the *average* number of deaths by one, at a cost of about $5,000,000. Those average values do not indicate whether more, or less, care is desirable. It's the marginal cost—the additional cost of saving one more life—that is relevant for decisions on efforts to avoid *additional* deaths.

WHAT KIND OF CATASTROPHES ARE INSURABLE?

No insurance is available for business losses, or divorce, or grades in your class. We are looking at insurance where *you* can choose whether or not to be insured by an insurer who, in turn, can choose whether or not to insure you.

The premium for life insurance is lower for younger adults whose risk of death is lower than for elderly people. The risk of death in the next year for a twenty-year-old is roughly about 1.5 and .67 per thousand for white males and females, respectively. It rises to about 2.2 and .8 per thousand for nonwhite males and females aged twenty. At age 65, the annual risks are up to about 28 and 14 per thousand for white males and females, and 35 and 10 for nonwhites. Males suffer a higher probability of death at equivalent ages. (Nature ignores any legislation about discrimination.)

Life insurance comes in two basic forms — *term* and *straight life*—with many combinations in between. Term insurance is usually renewable at the end of each term—though with higher premiums at older ages. The *predictability* of risk permits a constant annual premium called straight life insurance. You pay more for straight life insurance than for term insurance at a younger age, with the earlier payments being invested by the insurance company in a fund that covers the deficiency of the constant premium relative to the higher risks at older ages. That's a method of saving earlier in life and drawing on the accumulated wealth later to continue the insurance.

SOME NECESSARY CONDITIONS FOR VOLUNTARY INSURANCE

For viable voluntary insurance to be provided by insurance firms, some of the necessary conditions are: (1) the premium must cover the cost of operating the insurance arrangement as well as the risk of loss; (2) independence of timing and size of successive risked events; (3) reliable measurement of the probabilities and size of economic losses for each participant; (4) avoidance of adverse selection; and (5) control of moral hazard.

Fair Bets and Full Payoffs

The collected premiums (revenue to the insurance company) must exceed the insurance payouts for losses. Every insured person appears to be engaging in an unfair bet—paying more than the expected payback. Consider a wager of $1 on a coin toss in which $2 is won on heads and $0 if a tail. The *expected payoff* is the probability-weighted average of all the possible results. The probability of heads or tails is .5. The possible results are $2 and $0. The expected payoff value is $1 (= $2 × .5 + $0 × .5). A *fair bet* is one in which the amount bet ($1 in the coin toss) equals the expected value of all the possible outcomes (payoffs). Anyone who pays more than the expected value is said to be making an unfair bet. If the price of the bet is less, it's called a more than fair bet for you, and an unfair bet for the opposite party.

The owners of an insurance company do not bear the loss caused by the occurrence of the risky event against which the insurance is sold. An amount equal to the expected loss is spread over all the insured parties in the form of the annual insurance premiums. The owners of the insurance company—the insurers—bear a different risk. They must cover any losses that exceed the expected loss. They earlier will have invested wealth in the company as a *capital reserve* for larger than expected losses. If losses occur that are very much larger than the expected loss, the company may become bankrupt, but it usually, in turn, has insured against that risk by buying insurance from some other insurance company — called a *reinsurer*.

Independence of Risky Events among the Insured Persons

The spreading of the risk among many people is possible only if the accident, say, a fire, does not occur to everyone at the same time. If the disaster, such as an earthquake or hurricane, were so broad in its effects that many people would be affected by the same disaster, insurance may not be possible. Everyone would have to pay premiums that equaled their own expected loss. Instead of insurance, that would be merely a sort of advance saving to match the future expected loss. The larger the fraction of the insured people who suffer a loss simultaneously, the less likely is insurance to be feasible.

The Amount of the Expected Loss

The probability of the event and the loss must be objectively measurable for each insured person. If nothing is known about the probability of the event and resulting economic loss, the premium that would cover the expected loss can't be predicted. Voluntary insurance would not be feasible. No insurance is available to protect against being hit by an asteroid.

Adverse Selection and the Probability of the Disaster

Adverse selection is a factor faced *before* the insurance is obtained. Some are high-risk applicants with information they do not reveal to the insurer. This is *asymmetric information*, which permits *adverse selection* that would undermine the ability to maintain insurance.

If people or events cannot be classified according to their risks with appropriate premiums, and if all were charged the same insurance fee, only the highest-risk people would tend to join at those fees, while the lower-risk people would not. The insurance company must find ways to detect applicants with poorer qualities. Otherwise, premiums paid by the insured customers will not cover the higher risk and larger losses caused by the riskier people. This asymmetric information and adverse selection problem is present in all exchanges, lending, and investing, as well as in all social affairs, even (or especially?) in romancing and marriage.

Proxies for indicators of higher-risk people seeking driver insurance are: past driving records, age, and gender of the driver. Old people pay higher life insurance premiums than middle-aged people, and wood buildings have higher insurance premiums than steel fireproof buildings.

If you're a man, you will complain when you discover that women pay less for the same life insurance. In some states, students with good grades get cheaper auto insurance; so do nonsmokers. Yet some smokers are better drivers than are some nonsmokers — even for the same age, gender, and locality. Classifying people into risk classes on the basis of imperfect criteria is often criticized as unfair or biased. Do not confuse imperfection with bias.

Tests in your classes may be imperfect, but are they biased toward women versus men, or young versus old, or taller versus shorter people? So long as young males do have higher probability of automobile accidents than do young females, a higher premium for males is necessary for insurance. Otherwise, adverse selection would undermine insurance. Yet legislatures have passed laws declaring it illegal to use some unbiased indicators of risk and adverse selection, such as gender, academic grade records, and age.

A majority of California voters imposed legislation reducing the permissible insurance premiums for auto insurance. The result was that the voters then received no, or poorer, driver and auto insurance — unless the person seeking that insurance also purchased house insurance from the same insurance company. The tie-in of house and automobile insurance in one policy avoided the imposed limits on auto insurance. (Remember the effects of rent controls on renting arrangements?)

Moral Hazard — Risk Enhancing after Insurance Is Obtained

Moral hazard means the tendency to take additional actions that are personally beneficial if more of the costs will be borne by someone else. In contrast to adverse selection, it's a problem to be faced *after* the insurance is in place. If you have driven a car without insurance, you probably drove more cautiously and slowly than when driving with insurance. Therefore, insurers impose some explicit restraints. You tend to be more careful to avoid fires in your home if you don't have fire insurance. But *full-cost* (including added care and anxiety) is greater when driving or living in a house without insurance than with insurance.

Moral hazard often can be sufficiently controlled by including restrictions like deductibles and sharing of costs, to avoid claims for trivial items, as well as to establish good faith claims for service or payment of insurance. A claim for treatment for a cold, or strained ligament, or a claim for a dented automobile fender, may require the insured party to pay up to $500, a *deductible*, of any claimed insurance amount. This restrains relatively frivolous claims. Deductibles, and exceptions for special kinds of losses, are common, especially for hazards the risk of which are affected by the behavior of the insured party. Another arrangement is for the insured party to bear a fraction of the loss, say,

20 percent. That is *coinsurance*. Otherwise, the insurance premiums would be higher.

Some manufacturers or retailers provide a form of insurance, called *warranties*, for the goods they sell. They do that for failures that are relatively independent of the way the customer used the item. Automobile warranties (insurance) apply primarily to failures unlikely to have been caused by normal driving. Damage from failure to change or replenish oil is not covered by insurance, but failure of a generator is about the same for all the buyers, so it's covered. Those warranties (insurance) are paid for in the price of the auto.

MORAL HAZARD OF EMPLOYEE BEHAVIOR

In general, acceptable morally hazardous behavior of, say, an employee is behavior that is fully anticipated. It is permitted if the employer's cost of detecting, monitoring, and restraining that anticipated behavior would exceed the worths of that morally hazarded behavior. University administrators, who find it too expensive to monitor professors perfectly, tolerate professors' use of university pencils, paper, telephones, and offices for personal purposes. The full wage is comprised of less money but more nonmoney benefits to the employees.

WHAT ELSE DO YOU GET WHEN YOU BUY INSURANCE?

Insurance does more than spread economic losses over the insured parties. Insurance relieves one of anxiety and worry. It permits peace of mind and better planning for the future. Taking account of the *full* payoff, people are willing to pay a bit more than for only the *money* payoff in the event the insured disaster happens.

Reduced risks and more safety arrangements are imposed on the insured parties by the insurer. Insurers that are better at finding ways to lower risks are more likely to be profitable. Insurance companies provide and insist upon more reliable precautions. In fact, large publicly owned corporations take out insurance primarily to obtain those risk-reducing services, rather than merely to insure against the large catastrophic economic losses.

After a disaster, insurance companies supply legal services in arranging settlements between the parties. How quickly they settle claims, and how well they defend their insured customers, is part of what should be considered when deciding where to buy insurance. The concept of full price is appropriate for a more complete understanding of price, so a *full-product* concept is appropriate for analyzing the product.

INSURANCE THAT WAS NOT INSURANCE

Some major schemes that were supposed to be insurance largely failed. During the Great Depression of the 1930s — a time of many bank failures — Congress established two systems of deposit "insurance." One was the Federal Deposit Insurance Corporation (FDIC), which was to insure checking account and time deposits in commercial banks. The other was the Federal Savings and Loan Insurance Corporation (FSLIC), which created an insurance system for consumer balances held at federal savings and loan associations.[1]

Banking companies are assessed a small fee as a percentage of deposits to be paid into the FDIC to serve as a *reserve* against losses, but the reserve has been inadequate to cover significant losses by banking companies. Also, an unintended consequence of such government guarantees of deposits has been to increase *moral hazard* — banks are encouraged to incur greater risk.

Before federal legislation creating bank-deposit insurance, depositors had a strong incentive to place their funds with companies which had established and maintained good reputations for prudent lending and investing in order to minimize risks of losses. With the federal government providing guarantees against losses to depositors, bank customers were less concerned about the risks being taken by bank management. On the contrary, in order to attract deposits, banks could offer ever higher interest rates with the intention of lending to or investing in ever more risky ventures.

For many years, a highly profitable business for the savings and loan associations was to attract short-term savings deposits of consumers — guaranteed against loss by the government "insurance fund"— then lend to borrowers who wanted long-term, fixed-rate mortgages. A problem arose for these companies when inflation began to accelerate in the 1960s and 1970s because the depositors demanded ever-higher interest on their savings to compensate them for loss of purchasing power. However, because their deposits had been lent to homeowners at fixed rates for up to thirty years, it wasn't long before the interest paid to depositors exceeded the interest received from the mortgages, causing enormous losses and even bankruptcy for the savings and loan companies. Eventually, taxpayers had to cover the extraordinary losses.

The good intentions of protecting bank customers against losses became a system that greatly increased the risks to taxpayers of losses as a result of bailouts of companies that take on excessive risk in their lending and invest-

---

1. The FSLIC was later absorbed into the FDIC.

ment decisions. For bank management, it has become a *heads-I-win, tails-the-taxpayers-lose* system. If the risky investments return high yields, salaries and bonuses of bank executives are very generous. If losses result, first the FDIC and then the taxpayers suffer losses.

TRANSFORMATION OF INSURANCE
TO DAMAGE COMPENSATION

Some states have passed laws restricting permissible automobile insurance rates. As a result, some insurance companies have been withdrawing from automobile insurance. To provide insurance to higher-risk drivers, who can't get insurance at the lower mandated rates, state governments have instituted compulsory state-insurance arrangements, which means that taxpayers, or safer drivers, are paying for some of the damages caused by high-risk drivers. That's not insurance. It's tax-financed relief and damage compensation.

Another example of the partial transformation of insurance into tax-supported compensation is the federal *unemployment insurance* system. Employees pay monthly an unemployment insurance premium to the federal government. During spells of unemployment, the unemployed person receives benefits for specified lengths of time. The premiums charged are not closely matched with the class of risk of unemployment in various industries. As a result, employees in industries with chronically higher unemployment rates pay too little.

The mismatching of risks and premiums converts the so-called unemployment insurance into unemployment relief. Congress typically extends the compensation beyond the lengths of time initially promised. However, we will see that this does not mean unemployment relief is economically wasteful or undesirable.

RELIEF FROM LOSSES IS NOT THE SOLE
PURPOSE OF INSURANCE

Some losses aren't insured. Tax-supported or charitable relief is often granted to people suffering some large loss. Examples are losses from hurricanes, floods, tornadoes, and earthquakes, which are not readily insurable risks. Then, why is relief granted to those who choose to live in hazardous areas for which insurance is not obtainable?

People who buy beachfront or earthquake-risky property in Southern California did know or should have known that the price at which they bought the land was lower to compensate for the expectation of loss or damage to the land. Hillside property, known to be subject to slides and water drainage erosion and fires or earthquakes, sells at a lower price than if those risks were absent. The lower price of the land compensates the buyer for bearing the risks of those losses. Yet, if the loss does occur and several homes slide or burn, taxpayers give compensation in the form of *emergency relief*, despite the *advance relief* obtained in the lower initial purchase price of the land. (If only one or two homes are damaged, governments don't provide relief. It takes a significant number of victims to trigger the relief. The answer to why the number suffering makes a difference is left to political scientists.)

On second thought, do those who receive compensation really get a *gift*? Or did they pay for it earlier? If the buyers anticipate future damages will be compensated by relief payments, the purchase price they offer will be higher — higher by the present value of the expectation of that future compensation. The buyer gets no *net* benefit when later getting that compensation, for he paid more in anticipation of the potential relief. The beneficiary is the *former* owner who owned the land at the time the prospects of relief first were created, which then raised the price.

LOTTERIES — INCREASED RISK

People appear to be inconsistent in displaying risk preference — making unfair bets — while at the same time taking life, auto, and fire insurance. They prefer risk — make unfair bets — when they play state lotteries and gamble, where the price of a lottery ticket is far in excess of the expected winnings. But when they buy stocks and bonds, they display risk aversion. The prices of securities have to be lower than those of less risky bonds to induce people to buy the riskier bonds.

A solution to this apparently inconsistent behavior of poor people increasing their risk by buying lottery tickets (unfair bets) lies in the concept of the *full payoff* of a lottery ticket. A poor person buys the contemplation of a possible drastic, spectacular change in lifestyle. For many poor people, there is no way other than by a lottery to obtain such a possibility. But the rare winners, immediately upon winning, shift their behavior toward risk reduction by investing the winnings.

INSURANCE, ASSURANCE, AND
GAMBLING: A PLAY ON WORDS?

Gambling

Two aspects of the returns — the *expected value* and the *range (variance)* of the actual returns — are elements of choices. Gambling means the choice of a *wider* range of possible future wealth, regardless of whether the expected value is greater than the amount paid. As always, the expected value means the ordinary average — the sum of the probability-weighted values of possible outcomes. Thus, the expected value of a $1 bet on the toss of a *fair* coin, where a head wins $3 and a tail brings nothing, with .5 probability of each, is $1.50 = ([$3 × .5] + [$0 × .5]), which exceeds the investment. But accepting that action would still be gambling, because of the increased spread of one's future possible wealth, from (a) $1.00 for sure to (b) equal .5 chances for $0 or $3.

Incidentally, with gambling on sporting events, the owners of the betting establishment do not bet with or against the bettors. Instead, the owner earns an income by enabling people to bet against each other. The owners take a percentage of the total amount bet as their earnings.

Assurance Provided by Gamblers

Most feasible *insurance* arrangements, such as for life, or fire, or auto accidents are for events that occur as if at random and independently of each other. But what is usually obtained when one is said to *insure* a musician's hand or voice or when an athlete insures against an injury is basically a promise of compensation from some reliable *gambler*. That is not insurance — in which there are premium payments invested in a fund from which payments are made for losses against which insurance was provided.

Insurability of some kind of event requires its having a predictable probability of random, independently occurring losses. Otherwise, what's called *insurance* is sheer gambling or *assurance* — which is what the members of the famous Lloyd's of London insurers provide. More precisely, the members of Lloyd's of London provide assurance of compensation for loss, but not by insurance. The payments came from the wealth of the members of Lloyd's, rather than from a true insurance fund.

QUESTIONS AND MEDITATIONS

1)   In what sense is insurance a one-sided hedge?
Answer:
    It usually protects against large losses, without giving up rights to large gains.

2)   For what events is the distribution of risk the same in socialist and capitalist systems?
Answer:
    How about divorce, cancer, baldness, homeliness, having only male children, being left-handed?

3) Our laws and customs reflect the assignments of risk bearing. A person who owns land as private property must bear the consequences of changes in the value of that land if people move away or no longer value that location so highly. Similarly, if a person catches cold or breaks a leg or becomes hard of hearing and can no longer earn so large an income, the person must bear the consequences. Meditate on the following:

   a. Would you prefer to live in a country where people bear the wealth losses to their private property regardless of cause (aside from legal recourse to violators of property rights)?

   b. Would you want a homeowner to bear the consequences of a meteorite's falling on his house? Fire from using gasoline in the house? Floor damage to houses near rivers? Income loss from cancer? Blindness?

   c. Who do you think should bear the loss if the individual does not?

   d. Why would you draw the line differently in different cases? What is your criterion?

   e. In each case, do you think people's behavior would be affected according to the risk-bearing involved?

   f. Would you allow people to agree to take on certain risks in exchange for not bearing other risks, if two people could make a mutually agreeable partition and exchange of such risks? How would that differ from a system of private property rights?

Answer:

Think about the implications of the initial answers you give to the questions above. Can an objective probability be attached to such events involving risk? If so, the risk can be quantified, and a potential exists to insure against loss. Is the pool of potential risk bearers large enough and diversified enough to have premiums pay for the expected losses? Can a private individual's personal choices affect the probability of the event? If damages from such choices are compensated, how might this affect the likely level of compensation? What gains can you conceive might accrue to society by taxpayers' bearing the cost of harm done by the private decisions of others, or can that harm be more effectively covered by civil damages for negligence in a court of law? If society bears the cost and pays for catastrophic damages out of tax revenues, could the *total* cost to taxpayers exceed the *total* return to those individuals who by private decisions knowingly place themselves in harm's way? How does such taxpayer compensation affect the risk prevention and reduction decisions of individuals? How will this ultimately affect the total cost of compensation to taxpayers? Is taxpayer

compensation likely to increase or decrease the overall riskiness of decisions taken in that society? Are these the kinds of risks that are likely to
enhance or decrease the total well-being of that society?

Economics does not provide individuals or their elected representatives
the proper social choice they should make, but it can tell them some of
the consequences that can be expected from the particular choices that are
made.

4) "The fact that some airplanes sometimes collided in midair is evidence
    that there was too little air traffic control." Evaluate.
Answer:

The mere statement of the fact does not justify the conclusion. It may or
may not be reasonable to judge that there was too little traffic control, but
to remove all risk of all accidents costs more than it's worth — that is, the
only way to eliminate all such risk of accidents would be to ban flying.

5) Individuals and businesses that make deposits in a bank are making a
    loan to that bank. In return, the individuals and businesses earn interest
    and are provided services such as clearing checks and making payments
    by transfers. In the United States since the 1930s — and in most countries
    up to some limit — governments provide insurance or guarantees against
    any losses by those who lend money to the bank. Why have governments
    done this, and how is behavior of depositors affected?
Answer:

Before deposit insurance (guarantee against loss up to some maximum
amount held in each account), fears of bank failures such as happened
in the 1930s could cause a "run" on the bank. If all or most depositors
tried to make withdrawals in a short amount of time, the bank (even if
solvent) could not liquidate assets sufficiently rapidly to provide the cash
demanded by customers. The idea of deposit insurance or guarantees was
to minimize these "panic" runs by small depositors. The consequence has
been that small depositors have little reason to be concerned about the risk
being incurred by bank management in their lending and investment decisions. Bank managers, knowing that the insurance fund will protect depositors, take on greater risk than would be prudent if losses were incurred
by all depositors as well as equity and bond investors. In economics, this is
known as *moral hazard* — the potential losses of engaging in risky behavior
are not fully borne by those making the decisions.

6) In order to stimulate more investment in "green energy" such as solar-panel and windmill generation of electricity, governments in North America and Europe provided guarantees against loss to investors who would lend to such enterprises. What does economic analysis suggest would be the consequences of such taxpayer-provided guarantees?

Answer:

The risk premiums in such guaranteed loans have been much lower than otherwise, so the interest expense to borrowers has been artificially low. Decision makers in the solar and windmill businesses borrowed much more than otherwise and approved projects that had low probability of profitability. Over-investment (in economics, often called mal-investment) in energy-generating projects that require taxpayer subsidies results in lower standards of living. Losses incurred by such projects are paid by taxpayers. Also, the resources employed by money-losing projects could have been employed in more productive ways. Economics does not say that such choices are bad or undesirable, only that people will be poorer as a result.

7) Political leaders in less-developed countries of the world — sometimes referred to as the "third world"— occasionally decide that a good way to attract the greater investment necessary to grow more rapidly is to adopt a policy of government-provided guarantees of loans made by foreign investors. Governments in Asian countries —Thailand, Taiwan, South Korea, Indonesia, and the Philippines, for example— offered 100 percent guarantees for foreign loans to build new cities, office buildings, shopping centers, and hotels. Entrepreneurs found they could borrow in Japan at an interest rate of only 1 percent and lend to projects in Thailand for 15 percent— and the loan was fully guaranteed. What would economics suggest would be the consequences of such policies?

Answer:

The extraordinary profitability of borrowing at 1 percent and lending at 15 percent, while incurring no risk of loss because of the government guarantees, meant the lenders had no incentive to be concerned about the economic viability of proposed projects. Massive new construction projects created mini-booms of economic activity, but it all turned out to be the "healthy glow of a fever in the early stages of serious illness." As the projects were completed and it was found that there were few buyers and renters, many projects entered bankruptcy. The governments found they had provided guarantees for far more loans than their tax systems could afford to pay. The consequent "Asian Debt Crisis" occurred when governments and central banks in the borrowing countries defaulted on the guaranteed loans.

8) If you own and drive an automobile, you are required by law to have some minimum amount of insurance in case of accident. Suppose the law in the state where you live were changed to require all minimum automobile insurance policies to include a quarterly oil change and tire rotation. Is that really "insurance"?

Answer:

No, the requirement for "insurance policies" to include such routine pre-paid maintenance is not a feature of insurance. The cost to you of such a policy will reflect the costs of these services. Similarly, when government requires that "health insurance" policies include such services as regular physicals, mammograms, birth control, and so forth, that is not insurance. Even if you do not make a payment to the doctor for these services, they are not "free" to you. You have already paid for them in the higher price you pay for the insurance policies that include these services.

APPENDIX TO CHAPTER 34: VIABLE INSURANCE

Table 34.1 illustrates moral hazard, and why it can be mutually acceptable by the insured and the insurer. It shows how insurance can reduce the full cost of bearing uncertainty.

The first set of data shows the costs without insurance. The actions are valued here at $1,250. In the second part, if insurance is available and if monitoring of behavior were costless, the insurance fee of $50 would reduce anxiety and reduce the extent of private cautionary actions and care.

With insurance, a person takes less precaution, equivalent to precautions costing only $100, rather than the $200 without insurance. But if you have driven a car without insurance, you probably drove more cautiously than when you had insurance. Without fire insurance, you are likely to be more careful to avoid disastrous loss than if you are covered. That extra care is not free. So it is consistent to think that full costs of care are higher without insurance.

The third set of data shows the possibility when, realistically, there are costs of monitoring. Voluntary insurance is feasible so long as the cost of monitoring behavior of the insured person does not raise the insurance premium above the savings in anxiety and personal precautionary actions.

Table 34.1 *Reduction of Full Cost by Insurance, despite Moral Hazard*

Without insurance costs

Fire protection devices	$1,000
Care	200
Anxiety: Risk aversion	50
Full costs	$1,250

With insurance: if costless monitoring

Fire protection devices	$900
Care	100
Insurance fee	50
Anxiety: Risk aversion	10
Full costs	$1,060

With costly monitoring

Fire protection devices	$950	
Care	70	(e.g., reduced care worth only $70)
Insurance fee	100	($50 more for better monitoring)
Anxiety	10	
Full costs	$1,130	

Insurance fee must not exceed expected-loss premium by more than:

Anxiety reduction	[$50 – 10] = $40
Reduction in carefulness	[$200 – 70] = $130
Greater fire protection cost	[$1,000 – 950] = $50
Total	$220

CHAPTER 35

THE FULL EQUILIBRIUM:
EQUALIZED RATES OF RETURN
WITH INTERMEDIARIES

"Competition drives risk-adjusted rates of return on all resources toward equality."

That powerful statement includes financial instruments, which often are claims to returns on real productive resources. There are several important implications of this law.

1) Arbitrage among prices of securities and resources exhausts sure-profit prospects.
2) Observed prices are unbiased estimators of the future prices, because
3) News about events comes at random, though occurrences of the events are not.
4) A wider range, or *variance*, of prices of a security — within which its price varies — lowers the price paid for it, thereby raising the percentage rate of return to the *risk-adjusted* rate of return.
5) These adjustments result in an efficient *mean-variance trade-off* between (a) a riskier, higher-mean rate of return prospect and (b) a safer prospect with a lower-mean rate.
6) The path of resulting successive prices of securities has been characterized appropriately as a random walk down Wall Street.[1]
7) For a chosen expected mean value, the portfolio of securities with the lowest risk is a uniform percentage of shares of each security on the stock exchange with an appropriate amount of borrowing or lending of money.
8) Finally, a variety of new securities and firms are created appropriate to new economic circumstances.

ELIMINATION OF SURE-PROFIT ARBITRAGE

The first of the listed implications of the law of competition means that no opportunities will remain for arbitrage profits by assembling combinations of securities worth more as a package than individually. The value of each security

---

1. Burton Malkiel, *A Random Walk Down Wall Street*. Norton, 1995.

will already include the arbitraged value in its price. Since relative prices of securities vary from day to day, there's an ongoing profit-seeking adjustment of prices. *News can give profits to people who first make these arbitrage adjustments.* The race for profits by being first is so swift there's no profit in trying to win it. Those who do run the race cannot expect to earn more than the *wages* they could earn elsewhere.

No one has perfect foresight. Nevertheless, we know that the *changes* in successive prices of a security are random values with a zero *mean*, except for the trivially small interest over so short a time. In other words, for financial securities in a well-functioning securities exchange, a *current* price serves as an *unbiased estimator* of the *next* price.

UNBIASED ESTIMATOR

"Unbiased" means that while the estimates are likely to be wrong most, or all, of the time, the *average* of the errors tends to *zero* — neither too high nor too low. If the current price were $3, the next price might be $2 or $4 and never $3. But the *expected* value still is $3. Saying the current price is an unbiased estimator of the next price means that *zero* is the average of the *changes* in successive prices.

An unbiased estimate of the future price can be based on the current price, because investors have no demonstrated bias toward estimating *future news* to be better or worse than the most *recent news*. The successive percentage changes in a price are like *randomly drawn* values from a distribution with a mean that increases at the rate of interest. Both effects, unbiased estimator and random changes, are disbelieved or ignored by many investors and stock market "experts," though the propositions were formally recognized many years ago.

NEWS, NOT EVENTS, IS RANDOM AND ALWAYS SURPRISES

In equilibrium, prices of securities change *at random* times and amounts — but not because the events occur at random. Though events may be predictable in timing and in effects, prices change when *news* about those events is obtained. *News* is new information; else it's not news.

One day of rain in California is a good predictor that it will also rain the next day. Storms usually persist for a few days, so the second day's rain is not a total surprise. If it does rain that next day, the prices of crops affected by the rain don't change as if that subsequent rain were a total surprise. All foreseen, predictable future events and forces are taken into account now and capitalized into the *present* market price.

Predictable changes in prices are not sources of profits. The predictable changes in prices reflect cost-based differences, not profits. The seasonal variations in the price of tomatoes or lettuce offer no prospects of profit by buying when prices are low and selling when prices are higher, because those differences are cost-based differences. The cycle of seasons is not news! Thousands of people in financial houses around the world are racing to be first to detect future events that will change a price, so that they can gain by arbitraging between the present price and the next impending price. Anyone a few seconds later is too late.

RISK

The risk of a price is measured by the size of the range within which the future price is expected to be with some probability, say, 0.9, of the time. The wider that range, or variance, the greater is the risk said to be.

Compare two investments. One will certainly yield exactly $1.05 in a year. The other is known to yield some value between $.80 and $1.20, and is therefore riskier. What is called the *expectation* or *expected value* does not mean a psychological or mental expectation. A statistical measurement concept, it is the mathematical average of the distribution of possible future values, one of which will be realized.

If someone announces you will get a higher mean or expected rate of return on some investment, contemplate also the variance of the possible returns. It will surely be wider for the higher mean or expectation. In general, a smaller risk (variance) is preferred to a larger risk. In a competitive market for securities, the lower price offered for a riskier (larger variance) security raises its expected rate of return on the dollar price.

TRADE-OFF BETWEEN MEAN AND VARIANCE

What you are willing to pay for a resource now depends on: (a) what you expect to get from it in the future and (b) by how much the realized results are likely to differ from the expected amount. You prefer a higher expected value around which the variance is smaller. But competition in the market eliminates the option of having both a smaller variance and a higher average.

You are offered opportunities for a higher expected rate of return on riskier (larger variance) investments or for a lower, more certain, expected rate of return (smaller variance). You can't expect to find an alternative investment with both a higher expected value and a narrower range of possible values around that expected value. All such opportunities, if they exist, will quickly be repriced by competition to where the expected rate of return on the alternative investment adjusts to the expected variance.

People prefer a prospect that offers a higher average of potential gains, while they also prefer a *narrower dispersion*, or variance, of the potential gains around that expected average. The smaller the variance of probable outcomes, the higher the price offered, and therefore the lower is the expected average rate of return on safer investments.

Consider the *mean-variance trade-off* for two securities, A and B, differing in their variances and in expected rates of return. Assume that initially they have the same price because the riskier B has a sufficiently higher expected return to be equally preferred with the safer A. Which do you choose?

Security B is a riskier investment than Security A because the potential deviation from the expected value of B is greater. Yet, with either security, on any given day, tomorrow's value is expected to be the same as today's value (that is, the expected change in price from today to tomorrow for either security is o percent). However, if there is new information causing tomorrow's values to deviate from today's values, it is likely that riskier Security B's percentage deviation will be larger than Security A's percentage deviation. If that new news is negative, the price decline of B will be greater than the price decline of A. That's what is meant by saying Security B is "riskier" than Security A.

The capital valuation of Securities A and B will change until the expected annual rates of return are adjusted to reflect the relative difference in risk between any two securities. Security B has a greater expected variability in return than Security A, making it less attractive in that respect. Consequently, the expected annual rate of return on B, say, 15 percent, will be higher than the expected annual rate of return on A, say, 10 percent, by just enough to compensate owners for the risk differential. A smaller variance and risk factor is offset by a smaller mean or average return, while a higher average return is offset by a larger variance and risk factor. Younger people tend to choose Security B, while older individuals tend to choose Security A. Why?

Diversification to Reduce the Variance without Reducing the Mean

You can reduce the variance of your investments if you diversify. You could buy stocks in several different firms and industries, and you can diversify by holding bonds of different borrowers. The value of a portfolio of diversified corporate stocks will tend to vary less than the value of single stocks with the same expected average rate of growth of value. In that sense, diversification reduces risk.

Some investment strategies involve deliberately choosing to hold shares of companies that are affected in opposite directions by certain events. While tomorrow's price of oil is uncertain, the effects of higher or lower oil prices on a certain firm or industry is less uncertain. Companies that are energy intensive in their production process benefit from lower oil prices and are adversely affected by higher oil prices. An oil exploration and development company benefits from higher prices but is harmed by lower prices. An investor may choose to diversify by holding shares of companies in both, knowing that favorable effects on one are adverse to the other. The expected average return on the combined holdings is less than on either investment by itself, but the expected variance of returns is also smaller.

Diversification by Investing in a Cross-Section of the Market

Now we put together two principles in investing — (a) diversification reduces the risk (variance), and (b) prices of stocks move at random with an expected rise equal to the rate of interest. In a competitive equilibrium market, you cannot consistently do better than with a cross-section of the entire market. "Better" means a higher mean for given variance or a smaller variance for a specified mean.

You will not have to select and buy stocks to create your optimal portfolio. Investment firms have created many of those portfolios, called *market-indexed funds*, each being a representative sample of the entire set of stocks and bonds traded on the stock and bond markets. Some investment funds hold a cross-section of all corporations the stocks of which trade on the major stock markets, creating considerable diversity by business sector, industry, and region.

RANDOM WALK: THE PATH OF SUCCESSIVE PRICES — MARTINGALES

Consider the behavior of a series of equilibrated market prices of a security over time. Toss a coin. For a *head*, add a dollar to a hypothetical fund, starting at $50. For every tail, reduce the fund's value by one dollar. Continue for 50 tosses. Record the sequence of accumulated values of that fund. Examples of such series are shown in the diagram below. The successive changes in each of these series were random and independent of the preceding change. Each sequence wanders up and down. After 50 tosses, you could have nothing (50 successive tails) or you could have at most $100 (50 successive heads), but each of these results is extremely unlikely. The longer the sequence, the farther up or down it is likely to have spread. Values generated with this process are the *Martingale* series, the name assigned a couple of centuries ago to a gambler's path to wealth.

Wherever such a series of successive values happens to wander, it does not have any tendency to return toward its initial value. The successive changes are uncorrelated. Increases aren't more likely to be followed by decreases than by increases, nor are decreases more likely to be followed by decreases than

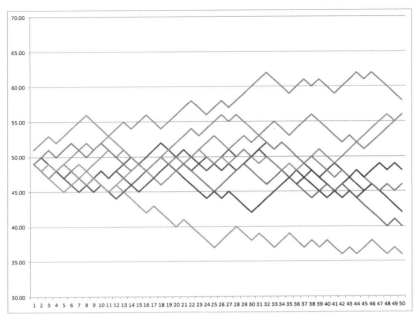

Figure 35.1 *Paths of Series of Accumulated Random Independent Changes*

Each series starts at fifty. By sheer luck, some have more ups than downs and move up, while others with less luck move down. The differences at any time — between the biggest gainers and the worst losers — are not a result of any persisting factor that made the gainers more likely to move up and the losers to move down. If we had asked fifty persons each to draw a series of accumulated sums of the random changes, the person who happened to achieve the highest value at any particular future moment would have displayed no more talent or skill than the worst.

by increases. The expected gain or loss is zero; the current value is an unbiased estimator of the value at any future time. This sort of random, wandering sequence of accumulated values mimics a corporation's common stock price over time, except that:

a. Stock prices are likely to be increased by retained earnings of the firm, making the fan of possible paths slope upward slightly, rather than spread with no upward or downward bias.
b. The spreading of the possible paths of values depends on the riskiness of the stock prices. The extent of the spreading is greater for riskier stocks, but which one will tend to move more can't be predicted.
c. A change in a stock's price, though usually small, can sometimes be so enormous and surprising that it creates a search for some dominant event, when the big change could have been a result of a rare chance alignment of the usually otherwise offsetting causes of changes. Another possibility is herd behavior with people responding to what

other people are doing as a guide to their own actions, which can be sensible. However, the major changes or swings in stock prices may more likely be responses to recoveries from, or onsets of, recessions in the larger economy.

AN EFFICIENT MARKET PORTFOLIO

Unless there is some specifiable future event on which the value of your wealth depends (inflation, pending legislation, war, foreign exchange rate fluctuations, etc.), a popular and sensible procedure appears to be to hold a portfolio that is (a) a random sample of the whole market plus (b) some secure bonds or some borrowing by you plus (c) some money. You must increase the variance if you seek a higher expected mean rate of return. The fractions of your wealth you hold in stocks, money, bonds, and debt to others will depend upon your preference for (a) a higher expected mean rate of return versus (b) a narrower variance. One of the effective ways to do that kind of investing is to buy a share in an investment fund that is a cross-section of the stock markets — usually called a *market-indexed fund*. These market-indexed investment funds are even more attractive when the fund managers promise not to waste money on research futilely trying to select stocks that would do better.

No Profitable Past Patterns of Prices

The *equilibrated financial market* denies a widely held belief that charts of past prices may reveal patterns that can be exploited for profits. That's like trying to find a rule for increasing predictability of heads and tails by looking at past sequences. No rule can profitably predict a series of independently random changes. A few unusually steady winners (and a few such losers) are consistent with sequences of random price changes.

If 1,000 people each toss ten coins, the chances are that about one person will get all heads and one would get all tails. You could not say that one in a thousand lucky persons had displayed skill rather than merely being the luckiest of many people using various systems, all of which can be equally good — worthless. You might as well select a stock at random by throwing a dart at a list of all stocks and bonds.

Growth Stocks Are Not Exceptions to the Principles

Growth stock is the name usually associated with a stock the price of which has tended to rise year after year and is presumed to continue to rise, because of the expectation that its products will be more widely used. The stock price is expected to have a greater than fifty-fifty chance of a rise by more than the interest rate and rate of inflation. But despite that greater than fifty-fifty chance of a gain, the changes in the price of a growth stock have an average of zero. Though the chance of a rise is, say, 90 percent after a fall occurs, the fall is likely to be larger, maybe by more than nine times, than the more frequent smaller increases.

Market Risk, Industry Risk, Firm Risk

Events that affect the stock value of only a particular company are firm-specific risks. The health of the owner or chief administrator is a risk specific to that firm. A risk associated with products of all the firms in one industry is an *industry-specific* risk. Events (e.g., inflation or deflation, interest rate changes, recessions, new taxes, wars) that affect all firms are *market risks*.

The range of effects on one's wealth can be reduced by investing in bonds as well as in stocks — or by holding your wealth in the form of money (which exposes you to the market risk of inflation). Several bonds of the US government are protected from the risk of reduced purchasing power of money caused by inflation. The principal of the bond is adjusted upward periodically by the rate of inflation, but not downward in the event of deflation. Unfortunately, measuring the rate of inflation is ambiguous, because of unresolved disputes about appropriate conceptions of exactly what is meant by *adjusting for inflation*.

SPECIALIZATION AND INTERMEDIATION
IN THE CAPITAL MARKETS

An equilibrated market is facilitated by a variety of specialist intermediaries. Lenders who buy bonds may later decide they want money for some sudden expenditure. In that event, they can sell the bonds. Salability of bonds is sometimes called "negotiability." The ability to sell a resource quickly, cheaply, and at a relatively predictable price is *liquidity*. Bond brokers who maintain inventories of bonds of well-known corporations and governments facilitate liquidity. These dealers rely chiefly on electronic networks for communicating and recording the transactions — a network often called *over the counter*.

Most bond market transactions are resales, rather than new (original) issues. Markets for resale of bonds and stocks are as important as used-car dealers are to new car sellers and buyers, or real estate agents for houses and buildings. Fewer people would buy used cars if cars could not be resold through used-car agencies. Search and transactions cost for both sellers and buyers of houses would be much greater without the services of realtors. Without intermediaries for resale of bonds and securities, the flow of savings to investors would be smaller, less effectively directed, and more expensive.

Stockbrokers

Stock firms (such as Fidelity, Merrill Lynch, and Schwab) can facilitate purchase and sale of stocks and bonds. Details must be specified, arranged, and recorded to ensure the proper transfer of title and payment. Brokers can inform you about common, preferred, and participating preferred stocks, bonds and Treasury bills, the rights and obligations of each, where the markets are, and how to place an order to buy or sell. They give you quicker, cheaper, and more reliable access to the stock and bond markets, collect dividends for you, hold your stocks securely, and maintain your records.

Investment Portfolio Advisors

Investment portfolio advisors can help *diversify* a portfolio effectively and identify securities as effective hedges against some potential obligations you may have, for example, pension investment funds for employees of a corporation. Investment portfolio managers don't know which stocks are likely to do better than others. Instead, they rely on knowledge of the different kinds of securities and how the price movements of those securities are related to each other. They know something about which stocks tend to move together or move in opposite directions. They also know to what future events a stock is more sensitive. That helps them select a portfolio that reduces your exposure to loss from some specified type of risk (war, drought, recession, proposed law, monetary policy changes, and interest rate variations).

Insider Trading and Insider Information

Inside information is news supposed to be secrets known only to a specific group. Usually, it is *inside* for only a brief moment before others learn. The insider trading that is regarded as *undesirable* is trading with inside information at the expense of people for whom that insider is an agent, or trading by one of the insiders before the information is revealed to any outsiders.

A commercial bank's officer often becomes an insider when business borrowers go to the bank for funds. The transfer of private information to the banker creates a tempting opportunity for the banker to sell or buy stock in the borrower's firm. That is usually considered *trading on inside information*, and declared to be illegal as well as being regarded as unethical. To avoid such undue influence of self-interest, bank officers usually are prohibited from owning shares in firms to which loans are made by the bank.

Financial Intermediaries

The stock exchanges facilitate trading of corporation stocks and bonds. Other financial intermediaries (savings and commercial banks) facilitate saving and the making of new productive investments—a key to economic growth. These financial intermediaries reconcile the desires of savers (lenders) and investors (borrowers). If savers want to lend for a short term while borrowers prefer long-term loans, the commercial banks borrow on short-term agreements from savers who provide the funds to the bank. The bank then lends to borrowers on longer-term agreements.

For this to be feasible, the commercial banks and other savings and loan banks must have a reliable flow of short-term lenders or lenders who maintain their deposits. The interest rate obtained by the banks on long-term loans to borrowers are higher than the interest rates paid to the depositors on their short-term deposits. From that spread between the higher interest rate paid by the borrowers and the interest rate to the lenders, the bank's intermediation costs are covered. That spread is much smaller—to the benefit of both the saver and the borrower—than if they themselves had to arrange the transactions.

Financial intermediation is widespread. It occurs between the manufacture of automobiles and the final purchases by consumers. An auto producer's employees and suppliers must be paid at the time they provide their services, rather than wait until the cars are finally sold to consumers. To do that, the auto producers borrow to *finance* the earlier payment of wages and material costs, as well as to tide them over times of low seasonal sales. Also, the auto retailers finance their inventories by borrowing from commercial banks, finance companies, and commercial credit companies—all of which are institutions for collecting and channeling savings from many sources to business firms.

When you buy a car and pay in an installment plan, you borrow from a lender associated with the car retailer. That's typically a bank or finance company. What you borrow is paid directly to the car dealer, who pays most of that to the auto manufacturer. The ultimate suppliers, who finance your installment plan purchase of a car, are ordinary savers whose savings are channeled to you by the financial intermediaries.

QUESTIONS AND MEDITATIONS

1) You decide to play a coin tossing game; you will be given $1 every time the coin comes up heads, and you will lose $1 every time it comes up tails. You start with $100 and get to flip the coin 100 times. If you get 100

heads in a row, you double your money. If you get 100 tails in a row, you
lose all your $100.

   a. Before you start, what is the best prediction of what your wealth will
be after your 100 tosses?

   b. After 50 tosses, you have had more heads than tails, so you now have
$110; what is the best prediction of what your wealth will be after the
next 50 tosses?

Answer:

   a. $100; you should expect to have an equal number of heads and tails.
No matter how many heads or tails you have tossed in a row, it is still
fifty-fifty that the next toss will be heads or tails.

   b. $110; in the final 50 tosses, there is no reason to expect you will either
gain or lose, regardless of the results of the first 50 tosses.

2) You have been following the stock prices of a company you like, and
are trying to decide whether to purchase the stock. You decide to call
different stockbrokers and investment advisors to ask their opinion of
the current price. One half think the price is too high, and one half say it
is too low, and not one says the current price is just right. Does that make
any sense?

Answer:

Yes. A prevailing market price does not mean that a single person on the
planet thinks that price is in any way "correct." The current price always
means that one half of market participants (weighted by amount invested)
think it is too high, and one half think it is too low. New information will
cause some to revise their opinion, and the price will rise or fall.

3) You are interested in buying the stock of either one of two companies.
You look up the history of their respective prices over the past year and
find that one has risen 10 percent, so it is now more expensive than it
would have been a year ago, while the other has fallen 10 percent, so it
is now cheaper to buy than it would have been a year ago. Does this help
you in deciding which stock to buy?

Answer:

The past history of the stock prices is not helpful information; the prevailing price of each stock reflects the collective judgment of market participants about the future of the companies. Buying one stock because "it is
now cheaper" or buying the other because "it rose a lot last year" would not

be valid reasons for choosing between the two. Only new information will cause either stock price to rise or fall from today's price.

4) Your uncle has died, and your aunt has collected his life insurance and asks your advice on investing the money. She wants to buy stock in a company that will give her a very high return, and she does not want to take any risk. What advice do you give her?

Answer:

Patiently and gently, explain that there is an unavoidable trade-off between risk and expected return. It is not possible to find an investment that promises to give her a higher-than-average return and a lower-than-average risk. Her best choice would be investment in a diversified mutual fund of many different companies.

5) The stock exchanges, with the sanction of the US Securities and Exchange Commission, occasionally prohibit (suspend) trading in a certain common stock, especially when some spectacular bad news about that company is heard. For example, if the president of a corporation is sued for fraud by some government agency, with a consequent rush of sell orders by common stockholders, the exchange suspends trading to permit time for the full news to be digested and to prevent wild swings in the price of stock. The defense of the suspension is that it protects some stockholders from selling in panic at the developing, but as yet unsubstantiated and unweighted, news. These sellers could later find the price had recovered — that they had sold at exceptionally low transient prices.

Does that reasoning — as a defense of suspension of trading of the stock — convince you that it would be risky for you to deal in an exchange that could stop trading in stocks you own? Consider the risk that the news will turn out to be accurate and the swing will not be temporary. Consider also the effect on potential buyers who are restrained from buying.

Answer:

Each is to judge what is best for himself. As for us, we would prefer formal exchanges not to shut off trading in particular securities, thereby reducing exchange opportunities. Under a system where suspension can occur, presumption is built up that stock exchange officials are good judges of what price changes are justified or what news ought not to be allowed to affect decisions of individual investors — a presumption which not even the stock exchange officials will defend. The rationale for trade restrictions is that wide price swings resulting from news that turns out to be incomplete or exaggerated are often blamed on the stock market, with the suggestion that stock market officials were responsible or that they ought to have prevented such unjustified (with hindsight) swings. In fact, these major, abrupt price falls are the result of incomplete information, which no one can improve on at the time. Stopping trading during those times locks existing owners into continuing ownership even though they would prefer to shed the uncertainty by selling to others who are more willing to bear it. Bad news is made more damaging for existing holders in that they cannot sell out as early upon the suggestion of worsening conditions.

6) The chapter considers the inescapable trade-off between mean rate of return and variance of price: do not expect to find investments that are both high return and low risk. Is this frustration largely a financial conundrum, or is it a commonly found problem of evaluation and choice in other aspects of living?

Answer:

There are myriad circumstances in which one must compare competing virtues and criteria, and decide which is preferable. The dessert is to die for — and the massive number of calories will contribute to early demise. She is gorgeous, but would she be a great mother for the children I hope to have? He is a hunk, but wants to lie on the beach while I prefer mountain hiking. It goes from 0 to 60 in five seconds — and gets only 8 miles per gallon. You are inspired by medieval poetry — but how many employers are interested in a graduate with a major in that field? You are the general manager of a baseball team who can acquire either a slugger who is likely to hit 35 home runs but strike out 200 times — or a nonsteroid type who may hit only .260 but will steal 40 bases in a season.

CHAPTER 36

DETERMINANTS OF THE INTEREST RATE

Changes in the interest rate will alter accumulated wealth in ways that can be surprising and undesirable. This chapter explains how the interest rate is the price of *current income obtained in exchange for future income*. We'll be puncturing the popular myth that the demand and supply for money determine the interest rate.

DEMAND FOR MORE CURRENT INCOME
RELATIVE TO FUTURE INCOME

You want to buy things now and pay for them later. You'll borrow rights to current income and pay with claims to future income. We say *rights* because money is recognized as a reliable way to obtain (*claim*) goods and services. Borrowing means obtaining *now* rights to income in return for promising to pay the seller (lender) rights to income in the *future*.

THE PRICE OF CURRENT INCOME: THE RATE OF INTEREST

One difference between a loan and a normal rental of some nonmoney good is the way the price is expressed, measured, and paid. On a loan, the price is expressed as a percentage, such as 10 percent per month, while on a nonmoney good the price is expressed in dollars per month. The price of a dollar of current income with payment a year later is expressed as the *percentage* future (one year) amount of income paid in *excess* of the current amount obtained now. But if you borrow (rent) a house, the rental payment is not expressed as a percentage of the value of the house. Instead, it's expressed as a definite number of dollars paid each month.

That doesn't explain why the price paid in the future is greater than the amount paid now. Why is the future payment for borrowing current income larger than the amount borrowed now? Two reasons are usually cited: (1) productivity of investing current income and (2) compensation to the lender or investor for deferring consumption to a later time.

Productivity of Investment of Current Income

Our innovative ancestors discovered how to save and invest income to obtain even more income later. Saving, by itself, would merely delay use. Investing the saving can result in more than was saved. A pipeline is constructed to avoid

carrying water in a bucket. The pipeline will move more water than was forgone by taking time away from carrying buckets in order to build the pipeline.

The construction of a concrete building requires an initial investment,
which means that someone diverts some current income (goes without consumption now) in order to invest in the building. The future services of the
building are expected to exceed the earlier savings, the forgone consumption.
Though the future yield of an investment may be *measured* as if it were in the
same kind of services that are invested now, it's likely to be in a different, more
desirable form of income.

People learned how to convert grain into beer, grapes into raisins and wine,
milk into cheese, olives into olive oil. Those productive investments yield future
goods worth more than the worth of what was forgone. That improved quality
or condition of the resource is a yield, though the physical form is different.
People will be willing to pay a premium (interest) to get more current resources
to invest for future increased income. It's profitable if the future increased production exceeds the current investment by the rate of interest.

Parents are major investors. They and you are investing in education. You
expect to create more future income than is currently saved. That's an investment in creating *human capital* as surely as constructing buildings, machinery,
or a business.

Though you may not know of prospective profitable investments, people
who do will compete to borrow your income to make the investment. Or if
you know (or believe you know) of prospective profitable investments and if
some other people share your confidence, they will compete to lend to you.
Your knowledge will be salable. Initially, we'll presume the investment is a sure
thing. Later, we'll allow for *uncertainty*.

As for all goods, the demand for more current income is negatively sloped
with respect to the price paid. Larger amounts of current income are demanded
at lower rates of interest, for two reasons. One is that at lower rates of interest,
the interest payments on debt are smaller. So borrowing against future income
is more attractive. There is a more important reason that has a widespread effect on all resources. Their increased profitability is caused by a fundamental
process of *capital pricing*— remember how the value of a tree and optimal time
to cut it was a function of both the growth of the tree and the interest rate to
discount its future value.

Time Preference

A second reason for being willing to pay a premium to the lender, even if the
borrowed income is for just more current consumption, has been labeled
time preference. But it's not a result *only* of preference to have something earlier

rather than later. It's a preference also to have something *for sure now* rather than merely expecting it later, when it might not happen. Rather than calling that reason time preference or shortsightedness or impatience, it could be called *certainty preference*. Future receipts are not *sure* things. Even if the future repayment is made, there was always the possibility you might not have survived to that time. *Having* it now rather than *expecting* to get it later is a real difference.

WHETHER FOR CONSUMPTION OR INVESTMENT IS NOT PERTINENT

Because of both net productivity and uncertainty about the future, people demand a premium when lending and offer a premium when borrowing. Whether the current income demanded is for profitable investment or riotous current consumption is irrelevant in determining the interest rate. Indeed, it's often difficult to distinguish between consumption and investment.

Couldn't we consider expenditure for medical bills and health care as an investment in one's body? And is a college education investment or consumption? Might a vacation be an investment in maintaining or restoring one's future personal productivity or in memories that are valuable? If a community spends for roads, schools, and research, should that be called investment or consumption? The US government's measure of investment excludes such expenditures, calling them consumption. In Japan, education is counted as investment.

THE SUPPLY OF CURRENT RELATIVE TO FUTURE INCOME

The supply of current income in exchange for future income is provided in several ways. (1) One person can obtain more current income by borrowing from someone else. (2) A second method is to own shorter-lived resources that pay more of the income immediately rather than later, such as annual plants rather than perennials, tar-covered instead of concrete driveways, wood instead of cement block fences. (3) A third is by more rapidly consuming existing resources to get more of the services sooner rather than later.

The first two arrangements for more current income are by market exchanges from one person to another of current and future income. They do not alter current income, but the third increases consumption now and leaves less for the future. Of these arrangements, the easiest to measure is the first, the market for new loans of current income and for existing bonds. However, they all establish the interest rate through their effect on the demand for current income power relative to future incomes.

BORROWING IS SELLING FUTURE INCOME; LENDING IS BUYING FUTURE INCOME

In the financial markets, what is being traded or exchanged are rights to current and to future income. A borrower sells a bond to a lender. An increased *supply* of bonds is an increased *demand* for current income relative to future income. The demander of current income — the borrower — supplies a bond, which is a promise to repay in the future.

THE MARKETS FOR CURRENT INCOME RELATIVE TO FUTURE INCOME

Lending and Borrowing

Competition in the loan (bond) market is represented, in figure 36.1, by familiar demand and supply curves. The demand curve represents the demand for more dollars now, obtained by borrowing money to spend for goods. The supply curve represents the supply of dollars now.

The horizontal axis measures the dollar value of the rights to current consumption being transferred. The price, on the vertical scale, is the rate of interest — the percentage excess of future income paid per dollar of current

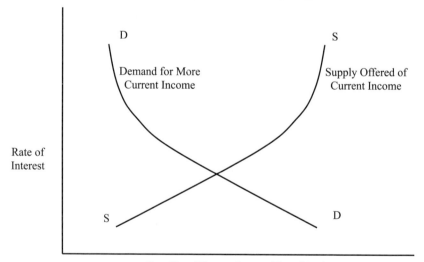

Quantity of Current Income Transferred

Figure 36.1 *Income Transfers of Loanable Current Income (in "Loanable Funds" Markets)*

The horizontal scale measures current income (claims to consumption) measured in dollars. The vertical scale measures next year's income, as the percentage by which next year's available income would exceed the current income offered. Six percent means that $1.06 of next year's income is exchanged for $1 of current income. Competition in demand and supply for current relative to future income (claims to consumption) determines an equilibrating interest rate.

income obtained now. A measure of 6 percent means that $1.06 of one-year-later-income is the price paid next year for $1 of current income. The rate of interest depends on the demand and supply of current income relative to future income, that is, demand for and supply of current consumption in exchange for rights to future consumption.

The amount of current consumption demanded relative to future consumption is smaller at higher rates of interest. From the future consumption side, the amount of future consumption offered in exchange for a current dollar is larger, the higher the interest rate. The market clearing interest rate is the rate at which competition among borrowers and among lenders equates the amounts demanded and supplied. As with other goods, changes in the price (market rate of interest) permit achievement of more of the mutually desired transfers of rights to current from future claims to consumption.

Adjustments of Prices of Short- Relative to Long-Lived Bonds

Another activity included in the market for current relative to future income is the buying and selling of bonds issued sometime in the past and still outstanding, that is, before they reach maturity and are paid and retired. Changes in the interest rate are observed as changes in the prices of longer- relative to shorter-lived bonds. One way to get more current relative to future income is to own shorter-lived rather than longer-lived bonds. You will get your returns earlier. An increased demand for shorter-term bonds raises their prices relative to prices of longer-term bonds.

In table 36.1, the times to maturity of the bonds run through 1, 5, 10, and 20 years. Each pays $50 a year in interest, a 5 percent explicit interest rate on the bond's principal amount due, $1,000. Each column shows the bond prices that would exist at that column's market rate of interest. The prices of longer-term bonds change by larger proportions than do the prices of shorter-term bonds,

Table 36.1 *Present Values of Fixed-Coupon, $1,000 Principal Bonds at Alternative Market Rates of Interest, Alternative Maturities*

Life of Bond	Coupon	Market Rates of Interest			
		3%	5%	7%	10%
1 Year	5%	$1,019	$1,000	$987	$956
5 Years	5%	$1,089	$1,000	$915	$810
10 Years	5%	$1,167	$1,000	$861	$698
20 Years	5%	$1,294	$1,000	$790	$576

when the interest rate changes. This is seen by comparing the prices in any one of the columns of values for a given interest rate.

A change in the rate of interest from 5 percent to 10 percent is the same thing as a reduction in the price of a one-year bond paying a specified rate of 5 percent from $1,000 down to $956. A 20-year-to-maturity bond paying a 5 percent coupon rate moves more—from $1,000 to $576. Competition to get a higher-yielding bond at the current prices would drive up its price to where the percentage yield would be no greater than on any other bond.

An increased demand for current relative to future income would imply a price structure more like the prices in the last column (10 percent), with shorter-lived bonds being priced higher relative to longer-term bonds than at a lower market interest rate. A reduced demand for current (relative to future) income would reduce prices of shorter-term bonds relative to the prices of longer-term bonds. The pattern of prices would be like that in the column for 3 percent.

This entire table illustrates the proposition that the interest rate is determined by the relative *prices* of longer- and shorter-lived resources, which is determined by the demand for current relative to future income. It's misleading to say long-term bond prices fell relative to prices of short-term bonds *because* the rate of interest rose. Both the prices and the yields to investors are responses to the same change in demand for current relative to future income. (*See shaded item on p. 578 to explain data in table.*)

ADJUSTMENTS IN PRICES OF RESOURCES

Analysis, Not Predictions

We have not inquired why the demand for current relative to future income shifted. We explained only how that shift would change the rate of interest and how the relative prices of resources would change. The analysis is applicable whether the change in demand was caused by an increased desire to consume more now rather than later, or because people expected to die earlier, or people thought they had found more profitable ways to invest current income. But, as warned earlier, there are two effects. One is the initiating event (which economists often call the *exogenous* event); the other is the responsive price change and its effects (the *endogenous* effects).

It is ill-advised to try to deduce the effects of a change in a price or the market rate of interest (the endogenous effect) without identifying what was the prior initiating (exogenous) event. The interest rate change is a result—an adjustment to a new set of demands or supplies of current relative to future income. And there's always the question of whether the change in the interest rate was a change in some add-on in the package called the nominal interest or a change in the pure rate. We'll not often know the answer.

THE MONEY SUPPLY AND THE INTEREST RATE

"Interest rates would be lower if the quantity of money were larger." This is a common error in the news media and even in high levels of the banking and political community. It is based on a misconception that interest is the "price of money," which suggests the interest rate is the price you pay to get more money. However, you can get more money in two ways, as with any other good: You can (a) buy the money or (b) borrow it. In the following discussion, keep an eye on the distinction between the *purchase* price and the price of *borrowing* money, usually called the rental price when borrowing anything except money.

THE LANGUAGE OF BUYING AND SELLING MONEY — INSTEAD OF LENDING AND BORROWING INCOME

We have seen that you can be said to *buy* money by selling your tennis racket, or old clothes, or your labor by working for *wages* paid in money. But we normally don't think of selling a good as *buying money*. When a grocer sells Cokes for $.50, the price to that grocer for *buying* a dollar is 2 Cokes. Our normal language says the *goods* are bought and sold, not the money, but the money *is sold* and bought in exchange for the goods.

LENDING, BORROWING, OR RENTING?

There is similar conventional language in whether it's called *renting* or *borrowing* or *lending*. In most social affairs, borrowing often means a loan with no expectation of a rent paid by the borrower. After you have used your neighbor's wheelbarrow, you return it and say thanks. (And there's no expectation of interest on a delay in payment for a rented/borrowed item.) But *borrow* in the business world implies an expected reward or compensation, called *rent* if the borrowed item is some good or *interest* if money is borrowed. However, more accurately, rent is the payment for services of borrowed goods. When you rent a car or an apartment, you rarely say you borrowed a car or an apartment, although you really do. But if you obtain some money and promise to repay, you never say you have rented some money, though you have.

A borrower of money sells a promissory note or a bond. When you lend me $100 and I hand you a written promise to repay you $100 (plus interest), you are said to have *bought* my promissory note, which I *sold* to you. A lender then is called a buyer of bonds or of promissory notes, and the borrower is their seller.

BOND YIELDS AND PRICES

Unlike interest rates on bank deposits, market interest rates are not *set* by anyone. The interest you earn on a certificate of deposit in a bank is "posted" by the bank and you can accept it or not. If you have $10,000 in your account and the bank announces they are raising the interest rate you will earn, you still have your $10,000.

The same is not true of the market yield on a bond traded in security markets. The initial issuer of a typical bond will set a "coupon" amount to be paid at regular intervals to the bondholder. The actual yield earned by the bondholder will depend on the actual price paid for the bond; that price is determined by supply and demand in the secondary market for such bonds.

There are two components to the actual interest rate earned by the bondholder—the present value of the stream of coupon payments received over the life of the bond plus the present value of the return of the face value of the bond when it matures. In table 36.1, all the bonds carry a 5 percent coupon, meaning that a bond with a principal or "face" value of $1,000 will pay to the holder $50 every year for the life of the bond.

If the bond has ten years to maturity and is trading in the market for $861 we use tables in earlier chapters to confirm that a bondholder would earn a yield of 7 percent. From table 30.2 we see that the present value of $1,000 to be received ten years in the future is $510 today. From table 31.1 we see that a stream of $50 received at the end of every year for ten years is worth $351 today. The buyer of the bond is acquiring the combined present values of the stream of coupon payments and the eventual return of principal, both of which are fixed. Because the price of the bond fluctuates in the market, the yield to the bond buyer must vary inversely with the price paid. That is, falling bond prices mean higher yields to new buyers, and rising bond prices mean lower yields to new buyers.

WHEN IS THE RENT PAID?

If you rent a house and pay the rent at the end of the month, you are paying for three things: (a) the wear and tear on the house, (b) the services of the house during the month, and (c) interest for the month's delay in payment. If you pay the rent at the end of the month, instead of the first of the month, you face a higher rent. One month's interest on a $1,000 monthly rent with the nominal interest rate of 12 percent is about $5 (the delay is an average of 15 days in a 30-day month).

CHANGING THE SUPPLY OF MONEY TO
AFFECT THE RATE OF INTEREST

Consider how the method of changing the supply of money can affect the rate of interest. More money in the economy means the purchasing power of a dollar will be lower. More dollars are chasing the same amount of goods. The price level will be higher. Each dollar will be worth less, but the interest rate will not be lower. More money and a higher price level don't change the relative supply of current to future income, nor the worth of current income relative to future income. The percentage premium (interest rate) paid later for the dollar amount borrowed now does not depend on the amount of money in the economy. But the *method* of increasing the quantity of money held by the public can affect the rate of interest.

INCREASING THE MONEY SUPPLY RANDOMLY

As a method of increasing the money supply, *new* money may be sprinkled from helicopters. The social supply of money is now larger than the desired *proportion* of money relative to the wealth and income of the public. The public doesn't necessarily *immediately* spend the excess amount of money. Initially, they lend it to a bank (a deposit) or buy existing short-term interest-bearing notes and bonds. The market implied interest rate on very short-term loans falls as the new money is used to buy those securities. But when people have decided what goods they want to buy with the added money, they start to sell the notes. The reduced demand for the short-term securities and their fall in prices raises the interest rate to the former level. After the initial increased demand for short-term bonds is reversed, the interest rate on short-term bonds rises back to its former level despite the now larger amount of money held by the public. The lasting effect is a *higher price level*, not a change in the interest rate.

INCREASING THE MONEY SUPPLY BY PURCHASING BONDS

There remains a way in which a different *method* of changing the quantity of money can change the pure interest rate. This effect is a result of what the central bank first buys with its newly created money, instead of randomly distributing it. A central bank can issue more money by first using that money to buy bonds, primarily government bonds, notes, and bills. This increased demand for bonds raises their price, so the stated interest paid on the bonds becomes a smaller percentage of their higher market prices, lowering the market rate of interest on those bonds.

This lower market rate would not be an effect of more money, but stems from what the new money is first spent on by the central bank. The price level would rise as the increased amount of money later is spent for purchases of all goods. A rising price level will cause people to anticipate further rises, so lenders of money will demand (and borrowers of money will pay) an "inflation premium" in the add-ons in market interest rates. This phenomenon will be discussed further in chapter 42.

QUESTIONS AND MEDITATIONS

1) Drying grapes to convert them to raisins is investing. Why is this investing, since it merely changes one form of consumption good to another form?

Answer:

It permits more future consumption at the cost of less current consumption. But consider carefully what is meant by "more" and "less." One grape makes only one raisin, and drying the grapes removes water, so 100 raisins weigh less than 100 grapes. But in economics, more refers to value or worth to the consumers — not a physical amount of something.

2) Instead of playing computer games, a man works around the house painting and refinishing the walls. Explain why this is a form of investment.

Answer:

Current consumption (leisure, watching TV) or some alternative, less-valued investment activity (reading an economics textbook, picking stocks to purchase) is forsaken for future income from the preserved house.

3) By giving up $100 of present income for $105 of consumption rights available in one year, a person gets what rate of interest?

Answer:

5 percent.

4) "Roundabout, more capitalistic methods of production are always more productive than direct methods using less capital equipment. Therefore, any country that wants to develop should start increasing the amount of capital goods it has." Evaluate.

Answer:

Not all roundabout, capitalistic methods are more productive. But many forms are. The right forms of capital-goods accumulation, used in appropriate amounts with other inputs, will enhance wealth in the future.

5) Goods differ in their yield of consumption services, or in their "durability." Pine lumber naturally deteriorates more rapidly than redwood. If demand for future consumption rights should rise relative to present consumption rights, would pine or redwood experience the greater rise in present price? Show why this is expressible as a fall in the rate of interest. (Hint: The interest rate is the exchange rate between present and future consumption rights.)

Answer:

Redwood. A fall in interest rate is a rise in the value of long-lived goods relative to short-lived goods. At lower interest rates (or discount rates) the present value of something in the distant future is greater than it would be with higher interest rates.

6) Changes in the rate of interest are detectable in the changes in the structure of relative prices of various types of goods.
    a. If the price of raisins (relative to grapes), of prunes (relative to plums), of whiskey (relative to corn), of cider (relative to apples) should rise, would that mean a change in the rate of interest? In what direction?
    b. What effect would that have on the profitability of producing raisins, prunes, whiskey, and so on?
    c. Ultimately, what effect would the revised production have on the relative values (for example, of raisins and grapes)? What effect would that have on the rate of interest?

Answer:

    a. Yes. A fall in the rate of interest.
    b. Increase the profitability.
    c. Reduce the ratio of the price of raisins to grapes. Raise the rate of interest.

7) As we have seen, the demand curve for investment is negatively sloped with respect to the rate of interest — that is, at higher rates, investment will be less profitable. Why is this implied by the earlier propositions on behavior of costs?

Answer:

> A higher rate of investment means a higher rate of production of some goods which involves using existing resources more intensively or for longer intervals and hiring more less-productive (higher marginal cost) resources. This implies a higher cost per unit of those goods.

8) "If savings is defined as an increase in wealth and if investment is defined as an increase in wealth, then savings by definition is always equal to investment; for it is merely the same thing looked at from the point of view of two different people." Since this statement is correct, how is it possible to speak of equilibrating the rate of investment and the rate of savings?

Answer:

> Investment is defined as that rate of conversion of present income to wealth which can be profitable. That rate is related to the rate of interest in the investment-demand function. Saving is defined as the rate of conversion of present income to wealth that the community wants to engage in. The rate at which the community is *willing* to divert income from current income to wealth accumulation is a function of the rate of interest (among other things), and this relationship between the savings rate and rate of interest is the supply-of-savings function.
>
> Note, though, that the *intention to invest* does not mean that a project will be successful. Wealth increases only as a result of positive-value-added investment activity. Economists use the term "malinvestment" to refer to negative-value-added investment activity. That is, if the project incurs losses and must ultimately be abandoned and written off, it was consumption activity (destruction of wealth) in spite of the best hopes and intentions.

9) "The most important fact about saving and investment is that they are done by different people and for different reasons."
   a. Is that why savings must be equilibrated to investment via a demand for investment and a supply for savings function?
   b. Suppose that everyone who invested had to do his own saving and could not lend or borrow or buy capital goods from other people. Would that destroy the principles of demand-and-supply analysis for growth of wealth?

Answer:

> a. The distinction between saving and investment is not that they are done by different people; some do both, although the bulk is done by differ-

ent people, and that is why we need markets to coordinate saving and investment. Saving is the rate at which people are willing to divert some of current income from current consumption to future wealth or capital accumulation. Investment is the maximum rate at which people think they can convert current income to wealth accumulation at different net rates of return. It's the rate of interest that coordinates the two — more is saved at higher interest rates, while quantity demanded for investment is less at higher rates. An equilibrium occurs at an interest rate where saving and investment are equal.

b. No, the principles remain unchanged. What would be different is the potential gains from exchange.

10) "The rate of interest helps to equilibrate investing and savings, and the demand for borrowing and the supply of savings; it is the relative price of current consumption rights over future consumption rights; it is the price of money; and it equates the demand and supply of assets." Explain how it is all these things at once.

Answer:

"Interest rate" is associated with several different concepts. First is the net rate of increase in wealth from a dollar more of investment, or the net productivity of investment. Second is a personal, subjective valuation of present consumption rights, measured in terms of the amount of future income that is valued as equivalent to one dollar of consumption now. Third is a market rate of return on loans — called *a rate of interest on credit* — on bonds or promissory notes. If this third rate is greater than the second, people will reduce present consumption (save more). If the second is less than the first, investment will increase. Fourth is an interest rate that is implicit in the relationship between present prices of capital goods and their future income streams. All these rates — (1) the net productivity of investment, (2) personal valuation of future income relative to current consumption, (3) return on bonds or loans, and (4) the interest rate implicit in relative prices of capital goods — are brought toward equality by switching activity among the various markets and goods. When all are equal, the common value is the interest rate. If any are not equal, then arbitrage (the simultaneous buying and selling of the same thing by the same person) will induce adjustments of profit prospects in the various markets, pushing them all toward equality. Since the most easily perceived and measured rate is the rate in the market for *secure bonds*, we usually look at the rate in that market to measure the interest rate. This explains why the interest rate is referred to variously as the price of "current consumption," the price of "credit," the price of "savings," the price of "loans," the "rate of time preference," the "net rate of investment productivity," and the "price of money." Properly interpreted, it is a measure of all these things in equilibrium.

11) Suppose you must consume only from current wealth, which is $100,000 (consumption occurs at year end, and no other source of income).
   a. If the interest rate is zero, what is the income (amount you consume) available in each of the next two years?
   b. If the interest rate is 10 percent, and you must consume only from wealth for an indefinitely long period, what is the maximum annual maintainable rate of consumption?

Answer:
   a. $50,000 per year.
   b. $10,000.

12) You are a visitor in some underdeveloped country in which all lending and borrowing are effectively prohibited.
   a. Is there a rate of interest?
   b. If so, where could you get data to compute it?
   c. How could you tell when it changes?

Answer:
   a. Yes.
   b. Relative prices of capital goods and earnings.
   c. Changed price of capital goods relative to current consumption goods; prices of capital goods relative to earnings.

13) "Large corporations have so much of their own funds that they do not have to borrow in the capital funds markets in order to make new investments. They are therefore immune to interest rates in the capital markets." Explain the error in that analysis.

Answer:

Corporation managers do not have to invest all funds within the corporation. They can invest in other companies; they can lend the money to others. So long as they consider possible alternative investments, they will use funds within the firm only if that looks more profitable, as would be the case if the funds were to be borrowed from the market.

14) For a long time, many states had restrictions on the rate of interest that could be contracted for in the absence of special authorization for higher

rates. During high inflation (and therefore high market interest rates), such state-mandated interest ceilings were below market-determined interest rates. Loans to corporations were generally exempt. Who was helped and who was hurt by these laws if they were effective?

Answer:

Among those hurt were people whose credit was so poor that they were unable to borrow at the low rates. Among those helped were the better-credit borrowers, since some funds that would have gone to high-risk borrowers were now diverted to the safer borrowers with a consequent lower interest rate to them; corporations were benefited.

15) Interest rate ceilings have sometimes restricted veterans from obtaining home mortgages. Here is one of the devices used to circumvent the ceilings: You propose to buy a house for $200,000. You have $30,000 in cash now, so you seek to borrow $170,000 from a lender at a 5 percent rate of interest. (The law will guarantee your loan so long as the lender does not get over 5 percent.) Unfortunately, no one will lend to you at that rate, because a yield of 6 percent is available to lenders elsewhere. But you are clever enough to find a lender who will lend to you at 5 percent, *after* you make the following proposal: If he will lend to you $170,000 at 5 percent (1 percent less than the 6 percent rate he could get elsewhere — and thereby costs him $1,700 a year interest otherwise available, that is, 1 percent of $170,000 is $1,700 per year), you will buy from him insurance on the house, your car, and your life. You may or may not realize that you could have bought the same insurance at a lower rate elsewhere.
a. Why do you make this agreement with him?
b. Is he being unfair or unscrupulous or unethical? Are you?
c. Who is aided or hurt if such tie-in agreements are prohibited?
d. Do you think tie-ins to get around price ceilings can be effectively and totally prohibited by laws? Why?

Answer:
a. To evade the 5% interest limit in order to get the guarantee.
b. Is this economic analysis or name-calling?
c. The veteran is precluded from getting a loan.
d. No. Tie-in sales are literally impossible to prohibit completely. (Once upon a time, a man rented his house, under rent control, at the legal maximum rent to the renter who had offered to buy his ailing cat for $1,000.)

CHAPTER 37

FUTURES MARKETS

Don't be surprised if you hear an aspiring politician or financial regulator say something like, "Futures contracts are speculative contracts for gambling on the price of commodities, like wheat, oats, corn, cotton, beef, and pork. Speculators destabilize those prices, driving them up or depressing them and causing producers to bear higher risks. That ultimately raises costs to consumers." Don't believe that: In futures markets risks are in fact reduced. In this chapter we'll first identify the kinds of *current* risks against which *futures* contracts provide protections.

The present owner of large amounts of wheat wants to avoid uncertainty about the price of wheat at the time it is to be sold for processing into consumption goods. Similarly, someone will now buy wheat for future delivery to reduce the risk of a rise in the price of wheat in that interval. Or a German who agrees to pay an American film producer some of the proceeds from exhibition next year of an American film in Germany will then have to pay European euros to get US dollars. To avoid the risk of a rise in the price paid in euros to get dollars, the German can now buy a futures contract for dollars to be obtained at the time dollars are to be paid.

And futures markets provide a social service. No central planning agency decides how much wheat, or other commodities, to save from month to month for consumption before the next harvest. Somehow the crops and supplies of goods are consumed at a rate that ensures smoothed consumption from harvest to harvest. Futures markets (1) provide a way of allocating and bearing the uninsurable risks of changes in market prices over time and (2) smooth consumption of goods between harvests, reducing the risks of wild gyrations in the prices of the available supply from moment to moment.

CONTROL AND SMOOTHING OF
CONSUMPTION BETWEEN HARVESTS

Farmers sell harvested wheat to specialists who store the wheat in grain elevators. Elevator operators earn income by providing efficient storage — not by speculating on what the price of wheat will be in the future. They want to *avoid the risks* of price changes while the wheat is stored. So they could immediately sell the wheat for future delivery to millers who will then mill the wheat into flour to be sold to bakers. But that would then put the millers at risk if the wheat price were to fall before they sell to bakers. No matter who owns the wheat, there's a risk of changes in its value.

Suppose the millers own the wheat. What's the price they paid? It's the price at which no profit or loss will be expected (on average) from future changes in the price. If the present price were lower than the expected future price, a profit would be anticipated; if it were higher than the expected price in the future, a loss would be anticipated. Competition for profits would drive the price toward the zero-profit-expectation price — the price expected to prevail in the future. Expectations about prices in the future control the present price.

The *current* price of wheat will necessarily depend on the expected *future* price, which, in turn, depends on (1) how rapidly the current stocks of wheat are being consumed and (2) how much will be left for consumption until the next harvest. The competition for profits drives the price toward constancy; otherwise, profits or losses would be in prospect. But that price, if it's to be relatively constant, must be one that results in a rate of consumption that will exhaust the stockpile at the time of the next harvest.

If the price in the interval from harvest to baking were higher, consumption would be smaller and too much would be conserved. If the price were lower, too much would be consumed too quickly, and the supply would be depleted before the next harvest. The competitive search for profits from price changes of wheat *between harvests* drives the price toward that at which the rate of consumption exhausts the stockpiles just at the time of the new harvest.

The first point is that this process of determining the rate of use of the wheat is aided by *contracts in futures markets*. They do so because the prices of contracts in futures markets for wheat reflect predictions of the price that will prevail in the future. Second, the undesired consequences of unpredictable changes in the price of wheat are avoided by use of futures contracts. For farmers, grain-elevator operators, millers, and bakers, the contracts in a futures market are effective ways to *hedge* against the consequences of those price changes. This chapter concentrates on how futures contracts provide predictions of the future price and also serve as hedges against changes in the market price.

HEDGES

A hedge is an arrangement whereby a future unpredictable and unfortunate event is automatically made to result in a favorable effect as an offset. It is like betting heads with one person while simultaneously betting tails with another person on the same toss of a coin.

WHAT IS A FUTURES CONTRACT?

A futures contract is an agreement in which the buyer of the contract agrees to pay the seller of the contract a *specified price* at a specified future *time* for a specified *amount* of some good, say, wheat, to be delivered at that future time. A baker of bread can know now how much he will have to pay for a certain amount of next year's wheat crop.

EXAMPLE OF HEDGING AGAINST CHANGES
IN THE PRICE OF WHEAT

The Contract's Buyer: A Miller of Wheat into Flour

Mr. Miller is a miller of wheat into flour. He promises in January to deliver flour in six months to bakers at a prespecified price, $12 per bag, based in part on the raw materials cost of $10 a bushel for wheat (assume a bushel of wheat yields a bag of flour), plus the costs of milling, transportation, and so on. If Mr. Miller waits until July to buy wheat, the price may rise above $10, which would result in a loss. If the price of wheat fell, Mr. Miller would gain with the lower cost. Since Mr. Miller is in business to earn income by efficient milling — not by relying on lucky changes in the price of wheat — he uses a *futures contract* to avoid the risks of changes in the price of wheat.

Mr. Miller, who does not currently have any wheat, could in January buy a *July wheat futures contract* from the Chicago Board of Trade. He has bought an *option* to receive wheat in July upon payment in July of the agreed price, say, $10 a bushel, or $100,000 for 10,000 bushels. It's an option because Miller doesn't have to buy the wheat. He can let the futures contract expire. Buying a *futures contract* is an advance agreement on a prespecified price of wheat — not requiring the purchase to be made, but requiring the seller to deliver if the option buyer demands. If the market price falls below the specified price, the option to buy at the specified price loses value, and may not be worth exercising.

If the Market Price of Wheat Rises

Suppose the market price of wheat rises to $11 by July. Mr. Miller will lose on the initial flour contracts which he had made with bakers to deliver flour at the $12 prespecified price of flour (based on a $10 price for wheat). That rise in the price of wheat from $10 to $11 would result in a loss to Mr. Miller of $10,000 on 10,000 bushels. However, the futures contract comes to his rescue. He will gain on the futures contract, which will provide the wheat at $10.

If the Market Price of Wheat Falls

A fall in the price of wheat from $10 to $9 would result in a gain to Mr. Miller of $10,000. On the futures contract, which stipulated a price of $10, there would be a $10,000 loss if he exercised the contract. So he opts out of the contract, letting it expire.

The purpose of the futures contract was to protect Mr. Miller against an increase in the price of wheat until July. The cost of the futures contract was a form of insurance; like the cost of fire insurance on his buildings, it is a cost of doing business and he does not regret spending the money because his buildings did not burn down.

THE SELLER OF THE FUTURES CONTRACT

A person who stores wheat—the grain-elevator operator—also bears risks of changes in the price of the stored wheat. When the market price rises, the holder of wheat inventories gains, but loses when it falls. He will sell July wheat futures contracts, thereby becoming obligated to deliver wheat in July at the prespecified price to the *buyer* of the July wheat futures contract.

The contracted commitment of the operator to supply wheat in the future at a price stipulated now precludes the operator from benefiting from a rise in the price of his inventory. But the contracted price protects him from a fall in the price of his holdings.

The purpose of futures contracts is to hedge against risks of changes in the market price. From farmers to bakers of bread, it is worth it to give up the chance of gains from some price fluctuations in order to avoid the potential for losses arising from other fluctuations. For them, futures contracts *reduce* risk, and allow them to focus on making money in their primary business.

STRUCTURE OF FUTURES CONTRACTS
AND INTERMEDIARIES

A large wheat *holder* would have to sell wheat futures contracts to many millers, and that would involve many detailed problems of contract arrangements and enforcement. Similarly, the millers would have to enter into contracts with many bakers. Boards of trade are intermediaries who arrange and enforce the contracts. Three parties are involved in every purchase or sale of a futures contract—a seller, a buyer, and an intermediary with whom both the buyer and seller deal.

A futures contract is only half of the full contract, one half being that between the board of trade and the buyer, and the other between the board of trade and the seller. This intermediary (the board) is responsible for full performance of the futures contracts.

GAMBLERS IN FUTURES CONTRACT MARKETS?

Farmers, grain-elevator operators, millers, and bakers are not gamblers who enter into futures contracts for the sake of speculating by predicting prices of the future. They don't buy or sell futures contracts because they hope to gain, but because they want to avoid loss. Both the buyer of the futures contracts and the seller were seeking to reduce a business risk they were unwilling to bear. In futures markets, the exposure to one risk is created in order to offset an exposure to another opposite direction risk, thereby forming a *hedge*.

EXAMPLE OF A FOREIGN EXCHANGE FUTURES CONTRACT

Consider the futures market for foreign exchange. A US purchaser of automobiles from Japan must pay Japanese yen, and will, we assume, pay later, say, in three months. When ordering the cars, if the exchange rate is 100 yen for one dollar (cost of 1 cent per yen), then a car priced at 1,000,000 yen would have a dollar equivalent price of $10,000 (= 1,000,000 yen/100). But three months in the future, when the auto is to be delivered, suppose the exchange rate has changed to only 90 yen per dollar, equal to 1.111 . . . cents per yen. It would then cost the US importer $11,111 (= 1,000,000 yen/90) to pay the Japanese manufacturer. The fall in the foreign exchange value of the dollar (fewer yen per dollar, or more dollars per yen) raises the costs to the US purchaser.

On the other hand, the yen-to-dollar exchange rate might have moved up to 110 yen per dollar. That would require fewer dollars, only $9,091 (= 1,000,000/110) to buy the 1 million yen.

The US auto buyer could avoid the risk of having to pay more dollars for the same number of yen by buying a *3 months yen futures* contract from the foreign exchange futures market operators. That futures contract gives the American a right to receive yen later at a prespecified price of 100 yen per dollar.

Who would use the Chicago Mercantile Exchange to sell a futures contract for yen? It might be some American apple grower who has agreed to ship apples to Japan for which 3,000,000 yen are to be received 3 months later. In the interim, the value of a yen in terms of dollars may change to where each yen is worth less than one cent, or may rise to be worth more, thereby altering how many dollars the apple exporter will actually get in 3 months for the 3,000,000 yen. The US apple dealer wants to avoid that risk.

Both the US apple exporter and the US importer of the cars can be protected from changes in the value of the yen relative to the dollar. The US importer *buys* a futures contract (getting the right to acquire yen at a prespecified price), and the apple exporter *sells* a yen futures contract (getting the right to deliver yen for a prespecified number of US dollars). The US auto importer and the US apple exporter have agreed to exchange dollars and yen with each other through the futures market — even though they don't know one another!

What the US importer of cars would gain by a fall in the market value of yen (fewer dollars per yen) is lost on the purchased futures contract. What the US exporter of apples would lose by a fall in the value of yen is gained on the sold futures contract. Both parties are hedged against changes in the foreign exchange rate. Both parties are Americans, and both used futures contracts to reduce risk, not to gamble. In Japan, the auto seller and the apple importer may be making similar arrangements on the Japanese foreign exchange market.

WHAT DETERMINES THE PRICE OF
THE FUTURES CONTRACT?

The price at which a pair of futures contracts is bought and sold by the Board of Trade is the futures price. As in other markets, it is set by competition among buyers and sellers. If an offered future price of wheat is higher than expectations of what the market (cash or spot) price will be at that time, more people will seek to sell such futures contracts. That would drive down the contract price. The reverse would happen if the proposed offer were lower. As a result of the search and competition for profits by buying low and selling high, the futures contract price will be driven toward the price expected to prevail at the contract's later ultimate delivery date. Competition for *expected* profits wipes out *expectations* of profits.

PREDICTOR OF THE PRICE IN THE FUTURE

The price in the futures contract is a predictor of what the price of the good will be at the delivery date — else a profit prospect would remain. If the price in a futures contract were persistently lower than the future *realized* price, profits could be made by buying wheat in futures contracts at the *too low* price. But, of course, if this were known, the price would be driven up, and there would be no expected profit or loss in buying or selling futures contracts. They would be useful only for hedging.

Observed futures prices may be wrong every time, but on average they are correct, in the sense that the average of the prices in those futures contracts will approximate the average of the realized prices. The plus and the minus errors will average out to zero. The price in futures contracts is the best estimate or predictor of the market price in the future. That leaves no sure profits by dealing in futures contracts as a speculator.

VARIETY OF FUTURES MARKETS

Financial Instruments

Several futures markets exist for a great variety of commodities and currencies. Futures contracts for financial instruments, such as bonds and stocks, are expressed in slightly different forms. In one form of contract, called a *put*, a buyer purchases the *option* of later requiring the seller to buy a specified security at the initially agreed-upon price — the *strike price*. There also are *calls*, whereby the buyer of the call obtains the right to buy a share of common stock of a specified corporation from the other party during some specified future interval at a pre-specified price — the strike price. Investors who hold the stocks or bonds and want to hedge the risk of big rises or falls in the value of those holdings can do so with puts and calls.

Put: You own some XYZ stock, and you buy for $10 a one-month option to put a share at the strike price of $110, the current price of one share. A put gives you the right to force the seller to buy a share of XYZ from you at $110, no matter how low its price falls during the life of the put. If the price fell to $100, then you would have recovered your $10 cost of buying the put option. For decreases of more than $10 a share, you would be recovering more than the cost of the insurance. You'd be getting insurance for those losses that exceed 10 percent of the current value of your shares, similar to the deductible on your insurance for damage to your automobile.

On the other hand, if the price of XYZ goes up to $115, you certainly won't force the buyer to buy your shares at the strike price of $110. The put would appear to have been worthless if the price of XYZ never fell below $110. But the put served as *insurance against a fall* in the price of the shares you were holding. If the price doesn't fall, you don't make any profit on the put, but, as with all insurance against loss, not having the loss doesn't mean the insurance was a waste.

Call: You could have bought a call for $8 on 1 share of XYZ stock, now priced at $100. A call is a right to buy a share of XYZ at any time in the next month at a price of, say, $110, the strike price. Your payment of $8 for the call with a strike price of $110 would mean that the price of a share would have to rise above $118 in order to make money. Of course, puts and calls can be used for the pleasure of gambling. But a market for puts and calls survives only because they are ways of obtaining protective insurance against losses.

SOME SOCIAL AND ECONOMIC EFFECTS OF FUTURES MARKETS: COFFEE

To see some other, wider-ranging effects, such as how futures markets help determine the *rate of consumption* of crops that are stored between harvests, we pursue a scenario in coffee futures.

Suppose a rumor spreads that unseasonably cold weather has damaged the coffee crop blossoming in Colombia. Owners of existing coffee beans can profit by withholding more until next year's expected higher prices. As less of the existing beans are released for current consumption, the current price of coffee to consumers will rise, though just as many coffee beans exist now as before the rumor, leading some legislators and consumers to demand an investigation as to why "greedy speculators" have driven up the current price.

If you were a coffee processor who used the coffee futures markets, or if you were simply a speculator, your defense might run like this:

"News of cold weather suggested a reduced supply and higher prices next year. No one would sell existing stocks at a price less than was expected for next year (allowing for storage and interest costs). Quite unintentionally, such actions — like those of many other processors or speculators — *enlarged* the *future* supply of coffee by holding part of this year's crop for later consumption, when the price would otherwise have been higher. As a result, consumers next year will have more coffee at prices *lower* than if we had not carried more coffee over.

"We did not cause the frost. There is going to be less coffee next year, no matter what. The choice is: Shall we continue consuming coffee today as if unaware there is going to be less next year? If so, we all would have to reduce consumption next year by the full reduction in the harvest. Or shall we start to reduce consumption this year and conserve some in order to have not as great a reduced amount next year? *When* shall the reduction in consumption occur — some this year, or a lot more next year?

"We speculators helped people to be better off. With next year's prices predicted to be higher than this year's, we believe that people prefer to give up a pound now to have one more next year. If our belief about their preference and our forecast about the reduced coffee harvest are correct, we will make a profit; if wrong, we will suffer a loss.

"We are anticipating the unfavorable consequences of the future crop, and enabling people more cheaply to adjust to it in ways they prefer. They will be better off than if the news of the coming failure were hidden until even more of the current crop were consumed.

"But what if our predictions were wrong? Suppose only a few buds are damaged; or the cold snap did no damage at all; or maybe the news was simply false. We who bought and stored more coffee this year would lose wealth to the rest of the public. We would have paid more for the coffee than it will be worth in the future. The damage done to other people by our incorrect forecasts—in the form of higher present prices and lower prices in the future than otherwise—is in part made up to them by our losses. Still, our incorrect forecasts do some damage to the rest of society, because if our forecasts had been more accurate, everyone could have achieved a more desirable adjustment in consumption patterns over time than was in fact achieved.

"Obviously, more accurate forecasts would be better for us and everyone else. However, the issue is not whether the forecasts are correct or incorrect, but whether they are more correct (or less mistaken) than would have existed without futures markets."

PRICE-FORECASTING ERRORS AND
RISKS IN FUTURES MARKETS

Do futures market contracts predict future prices more accurately than other possible schemes? Comparing behavior of prices with and without futures markets, the record is clear: With organized futures markets, prices varied less between crops. Futures prices more accurately predict future prices and enable less costly adjustments to be undertaken earlier and more completely.

Freezing or fixing prices does not remove the risk of changes in the market values. That would restrain desired adjustments in consumption over time and result in shortages or surpluses. No society can escape the profits and losses consequent to unforeseen changing supplies and demands for goods. Only the method of assigning risks and bearing of losses or gains can be changed. In a capitalist, private property system, ordinary individuals can negotiate among themselves, offering to exchange this risk of loss or gain for that risk. Although the extreme option of never bearing risk is not available, the risks one will bear are negotiable in the market according to what goods one chooses to own—or crops one chooses to grow.

Futures markets for US government bonds serve as predictors of future interest rates, and commodities futures prices are predictors of commodity prices in the future. No other predictor is known to surpass those futures markets.

QUESTIONS AND MEDITATIONS

1) Recently, the Chicago Board of Trade reported the prices ($ per bushel) of wheat futures contracts for the following months:

May $7.25
July $7.20
Sept $7.24
Dec $7.34

In what month does it appear that the new crop is harvested? Explain the basis of your answer.

Answer:

The prices of the contracts suggest supply will increase in July (relative to demand), resulting in a lower price. The higher price in December suggests this market is pricing in a relative decline of new supply versus demand.

2) Does storage from one crop season to the next season occur because people are farsighted and contemplate their own future demands, or is it done because people think they can make a profit?

Answer:

Primarily for profit. In pioneer days, households canned fruits and vegetables in harvest season for their own later consumption. Commodity exchanges achieve a similar outcome for an entire economy, although the motives of the "speculators" are merely to earn profits.

3) Which good will have a greater fall in its price as the crop is more fully harvested: one that will store readily or one that is more perishable? Why?

Answer:

Perishable. High storage costs (high perishability) imply larger present consumption supply and smaller future supplies. Increase in new supplies will be greater relative to carryovers, enabling greater increase in the rate of consumption and lower prices.

4) What is the difference between a "futures" price and a "future" price?

Answer:

Futures price is a price agreed to *now* for claim to a future good in the form of a futures contract. A future price is the price that will be formed in the future.

5) In May, what is the September futures price a measure of?

Answer:

It is the price one would pay in May for delivery in September after the harvest.

6) "That speculators push up the price of a good is evidenced by the fact that the price often rises before there is any change either in the rate of consumption or the existing supply." Do you agree?

Answer:

No; in a system with secure private property rights and open markets, prices rise or fall at the time expectations of the effect of a future event on a resource change — not at the time the event occurs. It's not that the speculators "push up the price"; it's the events that cause the change in expectations that cause the higher prices.

7) "If forecasts are correct, speculators who anticipate a rise in the price of a commodity will reap a profit. Also, they will have pushed up present prices, which will reduce current consumption and give a larger carryover to next season, so that prices in the future will be lower than they otherwise would be; but current prices are higher than they would have been had foresight been less perfect." In what sense can it be argued that this is "preferable to a higher price later and lower price now?"

Answer:

Most would agree that very wide swings in price are confusing and inconvenient. By supporting the current price and dampening the future higher price, the degree of price variation over time is modified — and seasonal variations in amounts available for consumption are dampened.

8) I own $1,000, and tomorrow I will own either $2,000 or nothing depending upon whether an oil well I am drilling strikes oil. You own $1,000 in wealth, and it is all in cash. Who bears the greater risk for the next twenty-four hours?

Answer:

I bear the greater risk — and have the much higher probability of a large gain.

9) Markets in which people can bet with each other can result in (a) exchanges of risk, (b) reductions in risk, or (c) increases in risk. If a participant in such a market increases his own risk, is that bad?

Answer:

Think of risk as being like what the physicists say about matter — it can be neither created nor destroyed. Risk can be quantified, and it can be exchanged between parties; it can be transformed (exchanging one type of risk for another); and an individual can hedge against a known risk. Do not confuse risk with uncertainty. The latter cannot be quantified, and it cannot be exchanged or hedged. Some like to say that risk is the "known unknown" while uncertainty is the "unknown unknown."

10) The Los Angeles Dodgers and New York Mets are tied for the National League baseball title. They are to have a play-off game in a neutral stadium. The winning team will then host part of the World Series, with consequent receipts to the owners of neighboring parking lots. I own a parking lot near the Dodgers' stadium, and you own one near the Mets' stadium. If the Mets win the play-off, you gain; if the Dodgers win, I gain.
   a. Into what kind of contract can we enter to reduce the risk each of us bears?
   b. Have we exchanged or reduced risk? Can you construct a kind of "futures contract" that would accomplish the same effect?

Answer:

   a. I bet on the Mets, and you bet on the Dodgers.
   b. We have shared some risk and reduced the range of our resultant wealths; in that sense, we have reduced our individual risk. I buy (half) rights to your parking lot and you buy (half) rights in mine for the World Series days. Neither of us expects to help the other operate the parking lot. Instead, each gets half the receipts regardless of which team wins the playoff game.

11) There are no speculative futures markets in some countries. Does that mean there is no speculation? Explain.

Answer:

The future is largely unknown everywhere and at all times. People "speculate," "gamble," and "experiment" in myriad ways in order to try to buffer themselves against outrageous fortune. But some communities are denied efficient, organized, institutionalized futures markets.

12) A US Senate Agriculture Committee once recommended the prohibition of futures trading in potatoes in formal speculative markets.
   a. Would such a prohibition stop speculation in potatoes?

b. What would be its effect?

c. Who do you think encouraged (lobbied) the senators to advocate the prohibition of futures markets in potatoes?

Answer:

a. No.

b. Less hedging, poorer price forecasts with greater price fluctuations, more erratic supplies to consumers.

c. A few middlemen who stood to gain because their private information about crop conditions and supplies is not as readily available to outsiders.

13) "Short selling" consists of selling promises to deliver at a specified date in the future some goods that the seller does not now own. Newspapers sell short when they take advance payment for subscriptions to deliver papers in the future. A house buyer sells short when he borrows money, for he is promising to pay money in the future — money he does not now have. A college that charges tuition and room and board in advance is engaged in short selling; it sells something it has yet to produce. I sell short if I sell a promise to deliver 1,000 bushels of wheat to you next year for a price currently agreed upon and in receipt for payment now from you. Why is short selling often regarded as immoral, improper, or bad?

Answer:

Ask those who consider it immoral. Some say, "Selling what you do not already have is immoral." But a contractor who bids on building a structure at a fixed price sells what he doesn't yet have. He has sold a promise or commitment to build a building. Short sellers do the same thing.

14) Things similar, but not identical, to futures contracts exist for stocks and bonds. These are known as "puts" and "calls." A call is a purchased *right* (but not an obligation) to buy a stock within the next six months at a prespecified price, regardless of how high the price of that stock may rise in that period. A call is guaranteed or sold by a party who, in effect, has sold "short" (the person does not currently own the stock). This second person is betting that the stock price will fall in the interim. If it does, this person will not have to fulfill his promise to sell at the higher specified price, since the buyer of the call can buy more cheaply on the market and will not exercise his right to buy at the higher price. If the stock price rises, the guarantor of the call will have to buy the stock on the market

at the higher price and deliver it to the holder of the call for the lower contract price in the call contract.

The buyer of a put buys the right to sell a stock at a prespecified price within some period of time regardless of how low the price may have fallen in that interval. The other party to the agreement (the seller of the put) agrees to buy later at the specified price. Thus, persons currently owning a certain common stock can protect themselves against a significant decline in the value of the stock by purchasing a put. If the stock price falls, the owner of the stock (and the put) exercises the right to sell the stock to the seller of the put at the higher contracted price.

On August 1, you can purchase a call for Omnicorp stock giving you a right to purchase 100 shares of Omnicorp stock at $50 per share (its current price in the market) at any time during the following six months. That call will cost you $600. How much would Omnicorp stock have to rise for you to make money by purchasing that call? If the price rose $1 per share, would you exercise your option? Or if the price fell $1?

Answer:

The price of the stock would have to rise by $6 per share for me to break even — paying $600 for the call plus $5,000 for the stock that is now worth $5,600. If the share price falls, I'm out my $600, because I can buy the stock cheaper in the market.

15) "Open speculative markets are defended on the premise that it is better to be aware of impending events than to be unaware of them. But for events like impending crop disasters, earlier news merely shifts forward the effects and thereby spreads them over a longer interval, to no one's benefit. People might prefer to experience a short, intense period of less coffee in the future rather than have an earlier, longer-lasting though less intense reduction in consumption." What does economic theory say about this?

Answer:

Bidding up present prices reduces the quantity currently demanded, leaving more to be consumed in the future at lower prices than if the earlier prices were unchanged. A speculator can choose the combination of risk he wishes to bear. The more the speculator chooses to buy and hold for the future, the more he stands to lose if prices do not rise.

PART FOUR

EMPLOYMENT AND INFLATION

CHAPTER 38

UNEMPLOYMENT: WHAT AND WHY

We live in a world of scarcity of *goods* — not of jobs. It takes work to produce the goods. That means infinitely many tasks are available. Then why are some people unemployed? Indeed, what is *unemployment*? Though no unambiguous definition has been universally adopted, the commonly used conception does *not* refer to a retired or wealthy person who chooses not to work. Nor does it mean spouses maintaining a household and therefore not working *in the market*, nor persons with severely handicapped bodily or mental ability, nor people who have grossly inflated beliefs of what they should be paid.

The distinction is between being *not* employed and being *unemployed*. The former includes lots of people who choose for one reason or another not to seek employment. We will be talking here only about the latter — people who would like to be employed and are doing something to find suitable employment.

What would the world be like if no unemployment were permitted; that is, if it were illegal to be unemployed? Everyone would work *full time*, as in a captive labor system. In the old Soviet Union, it was illegal to be unemployed, so the joke among workers was, "We pretend to work and they pretend to pay us." But we aren't forced to earn a paycheck. You won't want to take any job at random. You generally want the most valuable one you can perform. People sensibly choose to be without a job at some times, rather than perform any immediately available job no matter what the pay. People become unemployed in order more effectively to assess alternatives before choosing the best of the available jobs.

The governmentally reported index of unemployment has commonly wavered between about 4 percent and 6 percent of the people in the market labor force — when it is asserted that there is *full employment*. During recessions, that rate has increased generally to around 8 percent to 11 percent of the market labor force. Unemployment that occurs during normal, nonrecessionary times is called *frictional unemployment* or the *natural* rate of unemployment.

SEARCH FOR BEST JOB IN A WORLD OF CHANGING
TASTES, DEMANDS, AND CAPABILITIES

More goods and services are desired than are available; human wants are insatiable. That's what scarcity means — plenty of work needs to be done to provide what others want! But people don't agree to do something just because someone else wants them to. They look for the *best* of the many things that they can do.

In an idealized (and fictional) world, everyone has full information about everything, so people would *instantly know* the best of the available jobs. There would be no unemployment, because we could switch to new and better jobs without appreciable intervening spells of unemployment. In reality, reliable information about the best jobs available at the moment is expensive and difficult to obtain. Unemployment is a time of collection and evaluation of information about different possible jobs.

If the demand for your services in your current job falls, how do you adjust? You are physically and mentally as able as you were yesterday. You don't take the first job available, without regard to the prospective alternatives. *What,* and *where,* would now be your best job? Employment agencies offer help in assessing jobs. Want ads are reviewed. Firms are visited, and applications are submitted. Such search and assessment takes time and can be expensive. An interim spell of unemployment is a part of a rational response, however unfortunate the initiating change may have been.

The task of adjusting by searching and evaluating options permeates everyone's life in all areas. You spend a substantial portion of your time shopping — on foot or online — which would be a waste of time if you were willing to settle for the first item discovered, no matter how poor compared to what you expect to be able to find. The same is true for employers looking for employees and workers looking for jobs — a lot of shopping takes place. If information were costless (meaning that there was no uncertainty about the future), employers would hire the first person who walked in the door, knowing that no one better might appear. Workers would not engage in search and evaluation before accepting a job (no matter how unattractive it may appear) because they would know that there are no better alternatives. But that is not the world we live in.

The fact that information is not free to either employers or to prospective employees is the reason there is always a rational amount of unemployment and simultaneous job vacancies, even if government is not introducing artificial frictions in labor markets.

All shopping is time committed to reducing uncertainty and inadequacy of information about many possibilities. Of course, all that time you are unemployed means you must forsake income you could have had by immediately taking the first available job. Well-utilized periods of unemployment can be thought of as *investment* in information.

How long you choose to remain unemployed reflects your beliefs about the range and variety of options that exist. You'll refuse any known options so long as you expect to find a better one in a reasonable amount of future search. The length of time spent searching depends also upon the amount of welfare assistance and unemployment insurance you'll be receiving. Once you believe it doesn't pay to search further (or your unemployment assistance runs out), you will take the best job available. But during the period of search and evaluation of prospects, you are classified formally as unemployed rather than investing in the gathering of information. An effective job search can be *productive*, and in an important sense you are *employed in wealth-maximizing activity*, but the statisticians will count you as unemployed.

It is necessary to distinguish between the *initiating* event causing a loss of employment and the costs of adjusting to the unhappy circumstance. An interim spell of unemployment is not the *cause* of a loss of wealth. It's the earlier event or shock that eliminated or reduced the value of the prior job. The spell of unemployment, if rationally utilized, helps make that loss *less* severe.

In the distinction between (a) *the loss of earnings during the period of unemployment* versus (b) *the gain in wealth enabled by an interval of search*, attention is usually focused on the former. But the gain enabled by the interval of search is the present value of the earnings that are *higher than they would have been* with less effective search or if unemployment had somehow been prohibited. It is possible that the loss of earnings during the unemployment interval can be trivial compared to the wealth benefit of accepting an interim of unemployment in order to search and assess other opportunities.

Some firms do well and others fail in the normal processes of competition and shifting technologies and consumer tastes. Adaptations to those changes involve business failures and loss of value of jobs. The rate at which old businesses fail and new businesses start up is much greater than commonly realized. Also, the rates at which people lose a job and find a job can be high in a market economy. In the United States, government statistics show that millions of people lose a job and find a job *every month*.

People who voluntarily quit a job in order to search for better opportunities expect the temporary loss of a paycheck will be worth it later when they earn a bigger paycheck or enjoy a more satisfying employment. For people who are involuntarily terminated or were working for a business that failed, unemployment insurance is one method of bearing some of the costs of adapting to changing employment opportunities, even in an expanding economy.

At times, the economy experiences recessions, when aggregate production and employment fall and the rate of business failures is greater. The declines of employment occur in many firms at the same time, and the pace of new business startups is slower. During such times, the search by workers for the best alternatives becomes longer because those alternatives are fewer.

UNEMPLOYMENT INSURANCE OF NONHUMAN RESOURCES

We have concentrated on unemployment of people rather than nonhuman resources like machinery and buildings. Yet the same economic forces cause unemployment of those other resources — commonly called *idle resources* or *excess capacity*. The owners of productive resources face tasks, as do unemployed people, of informational search and assessment for best alternatives. But since machines, buildings, and objects are unemployed — rather than the people who are their owners — no one bothers to compute a rate of unemployment of nonhuman resources. Nor is unemployment relief proposed for the owners of, say, vacant shopping centers.

JOB CREATION: THE NONSENSE OF CREATING JOBS TO REDUCE UNEMPLOYMENT

Creating jobs is an ambiguous, misleading objective, as if there already were not an infinite variety of jobs still waiting performance. While there are plenty of jobs to be done, what are wanted are *more valuable* jobs. The unfilled jobs are considered not to be sufficiently valuable. They do not create enough wealth to be worth doing, compared to the believed alternatives.

When an earthen dam was built in China with thousands of people using hand shovels, many jobs were created. But still more jobs would have been created if the laborers had used teaspoons.

Building the dam — creating wealth — is the goal, not finding *work* for people to do. The problem of *unacceptably high unemployment is insufficiently productive* people or a mismatch between the skills of the unemployed and jobs that are unfilled. The unemployed must be made more productive by (a) increased training and education, or by (b) additional productive equipment with which to work, or by (c) making the search and evaluation of alternative jobs less expensive.

CREATIVE DESTRUCTION

Achieving higher-valued output for more income and wealth often destroys or reduces values of some existing jobs. The new, more valuable jobs attract people and resources from the now less valuable *displaced* work, destroying the less valuable jobs. That's been felicitously described as *destructive creativity*.

The invention of refrigeration destroyed (meaning it *lowered the value* of) tens of thousands of jobs of cutting, storing, and transporting ice from northern lakes in winter. But new jobs were created in making, installing, and repairing refrigerators — and later creating higher-valued jobs in air-conditioning — while also improving working and living conditions that are conducive to greater productivity.

The invention of steel destroyed the jobs of stone carvers and masons. The invention of the automobile destroyed the jobs of horse groomers and buggy manufacturers. Zippers and Velcro destroyed jobs of some button makers. The invention of movies and television destroyed jobs of many touring actors. The invention of synthetic fibers destroyed jobs of shearing sheep. When the airplane displaced railroads for passenger travel, the railroad jobs were replaced by the more valuable jobs of airline pilots and aircraft maintenance engineers.

Increased productivity is desired. Automobiles are more productive than horse-drawn wagons. Jobs making automobiles are more valuable than making buggies. Industries with higher rates of *job destruction* also have higher rates of creation of *more valuable* jobs. Indeed, the creation of more valuable jobs means the destruction (reduction in value) of other jobs.

NEW ENTRANTS TO LABOR FORCE

During the first five years after entry to the workforce, job testing and switching are most frequent. In time, jobs and people are better sorted into more satisfactory matches. Teenagers would still have the highest rate of unemployment and job switching, even if statutory minimum wages did not reduce job openings available to them. After age forty, on average only about one job switch has occurred for most people before retirement age is reached.

A MEANING OF THE MEASURED RATE OF UNEMPLOYMENT

In a commonly used measure of unemployment, the Unemployment Index (published monthly by US Department of Labor Bureau of Labor Statistics), a sample of the adult population is asked if they are employed in a market job. If not employed, are they *actively* searching for a job?

Actively searching means activities such as: contacting an employer directly or having a job interview; contacting public or private employment agencies and friends, relatives, and employment centers; distributing resumes; placing or answering advertisements for employment in newspapers or online; checking union or professional registers.

If actively searching for work, they are counted as unemployed. If they are not employed, but are not actively searching for a job, they are considered not to be in the labor force. If the search for a job stops without a job being accepted, unemployment and the size of the labor force both fall. If not retired, such people are said to have *dropped out* of the labor market, and may be classified as *discouraged workers*.

Alternative conceptions of unemployment are reported by the Bureau of Labor. It publishes measures based on six different categories of unemployment. The measures are the successive sums of the following six categories of people who are *not working*, but only some of whom are considered to be *unemployed*.

1) people who have no jobs and have been actively looking for fourteen or more weeks;
2) people who have lost jobs during the past two months;
3) people who were available for work and searched for their best work during the past month;
4) people who are discouraged from believing a job exists at wages they are willing to accept;
5) people considered to be discouraged from even looking for work;
6) people working part-time, but who would prefer full-time jobs.

TRANSITION TO AND FROM THE MARKET LABOR FORCE AND TO AND FROM EMPLOYMENT AND UNEMPLOYMENT

Data collected by the Bureau have indicated that about 10 to 15 percent of the workforce change jobs during a year. The data for each month include a large number of employees who quit or are laid off, as well as new hires. About 20 percent of the labor force experience unemployment at some time during a typical year, divided roughly equally in most years between job-*losers* and job-*leavers*. Of the job-losers, about 40 percent returned to work within two to three months, and the average for the other 60 percent has been between about four and six months.

PERSONAL AND GENDER DIFFERENCES
IN UNEMPLOYMENT RATES

A single population-wide measure of an *overall* unemployment rate can be misleading, because the labor force is composed of diverse groups with different typical probabilities of unemployment. The average rate is always highest for youngest, newest entrants and falls rapidly during the first ten years in the labor market. The unemployment rate of college graduates fluctuates usually in the range of 1 to 3 percent, while roughly 5 to 10 percent is the range for high school graduates. During the past fifty years, the ratio of the female unemployment rate relative to men (for persons over nineteen years of age) has steadily declined from 50 percent higher down to equality.

SPELLS OF UNEMPLOYMENT OR REDUCED EMPLOYMENT

Some occupations have relatively great predictability of spells of unemployment—such as temporary layoffs while awaiting recall which are common in agriculture, construction, theatrical, automobile assembly, and other strongly seasonal or cyclical jobs. Jobs with predictably higher probabilities of layoffs due to seasonality or weather conditions or job lengths on specific projects generally have compensating higher wages.

Schoolteachers who are out of the classroom for two or three months of the year are not counted as unemployed. Similarly, people in occupations such as real estate brokerage may experience lengthy seasons of slow or nonexistent sales, but they are not considered to be unemployed even though they aren't receiving a paycheck. Governments sometimes report on the number of *under-employed* people when they collect data on the people who are working only part-time, but report that they would prefer to have a full-time job.

A RISE OF NONRECESSION NORMAL RATE OF
UNEMPLOYMENT: CHANGED COMPOSITION
AND UNEMPLOYMENT BENEFITS

So-called *frictional* or *normal* rate of unemployment during nonrecessionary episodes has increased during the past few decades. That's a result of changes in the composition of the labor workforce. More people in the labor workforce are women and immigrants, who on average engage in more short-term exploratory jobs, as is typical also for the younger entrants, male or female. That's why the increasing unemployment rate is not necessarily a result of a sluggish or less rapidly growing economy nor of the educational system, nor unionization, nor of increased labor-saving devices, nor of greater imports of goods and services.

The availability of long-term unemployment benefits also causes the reported rates of unemployment to be higher over time. Consider the cost of remaining unemployed, especially for low-wage-rate earners. Suppose an unemployed person formerly earned $10 per hour. If, as is typical, the unemployment insurance benefit is equal to about to 55 percent of the former wage rate, that person receives $5.50 (= .55 × $10) per hour. Net of taxes (assuming a 15 percent tax rate), the benefit would be about $4.50 (= $5.50 per hour minus taxes of [.15 × $5.50]).

Compare that to working at $10 per hour, and paying 15 percent federal income tax, and a tax of 7.5 percent for Social Security and Medicare, and perhaps a 3 percent state income tax. That leaves about $7.45 per hour (= $10.00 − [.15 + .075 + .03] × 10). The gain by working at a wage $10 an hour rather than collecting unemployment benefits is only about $7.45 − 4.50 = $2.95 per hour.

This effect of unemployment benefits on the length of unemployment is stronger for people whose jobs involve frequent, intermittent spells of work — for example, casual laborers, actors, musicians, teenagers recently entering into the workforce, and older retired people. More sensitive to the trade-off are younger and less-skilled people, because unemployment benefits are equal to a larger proportion of their earnings. Unemployment among the young has tended to be higher and persist longer than when unemployment benefits were smaller. European countries have longer unemployment insurance benefits and also higher unemployment rates.

UNEMPLOYMENT — A BENEFICIAL PHENOMENON?

The involuntary loss of a job may result in your having to accept a lower-paying job. Being *unemployed* can help discover a higher value alternative, which may not have happened if that job search were not possible. The *decline in values of current jobs* — not the interval of search to find the best of possible alternatives — is what reduces personal lifetime earnings. Does a period in the hospital or on crutches reduce your well-being, given that you have suffered an illness or injury? Major recessions induce unusually extensive unemployment and reduced output. It's the recession that causes the damage.

QUESTIONS AND MEDITATIONS

1) The usual criterion of an unemployed person is "not employed and actively looking for a job." It says nothing about the range of jobs or the wages the person seeks. What seems to be implied by "actively looking for a job"?

Answer:

A person should be able to get an appropriate job at a salary close to his last salary without a significant cost in finding it. For there are always some jobs available at some sufficiently low wage — a wage the person rejects as ridiculous and thus unacceptable.

2) "A man who loses his job through no fault of his own should not have to bear the losses of unemployment. The government must see to it that he does not." This was a candidate for governor of California.
   a. Was the candidate proposing that there be no unemployment or that anyone not currently employed should be given an income perhaps equivalent to what he was formerly getting?
   b. How can either of these be accomplished, and who would pay for it?

Answer:

   a. Both bits of poetry are possible interpretations.
   b. One way to guarantee employment is to "draft" people into jobs (i.e., use force). Another is for the government to hire enough to guarantee existing jobs (which taxpayers subsidize). What might that do to incentives of people to seek their most productive and rewarding employment?

3) Is a person who loses his job through no fault of his own also unemployed thereafter through no fault of his own?

Answer:

No. He chooses not to accept the best alternative job he has so far discovered, and is instead looking for options, which is not to say that he is lazy, irrational, or deserves to be poorer. Time spent searching for employment can be wealth-enhancing.

4) "Unemployment is a wonderful privilege. Without it we would all be slaves to tyrants."
   a. Can you interpret this "ridiculous" statement so as to make it not ridiculous?

   b. Would you prefer to live in a community in which unemployment
   is forbidden? (Later, we analyze ways of reducing unemployment
   without forbidding it.)

Answer:

   a. Of course, losing a job can be wrenching, both financially and psy-
   chologically. But if there is to be *no* unemployment, everyone must be
   assigned at every moment to a job. The assignment would have to be by
   social (government) decree. No one would be free on his own volition,
   in a changing economy, to leave a job to seek another through gathering
   costly information and pursuing possible options of activity and reward. Carried to a literal extreme, you would not be allowed the fifteen
   minutes of unemployment to leave a job and walk across the street to
   take a new job.

   b. If you answered yes, does that mean you would work at any job at any
   wage you are forced to take?

5) What different kinds of unemployment (with respect to why
    unemployment exists) do you think it is relevant to distinguish?

Answer:

   Unemployment from relative demand shifts versus general money demand
   shifts — possibly reflecting inappropriate monetary, fiscal, and regulatory
   policies, creating confusion and uncertainty. Or unemployment caused
   by specific barriers to employment, such as minimum wage laws or construction projects where only high-wage unionized workers are allowed
   to compete.

6) When requesting a Congressional investigation into the methods,
    charges, and quality of services of private employment agencies, a
    former president of the United Steelworkers of America said, "A man or
    woman should not have to pay — often a large sum — for the privilege
    of obtaining a job." He also asserted that society and government had an
    obligation to make it possible for "every willing and able individual to
    work at or near his highest skill." Evaluate those remarks.

Answer:

   The unemployed can obtain jobs rapidly — at sufficiently low wages.
   However, most workers do not take the first job offer if it is below their
   reservation wage (what they think they can get). Obtaining reliable information about available jobs is expensive for job seekers (as is obtaining information about employees for employers). What job seekers pay

employment agencies for is costly information. In an open-market, free-enterprise society, the unemployed have the opportunity to search among potential employers for the best opportunity available to them, given their competence and accomplishment.

7) Almost every year, someone proposes that Congress enact legislation "to create more jobs." Of course, Congress doesn't create jobs: there are already too many jobs to do, and the jobs it presumes to create already exist as useful things to do. What is Congress really being asked to create by that legislation?

Answer:

Higher wages than are now available for those jobs.

8) During periodic energy "crises," people are told that unless more energy is conserved or made available, jobs cannot be preserved. Such statements are incorrect. Certain jobs would in fact be increased by a reduced supply of energy, for there would be more work for people to do! What do you suppose people mean, or should mean, by saying that jobs cannot be preserved?

Answer:

At higher energy costs, some jobs would be less valuable. Payment for those labor services would fall as the value of those jobs were revised downward. Some people could be laid off as the firms downsized in response to rising energy costs. More, not fewer, jobs would be available — however, most would pay less. The speakers/writers mean that fewer jobs would be available at the higher wages associated with the prior lower energy costs. With more costly energy, the community would be poorer.

9) "Automation is destroying jobs." Is destroying jobs socially good or bad? Explain why it does not mean that anyone will be left without a job.

Answer:

Earlier labor used in creating capital equipment is being substituted now for workers who used to perform the tasks. The displaced workers are available to work at other jobs, which may be less valuable jobs and have lower wages. The high-wage people who designed, built, and programmed robots to ice cookies in the bakery displaced the lower-wage people who formerly iced cookies by hand.

CHAPTER 39
YOUR EARNINGS: HOW AND WHEN

Economics explains much of how you are pushed, pulled, and guided in decisions about consumption and investment. But we have ignored two major economic choices — marriage and earning an income. Economics can help you make a more informed selection in both matters — but we leave one for you to think about on your own.

As for the other, we imagine that when you have your first paycheck on your new job paying $500 a week, you'll see your paycheck is for only $410 — $90 less! Social Security, union dues, pension contribution, health insurance, and income taxes, to name a few of the likely deductions, were withheld. Some are prepayments of obligations you incurred by taking a job. Some are withholdings of current earnings for your later retirement and insurance. They are allocations, not reductions, of your *current* earnings.

We look in this chapter primarily at how your earnings are related to your performance, and how it is paid to you. We will then see why earnings are paid sometimes earlier and sometimes much later.

FULL EARNINGS VERSUS MONEY EARNINGS
Your earnings will include more than money payments. The add-ons, or benefits, include paid vacations and sick leave, as well as employer costs for medical care, health insurance, subsidized lunch, coffee breaks, parking space, pension, maternity leave, paid time for voting and jury duty, Social Security contributions (by employers), recreation facilities, child and elder care, educational grants, severance pay, workplace amenities, reemployment assistance — to name some.

In a competitive open-market economy, your full earnings are pushed toward what *you add* to the social output. Whatever the composition of earnings, how do employers assess productivity of employees?

TYING EARNINGS TO PERFORMANCE: PAY LATER
WHEN WORTH OF THE WORK IS KNOWN

Direct Wages per Hour of Work

You receive wages based on the employer's estimate of your marginal productivity to the employer. How does the employer measure or estimate that worth? And how is the wage paid to the employee? Sometimes worth is most easily measured by *piecework*, with a payment by the employer for each unit of product or unit of service. The workers in the fields harvesting crops are usually paid by the number of boxes they fill.

Part of the compensation may be in the form of *commissions* based on a percentage of revenue generated. Sometimes an employer allows the ultimate customer of the product to judge the product and pay at least part of the employee's wages by *tips*.

Tips

A *tip* is a way of inducing *expected* performance by the employee. Tips are used when the person best situated to monitor the employee's performance is the customer, rather than the employer. The customer completes the wage payment, if the service is as *anticipated*. A restaurant waiter may be paid a salary that is some 10 percent to 15 percent less than the wage for the normal quality of service.

That underpayment is to be covered by payments — tips — from the customer if the service is of standard quality. A tip can be considered *not* to be a payment for extraordinary service; instead, it completes the wage payment at about the competitive full-wage level. Arrangements for sharing tips with *busboys* and others who assist in serving the customer reflect this.

There are then two reasons for tipping as a means of completing payment for services that can be best judged by the customer. (1) Tipping is a method of improving the monitoring and completing payment of the full money wage for standard service. (2) Tips also permit differences in rewards to employees who provide different levels of service among customers. That is, two employees receive the same base pay, but the one who provides better service to customers receives a greater full wage.

Payments for Services Delayed for Years until
Worth of Services Is Fully Assessed

Part of the wages for current services may be delayed for many years until the value of the current services are more reliably evaluated. Services of some young professors are worth more than the wages they receive when beginning to teach. The appropriate wages can be ascertained more reliably much later. At that future time, their wages will include a payment for underpaid earlier services. But if it's discovered the quality of earlier services was lower than expected, the employer will terminate the professor. This *up or out* system of delayed evaluation and then either overpayment or termination tends to tie the successful employee to the employer until that time of more accurate evaluation.

Up or Out and Tenure

The up or out system is typical in universities and in law firms. A new employee is promised employment for a stated number of years. At that later time, the employer will judge whether to terminate employment or retain with assurance of a permanent job — tenure.

Up or out protects the junior member from senior members' opportunistic delaying tactics in making a decision. One force tending to ensure fulfillment of actions at the promised time is that an employer who becomes known for not fulfilling promises will have higher costs of employing new workers.

Premium Earnings or Efficiency Wages

In chapter 24, the premium pricing of Coors beer was an example of providing a retailer a margin that is *more* than a competitive amount, in order to assure expected performance. An employer can pay the employee a *bonus* for performing as expected. The anticipated loss of that bonus, if the employee were detected not to be providing the promised services, would help maintain the promised performance. The employer would be paying more but would be avoiding greater costs of other methods of monitoring the employee's performance. This form of wages is misleadingly called *efficiency wages*.

The ability of people to control the level and reliability of their services is a reason the concept of a *quantity of labor* is, at best, a very general concept with little analytic value. *Labor* usually means *number of people* from whom labor services are available for specified intervals of time, rather than the *amount of services*. We can refer to the *market value* of an hour of labor, but that may not measure the amount of labor services actually performed during that hour.

Stock Options to Employees

Lifting boxes or sewing shirts or typing is more easily and accurately measured than the performance of a manager. One way of tying reward to performance of employees, especially the top management of corporations, is by the grant of a *stock option*. A stock option is the right (option) to buy in the future newly issued stock from the corporation at a currently specified price — called the *strike* price — usually set equal to the market price at the time the stock option is granted. The value of the option reflects the probability the stock's market price will rise in the future.

To a top manager whose individual actions are expected to have an effect on the corporation's market value, the option is a strong incentive to perform well. It helps align the manager's interests with those of the firm's owners, the common stockholders.

The changes in the value of a corporation's stock are caused not only by the performance of the managers. The market interest rate may fall, which would raise the stock value and the option's value. Inflation may occur and raise the stock price and the option price disproportionately more. To discriminate between the effects of the manager's performance and these other events, one procedure is to tie the option value to the extent to which the corporation's stock price changes *relative* to the whole market or to the firm's competitors.

Pensions

Pensions, which are *delayed* payments of earlier earnings, can constitute a substantial part of one's lifetime earnings. Usually, after a specified number of years of employment with the same employer, an employee becomes eligible (*vests*) for rights to retirement pension benefits from that employer. At that time, the employee becomes eligible to receive either a *defined-benefit* or a *defined-contribution* pension upon retirement.

A defined-benefit pension specifies (*defines*) the *amount* of benefits to be paid, such as $1,000 a month, from retirement to death. The amounts of the defined-benefit pension usually depend upon earnings and length of employment. Under a defined-contribution benefit retirement system, the benefits received depend upon how much the employee (and maybe the employer) contributed during the period of employment to the retirement fund. At retirement, the accumulated value of the retiree's (and employer's) employment career contributions is paid to the employee as a series of monthly pension benefits, based on expected life length.

The employer may create and manage a *fund* or may outsource that activity. A corporation's employee retirement fund may be a collection of common stocks and bonds of other corporations as well as government bonds, the earnings from which are to pay the promised employee pensions.

Until a few decades ago, employers often had little or no fund of investments set aside for employee retirement. Their fund was their promise to pay employee retirement benefits from the employer's future revenue. If the firm's future income or wealth was insufficient, the pensions could not be paid. Legislation at federal and state levels now requires private companies to make regular contributions to investment plans, and to report regularly on the assets of such plans. In contrast, state, city, county, school district, and other government-employee pension plans often depend mostly on the expectation that future tax revenue collected from future workers/taxpayers will be a major source of the funds to meet pension promises.

The defined-contribution pension plan is somewhat similar to a 401K pension plan available only for self-employed business owners or top-level managers of a firm. It permits the self-employed and executives to pay monthly contributions from their salary toward retirement by investing in stocks or bonds until time of retirement—and not pay current income taxes on that deferred income. Deferral of the income tax is the major reason for the popularity of the *401K pension plans*. (The 401K refers to the number of the authorizing section in the income tax law.) At retirement, retirement benefits may be taken from one's personal fund at rates of withdrawal set by federal law, at which time taxes must be paid.

With the defined-*contribution* plan, the value of the accumulated *retirement wealth* increases relatively smoothly from the beginning of employment to retirement, closely conforming to the gradual increase in a person's annual earnings. But for the defined-*benefit*, the accumulated *retirement wealth* is zero until an employee's pension rights are *vested* (i.e., right to a pension is established), usually at about five to seven years of employment with the same employer. Then, the present value of the right to a future pension is an increase in the employee's wealth.

PITFALLS IN PERCEPTIONS OF HOW MUCH EVERYONE ELSE EARNS

Self-esteem is a powerful motive. Your supposed *relative* income and wealth affect your social relations. But there are pitfalls in perceived measures of current and potential earnings and wealth relative to those of other people.

Data reporting on "income inequality" provide a deceptive impression of the degree of inequality of personal earnings. First, such data measure earnings only during a short time, one year. Second, adjustments must be made for differences in ages of the income earners. Most people move from low income to greater income as they get older. That's why *lifetime* incomes are less unequal than suggested by earnings in one calendar year. And lifetime *consumption* is more constant over the years than are annual earnings. We smooth our consumption, borrowing and investing when young, then repay from larger earnings when older. We must look at lifetime patterns of investments in education to help account for earnings.

AGE-RELATED ANNUAL EARNINGS VERSUS
TOTAL LIFETIME EARNINGS

High school–only people earn earlier with less investment and receive a longer, lower stream of earnings than do college students who invest more in human capital to obtain higher earnings later. When attending college, you incur two forms of investment costs: (1) tuition and college fees and (2) forgone income that could have been earned during that time.

Earnings in some professions, such as physicians, come much later after extensive investment and very low consumption, than for high school and college graduates. The *capital value* of *lifetime earnings* permits a more complete comparison of earnings of people with different lifetime patterns of investment and consumption.

Clearly, there are substantial upward and downward movements over a span of a few years, reflecting transient movements associated with job shifting and the year-to-year changes in demands for types of services and skills. It is important also to make adjustments for household size and number of income earners in a family or household.

SHIFTING DEMAND AND SUPPLY

One reason for inequalities in earnings is that current demands and supplies, which determine current wages, are shifting. Equality of average lifetime earnings across people is never achieved, partly because of unpredictable changes that raise values of some jobs and lower others.

Inventions, such as computers, create and raise the demand for technical specialists. New medical procedures and an increasing fraction of older people in the population alter the demand for medical services. Genetic knowledge brought an increased demand for genetic biologists and chemists. Earnings have leaped in those jobs, but in time they will fall toward equality with the fully adjusted average in other occupations.

Some industries suffer declines in earning as radio and movies did initially when television entered our lives. In recessionary times, people retire or leave some occupations to the point where the reduced supply results in restored rates of earnings for the fewer people in that industry during economic recovery.

People *already* in jobs where demand has recently increased enjoy *fortuitous* and *transient* rises in earnings. A high cost of quickly moving to another job with appropriate skills is a reason unusually high earnings in an occupation aren't immediately eliminated by new entrants. Still, the excesses are eroded by competition for entry to the higher-paying jobs, and the deficits are eroded by exits and reduced entry.

RICARDIAN SUPERIORITY

Regardless of educational and employment opportunity, genetic differences in *inherited natural* talents cause differences in ability, which affect earnings. People differ in natural features because of their genes. Once you are born, they can't be acquired by study, investment, or effort, though a more effective use of those you have is gained through investment and practice. Economists label that natural, nonreproducible superiority Ricardian superiority, in honor of David Ricardo — an influential economist of the early nineteenth century — who emphasized it. Ricardian superiority can be important in work habits, reliability, responsibility, perceptiveness, and honesty. Natural superiority of some talents results in differences in economic performance and earnings.

SENSITIVITY OF EARNINGS TO DIFFERENCES IN TALENT

Differences in abilities have less effect on earnings of carpenters, truck drivers, or accountants than for surgeons, lawyers, or musicians. The best janitor does not have a much greater value effect than an average one.

In contrast, the value of service of the best surgeon is relatively much higher than for an average one. In composing music or managing a large firm or handling a complex law case, differences in talent can have enormous differences in effects. In professional sports, the physical superiority of the best players may be small, but that makes much difference in the values of their services. However, the *average* of talents in the different occupations will tend toward equality — *net of costs of educational investment.*

WHY LARGE-FIRM CEOS EARN MORE
THAN SMALL-FIRM CEOS

The preceding principles imply that top executives in larger firms have greater salaries than those in small companies. The strong relationship between the size of firms and the top managers' salaries does not carry over to other employees, because the managers' decisions have a larger range of unpredictable effects on the firm's values.

Differences in managerial ability are multiplied in their value effects in larger firms. Wages for nonmanagerial employees, whose individual effects on the firm's resources are more predictable and smaller, will be less related to the size of the firm. Better lawyers work on "big" cases, and better architects design the more expensive projects. It's not that big firms have "deep pockets" and profligately pay more to managers, like careless spenders. Instead, the differences in managerial skill make more difference in the larger firms.

The importance of the range of potential effects of a manager on the firm's value is evident in the smaller salaries of managers of *highly regulated* firms, such as public utilities, where the managers don't have as wide a range of value consequences as do managers of unregulated firms. Public utilities are more likely to function with established routine actions.

In contrast, for less regulated enterprises and those where decisions about new projects are highly discretionary with a very wide range of potential consequences, the CEO's salary will be large and with a job tenure closely tied to the resulting performance, measured by profits or changes in the firm's stock value. Compared to a regulated utility company, more will become very rich, and more will be fired more quickly. After deregulation of airlines, the airline CEOs' decisions had a wider range of consequences on the firm's wealth. As a result, more airline CEO wage contracts began to include changes in stock prices as determinants of executive compensation.

REPLICABILITY OF SERVICES CONCENTRATES REWARDS TO THE BEST OF THE COMPETITORS

Recording and reproduction devices, such as records, tapes, discs, film, radio, and television, enable the services of superior-ability performers to be enjoyed by almost everyone. As a result, demand for the less talented performers has been relatively reduced. The reward is now obtained by the best few performers, rather than by a wide range of many performers each supplying a few customers. Minor league baseball teams were, once upon a time, the only source of professional baseball games for much of the population. Now a few teams of the best players supply virtually all the nation by television. The fewer top earners now earn enormously larger incomes. Very large incomes to the few best performers attract many aspirants, each with a very small probability of success. The failures move on to other work.

PRIZE FOR BEING THE *BEST*

In some activities, especially sports, the worth of a performer often depends on the rank among all the competitors. The winning team of the baseball World Series or the football Super Bowl or the US Open tennis championship is rewarded by virtue of being the best, regardless of the absolute quality of performance. No matter how close or good are the contestants, the winner's prize is substantially larger than for second place. Though contestants may barely differ in quality, the difference in the reward for winning is great.

Youngsters, especially in sports, are motivated to practice intensely in a specialized activity beginning at the earliest ages. Such specialization increases the probability of earning less than the average of the population. The odds are great that the specialization gamble will fail, with only occasional spectacular successes. Other young people who invested more broadly in learning in academics have a higher and wider variety of skills.

GENDER-RELATED EARNINGS

Historically, there has been much discrimination by males against females, and by females in favor of home rather than market employment. Even today, in some societies women have virtually no rights against men.

Free-market competition, with private property rights to one's self (i.e., no slavery or serfdom) and the right to choose occupations, tends strongly to reduce gender-earning differences. An employer who refuses to employ women who can do what men do, and do it at a lower wage, would be throwing away potential profits. (The difference in pay persists in spite of anti-discrimination laws.)

Can some nonprejudicial forces be strong enough to maintain a gender differential in wages? Are the costs of employing women greater than for employing men? Childcare and maternal leave are two extra costs. Access by women to market employment opportunities has been hindered by contrived restrictions in several industries. Permissible working hours, for example, have not always been the same for men and women.

Some self-selective *discrimination* or *choice* by women is present. Independent of prejudices against women, there are reasons for their voluntarily clustering in certain kinds of work. A woman could reasonably enter a profession or occupation in which acquired skills and knowledge do not depreciate if she leaves the occupation for a while, and sensibly hesitate to specialize in an occupation where research and technological ideas are advancing rapidly.

HUMAN AND NONHUMAN WEALTH

Nearly two-thirds of all families own their homes, which on average accounts for almost half their wealth. A business owned by the family head is the next largest form of wealth, though on average that is only about 10 percent of the householder's wealth, with substantial variations from the average. These reported measures of wealth do *not* include human capital. If *human wealth* — measured as the present value of the future earnings of personal labor — were included in the formal measures, the young would be richer than the old, whose human capital is almost exhausted.

POVERTY

Poverty as stipulated by the US government does not mean the extreme destitution that billions of the world's population endure. As the label is applied in this country, about 15 percent of the population is in poverty. The poverty line in the United States is now defined as an annual family earned income less than three times the annual cost of a stipulated *food basket*, adjusted for family size.

When the government's Office of Management and Budget first officially indicated a poverty level, some studies indicated that low-income families typically spent one-third of their cash income on food, so the upper limit of poverty income was taken as three times the food cost.

The poverty level is defined in terms of money income, not in terms of consumption. This ignores some forms of income or consumption power, such as *in-kind* benefits like housing assistance, food stamps, consumption of prior savings by the elderly, and charity.

Poverty can be in substantial part a result of not working, rather than working at a low wage. Not working is not necessarily a matter of laziness. Poor health, caring for children, and absence of a breadwinner are common obstacles.

NONMONEY FORMS OF INCOME AND AID

The formal measure of poverty that qualifies a person or family for government special poverty aid excludes from the measure of income other government noncash benefits, such as food stamps, Medicaid, unemployment insurance, subsidized housing, and public school lunches for people regardless of income levels. Also excluded are personal *nonreported* money receipts. A study of families in officially defined poverty has indicated that on average families had non-officially-measured earnings and receipts equal to about 40 percent of their poverty thresholds.

Covert jobs and aid from friends provided nonmoney sources of increases in consumption. When omitted forms of consumption and aid are included, the average full consumption power of families in poverty has been estimated to be above the official poverty line by 40–50 percent, so the percentage of families in poverty based on the consumption criterion is about 8 percent.

POVERTY, HOW LONG? TRANSITIONS
TO AND FROM POVERTY STATUS

For some, poverty is long-lived, and to others, it's a short, random event. It appears from past behavior that about half of those in poverty will in one year rise above that state, while about 80 percent will have left within five years.

Actors between jobs and seasonal-type workers and those on contract jobs are classed as in poverty while unemployed. Some in the poverty class are the young starting to earn income or are self-financing college students.

Grouping people by income quintiles and looking at seven-year spans of time, about 6 percent of the lowest-income quintile (20 percent) of families in poverty in year one moved up to the richest quintile by year seven. And about half of the families in the richest quintile moved downward, with about 4 percent of them moving all the way to the poorest quintile.

Of those in the middle quintile, about one-third reached it by moving up from a lower quintile, while about one-third entered with a downward fall from a higher quintile. Obviously, movements and shifts within the income distribution are not trivial. But many retired people living on accumulated wealth are recorded as low-income earners, and probably will remain in that status. Those suffering from disadvantages in natural competence, education, and training tend to stagnate.

FEMINIZATION OF POVERTY?

About one-third of female-headed families have measured incomes placing them in poverty in a given year. Unwed mothers head a substantial portion of these households. The rise in the proportion of women living independently and working in the labor force has contributed to the increase in poverty. Women are often temporary entrants to the workforce with lower incomes, at least initially. From 1970, married couples form a smaller percentage of the poverty group, while single-parent and single-person families have increased.

None of these facts mean that being in a state of poverty is merely a passing inconvenience. Economic principles and analysis can help only to clarify problems. Does unemployment insurance increase unemployment? Yes, the extent and length are increased. Does it help get better job matches at the selected new job? Yes. Does aid to single female parent families increase the creation of single-parent families? Yes. Are food stamps essentially equivalent to cash grants? Very largely. Does administering government welfare cost more than private charity? Yes. Does government aid to the homeless increase homelessness? Yes. Do these answers imply that the income redistribution welfare programs should be reduced or eliminated? No, more than economics is involved.

QUESTIONS AND MEDITATIONS

1) "Different workers receive different wages because the workers are different, the jobs are different, and workers can't move to other jobs easily." On the other hand, "Workers are different but get the same pay

in many jobs; many different jobs pay the same wages; and it is about as 'easy' to move across the country as it is to move next door." Where lies truth? Write a better version of the line of thought.

Answer:

People differ in their productive abilities and in their costs of acquiring skills. The cost of acquiring skills (cost factors that restrain one person's ability to duplicate that of another) are such that wage differentials can exist. These wage differentials commonly will be smaller than the costs of acquiring skills that would enable lower-paid workers to do the work of higher-paid people. Except for fortuitous matching of demands and supplies at wages equal in all tasks, differences in wages will persist, but they will be less than the costs of acquiring skills of higher-paying jobs and/or transfer costs.

2) Are higher costs of training the reason why earnings in some occupations are higher?

Answer:

Costs of training affect both the demand for the services in question and their supply. Potential buyers (employers) will assess the likely value to them of the services partly in light of what is known about the previous training of the employee, with increased demand in light of greater training. And higher costs of training restrict supply, shifting the supply curve to the left, intersecting the demand curve at a higher wage. The wage is given by the demand price at the amount supplied.

3) The 2017 US national income estimate of over $16 trillion annually does not include the value of women's services in the family household. Is that a significant omission?

Answer:

Consider the wages for someone hired to perform all the tasks of a housewife and mother, and do not forget the problem of monitoring an employee's performance to see that it is as efficient and motivated as the housewife's. One reason, possibly minor, for so much self-performance in the home is that the value of that performance is not subject to income tax, whereas if performed by a hired employee, taxes would have to be paid.

4) Long ago, few could read or write. Those who could were called "scriveners." They were well paid compared to the masses. Those skills were so valuable that now almost everyone invests in acquiring them. If

specialization is so valuable, why does everyone learn to read and write as a self-sufficient supplier of those skills? We do not all invest in extensive medical and legal knowledge rather than having others supply it for us. But what about driving a car or preparing meals? What determines in what activities we tend to specialize less but do it ourselves in driving, cooking, reading, and writing?

Answer:

Generalized skills can be acquired relatively quickly and cheaply, applied to a wide variety of consumption and production activities, and maintained in value or usefulness over time. In contrast, specialized skills are more expensive to acquire, more narrow in use and application, and their value may fluctuate more widely over time intervals.

5) "The presidents of some big corporations are paid over $1,000,000 in one year. They make the kinds of decisions that are made in thousands of other companies by much lower-paid people who are as intelligent, but who haven't had a chance to get those fancy jobs and who aren't as well known. Salaries are based primarily on past experience, reputation, and pull. Therefore, marginal productivity — which is an academic, unrealistic abstraction of an imaginary world — is misleading at best and false at worst." Explain why the last sentence is not implied by the preceding sentences.

Answer:

Marginal productivity of a resource affects its reward, and the amount of capital used with it affects its marginal productivity. Consider two managers, one of whom has the ability to make correct decisions about 5 percent more of the time than the other. For a $1,000,000 company, this difference would amount to about $50,000, whereas for a $100,000,000 company, this difference would amount to about $5,000,000. Clearly, the larger company will gain more with a superior manager than would a smaller one. Standard workers would not be making decisions that affect company wealth as much as do top executives, so the difference in their talent would not be magnified as much as those of top executives. As a result, pay of nonmanagerial personnel would be about the same in small and large companies while pay of top executives would be related to the size of the company.

6) Which of the following are occupations with differential earnings due to superior productivity and which are from monopoly sources?

a. Star athlete in a major sport
b. Movie star
c. Conspicuous television performer
d. Widely syndicated newspaper columnist
e. Powerful politician
f. Highly successful financier
g. Popular singer
h. Inventor of something everyone wants
i. Author of serial best-selling novels

Answer:

Probably all are returns to productivity deemed highly valuable by the community rather than monopoly-protected incomes. We know of no evidence that any have power to exclude competition by methods not related to superior performance.

7) Suppose that for all the people in the bottom quartile of incomes in one year, you computed their average income that year and compared it with the average of those *same individuals* in the next year. Do the same for the top quartile. Which group will show a rise and which will show a fall?

Answer:

The average income of those people who were in the lowest quartile will be higher in the next year, while the income of the individuals who had been in the top will fall on average. This reflects the universal regression effect.

CHAPTER 40

LABOR-MARKET COALITIONS

"The high wages of the American worker are a result of a strong labor-union movement." If that were true, the path to higher income for all workers would seem to be: "Unionize and strike for higher wages!" Neither economic reasoning nor evidence supports that prescription. The *productivity of labor* explains wages.

If a community has relative abundance of modern capital equipment, high educational levels, skilled workers, and an efficient system for organizing productive activity, productivity of labor will be relatively high. That and nothing else is the foundation of high wages.

What labor unions can do is help smooth grievance procedures, provide increased information about job opportunities, help workers improve their skills, and monitor payment of benefits like insurance, retirement, and so forth. These are not trivial functions. How are those benefits obtained and at what costs? Who pays for benefits provided to union members? Are there similar organizations among employers?

HISTORY AND ORGANIZATION

A labor union is a formally organized coalition of employees, recognized for the purpose of helping them to negotiate with employers. The process is *collective bargaining*. Union officers/agents negotiate, monitor, and enforce the terms of the employment contract. A union that represents those with specific skills, such as musicians, carpenters, electricians, plumbers, or painters, is a *craft* union. An *industrial union* contains employees of all firms in one industry, such as textiles, steel, automobiles, or chemicals.

Both types of unions are now allied in a large umbrella labor organization, the American Federation of Labor and Congress of Industrial Organizations (AFL-CIO). Guiding this structure is an Executive Council composed of the heads of many of the major unions.

Officers of a *local*, consisting of union members at one firm or one locality, are usually elected by the members to administer union affairs, resolve employer-employee disputes, manage pension funds, etc. A union *shop steward* at each enterprise helps settle disputes about job grievances concerning issues like discipline, interpretation of the union contract, and safety rules. Unions are financed by *dues* paid by members. Although it is illegal in the United States to have *union shops* in which new employees must join the union, union contracts are permitted under which all employees must at least pay union dues as a condition of employment, whether or not they choose to join the union.

In the United States, close to 15 million people belong to unions (including those in government employment — now the fastest-growing union sector). The percentage of the labor force in unions had hovered around 5 percent before the 1930s, but after the Wagner Act in 1935, it rose to around 30 percent by the 1950s. Since then, it has fallen relatively steadily to under 12 percent. Apparently, union membership is less popular in more rapidly growing and *high-tech* industries. Decline has been most severe in industries affected by imports from abroad, such as for textiles, clothing, shoes, electronics, and other products relying on less skilled workers.

City, state, and federal government employees are now more likely than private sector counterparts to be union members. Local government workers, including police, have been the most likely government employees to be union members. Government workers have a rate of unionization of almost 40 percent, compared to under 7 percent in the private business sector. Relatively high unionization of over 20 percent in the private sector occurs in the transportation and utilities sectors. Low unionization in the private sector occurs among sales workers and in farming, fishing, and forestry occupations. In the computer and high-technology sector, union membership is rare.

Why has union membership increased for government employees but not for employees of privately owned firms? A major reason is that an imposed wage that exceeds competitive market-determined wages cannot be maintained by private firms. Private employers, unlike government agency administrators, must pay employees and other resource owners out of their sales revenues, which reflect the values consumers are willing to pay for goods and services. A private employer can't call upon taxes to finance losses, as government agency administrators can, so administrators of government agencies are less resistant to union demands.

RISE OF UNIONS

In early American history, unions were considered to be *conspiracies*, a coalition with an illegal objective. Later, when unions were legal, employers often refused to deal with union representatives. However, Congress in 1935 passed the National Labor Relations (Wagner) Act compelling employers to *negotiate* with a union, if a majority of employees in an *appropriate bargaining unit* (which could be a department, a craft, or an entire plant) voted to join or form a labor union. Congress thus affirmed the right of employees to form or join unions without coercion or interference by an employer.

The union selected by a majority of employees would be the *exclusive* representative of employees (other than supervisory or management personnel), whether or not they were members of the union and whether or not they wanted to be represented by that union. This is known as *exclusive compulsory collective bargaining*. (a) It's exclusive in that the only representative for the employees is the designated union agent. (b) It's compulsory in that the employer must negotiate, on request, with that union with the object of arriving at an agreement (union contract). (c) It's collective in that all the employees of the bargaining unit, whether or not members of the union, are bound by the contract. An employer cannot legally make other agreements with different employees in the union.

THE NATIONAL LABOR RELATIONS BOARD (NLRB)

The NLRB, created at the time of the National Labor Relations Act of 1935, supervises elections determining which union, if any, is to be the sole authorized union for all the employees in a bargaining unit. That board also can issue orders to restrain *unfair labor practices* — activities stated by the NLRB to be attempts by the employer to obstruct unionization or to refuse to bargain and negotiate with the designated union.

In reaction to the one-sided effects of the Wagner Act, the Taft-Hartley Act of 1947 defined, and forbade, some union unfair labor practices. Unions were forbidden to interfere with the employees' freedom not to join the union, and certain traditional union weapons like secondary boycotts (against third parties doing business with an employer with whom the union has a dispute) were prohibited.

The Taft-Hartley Act banned the closed shop in which all employees must belong to a union. However, it permitted union contracts under which a dissenting employee no longer is required to join the union, but still is required to pay the union dues.

Some kinds of political activity and contributions to political candidates were banned. The Taft-Hartley Act also authorized the president of the United States to declare that a strike was creating an *emergency* and imperiling the *national health or safety*. Such a strike had to be delayed for a *cooling-off* period of eighty days. The Taft-Hartley Act preserved the right of the states to pass *right to work* laws where state constitutions could forbid union contracts that made membership in a union a condition of employment. At present, 28 states have *right to work* laws.

An *industry union* with members among the several firms in one industry —

for example, auto, steel, truck-driver, sports league—negotiates for the union members with those firms. Since the negotiations are for employment and wage conditions for all the firms in an industry, the employers must inevitably negotiate as a group. This led to accusations that the employers were colluding. Collusion of the employees through the union is legal, as authorized by the Wagner Act and related legislation.

Not until 1996 was joint action by employers declared legal (that is, not subject to the antitrust laws) by the Supreme Court. The Supreme Court stated also that only the National Labor Relations Board should decide exactly what joint actions of employers concerning employment conditions would be legal. The board, which initially was a protector of unionization by employees, must now act also as a protector of collusion by employers.

UNION OBJECTIVES VIA MONOPOLY STATUS

While the legal right of unionized employees to restrict competition from nonunion labor was a congressional intent, that right to monopolize does not guarantee success. The degree of success is strongly limited by the similarity and substitutability of workers and products and production techniques. If unions raise labor costs in one area, production in lower labor cost areas will expand and supply more of the market. As unionization raised labor costs in the northern states, southern states could underprice the northern products—as in automobile production, which moved more to the South.

What guides union leaders and officers in determining what wages and working conditions to seek? Do they want to maximize the total wage earnings of all members, or is the objective to raise the average of those who retain jobs? Do union agents serve as intermediaries to depersonalize negotiations, as real estate agents do for purchase of homes? Do they help enforce employment contracts so that neither the employer nor employee can expropriate values dependent on the other party? We will address these questions below.

LABOR UNION EFFECTS ON WAGES

The median money wage of unionized laborers is often higher than for nonunionized labor in a specific industry—such as retail clerks or auto parts manufacturers. To be sure, that excess reflects a variety of nonunion features, such as skills, ages, types of industries, areas of the country, and size of firms. And more than the wage level is involved in unionization. There's the degree of job security, working conditions, and assurance of contractual performance by the employer and the employee. The benefits to individual employees are in part offset by union dues and time lost during periodic strikes or "lockouts."

PROTECTION FROM EMPLOYER
OPPORTUNISTIC EXPROPRIATION

Unions can help protect employees from employers who would renege on promised future rewards, like promotions, pensions, insurance, and vacations. Without an employment contract, once an employee takes a job in anticipation of those future events and has accumulated some rights related to length of work for that employer, a threat of dismissal may be sufficient to persuade an employee to accept a wage cut to retain the job and the promised future benefits.

At the time of the initial hiring, both the employer and employee anticipate that possibility, and each wants that possibility reduced, which creates an incentive to enter into a contract. That reduces the employer's cost of attracting employees, and the employee is more willing to work for a more reliable employer.

A worker representative of a union serves as a central monitor and clearing-house for information on employee benefits and as an agent to ensure employers fulfill those obligations. The union can mobilize concerted employee action. It can also help restrain improper actions by employees. Sometimes an employee acts irresponsibly and indirectly harms the interests of all the other employees. The disruptive employee can often be restrained by the union more effectively than by the employer.

Some employers promote internal *company unions*, encouraging group employee actions, credit unions, and employee representation, although they aren't recognized or supported by outside unions in the event the employees venture to strike. Most important, they lack exclusive, compulsory negotiating authority for all the employees.

An employer known to have good prospects of continued future growth will be more hesitant to renege on promised benefits. Loss of reputation would raise costs of getting future employees, which is of less concern to a declining firm. If, at a later time, growth prospects were to decline and create the expectation that few new employees would be hired, the reputation value of being a reliable employer helps assure fulfillment of promises.

HOW DOES UNIONIZATION ACHIEVE ITS OBJECTIVES?

Negotiations and Employee Representation

Intermediary agents providing disinterested representation facilitate personal negotiations about jobs, the same as agents do for purchasing a house or settling terms of a divorce. Agents can also monitor subsequent performance to allay or resolve misunderstandings, confusions, and disputes arising with ambiguities from incompleteness of written contracts. However, a uniform contract to cover many employees limits accommodation to individual preferences and differences in abilities, performance, tastes, and full-wage packages. That egalitarian common denominator is a deterrent to unionization — particularly of some better-educated professional or technical employees.

Exclusive Collective Bargaining

Often it is said that employees individually lack sufficient bargaining power and must accept lower wages than otherwise in the absence of collective bargaining. However, bargaining power reflects alternatives. An employer has to beat competing employers. If the employees' alternatives are good, bargaining power is strong. If alternatives are poor, bargaining power will be lower.

Employers pay the wages they do because they must match what the employees could earn elsewhere. Employers face competition from other employers, and employees face competition from other employees. Buyers compete against buyers and sellers against sellers, not buyers against sellers. This is not to deny that unions often manage, backed by the strike threat, to raise wages above market levels. The expressed or implied threat of a strike, shutting down the business, can induce an employer to yield to union demands, which might otherwise be rejected. However, to the extent that he does, the employer's ability to compete successfully in the market is diminished.

The Strike

A strike is a collective refusal by employees to work and prevention of others from taking their places, permanently or temporarily. A third element is that, under current labor relations laws, the employer may not be able to fire employees for striking. However, if the strike is *economic* (as opposed to one that protests *unfair* labor practices), the employer can replace the strikers with newly hired workers and (if necessary to attract them) promise permanent employment. This right to replace strikers — and to replace them permanently, if necessary — is the employer's counterforce to the strike, and has sometimes been accompanied by violence.

The *lockout* is often called the counterweight to the strike, but it is not highly effective unless accompanied by the right to replace the locked-out employees. The National Labor Relations Board has tried over the years to protect the position of the strikers and to limit the ability of the employer to replace them. The right to strike, the right to try to prevent replacement, and the inability of the employer to fire strikers, all are critical to the union's exercise of its right of exclusive collective bargaining.

Picketing during a strike, while superficially directed at the employer, is basically directed at deterring potential replacements for the strikers from entering the plant. Often a strike is accompanied by an attempt to convince customers not to purchase from the struck firm and by attempts to discourage deliveries of materials to the struck plant. Strikers sometimes resort to violence in their efforts to discourage others from taking the jobs and to prevent the employer from trying to operate despite the strike.

Lest the preceding make the strike and exclusive bargaining appear to be immoral, note that Congress has approved the right to strike and monopolize by unions the sale of labor services. There are other state-supported monopolies. There is no apparent reason why people who seek successfully to restrict competitors should be only tobacco growers, milk producers, liquor retailers, taxi owners in New York, morticians, doctors, and teachers, but not teamsters, carpenters, auto assemblers, dockworkers, or butchers.

SELECTIVE MONOPOLIZATION: LABOR AND WAGE EFFECTS

An indirect way for a union to obtain monopoly rents is to help a favored employer achieve protection from or an advantage over other employers, which is then shared with the union. If costs of the other firms can be raised, or their access to customers restricted, the advantaged employer could share some of the resulting monopoly rents with those who helped impose handicaps on competitors. Or if different firms employ labor in different ratios to capital, the firm with the highest ratio of labor to capital would find its costs raised most by an increase in wages. A construction firm with much capital equipment that substitutes for labor would have a minor increase in labor costs, and hence a minor increase in total costs from generally higher market wages. A department store with only a few clerks and relying on customer self-help would have a smaller percentage increase in total costs, compared to a full-service retailer with many more clerks to help customers. This differential impact helps explain why employers in an industry often disagree among themselves about new contract terms with a union.

Opportunistic Expropriation of Dependent Resource Values
Another tactic, probably most feared by employers, is the possibility of a union's attempt to destroy the employer's wealth that is dependent on the union action. Farmers are especially vulnerable, because a union could at the moment before harvest refuse to work unless paid some of the farmer's value of the harvest. (Recall the Codlandia fishing boat winch.) A strike by steel-workers — in contrast to farm crop harvesters — would be less capable of

effective opportunism because, unlike ripening crops, steel can be stockpiled and production can be delayed.

Union influence can be exerted for three objectives: (a) productivity-enhancing negotiation and stabilizing arrangements, (b) monopoly wages, and (c) expropriation of the employer's employee-dependent values. Economic analysis does not imply that any of these are unethical or illegal. As mentioned earlier, Congressional legislation declared that (a) and (b) can be desirable and therefore lawful. No objective basis exists for judging merits in terms of whether costs of reduced national income are worth it.

WHY DO PRIVATE EMPLOYERS RESIST UNIONIZATION?

Rise in Wage Costs

If customers ultimately pay for higher costs, why do private employers resist unions that raise wage rates above the competitive level? Ultimately is not the same as completely or instantly. The higher costs result in higher prices, not when the costs rise, but only when the higher costs result in a smaller amount supplied to the market. In the interim, current owner/employers with existing production facilities suffer a loss of wealth, and current employees get a short-lived transient gain in wages. The higher costs reduce the profit margin, reducing the value of the enterprise's existing and nontransferable resources.

That loss is borne by the employers. It's a permanent loss of wealth. (Wealth losses are permanent because current wealth is the present value of all future foreseeable events. Therefore, any future rise in prices is already taken into account in the market measure of wealth. The reduction of wealth now reflects the fact that the future rise in product prices will not completely offset the current rise in costs.)

In the longer run, as the nontransferable resources wear out and are ready for replacement, the new investments will be made only if they look profitable. Thereafter, the product price must cover the full costs, including the higher wages. That permanent loss of wealth, a loss equal to the present value of the interim decline in earnings, is a reason employers object to unions that might raise wages above the competitive level. But it's not the only reason, nor necessarily the most important reason.

Labor Supply Monopolization and Exclusive Bargaining

Exclusive bargaining is a reason private employers resist unions (others are the cost of strikes and wasteful work rules). The union has the potential, as the exclusive bargaining agent for all existing and potential employees of the firm, to (1) engage in monopolistic pricing of wage rates and (2) opportunistically capture some of the employer's wealth.

Which Is Set? The Price or the Amount?

There are two ways to try to control the price of labor. (a) One is to curtail the supply of labor and let employers bid up the wages. (b) The other is to negotiate a higher wage, letting employers hire as many as are demanded at the controlled wage. In principle, the results should be the same, because controlling the amount supplied controls the price, while controlling the price determines the amount demanded and hence the amount produced.

Governmental members of an international coffee cartel once thought they had to control both how much coffee to supply and also the price. At any rate, controlling the price is extremely difficult, since each party has an incentive to violate the cartel agreement. Similarly, controlling the amount supplied is difficult since each party has an incentive to supply more.

DIFFICULTY OF MAINTAINING CONTRIVED MONOPOLY RENT: THE VALUE OF MONOPOLY RENT IS COMPETED AWAY EVEN IF PRICE AND SUPPLY ARE EFFECTIVELY CONTROLLED

Nonmoney Components of Full Wage Are Competitively Adjusted

Even if a union successfully negotiates for a higher money wage, the full wage may not be increased.

If competition for the higher money wage jobs is not controlled, competitors will offer to work for fewer nonmoney attributes, for example, with less safe, dirtier, and more strict work standards or with shorter coffee breaks, until the full wage of higher money wages — but less nonmoney components — is competed down to the market-clearing level.

If the full wage is not competed down, employers will be more selective in who is hired and laid off. The quality of employees will be higher, meaning that they will correspond more with the employer's tastes. At the higher imposed money wage, more weight and discrimination will be given to such qualities and characteristics as gender, ethnicity, education, personality, and age.

Monopoly rent is not easy to maintain. Only if the amount of labor supplied and the aspects of the service and working conditions are controlled can the effective full price of any good or service be maintained above the market-clearing rate. But people will try to get such rent, and that creates wasteful activities in merely transferring wealth rather than increasing it.

Competition through Product and Input Substitutions

Even if the union were successful in controlling both the money and nonmoney aspects of the effective full wage, the rent of a closed-market monopoly could still be competed away over time through product and input substitutions. If basketball game prices were raised too much as a result of higher costs of players, people would tend to substitute watching other sports. If carpenters were able to create an effective closed-market monopoly, that would not eliminate product competition through substitution of materials other than wood. An attempt by physicians to raise fees would be restrained by nonprescription drugs, advice of friends, nurses, pharmacists, and faith healers.

Competition among Union Officials

Another way in which the rent of a closed-market monopoly has been competed away is by the union officers themselves. A notorious example arose from union officials' management of union pension, health, and recreation funds. When the officials invested the funds at less than competitively available interest rates, favored borrowers offered some of the difference to union officers as favors, commissions, or business purchases from firms with which the union agent was associated. Low-interest-rate loans have been frequent in union pension fund management.

Competition for Government Favors

During a period of great government regulation, commercial airlines obtained revenues far in excess of what they would have received had the industry been open to new entry. That larger revenue, the source of monopoly rent, was competed for and distributed in several ways. Part went to political campaign funds to maintain favorable government regulations; some to subsidize local air service to small towns of interest to members of Congress; some for better, fancier airplanes and service than the public would have supported if they had had a choice of lower-cost service; and some went to the airline employees — largely to the pilots, who had a strong union.

When the restriction on airline entry ended, airlines could not maintain that high-cost service. Pilots' wages were reduced as new airlines hired nonunion pilots, so all pilots later had to agree to wage reductions. The aircraft mechanics' unions shared in little of that monopoly rent, and they refused to suffer wage reductions consequent to airline deregulation.

CLOSED-MARKET MONOPSONIES OF BUYERS OF LABOR

Employers, also, have colluded to *monopsonize*. Monopsonizing, as explained in a preceding chapter, is the counterpart to monopolizing—buyers collude to restrain competition from other buyers.

Military Draft

The most spectacularly successful monopsony was the military draft. From World War I into the 1970s, the US Army obtained enlisted men by a draft both in peacetime and during wars. A draftee had to serve at below-market wages set by Congress, though there is no law requiring people to serve as local police, sanitation men, or firemen. That is an *implicit* form of tax, and is not included in any government budget records.

After Congress ended the draft, the military has moved toward higher competitive wages with an all-volunteer basis for enlistees. That has raised the *official* budget expenditures and has required an explicit tax on the rest of the public, making the official budget of government expenditures larger. However, there is really a *reduction* in the total cost (i.e., the effect on national income).

People whose productivity is higher in the private sector than in the military will not be attracted to enlist. With a draft, people with alternative productive values higher than they are paid in the military suffered a loss — they sacrificed that alternative higher income. Without a draft, the loss that had been imposed on the draftees will be paid by the rest of the population explicitly to the people enlisted into the military.

For the Union Army in the Civil War, the draft was used, but draftees could (and very many did) hire someone to take their place — at competitive wage rates. The draft was a means of assigning the tax obligation, not only as a way of specifying who would serve in the military.

QUESTIONS AND MEDITATIONS

1) "Technically speaking any labor union is a monopoly in the limited sense that it eliminates competition between workingmen for the available jobs in a particular plant or industry. After all, all unions are combinations of workingmen to increase, by concerted economic action, their wages, i.e., the price at which the employer will be able to purchase their labor" (Arthur Goldberg, Justice, Supreme Court of the United States, and formerly Secretary of the Department of Labor and counsel for the United Steelworkers; quoted from *AFL-CIO: Labor United*, New York, McGraw-Hill, 1956, p. 157). Why did he write "technically speaking" and "in the limited sense"? Is there some other mode of speaking, and is there an unlimited sense of monopoly? Does a monopoly (closed or open?) eliminate competition?

Answer:

"Technically" often means "accurately and unambiguously." All monopoly is limited in some sense to some class of goods. Monopoly does not eliminate competition. It eliminates certain forms of competition and increases reliance on other forms. In the present case, it reduces the scope of wage-rate competition but increases the relevance of nonwage competition such as age, seniority, and so forth.

2) At one time it was said that the steelworkers' union and the US Steel Corporation were both monopolies. In terms of the closed and open monopoly distinction, was that correct?

Answer:

Yes, but the union is not an open-market monopoly and US Steel was. (With respect to the world open market, both are closed-market monopolies as a result of immigration laws and tariffs on imports.)

3) You work for a television manufacturer as a welder, and two unions contend for recognition as the sole bargaining unit for welders. One, a "craft" union, would be composed only of welders; the other, an "industrial" union, would admit all employees who work for television manufacturers.
   a. In which type of union do you think you will be able more effectively to raise your wages by imposing apprenticeship conditions and other devices to restrict the number of people who can seek jobs in competition with you?
   b. Which union do you think will be more able to impose a wage-rate increase upon the employer, or negotiate additional benefits, without first restricting union membership?

Answer:
   a. Craft union of welders.
   b. We don't know. Both types of unions depend on their ability to restrict membership in their negotiations with management.

4) Barriers to labor competition:
   a. Labor groups were strong advocates of raising barriers to immigration in the nineteenth century. Employers objected. Why?
   b. Labor groups were less enthusiastic in support of tariffs (taxes on imported goods), but some were in favor of them. Why?

Answer:
   a. It would have reduced the number of laborers and raised wage rates. Today, many unions continue to oppose "guest-worker programs" for immigrants to temporarily work in the United States.
   b. Producers (employers and employees) of goods that could be obtained

more cheaply by importation wanted tariffs. Tariffs would raise the price of the imported products relative to domestically produced products. In some industries, unions claimed that it was "unfair" that their members had to compete with less-well-paid foreign workers.

5) A former head of the auto workers' union contended that automobile producers should lower their prices to benefit the public.
    a. Why did he not propose that the tax (tariff) of 12 percent on importation of foreign cars at that time be abolished as a means of increasing domestic supply?
    b. Why did the union leader want lower prices for products produced by members of his union?

Answers:
    a. That would have lowered the price of foreign imported cars relative to autos produced by US manufacturers. At those lower prices, foreign manufacturers would have sold more autos in the United States. Members of his union would have to switch to lower-paying jobs.
    b. At relatively lower prices consumers would purchase more cars produced by union members. While the advocacy of lower prices was said to be for the benefit of consumers, it actually was intended to benefit producers (workers) who made cars.

6) Some employers welcome the growth of powerful unions that will be able to raise wages and control the number of employees admitted to the union. Why?

Answer:
    If the union can eliminate low-wage sources of labor, then competing firms — that would survive only with low-wage, low-productivity labor — can be eliminated from competition against the firms with higher-cost labor.

7) "Any craft union that has to resort to the strike to get higher wages is not being operated efficiently. It should instead concentrate on control of apprenticeship rules and admissions in order to assure high-quality, reliable, skilled union members. And it will incidentally thereby achieve its higher wages in a peaceful, democratic way." Explain what the speaker, a successful union leader, mainly meant.

Answer:
    A smaller supply of labor raises wages, but that also means fewer union members. Restricting admission to the crafts unions by imposing higher

skill standards does raise quality and reliability of workers, but it also raises wages — which is what the union leader meant. The union leader's remarks suggest that he perceived that more productive (higher-quality) labor would see a greater amount demanded, even at the higher wage.

8) At a time when it was being debated whether to maintain the military draft or switch to a volunteer system, an official Defense Department study reported that the elimination of the draft by raising wages to enlistees would cost about $5–$15 billion annually. Therefore, the Defense Department in view of that prohibitive cost is recommending continuance of the draft.

   a. Explain why the first sentence is incorrect.
   b. Would you be willing to assert that raising wages to abolish the draft would *reduce* costs?

Answers:

   a. Draftees were forced (prison was the potential penalty for refusing the draft) to leave jobs, education, or other activities in which they would otherwise be engaged. The statement only meant that eliminating the draft would raise the *payments* the federal government would have to record in its budget. Real costs are paid by those who are drafted (and the consumers of products and services that the draftees would have created). By eliminating the draft, military personnel were recruited by paying adequate wages to attract men whose opportunity cost in doing other things was lower than their value to the nation as soldiers.

   b. You should, since it will. By better assignment of people to jobs in this country — resulting from using adequate wages for military personnel — the total productive efficiency and output was increased, so our sacrificed output became smaller. The draft system concealed costs — by making federal *expenditures* lower through the device of compulsory service — just as police-department costs could be made to appear lower if police were drafted.

9) "Long ago we stated the reason for labor organizations. We said that they were organized out of the necessities of the situation; that a single employee was helpless in dealing with an employer; that he was dependent ordinarily on his daily wage for the maintenance of himself and family; that if the employer refused to pay him the wages that he thought fair, he was nevertheless unable to leave the employer and resist arbitrary and unfair treatment; that a union was essential to give laborers opportunity to deal on an equality with their employer" (Charles Evans

Hughes, Chief Justice, Supreme Court of the United States, from the decision in *United States v. Jones and Laughlin*, 1937). Evaluate the above propositions for their meaning — or are they wrong or vacuous?

Answer:

All the statements are empty, wrong, or irrelevant. That many sentences written about unions are empty, wrong, or irrelevant in no way implies that unions are useless, wrong, or misunderstood. An employer must pay wages that are high enough to attract workers from other employers. The individual worker (price-taker) acting alone cannot change the wage rate by withholding his services; however, the employer must offer the worker wages and working conditions attractive enough to attract the worker away from other potential employers and offers.

10) "The strike is an attempt to deny some people the ability to sell their services at open-market prices." Explain why is this a true statement.

Answer:

When the government enforces the strike, employers are prohibited from hiring competing potential employees to replace the striking workers. The union is acting as a closed monopoly.

11) During a strike or labor-dispute negotiations, the government sometimes appoints an investigating panel composed of representatives from the union, the employers, and the consuming public. Which especially affected group is *not* represented on these panels?

Answer:

Those people who would be willing to work at open-market wages and who do not belong to unions.

12) Coalitions of employees called unions permit the members to have an agent to monitor the employer's fulfillment of promised services and working conditions for employees. Employers often welcome that kind of intermediary to smooth relations with employees. Indeed, if the employees don't form their own unions, the employer creates a personnel representative to perform similar services. If the preceding is true, and it is, then why do employers generally oppose unions?

Answer:

Employers are better able to monitor the behavior of "employee representatives" who are also employees of the company. Union leaders who are paid by the union from the proceeds of the dues collected from members are able to compensate themselves—both in salary and "perks"—in amounts and ways that are not in any way controlled by the company. If the union is not organized in such a way that the members can effectively monitor and determine the compensation of the union leaders, there is little effective control. It comes down to a question of who pays those who profess to represent the workers, and who is in a position to hold them accountable for their performance.

CHAPTER 41
LABOR-MARKET CONSTRAINTS

Labor markets are constrained by extensive legislation, usually intended to aid employees. Intent does not always determine effects. We will look at minimum wage laws, fair employment laws, mandated benefits, and *comparable worth* as bases of setting wage rates.

MINIMUM LEGAL WAGES OR LIVING WAGE

Congress sets a nationwide minimum legal wage rate. And almost every state has a minimum-wage law setting a lowest permissible money wage in *covered* industries — those to which the minimum-wage law applies. Noncovered industries are typically personal services, including hotels, agriculture, fast food stores, and babysitting. About 20 percent of working males between 16 and 19 years of age are in jobs in noncovered industries and receive less than the minimum wage per hour. The proportion of employees in noncovered industries who are young women is about 35 percent.

The legal minimums apply typically to only the money component, because it's difficult for outsiders to measure the nonmoney components of the full wage. *Full wages* include Social Security contributions made by the employer, medical insurance, paid vacations and holidays, coffee breaks, the value of on-the-job training/learning, tips, and mastering the skills of the trade while working. The legal money minimum is usually higher than the going money wage rate of *common unskilled labor*.

Almost always, the stated purpose of a minimum-wage law is to help low-wage employees obtain a better standard of living and reduce the number of people in poverty. But since the legal minimum is barely greater than the going wage rate, it tends only to displace the less able workers.

Why not set the minimum at \$30 or \$60 an hour, so employees can earn a really *living wage*? Like everything else, the amount of labor demanded is smaller, the higher the wage rate. However, since the minimum legal wage is usually only barely above the competitive wage for unskilled labor, the reduction in employment is not large enough to command national attention. The debate about raising the minimum legal wage is largely about whether the benefits to those who get the slightly higher wage in some sense compensate for the lost earnings of those who lose their jobs or never get hired into their first job.

Living wage proposals are merely proposals for higher wages. The higher the imposed wage, the fewer the jobs will be maintained. Though no one need be fired immediately because of the higher wage, fewer of those who retire or quit will be replaced.

Why has it received fewer objections from governments than from private employers? Higher costs, insofar as they exceed the competitive market-determined wages, cannot be maintained by market sales values of private firms. Private employers must pay employees and other resource owners out of their sales revenues (which reflect the values consumers place on their services). If voluntary consumer-determined revenues do not cover the costs, the employees will lose their current jobs. A private employer can't call upon taxes to finance its losses, as government agents can. This appears to be why during the past few decades unionization of government employees has grown. They are paid from taxes levied by the government, and not paid from personal wealth of the government administrators.

NONMONEY PRODUCTIVITY AND NONMONEY COMPONENTS OF FULL WAGES

The law specifies only the *money wage component*. The unintended consequence is that to get or retain jobs at the higher imposed wage rates, job applicants will tolerate less pleasant and stricter working conditions, less vacation, less insurance, less employer-supplied work clothing and tools, shorter coffee breaks, more intense labor, less job security, and more occasions of temporary layoffs when demand is transiently low.

Employees' individual characteristics — personality, gender, race, religion, age — become more important for the employer when making hiring decisions. Nonmoney wage components are competed down to offset the excess of the higher money wage — to where the full wage again approximates the competitive level. As in the case of rent controls, where the full rent is competed up to clear the market by including more nonmoney personal characteristics and attributes of the renters and reduced quality of the rented housing, the same adjustment occurs in employment.

Despite these adjustments in the full wage, the new full wage is more expensive for the employer and less desired by the employees. If the new working terms and conditions were just as good or better, they would already have been adopted.

SUBSTITUTION BY DEMANDERS OF LABOR SERVICES

Employers substitute some capital for the now more expensive labor. They substitute by buying more components made elsewhere and by substituting non-labor resources at the employer's premises. Labor-saving devices include power equipment, automated cash registers, and inventory-counting methods. With respect to selling, the firm switches to more *self-service* by customers, reducing the number of sales clerks and grocery baggers. The resulting situation after all the adjustments is less desired, but it reduces the proportion of resources paid for by wages.

OTHER MOTIVES FOR ADVOCATING HIGHER
MINIMUM LEGAL WAGE RATES

Many employees already earning substantially more than the legal wage, and some employers barely breaking even, advocate higher legal minimum wage rates. Why? Is it altruism and a concern for the benefit of low-paid workers? Perhaps; but there is another force — self-interest.

Suppose you were a trucking firm with the latest labor-saving equipment — big, faster, fuel-efficient trucks. Your competitors operate smaller trucks and have more employees per unit of service to customers. A rise in the minimum wage will raise your competitors' costs more than your own, and you will benefit relative to your more labor-intensive competitor. Or suppose you own a retail store with few sales clerks and customers engaging in much self-service. A competitor employs relatively more labor. In both cases, you would benefit at the expense of your competitor.

There has been advocacy by unions in Michigan (where wage rates are relatively high compared to the South) for higher *national* minimum wages, ostensibly to help the "underpaid" Southern workers. Suppose you were an employee in a Michigan auto factory competing against employees with lower wages making cars in Alabama. A higher required wage would raise costs of all firms, but yours would be raised less. You'd then have a competitive edge over the more *labor-intensive* firms that then would have higher total labor costs relative to sales value. You could advocate higher minimum wages "to help the lower-paid employees of your rivals" — though in fact your advocacy is hurting them and benefiting you.

Though employers compete against other employers for customers, it's largely a situation where employees in one firm compete against employees in other firms for customers, using the employers as the agents of the employees.

The pressure for minimum wage enforcement is especially strong in the unionized garment industry, which wants to restrain competition from garments sewn by recent immigrants, primarily women, in what are called *sweatshops*. If their wages were raised to more closely match those in larger firms, the women would lose most of those jobs; they have no equally desirable alternatives. Supposedly to protect immigrants from "exploitation," the higher-paid garment industry sector proposes that the sweatshops be closed or forced to pay higher wages. The minimum-wage laws benefit white, middle-aged, higher-paid employees. The same effect occurs for men relative to women. Women's wages, being on average below wages of males, would be more affected by the minimum-wage law.

EQUAL PAY FOR EQUAL WORK

Compensating wage differences reflect differences in employees' abilities and attractiveness. Acceptance of lower wages enables employees with unattractive features and characteristics to offset competition of people with preferred attributes. Males might be hired in preference to women in a certain occupation, but lower wages to women enable them to match the competition of males for the jobs.

To be sure, employers must pay higher costs to indulge in such preferences, if there are no market value differences in productivity. The same principle applies to minimum-wage laws. People who are fortunate to have more of *desirable* nonmonetary attributes will have a better chance of being hired (or promoted) when wage differentials are restricted by legislation. People with less desirable attributes will not be able to offset them as easily through wage differentials, so they are more likely to be employed in lower-valued jobs or be self-employed or engaged in more criminal activity. In sum, with open-market pricing, differentials in nonmonetary attributes and in market-valued productivity are most easily offset by money-wage differentials in seeking employment.

FAIR EMPLOYMENT LAWS

Fair employment laws are intended (a) to restrain the increase in nonmonetary, invidious discrimination caused by minimum-wage and equal-pay laws, and (b) to eliminate certain kinds of discrimination that occur even without wage-restricting laws. There are prejudices against immigrants, persons of color, women, Jews, and Mormons, among others. Where feasible, there is common acceptance of lower wages to offset those "disadvantages." But if such employees are laid off, they may well charge the employer with unlawful discrimination, thereby imposing disincentives to their initial employment.

The cost of discrimination is higher for a private employer than for a government bureau agent. A private employer indulging a personal preference is paying higher wages for labor that is not more productive of market revenue. A public agency manager does not depend as much on the market value of an employee's services, and therefore does not directly incur a cost for indulging in one's personal preferences about an employee's non-market characteristics.

The dominant situations of discrimination in employment are in government agencies and in public utilities, which are subject to government control of pricing and profits. A public utility manager can tolerate the higher costs of his discriminatory behavior, which can be covered by subsequently higher prices (permitted by public utility regulation) or by taxes. And if such managers are told to hire according to some non-market-related criterion, say, to have equal proportions of males and females, they are more willing to do so, because, again, their institution's income is less dependent on the market value effects of the new mandated policy.

A similar effect occurs with respect to unionization of employees. Government agents, as employers, bear less of the costs than do private employers when agreeing to union demands. The government can resort to taxes to finance the raise. One can surmise why unions in the public sector are more likely to be strong and supported by the political authorities.

LEGISLATIVELY MANDATED BENEFITS

Suppose a benefit were mandated by legislation, rather than voluntarily agreed to by employer and employees. Only in the short run, before competitive forces have been completely felt, would the employees who want those benefits have gained.

If maternity leave or childcare centers are mandated, the currently employed mothers will gain initially, while future women employees will not gain. (1) The gain to the employees favored by the legislation comes at the expense of the resources that are immobile and now less valuable elsewhere. (2) In time, as competition increases among job seekers for jobs with bigger benefits, the money wage will be competed downward.

The new competitive market-clearing full-wage package will be loaded with elements more favorable to working mothers. After full adjustment in wage scales, the effects won't differ much from levying a tax on all employees and using the tax proceeds to provide childcare centers. But initially the employees will have obtained a short-run gain at the expense of the employers, who suffer a loss of value of resources.

EXAMPLES OF EVIDENCE OF THE DEDUCED IMPLICATIONS

A study of legally mandated health insurance indicates that money wages fell by about 85 percent of the cost of mandated health insurance *paid for by the employer*. If your monthly salary were $2,000 and the monthly premium for the mandated health insurance were $80, your monthly salary would be reduced from $2,000 to $1,932 (= $2,000 − $80 × .85), a decrease of $68. The legally mandated benefit costs $80, but the employees take a reduced wage of only $68 to get it.

Who will have benefited? Possibly no one. Each employee to whom the insurance is worth less than the $68 will have lost compared to being paid $68 more. If any employees value the insurance at more than $68, they will have gained. If the aggregated costs for the insurance for all the employees were less than the aggregated worth to the employees, the insurance would not have to be mandated.

When the cost of the mandated benefit exceeds the worth of the benefits to the employees, the current employees may get a short-lived gain. Suppose an employer were required by law to provide *free* haircuts to employees each two weeks at a cost of $20 per haircut. Probably few employees would regard that "free" haircut as worth $20 reduced pay. Money wages would not be competed down by $20. The employer, faced with the higher net costs, would have to reduce output and employment, and jobs would be lost. Employees would have to transfer to producing less valuable goods elsewhere.

If the mandated benefits cost more than their worth to employees, employees are hurt, not benefited. And the resultant higher costs and reduced output here, and less valuable increase in output elsewhere, will harm consumers.

If the mandated action is worth more to employees than the costs, the employees pay the full cost as people compete for those better jobs. They offer to work at a reduced money wage. If the mandated benefit is worth less than its costs, the employees get a temporary gain, except that some will lose their jobs at the higher full cost of labor. But the gains are temporary: in the long run, competition for the jobs establishes the competitive wage. Competition for jobs with larger benefits ultimately pushes down the money portion of the wage to make the full wage a competitive equilibrium wage, composed of revised proportions of money and benefits.

All costs of mandated actions can be treated as *implicit taxes*. The funds could have been collected by the government and then spent for the mandated actions. But when mandated as obligatory expenditures, the employers make the expenditure. The money to pay for the mandated actions is not collected by the government as taxes and then used to pay for the benefits.

WHY WOULD EMPLOYEES OR EMPLOYERS OBJECT TO MANDATED BENEFITS?

Why should employees object to mandated benefits? Don't they get at least a temporary gain, at the employer's expense? If the employees, not the owners (stockholders) of the firm, are paying for the mandated benefits, why do employers object to employer-paid benefits? Aren't the costs of the mandated nonmoney benefits to employees offset by lower money wages or covered by higher prices to customers?

The higher labor costs squeeze the profit margin. Production would continue until the resources wear out. Then, reinvestment would occur only to the extent that the higher costs are covered. At that time, the higher labor costs would restrain investment, resulting in smaller output and higher prices to consumers.

Future investors won't complain about the earlier mandated employee benefits. Later investors will invest only to the extent their investments are expected to be profitable despite the higher labor costs. At the higher labor costs, a larger part of the investment will be toward labor-saving equipment. Consumers will be paying higher prices for a reduced output. Some employees must then accept lower full wages at the existing job or transfer to a lower-paying job elsewhere, or be unemployed, or leave the workforce. At that time, the free ride of employees on the lost value of the employer's earlier investment is ended.

COMPARABLE WORTH AS A BASIS OF WAGE RATES?

Some years ago, wages set according to comparable worths were commonly advocated. It was argued that some employees were underpaid relative to others doing work of comparable worth. To eliminate those inequalities, comparable wage rates were to be set on the basis of evaluating jobs according to various requirements and characteristics of the jobs (experience, aptitude or intelligence, physical effort, education, etc.). These features were assigned weights, and the total of the weights was to determine the relative pay levels.

For example, the social worth of garbage collection was to be given weight in determining the wage. If nursing had the same total weight, then each nurse and each garbage collector should get the same salary. The advocates also proposed that some adjustments should be made to allow for degrees of effort and costs of training and the difficulties of doing the work. No great imagination is required to discern the extraordinary vagueness and lack of objectivity in those adjustments.

If the wage rates were set on the basis of those proposed measures of comparable worth, the results would be shortages of some employees and surpluses of other workers. The wage rates would not be market-clearing wages.

Comparable worth proposals imply a fundamental change in the economic and social system, from private property, competitive exchange systems toward governmental administrative setting of resource allocations and rewards. Such proposals would prompt a greater reliance on taxes instead of sales revenues. If applied, they would reduce market output, and would reduce inequality of incomes, with employees being assigned to jobs by a central authority.

QUESTIONS AND MEDITATIONS

1) "The higher the legally constrained minimum-wage rate, the greater the amount of unemployment of unskilled workers." Is this correct?

Answer:

Those who cannot provide labor services worth as much as the minimum-wage rate will lose wage-paying employment and will have to work as self-employed or commission-basis employees. Thus, in saying that a higher minimum wage reduces employment, we mean employment for wages — not work in industries and sectors not covered by minimum-wage legislation, or where labor services can be offered by "self-employed" contractors.

2) As a beginning lawyer, would you benefit if fees for the following were set by the bar association: drawing up someone's will, serving as an executor of an estate, arranging for a divorce?

Answer:

It would be made harder for less experienced and less established lawyers to get business if the fees were uniform among all lawyers. But if fees are set at a point that maximizes total net revenue from this kind of business — as in collusive price-setting — the present value of the future receipts may be higher.

3) A representative of the Congress of Racial Equality advocated raising the minimum legal wage in order to help black people get higher wages.
   a. Would black people benefit from a higher minimum wage?
   b. Would it reduce or increase discriminatory hiring?
   c. Why didn't they suggest tripling the minimum wage?

Answer:
>   a. Some would. But we conjecture most would not.
>   b. It would increase revealed discrimination by color, reducing the possibilities of black people to compete by taking lower wages to get jobs. (Do you think a law prohibiting choice of employees by color or race would be effective enough to offset increased incentives to discriminate? What would be the monitoring and enforcement cost of legislation or regulations designed to prohibit discrimination on the basis of race, religion, sex, age, and other nonmonetary criteria, versus allowing money wages to be freely determined in labor markets?)
>   c. We must be "reasonable."

4) If in some town the minimum wage rate for taxi-driver employees were raised to $50 an hour, what would happen to the ratio of cabs driven by the owners to cabs driven by employees of cab owners?

Answer:

Increase. Self-employment is a way of evading wage regulation.

5) You are an immigrant. Would you prefer laws insisting on equal pay for equal work, minimum-wage laws, or apprentice laws that might be effective in raising wages above the open-market level?

Answer:

We would be dubious of all those laws, since they restrict the opportunity of an immigrant to compete against more popular types of residents in seeking jobs.

6) As a summer-job-seeking college student, are your chances of getting a job increased or decreased if the wages you can get in a summer resort, as a babysitter and so forth, are enforced by a union comprised of current full-time employees?

Answer:

Decreased. The union will seek higher wages to keep only full-time employees (its members) at work, with less interest in casual, inexperienced, seasonal laborers. And a higher wage will lead employers to shun less productive workers.

7) As a college-age babysitter, would you benefit if an association of babysitters were organized and a minimum wage of $20 an hour enforced?

Answer:

Depends in part upon whether parents prefer high school–age people or older people for babysitters. Junior high school students will suffer, since they are generally thought to be of poorer quality (younger, less experienced, less responsible) and manage to compete by offering to work at lower wages.

8) Some employment contracts provide the employee with the following: paid time off for jury duty, funerals of relatives, voting, sickness, and vacations; free parking space and work clothes; retirement; two weeks' severance pay; seniority rights over new employees; no discharge for union activities; no discharge if job is displaced by new machinery.

a. Suppose you were to offer to work for some employer who did not give any of these provisions and who insisted on the right to fire or discharge you at any time for any reason. Would you consider working for him at the *same take-home pay* as for employment with such a contract?

b. Would the employer be willing to pay you a higher take-home salary for an employment contract without all those provisions listed earlier?

c. In the light of your answers to the preceding questions, who do you think pays for those benefits listed earlier?

Answer:

a. No.

b. He would offer higher wages.

c. Employees.

9) At one time, the National Teachers Federation, a teachers' union, advocated a single salary scale, wherein every teacher, regardless of specialty, gets the same salary in the first year of teaching, with salary thereafter tied strictly to years of service. Who would benefit and who would suffer if that were made universal: Men or women? Superior or inferior teachers? Mathematics or physical-education teachers?

Answer:

The losers are those who would have advanced more rapidly because of personal superiority in job performance as judged by superiors. We conjecture those who would have advanced relatively rapidly are men, superior teachers, mathematics teachers. (What is your conjecture? If we differ, is it in principles of analysis or in estimation of attributes that would lead to more rapid advance?)

10) Laws have been passed designed to prohibit employers from discriminating among potential employees according to race, religion, and, in some instances, age. Why are there no laws prohibiting *employees* from similarly discriminating among employers for whom they choose to work?

Answer:

Perhaps employee discrimination is regarded as acceptable. At any rate, it probably would be incapable of being enforced even if prohibited by law.

11) Assume that you are a member of a minority group in some country and have reason to doubt that your private property rights would be enforced and respected in that community.
   a. In what forms of capital would you invest?
   b. What kinds of skills (as forms of accumulations of wealth) would you encourage for your children?
   c. Do you know of any evidence of such actual behavior of minority groups?

Answer:

   a. Human capital through education and increased skills, because it cannot be confiscated or expropriated as easily as real property — such as buildings and machinery.
   b. Professional skills — such as doctors, lawyers, teachers, accountants.
   c. Jews, Armenians, and other ethnic and religious minorities.

12) At some colleges, students seek membership on committees that appoint or terminate faculty members. The faculty usually contends that employment is a matter best judged by qualified people like other faculty members. Students contend that the faculty chosen affects their lives, and hence they should have a say in the matter. Perhaps students already have more power than the faculty. Explain.

Answer:

Students as a group (and parents who pay most of their expenses) have more power than faculty in the sense that they select which colleges to attend, what fields to major in, and which classes (professors) to take. Payments for tuition, room and board, textbooks, and other expenses reflect these decisions. Over time, colleges that are not responsive to the demand of the students and their parents will lose applicants and enrollments. The quality of applicants and enrollments of these schools will decline, further affecting the school's reputation and ability to raise funds. All of this will affect hiring of new faculty and the advancement of existing faculty members. As students switch majors from one field toward another, the faculty in some fields will be expanded relative to others. Within a field of concentration, word spreads among students who the better teachers are, and more students register for those classes and try to avoid "unpopular" teachers, ultimately affecting which classes are expanded and which are cut back over time.

13) In feudal England, there was no unemployment—only work or leisure. Employment for wages was rare. But the rise of the commercial system introduced markets for labor services and induced peasants to sacrifice feudal security (laboring as serfs on the land of others) for the hazards of private contractual employment and unemployment. By the sixteenth century, employment for money wages was well established, but maximum permissible wage rates were set by government, and potential employers were exhorted not to offer more and were punished if caught paying more than the legal maximum wage.
   a. What devices do you think developed as a means of paying more than the maximum-wage ceilings?
   b. Why would the government have imposed *maximum* limits to wages?

Answer:
   a. Employees were also paid in nonmonetary ways, such as "free" or "low-cost" clothing, food, or housing.
   b. Feudal lords wanted people to remain tied to their estates, so they tried to prevent industrial employers from luring them to more attractive industrial activity.

14) During World War II, men were conscripted into the armed forces, so women were needed to work in the factories, especially to build airplanes and other military equipment. However, war-time controls on wages and prices prevented employers from offering higher incomes to women to join the workforce. One consequence was employers began offering "free" health care benefits to the women and their families. This legacy, the "third-party payer" form of medical insurance, is still common and is often a major objective of union labor negotiations. What have been the long-term consequences of this "historical accident" of wage controls giving rise to employer-provided health care?

Answer:
   During the decades following the end of the war, employees became less and less concerned about the prices charged by doctors and hospitals be-cause the insurance provided by their employer was paying most, or all, of

the bill. Doctors and hospitals had less incentive to compete on the basis of best medical services at the lowest prices. Costs of many medical services covered by insurance rose continuously, even where new medical technologies would have suggested falling prices. In contrast, non-insurance-covered medical services — such as laser eye surgery or elective cosmetic surgery — have seen continuously falling prices as new technologies and procedures were developed.

CHAPTER 42

MONEY, PRICES, AND INFLATION

MONEY AND PRICES

Changes in the money prices of goods and assets convey information. If an economy's monetary unit is known to be a stable standard of value, then changes in money prices will accurately reflect changes in the relative values of goods and assets. That is, price fluctuations signal changes in the demand for, and supply of, goods and assets; resources are then shifted toward more valued uses and away from those less valued. This is essential in order for the economy to achieve the most economically efficient aggregate output. In other words, standards of living will be highest when all price changes can be interpreted as relative price changes. Similarly, all changes in interest rates would be changes in real interest rates — a reflection of changes in people's preferences about time, changes in the pace of innovation, or changes in the economy's endowment of productive resources.

When innovation occurs and new goods are invented, the average well-being of the society is improved but not because the information content of money has changed. Innovation involves *creative destruction* — the economic value of something old is reduced by the discovery of a new product or more efficient way of producing an old product. Relative prices change; a market system treats such changes as signals that resources are better used by shifting away from the old and toward the new.

Unfortunately, in the world of fiat money, one can never be certain that observed changes in the prices of specific things or changes in interest rates reflect real events — crop failures, for example — so mistakes are made in the allocation of productive resources. As a consequence, the well-being of the society is less than optimal.

When the standard of value — money — does not mean the same thing over time, we say there is noise or static in the pricing of goods and services. This static means the signals that are coming to decision makers from observed price changes cannot be relied upon to indicate that the use of productive resources is shifting.

In economies where changes in money prices are contaminated by the changing purchasing power of money, false signals are being sent to businesses and households. Erroneous decisions are being made, and resources are being misallocated. Standards of living — real incomes — fail to rise at their potential rate.

Since nominal interest rates (the kind seen quoted every day) respond to shifting expectations about the future purchasing power of money, changes in *real* interest rates are obscured, so resources are misallocated. Saving and investment decisions are affected; growth is impaired.

INFLATION

It would be hard to get agreement on a definition of inflation and even more difficult to get agreement on an acceptable measure of inflation. Economists are better able to describe the conditions that would prevail when there is an *absence* of inflation or deflation. Common usage of the term *inflation* is misleading because it confuses cause and effect. Often people think that inflation occurs because *prices are rising*. That is too simple. Such a diagnosis often leads naive politicians to think the appropriate prescription is either to put controls in place to prevent prices of things from going up or to ensure that incomes rise at least as rapidly so that standards of living do not erode. Both prescriptions are wrong.

To inflate certainly means *to make larger*, but what is increasing is the number of money units required to purchase the same basket of goods over time. The diagnosis should be that money units are being created at a faster rate than people want to add to their holdings of them. *Too much money chasing too few goods* is the familiar definition of the cause of inflation. The appropriate prescription would be to avoid creating money at a pace that is faster than people want to add to their money balances.

The obvious political risk of talking as though inflation means that prices and wages are rising is that people come to fear that policymakers are out to deny them the deserved wage increase or higher price for their products that other people seem willing to pay. Public surveys reveal that people form ideas about inflation based on prices of things they *buy*. They rarely see higher prices of things they *sell* as anything other than just rewards for their labors.

The expressions *price stability* or *stable prices* are not any more helpful. Prices of things — both goods for current consumption and investment assets — are constantly changing. All innovation implies lower (relative) prices for previous goods and technology. The familiar pattern for all newly introduced goods is for their prices to fall as methods of production and distribution are improved and as economies of scale are achieved.

Conversely, as wealth rises, people spend a declining *share* of their income on certain goods thought of as *necessities* and larger shares of their income on goods thought of as luxuries. Such shifts in consumption patterns may be associated with rising prices of the more sought-after goods. These are natural manifestations of a market economy. It would be highly undesirable to have policies designed to maintain stable prices.

People know that the money prices of some things will rise (cars, concert tickets, impressionist paintings, greens fees, tuition, etc.) even though they cannot be sure by how much. Money prices of other things will fall (refrigerators, telephone calls, computers, televisions, DVD players, carpets, microwave ovens, etc.), even though they cannot be sure by how much. Most of the time for most things (food, gasoline, clothing, prescription drugs, etc.) they cannot be certain whether the money prices in the future will be higher or lower. Such uncertainties cannot be eliminated from a market economy. As a consequence, people have always chosen to use *as money* (subject to the effectiveness of criminal prohibitions by governments) the entity that their own experience suggests is more likely to be exchangeable in the future for known quantities of things they desire.

Uncertainty about present and future relative values of things is precisely why people hold money balances at all. When alternatives are available, they will choose to use as money the currency they are least uncertain about with respect to future money prices. People know they get hurt by inflation so they naturally seek assets and alternative monies that are expected to better maintain real value. However, for over forty years — from 1933 to 1974 — the US government made it illegal for American citizens to hold gold as a way of protecting themselves from falling purchasing power of the US dollar.

Time and other resources are required to shop — to gather information about relative prices of various goods, services, and investment assets. People will naturally prefer to use the monetary units that economize best on the use of their time and productive resources to gather information about relative prices and to conduct transactions.

In recent decades, the world has had ample opportunity to observe ordinary people in Latin America, the former Soviet Republics, and central Europe choose to use US dollars rather than the currency supplied by their own governments. Obviously, they do so based on an expectation that the information available to them regarding the relative values of things is more reliable when denominated in dollars than in pesos, rubles, dinars, or bahts.

Bad experiences have taught most people that neither inflation nor deflation enhances economic performance. What also occurs, but is not as easy to observe, is that unanticipated inflations and deflations induce redistributions of wealth — especially between debtors and creditors — and they leave the average standard of living lower. According to a former governor of the Federal Reserve, "a place that tolerates inflation is a place where no one tells the truth." He meant, of course, that true changes in the relative values of things cannot be observed from stated prices when the purchasing power of money is not stable.

Nevertheless, inflation, like death and taxes, appears inevitable. We know of no nation that hasn't experienced it. Inflation is a tax — of a special kind — on money. It's easy to impose, and it's usually not even thought of as a tax.

HOW IS INFLATION MEASURED?

Inflation is a continuously *rising level* of money prices of goods and services. The general upward long-term trend of prices is usually measured by the *CPI* — the Consumer Price Index computed by the Bureau of Labor Statistics of the US Department of Labor. It is intended to measure what is happening to a *basket of goods* purchased by a typical working family. Several variants of the CPI are computed for different groups of people, such as the elderly and for geographical regions.

It is common to hear references to measures of consumer prices as the *cost of living* or the *cost-of-living index*. However, these statistical measures are not intended to reflect what is actually happening to the economic well-being, or cost of living, of any one person or family.

The usual consumer price index reports the changes in dollar costs of a *fixed* basket of goods and services that middle-class urban residents or typical workers buy for day-to-day living — food, clothing, automobiles, housing, household goods, fuel, medicines, health care, repair costs, and movies, to name a few. The prices in that unchanged basket in successive months are used for computing the total costs, which form the Consumer Price Index series. The first date of a series is assigned a value of 100, and the cost is computed for each succeeding month of the same basket.

Not all prices increase at the same rate over time, and some may fall even when most are rising. But during persistent inflation, the *weighted average* of all prices of the goods and services in the basket rises.

THE CAUSE OF INFLATION

The dominant cause of every *persisting* inflation has been an increasing money supply relative to aggregate production. However, there also have been rises in the general level of prices that were very short-lived. A one-time increase in the

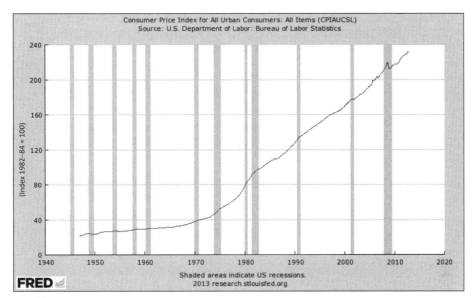

Figure 42.1

supply of money without a corresponding increase in aggregate production, or a decrease in aggregate production without a corresponding decrease in the money supply, would raise the average of prices, and they would stay at that new level.

A country can experience a rise in its price *level* if the price of a critical imported good or resource jumps up. If a country is heavily dependent on imported energy, such as oil or natural gas, then a reduced petroleum supply and consequent higher price would cause an increase in the country's price level. Because energy is an input to the production of many other products, the reduced supply of petroleum would also reduce the output of many final goods, and that reduction in output will, in turn, be reflected in higher prices. However, if the price of energy stabilizes at the new higher level, there will not be a continuing upward increase in prices. With fewer goods and an unchanged amount of money in the economy, the price level would not continue to rise, and what is called inflation will not persist.

There can be exceptions to the rule that persistent inflation has been a result of increasing amounts of money — increasing faster than the increase in real goods and services. Historically, there have been a few episodes when the increasing price level was the result of a persistent, long-term decline in the amount of goods being produced and consumed — such as the Irish Potato

Famine, Black Death, or Bubonic Plague in Europe. Such disasters are not the result of excessive money creation and are better described as periods of *wealth loss*, rather than periods of inflation.

The more common case of rising prices caused by the increased supply of money affects both the production of output in an economy and the distribution of wealth. The amount of wealth there is available to consume by an economy will be affected by an inflationary process because of the effects on relative prices. Less well recognized, the distribution of income in the economy also will be altered.

As described above, if all participants in a market economy — both producers and consumers — make decisions in the firm belief that there is no inflation or deflation, then they see all actual price changes (of assets as well as goods) as *relative* price changes. Recall that either the demand curve or the supply curve has to change in order for there to be a price change. Knowing that the higher price of coffee results from poor crops in coffee-producing countries will cause different — temporary — adjustments from a general change in preference for coffee versus tea.

Furthermore, if everyone believes that the purchasing power of money is stable, all *observed* changes in interest rates are changes in *real* interest rates, not the inflation premium *add-on* that lenders require during inflation. That belief tells producers that the best allocation of productive resources has changed, and it will affect consumers' *buy-versus-rent* and other decisions.

Once uncertainty about the purchasing power of money is introduced, signals about the meaning of changing relative prices and interest rates are no longer as reliable. Both producers and consumers will make mistakes they would have avoided had money been stable. Resources will not be allocated to their most effective and preferred uses, and wealth creation will be impaired. In the end, inflation will leave the economy less wealthy than it would have been with stable money.

THE CAUSE OF THE INCREASED MONEY SUPPLY

While the cause of persistent inflation is a continuous increase in the supply of money, the more fundamental cause can be regarded as whatever caused the money supply to be increased. Increasing the money supply is an easy, obscure, and effective tax levied by a national government, but it is not the sort of tax that is debated by a congress or parliament. Central banks are the vehicles governments use to increase the supply of money to produce inflation. When inflation does occur, it is common for politicians and news commentators to assert that foreign aid, agricultural price supports, labor unions, corporations, or an

excess of the federal government's total of expenditures over tax receipts —
deficits — caused the inflation.

Yet, none of those factors require an increase in the quantity of money in
the economy. More spending by the government is not the same as, nor does
it require, a larger supply of money in the economy. Still, governments do tend
to spend more by increasing the supply of money, which is usually politically
more feasible than by explicit taxation.

The Money Supply and Inflation of the Price Level

Suppose we awoke today with twice as much money as yesterday (both in our
wallets and bank accounts) and unchanged amounts of other goods, as if the
new money came from the tooth fairy. We would have too much money relative
to our other forms of wealth. That does not mean we would have too much
wealth. Instead, we would have more money than we prefer relative to other
forms of our wealth. We would each try to restore a desired balance in our total
portfolio of wealth by reducing our holdings of money by buying other goods
or assets. But that just passes the money to another person who sold us something, with no change in the total supply of money. Prices would be pulled
up, and almost everyone's wages, income, and wealth, all measured in dollars,
would appear to be higher. However, unless production of goods and services
is increased, the reality is that society would not be wealthier.

Prices of all goods, services, and assets will have risen to a level at which
the public will want to hold the larger amount of money that it has. We would
be wealthier in dollar terms, but not in aggregate purchasing power or the
amount of goods and services. While the average wealth of the economy in real
terms may initially be the same, some people will be made worse off and others
better off, as we will see.

HOW INFLATION IS DISRUPTIVE AND CONFUSING

We know that in a market economy, some prices are rising and others are falling and that, in the absence of inflation, the weighted average of the prices that
are rising will equal the weighted average of the prices that are falling. When
the weighted average of rising prices is larger than the weighted average of the
prices that are falling, there is some inflation. How much inflation is occurring
is never certain, so there be can be disruptions caused by confusion between
dollar price-level changes and relative price changes. Detecting changes in *relative* prices becomes more difficult and less reliable during inflation when all
dollar prices are rising.

Even for a given rate of inflation — say, 5 percent — not all prices will rise simultaneously or to the same extent, because demands and supplies of various goods are affected by many other factors in different degrees. During persistent inflations, comparisons must be made between many prices, which are changing at different rates. That is difficult, and there will be unreliable information, with confusion and mistakes in purchase, production, and investment decisions.

Another disruptive effect of inflation is the unintended transfer of wealth when interest rates fail to predict the inflation. And there's the popular belief that inflation is good in that it promotes higher employment and output.

MISTAKEN BELIEFS ABOUT CAUSES OF INFLATION

Confusing the Measure with the Cause

There's a tendency in the media to blame the inflation on the price of the good — perhaps gasoline or steel — which happens to have risen the most in a recent time period. That confuses cause and effect. A related confusion is associated with the word *deflation*. While in a general sense it means a persistent decline of the average price level, another way to think of it is as a persistent rise of the purchasing power of money. When nations based their money on gold and silver, there were long periods when the average of all prices in terms of this specie-backed money did decline.

It is possible, but rare, also to have persistent deflations when an economy uses a fiat — unbacked, *paper* — money. Yet in such a case it is important not to make the mistake of attributing the cause of the deflation to the prices that are falling the most. It is not likely that people would say that falling computer prices or cellular telephone prices *cause deflation*, because clearly it is technology that is advancing. Nevertheless, if farm prices are falling (maybe because of bumper crops), farmers will complain about deflation.

Transient Fluctuations of Prices of Goods Do Not Cause Inflation

Short-lived, transient fluctuations in the supplies of goods cause short-lived rises or falls in prices of those goods. Everyone understands that the prices of fruits and vegetables are lower in *season* than *off season*. Such price fluctuations are not related to a process that generates inflation.

Less obvious is whether higher prices of French wines sold in the United States are a reflection of inflation. If the price increases reflect the underlying supply of wine or the consumer demand for it, we do not call that inflation. However, if economic policies in the United States are causing general inflationary pressures on the dollar, then the foreign exchange value of the dollar will fall compared to currencies experiencing less inflation. That will cause the dollar prices of imported goods — like French wine — to be higher, so it is a reflection of inflation.

In summary, we distinguish between (a) transient, reversible increases in prices, caused by variations in supplies of particular goods, and (b) the persisting rising price level caused by increases in the money supply.

WEALTH TRANSFERS BY INFLATION

Inflation imposes a tax on the public — without legislation explicitly mandating the tax. Consider the ways.

1) Tax on Money

The creators and initial spenders of new money created by government obtain goods from the public. With *more received* money, the public's demand for goods rises, and the price level rises. The subsequent rise in the price level reduces the purchasing power of dollars held by the public. That reduction is what the new money gained for the government from the public. An inflation in the price level at a rate of 3 percent per year, as a result of increasing the supply of money, becomes a 3 percent tax on the public's money holdings — *a 3 percent loss of that money's purchasing power.* That's happened in many nations — enduring inflation caused by printing additional amounts of new money to buy goods and services for government agencies.

Printing more money to finance the government is not necessarily undesirable, at least from the point of view of politicians. Many less-developed nations do not have an effective system of explicit taxes. Income taxes and sales taxes require that government can reliably verify incomes and sales. If they are not able to do so, many activities are financed by printing money. Even when the public understands that the purchasing power of the paper money is falling, they have little choice but to accept it because it's the only way they can pay the explicit taxes they owe.

2) Taxes on Illusory Gains in Wealth of Resources

Besides taxing the public's holding of money, inflation increases taxes by creating illusory increases in income and values of resources, which are then taxed. That happens in several ways.

a. Graduated Income Taxes

The graduated (progressive) income tax means that each successive bracket of income has a higher *marginal tax* on the *marginal income.* Suppose incomes up to $10,000 annually are

taxed at 10 percent ($1,000), and the next $10,000 in income is
taxed at 15 percent ($1,500). A person earning $20,000 annually
would pay a total tax of $2,500, which is 12.5 percent of the income
(= $2,500/$20,000).

Now, look at the tax effects of doubling the price level, with a
$20,000 income rising to $40,000. Suppose that income above
$20,000 is taxed at 20 percent, or $4,000 (= .20 × $20,000). The total
tax is now $6,500 (= $2,500 + $4,000). That entire increase in taxes
is caused by being pushed into the higher nominal dollar income
brackets when inflation raised the *dollar* measure of income. The
overall effective tax rate is raised from 12.5 percent to 16.25 percent
(= $6,500/$40,000) without any change in the tax laws or rise in real
income. The government wins because its tax revenue has increased
more than the price level has increased.

b. The Capital Gains Tax

Taxes are levied on increases in market dollar values of any asset,
payable when the asset is sold. If you buy a painting or common
stock for $1,000, and three years later sell it for $2,000, while prices
of all goods have doubled on average, you are not wealthier in real
terms. But you must pay a tax on that $1,000 wealth gain — called
a capital gains tax. Though the $1,000 gain in dollar terms is an
illusory gain, the tax is not illusory.

c. Depreciation Replacement

Under business tax laws, the dollar costs of replacing
depreciating assets cannot be adjusted upward to reflect replacement
costs at the new price level. The reported dollar net earnings are
overstated, because the allowable costs (wear and tear of capital
equipment) are too low. Business firms must pay a tax on a fictitious
gain, reflecting merely a change in the price level. This is believed to
be a reason stock prices tend to dip when fears of inflation increase.

3) An Inflation Tax on Holders of Government Bonds

The inflation premium in the nominal interest rate package on
government bonds can be substantially below the inflation rate, and
bondholders have lost billions of dollars of wealth to the government.
Suppose the interest rate on government (or any other) bonds is 5
percent. If the price level rises 4 percent in a year, the bondholder
would lose 4 percent of the worth of a $10,000 bond, a loss of $400
in purchasing power of the $10,000 principal. The 5 percent interest
received in that year would be $500 (= .05 × $10,000). But that $500

interest would buy only 96 percent as much, or $480, a 4 percent loss from the 4 percent inflation. The bondholder's total loss in that year is the $400 loss pertaining to the $10,000 principal's purchasing power and the $20 lost purchasing power from the $500 interest, a total loss of $420. That $420 is the inflation-induced gain to the government, which is not officially recorded as a tax collected from bondholders. But the main point is that it's an *underanticipated* inflation that creates a tax on lenders to the government.

You can replace the government in the preceding analysis with any private borrower. What we called a *tax* by the government would be called a *wealth transfer* from the lender to the borrower.

WHY LEND IF INFLATION IS EXPECTED?

That raises the question: Why lend to anyone else, government or not, if a prospective inflation can be accurately predicted? If a 4 percent rate of inflation were anticipated, the lender could require the borrower, on a one-year loan, to pay interest of 5 percent and to increase the total principal to be repaid by another 4 percent to adjust for the higher price level. The borrower would repay $1,000 plus the $50 interest of 5 percent on the principal, and then increase that total of $1,050 by 4 percent to adjust for the price level rise. That can be written: Repayment = $1,000 × 1.05 × 1.04 = $1,000 × 1.092 = $1,092.

The term 1.092 tells us the nominal interest rate is 9.2 percent per year, covering the 5 percent pure interest and the 4 percent inflation rate. (The additional 0.2 in the .092 is the 4 percent interest on the 5 percent growth of the principal during the year.) The lender gets back $1,092, which has exactly 5 percent more purchasing power at the 4 percent higher price level than the purchasing power initially loaned to the borrower. There's no wealth transfer as a result of the inflation, because it was *correctly anticipated*. If the inflation is overpredicted, the borrower will lose.

INTERPERSONAL WEALTH TRANSFERS AS A RESULT
OF *INCORRECTLY* ANTICIPATED INFLATION

If the nominal interest rate on government bonds, or any other bonds, reflects a correctly predicted inflation adjustment premium (which will match the realized inflation rate), both the lender and borrower are protected from unintended *interpersonal* transfers of wealth. We emphasize interpersonal, because the government gains by the tax on money, whether or not the inflation was predicted. There is no way individuals can avoid that—as long as they hold any money that loses purchasing power. But transfers of wealth to other persons can be avoided by being neither a net monetary creditor nor debtor and therefore being neutral.

If the amount of money owed to you (your monetary creditor side) is equal to the amount you owe to others (your monetary debtor side), you'll be neutral. What you gain or lose on your debts (money you owe) will be exactly offset by what you lose or gain on your credits (money owed you). (Appendix B provides an example of what happens if you have debts of money not equaling credits.) But this neutrality will not protect the public from the tax on money.

SUMMARY

1) Inflation is a persisting increase in the money prices of a group of goods.
2) Almost every significant inflation has been caused by an increase in the absolute quantity of money. Exceptions are rare events like the Black Death during the Middle Ages, which reduced populations and raised wage rates.
3) The effects of an inflation depend on how accurately it was anticipated. If anticipated, no transfer of wealth would go from creditors to debtors, because the interest rate on debts would have been fully adjusted. However, because government-issued currency bears no interest, money holders lose during all inflations.
4) Wage and price controls do not reduce inflation, and cannot prevent the loss of the purchasing power of money. The exchange value of money is reduced by restrictions on the right to offer money in the market. Suppressing prices is usually followed by political controls, such as government allocation of price-controlled goods — rationing.
5) By pushing dollar incomes into higher tax brackets of the graduated income tax schedule, inflation creates an automatic, nonlegislated increase in income taxes. The tax on capital gains (the gains in the nominal values of assets) is similarly increased.

QUESTIONS AND MEDITATIONS

1)   Which of the following would not serve as money: tobacco, sugar, salt, cattle, nails, copper, grain, beads, tea, cowrie shells, fish hooks, chocolate, cigarettes, feathers, silver, gold, printed paper, stones, promissory notes, debt?

Answer:

All have served as money at one time in various countries.

2) "Money is a medium of exchange. It is a common denominator or measure of value. It is a store of value. The first two are relatively unique to money, whereas the last is not." Explain what is meant by each sentence.

Answer:

Most exchanges involve money as one of the goods, and the exchange rates are expressed in terms of money. Use of money prices makes it easier to compare the worth of disparate items, like a pair of shoes and a loaf of bread. But many nonperishable goods have values that persist over time.

3) What are some desirable physical attributes for a commodity if it is to serve as money? Its usefulness as money is affected by its recognizability, portability, divisibility, durability, and resistance to counterfeiting. Why?

Answer:

These physical features help to reduce the transactions cost of the commodity that serves as money, but are not all essential. The Pacific Island of Yap used very large stones that were not transportable, but change of ownership occurred as a result of transactions.

4) What is legal tender? A $10 Federal Reserve note says, "This note is legal tender for all debts, public and private, and is redeemable in lawful money at the United Sates Treasury or at any Federal Reserve Bank." If you ask the Treasury to redeem that note for lawful money, what will you be given?

Answer:

If the courts of a country will require payment in a certain currency as a result of a judgment or settlement, that currency is legal tender. If you win a court case in which a seller defaulted on his agreement to deliver gold to you, the court will require simply that you be paid an amount of US dollars in settlement of your claim. So the court is not treating gold as money—legal tender. The Treasury might give you another $10 Federal Reserve note, or two $5 notes.

5) Does the value of money depend upon what it is made of or upon its quantity?

Answer:

Value of money is what you can exchange or trade 1 unit of the money for—you could trade one dollar for one quart of ice cream, or one cup of coffee, or one loaf of bread. The value of money depends also on the total quantity of money in existence. If the stock of money doubles, after adjustments occur, prices would about double. Then one dollar would trade for only half as much as before.

6) What serves as money:
   a. Do you think bus and subway tokens should be counted in the money supply? Why?
   b. Would you consider time deposits or savings accounts to be money? Why?
   c. Traveler's checks?

Answer:
   a. No. They are used only for exchange for a particular good. Normally, such tokens cannot be used for general purchases. They are receipts for prepayment for a special kind of service to be rendered to you.
   b. We would not, because they are not used generally for purchases; instead, they are first converted to currency or checking accounts. But they are so readily transferred to money that for some questions it may prove more useful to consider them as money.
   c. Traveler's checks issued by companies such as American Express are considered currency, and counted as part of the stock of money.

7) What is meant by "the demand for money"? Money itself is not eaten, worn, or otherwise consumed; so, except for the miserly joy of running through it in one's bare feet, what gains can there be in *not* spending all money on consumption as soon as it is received?

Answer:
   Money is used to facilitate trade by economizing on transactions costs (so you don't have to carry around other items that other people may want in exchange for what you want to purchase), it's a store of value, it's easily recognizable, it's portable (easy to carry around), and it's durable. Sometimes the terms of an exchange are different when it is "all cash" from the buyer to the seller.

8) Money and wealth:
   a. Why should you be happy to wake up and find you have twice as much money, but not if other people also have that lucky experience?
   b. Would you behave differently if you were the only one who luckily

doubled his money stock than if everyone else also got twice as much overnight? Why?

Answer:

   a. If you are the only one with twice as much money, you are richer and you can buy twice as much. But if everybody's money holdings double, as the larger money stock is spent prices would rise and about double, so you would end up with the same amount of real goods as before the money stock doubled.

   b. Probably; you would be wealthier than before and relative to everyone else.

9) Twenty years ago, you paid $5,000 for a gadget. Now you have to replace it with a new gadget, and today's price is $10,000. Is it obvious that the new item is twice as expensive as the one bought years ago?

Answer:

The money price has doubled. But (a) there may have been quality changes — today's gadget is better (or worse) than the old, and (b) the general level of prices may have more than doubled, so you now must give up less of other products to buy a gadget than you had to forgo in the original purchase.

10) You are trying to compute a price index. The price of some good is reported as $100; however, the amount available in shops is less than the amount demanded, and shops often report they are "sold out." I offer to sell you a vintage 1970 Ford Mustang for $1,000, whenever I happen to have one in stock, but I don't have one available now, nor is it likely I shall ever have one. Apartments are subjected to rent controls, and, at present rents, there is a long waiting list of potential renters at that price. How relevant are these prices in formulating your price index?

Answer:

The relevant price is the transactions price at which buyers can purchase the amount they want to buy and sellers can sell the amount they want to sell. "Posted" prices at which none of the goods are available, or are so high that there is little demanded, are not meaningful.

11) "The progressive deterioration in the value of money throughout history is not an accident, and has behind it two great driving forces — the impecuniosity of governments and the superior political influence of the

debtor class. . . . The power of taxation by currency depreciation is one
which has been inherent in the State. . . . The creation of legal tender has
been and is a government's ultimate reserve; and no state or government
is likely to decree its own downfall, so long as this instrument still lies
at hand unused" (J. M. Keynes, *A Tract on Monetary Reform*, London:
Macmillan and Co., Ltd., 1923, p. 9). Explain in more detail what Keynes
meant.

Answer:

According to the quotation, two groups — the government and other debtors (net monetary debtors) — benefit from inflation and are the driving
forces behind it. Inflation is a tax on money. Inflation is caused by increases
in the supply of money (currency), which is controlled by the government.
If the money stock doubles and the amount of goods and services remains
about the same, prices eventually double. The government, which makes
purchases with the new money before prices rise, benefits from the inflation tax since real resources are transferred to it at the lower prices. The
government and all other debtors benefit from inflation to the extent that
it is unanticipated. If loans were made and bonds issued while assuming
no inflation (so that no adjustment could be made in the interest rate for
the inflation), the dollars repaid to the creditors after the inflation would be
worth about half of their original value — they would purchase about half
the real goods and services they would have before the inflation. There is a
shift in real resources to net monetary debtors from net monetary creditors.

12) Suppose that all colleges were forced to pay professors a minimum salary
of $300,000 per year. Many professors will soon find themselves without
jobs. Being of influence in government, the professors tell the politicians
that the basic trouble is insufficient demand. To increase demand, the
government can increase its expenditures to colleges to enable them to
hire all the professors at $300,000. If it finances this by taxes, demand
will fall elsewhere and unemployment will result until wages and prices
fall in other professions to keep resources employed. The fall in prices
elsewhere offsets the rise in professors' wages.

Alternatively, the government could embark on general-demand
expansion by spending more and taxing less, meeting the deficit with
money creation. If the government assures college professors that they
will have full-employment demand conditions without wage cuts and
without causing unemployment elsewhere, is inflation the inevitable
consequence?

Answer:

Yes. Inflation is the only method of fulfilling that assurance — but the increase in the money wages of the professors will not be matched by an increase in their real (purchasing power) wages.

13) A monetary asset is one whose price can change although the asset is a claim to a fixed value in money terms. Give an example.

Answer:

A bond is a monetary asset. It is a claim to a fixed stream of interest payments over the life of the bond and a return of a certain number of dollars at maturity. However, the market price of the bond at any one time can fluctuate as prevailing market interest rates are higher or lower.

14) Which of the following are monetary? Are they assets or liabilities?
   a. Money; checking accounts
   b. Charge account at a department store
   c. Prepaid subscription to the *Wall Street Journal*
   d. Long-term lease for land
   e. Rental arrangement whereby tenant pays 1 percent of monthly sales as rental to the building owner
   f. US bonds

Answers:

   a. Monetary asset to creditor (depositor); monetary liability to debtor (bank).
   b. Monetary asset to creditor; monetary liability to debtor.
   c. Real asset to subscriber; real liability to publisher.
   d. Real asset to leaseholder; real liability to lessor.
   e. Monetary liability to leaseholder; monetary asset to lessor.
   f. Monetary asset to bondholder; monetary liability to bond issuer.

15) If, during an inflation, you held all your wealth in the form of real goods, would you gain or lose wealth relative to the price level?

Answer:

Are you a monetary debtor? Answering the question requires information about your liabilities.

16) Emperor Julian exhorted the merchants of ancient Antioch to practice self-restraint in pricing their wares. In modern times, government leaders sometimes exhort business and labor leaders to "exercise

statesmen-like self-restraint." Why is such exhortation worse than useless?

Answer:

Market prices facilitate exchange by revealing relative supplies and demands for everything, including labor services. Such exhortation diverts attention from causes of inflation (the government increasing the money stock) to consequences.

17) During the period of rapid inflation in the United States in the late 1970s, interest rates on loans and bonds were adjusted accordingly, to about 15 to 20 percent. Two decades later, inflation was substantially reduced to about 2 percent. Who gained and who lost during the transition from high to low inflation?

Answer:

Those who bought bonds when inflation and the coupon interest rate were high experienced a considerable wealth gain with lower interest rates from falling inflation. Those who issued the bonds when inflation and interest rates were high suffered a wealth loss.

18) Explain how bank owners (stockholders) as a class suffer from inflation.

Answer:

Banks are net monetary creditors. Part of the equity or net wealth, represented by this amount of net monetary assets, does not rise in proportion to the price level.

APPENDIX A TO CHAPTER 42: ADAPTING TO INFLATION

Data Inadequacy: Substitutions among Goods When Relative Prices Change

The CPI does not include adequate adjustment for how people react to higher prices. Consumers and businesses economize by substituting away from goods whose prices have risen relative to prices of other goods. If the price of beef rises relative to the price of chicken, people save in costs by shifting toward more of the now relatively lower-priced chicken or more nonmeat foods and away from the more costly beef. That substitution toward lower-priced items and away from the higher-priced ones reduces the dollar cost of the basket below what it would be if customers stubbornly persisted in buying an unchanged amount of beef.

Since the CPI does not take account of that shifting, and instead measures the cost *as if* people continued to buy the original amounts, it tends to overstate the cost of living when relative prices change, as they do whether or not there is inflation.

Fixed Standard of Living Despite Quality
Improvements at No Higher Prices?

Another problem arises as the CPI attempts to measure the rise in the dollar cost of the *same constant standard of living*, no worse and no better, over time.

Every few years the basket is revised to be better aligned with the kinds of goods people actually consume. But in that time, many improvements develop, as a result of normal technological and entrepreneurial innovations, part of which comes to consumers *at no higher price* for the improved goods. Examples are plentiful — computers, Internet, television, medicines and medical techniques, Velcro, zippers, plastics, graphite materials. The discoveries were costly to the innovators, but often the price to consumers is no higher than for the now obsolete and cheaper items. Competition among suppliers passes some benefits to consumers at unchanged prices.

These normal, zero-priced improvements offset some of the erosion of the dollar caused by inflation. The actual fall in the purchasing power of a dollar is not fully measured if the measure of inflation doesn't adjust for the zero-priced increase in the purchasing power of a dollar. In other words, the rate of actual inflation is less than the measure reported in the CPI.

Taxes That Mistakenly Can Raise the Measure of Inflation

On some goods, taxes are hidden in the price. For example, increased tariffs on imported goods reduce the supply and raise the prices of the imported goods. The resulting higher market price is a price of two things — the good and the tax. Because the higher price is attributed to the imported good, that overstates inflation. If the government had levied an income tax, instead of taxes on goods, no price of any good would have been raised by the income tax. It is a hopeless task to adjust all measures of inflation so as to not confuse higher prices due (a) to higher taxes with those due (b) to inflation.

Governmental Futile Attempts to Prevent Effects of Inflation

Though governments (representatives of the voters) create inflation, they also try to prevent the consequences. The attempts take many forms — often creating more burdens. Consider a few.

Price and Allocation Controls

Politicians, media columnists, business managers, laborers — almost everyone — asserts that the way to control inflation is to impose wage, price, and allocation controls. This means to replace market prices in directing resources. It is euphemistically labeled "incomes policy," and it is often initially described as voluntary. The imposed controls may stem from the mistaken impression that inflation is caused by greedy, powerful businesses and labor unions seeking higher prices and wages.

Far from preserving the value of money, price controls impair the function of money by making it less relevant for exchange. Controlled prices below those that would exist in open markets make money less effective in signaling information about changing supplies and demands for goods. Inevitably, shortages, outages, and delayed deliveries show the reduced power of money to command goods. Other forms of competitive behavior or rewards to the seller increase political power or status, the appeal of personal characteristics, the existence of waiting lines, and so forth. The effects on standards of ethical, proper behavior and customs soon become evident.

In Germany, three years after World War II, price controls were removed. The immediate and predictable responses were increases in production and disappearance of shortages, queues, and arbitrary allocations. The same results occurred in Japan and Italy when controls were removed there. The ending of price controls did not result in more inflation. Instead, market-determined prices caused more efficient uses of resources.

Other clear lessons about controlled prices versus market prices can be learned from government involvement in energy prices around the world. In the United States, for example, domestic price controls on gasoline in the turbulent 1970s resulted in shortages and rationing. At one point, it was legal to buy gas for your car only on odd or even days, depending on the last letter or number in your license plate. In early 1981, all price controls on domestically produced oil were ended — and oil prices immediately fell as production increased. The shortages disappeared, and rationing of gas ended.

APPENDIX B TO CHAPTER 42: GENERALIZATION OF INTERPERSONAL WEALTH

Redistribution of Unanticipated Inflation

Whenever inflation is not fully anticipated, some people in an economy gain wealth while others lose. This statement applies to individuals, households, businesses, governments, and even charity organizations. By "*not fully anticipated*" we mean that while *some* inflation may be expected by many, or even most, people in the economy, the actual rate exceeds the rate that is reflected in the *inflation add-on* in market interest rates.

Who gains and who loses can be illustrated by looking at some simple balance sheets. The *interpersonal wealth distribution* effects of unanticipated inflation can be summarized by the concepts of monetary and nonmonetary assets and liabilities.

Monetary and Nonmonetary Assets and Liabilities

The markets for goods discussed in earlier chapters were markets for nonmonetary assets — often called *real assets* — because their market values can change. They are not claims to fixed amounts of money. The dollar prices of houses, rare paintings, eggs, and cars change on average in proportion to the rate of inflation, although some of them will rise in price and some will fall, as they would without inflation.

Monetary Assets and Liabilities

Monetary assets are resources the values of which are fixed in a *specified number of dollars* — regardless of whether there is inflation or deflation. Money (currency and coin) is certainly a monetary asset; a checking account with no interest (or interest that does not change with inflation) is also a monetary asset. A bond — a claim to a specified number of dollars of interest and principal — is a monetary asset. Promissory notes of fixed-dollar payments and constant-dollar retirement pensions are monetary assets to the recipient. Monetary liabilities are the other side of these clams: obligations to pay those fixed amounts of money.

Everyone's monetary asset is a monetary liability to someone else. If you or the pension plan you contribute to holds long-term, fixed-rate government bonds, those are monetary assets to you and monetary liabilities to the government that issued them. Banks may hold fixed-rate mortgages as monetary assets, and the checking deposits of customers are monetary liabilities. As a homeowner, your mortgage is a monetary liability (unless the interest rate varies with inflation).

All currency issued by governments is a monetary liability to the government and a monetary asset to money holders. In the case of the United States, people around the world now hold $1.5 trillion dollars — the paper kind.

Nonmonetary Assets and Liabilities

Almost everyone has some nonmonetary assets and liabilities — also called real assets and liabilities — which are claims to, and obligations to deliver, goods and services whose dollar values are *not fixed* in dollar terms and can change with inflation. Owners of real assets on average do not suffer a loss from inflation, because real asset prices rise with inflation. An example of a real liability would be a long-term contract to deliver a real product — say, a newly manufactured Boeing airplane — many years in the future.

Real assets and real liabilities do not determine whether there are gains or losses of wealth by unanticipated inflation since their values change in proportion to the inflation. Monetary assets and liabilities determine the wealth redistributive effects.

Net Monetary Creditor

This is a net monetary creditor, holding more monetary assets, $10, than monetary debt, $6.

Before Unanticipated Inflation

	Assets		Liabilities	
	Cash	$10	Debt	$6
	Inventory	4	Equity	8
Total:		$14		$14

If the price level doubles, the result is:

After Unanticipated Inflation

	Assets		Liabilities	
	Cash	$10	Debt	$6
	Inventory	8	Equity	12
Total:		$18		$18

Equity has increased only 50 percent while the price level has doubled. This entity has lost wealth in purchasing power.

Neutral Monetary Status

Here is a neutral entity, with monetary assets equal to monetary liabilities (and net real assets equal to equity).

Before Unanticipated Inflation

	Assets		Liabilities	
	Cash	$6	Debt	$6
	Inventory	8	Equity	8
Total:		$14		$14

After a doubling of the price level, we have:

After Unanticipated Inflation

	Assets		Liabilities	
	Cash	$6	Debt	$6
	Inventory	16	Equity	16
Total:		$22		$22

Equity doubles to $16 when the price level doubles, so there is no gain or loss of purchasing power equity. Equity can increase proportionally to the general level of prices only if equity is equal to net real assets, that is, there is a zero net monetary status.

The only way to gain — for equity to increase by a proportion greater than rise in the price level — is to have a net monetary debtor status.

Net Monetary Debtor

Before Unanticipated Inflation

Assets		Liabilities	
Cash	$4	Debt	$6
Inventory	8	Equity	6
Total:	$12		$12

If prices double, the balance sheet becomes:

After Unanticipated Inflation

Assets		Liabilities	
Cash	$4	Debt	$6
Inventory	16	Equity	14
Total:	$20		$20

Equity has more than doubled, from $6 to $14. An increase in equity can be obtained only by being a net monetary debtor. Merely having some monetary debts is not sufficient. Nor does holding more inventory (by itself) generate a gain. It is excess of the monetary debt over monetary credit that generates a gain when the inflation was underanticipated.

One of the ways to be a net monetary debtor has been to buy a house with a large mortgage — with subsequent inflation higher than anticipated!

Before Unanticipated Inflation

Assets		Liabilities	
Cash	$1,000	Debt	$200,000
House	200,000	Equity	1,000
Total:	$201,000		$201,000

The balance sheet shows a very large net monetary liability, relative to the borrower's equity. The net monetary status is a net monetary liability of $199,000 ($200,000 – $1,000).

After Unanticipated Inflation

Assets		Liabilities	
Cash	$1,000	Debt	$200,000
House	400,000	Equity	201,000
Total:	$401,000		$401,000

Equity has increased from $1,000 to $201,000, or $100,500 in price-level-adjusted terms, an increase by a factor of 20 when the price level doubled.

There have been periods in the United States and other countries when owners of homes with large, fixed-rate mortgages reaped large gains when the ensuing inflation was greater than earlier anticipated. More generally, governments that have incurred deficits that were financed by the issuance of long-term, fixed-rate debt gain at the expense of the general public when inflation exceeds expectations. That is a primary reason economists refer to inflation as an *unlegislated tax*.

To review:

1) Equity (Net Wealth) = Assets – Liabilities
2) Equity = (real assets + monetary assets) – (real liabilities + monetary liabilities)
3) Rearranging the terms, we get:
   Equity = (real assets – real liabilities) + (monetary assets – monetary liabilities), which becomes
   Equity = net real assets + net monetary assets

To summarize the results, real assets and real liabilities do not affect the interpersonal distribution of wealth caused by an incorrectly anticipated inflation. There's no gain (nor loss) by any disparity between real assets and real liabilities, because both change in the same proportion to the price level.

However, a change in the price level leaves the *monetary* assets and liabilities at their prior dollar values — unadjusted by the inflation, and not augmented by any add-ons in the nominal rate of interest earned on the monetary assets.

GLOSSARY

ABSOLUTE ADVANTAGE: A comparison of the output/input (productive efficiency) ratios of two producers of one commodity, with the possibly *compared* producers ranging from individual workers to entire economies. Cf. COMPARATIVE ADVANTAGE.

AGGREGATE DEMAND: The sum of all individual demand schedules.

AGGREGATE SUPPLY: The sum of all individual supply schedules.

ANNUITY: A series of annual yields or payments for a specified period.

AVERAGE EXPENDITURE: Price per unit of production INPUT.

AVERAGE REVENUE: Money price of a unit of a good; sales revenue per unit: total revenue (TR) divided by number of units of product (TP): AR = TR/TP.

BARGAINING POWER: A measure of the ability of parties in negotiations (such as labor unions and employers) to achieve their goals.

BASING POINT PRICING: Price of a good in a particular market is the sum of a price at some designated geographic base plus costs of transport from the base to the market, even if the supplier is not located at the base site.

BOND: A promise, usually by a business firm or a government, to repay, with interest, a borrowed amount at the end of a specified period.

BOYCOTT: An organized refusal to buy, and an effort to persuade others not to buy, the product of a particular firm.

BUSINESS FIRM: A group of productive resources, a team, jointly producing goods and services for sale to others.

CAPITAL: A durable "factor of production" which contributes to a future stream of output; commonly referred to as a "capital good" and associated with such nonhuman inputs as machinery and inventories but also part of "human capital" of knowledge and skills.

CAPITAL GAIN: Increase in market value, sale price over purchase price, of an asset.

CAPITAL GOODS: Durable goods producing a stream of future goods or services that have market value at the time of production.

CAPITALISM: Essentially the same system as a market, price-directed, economy of private ownership of assets. Cf. COMPETITION.

CAPITALIST: The individual who makes wage or rent payments to inputs of production; commonly, a manager, an organizer, a risk-taker.

CARTEL: A coalition of sellers, sometimes legal, who agree to restrict output or reduce quality of product and to raise prices while restricting entry of potential competitors. Cf. COLLUSION.

CLOSED SHOP: A firm in which only union members can be hired.

COLLECTIVE BARGAINING: Negotiations on contract terms and working conditions that are conducted by employees as a group, usually through a representative, such as a union official.

COLLUSION: Joint action of producers of a good to equate the group's marginal revenue to marginal cost, raising price and reducing output; not to be confused with a COALITION, which can reduce price, increase output, or reduce costs.

COMMAND ECONOMY: An economy in which production and distribution of goods and services is organized and directed by a central authority.

COMPARATIVE ADVANTAGE: A comparison of different output/input (productive efficiency) ratios of two producers of two commodities, with one of the producers absolutely superior in both commodities, but by different degrees; one producer may be absolutely superior in both goods, but he can be comparatively superior in only one of them. Cf. ABSOLUTE ADVANTAGE.

COMPETITION: Rivalry among sellers and among buyers for goods and services, a method of coordinating economic activity through free exchange of productive resources and final goods and services under a system of private property.

COMPETITION MARKET CLASSIFICATION: Many firms, each supplying such a small proportion of an undifferentiated product that it cannot affect the market-determined price; price-taker, with horizontal average revenue curve.

CONSTRAINED MAXIMUM: Maximization of some variable (like output of a good) subject to some constraint (like a given output of another good); the production possibility boundary represents constrained maximization.

CONSUMER PRICE INDEX: A measure of changes in money prices of a typical market basket of goods and services for average-income people, compiled by the Bureau of Labor Statistics of the US Department of Labor.

CONSUMER'S (BUYER'S) SURPLUS: Excess of personal valuation (use value) of a good over the price which must be paid to obtain it; the excess of total use value over market value (price times quantity); in a supply-and-demand diagram, the area under the demand curve and above the level of price per unit. Cf. PRODUCER'S SURPLUS.

CONTRACT CURVE: A curve in an Edgeworth Box connecting points of equal marginal rates of substitution of the two people; moving toward the curve generates mutual gains of exchange; if the parties are on the curve, there can be further exchange only by one party being made worse off (moving to a lower indifference curve). Cf. EDGEWORTH BOX.

COPYRIGHT: The assignment of an exclusive right to commercial use of written or published material.

CORPORATION: A business firm jointly owned by shareholders, whose liability is limited to their stock; the organization continues despite death of owners or sale of their stock.

COST: The highest-valued opportunity necessarily forgone to obtain, attain, or produce something; the most-valued forsaken option in a choice. Cf. FIXED COST, VARIABLE COST, MARGINAL COST.

CRAFT UNION: A labor union whose members are practitioners of a particular skill, like carpentry or bricklaying, though they may work in different industries.

DEMAND: Schedule of quantities demanded at alternative prices; inverse relation between price per unit and the number of units demanded, with a downward-sloping curve; change in demand refers to a shift in the curve.

DEPRECIATION: The predictable reduction in the value of a resource as it deteriorates with use or with aging.

DEPRESSION: A decline in production, income, and employment that is more severe, and may be longer lasting, than a recession.

DERIVED DEMAND: The demand for productive resources derived from demand for the output those resources can produce.

DIFFERENTIAL EARNINGS: The earnings to a superior talent or more efficient resource; a Ricardian rent (but not a monopoly rent).

DIVISION OF LABOR: The coordinated division of production of some output into a number of different tasks in which people specialize.

DOMINANT FIRM: A seller controlling a sufficient amount of supply to act as a price-searcher, while competitors are price-takers of the price established by the dominant firm. The dominant firm controls not only current supply but also sources of expanded supply in the near future.

DUOPOLY: Two sellers in a well-defined industry; price-searcher, downward-sloping average revenue curve.

EARNINGS: The accounting conception of profits as the margin of revenue over accounting cost, as opposed to economic profits, which are the margin of revenue over economic costs (including a "normal" profit).

ECONOMIC EFFICIENCY: The condition of an economy that is operating with productive efficiency (that is, is on the production possibility boundary) and is maximizing consumer welfare such that no change in resource or output allocation could make someone better off without making someone else worse off.

ECONOMIC GOOD: A good that is scarce, of which less is available than people want; not a "free" (nonscarce) good.

ECONOMIC GROWTH: Substantial and sustained increase in the output of an economy.

ECONOMIC RENT: Any price that is unnecessary to keep a good in existence; hence any price in excess of resource cost. Economic rent may, however, be necessary to allocate goods to their highest-value uses.

EDGEWORTH BOX: A geometric construct with indifference maps of two people, one map rotated 180 degrees and superimposed on the other so that the width and the length of the rectangle measure the total amounts of the two commodities held by the people; the possibilities and limitations of mutually beneficial exchange are seen as potential movements within the box. Cf. CONTRACT CURVE.

ELASTIC; ELASTICITY NUMERICALLY GREATER THAN UNITY: A degree of responsiveness of a dependent variable which is greater than the proportionate change in the independent (initiating) variable.

ELASTICITY: A measure of the degree of responsiveness of a variable which is functionally related to another variable which changes in value, for example, the proportionate change in quantity demanded of a commodity in response to a given proportionate change in the price of the commodity.

ENDOWMENT EFFECT: The effect that change in a good's price has on demand for that good by a person whose income or wealth is partly derived from that good.

EQUILIBRIUM: A level, rate, or condition which tends to persist, with no external net forces promoting change, for example, equilibrium commodity price or rate of production.

EQUILIBRIUM PRICE: A market-clearing price, with quantity demanded equal to quantity supplied. Cf. EQUILIBRIUM.

FAIR-EMPLOYMENT LAWS: Laws regulating the hiring practices of employers, with the stated intent of prohibiting discrimination.

FEDERAL RESERVE SYSTEM: The central banking system created by the US government; the major agency of monetary policy.

FIRST LAW OF DEMAND: At any given price, there is some higher price at which less of a good is demanded and a lower price at which more is demanded.

FISCAL POLICY: Government use of expenditures and taxation to attempt to affect general economic activity.

FIXED COST: Unavoidable cost of a producing unit which is not a function of the rate or volume of output, for example, rent on facilities, interest on bonds and other borrowing, which must be financed regardless of the level of operations.

FREE ENTERPRISE: Another term for private property, market-exchange system.

FREE GOOD: A good (such as air) the availability of which is sufficient to satisfy all wants, even at a zero price. Some goods that are "free" to their consumers, like public education, are not free to the economy in general. Cf. ECONOMIC GOOD.

FRICTIONAL UNEMPLOYMENT: Unemployment arising from normal shifts in demand and supply in the labor markets. It is a method of adjusting to changing market conditions by providing for search of the best available alternative employment.

FULL EMPLOYMENT: The condition in which the entire labor force is working except those who are temporarily between jobs.

FULL PRICE: The money price of a good or service plus all other costs incurred in making the purchase, such as time, inconvenience, and the like.

GAINS FROM TRADE: The difference between seller's or buyer's marginal personal use value for each unit of a good traded and the price of that good.

GOOD: Anything that someone desires.

GOODWILL: A specialized asset of a firm, which earns a rent equal to the excess of the value of the firm over the sum of the value of each of its productive resources if those resources were used elsewhere.

GROSS NATIONAL INCOME: National income including wages, rents, profits, interest, and the value of capital equipment used up through depreciation.

IMPORT QUOTAS: Limits on the amount of a good suppliers from other countries are permitted to sell in the country imposing the quota.

INCOME ELASTICITY OF DEMAND: The responsiveness of the quantity of a good demanded to changes in the incomes of buyers of the good; the ratio of the percentage change in quantity demanded to the percentage change in income.

INCOME RELEASE EFFECT: An effect of a lower price, which releases some of the income formerly spent on that good at its higher price. There is usually a negligible effect on demand for the good in question, the released income being spread out over all goods purchased. The opposite effect occurs when the price of the good increases.

INDUSTRIAL UNION: A labor union whose members work in a particular industry, such as steel or automobiles, though there may be numerous different skills practiced by its members.

INELASTIC; ELASTICITY NUMERICALLY SMALLER THAN UNITY: A degree of responsiveness smaller than the degree of change in the first variable.

INFERIOR GOOD: A good of which a smaller proportional increase is demanded by an individual as personal income rises, all other things affecting demand for that good remaining unchanged.

INFLATION: A persisting, uniform rise in the average of all money prices (not changes in relative prices); reduced purchasing power of a dollar — in contrast to "deflation," a fall in the average of all prices.

INTEREST: The anticipated rate of growth of wealth when income is reinvested; the amount of wealth that could be consumed in a given year without reducing one's stock of wealth below its original value. Hence, it is the price of borrowing money.

INVESTMENT: Transforming saved resources into productive capital for future use.

JOINT OUTPUT AND COMMON COSTS: A firm of different operating divisions or types of customers can have common (overhead) costs for the whole firm, and those costs which do not vary with the operations of each division cannot be distributed among the several divisions, and are not pertinent to output decisions.

LABOR-MARKET PARTICIPATION RATE: The proportion of the adult population that is in the market labor force (which excludes the nonmarket labor services of the military and of spouses in the household).

LABOR UNION: A coalition of employees of a firm, or of many firms, to monitor and affect wages, benefits, employer-employee relations, and working conditions.

LONG RUN: Either (a) the interval in which all productive resources can be changed to adjust optimally to a given level of output or (b) a long-lived activity.

LONG-RUN PERIOD: The period in which all desired adjustments to market conditions have been made, including changes in any and all productive resources and in prices and output.

MARGINAL COST: Change in total cost (which equals change in variable cost) when output (total product) changes: $MC = \Delta TC / \Delta TP$. Cf. MARGINAL EXPENDITURE.

MARGINAL EXPENDITURE: Change in total production cost (expenditure) when quantity of inputs (N) changes: $ME = \Delta TC / \Delta N$. Cf. MARGINAL COST.

MARGINAL PERSONAL USE VALUE: The value a person places on one additional unit of a good, measured as the amount of some other good the person would forsake to get that unit.

MARGINAL PRODUCT: The increase in total output from the addition of one unit of some input, with all other inputs used in the production of that good held constant.

MARGINAL REVENUE: Change in total revenue (TR) when sale of a product (TP) changes: $MR = \Delta TR / \Delta TP$.

MARGINAL REVENUE PRODUCT: Change in total revenue with a change in variable input: $MRP = \Delta TR / \Delta N$; equivalent to $\Delta TR \Delta TP \times \Delta TP / \Delta N = MR \times MP$. Cf. VALUE OF THE MARGINAL PRODUCT.

MARKET CLASSIFICATIONS: Price-searchers. Cf. MONOPOLY, DUOPOLY, OLIGOPOLY, MONOPOLISTIC COMPETITION; price-takers. Cf. COMPETITION.

MARKET-CLEARING PRICE: A price at which quantity demanded equals quantity supplied, with neither "surplus" nor "shortage." Cf. EQUILIBRIUM, SURPLUS, SHORTAGE.

MARKET ECONOMY: An economic system in which individuals have rights to control and use private property and to exchange such property at market prices.

MARKET PERIOD: The period in which the supply of a good is unchanged regardless of the change in the price for which the good can be sold.

MARKET POWER: Power to affect selling price by changing the amount sold; a price-searcher, with negatively sloped average revenue curve. Cf. PRICE-SEARCHER, MONOPOLY.

MARKET VALUE: The total value of an amount of a good at its market price: the price of the good times the quantity sold at that price.

MERCANTILIST SYSTEM: A system in which access to private property and markets is limited by government to certain individuals; both government restrictions and discriminatory subsidizations of business enterprises.

MERGER: The combining of two firms into one, either by one firm's buying the other or by the two being aggregated under common ownership of the original owners, who form the new ownership of the merged firm.

MINIMUM-WAGE LAW: A mandated rate of pay below which employers are forbidden by law to pay employees, whether or not individuals are willing to work at that lower wage.

MONETARY POLICY: Government use of expansion or contraction of the money supply to affect the general level of economic activity.

MONEY: A recognized, divisible, storable, and exchangeable good used in facilitating virtually every exchange. It serves as a medium of exchange, unit of account, and store of value.

MONOPOLISTIC COMPETITION: An industry of "many" firms, with differentiated variations in the product and/or conditions, circumstances, and tactics of sale and distribution; price-searcher, with downward-sloping average revenue curve.

MONOPOLY: Single seller of a product with no close alternatives (substitutes); price-searcher, downward-sloping average revenue curve.

MONOPOLY DISTORTION: The failure of a monopolist to produce goods for which the value to buyers exceeds the costs of production, because marginal revenue is less than marginal cost for units not produced.

MONOPOLY RENT: The higher income of a protected seller from a price higher than would be received without legal restrictions on other sellers; gain from all suppliers restricting output and selling a higher price; not PROFIT from shifting resources from lower-valued uses to higher-valued.

MONOPSONY: A monopoly held by a buyer rather than a seller.

MORAL HAZARD: Actions with inadequate contracts, with resulting conflicts between an agent and others; maximizing one's well-being at the expense of others and not bearing the full consequences of those actions, thus inducing excessive carelessness and risk-taking.

MULTIPART PRICING: The selling of additional units of a good at successively lower prices as larger quantities are produced but with no lowering of prices of the earlier units.

NATIONAL INCOME DEFLATOR: A measure of inflation — usually lower than the Consumer Price Index — calculated according to the rise in money prices of all national income. By including all goods and services, it provides a more reliable measure of inflation than the CPI, which uses a rigid market basket that does not allow for substitution among goods whose relative prices have changed.

NATURAL MONOPOLY: A firm whose costs decline as output increases such that one firm is more efficient than two or more could be.

NET MONETARY DEBTOR/CREDITOR: Monetary assets are claims to a fixed number of dollars, including money and fixed amounts of money; monetary liabilities are obligations to pay fixed amounts of money; equity for net monetary debtors increases from inflation, and net monetary creditors lose wealth during inflation.

NET NATIONAL INCOME: The sum of value added over the entire market economy; the sum of wages, rents, interest, and dividends for the economy.

NET OF TAX: The price of a good a seller receives after taxes on that good have been subtracted.

NET PRODUCTIVITY OF INVESTMENT: The increase in future income created by investment today to transform some resource into a more highly valued form for later use, a form more highly valued than the present value of the funds invested.

NOMINAL PRICE: The amount of money, rather than the amount of other goods, that must be given up to obtain some of a good.

NONPROFIT CORPORATION: An enterprise, usually nongovernmental, holding assets the return from which is not distributed to any individual (as they are under private property arrangements) but is reused to further the stated goals of the enterprise.

OBSOLESCENCE: Reduction in the value of a productive resource from development of a new, superior competing resource.

OLIGOPOLY: An industry of "a few," but more than two, dominant firms; price-searcher, with downward-sloping average revenue curve; each seller makes pricing and output decisions in light of anticipated responses of other sellers.

OPEN MARKET: Markets to which all individuals have access without legal or artificial barriers. All individuals are permitted to buy or sell goods or services at market prices.

OPPORTUNITY COST: The most valuable alternative that must be forsaken to undertake a given act; often referred to as "alternative" cost.

PARETO-OPTIMAL ALLOCATION: Output allocation such that any change to make someone better off would make someone else worse off.

PARITY PRICE: A government-guaranteed minimum price for agricultural output—essentially, a price floor on agricultural products. These are said to bring "parity" with the costs of farm output.

PARTNERSHIP: A form of proprietorship involving two or more owners, each liable to the extent of his wealth. A partnership dissolves upon the death of a partner.

PATENT: Assignment of an exclusive right to commercial use of an invention not previously known. The patent usually has a limited life and protects only the commercial rights to the good or service; private production and consumption aren't limited.

POVERTY LINE: A level of income, chosen by the Social Security Administration, below which families are said to be in poverty. The line is based on family size and includes no in-kind income, such as government-provided medical services or food stamps.

PREDATORY PRICING AND ACTIVITY: Allegedly unethical charging of prices which are "too low" in practices of "unfair" competition; the term is generally, if not invariably, undefined or ambiguously applied, with relevant costs misunderstood or price incorrectly perceived.

PRESENT VALUE: The current value of the future stream of goods or services that an investment will yield; it is derived by discounting the value of that stream at an appropriate rate of interest.

PRICE: What is paid by the buyer and received by the seller in purchase and sale of a unit of a good or other asset. Cf. AVERAGE REVENUE, PERSONAL VALUE, DEMAND SCHEDULE.

PRICE DISCRIMINATION: Selling goods at different market prices to different groups, reflecting differences in demand among the groups rather than differences in the costs of providing those goods. It is undertaken to capture some of the consumer's surplus that goes to consumers under uniform pricing.

PRICE ELASTICITY OF DEMAND: The responsiveness of the quantity of a good demanded to changes in the price of that good; formally, the ratio of the percentage change in quantity demanded to the percentage change in price.

PRICE-SEARCHER: A seller or a buyer in a "noncompetitive" market; a seller of output facing a downward-sloping average revenue (demand) schedule (greater than marginal revenue); buyer of inputs with an upward-sloping average expenditure schedule (less than marginal expenditure); a price-searcher is large enough relative to the market to affect price. Cf. AVERAGE REVENUE, MARGINAL REVENUE, AVERAGE EXPENDITURE, MARGINAL EXPENDITURE.

PRICE-TAKER: A seller or a buyer in a "competitive" market; a seller of output facing a horizontal average revenue (demand) schedule (identical to marginal revenue), able to sell any desired amount at the price established by the entire market; a buyer of inputs with a horizontal average expenditure schedule (identical to marginal expenditure), able to buy any desired amount at the market-determined price; a price-taker is too small relative to the market to influence price. Cf. AVERAGE REVENUE, AVERAGE EXPENDITURE.

PRIVATE PROPERTY: Economic goods that can be controlled, used, and exchanged by individuals without political restrictions.

PRODUCER'S (SELLER'S) SURPLUS: Excess of market receipts from selling a good over marginal production costs; in a supply-and-demand diagram, the area under the level of price per unit and above the supply curve. Cf. CONSUMER'S SURPLUS.

PRODUCTION EFFICIENCY: Production of the maximum output possible at given levels of resources and technology; it is described by the points along the production possibility boundary.

PRODUCTION POSSIBILITY BOUNDARY: The locus of points describing the maximum amount of one good that can be produced given production levels of a second good with given resources and technology.

PROFIT: Any increase in wealth above and beyond that accounted for by investment of savings out of standard income; increases in an economy's stock of wealth that are not anticipated in the market.

PROMISSORY NOTE: A legal contract promising to repay a debt at some point in the future at a stated rate of interest. "Buying debt" is the purchase of a promissory note.

PROPRIETORSHIP: A business owned by one person who has full liability for all the firm's debts to the extent of his or her entire wealth. The firm ends upon the death of the proprietor.

PUBLIC GOOD: A good that can be consumed by any one person without there being less available for others to consume. The value of a public good is thus the sum of the value all individuals who consume the good place on each unit.

QUANTITY DEMANDED: Amount demanded at a specific price, with more demanded at lower prices and less at higher prices; a shifted position on an unchanged demand curve reflects only a change in price.

QUANTITY SUPPLIED: Amount offered for sale at alternative prices, generally with more supplied at higher prices and less at lower prices; a changed position on a given supply curve reflects only a change in price, with supply constant but quantity supplied increasing or decreasing (except with a vertical supply curve).

QUASI-RENT: Any part of a price that does not affect the amount of a good available now but will affect the future amount of that good available; a temporary rent.

REAL ASSET: Any asset (such as land) the real value of which remains unchanged by inflation, although the money value of such assets will change.

REAL LIABILITY: Any obligation the real value of which is unchanged by inflation, although the dollar value may change.

REAL PRICE: The same as relative price.

REAL WAGES: Wages measured against living costs — the actual goods and services that can be purchased with the wage.

RECESSION: A transient decline in the general level of employment, income, and production from some shock to the economy. Cf. DEPRESSION.

RELATIVE PRICE: The price of a good compared to the price of all other goods. The amount of other goods (other than money, itself a good) that must be given up to get a good. If all money prices change by the same proportion, relative prices are unchanged.

RENTS: Earnings paid for the services of nonhuman resources, such as land. Cf. MONOPOLY RENT, QUASI-RENT, RICARDIAN RENT.

RETAIL PRICE MAINTENANCE: An agreement between manufacturers and distributors of a product that the price cannot be above some maximum or below some minimum.

REVENUE SHARING: Distribution of federal tax revenues to state and local governments.

RICARDIAN RENT: Higher income attributable to superior productivity, for example,

greater talent of a person, more fertile land; not a MONOPOLY return gained by
contrived exclusion of competition.

SAVING: The nonconsumption of standard income, thus adding to an economy's stock
of wealth and increasing that economy's future standard income.

SCARCITY: Any asset — commodity or resource — is scarce when the amount available
is less than the amount demanded — not to be confused with "shortage."

SECONDARY BOYCOTT: A boycott against a firm that deals with a firm being
boycotted.

SECOND LAW OF DEMAND: In the long run, demand is more elastic for any given
good as substitutes for that good become more readily apparent and available.

SHORTAGE: An excess of quantity demanded over quantity supplied because price is
below its market-clearing level, for example, a shortage of apartments because of
rent control; anything in short supply is scarce, but not everything which is scarce is
in short supply. Cf. MARKET-CLEARING PRICE, SCARCITY.

SHORT RUN/LONG RUN: Short run is a period in which some production facilities
cannot be economically varied; it encompasses a range of possible adaptability of
variable factors while other factors are currently fixed; in a sufficiently long period,
all inputs can be varied, permitting full adjustment to circumstances.

SLOPE: Ratio of vertical change to horizontal change — positive, zero, or negative — at
a point on a curve. Cf. ELASTICITY — demand elasticity = $1/\text{slope} \times P/Q$.

SOCIALIST ECONOMY: A system in which income-producing goods and durable
consumer goods are controlled by the government and are not salable at market-
clearing prices.

SPECIALIZATION: The production of more of a good than one consumes, the
unconsumed portion being sold for other goods.

SPECULATION: The buying of a good in the hope of making a future profit on its sale.

STABLE EQUILIBRIUM: An equilibrium which tends to correct or reestablish itself if
it is upset.

STANDARD INCOME: The increase in an economy's wealth, analogous to the interest
rate, that the economy can consume in a year without detriment to the original stock
of wealth. The market-forecasted sustainable rate of increase in wealth.

STRIKE: A concerted refusal by employees to work for a particular employer with which
a union has a grievance, attempting to prevent others from taking jobs with the same
employer in their absence.

STRUCTURAL UNEMPLOYMENT: Unemployment caused by very large and long-
term or permanent shifts in labor demand in a few industries, often forcing those
unemployed to accept lower wages or rents in other industries where their skills in
the declining industry are not as valuable.

SUBSTITUTION EFFECT: The effect of a change in price of a good on the quantity of
the good demanded; when the price of a good rises, other goods will be substituted

for it and the quantity demanded will fall, all other things affecting demand for that good remaining unchanged.

SUPERIOR GOOD: A good of which a more than proportional increase is purchased by an individual as personal income rises, all other things affecting demand for the good remaining unchanged.

SUPPLY: Schedule of quantities offered at alternative prices; generally direct relation between price per unit and the number of units supplied, with an upward-sloping curve; for a price-taker (competitive) seller, supply is the marginal cost curve above its intersection with the average variable cost curve; change in supply refers to a shift in the curve.

SURPLUS: An excess of quantity sellers wish to supply over quantity demanded because price is higher than its market-clearing level, for example, agricultural surpluses because of stipulated food prices above equilibrium. Cf. MARKET-CLEARING PRICE.

TIE-IN SALES: One good is sold on the condition that some other specified good also is bought at a price covering both goods.

TOTAL PERSONAL USE VALUE: The total amount of other goods and services one would be willing to give up to obtain some amount of a good.

TRAGEDY OF THE COMMONS: Waste of resources not individually owned; private property is economized through incentives of private gain, but in the absence of individual ownership and protection, resources commonly held are exploited inefficiently in the short run and at a rate which cannot be sustained in the long run.

UNEMPLOYMENT: The absence of employment acceptable to the unemployed in terms of wages and working conditions.

UNION SHOP: A firm in which one need not be a union member to gain employment, but must pay union dues.

UNSTABLE EQUILIBRIUM: An equilibrium which is not self-correcting, continuing to move further from its initial condition when disrupted.

UTILITY-MAXIMIZATION THEORY: The theory that individuals seek the highest possible satisfaction from the goods and services they consume and from other activities they undertake.

VALUE ADDED: The value of a product in excess of the cost of materials and services purchased by a firm to make that product. The sum of values added, rather than the value of sales at each step of production, is the proper measure of national income.

VALUE OF THE MARGINAL PRODUCT: Market value of marginal product: price (AR) times quantity, AR × MP. Cf. MARGINAL REVENUE PRODUCT.

VARIABLE COST: Cost of producing a unit which is a function of the rate or volume of production, for example, wages of employees, expenditure on raw materials.

WAGES: Earnings paid to providers of labor services.

INDEX

Figures and tables are indicated by "f" and "t" following the page numbers.